A PEOPLE'S CHARTER

A PEOPLE'S CHARTER

The Pursuit of Rights in America

James MacGregor Burns

AND

Stewart Burns

ALFRED A. KNOPF NEW YORK 1991

THIS IS A BORZOI BOOK
PUBLISHED BY ALFRED A. KNOPF, INC.

Library of Congress Cataloging-in-Publication Data
Burns, James MacGregor.
A people's charter: the pursuit of rights in America / James MacGregor Burns
and Stewart Burns.
p. cm.
Includes bibliographical references and index.
ISBN 0-394-57763-9
1. Civil rights—United States—History. 2. Human rights—United
States—History. I. Burns, Stewart. II. Title.
JC599.U5B87 1991
323'.0973—dc20   91-52855 CIP

Manufactured in the United States of America
First Edition

For the children of the third century

Let me give you a word of the philosophy of reform. The whole history of the progress of human liberty shows that all concessions yet made to her august claims, have been born of earnest struggle. The conflict has been exciting, agitating, all-absorbing, and for the time being, putting all other tumults to silence. It must do this or it does nothing. If there is no struggle there is no progress. Those who profess to favor freedom and yet depreciate agitation, are men who want crops without plowing up the ground, they want rain without thunder and lightning. They want the ocean without the awful roar of its many waters.

This struggle may be a moral one, or it may be a physical one, and it may be both moral and physical, but it must be a struggle. Power concedes nothing without a demand. It never did and it never will. Find out just what any people will quietly submit to and you have found out the exact measure of injustice and wrong which will be imposed upon them, and these will continue till they are resisted with either words or blows, or with both. The limits of tyrants are prescribed by the endurance of those whom they oppress.

FREDERICK DOUGLASS
Canandaigua, New York, August 3, 1857

CONTENTS

PART FIVE

A PEOPLE'S CHARTER

OVER THREE MILLENNIA AGO, in a war-scarred land of hills and
desert called Canaan, there arose a legend that came to have a powerful
impact on the hopes and visions of suffering humanity around the world.
That legend told of a people who had lived as slaves in Egypt, rebelled
against their masters, fled to Canaan, and established there a new society
and a new covenant, their struggle catalyzed by the leadership of a phe-
nomenal visionary, organizer, revolutionary, and lawgiver named Moses.
The literal-minded have sought to sift the "historical truth" from the
biblical story of Exodus. But the legend itself has had a far greater influence on human thought and action than the "real truth," however well
documented, could possibly have had. Sages, storytellers, priests, poets,
slaves and other downtrodden people have fashioned the legend to fit
their own needs and dreams.

On a tomb at Thebes we see images of slaves at forced labor, carrying
stones and bricks on their heads and their backs, on bows over their
shoulders, on poles between two men. Elsewhere we view them at work
in vineyards, on plantations, in mines. They are essentially beasts of
burden. What we cannot see from these images—what the nonslave can
rarely know—is what these toilers in Egypt were thinking. Did they accept
their lot? Did they become slaves psychologically to their slave condition?
If they struck back, did they do so instinctively, as an overburdened
workhorse blindly kicks off its harness? Or did they rebel in the conviction
that they had a right to a better life?

Among the slaves in Egypt were people called Israelites. According to
legend they had not always been slaves, but had come to Egypt as a guest
people and worked for wages, then were denied their pay and forced into

bondage. In likely historical fact some of them rebelled in the thirteenth century B.C., escaped from Egypt, fought their way through hostile lands, and eventually settled in Palestine. But once again, legend transcended known facts in historical impact.

"And it came to pass, when Pharaoh had let the people go, that God led them not *through* the way of the land of the Philistines, although that *was* near; for God said, Lest peradventure the people repent when they see war, and they return to Egypt: But God led the people about, *through* the way of the wilderness of the Red sea: and the children of Israel went up harnessed [equipped for battle] out of the land of Egypt. . . . And the Lord went before them by day in a pillar of a cloud, to lead them the way; and by night in a pillar of fire, to give them light; to go by day and night." And Pharaoh pursued them with five hundred chariots, and the Israelites cried out in fear, and Moses told them to trust in the Lord, and the Lord caused the sea to go back by a strong east wind, and His children crossed over the dry ground while the Egyptians and their chariots were caught in the returning waters and "there remained not so much as one of them."

Who led Exodus, God or Moses? According to biblical legend, God was the leader, with Moses as His agent. But it was Moses who inspired the Israelites, Moses who commanded, implored, disciplined them, and when he faltered in his leadership, God chastised him: On the banks of the Red Sea, Moses said to his terrified people, "Fear ye not, stand still, and see the salvation of the Lord. . . . The Lord shall fight for you, and ye shall hold your peace," but the Lord said to Moses, "Wherefore criest thou unto me? speak unto the children of Israel, that they go forward."

For such a desperate venture to succeed, however, disciples were needed among the rebelling and fleeing people, men and women who would urge on the weary and the fainthearted. Although they are un-recorded in history, such subleaders had to exist. And the followers had their own demands. When they came to Marah and found the water there too bitter to drink, they "murmured against Moses," demanding, "What shall we drink?" until Moses cried unto the Lord, who showed him a tree that could be cast into the water to sweeten it. Exodus is the saga of a people overcoming generations of external and internalized oppression. The wandering in the wilderness becomes, in Michael Walzer's words, "a march toward a goal, a moral progress, a transformation."

As the Israelites developed into a united purposeful force, headed toward the promised land, Moses became the archetypal revolutionary leader, empowering his followers even as they empowered him. Like many later revolutionary leaders Moses himself never made it to the promised land—to Canaan—but his faith was implemented along the way, in Sinai. There he met the harshest test of the revolutionary and transforming leader—as consolidator of the revolution, builder of a new society, lawgiver in a new state. He would brook no deviation: when he descended from the mountain carrying the tablets of the law and found some of his people worshipping an idol, a golden calf, he reviled them in the name of the Lord.

What kind of promised land, what kind of new nation, did the Israelites want? Having rebelled against Egyptian gods, hierarchy, and oppression, their deepest yearnings were for their own God, for freedom under God, for equality before Him. In the Exodus, according to J. Severino Croatto, Israel "grasped a liberating sense of God and an essential value in its own vocation, namely, *freedom.*" Thus the fundamental consciousness of Israel was freedom "at the communal level of the Covenant, or as a people, and at the level of the person."

The two documents from these legendary days, the Decalogue and the Covenant Code, are embedded in the American heritage and remain compelling for us today. The Decalogue we might view as a kind of embryonic "bill of rights," while the Covenant is more like a constitution, founded in the principles of the Decalogue and dealing with such matters as property, usury, and the impartial administration of justice. Tying the great documents together is a form of social contracting, a free binding of people to laws and society that puts the community into a condition of "moral equality," in Walzer's term. "The covenant reflected what we might usefully call the general will of the Israelites," Walzer concludes, but a general will fashioned from "the wills of independent, noncommunicating individuals." The people—or at least the leaders or heads of families among them—were involved, by voicing assent to the terms in these documents and by taking part in the ceremony that formally ratified the lofty pronouncements.

What kind of rights did the manifestos proclaim? Can they be called rights at all, in our modern usage? If rights, were they individual rights or communal rights? Were they to be applied to all the Israelites, without distinction of class, status, or gender? We cannot give historically satisfactory answers to all of these questions, but we do know that the issues they raise, with their implications for the theory and the practice of rights, challenge and haunt us to this day.

Eventually this people of ancient Israel and their rulers, as with so many other societies before and since, would come to exhibit autocratic, inegalitarian, and aggressive tendencies. But the lasting image of the long march out of Egypt would be a noble one. Oliver Cromwell found a precedent for his Puritan Revolution in Exodus, the "only parallel of God's dealing with us that I know in the world." The trek inspired the preachings of the ascetic monk Savonarola against religious corruption and political tyranny; it was cited in the pamphlets of the sixteenth-century German peasant uprisings; and it "underpins the radical contractualism" of the Scottish Presbyterians. And it helped define and establish "God's new Israel" in America.

The enduring mythic influence and political power of this legend comes in part from its story of the piercing of the slave consciousness of a subjugated people, who were drawn out of their internalized oppression toward an understanding of their right to a better life, a life that offered them a measure of liberty and material welfare, and who then *acted* to escape their oppressors and to establish that better life. This summons was framed not in drab legalistic terms but in a clarion call for liberation and a glowing portrait of the promised land. The story of Exodus has animated ideologies that awaken a people's sense of grievance, focus their discontent, and incite them to action, all in the name of higher moral goals.

Exodus, then, is the story of revolution, the most decisive, the most portentous, and often the most poignant of human actions, and the story also of transforming leadership, the most difficult of all forms of leadership—leadership that not only preaches change but accomplishes it, not only guides followers to the promised land but fashions a new covenant there, not only arouses people's hopes but brings about concrete betterment in their daily lives. Such leadership requires subleaders who help mobilize followers among the masses and then serve as the counselors, managers, and guardians of the new society. The practice of creative leadership is tested by the ideals and principles—for the Israelites, the human right to liberty and equality—of the cause that inspired it.

Could American revolutionaries remain immune to the legend of Exodus? Benjamin Franklin could not: he wanted the Great Seal of the United States to picture Moses with his rod held high and the Egyptian pursuers dying in the sea. Thomas Jefferson could not, though his design for the Seal was a gentler one, showing the Israelites marching through the wilderness with the vision of God's pillars of cloud and fire. The slaves on American plantations could not. Their mournful spirituals rendered the Israelites' plea:

> *Leader:* When Israel was in Egypt's land,
> *Chorus:* Let my people go!
> *Leader:* Oppressed so hard they could not stand,
> *Chorus:* Let my people go!
> *All:* Go down, Moses, 'Way down in Egypt's Land,
> Tell ole Pharaoh, Let my people go!

Union soldiers marching to war sang hymns of exodus and liberation. Later, Lincoln Steffens in *Moses in Red* contended that Exodus was the model for all revolutions.

If Exodus was the legendary prototype for awakening the minds of the exploited, mobilizing them for action, vanquishing oppressors, and leading the revolutionaries to a promised land of freedom and justice, the long march set the agenda of questions for those who would continue the struggle for human rights. What rights? Whose rights? Measured by what values? Validated by what philosophers? Enforced by what institutions and processes? Tested against competing rights by what standards? And with what impact on the wants and needs, the hopes and expectations, and ultimately the daily lives of humankind?

PART ONE

CHAPTER ONE

THE BIRTH OF RIGHTS

TO SEE RIGHTS CLEARLY, we must begin not with laws and institutions but with people. And if we begin with people we must begin with the newborn child. For with that child rights begin.

By the act of being born, of becoming a person, the infant unknowingly presents its basic wants as claims against the rest of us—claims to nourishment, shelter, comfort, to survival and growth. These claims will remain unanswered unless other humans respond to them, first of all the mother. The mother meets the child's wants with her warm body, with milk from her breasts or a bottle, with protection against cold or heat, with hugs and caresses.

The mother's response to the wants of her child depends both on what she judges to be necessary or good for the infant and on her resources. This is the recognition of needs, defined as legitimated wants. Needs entail rights, however, only when articulated and justified as such. If needs are legitimated wants, rights are justifiable moral claims to those protections or resources that fulfill human needs. In satisfying the infant's needs and rights, the mother most often does not act alone—the child might also be nurtured by its father, older siblings, grandparents and other family members, neighbors and day-care providers. All involved are nurturing persons.

This can be a compelling sight—a small, vulnerable human being whose wants are recognized, whose needs are met, whose rights are respected. But as infants emerge from the cocoon of parental protection, unsettling changes may disrupt this pleasing image. Children yield to new arrivals whose needs and rights may now take priority. Older children may be expected to protect the rights of their younger siblings. Rights come increasingly into conflict, both within and outside the family.

Nor does it suffice that wants are recognized as needs and are met as rights; rather the satisfaction of needs brings a dynamic force into play, for new wants arise as earlier ones are largely satisfied. If the youngsters have been adequately nourished, clad, and housed, they may come to desire more freedom of action and expression, even in defiance of parents and other authority, or more opportunities for self-fulfillment. That the satisfaction of needs often leads not to their extinction, but to fresh, more urgently felt wants—this is a fundamental dynamic in the pursuit of rights, as well as an essential aspect of human existence. But rights may be blocked or diminished as well, leading to resignation—or to new and more vigorous assertions of rights.

Rights vary according not only to ever-shifting wants but also to the social contexts in which rights are claimed and the nature and pliability of the dominant ideology and authority. In school youngsters enter into a new complex of wants and needs, with their fulfillment as rights or their frustration dependent on power relations with and among peers, teachers, and administrators. Later, people's experiences in their workplaces arouse still newer wants, in turn provoking further assertions and denials of rights.

People possess certain rights on the basis of citizenship, such as voting, but such rights are often not very relevant to everyday needs. Some citizens live in communities where rights are as circumscribed as in school or on the job, or where basic rights are violated, as still with many people of color in the United States. Yet citizenship offers the prospect, at least, of a broader range of rights claims to protections and resources.

As citizens recognize needs—for good jobs, schools, housing, health care, social security, cultural expression, and the like—some of them become activists who articulate these needs as entitlements and organize community action for their realization. The more effectively that activists are able to advance claims for rights, the more citizens will assert them in their everyday lives. Politicians competing with rival vote-seekers may respond to pressures from citizens by assuring them that they are entitled to the things demanded. Political leaders might then enact into law such rights claims, spurring new and still higher assertions of entitlements. While this process will vary widely from one society to another, it encompasses reciprocal and mutually stimulating relationships among the citizens' need for rights, the recognition of that need by activists, and the response of political leaders to citizens and activists.

Our approach to rights in this book is unorthodox. We have begun with people, with the wants of infants that expand into more varied and intense claims to rights and that culminate in historic rights movements in which all participants are engaged in forging a dynamic and evolving people's charter of rights. We make several assumptions about rights: that political, civil, economic, and social entitlements are not primarily the creations of philosophical, political, or legal establishments; that, on the contrary, rights are created far more by those who actively shape them and live them in the thick of personal and social struggles, often in conflict with other groups; that rights are not static concepts but dynamic moral forces—"grounds for action" that do not exist apart from cultural, economic, and political environments; that these environments will choke off some rights and enhance others, serving variously as an opportunity course of possibilities for growth and self-fulfillment, or as an obstacle course of gender, racial, caste, and class barriers; and therefore that the human environment must be altered, or even transformed, in order for rights to be actualized.

This approach is alien to most political and social theorists and to most of those who exercise political power. The former tend to describe their fellow humans as merely calculators in self-interest, traders in influence, transactors in economic and political marketplaces. For the latter, the popular demand for rights is often not the expression of true human needs but a threat to their power or to their economic or social interests. Thus is posed a fundamental moral and political conflict. Elites typically consider the masses irrational, demanding, fickle, contentious—and hence dangerous to the state; while rebels and iconoclasts among the masses see their rulers as power-mad, oppressive, corrupt—and hence dangerous to the people. To control the populace, elites preach and enforce the virtues of authority, hierarchy, stability, continuity. To thwart their rulers, rebels demand their rights in the language of liberty, equality, and justice.

The balance of power between these two sides is inherently uneven. The elites control armies, courts, bureaucracies, educational and religious establishments, channels of communication, and dominant sectors of the economy, while their adversaries marshal their power in factories, classrooms, print shops, taverns, and in the streets—in the "unsteepled places," E. P. Thompson called them. This imbalance can be righted somewhat by the capacity of rebels to appeal to political philosophy, Scripture, the national heritage, the founding values of the polity, principles of justice and rightness—to sources of authority that might bring great moral and intellectual force to their cause.

Among such sources of authority are the intellectual leaders, the influential philosophers and theorists whose concern is with issues of human nature and the nature of human society and whose writings might be powerful weapons in the struggle to shape a people's charter of rights. But where have these leaders stood in the defense of people's rights?

Where have they thrown their intellectual and moral weight in the millennia-old conflict between those claiming rights and those suppressing them, between those, like Moses, who subvert order for higher purposes and those who enforce it? The answer seems clear: the voice of intellectual authority has usually resounded in the service of power and privilege.

DEFENDERS OF THE RIGHT

DEMOCRATIC MAN, wrote Plato, "lives from day to day indulging the appetite of the hour; and sometimes he is lapped in drink and strains of the flute; then he becomes a water-drinker, and tries to get thin; then he takes a turn at gymnastics; sometimes idling and neglecting everything, then once more living the life of a philosopher; often he is busy with politics, and starts to his feet and says and does whatever comes into his head. . . . His life has neither law nor order; and this distracted existence he terms joy and bliss and freedom; and so he goes on."

No statement could sum up more tellingly the fundamental distrust of the people and popular rule held by most of the Greek philosophical eminences, or the concept of human nature that underlay that distrust. The Greek "greats" broadly agreed that people were grossly unequal in birth, abilities, industry, and virtue; that the kind of individual produced by democracy was a self-indulgent drone, purposeless, easygoing, childish; that true virtue was found only in the upper class. And they shared a deep fear of the masses as potentially threatening to the values they prized: harmony, order, stability, continuity, hierarchy. Whatever their disagreements on particulars, the political philosophies of Socrates, Plato, and Aristotle were all deeply antipopular and antidemocratic.

The Greek thinkers embodied and sanctioned the dominant values of the world in which they lived. Their Greece was a stratified society in which rights and duties were allotted in accord with hierarchical position. Clearly, magnificently, at the top were the *aristoi*, meaning literally the "best people," a landed, hereditary aristocracy with the leisure, gained from their possession of property, to govern, to philosophize, to cultivate virtue. Beneath them was the populace—the commoners, craftsmen, herdsmen, peasants, landless laborers, traders, slaves. Women in general were of course subordinate.

Among the populace were the Athenian citizens, who did not fit easily into the hierarchy. They were, on the one hand, a somewhat exclusive and even cliquish group, composed only of adult males, and numbering in 450 B.C. between 30,000 and 40,000, or approximately 15 percent of the population. To the *aristoi,* however, they were scarcely distinct from other elements in the great *demos,* the large mass of "ordinary" people. What distinguished the citizens of Athens was their possession of certain rights, particularly political rights—to attend meetings of the assembly, to speak and vote there, and after the age of thirty to seek election to the Boule—the Council of 500—and to stand for state offices. In short, these men had the right to participate in major public decisions and the administration of the *polis.*

Possession of these and other rights set citizens apart from another large body of Athenians, perhaps a third of the city's population—the 80,000 or more slaves who were owned privately or by the *polis* and who toiled in silver mines, in shield factories and other workshops, in households, and in such skilled work as knife-making and vine-dressing. Most Athenian slaves were probably better off than black slaves later would be on North American plantations. It was not always easy to distinguish an Athenian slave by either dress or demeanor from citizens working on the same construction project, and it is said that the slave would not step aside for the citizen in the street. But slaves lacked *rights.* Their masters might sell them, bequeath them, give them away; they were property. "The Athenian could beat or maltreat his slaves (and their only protection was to seek asylum at the shrine of Theseus or the altar of the Eumenides)," according to R. K. Sinclair, "while a master who killed a slave seems to have been required to do no more than submit to the ritual act of purification." And the slave, except by another's action, could never be free.

If the vaunted civilization of Athens legitimated so many violations of liberty, it could hardly be expected that the Romans would move much beyond the Greeks in defining and protecting rights, nor did they. Rome's established thinkers drew heavily on the Greek philosophers and shared the Greek view of human nature—that people were fundamentally wicked and needed to be contained. And the Romans had their own rigorous differentiation of social orders: the patricians and their dependent "clients," the "equestrian" class of businessmen and landowners, the plebs, the freedmen, all bottomed on the slave caste. While Cicero wrote or orated brilliantly about the natural equality of all men before the "one eternal and unchangeable law," and while early Rome offered some legal rights to a citizen of Roman birth, these in general did not apply to the rapidly mounting number of alien residents, and far less to slaves.

Dedicated to law and order, the Romans effectively and brutally put down the sporadic revolts against their rule. They could not so easily suppress a mysterious insurgency that slowly emerged 1,500 miles south-east across the Mediterranean in Palestine against the Romans and the Jews who ruled the land as Rome's surrogates. An electrifying legend was sweeping the eastern shores of the Mediterranean about a man named Jesus who wandered the land healing the sick and living on charity, fraternized with social outcasts and the oppressed, later marched to Jerusalem with his followers, and there excoriated the Pharisees for pious hypocrisy, ousted the moneylenders from the Temple, and was executed. To a marked degree Christianity rose in response to basic human spiritual and material needs that Jesus and his disciples brought to consciousness.

They were men who preached love, charity, kindness, and turning the other cheek to enemies, values that lay at the heart of the Christian doctrines that came to predominance in the West during Rome's long decline. But just as the rebellious ideas of Moses were transmuted into doctrines of obedience and order and given the authority of law, so were the spiritual values of Jesus politicized and institutionalized in the Papacy and European monarchies. Popular aspirations and beliefs that had grown from the pasturelands of Canaan were superseded by dogmas and practices that harshly subordinated the great number of people—the subjection of soul and body to higher temporal authority, the obligation to obey civil laws whether just or unjust, the abrogation of the right to resist even the most tyrannical king.

In the long and often silent struggle of populist expression of rights against political and religious absolutism, what position did intellectual leaders take? No thinker achieved higher or more lasting intellectual and moral standing in early Christendom than Augustine, nor was any thinker more aware of human needs and human error. After a wild youth during which he rejected his Christian upbringing and passed through extremes of spiritual turbulence, he wrote his *Confessions, The City of God,* and other profound works.

There was little solace for the oppressed, however, in the preachings of this great theologian. To be sure, he believed that before the Fall people were created free and equal in their goodness. But after the Fall human sin burst through the original innocence—pride, egotism, violence, the lust for power and money. Whereas people originally took delight in not sinning and used their liberty to do right, now they pursued a fruitless quest for happiness, possessed by one vain desire after another.

The fallen were indeed born equal, but as sinners, and harsh and repressive civil institutions were both punishment and remedy for their sinful condition. For a millennium after his death in A.D. 430, the intellectual foundations of Christian states and the Papacy were bolstered by such Augustinian concepts as humanity's essentially evil nature, the fundamental need for order and harmony, the use of coercion if necessary to prevent disorder, the rightful resort to state power in order to suppress heresy, and above all and encompassing the others, the obligation to obey church and throne.

Some in the Middle Ages did speak for popular needs and rights—rebels and heretics and agnostics—but these could not speak with the voice of authority. It was not until some eight hundred years after Augustine that another intellectual leader spoke with such a powerful voice. This was the Italian philosopher and theologian who became a saint, Thomas Aquinas. The son of a landed family of soldiers and civil officials, he studied in Naples, Paris, and Cologne during the 1240s and 1250s, a time of great doctrinal conflict in the church. An avowed Aristotelian, he combined a Greek faith in reason with a Catholic faith in faith. A man of spacious intellect, he probed the nature of truth, the existence of God, the ethical bases of the state, the sources of and paths to virtue, the uses and abuses of law, the nature of natural law.

Yet all these wise and often benign writings offered little beyond perfect faith and quiet obedience to the populace looking up from peasant homes and narrow streets to the eminences towering above. In Aquinas, there was the familiar emphasis on authority, on the subordination of the individual to the state and of rights to duties, on the necessity for authoritarian government. To be sure, he insisted that authority must be legitimate, that unjust laws did not bind in conscience, that means might be found to deal with a tyrant, but in the final test people had no natural right to resist, unjust laws must be obeyed in behavior, and the best way to deal with even the cruelest tyrant was not to pull him down—this would threaten order—but to endure him and pray.

Still, as a product of changing times and intellectual conflict, Aquinas served as something of a tentative transition from the authoritarian, highly anti-individualistic doctrines of the Middle Ages to new ideas emerging slowly throughout the West.

Mounting hostility to corruption and arbitrary power in the Roman Catholic Church, dramatized in the fourteenth and fifteenth centuries by John Wyclif and the martyred John Huss, rose to a pitch in the sixteenth with the religious "reformation" led by Martin Luther. The young German monk not only attacked indulgences and other excesses of the papal establishment but defended the rights of believers to full participation in sacramental practices and urged the restoration of "our noble Christian liberty." Luther helped precipitate a great popular rebellion. "Politics were hammered out on the roads," Richard Friedenthal notes. "Conversations on the highroads—between a peasant and a nobleman, a mendicant friar and an abbot on horseback, a brothel keeper and a university scholar—were the sources from which sprang the inflammatory writings and dialogues."

A revolution for people's religious rights—but what about their political and economic rights? Luther did not challenge authority, only Catholic authority; he did not oppose order, only Catholic order. Indeed, secular political order had to be imposed from the top, he came more and more to believe, both to check the power of the Papacy and to enforce "outward peace and protection." While condemning hierarchical distinctions in the realm of faith, Luther held that social hierarchies were natural and should, if necessary, be maintained by force. And if Luther paved the way for an authoritarian Protestant regime, John Calvin institutionalized one in Reformation Geneva. Once again the peoples of Europe were confronting a religious, political, and intellectual oligarchy against which they would struggle in vain for their rights. And once again revolutionary leaders had become the guardians of a new oppressive order.

Was there no one or nothing, then, in all these centuries, no eminent theorist, no intellectually impressive creed or lasting philosophical school, to offer support to the cause of human rights for the populace, for the great majority of the less privileged? Throughout these centuries there were indeed freethinkers, dissenters, iconoclasts. Sophists and other Greek "liberals" showed some grasp of the wants and needs of the *demos* and took a somewhat egalitarian, democratic line in politics, offering a variety of prophetic contentions—that the rich should share their wealth with the poor, that all men were naturally equal and equally educable, that poverty in a democracy was preferable to prosperity under an oligarchy—but these never culminated in a coherent body of democratic thought capable of challenging Platonic authoritarianism. During the Middle Ages, while philosophers for church and state preached doctrines upholding these establishments, the populace was living its own life, claiming its own day-to-day rights, fashioning its own common law. But again, the theoreticians of the Middle Ages offered little intellectual support and no powerful vision to common men and women locked in peasant villages and urban hovels. There were ample Defenders of the Right, few defenders of people's rights.

RIGHTS FOR ALL?

"IN THE CENTURY of the Enlightenment, educated Europeans awoke to a new sense of life," wrote Peter Gay. "They experienced an expansive sense of power over nature and themselves," over "the pitiless cycles of epidemics, famines, risky life and early death, devastating war and uneasy peace," over "the treadmill of human existence."

A dynamic new sense of life and ideas, yes—but this was no overnight development. The changes that came to a climax in the Age of the Enlightenment—roughly the span of the eighteenth century—had their immediate origins in the two preceding centuries, a time of brutal warfare and hardship but also of fresh and liberating ideas, and the extension of the technology of printing permitted the wide diffusion of those ideas. A revolution in scientific thought, highlighted by the publication of Copernicus's *De Revolutionibus Orbium Coelestium* in 1543, Galileo's *Dialogo sopra i Due Massimi Sistemi del Mondo* in 1632, Newton's *Philosophiae Naturalis Principia Mathematica* in 1687, had opened minds to dazzling new concepts of time and space and of the place of humankind in the universe, just as Columbus and his fellow explorers were testing the frontiers of the earth. Politically it was an era of increasingly powerful nation-states that slowly established dominion over the principalities and city-states of the Middle Ages. Culturally it was a time of striking ventures in art and literature and theater. Informing all these new departures was a sense that humankind, long confined fatalistically in religious and social enclaves, could take possession of its own fate—could make man the "lord and master of nature," in Descartes's phrase, or the "architect of his fortune," in Bacon's.

It was no "age of the common man." Not only did war and pestilence continue unabated but they fell as heavily as ever—probably still more heavily—on the poor. The rich could move from cities to country estates as epidemics neared; they could hire the poor to do their fighting; they could employ soldiers to guard their property and themselves. The great drift of populations into political and commercial centers left onetime peasants displaced in their urban hovels, still illiterate, uneducated, and often jobless. And as for any protection or enhancement of their economic or social or political rights—philosophy was still largely silent by the early 1600s.

Still, as the rural and urban poor became more numerous, more restless, and occasionally even rebellious, philosophy moved toward a more enlightened view of humankind and its potential, a change most dramatically reflected in the political thought of two Englishmen who stood astride the two centuries like philosophical colossi, Thomas Hobbes and John Locke. Both grounded political theory in assumptions about human nature. Hobbes, born late in the sixteenth century, saw human beings as selfish, contentious, at constant war with one another, and when in a state of nature living a life that was inevitably—in his most famous phrase— "solitary, poor, nasty, brutish, and short." The implications for politics and statecraft were clear to Hobbes: people's most vital need was for order and security, the protection of life, which required submission to the absolute authority of a sovereign. Clearly there was little place for popular rights in the lexicon of this great Oxonian. Even worse, the situation would never change, for the human character was not malleable.

It was on this last point that Locke's assumptions about human nature differed most from Hobbes's. In *Some Thoughts Concerning Education,* Locke opined that the mind is born open and blank, then to be written on via the five senses. Schooling made the crucial difference. "Of all the Men we meet with, nine Parts of ten are what they are, good or evil, useful or not, by their Education." The child was not born good or bad; unlike Hobbes, Locke believed that in the original state of nature men were equal, independent, and happy. All had the right not to be injured in their lives, liberties, or possessions; hence none had the right to injure another. The rights found in nature—rights that were difficult to protect against intrusion—were safeguarded in organized society by government under the Social Contract. By this wholly theoretical contract rulers and ruled joined in compact to establish and preserve a society's political principles and institutions.

John Locke might have appeared to open the floodgate for the declaration or assumption of a wide array of human rights for all. The very idea of human malleability was revolutionary for the time, as it implied that even those born to no rights but able to learn might win both the right to rights and the capacity to make use of them responsibly. Locke, moreover, held that people had the right to resist, even to rebel against, tyrannical rule. Yet Lockean rights tended to dissolve when read in the fine print. Instead of offering a panoply of rights that might be claimed by all people, Locke concentrated his attention and affection on property rights—and his philosophy accommodated both sharp disparities in income and holdings and the unregulated economic competition that tended to intensify them. And the right of revolution, the eminent philosopher concluded, was reserved to society, not to the individual. Since revolutions are started by individuals, or groups of them, not societies, Locke's right to revolt seemed to amount to a duty not to revolt.

The era of Hobbes and Locke produced a rich array of philosophical notables—among them, Robert Filmer, James Harrington, Richard Hooker—who in their books and tracts reflected the intellectually exciting departures of the age. While they differed keenly among themselves, they formed a kind of philosophical establishment that stood united on such fundamental questions as the crucial role of human nature, the need for order and the protection of property, and the future possibilities of humankind, about which they held mingled hope and skepticism. They argued interminably about doctrines remote from the wants and needs of the people. Oceans of ink were spilled on a fiction, the Social Contract, that was nowhere to be found in history nor was an especially useful analytical construct; it served largely as an intellectual buttress to the status quo.

The people in city streets and country fields would not have recognized a Social Contract if it was posted in the marketplace by the Lord Deputy Mayor himself. What they needed was the securing of their rights, not philosophical abstractions. So what they further required was intellectual leadership that would recognize their political, social, and economic needs and make them conscious of rights that might meet those needs. And outside the philosophical establishment, some thinkers and activists were listening to the people, recognizing their needs, and preparing to lead them.

I F C O N F L I C T is the vital engine of great ideas, it is not surprising that both ideological and political combat came to a head in England in the first half of the seventeenth century. In England, because this was the land of a burgeoning mercantile and trading class eager to throw ancient constraints off its enterprise. In England, too, because of the tradition reaching back four hundred years to Magna Carta that defined government as a pact between sovereign and subjects and placed royal authority under the restraints of law. An agreement between king and barons, the great charter nevertheless provided the foundations for the evolution of the common law and of a House of Commons in Parliament and so for the extension of "fundamental liberties"—protections against arbitrary power—to the populace. When an Englishman invoked his "birthrights," it was to this tradition above all that he appealed.

The long-simmering conflict between Parliament and Crown over the tradition's meaning reached a climax in the seventeenth century. Parliament approved in 1628 the Petition of Right, a statement of civil liberties and an assertion of its own prerogatives, grounded in Magna Carta. The following year, when the Commons charged Charles I with flouting the Petition's limitations on his power, he suspended Parliament indefinitely, creating an eleven-year interregnum of "personal rule" and sharpening the confrontation that would end in civil war and the execution of the king.

During the years of crisis, the presses turned out hundreds of pamphlets of political and social protest that incited commoners and provoked authorities. Royalist, parliamentary, and radical ideas fought it out in the streets as well as in Court and Commons. Once again philosophical authority was mainly silent on the upheaval's crucial, wide-ranging issues.

In 1640, at the start of the decisive decade, Hobbes evaded the Civil War, which was to give such dark urgency to his political thought, by taking refuge in France for eleven years. He himself made the claim—for which he was later jeered—that he had been "the first of all that fled." Locke, a youth in these years, would come to justify revolution under certain narrow circumstances, but only long after Oliver Cromwell had seized power and even after the "Glorious Revolution" of the late 1680s.

Not the philosophers, not even Cromwell himself, but the rank and file—the common soldiers—of Cromwell's army raised the banner of popular rights in the late 1640s. Trusting neither king nor Parliament, fearing that even their leader might barter away the rights they hoped to gain through reforms, these soldiers and their immediate superiors formed the heart of a movement that has been called England's first left-wing party. Having overcome Charles I in earlier battles, the farmers, small tradesmen, craftsmen, tenants, and artisans who made up Cromwell's officers and foot soldiers now opposed as well many of the landed gentlemen and wealthy merchants who had triumphed with the general. Organizing their own "regimental committees," they set up presses, printed pamphlets, circulated mass petitions, and confronted Cromwell himself in debates within the army. These extraordinary debates, preserved almost verbatim in army records, provide today an authentic portrait of the mind of the *demos.*

> *Mr. Wildman:* . . . in case a Parliament, as a true Parliament, doth anythinge unjustly, if wee bee engaged to submitt to the Lawes that they shall make, if they make an unjust law, though they make an unrighteous law, yett wee must sweare obedience. I confesse to mee this principle is very dangerous. . . .
>
> *Mr. Pettus:* Wee judge that all inhabitants that have nott lost their birthright should have an equall voice in Elections.
>
> *Col. Rainborow:* Really I thinke that the poorest hee that is in England hath a life to live as the greatest hee; . . . and I doe thinke that the poorest man in England is nott att all bound in a stricte sence to that Government that hee hath not had a voice to putt himself under. . . .
>
> *Mr. Sexby:* Wee have . . . ventur'd our lives, and itt was all for this: to recover our birthrights and priviledges as Englishmen, and by the arguments urged there is none. There are many thousands of us souldiers that have ventur'd our lives; wee have had little propriety in the Kingedome as to our estates, yet wee have had a birthright. . . . I shall tell you in a worde my resolution. I am resolved to give my birthright to none. . . .

What did these citizen-soldiers want? Abolition of monarchy and aristocratic privilege, a written constitution, a representative Parliament
elected on the basis of proportional representation. These were the crucial means to the realization of their ultimate goals—religious and political equality. Caricaturing this belief in equality, their enemies claimed
they held that "commoners by right, are equal with the lords," and that
by "natural birth all men are equally and alike born to like propriety,
liberty, and freedom." Branded "levellers" by the opposition, Cromwell's soldiers proudly took on that name.

For all their comradeship in war and peace, the Levellers had their
political and intellectual differences. The sharpest of these—whether the
poor and "dependents" should have the right to vote—anticipated three
centuries of conflict over the issue. Among the soldiers this debate was
both eloquent and sophisticated. When Colonel Rainborow declaimed
that he did "nott finde any thinge in the law of God, that a Lord shall
chuse 20 Burgesses, and a Gentleman butt two, or a poore man shall
chuse none," he shrewdly added that some of the most zealous soldiers
of freedom might end up too poor to vote. But many of the Levellers
agreed with Cromwell that servants and apprentices and alms-takers
should be denied the vote not because of inferior intelligence but because
they were dependent on the will of their masters—and hence could not
control their own voting.

The oratory could not conceal the real issue—property. Cromwell's
protégé and son-in-law Henry Ireton orated boldly about the "Divine
Law" of property—"Thou shalt nott steale"—while the more subtle defenders of property rights contended that the qualification for suffrage
was not property in land or money but in labor, for labor was property,
and that when persons were dependent on others they lost the proprietorship of their labor and hence their full rights as members of the
community. To such arguments Mr. Pettus could only reply that the way
to preserve property was through free government and free suffrage, and
Colonel Rainborow's younger brother, a major, that the "cheif end of this
Government is to preserve persons as well as estates, and if any law shall
take hold of my person itt is more deare than my estate." An army
compromise authorized Parliament to judge the issue of suffrage, on the
clear but inexplicit understanding that the Commons would sustain a
property qualification—a defeat to the more radical Levellers. They had,
as consolation, the guarantee that all who had served in the army would
be exempted from "the qualifications to bee sett downe."

While Cromwell was becoming famous throughout Europe, the Levellers generated leaders from their own ranks. The most noted was John
Lilburne. Fearless to the point of foolhardiness, contentious to the point

of pugnacity, an antiroyalist who called for the expiatory execution of the king but protested the "illegalitie" of the parliamentary proceedings that condemned Charles to death, this man of self-contradictions was consistent on one supreme issue—"the rights of the people." Repeatedly jailed or exiled, until his death in his forties he published a steady stream of writings—pamphlets, tracts, denunciations, self-defenses, though no formal treatise—that made him for years the hero of the English poor. Even a left-wing democratic Leveller like Lilburne, however, would press for the erasure of inequalities in political rights while leaving intact the economic and social inequalities that scarred English society.

LAWS OF FREEDOM AND HAPPINESS

IN 1649 there arose a new and audacious movement—audacious because it called outright for a communist society in England, new because its communist ideas had not been voiced before in Europe, not even in the desperate peasant rebellions in Germany and elsewhere. The members of this movement were called Diggers after militants among them tried to seize and cultivate some unenclosed common land whose harvest they meant to give to the poor. The occupation never amounted to much, as the occupiers abandoned their experiment in the spring of 1650 after harassment by neighbors and the law, attacks by mobs, and death threats. But though their enemies destroyed their community, they could not destroy their idea, which would resonate in England for another two centuries and round the globe for over a century after that.

That idea was, then as now, boldly subversive of order and property. Concerned for the poor and the propertyless, the Diggers understood the law of nature to sanction a communal right to the means of subsistence—essentially land—with all partaking of the product of the common land and labor. Whereas the Levellers had defined the law of nature in a way that supported their doctrine of individual rights, including the individual's right to property, the Diggers discovered in natural law the right of the poor to seize and share that property as God or nature had meant it to be shared.

The Diggers' commanding voice was that of Gerrard Winstanley, one-time mystic and pantheist, later materialist and rationalist, and finally practical communist. According to Perez Zagorin, Winstanley was the first theorist "to give a reasoned elaboration to the doctrine which upholds the eternal inseparability of political liberty and economic equality." Winstanley himself, to be sure, did not express his ideas in such dispassionate terms. Rather he inveighed against property as inherently diabolical. "Most Lawes," he wrote in one of his many tracts, "are but to enslave the Poor to the Rich, and so they uphold the conquest, and are Lawes of the great red Dragon." And he attacked the enemy personally, with biblical wrath: "O you *A-dams* of the Earth, you have rich Clothing, full Bellies." But the day of judgment had begun. "The poor people whom thou oppresses, shall be the Saviours of the land." He excoriated landlords, clergymen, and lawyers with equal fervor and a fine impartiality.

Winstanley's cry—expressed most keenly in *The Law of Freedom,* a book addressed to Cromwell—was for equality not only as a matter of justice but as the essence of freedom, for the root of all bondage was poverty. His passion for equality anticipated—though probably did not influence—the writings of the French philosopher Jean Jacques Rousseau. A deeply conflicted man intellectually and psychologically, Rousseau wrote so ambiguously on the ancient issue of individual liberty and independence from the state as to set astir a thousand subsequent tempests in philosophical teapots. His portrait of liberty as an absolute but subject to the will and authority of the community, of individuals holding rights only as members of the community and not in opposition to it, culminating in his ultimate paradox of freedom—that "whoever refuses to obey the general will shall be compelled to do so by the whole body" and thus must be "forced to be free"—reflected the confusions in Rousseau's mind about individual and communal rights, but at the same time anticipated crucial dilemmas and dichotomies of the two centuries that lay ahead.

From Rousseau's intellectual murk there emerged a central value of unmistakable power—that "every man has naturally a right to everything he needs," that in an ordered society no one would have much less or much more than what he needed, that no citizen would be rich enough to buy another or poor enough to have to sell himself. In his *Discourse on the Origin and Foundation of Inequality among Men,* Rousseau wrote that wealth ruled where property was enthroned, but added that the few who were rich and powerful were in fact fellow prisoners with the many poor and weak. "The usurpations of the rich, the brigandage of the poor, and the unbridled passions of all, stifling natural pity and the as yet weak voice of justice, made men avaricious, ambitious, and evil." Large property holdings, side by side with wretched poverty, were at the heart of the problem.

At last it seemed that the rights of the poor had found a voice of intellectual authority to defend them. But Rousseau was at odds with the philosophical establishment in Paris, and after he emerged as a religious as well as an economic and political iconoclast, he was proscribed by the

Parlement of Paris, censored by the Sorbonne, and condemned by the Papacy. Having won little support from either the bourgeoisie or the poor, he died in poverty and semiobscurity. It took sixteen years and the coming of the revolution he so profoundly influenced before his remains were transferred to the Pantheon.

Yet the eighteenth century—the century of the Enlightenment—was fit for the advanced political thought of a Rousseau. In France, in the early decades of the century, Montesquieu and Voltaire presided over philosophy. Diderot and his colleagues published the first volume of the *Encyclopédie* in 1750. It was an age of relative, though perhaps only superficial, political stability. The civil strife in England was long since over; the revolutions in America and France were yet to come.

This era of surface harmony, however, was a time of intellectual ferment—a rare occasion in Western history when revolutionary ideas erupted in the lull between periods of political turbulence. And nowhere could one have found a place of greater philosophical creativity than in Scotland—a country that English and continental thinkers viewed as backward and impoverished. Its most prominent city, Edinburgh, had an urban population of perhaps 57,000 in mid-century—and it also had a flourishing university. An English visitor, more tolerant than most of his countrymen, observed that he could stand "at what is called the *Cross of Edinburgh,* and can, in a few minutes, take fifty men of genius and learning by the hand." Not many miles to the west, Glasgow, another port city, could boast that it too was a "hotbed of genius"—a center of teaching and learning not only for moral and political philosophers but also for economists, geologists, physicians, biologists, legal theorists, inventors, architects, historians, theologians.

It was in this city, smaller even than Edinburgh, that the eighteenth century's Scottish Enlightenment can be said to have commenced. It began not with a Winstanley writing revolutionary tracts for the masses or with a Rousseau struggling with his own demons but with a genteel, middle-class academic who had been born in Ireland and had taken up a post at the University of Glasgow, where he had earlier studied theology. One of "fortune's favorites," he was popular with students and colleagues, contentedly married, a man who exuded happiness, warmth, and benevolence.

Benevolence—this lay at the heart not only of Francis Hutcheson's character but of his evolving philosophy. In the teeth of the widespread Hobbesian belief that people were selfish and aggressive, Hutcheson contended that humankind was naturally faithful, kind, virtuous, and above all benevolent. In his *Essay on the Nature and Conduct of the Passions and Affections* Hutcheson maintained that Hobbes's version of human nature had created great difficulties, "since many have been discouraged from all Attempts of cultivating *kind generous Affections* in themselves, by a previous Notion that there are no such Affections in Nature, and that all Pretence to them was only *Dissimulation, Affectation,* or at best some *unnatural Enthusiasm.*" To Hutcheson "*kind generous Affections*" were neither false nor insipid qualities but potent sources of human bonding and the good society.

An arresting quality of Hutcheson's thought was the capacity to apply reason and logic to morality and benevolence. We are led by "*our moral Sense of Virtue,*" he wrote, to choose among actions on the basis of the "degrees of happiness expected to proceed from the action." Virtue was "in proportion to the *Number* of Persons to whom the Happiness shall extend . . . so that, *that Action* is *best,* which procures the *greatest Happiness* for the *greatest Numbers;* and *that,* worst, which, in *like manner,* occasions *Misery.*"

Hutcheson was no "number-cruncher" but he did offer charming if unworldly algebraic formulae to measure quantities of Benevolence and Hatred in an action, putting A (for Ability) in the denominator and qualities such as "*Moment of Good*" and "*Moment of Evil*" in the numerator. Robert Shackleton concluded that "when Hutcheson writes of 'the greatest happiness of the greatest numbers,' he is using the words literally and mathematically, and is by no means coining a propagandist slogan, and he is led, through his innovating ingenuity, into extremes of naïveté which one would expect to prove sterile." So sterile that Hutcheson's marvelous phrase about happiness survived while his formulae were forgotten.

Indeed, Western humankind had at last found its philosopher of happiness. Not that Hutcheson or anyone else so conceived of him at the time, but his philosophy of benevolence had profound libertarian and egalitarian implications for the human rights of great numbers of people. For benevolence was collective and social, as people were both givers and recipients of benevolent acts and were motivated to further benevolence by the sight of others' benevolent acts. Similarly, by pursuing one's own happiness, one spread happiness to others and came "to desire the greatest happiness and perfection of the largest system within the compass" of one's knowledge. Hutcheson's term "the *greatest Happiness* for the *greatest Numbers*" in time would become an explosive idea and slogan for Western peoples.

Hutcheson's immediate influence should not be exaggerated. Though he directly influenced such other members of the Scottish Enlightenment as David Hume and Adam Smith, as well as a host of French and English thinkers, dominant attitudes toward rights during and after his time were in sharp contrast with the Scottish philosopher's benevolence. The great passions and revolutionary thoughts unleashed during the seventeenth and early eighteenth centuries settled into gradualism, incrementalism, rationalism. Rights were no longer to be won through revolution in Britain, but rather through electoral and parliamentary action; thus Parliament passed the Reform Act of 1832 after years of factional conflict and party debate. Progress, sometimes glacial, came through an evolving common law. Rights were broken down into categories—libertarian, such as freedom of speech; political, such as the right to vote; economic, such as property rights.

All the while, Hutcheson's benevolence stood as a contrasting idea of human rights transcending narrow categories of thought. That idea, picked up by other thinkers and by actors, helped shape British and European thought through the eighteenth century and thereafter. But the Scots themselves faced one poignant, even tragic, fact. They could not translate liberty and equality directly into public policy on their own. For they were under the British Crown, governed by a Parliament located in London and ruled by men far more responsive to the ideas of Hobbes and Locke than to those of the philosopher of happiness up north. And even if they had attempted to administer benevolence, Hutcheson would not have long been there to brain-trust the operation. Fortune's favorite died at fifty-three.

CHAPTER TWO

THE NEW WORLD
OF RIGHTS

As European explorers penetrated ever more deeply into the Americas during the centuries after Columbus, mesmerizing reports and rumors, often tinged with superstition and racism, came back about the marvels of the New World. Tall tales from Brazil told of cannibals twice the size of ordinary men, of single-breasted Amazons who hunted down and ravished cowering males in order to perpetuate their species, of hermaphrodites and Cyclopes and dog-faced men. And from the icy north came stories of pygmies who lived in holes in the ground but used tools fashioned from gold and silver, of a place whose natives were one-legged, of albinos who could see only at night. As late as 1707, the scholarly Cotton Mather was warning of "Dragons, Droves of Devils, and Fiery Flying Serpents" in New England forests.

In time, new images of America replaced the old. The most enthralling for some Europeans were created by reports of settlers living freely in the wilderness, in a virtual state of nature, enjoying the natural rights that Enlightenment philosophers and savants had idealized. But for the most part these accounts too were tall tales. Settlers in North America often struggled for survival not in serene Lockean individual freedom and autonomy but in a Hobbesian world where life was nasty, brutish, and short. As they encroached on Indian lands, provoked resistance, and then engaged in murderous little battles with the original Americans, they came to prize security and order above liberty and independence.

Other myths emerged. The English in particular followed the adventures of the Pilgrims, who to some appeared to be inaugurating a Golden Age of religious liberty and assured rights in the New World. Had not the hardy band, even while still on board the *Mayflower,* drawn up a compact to protect religious freedom and to make possible "just and equall laws"? But the Pilgrims and other Puritans who flocked into Boston and Salem soon established a theocracy that sought to control every aspect of human behavior, to crush individual autonomy. Those who would not conform, said a Puritan leader, still had their liberty—to stay away from New England. By the end of the seventeenth century the Puritans were hunting and hanging witches. Once again a band of heretics and dissenters had gained power and metamorphosed into a dictatorship by the select few.

During the eighteenth century still another image brightened the European perspective on the New World—of an America led by men of intellectual genius. As new dissenters rose to inveigh against theocratic orthodoxy, the writings and examples of such rebellious ministers as Roger Williams, expelled from Massachusetts for "divers dangerous opinions," or John Wise and Jonathan Mayhew, were carried back across the Atlantic to Old World preachers and philosophers. Later Benjamin Franklin, Thomas Jefferson, John Adams, and other emissaries and visiting luminaries would be lionized in European capitals.

Perhaps the Old World was too generous in this regard. America did not yet possess—perhaps it never would possess—philosophers and intellects comparable to the Old World eminences—systematic thinkers, framers of first principles, investigators of knowledge itself. Americans could not boast a Hobbes or Rousseau, far less a Plato or Augustine. Yet, with their soaring love of liberty and autonomy, they would need thinkers whose lack of systematic doctrine would be compensated by their offering what those eminences did not—ideas for the benefit of the "lower classes" of humankind.

Eighteenth-century Americans were not yet ready to deal with this question. They were so enamored of liberty—liberty from British and other colonial domination, religious liberty, political liberty, press liberty, as well as the individual and family autonomy so many had sought in the New World—that they were not prepared to pursue such values as equality, justice, communal solidarity, and those who most needed such pursuit, who would benefit most from the realization of such values and for whom liberty was an unredeemed promise without their realization, were those least equipped to fight for them.

Still, in a land dedicated to liberty, questions of justice and equality would intensify as the population increased, cities expanded, economic inequality and social class divisions hardened, or at least became more evident through free and open debate. Once again those holding power and profiting from the status quo would ultimately confront the protests of the discontented, and once again, as in Europe, people on both sides, or on all sides, would turn to political and religious thinkers for ideas and counsel that might appear to transcend individual ambition and naked self-interest.

RIGHTS—CORNUCOPIA FOR SOME

FROM THE VAST SEEDBED of European philosophy a profusion of ideas made their way to the British colonies across the Atlantic, scattering seedlets that would produce a cornucopia of political ideas, including some strange pietistic or radical blossoms. Some of the early escapees from oppression carried ideas of liberty and other rights in their heads or their luggage. Some ideas were brought later by teachers, ministers, tutors, and others planning to ply their trades in the New World. Most came in the form of weighty books, religious tracts, political pamphlets, journals, and popular magazines printed in London, Paris, and other intellectual centers. Within a century or so the resulting harvest of ideas would be shaped into revolutionary cannon aimed straight at royal authority.

The philosophical eminences of France and Britain perhaps dominated the political thought of colonial Americans even more than that of Europeans. The towering figure for Americans has long been seen to be John Locke, whose writings on natural and inalienable rights, including his vindication of the right of revolution, appealed directly to growing American needs. A later generation of historians, including Bernard Bailyn and Gordon Wood, questioned this emphasis on Lockean liberalism and individualism, arguing rather that multiple influences were at work, notably the British Whig or republican ideas called "civic humanism," English common law, Greek and Roman classical writings, and Puritan theology. More recently Garry Wills and others put forth the still more challenging argument that the Scottish thinkers—notably Hutcheson—had the most potent impact on prerevolutionary thought.

But the search for "original influence" is ultimately frustrating and even misleading, for the intellectual, political, psychological, and cultural forces at work are so complex and multiple, and the currents flowing from the work of a given philosopher are so elusive and subtle, that central causal influences can be portrayed only in the most general and inconclusive terms. And the identification of the origins and impact of ideas is made even more difficult by the fact that these ideas are constantly impinging upon, and being shaped by, men and women who seek to realize diverse personal and communal aims by applying ideas to everyday, practical needs in an ever-shifting social and political environment.

The most palpable, everyday fact of life relating to rights in early colonial America was the church and the religious liberty its ministers and parishioners demanded. The overwhelming majority of colonists were Protestants, splintered into Congregationalists, Presbyterians, Anglicans, and Baptists, roughly in order of their numbers, along with scatterings of German Reformed, Lutherans, Dutch Reformed, Methodists, and still smaller sects. These churches fought among themselves, or at least competed for adherents in the same community. But aside from such repressive church-state establishmentarians as the Puritans, they united in their cry for religious liberty. The Protestants of America, Edmund Burke would note with unerring insight, were "of that kind which is the most adverse to all implicit submission of mind and opinion." With its claim to natural liberty, he told Parliament in 1775, "all Protestantism, even the most cold and passive, is a sort of dissent," and American Protestantism "is the dissidence of dissent."

But Catholics, Jews, even Quakers? There was a limit to tolerance. Nine of the thirteen colonies eventually established a state church. Until almost the end of the eighteenth century Massachusetts Puritans barred a man from voting unless he belonged to the correct—often the only—church in town. Virginia's Anglican establishment long viewed campaigns for toleration itself as subversive. Even Rhode Island, otherwise the very model of religious liberty, limited political participation to Protestant Christians, thus excluding Catholics and Jews. And within the Protestant sects there were more subtle but still potent forms of discrimination. "The Bible as it was variously interpreted in America's proliferating denominations," Joyce Appleby noted, "provided the basis for justifying the inferiority of women, for explaining the differences among the races, and for structuring familial relations, not to mention for conveying the sexual taboos of western Christendom." Still, to survey the rights of religious dissenters, separatists, and nonbelievers in the context of the world's long history of savage religious conflicts is to admire the tolerance and restraint of men and women who took their Bible literally and felt their own faith profoundly.

The wide practice of religious liberty, moreover, buttressed respect for other rights. These were many, and closely interrelated. "The *Liberty of the Press,*" an anonymous reader wrote the New York *Weekly Journal* in January 1734, "is the *Foundation* of all our other *Liberties,* whether *Civil* or *Religious* and whenever the Liberty of the Press is taken away, either by *open Force,* or any *little, dirty infamous Arts,* we shall immediately become as *wretched,* as *ignorant,* and as *despicable* SLAVES, as any one Nation in all *Europe.*"

John Peter Zenger, German immigrant and printer of the *Weekly Journal,* had made his paper a mouthpiece for defiance of the unpopular royal governor. Though a grand jury refused three times to indict him, Zenger was arrested and charged with publishing seditious libels against the government. The trial turned on his attorney's bold use of truth as a defense—bold because under the English law of seditious libel, as the prosecutor told the jury, "their being true is an aggravation of the crime." Zenger's lawyer retorted that by the court's standard "truth is a greater sin than falsehood." His client had "a right—the liberty—both of exposing and opposing arbitrary power" by printing the truth about it. It was unjust for government to oppress the people, provoke them to cry out and complain, and then make those complaints the basis for new oppressions and prosecutions. The jury swiftly acquitted Zenger. While the law of seditious libel remained unchanged, the Zenger case came to be considered a landmark in the struggle for press freedom and for the idea, in Stanley Katz's words, "that personal freedom rests upon the individual's right to criticize his government."

Printers and writers spoke out for freedom of the press partly from conviction, partly from professional need. Newspapers grew in colonial America like mushrooms, and sometimes seemed as short-lived. Printing was a living. Presses ground out pamphlets, broadsides, sermons, speeches, resolutions; and editors and printers feared bankruptcy almost as much as arrests and horsewhippings. Most tried to play it safe by giving voice to all sides, and through such financial considerations, the principle of a free and open press was strengthened and expanded. "Printers are educated in the Belief," wrote the most famous printer of them all, Benjamin Franklin, in an "Apology for Printers," "that when Men differ in Opinion, both Sides ought equally to have the Advantage of being heard by the Publick; and that when Truth and Error have fair Play, the former is always an overmatch for the latter: Hence they cheerfully serve all contending Writers that pay them well, without regarding on which side they are of the Question in Dispute."

Printers'—and the public's—right to a free press was flanked by other rights that became more and more powerfully asserted, especially during the mid- and late eighteenth century. As these rights broadened they became more varied, and often more ambiguous. The most basic right, the right to life itself, was "so far above dispute," observed Clinton Rossiter after a mammoth search through colonial writings, "that authors were content merely to mention it in passing." Yet few doubted the right of the state to sacrifice men's lives in order to resist external attack or opposed capital punishment. The right of conscience was placed high on the altar of liberty—but how far could one act on the basis of one's conscience? Americans claimed a right of free speech broader than that of the press—but, as the Boston *Gazette* warned in 1767, "political liberty consists in a freedom of speech and action, so far as the laws of a community will permit, and no farther: all beyond is criminal, and tends to the destruction of Liberty itself."

But whatever its form, whatever its ambiguity, liberty was the supreme right. It was more than a right—it was the highest value, and it was a tangible, palpable thing, a "jewel," precious, even "darling." America was called the vineyard of liberty. Ardor for liberty acquired a momentum of its own as the struggle for it increasingly took the form of resistance to monarchical and colonial rule. And colonists turned to the English homeland for support in their resistance to its rule. They talked about— and partially invented—a Golden Age of liberty in pre-Norman Britain, and reminded Englishmen of their own Magna Carta, the Petition of Right, and what Americans called "that second Magna Carta," the 1689 Bill of Rights that reasserted the liberties of the people and secured parliamentary supremacy over the throne. The Americans were employing one of the most powerful of revolutionary weapons—they justified their protests against their colonial masters with the values the masters professed.

If colonial America offered a mixed picture of the extent to which Americans practiced liberty and other rights, we have imposing records of the extent to which they formally recognized rights. Orators could proclaim freedom and pamphlets might have such impact as readers wished to give them, but, as Richard Hillard notes, "a constitution, once adopted, was law," as indeed were statutes. The Maryland Act for the Liberties of the People, enacted in 1639 by the "Lord Proprietarie of this Province of and with the advice and approbation of the ffreemen of the same," held that "all the Inhabitants of this Province being Christians (Slaves excepted)" shall have "such rights liberties immunities priviledges and free customs within this Province as any naturall born subject of England." The Massachusetts Body of Liberties of 1641, which served as something of a model for New York's 1683 Charter of Liberties and Pennsylvania's Charter of Privileges of 1701, guaranteed freedom of speech and petition at public meetings, right of counsel, trial by jury, "the same justice and law" for every person, and—rather remarkably—free access to public records. The Fundamental Constitutions of Carolina of 1669 were notable not only for provisions safeguarding individual rights. They were drafted by John Locke himself, though the result was scarcely a noble paean to individual liberty but, in Bernard Schwartz's words, a baroque aggregation of "outmoded feudal conceptions" and "Graustarkian layers of nobility, with its palatines, signiories, baronies, manors, court-leets, landgraves, and caziques."

If liberty, however many-sided it was to the touch, stood at the apex of American ideals in the colonial era, another value, equality, was as evocative but even more shadowy in its meaning and effect. No one pretended that the colonists had achieved an egalitarian society in their first century and a half on American soil. The colonial aristocracy—the royal governors and their circles—towered over a pyramid bottomed on large numbers of women, white indentured servants, blacks, Indians, and children. In between were the colonial elites—political, economic, and social—the landed gentry, the ever-rising mercantile groups, professional men, and the great body of clerks, artisans, farmers, tradespeople, craftsmen.

American egalitarianism was more a dream than a purpose—an end to appeal to rather than to realize. Much depended on the kind of equality colonists had in mind. Some merely wanted social or status equality with their "English cousins"—but since England had a more rigidly hierarchical society than the colonies, this want reflected envy and resentment of the "cousins," not a desire to pursue equality at home. For some Americans, equality might encompass all or part of a series of separate but overlapping assumptions—that men were equal at birth, with their futures to be determined by circumstances, intelligence, and education; that no man had an inherent right to rule over others; that men were equally bound to duties by moral obligation; that men were equal before the law; that men were equally endowed with a moral sense as to right and wrong, good and evil; that men were equally disposed to do good. On this last score there was an echo of Francis Hutcheson, who had said flatly that in the disposition to do good "all men are originally equal."

Americans experienced inequality in a variety of ways. If the early settlers had been somewhat equal in land and money, economic differences developed with remarkable speed. By the start of the eighteenth century fewer than a dozen people owned three-quarters of the land in the colony of New York, and later seven persons would control nearly two million acres in the Virginia hinterland. Rich merchants and planters might have fortunes of over $100,000, lawyers might earn $10,000 a year, but farm laborers, common seamen, and unskilled workers subsisted on less than a dollar a day. As for political equality, perhaps half of the adult white male population in colonial America was enfranchised—but this left a huge majority of all adults without the vote. And social equality? America was supposed to be a less deferential society than England or France, but the situation was confused. "On one hand," Gordon Wood notes, "social distinctions and symbols of status were highly respected and intensely coveted," yet "on the other hand, Americans found all of these displays of superiority of status particularly detestable, in fact, 'more odious than in any other country.' " Legal equality? Most white males stood in ostensible equality before the bar, but financial resources and social position could make a crucial difference. In court as elsewhere inequalities bred and fed one another.

Perhaps the fundamental contrast in this variegated picture was one that would still be familiar three centuries later—between equality of condition and equality of opportunity. Few colonists favored the former as such—it was considered "leveling." Natural distinctions of "capacity, disposition, and virtue," in the words of "Democraticus," were thought inevitable and probably desirable. But equality of opportunity based on merit was considered the very essence of republican America. In such a society "even the reins of state may be held by the son of the poorest man, if possessed of abilities equal to the important station," said David Ramsay.

But where did this leave the dispossessed? Not even on the bottom rung of the ladder of opportunity. They had no place in the colonial legislatures or bureaucracies where decisions were made, nor even in the churchly ministries and newspaper offices, the clubs and taverns where white male networks buttressed local elites. Despite the growing legend of unlimited opportunity in America, very few of the large numbers of indentured servants graduated into the middle class as "sturdy yeomen" or independent craftsmen. In some colonies the legal rights of women— in property, inheritance, land conveyance, even marriage and divorce— were improving but progress was glacial. The perhaps nearly half a million African-Americans enslaved in the South on the eve of the revolution, the thousands of black chattel slaves in New York, Rhode Island, Connecticut, and other Northern states, had virtually no rights at all, no ladder to opportunity even in sight.

These persons, typically inarticulate in political affairs and often illiterate, did not generate the internal leadership that might have helped translate their wants and needs into political demands. Grass-roots leaders may have arisen to express grievances without leaving a historical record, and slaves in some localities burst up in sporadic and desperate revolts, but a comprehensive and sustained leadership was lacking. The very idea of a coalition of the dispossessed to promote their common rights was inconceivable. America was full of rebels and radicals protesting English rule, and many a lawyer or printer spoke out to preserve his freedom. But the people of the underclass needed more than liberty and independence from Britain; how could they be sure that they would be freer under American masters than under British?

Some states granted a degree of equality before the law in their constitutions but one would be hard put to identify any other significant egalitarian measures. Clearly the early Americans were far more interested in sheltering the individual against government than in guaranteeing certain positive rights through government. To most of those who drafted the state charters, the latter idea would have seemed outlandish. In short, between liberty and equality the priorities of white male Americans in this era were clear—it was individual liberty, first, last, and almost all the way in between.

This might have appeared natural and inevitable, except for one phenomenon—Americans *talked* equality. Americans have always had "a special link with the ideal of equality," the British political historian J. R. Pole has noted. Increasingly as they approached revolution, Americans spoke of equality almost as endearingly as of liberty. The principle of equality, wrote a Virginian in 1776, "alone can inspire and preserve the virtue of its members." All men, the philosophical James Wilson had written two years before, "are, by nature, equal and free," and no one "has a right to any authority over another without his consent." But Wilson's benign comment reflected the central dilemma—equality was merely equal liberty, and equal liberty fell far short of real opportunity.

WITH SHOCKING SPEED—after decades of migration, further settlement, rural and urban growth, punctuated by rising protests against British rule, wars against French and Indians, domestic political and religious conflicts—the growing pressure for independence erupted in violence. British troops spearheading into the country north of Boston shot down Minutemen on Lexington Common in April 1775; revolutionary militia swarmed in from the countryside and turned the redcoats back at Concord Bridge, picking them off by the scores as they retreated toward Charlestown; two months later the British disgorged from ships in the Charles River and drove George Washington's troops off Breed's Hill and then Bunker Hill. Over a year passed before the Second Continental Congress declared America's independence from the mother country.

We recall these events from our school textbooks, and perhaps we still have a little sense of surprise. For the sequence of events seems wrong. Why did not a declaration of independence precipitate the first clash of arms rather than follow it by a year? Also, the dominant forces that produced the move toward independence seem unclear. Were they economic? The colonies and Britain had bitter disputes over taxation, nonimportation from England, the costs of quartering troops, and much else. Geostrategic? Perhaps Americans were merely pawns in a much larger game among the European powers. Political? Domestic conflicts earlier in the 1700s had bred cadres of young zealots ambitious for power and position, and for issues that would inflame the public. Ideological?

Explosive ideas were abroad, aimed not merely against the elites in London but against some colonial leaders as well. Historians are thrashing out such questions to this day.

An extraordinary event in Philadelphia in early 1776 throws some light on the temper of the times. The event was a literary one—the publication of a book called *Common Sense* written by one Thomas Paine—and it took America by storm. Sold as an anonymous two-shilling tract of 47 pages, *Common Sense* was an almost immediate best-seller, with well over 100,000 copies purchased in the first three months. Yet the author of this work that catalyzed American feelings was a self-educated Englishman who had not published a syllable before leaving England in 1774 and had been settled in Philadelphia for hardly a year when he wrote his pamphlet.

How could this thirty-seven-year-old immigrant meet such instant success? In part because of the style of *Common Sense*. Paine was eloquent: "The cause of America is in a great measure the cause of all mankind." He was blunt: George III was the "Royal Brute." And he was radical: he declared that after Lexington and Bunker Hill everything was changed, "the last cord now is broken," a "separation between the countries" was inevitable, and for Paine separation meant revolution. But even more, in Philadelphia he had quickly reached to the heart of popular feeling, which had then crystallized his own attitudes, which in turn, as Jack Greene has noted, brought the American people to a higher, a revolutionary political consciousness. And he could do this because in his youth, as an impoverished apprentice corset-maker and as a common sailor before the mast who had experienced terrible sea battles, he had known misery and fear, impotence and poverty just as countless poor Americans had. So when Paine spoke of American rights to independence, self-rule, and freedom, and later when he urged Americans to "establish a new social order," he was speaking for American farmers, tradesmen, seamen, mechanics, laborers in terms they approved.

Many Americans, in villages as well as cities, in taverns as well as mansions, were already mobilizing against Britain, often under their own leadership. A year before Lexington, town meetings in Massachusetts were becoming so radical in their protests that the royal governor moved to curb them. Hundreds of committees of correspondence sprang up along the length of the seaboard. Local militias were growing more militant. Radicals in Virginia and Massachusetts attracted the most attention, but Pennsylvania radicals forced the most dramatic changes. Their colony had been notorious as the most placid of the thirteen, with a strong Quaker flavor of quietism, with an "elected oligarchy" in charge, and with neither a strong dissenting tradition nor sharply felt economic vexations. Yet from mid-1774 to mid-1776 hundreds of Pennsylvanians took over local offices and boards in Paine's Philadelphia and in rural sections of the colony, swamping the old regime of entrenched sheriffs, commissioners, and justices.

These radicals were typically young, aggressive, unmoneyed, and articulate. "Do not mechanicks and farmers constitute ninety-nine out of a hundred of the people of America?" a writer demanded in the *Pennsylvania Evening Post*. If such people were to be given no share in choosing their rulers in an independent America, why not accept the government of the gentlemen in the British Parliament? "Is not half the property in the city of Philadelphia owned by men who wear LEATHERN APRONS?" he went on. "Does not the other half belong to men whose fathers or grandfathers wore LEATHERN APRONS?"

Up and down America the leathern aprons were speaking out in churches and boardinghouses, fields and streets, and as agitators aired their grievances, it became increasingly clear what Americans were rebelling against. What were they rebelling for? What about that Philadelphia letter writer who saw no point in swapping rule by English gentlemen for that by American gentlemen? The man who best answered this question was a young Virginia gentleman who in some respects was even more radical than the leathern aprons.

With his sandy hair topping a long frame, his casual, lounging ways, his agreeable manner and disdain for oratory, Thomas Jefferson hardly met the stereotype of a revolutionary, even apart from his ownership of thousands of acres of land and scores of slaves. Nor was he a political outsider; he had worked his way up through local offices in his "country" of Virginia. But neither was he among the eminent colonial leaders—the fiery Patrick Henry of Virginia, the Adams cousins from Massachusetts, John and Samuel, Christopher Gadsden of South Carolina, and over fifty others—who met in Philadelphia in fall 1774, in the First Continental Congress, to denounce British actions as unjust and cruel, to proclaim American rights, and to recommend a course of action. Jefferson did not even attend, because of illness, a Virginia convention that had met earlier in the same year to debate the crisis, but he sent in a paper, later published as *A Summary View of the Rights of British America*, that grounded the American protest in such a broad view of natural rights as to place Jefferson among the most intellectually impressive of the rising revolutionaries. He almost missed the crucial Second Congress, convened in Philadelphia in May 1775, because of family and county duties, but he arrived in time to win a remarkable recognition in June 1776—election by the Congress, along with Benjamin Franklin, John Adams, Roger Sherman, and Robert Livingston, to a committee that would draw up a declaration of independence. His new colleagues in Philadelphia encountered the wielder of such a "masterly Pen" that soon the committee asked this thirty-three-year-old to prepare a draft of the declaration.

Writing with a goose-quill pen on the tilted top of his brass-handled folding desk, Jefferson labored over the statement on the second floor of his lodgings at the southwest corner of Seventh and Market streets. He claimed later that he "turned to neither book nor pamphlet while writing it," nor need he have, for his declaration embodied the widely known ideas of John Locke and other political philosophers, repeated the ideas and phrases of earlier colonial protests, and above all invoked hallowed English precedents. Americans, according to Edward Dumbauld, considered that they were acting in the militant intellectual and political tradition of "the patriots who decapitated Charles I in 1649 and deposed James II in 1689 for violations of the compact between king and people."

Not that the "Committee of five" lacked disagreements among themselves or with the other congressional delegates. Adams and Franklin in particular offered amendments to Jefferson's text, and then Congress made further modifications. Some of these Jefferson did not relish, but Franklin, sitting next to him during the debate, amused him with the story of John Thompson the Hatter who wrote an inscription for his shop's signboard and submitted it to friends for criticism—when they were through with it nothing remained but his name and a picture of the hat.

What remained when Congress was through with Jefferson's work began, "IN CONGRESS, JULY 4, 1776, *The Unanimous Declaration of the thirteen united States of America,*" and continued with a credo and then a long list of grievances. And the words of that credo were certain to appeal to the hearts and minds of countless Americans—especially those young radicals, those mechanicks and farmers and leathern aprons in Pennsylvania and elsewhere, who were ready to fight for independence, liberty, and something more.

AN ERUPTION OF RIGHTS

THE DECLARATION OF INDEPENDENCE has been called the first American Bill of Rights, but in fact a number of colonies long before 1776 had established rights in their charters and laws. The Declaration was not even the first colonies-wide assertion of rights, for the First Continental Congress in October 1774 had approved a "Bill of Rights" invoking the entitlement to "life, liberty, & property," and in May 1776 the Second Congress had asserted the rights of colonists to defend "their lives, liberties, and properties." But nowhere had American rights—and their violation by the British—been avowed so powerfully as in the Declaration of July 4, 1776.

The words rang out—that all men were created equal, endowed by their Creator with certain unalienable rights; that among them were life, liberty, and the pursuit of happiness; that to secure those rights governments were instituted among men, and that whenever a government became destructive of those ends, it was the right of the people to alter or abolish it.

The Declaration was the most radical document Americans had yet produced—radical in its declaration of complete independence from Britain and radical in the rights asserted. For a new phrase had burst into the old litany of rights, a phrase as fecund in potential as it was benign in appearance—"the pursuit of happiness." Jefferson of course reaffirmed the historic rights to life and liberty—rights that had emerged from epic struggles. But now he quietly dropped the third in the traditional trinity of life, liberty, and property, and substituted happiness for property.

Jefferson did not make this change because he opposed people's rights to property, including his to his own, or minimized the extent to which a man's ability to fall back on his property—on his house, his tools, his land, his little kingdom—helped buttress his possession of more fundamental rights. But happiness was not for Jefferson merely some kind of pleasant sensation. Rather this further end of mankind was grounded solidly in people's daily lives and welfare. In 1788 he would urge two young American friends traveling in Europe to "take every possible occasion of entering into the hovels of the labourers, and especially at the moments of their repast, see what they eat, how they are cloathed, whether they are obliged to labour too hard; whether the government or their landlord takes from them an unjust proportion of their labour; on what footing stands the property they call their own, their personal liberty &c." While minister to Louis XVI, he even advised Lafayette how best to know his own native France, that he must travel "absolutely incognito" and "ferret the people out of their hovels as I have done, look into their kettles, eat their bread, loll on their beds under pretence of resting yourself, but in fact to find if they are soft."

The "hovels" laborers lived in, the quality of their food, the taste of their bread, the very softness of their beds—such mundane concerns might appear to have but a remote connection to the high philosophical discourses of the past. But Jefferson, who had read extensively in the writings of the Scottish Enlightenment, was only going back to the school of Hutcheson, to the Scottish and French thinkers who had not only glorified happiness as the ultimate end but had quantified and applied it.

Jefferson had prefaced his advice to his young friends traveling in Europe with the significant plea to study the influence of politics "on the happiness of the people." And what if Jefferson's friends found that the hovels of the workers were wretched, that their food and clothing were inadequate, that they were obliged to labor too hard and too much of their labor was taken from them? What if it was found that government obstructed people's pursuit of happiness, denied them that right?

In defending the rights of colonies, Francis Hutcheson had written that "large numbers of men cannot be bound to sacrifice their own and their posterity's liberty and happiness, to the ambitious views of their mother-country, while it can enjoy all rational happiness without subjection to it." Jefferson put it more bluntly and broadly a generation later, in his Declaration: "whenever any form of government becomes destructive of these ends"—including the pursuit of happiness—"it is the right of the people to alter or to abolish it" and "to institute new government" that would secure the people's "safety and happiness." Both Hutcheson and Jefferson grounded the right of resistance in happiness, in government's obligation to assure the individual's free pursuit of happiness, and since that pursuit was, as Garry Wills noted, the "efficient motive force for spreading happiness to others," government must ultimately promote "the *greatest Happiness* for the *greatest Numbers.*" The "general happiness," declared Hutcheson, "is the supreme end of all political union." By replacing property with happiness in the ancient trinity, by making not merely the security of possessions but the larger quality of people's lives, the effect of government on their happiness, the "hard political test of any reign's very legitimacy," Jefferson transformed the American case against British rule into a deeply moral cause.

And also a radical one, as radical as the milieu in which Jefferson, Adams, and the other members of the Continental Congress worked. By July 4, 1776, staid old Philadelphia had been transformed by a whole new breed of leadership—the leadership of resistance committee members, of militiamen, artisans, mechanicks, of the leathern aprons. These were the men that Tom Paine's writings had helped bring to a fever pitch by the summer of 1776—and they had their counterparts throughout the colonies in the mobilization that, in Richard A. Ryerson's words, had "begun in a thousand taverns, streets, squares, and fields." Jefferson was writing amid the early eruptions of a potentially revolutionary mass movement.

The revolution reached only marginally, however, to the more remote members of the underclasses. It reached not at all to slaves. In his original draft Jefferson had denounced the king for violating human nature's "most sacred rights of life & liberty" by "captivating & carrying" Africans "into slavery in another hemisphere, or to incur miserable death" on the slave ships. This "CHRISTIAN king" had suppressed "every legislative attempt to prohibit or to restrain this execrable commerce." Was this a proclamation of emancipation? Not at all. Jefferson, in an outburst untypical of this philosophical radical, had gone on to charge the king with exciting slaves "to rise in arms among us, and to purchase that liberty of which *he* has deprived them, by murdering the people upon whom he also obtruded them; thus paying off former crimes committed against the *liberties* of one people, with crimes which he urges them to commit against the *lives* of another." But the final Declaration, as changed by Congress on this point, proclaimed simply that the king "has excited domestic Insurrections amongst us." Jefferson's "vehement philippic," as John Adams later called it, had not been acceptable to representatives in Congress of Southern slave owners or New England traders. Yet both versions were meretricious, for the Crown had vetoed Virginia's repeated efforts to enact a colonial tariff that would shore up slavery by maintaining the price of slaves and stabilizing the slave population.

The British were quick to expose such hypocrisy. "But how did his Majesty's governors excite domestic insurrections?" demanded John Lind, a pamphleteer for the royal government. "Did they set father against son, or son against father, or brother against brother? No—they offered freedom to the slaves of these assertors of liberty." Was it tyranny to bid a slave to be free—to "hold out as a motive to him that the load which crushed his limbs shall be lightened, that the whip which harrowed his back shall be broken, that he shall be raised to the rank of a freeman and a citizen?"

This brilliant retort to Jefferson and his fellow revolutionaries cloaked the fact that the British too had compromised on slavery. There was plenty of hypocrisy on both sides. But once again black Americans were the victims as white Americans and British prated about rights but refused to share them.

BY SOME GRIM PARADOX certain wars liberate even as they kill. As the struggle against the British widened during 1776, a contagion of liberty swept up and down the eastern seaboard. State after state adopted capacious bills of rights that nailed the protection of basic freedoms firmly into their newly adopted constitutions. Virginia had led the way weeks before the Declaration with what has been called the "first true Bill of Rights in the modern American sense," for it was the first protection of individual rights "to be contained in a Constitution adopted by the people acting through an elected convention."

The states' bills of rights were remarkably similar to one another, reflecting the pervasive impact of European theory, the long philosophical interchange among the colonies, and the unity forged by war against a "tyrannical" enemy. All established rights to free speech and freedom of religion, and the trinity of natural rights to life, liberty, and property. Only the specifics of freedom varied from state to state; thus freedom of speech might include freedom of the press or of legislative debate, and two states—Massachusetts and Virginia—proclaimed freedom of conscience but admonished the citizenry to worship God. Most of the states approved some form of equality before the law, but this right was left rather vague in application except for the proscription of titles of nobility. All the declarations spelled out rights of persons accused of crime, who were to know the nature of the accusation, to be confronted by the accusers, to receive a timely and public jury trial.

Was a social as well as a constitutional revolution under way—a revolution of the right to equality, to material and psychological happiness? "The stream of revolution, once started, could not be confined within narrow banks, but spread abroad upon the land," J. Franklin Jameson said in 1925. "Many economic desires, many social aspirations were set free by the political struggle, many aspects of colonial society profoundly altered by the forces thus let loose. The relations of social classes to each other, the institution of slavery, the system of land-holding, the course of business, the forms and spirit of the intellectual and religious life, all felt the transforming hand of revolution." But in reality the American Revolution at this stage fell far short of economic and social transformation; for many American leaders, the political revolution against Britain was revolution enough.

THE DECLARATION OF INDEPENDENCE glows in our historical memory. We celebrate it every July 4 when orators quote its stirring phrases and newspapers reprint the whole document in its original script (who reprints the Constitution?). We remember the long struggle that followed the Declaration, the trauma of Valley Forge, the final defeat of King George with the indispensable help of France.

But other images of the late 1770s and early 1780s emerge more hazily. We may recall how a national government was set up with the bland title of Articles of Confederation; how the state governments wielded far greater political power than the Confederation; and how they actually put up tariffs against one another, as though they were sovereign nations. We may remember learning how "weak" the Confederation was, how depressed economically, how vulnerable the little nation was to the predatory Spanish, English, and French flanking it south and north—until George Washington rode to the rescue.

Revisionist historians have challenged some of these notions. The Articles reflected a natural shift back toward state loyalties in the 1780s, they have contended; the country made substantial progress economically, considering the intractable problems it faced at home and abroad; state governments provided significant leadership and at least protected the liberties guaranteed by their bills of rights. And toward the end of its life the Confederation brought off a stunning achievement—the Northwest Ordinance, which, based in part on an earlier plan drafted by Jefferson, not only set up an enlightened and durable plan for admitting territories to statehood but contained a bill of rights that provided for "the fundamental principles of civil and religious liberty," and even banned slavery in the vast area north of the Ohio River.

Whatever the mixed verdict of history on the Confederation, there were those at the time who had no doubt about its failures. We know their names because history is written by the victors (and by the scribblers who admired them)—Benjamin Franklin, George Washington, James Madison, John Adams, Alexander Hamilton, John Jay, and several score other leaders of hardly lesser capacity. These men were accustomed to running state governments, commanding large bodies of troops, supervising plantations, conducting diplomatic negotiations, writing constitutions. They believed of course in liberty, in diversity, in bills of rights. But they also valued order, stability, security, continuity, efficiency. They believed that liberty and order buttressed each other—neither could survive without the other. They feared that the very weakness of the Confederation would invite disorder, even a return to "tyranny" imposed by hostile forces from within or without.

When Hamilton and other leaders from five states met at Annapolis in September 1786 to discuss commercial problems, we presume that there was much grumbling about the state of the Confederation. We know that the men of Annapolis called on all states to send delegates to a convention, set for Philadelphia in May 1787, to consider the steps necessary "to render the constitution of the Federal Government adequate to the exigencies of the Union." On this proposal, as on so many others, the Confederation Congress dawdled, as did most of the states, while the activists fretted and fumed. But by now word had come of an event that would shock the nation's leaders to action. A protest against hard money and high taxes begun in Massachusetts in August was by September taking on the character of an insurrection in the western part of the state. Farmers were defying sheriffs, occupying courts and driving judges off their benches, turning debtors out of jail. An army of insurgents was forming.

Washington received the news in Mount Vernon with consternation. What was man, he demanded, that there should be such perfidy? "For

God's sake tell me what is the cause of all these commotions," Washington begged of a friend. Were these real grievances? Were they
sheer licentiousness or the fruits of British machinations? In fact Shays's
Rebellion, so called after one of its leaders, was finally but a small affair.
Federal intervention was authorized, but the revolt was easily put down
in early 1787 by state troops from eastern Massachusetts equipped with
cannon. Yet the "little rebellion" was enough to galvanize men of affairs.
Here was the final proof—the Confederation was impotent. "Commotions of this sort, like snow-balls, gather strength as they roll," Washington wrote, "if there is no opposition in the way to divide and crumble
them." In February, with the rebellion all but crushed, Congress cautiously approved the proposed convention. By May, delegates were as-
sembling in Philadelphia.

The story of the Constitutional Convention of 1787 is not about liberty. It is about unity, stability, security—about *order*. The great majority
of delegates were resolved to build a stouter, more durable union. Unlike
the Confederation, the new federal government would govern individuals directly rather than through the states, with national leaders chosen
and dismissed not by states but by citizens in direct and indirect elections.
The chief executive, with the advice of the Senate, would direct foreign
policy, and the government as a whole would control the making of fiscal
policy.

Was there no concern, then, for the craving throughout America for
liberty against government? What about those tens of thousands of citizens who had fought King George and proclaimed in taverns and on
street corners that they did not want a whole new national government
"on their backs"? Delegates of course were sharply aware of this powerful
feeling. But they had a different agenda, to create a political order in
which, they convinced themselves, liberty would be all the better protected. Having all but sealed themselves off from the outside world, they
could hardly heed the clamor of the people. They received personal
letters, and a Philadelphia Jew managed to have a petition brought before
the convention opposing any requirement that a public official swear a
Christian oath, but the delegates worked in virtual isolation.

It was their very success in framing a strong central government to
replace the Confederation that prompted demands—made even in the
last days of the convention itself, by George Mason of Virginia and
others—for a federal bill of rights. The draft constitution protected such
individual rights as that of habeas corpus and of trial by jury in criminal
cases and proscribed religious tests, bills of attainder, ex post facto laws,
but skeptics maintained that this left vast fields of individual liberty un-
guarded against the proposed national power. "There is no declaration

of any kind," wrote Mason, "for preserving the liberty of the press, or the trial by jury in civil causes; nor against the danger of standing armies in time of peace."

To these complaints, the Constitution's proponents had ready rebuttals. "The State Declarations of Rights are not repealed by this Constitution," said Roger Sherman, "and being in force are sufficient." Nor would the new national government have power to violate liberties—why deny it authority to do what it had no authority to do? But opponents answered that the states could not be depended on to enforce their bills of rights, some of which were inadequate anyway. Further, as Mason noted, if federal law was to be supreme, then "the Declarations of Rights, in the separate States, are no security." And with the broad powers extended to the new government, hard experience had proved that guarantees of individual rights against it must be made explicit.

Yet the Constitution's defenders had a fundamental argument that, oddly, was scarcely articulated. The new charter introduced a careful and elaborate "separation of powers" among the executive, legislative, and judicial branches of the federal government, better described as checks and balances. The system set up barricade after barricade to action, veto after veto by one or more of the branches of government, including an absolute veto by House and Senate over each other. Thus the central power might prove so interlocked and even deadlocked as to delay and force amendment, defeat, or nullification of measures that might threaten individual liberty. "With regard to rights," a Massachusetts Federalist noted during the long ratification debate, "the whole Constitution is a declaration of rights."

So the Constitution was signed on September 17, 1787, with no bill of rights.

ALMOST ALL the nation's prestigious leaders—among them Washington, Franklin, Madison, and Hamilton—favored the new Constitution and were prepared to work and fight for its adoption. A second team of supporters was ready in virtually all the states to push for ratification. The Federalists, as they came to be called, had interior lines of communication based on old networks of correspondence, and on conferences too, often held at estates like Mount Vernon despite the long horseback journeys. They had access to the nation's opinion leaders—newspaper editors, clergy, jurists, state politicians. Writing in behalf of the Constitution were three of the finest theorists and proselytizers in the nation—Madison, Hamilton, and Jay—who prepared for New York newspapers a series of columns that later formed *The Federalist,* "America's greatest contribution to political philosophy."

The Constitution's opponents, called the Anti-Federalists, were widely dispersed, located mainly in the hinterland away from the Atlantic port cities. They had to defeat the Constitution in at least five states, for the foresighted Federalists had provided that the charter would go into effect when ratified by conventions in merely nine states of the thirteen.

By the end of 1787 Federalist prospects appeared strong. The Delaware and New Jersey conventions had voted unanimously for ratification. The key state of Pennsylvania fell in line too, though not without a sharp struggle. When the opposition boycotted a session of the Assembly in a delaying maneuver, the Federalist majority had the sergeant at arms and his minions hunt down absentee members, hustle them into the hall, and thrust them into their seats. The Constitution later cleared the convention by a two-to-one margin, but the Assembly's violation of members' liberties did not help the cause of those arguing against a bill of rights.

Early the following year the conflict turned noisy and bitter, as Anti-Federalists mobilized throughout the interior. In taverns and editorial offices and in the streets the refrain was becoming incessant: "Why no bill of rights? Where is the bill of rights?" Opponents pictured the Constitution as a "misshapened heterogeneous monster of ambition and interest," its authors plotting to erect on the ruins of liberty one "great and extensive empire" that would empower and enrich the rulers and enslave the citizenry. From the other side, Federalists urged "O my countrymen" to reject the "mad dictates" of anarchists who were "aiming, by every artifice and falsehood, which the emissaries of hell can invent, to effect your total destruction and overthrow."

Both the invective and the stakes reached a pitch when in January 1788 delegates gathered in the bellwether state of Massachusetts. In a large Boston meeting house a formidable phalanx of Federalists, headed by the likes of former governor James Bowdoin, confronted a cohort of Anti-Federalists, led by Elbridge Gerry, who had voted against the Constitution in Philadelphia and returned to Boston breathing fire against its lack of a bill of rights. The 350 delegates from all over the state and from its "province" of Maine soon were engaged in fiery debates between one side dominated by Boston and coastal politicians, lawyers, and businessmen and an opposition consisting mainly of farmers and country notables. So brilliantly did the outlanders take on the Boston celebrities that a Federalist defeat began to seem likely.

It was at this point that moderates on both sides shaped a compromise that represented a turning point in the Massachusetts convention and ultimately in the founding era. While many Anti-Federalists were now against the whole Constitution, others asked only that it be amended to include a bill of rights. Many Federalists would now support such a bill, but flatly opposed the procedure suggested by some of their opponents— holding a "second Philadelphia convention"—from fear that their foes would use it to amend and weaken the structure of the proposed national government. Why not add a bill of rights as soon as the new government was set up? Some Anti-Federalists refused to buy this pig in the poke, but enough accepted a compromise—to "remove the fears and quiet the apprehensions of many of the good people of this Commonwealth"—by which Massachusetts would send recommended amendments along with its ratification, and a narrow victory was won for the Constitution. High principle alone did not decide the issue; John Hancock was persuaded to offer the compromise, it was said, on the promise that he would be supported for the vice presidency of the new union.

Just as the Federalists had hoped, Massachusetts set the vital precedent for later ratifications. South Carolina and Maryland endorsed in the spring, both adopting recommendatory amendments, and other states were likely to go along. But nothing could be certain until conventions met in the two big states, Virginia and New York. In June 1788 the Virginians squared off against one another—the Federalists with the Constitution's principal author, James Madison, at their head and strengthened by such men of rising eminence as John Marshall, arrayed against a brace of young politicos, including James Monroe, as well as such veteran leaders of the revolutionary struggle as George Mason and Benjamin Harrison. The Anti-Federalists were led by the man from Prince Edward County, the indomitable Patrick Henry, who had lost none of his devotion to liberty. "The rights of conscience, trial by jury, liberty of the press, all your immunities and franchises, all pretensions to human rights and privileges, are rendered insecure, if not lost, by this change," he told the rapt convention.

"Liberty, the greatest of earthly blessings—give us that precious jewel, and you may take every thing else! But I am fearful I have lived long enough to become an old-fashioned fellow. Perhaps an invincible attachment to the dearest rights of man may, in these refined, enlightened days, be deemed old-fashioned; if so I am contented to be so."

The next day Madison, speaking in a low voice that sometimes failed to carry to the packed hall, met Henry head-on. Henry had suggested that "licentiousness has seldom produced the loss of liberty; but that the tyranny of rulers has almost always effected it. Since the general civilization of mankind, I believe there are more instances of the abridgment of the freedom of the people, by gradual and silent encroachments of those in power, than by violent and sudden usurpations," but Madison admitted as well that majorities trampling on the rights of minorities could generate factions and disorder that in turn might produce despotism. The Constitution, however, with its checks and balances, had been carefully contrived to prevent both ambitious rulers and popular majorities from usurping power.

The oratorical and constitutional battle was so evenly and brilliantly fought that the Constitution might not have prevailed on its merits. When the Federalists won on June 25 by a narrow 89–79 vote, the outcome was due in good part to local interest—all but one of the sixteen delegates from the Alleghenies voted aye because they expected a strong federal government to clear their lands of Indians. And George Washington, following matters closely from Mount Vernon, had lent his unparalleled prestige to the Federalist cause. But the Federalists had also been obliged to consent to the most sweeping package of recommendatory amendments adopted by any state.

The climactic convention, a few hundred miles north in Poughkeepsie, was already in session when the Virginians concluded in Richmond. Like other states, New York was divided between commercial-cosmopolitan spokesmen from the urban seacoast and rural and small-town politicos from the interior, and once again the issue of the absent bill of rights dominated debate. Would the Federalist strategy of promising amendments after the government was set up prevail over the Anti-Federalist strategy of demanding a bill of rights before the Constitution would be ratified? Word that New Hampshire had provided the ninth—and decisive—ratification did not deflect George Clinton's Anti-Federalists; it was news of the defeat in Virginia that crushed their last hopes. The everpractical Alexander Hamilton had arranged for express riders to bring the tidings from Richmond, and his virtuoso performance in the debates helped tilt the outcome toward recommendatory rather than conditional amendments. Even so, the narrow margin on July 26 for unconditional ratification, 30–27, attested again to the popular fear that the Federalists would not keep their promise.

The Federalists had won. Or had they? The most remarkable aspect of the whole ratification struggle was the ability of mainly hinterland people, lacking the prestigious leadership of the Federalists, to force their opponents to accept rights as the crucial issue. Once again rights had to be demanded, and once again lower-income, lower-status people had to demand them. But the question remained—with the Constitution safely enacted, would the Federalists honor their promise of a bill of rights?

JAMES MADISON'S POLITICAL SOMERSAULT

HOPES WERE HIGH late in 1788 for the enactment of a sweeping bill of rights. Surely Anti-Federalists who had demanded such a declaration and Federalists who had made the switch to it would combine to make rights the first order of business when the new government was set up. And after their delegates had fought for a declaration of rights in the ratifying conventions, the people expected it. But it would be three and a half years after New Hampshire ratified the Constitution in June 1788 before the Bill of Rights was finally adopted.

The difficulties were complex and shadowy. One was James Madison's early opposition to a bill of rights. At the 1787 convention he, like most of the other delegates, had had as his paramount concern the establishment of a strong and stable federal government. And he had watched with considerable annoyance as fellow Virginians like Mason and Henry had seized upon the lack of a bill of rights as their main cudgel for pummeling the new charter; Madison suspected, rightly in some cases, that opponents were more intent on protecting states' rights in economic matters than on protecting the people's liberties.

Still, he had to share the blame for what Leonard Levy, with the perspective of two centuries, would call a "colossal error of judgment" in omitting rights, then for his refusal to admit the error, and then for advancing "impolitic and unconvincing" arguments to justify the omission. And Madison played only a grudging role in the grand compromise, initiated in Massachusetts and consummated in Virginia, by which Anti-Federalists were induced to accept the Constitution on the promise of an added bill of rights. Indeed, at the Virginia ratifying convention Madison was still arguing that the Constitution as framed in Philadelphia was "infinitely more safe" than "it would be after introducing into it that long train of alterations" that the Anti-Federalists "call amendments."

Within a year of that stance Madison—this steady, principled constitution-builder—performed an intellectual and political somersault. He became the principal champion of bill of rights amendments. Why this flip-flop? In part the challenge posed by Thomas Jefferson, serving then as American minister to France, in an extraordinary transatlantic dialogue with Madison the intellectual. Even more, a desperate "appeal to the people" by Madison the ambitious politician.

The dialogue, made all the more remarkable by the months and sometimes the year it took their letters to cross the Atlantic, began with a long missive—over 5,000 words—that Madison penned to Jefferson late in

October 1787. It was the letter Jefferson had eagerly awaited, packed with information about the proposed charter. But he had to read through endless pages on procedures and powers before he came to the subject he was most interested in—rights. Here Madison was not forthcoming, even disappointing, referring to the subject mainly in terms of the Constitution's opponents. Of their fellow Virginian George Mason, Madison wrote: "He considers the want of a Bill of Rights as a fatal objection."

So did Jefferson. In replying to Madison he listed what he did like in the charter—a federal government that could stand on its own feet. He also pronounced himself "captivated" by a legislature that would give equal representation to small states and proportional representation to large states in its separate Senate and House.

"I will now add what I do not like," Jefferson went on. And what he did not like first and foremost was the "omission of a bill of rights providing clearly and without the aid of sophisms for freedom of religion, freedom of the press, protection against standing armies," and other securities. The ordinarily reserved Jefferson minced no words. A bill of rights, he went on, "is what the people are entitled to against every government on earth, general or particular, and what no just government should refuse, or rest on inference."

This rebuttal from his longtime mentor and friend must have upset Madison, since he responded rather disingenuously in October 1788. "My own opinion has always been in favor of a bill of rights; provided it be so framed as not to imply powers not meant to be included in the enumeration." But he had never thought its omission a "material defect," he went on airily, and had only favored it because it was "anxiously desired by others." Madison then trotted out the well-worn arguments against a declaration—that the new government would not be given power to violate rights, that the Constitution, by barring religious tests, "opened a door for Jews Turks and infidels," that state bills of rights had been only "parchment barriers" against overbearing majorities.

This last point, however, led Madison to the kind of analysis that had already marked him as a "profound scholar and philosopher." Responding directly to Jefferson, he wrote: "Wherever the real power in a Government lies, there is the danger of oppression. In our Governments the real power lies in the majority of the Community, and the invasion of private rights is *chiefly* to be apprehended, not from acts of Government contrary to the sense of its constituents, but from acts in which the Government is the mere instrument of the major number of the constituents. This is a truth of great importance, but not yet sufficiently attended to: and is probably more strongly impressed on my mind by facts, and reflections suggested by them, than on yours which has contemplated abuses of power issuing from a very different quarter."

What different quarter? Madison saw Jefferson, with his position at the court of the French king, as more concerned about tyranny by monarchs than by majorities. But wherever there was an "interest and power to do wrong," Madison went on, "wrong will generally be done, and not less readily by a powerful and interested party than by a powerful and interested prince." Madison appeared to be making a strong case for a bill of rights as the way to protect individual rights against overbearing government, but no, he saw little danger in the new government. He argued and worried the issue back and forth, and finally concluded with a masterly summary of the dilemma: "It is a melancholy reflection that liberty should be equally exposed to danger whether the Government have too much or too little power; and that the line which divides these extremes should be so inaccurately defined by experience."

To these brilliant equivocations Jefferson responded in March 1789 with sledgehammer certainties. A declaration of rights might not be broad enough? "Answer. Half a loaf is better than no bread. If we cannot secure all our rights, let us secure what we can." Limited federal power and opposition from jealous states would combine to protect liberty? "Answer": A declaration of rights would set a standard for both levels of government. Experience had proved that a bill of rights was not always an effective protection? "True. But tho it is not absolutely efficacious under all circumstances, it is of great potency always." Then Jefferson came to his own stunning argument. A declaration of rights, he granted, might "cramp government in it's useful exertions." But "the evil of this is shortlived, moderate, and reparable. The inconveniencies of the want of a Declaration are permanent, afflicting and irreparable: they are in constant progression from bad to worse."

Jefferson's belief in government by the people—in majority rule provided that individuals were protected against oppression—was buoyed early in 1789 by the rising revolutionary fervor in France. He was in close touch in Paris with an early leader of that revolution, his young friend Lafayette. Sharing Jefferson's disappointment that the new American Constitution contained no bill of rights, Lafayette drafted a ringing French manifesto that might take its place next to Jefferson's Declaration of 1776. As Lafayette later described it, he held at this time "an ardent wish" that "a Revolution might take place in this country founded on our American principles of Liberty and Equality." He showed his draft to Jefferson, who was impressed enough to send it on to Madison. Perhaps Jefferson hoped that his fellow Virginian might be inspired toward an even greater effort for an American bill of rights.

It was hardly necessary. By this time Madison had been thoroughly convinced not only by Jefferson but by events that a bill of rights must be added to the Constitution. And Madison in turn had persuaded Jefferson that the Constitution met his mentor's exacting criteria for popular government. It had been Jefferson's genius that three thousand miles away he could detect that the Federalists had made a huge mistake in omitting a bill of rights and that they must ultimately accept it, because the people insisted on it. Writing to another correspondent a week after penning his "half a loaf" letter to Madison, Jefferson maintained that "this security for liberty seems to be demanded by the general voice of America." It was Madison's talent that he could sense the shift in popular attitudes on the bill of rights issue and that he could respond to it in time.

A great strategist united with a brilliant tactician—this was the formidable partnership that stretched across the Atlantic. But Jefferson was more than a strategist—he was a moral philosopher who viewed a declaration of rights as a matter less of political expediency than of natural, inalienable human freedoms. And Madison was more than a tactician—he saw the threat to liberties from inflamed majorities and hence the need for a stable, orderly government to control faction. Both men recognized, however, that the moral claims of rights would not be enough in themselves to carry the day for liberty. Rights had to be fought for in every sector of the political battlefield, by thousands of grass-roots warriors led by able leaders with strong values.

POWERFUL though Jefferson's arguments were, they were not the principal reason for James Madison's somersault. As Paul Finkelman and other historians have pointed out, Madison was shifting his position even as key letters from Jefferson were making their slow oceanic crossing.

For reasons ranging from a high sense of moral duty to sheer ambition, Madison wanted to be a member of the federal government that would be established in New York in the spring of 1789. His great wish was to be chosen for the new Senate, but any chance of this went glimmering when a vengeful Patrick Henry, leading Virginia's campaign for a second convention, threw his decisive influence behind two Anti-Federalist partisans. Madison then considered a run for the House of Representatives, only to encounter again the animus of Henry, whose troops in the state legislature had carved out a congressional district that Madison would have a hard time carrying. So hard that Madison, despite the discomfort of travel through winter cold and snow and his dislike of electioneering, decided he must journey from New York to Virginia to fight for the seat. It was already rumored that the relentless Henry had fashioned another masterstroke—persuading the popular young James Monroe to oppose Madison.

Madison expected that he could beat Monroe, an old friend and another protégé of Jefferson, in a fair fight. But he had not anticipated the

strength of feeling against an unamended Constitution or the effectiveness with which the Anti-Federalists were broadcasting their charge that,
as he wrote to Washington, "I am dogmatically attached to the Constitution in every clause, syllable & letter" and that he would not vote for a
single amendment. "This," he added ominously, "is the report most
likely to affect the election." Touring key areas of his district, sometimes
sharing the platform with Monroe, Madison again and again pledged his
willingness to consider amendments. He also wrote letters of reassurance
to local influentials. Stung by accusations that he had "ceased to be a
friend to the rights of Conscience," Madison gave his "sincere opinion"
to a Baptist minister that the Constitution must be revised and that in
Congress he would work for "the most satisfactory provisions for all
essential rights, particularly the rights of Conscience in the fullest lati-
tude, the freedom of the press, trials by jury, security against general
warrants &c." Thus Madison sought to calm fears and hostility toward the
Constitution and himself as its chief defender, and voters responded in
February 1789 by giving him a convincing victory over Monroe. Baptists
in particular had supported him strongly.

Madison's campaign had exposed him to what he would much later
describe as the "desires of the body of the people." In his victory lay a
far greater significance than the election of one man, however brilliant,
from one constituency in the heart of Virginia. While we know even less
about the "making of a congressman" in other races for the first House
of Representatives than we do about Madison's, we can assume that
similar popular support for a bill of rights stretched through many districts. Here was the great opportunity for the people—at least for eligible
voters, white property-owning males—to speak out, and they did. The
unsung heroes of the Bill of Rights were the Baptists and other lovers of
liberty at the grass roots of American politics.

Madison's next political battlefield was the House of Representatives.
On his return to New York in March 1789 for the first sitting of Congress,
he began to draft a set of rights amendments. He had before him over
two hundred state proposals. Many of these expressed in similar language a common call for the protection of certain individual rights—six
states had demanded the inclusion of the rights of conscience, five had
asked for guarantees of press freedom, with three adding free speech,
four had insisted on the incorporation of due process and speedy trials
and bans on excessive bail or cruel and unusual punishment, three had
proposed the right against self-incrimination and the significant stipula-
tion that rights not enumerated in amendments be reserved to the people—reflecting, in Bernard Schwartz's words, "the consensus that had
developed among Americans with regard to the fundamental rights that

ought to be protected by any Bill of Rights worthy of the name." The roots of that consensus—the determination to secure the liberty of the individual against authority—lay in the English heritage, the long and often turbulent development of constitutional principles since Magna Carta, in the doctrines of natural rights theorists; it had been steeled in the revolutionary struggle, sharpened in the wars over ratification.

While Madison relied heavily on the comprehensive rights proposals of his native Virginia, his work reflected the national consensus: of the twenty-two amendments advanced by at least four states, fourteen found their way into his draft. But, as Schwartz noted, Madison was no "mere compiler." He had to sift through the state offerings, decide which merited congressional consideration, weigh which would survive the political gantlet through both houses of Congress and the state legislatures, and refine their language, making them "both an eloquent inventory of basic rights and a legally enforceable safeguard of those rights."

By early May, a month after the House convened, Madison was ready, and he gave notice that he would soon "bring on the subject of amendments to the constitution." But it would not be so easy. Despite George Washington's cautious encouragement of amendments the week before in his inaugural address—he had called, in a speech Madison had helped to draft, for a balance between "a reverence for the characteristic rights of freemen" and "a regard for the public harmony"—Madison's fellow representatives showed little enthusiasm for redeeming the Federalist promise. Rather, the "first congressmen" already were struggling over two issues that would preoccupy them for much of the next two centuries at least—taxes and tariffs. While Madison yearned to present his proposals for amendments, he had to listen as the representatives conducted a sometimes sordid debate over who got what, when, and how much—and, even more mortifying, he was compelled to step in and speak up for his own home interests and factions.

Again and again Madison requested the floor to introduce his proposals. Again and again he was put off with arguments that money to fund the government had to be raised first. Madison warned the representatives that continued delay "may occasion suspicions" among their constituents, who considered their rights "as not sufficiently guarded."

On June 8, 1789, Madison gained the floor, determined to offer his amendments. Once more he was told that it was premature, unnecessary, that "without revenue the wheels of Government cannot move." A gentleman from Georgia proclaimed grandiloquently that the Constitution was "like a vessel just launched," lying at the wharf untried, and any precipitous alteration might "deface a beauty, or deform a well proportioned piece of workmanship." But this time Madison regained the floor and plunged ahead. He was not an especially good speaker, and his address was neither very elegant nor very eloquent, but it can be ranked as one of the great public utterances, for he was reasonable, fair-minded, and above all explicit.

The rights seemed to take palpable form when he proposed that the "civil rights of none shall be abridged on account of religious belief or worship, nor shall any national religion be established, nor shall the full and equal rights of conscience be in any manner, or on any pretext, infringed." And when he proposed that the "people shall not be deprived or abridged of their right to speak, to write, or to publish their senti-ments; and the freedom of the press, as one of the great bulwarks of liberty, shall be inviolable." Madison did not, however, present these and his other proposals as a separate bill or declaration. Rather, they were to be scattered throughout the body of the existing Constitution—in the case of the above civil rights, "in article 1st, section 9, between clauses 3 and 4."

Still the House would not act. Madison had to wait more weeks while his colleagues, in time-honored parliamentary fashion, debated proce-dure rather than substance. It was not until late July that a select commit-tee was appointed, and mid-August before the lower chamber "resolved itself into a Committee of the whole" to take the amendments under consideration. Now at last the House got down to business.

The debate that followed, taking up each of Madison's proposals in its turn, was so intense and multisided that Madison himself confessed to finding it "exceedingly wearisome." But he and his allies remained in control most of the time, negotiating, placating, demanding, yielding. Madison could be firm too; he wrote Edmund Randolph that "it has been absolutely necessary in order to effect any thing, to abbreviate debate, and exclude every proposition of a doubtful & unimportant nature." Two thoughts weighed on him: that however much the House inclined to passivity, the people would demand action, and that Jefferson was follow-ing matters closely from Paris. "I like it as far as it goes," Jefferson said of one draft Madison had sent him, "but I should have been for going further."

By the required two-thirds vote on August 24, the House finally ap-proved a package of seventeen rights amendments, now in the form of articles to be attached to the end of the Constitution. These were read to the Senate the next day, and here the whole process had to be re-peated. But little of the Senate deliberation has come down through history because the upper chamber met behind closed doors. The sena-tors struck a blow against federal limitations on the power of states when they dropped the House amendment that prohibited the states from

BILL OF RIGHTS

Amendment I

Congress shall make no law respecting an establishment of religion, or prohibiting the free exercise thereof; or abridging the freedom of speech, or of the press; or the right of the people peaceably to assemble, and to petition the Government for a redress of grievances.

Amendment II

A well regulated Militia, being necessary to the security of a free State, the right of the people to keep and bear Arms, shall not be infringed.

Amendment III

No Soldier shall, in time of peace be quartered in any house, without the consent of the Owner, nor in time of war, but in a manner to be prescribed by law.

Amendment IV

The right of the people to be secure in their persons, houses, papers, and effects, against unreasonable searches and seizures, shall not be violated, and no Warrants shall issue, but upon probable cause, supported by Oath or affirmation, and particularly describing the place to be searched, and the persons or things to be seized.

Amendment V

No person shall be held to answer for a capital, or otherwise infamous crime, unless on a presentment or indictment of a Grand Jury, except in cases arising in the land or naval forces, or in the Militia, when in actual service in time of war or public danger; nor shall any person be subject for the same offence to be twice put in jeopardy of life or limb; nor shall be compelled in any criminal case to be a witness against himself, nor be deprived of life, liberty, or property, without

infringing on freedoms of conscience, speech, and press, and the right to a jury trial. To Madison this was "the most valuable amendment in the whole list." One right he opposed was the right of states to deny rights. It would be nearly a century and a half before federal protections of individual rights began to be cautiously extended as checks against repressive action by states.

due process of law; nor shall private property be taken for public use, without just compensation.

Amendment VI

In all criminal prosecutions, the accused shall enjoy the right to a speedy and public trial, by an impartial jury of the State and district wherein the crime shall have been committed, which district shall have been previously ascertained by law, and to be informed of the nature and cause of the accusation; to be confronted with the witnesses against him; to have compulsory process for obtaining witnesses in his favor, and to have the Assistance of Counsel for his defence.

Amendment VII

In Suits at common law, where the value in controversy shall exceed twenty dollars, the right of trial by jury shall be preserved, and no fact tried by a jury, shall be otherwise re-examined in any Court of the United States, than according to the rules of the common law.

Amendment VIII

Excessive bail shall not be required, nor excessive fines imposed, nor cruel and unusual punishments inflicted.

Amendment IX

The enumeration in the Constitution, of certain rights, shall not be construed to deny or disparage others retained by the people.

Amendment X

The powers not delegated to the United States by the Constitution, nor prohibited by it to the States, are reserved to the States respectively, or to the people.

Ratified December 15, 1791

The final passage of twelve amendments by Congress late in September testified to the brilliant legislative leadership of Madison and his colleagues. They had had to mobilize two-thirds support in two chambers and adjust differences between House and Senate. Madison must have reflected throughout the proceedings on the cumbersome legislative process he had helped father at the Constitutional Convention. Fearful of majority rule, he had favored the two-thirds requirement for especially important measures. He must have reflected further on the laborious process of ratification by state legislatures for constitutional amendments. The first two of the twelve amendments sent to the states—concerning the number of representatives and congressional pay—were not ratified, and over two years passed before three-quarters of the states approved the remaining ten. Massachusetts, Connecticut, and Georgia did not return formal notices of ratification to the federal government until they did so as a symbolic gesture on the 150th anniversary of congressional approval of the Bill of Rights, in 1939.

There were other ironies. The conversion, over Madison's objections, of the rights amendments into a separate series of articles attached to the Constitution—first proposed, ironically, by Roger Sherman, a persistent foe of enumerated rights—made the Bill of Rights far more visible and comprehensible than if they had been scattered through the body of the charter. And Virginia, home of the most eminent preachers of liberty and equality, was the state that erected the greatest barriers to passage, with bitter-end Anti-Federalists denouncing Madison's work as "inadequate," as well as the last to ratify. This reluctance too had its ironic edge: many Virginians who had opposed the 1787 document ostensibly because of its lack of a bill of rights had resisted in fact because they feared that the new federal power would threaten states' rights; later, when Madison & Co. moved toward adding rights amendments, some of these same Virginians resisted because they dreaded the loss of an issue around which they could rally their disparate forces.

A final and most costly paradox was that this great charter of liberty failed to—as it was never intended to—redress the injustices inflicted by the Constitution on three classes of Americans. Slavery was nowhere explicitly mentioned in the Constitution and thus was at the very least condoned. Madison in 1787 had said that it would be "wrong to admit in the Constitution that there could be property in men," but he had also assured the Virginia ratifying convention that "no power is given to the general government to interpose with respect to the property now held by the states." Slaves appeared in the document only by implication, as the "such Persons" with whose importation Congress was barred from interfering before 1808, as the "other Persons" valuated as three-fifths of "free Persons" in the apportionment of representatives and taxes, and as those "held to Service or Labour" who, if they succeeded in fleeing to "free" states, had to be returned to their owners. Despite Madison, the American Constitution indeed regarded slaves not as citizens or as beings endowed with unalienable rights but as articles of commerce, as property. And on this, the Bill of Rights was silent. Women were not mentioned in the Constitution, and as qualifications for suffrage were to be left to the decision of the separate states, states would continue to deny the voting rights of American women. Finally, the Constitution's reticence on suffrage empowered the states to maintain their property requirements, thus denying the right to vote and effective representation to the unpropertied. And for these too the Bill of Rights made no amends. Yet the very existence of a Bill of Rights ironically would give those who were not protected by it a potent focus and a resounding rallying cry in future struggles for their rights.

But practical purpose outweighed paradox. The enactment of the Bill of Rights was primarily the result of a ground swell of popular support throughout the states, of the rights consensus lying deep in a people fired by its love of liberty. That popular consensus was expertly marshaled by Madison and hundreds of other Federalist leaders, national, state, and local, propagandizing and politicking throughout the new nation. And Madison, demonstrating superb legislative leadership, pulled together scores of rights amendments proposed by the states and shaped, with the invaluable help of other members of Congress, the terse, no-nonsense Bill of Rights.

But Madison's role posed another paradox. The man who came down through history as the "Father of the Constitution," and particularly of its checks and balances and antimajority roadblocks, was almost defeated by those roadblocks, especially the convoluted amending process—but by overcoming them he earned the designation that truly fitted him, "Father of the Bill of Rights."

CONSENSUS AND CONFLICT

THE STORY of the ratification of the Bill of Rights by the states is a "black hole" of American history. The legislatures that slowly endorsed the amendments over a two-year period left virtually no records. Still, there is little mystery as to what happened. After the long process of framing the amendments, a powerful grass-roots consensus propelled them through the states. But consensuses do not make for much excitement, and it is no wonder that, when the Bill of Rights became part of the Constitution on December 15, 1791, there was no great national celebration and, so far as we know, few local ones. The historic battle over rights ended, at least for the time, not with a whimper but in a whisper.

All this was in sharp contrast with a scene across the seas. While Madison was looking for an opportunity to bring his rights amendments before the House, Louis XVI had convened the Estates General in Versailles to consider fiscal reform, and when it became clear that political and social reforms were also to be demanded of the royal government and the king dithered, representatives of the commoners' third estate, together with members of the clergy and a number of aristocrats, proclaimed themselves a National Constituent Assembly; on July 14, 1789, Parisian sansculottes—artisans, small shopkeepers, housewives—swarmed into the Bastille. As the American Congress debated the proposed bill of rights, the French Assembly was passing "decrees abolishing the feudal system," wiping out tax and other privileges, issuing a powerful Declaration of the Rights of Man and of the Citizen that laid out fundamental "inalienable rights"—liberty, property, security, equality of all before the law, freedoms of speech, press, religion, and assembly—and planning a constitution that would establish a limited monarchy ruled largely by property owners.

On most of this Thomas Jefferson gazed benignly, first from his post in Paris and then as Washington's secretary of state after the American government established itself in New York. The revolutionary skies darkened in France as war broke out with Austria and Prussia and later with Britain, as the monarchy was abolished, the Republic proclaimed, Louis XVI executed, and the Jacobin Reign of Terror inaugurated. Jefferson defended the Jacobins, despite their excesses, and even the Terror that devoured cadre after cadre of earlier revolutionaries, beheaded liberal and moderate sympathizers, and incidentally jailed for a time Jefferson's friend Lafayette, who had turned against the revolution.

Jefferson believed that higher stakes were involved. "The liberty of the whole earth," he wrote a friend, "was depending on the issue of the contest, and was ever such a prize won with so little innocent blood?" Yet even as more and more blood ran in the gutters of Paris, over the fields of the Vendée and elsewhere, Jefferson's faith in the revolution hardly wavered, nor did his fear diminish that if the revolution was defeated, especially by the hated British, the cause of liberty would be set back around the world.

Other Americans stared aghast at the Terror's crushing of liberty in the name of liberty. Washington, who had hailed the first renovation of the French constitution under Lafayette's influence as "one of the most wonderful events in the history of mankind," had also feared that France "would not be sufficiently cool and moderate" in securing its freedom. Now this preacher and exemplar of ordered liberty was seeing his worst fears realized. And as the Terror sundered French families, communities, and the revolutionaries themselves, it also helped to polarize Americans.

It had been relatively easy for the young republic to debate whether to have a bill of rights, what kind of rights, and how they were to be enacted; these were essentially domestic questions. It was something else to debate rights in what became a deadly context of, on the one hand, rising popular sentiment against "royalist" Federalist rule, with its suspected pro-British leanings, and on the other the most intense feelings against "Jacobins" at home as well as abroad. Soon this compound of domestic and foreign concerns flared into all-out ideological and political war—a time of such brutal strife that Washington claimed he did not see "how the Union of the States can be much longer preserved."

The war appeared to observe no polemical borders and to respect no persons. The President, once so universally revered, now writhed under savage assaults even from such old revolutionary comrades as Thomas Paine, who denounced Washington as "treacherous in private friendship, and a hypocrite in public life," and then asked "whether you have abandoned good principles, or whether you ever had any." Republicans labeled administration Federalists "blood suckers," monarchists, tyrants. Federalists labeled Republicans Jacobins, anarchists, "the French party." The war of words escalated as they took sides in the shooting war between Britain and France. Now each saw its opposition as conspiratorial and subversive. Thus within a few years after its birth the new republic was facing a problem that would harry it for at least two centuries further— the merger of fierce domestic political and ideological conflict with sulfurous foreign questions, leading to accusations of treason all around.

It was in this context that the Whiskey Rebellion of the summer of 1794 took on exaggerated significance for many Americans. As a revolt it was almost trifling: a small excise tax on liquor had inflamed western Pennsylvania farmers, who were cash-poor and found they would have to pay the tax even on what they drank at home. Some mobs destroyed excise offices and threatened to tar and feather tax collectors. Still, it was the first real challenge to federal authority, and evoked the President's worst memories of Shays's Rebellion and other disorders. In a massive overreaction he called up several state militias, which put the rebels to flight. European friends could now see, a satisfied Washington wrote to an old acquaintance, that under no form of government would "laws be better supported, liberty and property better secured, or happiness be more effectually dispensed to mankind" than under the American republic. Liberty yes, but order above all.

THE EXPERIENCED, well-read men and women of the 1790s knew the price of excessive order—a swing of the pendulum back toward anarchy. Nevertheless men like Washington and John Adams, who succeeded Washington in March 1797, and scores of other leaders who had fought for liberty as revolutionaries, only seven years after the adoption of the Bill of Rights were targeting the kinds of acts they themselves had once committed. In one four-week period in June and July 1798 a Federalist-dominated Congress passed measures that directly threatened freedom of speech and press and other liberties so recently enshrined in the ten amendments. The Naturalization Act almost tripled the five-year period of residence required for admission to full citizenship. The Alien Act authorized the president to expel aliens regarded as dangerous to the public peace and safety or suspected of "treasonable or secret machinations." The Alien Enemies Act empowered the president in time of war to imprison or deport aliens subject to an enemy power. The Sedition Act would punish by fine and imprisonment any alien or *citizen* guilty of "advising" or attempting "any insurrection, riot, unlawful assembly, or combination," or of uttering or publishing "any false, scandalous and malicious writing" bringing into disrepute the federal government, Congress, or the president.

The measures aptly mirrored Federalist fears of restless immigrants, of enemy conspiracies during wartime, Federalist hatred of blunt criticism, of factional opposition, indeed of the very idea of Opposition. Federalist constitutional justifications of the Sedition Act were based in a theory of press freedom that had advanced little since the prosecution of John Peter Zenger under English law. The Federalists interpreted the First Amendment narrowly, as protecting "liberty" of the press but not "licentiousness," "truth" but not "falsehood," and having no doubt where "falsehood" lay, they moved easily to criminalize criticism of their government. Printers, warned a Republican opponent, "would be afraid of publishing the truth, as, though true, it might not always be in their power to establish the truth to the satisfaction of a court of justice"—especially if that court was presided over by a Federalist judge.

Not that the Federalists were monolithic. Even the presidential couple was somewhat divided. Abigail Adams, furious over the "most wicked and base, violent and calumniating" attacks on her husband, called for a bill that would shut up obnoxious newspapers. Her husband neither fathered nor urged the Sedition Act, and later appeared to disclaim it; but he joined the Federalist clamor against the opposition's "profligacy, falsehood, and malignity in defaming our government," he signed the Alien and Sedition laws, and he backed up their chief enforcer, Secretary of State Timothy Pickering. In general, despite differences over details, the Federalists stood united, with Washington in Mount Vernon dispatching strong endorsements of the repressive measures.

The laws—especially the Sedition Act—were enforced by Pickering, one of the most rigid and punitive of the Federalist leaders, and by

Federalist prosecutors and judges with ferocious partisanship. The vigorous young Anti-Federalist "Lightning Rod" Bache of Philadelphia, after being barred from the floor of the House of Representatives, assaulted in the streets, and surrounded by mobs at home, was indicted for "libeling" Adams and his administration and very probably was headed toward a severe sentence when he died from yellow fever. Old Luther Baldwin, after morosely watching President and Mrs. Adams parade down Newark's Broad Street to the booming of cannon, remarked to a fellow drinker in a dramshop that he didn't care if they fired through Adams's "a—"; reported to the authorities by the tavernkeeper, Baldwin was given a $200 fine and sent to federal jail until fines and fees were paid. "Spitting Matt" Lyon, a Republican congressman from Vermont so named because he had shot a stream of tobacco juice into the face of a Federalist foe on the House floor, was later, and probably not wholly coincidentally, indicted under the Sedition Act for libeling the President. Found guilty and jailed, Lyon made the most of his martyrdom and won reelection from his cell. Thomas Cooper, who had fled British oppression to become an editor in Pennsylvania, aroused Adams's ire by calling the President a threat to liberty and the rights of man; Cooper, given short shrift in court before the notorious "hanging judge" Samuel Chase, was convicted by a well-directed jury that deliberated for all of twenty minutes.

Americans had feared a federal government with the power to invade the liberties of the people. They had rallied enough opposition to the new Constitution to force the great concession of a federal bill of rights; they had held Madison and the others to their promise to add that bill of rights; they had rallied to its support when their state legislatures had considered the amendments sent down by Congress. Now, just seven years after the amendments were enacted, the worst specters of the loudest fearmongers were being brought to life—the government was prosecuting and fining and jailing persons whose only crime was speaking up.

Protest against the Alien and Sedition Acts and the prosecutions erupted across the nation as people rallied once again to defend their liberties. But there was a double peril now: the key weapon for opposing repression—protest—might well be blunted by the repression itself. Apprehensive leaders cast about for other strategies. Some favored appeal to Congress—but Congress had passed the measures and remained under Federalist control. Others favored resort to the judiciary—but the benches were packed with Federalists. Still others demanded the most extreme resorts—nullification of the measures by the states or, that failing, secession. But this threat struck terror into the hearts not only of Federalists but indeed of most Republicans. All had to face an ancient truth: extremism begat extremism.

This dangerous and complex situation called for astute and committed leadership. In an unusual combination of national and local initiatives, such leadership had come forth with alacrity in both the new temporary capital, Philadelphia, and the bluegrass counties of Kentucky. Late in June 1798 the Lexington *Kentucky Gazette* had printed the menacing text of an early House version of the Alien and Sedition bills; a notice in the very next issue called for a mass meeting to discuss "the present critical situation of public affairs." This unsigned notice was the work of John Breckinridge and George Nicholas, two transplanted Virginians who had become active in Kentucky politics. As the two issued pamphlets and as the *Gazette* printed Congress's successive drafts of the bills, mass meetings of county folk issued ringing manifestos against the measures. In Lexington four thousand or more persons convened, amounting to three times the population of the city. When an audacious Federalist tried to defend the bills at this meeting and encountered sustained booing, Nicholas—along with a young politician named Henry Clay—urged the crowd to respect that right to free speech Federalists wished to deny their opponents.

From Monticello, Vice President Jefferson followed developments both in Congress and in Kentucky. In a display of skilled "hidden-hand leadership," he not only secretly counseled Breckinridge and Nicholas and his other friends in Kentucky but also drafted a resolution passed by the Kentucky legislature holding that where the national government exercised powers not specifically delegated to it, each state had "AN EQUAL RIGHT TO JUDGE FOR ITSELF AS WELL OF INFRACTIONS AS OF THE MODE AND MEASURE OF REDRESS."

At the same time Madison, riding the miles from Montpelier to confer with Jefferson at Monticello, engineered somewhat milder resolutions that passed the Virginia legislature; these held that states had the right and duty to "INTERPOSE FOR ARRESTING THE PROGRESS" of unconstitutional acts.

Once again the formidable combination of Jefferson and Madison was at work, in collaboration with state leaders south of the future capital on the Potomac. But this time their success was limited. All the states north of the Potomac strongly opposed the Kentucky and Virginia resolutions. Elsewhere in the South the Republicans were active enough to block disapproval by state legislatures but could not gain endorsements. It was impossible to mobilize nationwide popular opinion against the Alien and Sedition laws because that opinion was laced with conflicting sectional, partisan, and ideological attitudes. The result was a kind of stasis, as people and politicians eagerly awaited the election of 1800.

———

A FEDERALIST PRESIDENT and Congress governing in a high-handed fashion—Republican opponents attacking and stigmatizing those in national office as corrupt, unconstitutional, unpatriotic "monocrats"—Federalists seeking to shut up the "Jacobin Cabal" through repressive legislation—the "Jacobins" threatening to block or nullify the acts—the Federalists charging disunion, subversion, treachery. Prosecutions go on, martyrs bask in the limelight, people even speak of violence, at least in tavern whispers. Has the checked and balanced political system suddenly become rigid and oppressive? And what would happen to people's liberties in the chaos that might follow as a reaction to repression at the top?

The system, and liberty with it, would survive through a process anathema to the thoughts of President Adams and former Treasury Secretary Alexander Hamilton in 1798, and equally hostile to the earlier attitudes of Vice President Jefferson and former congressman Madison. This was the creation of a two-party system that would enable a majority to govern with legitimacy, and an opposition to oppose, with equal legitimacy.

It was not that Adams was unaware that he would have to fight to retain his office in the coming presidential election or that Jefferson, already ambitious for the presidency, hoped to climb the greasy pole without a vigorous effort. Both men after all had competed for the top post in 1796. But they shared the conventional wisdom of the day—that parties were merely large factions, that factions were dangerous to order and liberty, that factional conflict threatened national unity and survival. Federalist and Republican rivals did not see themselves or each other "as alternating parties in a two-party system," in Richard Hofstadter's words. "Each side hoped instead to eliminate party conflict by persuading and absorbing the more acceptable and 'innocent' members of the other; either side hoped to attach the stigma of foreign allegiance and disloyalty to the intractable leaders of the other, and to put them out of business as a party." They did not see how organized party competition could sustain both order and liberty; hence their bill of rights did not extend to freedom for parties.

So it was not party theory but personal and ideological rivalry that moved the leaderships of both "factions" in the late 1790s to build coalitions, to reach out to broader electorates, to recruit local and state leaders, to publish tracts and broadsides, to enroll voters—in short, to lay the rough foundations of the first nationwide popular parties. Slowly, and consciously, Jefferson assumed visible and militant leadership of the Republicans. At this point competitive party politics hardly moderated electoral tactics or language. Slander and invective were the keynotes of the day, while bitter anger was the mood.

That fact made all the more remarkable the great feat of American democracy in 1800—the completion of an essentially fair election, the acceptance of its defeat by the incumbent party, and, despite rumors of impending violence, the peaceful transfer of power to a despised and feared opposition. In the next two centuries many a developing nation would fail this cardinal test. Tolerance by the party in power of a "loyal opposition" and its acceptance of defeat by that opposition evoke Ortega y Gasset's famous description of liberalism as the "supreme form of generosity," as the right that "the majority concedes to minorities and hence it is the noblest cry that has ever resounded in this planet."

If history followed human logic, Jefferson might have become the "Bill of Rights President," considering his lifelong commitment to religious liberty, his opposition to the Alien and Sedition bills, his libertarian philosophy. Under the pressures of the Sedition Act, the Jeffersonians, according to Leonard Levy, had been driven to originate so expansive an interpretation of the First Amendment that they "advocated the exemption of political opinions from all legal restraints." And the new president did proclaim in his inaugural address: "We are all republicans; we are all federalists" and "If there be any among us who wish to dissolve this union, or to change its republican form, let them stand undisturbed, as monuments of the safety with which error of opinion may be tolerated where reason is left free to combat it." He let repressive Federalist acts expire and pardoned their victims.

But history follows its own logic, if any. Rather than merely tolerate the Federalist Party, President Jefferson hoped to kill it off by detaching moderate Federalists from their "monarchical" leaders and consolidating them in a new Republican coalition. And he proved almost as sensitive as Washington and Adams had been to the "lying press." He favored a few "wholesome" prosecutions by the states of the worst offenders in order to restore "the integrity of the presses," and he did not protest when Pennsylvania prosecuted an arch-Federalist editor for seditious libel against the state or when New York went after another Federalist editor for libeling the President.

Even in the Jeffersonian years, in short, the nation was still feeling its way toward a balance between majority rule and minority rights, including individual rights. Jefferson, during most of his life a strong majoritarian, recognized the need for this balance. All should "bear in mind this sacred principle," he had said at his inauguration, "that though the will of the Majority is in all cases to prevail, that will, to be rightful, must be reasonable: that the Minority possess their equal rights, which equal laws must protect, & to violate would be oppression." But who—or what—would speak for the minority when a majority party controlled presidency and Congress?

The potential answer to this question lay in an institution—the judiciary. Appointed for life or otherwise protected against partisan pressures, judges would uphold minority rights against the "political" branches. To be sure, there was much ambiguity over what kind of judicial review the courts might exercise—whether enough only to protect their own independence, or enough to maintain the constitutional balance between the national and state governments, or enough to curb a chief executive who exceeded his powers, or enough even—the broadest, most awesome degree of judicial review—to invalidate laws passed by Congress, the elected agent of the people. This whole question remained to be decided when Jefferson took office.

If Jefferson and his fellow Republicans tended to be cynical about the independence and neutrality of the judiciary, they had a right to be. Where had the judges been when men were thrown into jail for exercising their First Amendment rights during the Adams administration? They had been deep in the Federalist fold, obedient to the president who had chosen them. The Republicans were all the more furious when Adams, on the eve of Jefferson's inauguration, made a number of "midnight appointments" of judges and court officials under a recently passed judiciary act. And six weeks before, the lame-duck president had chosen John Marshall, a blood cousin but political foe of Jefferson, to be Chief Justice of the United States.

Once in the saddle, the Republicans deployed some counterweapons: not only pardons for the victims of '98, but also repeal of Adams's judiciary act and impeachment of the extremist Judge Chase. Still, there was little they could do in the short run about a federal judiciary packed with Federalists. And that judiciary had an undefined power to declare acts of the political branches unconstitutional.

No one knew better than Marshall that the judicial branch could not simply impose its will on the majority. When one William Marbury, however, having failed to receive the commission as a justice of the peace that departing President Adams had signed for him, asked the Supreme Court to compel delivery of it, the Chief Justice saw his opportunity to establish the judiciary's authority. In a brilliant political and judicial feat Marshall lectured Jefferson and his administration on the conduct of their offices in failing to give Marbury his commission, dismissed Marbury's suit on the ground that the Supreme Court lacked jurisdiction under the Constitution, and declared unconstitutional the section of the Judiciary Act of 1789 that had granted the Court jurisdiction and under which Marbury had brought his case. By invalidating a measure that had given the Court a small power, Marshall and his brethren established the vital precedent of judicial review of legislation—and there was no way that Jefferson could defy a decision that resulted in no court order he might disobey and that on its face limited rather than expanded judicial power.

Marbury was, of course, only a weak precedent for the later broad applications of judicial review. That precedent, however, would become a time bomb, ticking away for half a century, when it exploded and helped precipitate the gravest crisis in American history. By 1803, the year of *Marbury,* the American constitutional system had settled into its lasting form. The checks and balances of the 1787 Constitution, the forceful expression and "guarantee" of freedom through the Bill of Rights, the early building of a two-party system, and the establishment of the precedent for judicial review—all these formed the constitutional and political context in which the battle for individual liberty and human rights would be fought out.

Clearly this constitutional system would make it somewhat more difficult for the federal government to suppress a minority party or to deny individual rights. Whether it would make it far harder for popular majorities to use government to achieve social and economic rights was an even graver question for the future—but a question rarely asked in the halcyon days of the new century.

CHAPTER THREE

THE REVOLUTIONS
OF RIGHTS

ON NEW YEAR'S DAY 1792 a mob in Coventry, England, propped an effigy of Tom Paine, with *rights of Man* pinned to its chest, on a cart and dragged it through the main streets to Cross Cheaping, where a gibbet and a fire had been prepared and a big crowd waited. The effigy was let dangle for a time, then it erupted in flames. The spectators burst into loud cheers, as Paine's likeness was swiftly reduced to ashes, and all joined in a hearty chorus of "God Save the King." Later in the year Paine's writings were burned in other cities, and in November, it was said, almost as many effigies of the author were put to flame as of Guy Fawkes.

To what did Tom Paine owe such honors? All knew the answer: to his most recent book, *The Rights of Man.* The agitator who had electrified Americans a decade and a half earlier with his *Common Sense* and who had left the United States in 1787 for fresh adventures in London and Paris now roiled Britishers with a second tract. *Common Sense* had been a direct appeal to the people, but the new volume was a long and discursive critique of Edmund Burke's *Reflections on the Revolution in France.* Burke's pamphlet, subtitled *and on the Proceedings of Certain Societies in London Relative to That Event,* was a blistering attack on the French Revolution's destruction of the conservative values of hierarchy, tradition, and continuity—an attack too on those at home and abroad who were "so taken up with their theories about the rights of man, that they have totally forgotten his nature." The rights of men in civil society, Burke contended, lay not in absolutes but "in a sort of *middle,*" in balances and compromises between good and good, between good and evil, sometimes between evil and evil.

Page by page, paragraph by paragraph, Paine dissected Burke's argu-

ments. *The Rights of Man* was occasionally eloquent—as in its bold assertion that "Man has no property in man; neither has any generation a
property in the generations which are to follow"—and it was explicit in
broadening the rights of man to encompass economic as well as political
life. Paine urged that as a matter of right, not favor, public moneys be
used to educate all children, to fund old-age pensions, to provide maternity and funeral benefits, to aid newly wedded couples, to build combined
lodging-houses and workshops to help the jobless. He even advocated a
progressive income tax, set forth in elaborate grades and schedules.

Whatever its merits, Paine's tract was, on the whole, tendentious, dog-
matic, digressive, repetitious, and always chained to its target, Edmund
Burke. Yet it became a sensational best-seller. In a population of ten
million it sold at least 200,000 copies, E. P. Thompson estimates, in its
first two years. The book circulated in coalpits and potteries, cottages and
Cornish tin mines, in the Scottish Highlands, in northern Wales. The
Attorney General charged that *The Rights of Man* was "thrust into the
hands of subjects of every description, even children's sweetmeats being
wrapped in it."

The government struck back at this émigré, this adoptive American,
with a Royal Proclamation against seditious publications. Anti-Paine
meetings were organized, an anti-Paine pamphlet was secretly subsidized
by the authorities. The author, glorying in both the applause and the
attacks, settled in Paris to avoid arrest.

The wide distribution of Paine's work was testament to the yearnings
of masses of people for ideas and arguments touching their needs and
hopes. And the yearnings, too, of poets. William Wordsworth wrote of

> . . . the People having a strong hand
> In making their own Laws, whence better days
> To all mankind.

And Robert Burns wrote:

> Its comin yet for a' that,
> That Man to Man the warld o'er,
> Shall brothers be for a' that.

As the French Revolution swept toward regicide and fratricide, disillusion came in the wake—for Paine most keenly. Having been made a
French citizen by the Assembly, along with Washington, Hamilton, and
Madison, he joined the moderates, and despite his hatred of monarchy
urged at the trial of Louis XVI that the ex-king be imprisoned and eventu-

ally banished—to America, indeed—rather than guillotined. Then Citoyen Paine himself, an American now formally outlawed in his native England, was arrested in France as an Englishman. After almost a year in prison he was released, in part because the American minister claimed him—as an American.

Americans followed these events with avid curiosity and mounting passions. If the American Revolution served in a romanticized version as a model for the French, the French Revolution was proving to be at once a catalyst for American thought and a divisive, tearing force in American politics. Even as American, French, and English leaders and philosophers conducted their political and forensic battles, however, another revolution was proceeding relentlessly, almost stealthily, through the West— one that would pose problems and choices that advocates and adversaries of rights would have to face in good time. This pervasive economic and social transformation would later be called the Industrial Revolution.

INDUSTRIALIZING RIGHTS

AMERICAN HISTORIANS of the nineteenth-century "onward and upward" school tended to view the evolution of rights in the West as a long march toward the inevitable realization of liberty and democracy. The marchers, they conceded, had often been halted, or turned from their path, forced back or even annihilated, but others had come swiftly to the fore and the march had resumed. Thus, in Britain, liberty had broadened out "from precedent to precedent"; in America, despite many setbacks, freedom had advanced inexorably from the Salem witch trials to the passage of the Bill of Rights and then to the emancipation of the slaves seventy years later.

In fact, as we have come to understand in the twentieth century, the march can be diverted or stopped for decades. Or the advance toward rights in one of its dimensions, the political, for instance, can be overwhelmed by the denial or suppression of rights in another, such as the economic. This was the case with the Industrial Revolution.

Americans had a unique double exposure to this revolution. Lagging behind the Western Europeans by about a generation in economic development, they could study the European experience—especially the British—as a foreshadow of their own. And during the American era of industrialization they could measure their achievements against those of other industrializing nations in, among other things, the extension or protection of fundamental rights. They might analyze in particular the linkages among a medley of rights, the causal forces behind both the expansion and the narrowing of rights, and the impact of economic change on the attitudes of elites and masses, on social conflict and political movements, and on intellectual and political leadership in the development of rights.

Certain of these changes and their implications were of course hidden to the most interested Americans, even to those who happened to be on the scene, and many who looked to the Old World as it underwent industrialization were less curious to fathom the mysteries of social change than they were to learn the methods of economic growth; what excited the imaginations of would-be American capitalists was the profit to be made by importing the Industrial Revolution to the United States, not the price that was being paid by masses of Europeans.

Visible to the most casual eye was the alteration of Europe's physical landscape. Between the 1770s and the 1840s Britain and France changed from predominantly rural environments to darkening tableaux cut with rail lines and patched with industrial plants and rapidly swelling cities. Britain led the way, with its rising textile and mining industries and busy ports. One of the most striking physical changes there lay in the fields once unenclosed and held in common and now partitioned off to favored individual owners, often forming large farms worked by droves of hired hands.

Thrown off enclosed fields, or unable to survive on the tiny plots left them, thousands of farm laborers drifted into the cities. The lot of the urban poor in the early nineteenth century was well known, especially in Britain, because of protesting press sheets and reform-minded politicians and the findings of parliamentary investigations. Squalor, polluted water, disease, crowded conditions that pressed families of five into sharing a bed, extreme suffering in both cold and heat, sheer hunger—all this was dramatized also in the poetry and novels of Blake and Dickens and others.

In the "dark Satanic Mills" and mines, life for children, women, and men became truly hellish: boys five years old, chained around the waist, hauling trucks of coal in mines—girls of eight, called "trappers," waiting in perfect darkness twelve hours a day to open and close passages for the coal cars—milliners standing on swollen feet for fifteen hours, with twenty minutes for the midday meal and tea taken on the run—a hundred men or more working 1,200 feet below the earth in a great colliery, at the mercy of "an idle or mischievous Engine Boy to drown the whole of them."

Day-to-day, almost commonplace cruelties, degradations, pains accompanied the change from smaller enterprises to larger, more highly mechanized and impersonal ones. The grievances aroused by this change were movingly described by a "Journeyman Cotton Spinner" in an address to the public during an 1818 strike in Manchester. The Cotton Spinner noted, in E. P. Thompson's summary, "the growing distance between master and man: . . . the loss of status and above all of independence for the worker, his reduction to total dependence on the master's instruments of production: the partiality of the law: the disruption of the traditional family economy: the discipline, monotony, hours and conditions of work: loss of leisure and amenities: the reduction of the man to the status of an 'instrument.' "

In factories and coalpits throughout the industrializing world millions of men, women, and children were in a condition not of life, liberty, and the pursuit of happiness but of death, oppression, and the endurance of misery. These conditions were in blatant contradiction to what the radicals of the English Civil War had fought for, to what the philosophers of liberty and happiness had preached and were preaching, to eloquent voices raised in Parliament.

What, then, had happened to rights for humankind? Had these been but the empty phrases of philosophers and politicians? Or had they become the exclusive possession of the ruling and rising classes? Under the awesome pressures of industrialization, the English poor and their leaders began to speak openly, if somewhat ambiguously, of a concept that was both ancient and radical—their birthrights, which were held to encompass not only the historic freedoms *from* government but also more positive rights. In the 1830s the populist agitator William Cobbett, charging that the poor had been cheated of their rights, drew up a bill of particular deprivations: "the right to live in the country of our birth; the right to have a living out of the land of our birth in exchange for our labour duly and honestly performed; the right, in case we fell into distress, to have our wants sufficiently relieved out of the produce of the land, whether that distress arose from sickness, from decrepitude, from old age, or from inability to find employment." Social responsibility for meeting individual needs—here was a definition of an Englishman's birthright that reached nostalgically back into the past of settled farming villages and radically forward into a future of caring cooperation and human dignity achieved not through triumph in savage competition but through worthy membership in the community.

This "reactionary radicalism," in Craig Calhoun's phrase, was in violent conflict with the bewildering new order of capitalism and its individualist ethos. Both reactionary radicals and bourgeois individualists esteemed property and property rights, but where the latter saw ownership as the underpinning of invention and innovation, the foundation for investment and expansion, the motivation for hard work and the license for consumption, the reactionary radicals found the essence of property in their own labor—in the exertions of head, hands, feet, back, heart—and thus the right of property was supremely the right of the laborer to dispose freely of his own labor, to protection against the alienation of his labor and his reduction to the condition of an inertly functional and exploitable "instrument," deserving of no more consideration than plow or loom or pick. And it was for this reason—to protect their property in their labor and the human dignity it afforded them—that the reactionary radicals resisted a thin and narrow individualist version of legal and political rights that sanctioned untrammeled liberty in the economic sphere—laissez-faire—and they placed social and economic rights in a place of honor among English birthrights.

But would the English poor claim their birthrights? "The workmen in general are an inoffensive, unassuming, set of well-informed men," the Journeyman Cotton Spinner had said, "though how they acquire their information is almost a mystery to me. They are docile and tractable, if not goaded too much."

This docility was not to be wondered at, the Cotton Spinner went on, "when we consider that they are trained to work from six years old, from five in the morning to eight and nine at night." A significant part of this education was of their virtual powerlessness before the law and of the formidable obstacles they would meet if they tried to appeal to their "legal rights." The Cotton Spinner gave an example: If a dispute arose as to whether some spinning had been properly done and the overlooker rejected it, the worker's only recourse was to summon his employer before a magistrate, but "the whole of the acting magistrates in that district, with the exception of two worthy clergymen, being gentlemen who have sprung from the *same* source with the master cotton spin-ners"—the employers—"the magistrate's decision was generally in favor of the master, though on the statement of the overlooker only."

But worker tractability was also internal, psychological. With their re-spect for property and property rights, most workers did not doubt that proprietors and investors had the same rights in their factories and mines and machines and lands as they themselves had in their own little homes or plots, if they owned them. So gradually did big owners extend their holdings that workers were never confronted with a catalytic moment of realization that property had been transformed in its economic reach and social impact. Slowly but inevitably, relentlessly, the Industrial Revolu-tion enlarged, in Wolfgang G. Friedmann's words, "not only the diversity of the modalities of property but also, and above all, the function of property as a means of controlling the lives of others" who did not own property beyond their immediate personal needs and were dependent for their living on those who did.

IN ASSESSING the relationship between people's "objective" social conditions and their resulting attitudes, and between those attitudes and people's political behavior, historians face the most imposing tasks. Even if we are able to describe with some degree of objectivity conditions of life at home and work, it is difficult to measure just how people respond to their conditions—whether with feelings of contentment or anger, happiness or dejection, hope or despair—and why they do so. And it is especially difficult to describe precisely how and why such feelings are— or are not—transformed into individual or collective actions aimed at changing those conditions of life.

The plight of the English poor is an arresting case in point. For their "objective" conditions—the existence of pervasive and almost unmitigated misery—we have well-authenticated data. But what and how the impoverished masses felt is elusive, as is the link between those feelings and the actions of the poor. Despite the explanations of the Cotton Spinner, it remains a mystery why millions accepted their lot with relative passivity, while others were stirred to fight for their rights.

That some did stir we have ample evidence. The first and most enduring protest actions in England had their beginnings no later than the 1520s and accelerated during the sixteenth and seventeenth centuries. These were food riots—demands for the most basic of rights, the right to live. The centuries of food riots culminated in the 1790s. Harvest crises provoked attacks on corn dealers and middlemen. In September 1800 a thousand Londoners met in a corn market to hiss and pelt mealmen and factors; later the crowd swept through the streets smashing shopwindows and streetlamps. The rioters' posters and handbills appealed to wider feelings with slogans such as "Liberty or Death" and "defend your rights."

Behind every such form of popular direct action, Thompson noted, "some legitimising notion of right" was to be found. Even so, the hunger riots were too ephemeral, too dependent on bad harvests, too spontaneous and disorganized to have deep and lasting impact on the struggle for people's rights.

As mines and mills expanded and workers encountered more hardships on the job, their militancy also took the form of direct action. This could be rather elementary. William Kershaw, who had started in a mill at the age of eight, testified at a parliamentary inquiry that after a "slubber" had beaten him over the head with a long "billy-roller," he told his mother, but entreated her not to complain. Nevertheless she gave the slubber a sharp lecture. As soon as she left, the boy was beaten again. When his mother learned of this, she returned to the scene and seized the same billy-roller "and beat it about the fellow's head, and gave him one or two black eyes." Yet most parents could not or dared not protect their children or spare them twelve-hour days, whether from ignorance, fear, or need for their wages.

Early trade union action was often equally elementary, usually spurred by desperation and frequently accompanied by violence. As industrial action became more prevalent in the early nineteenth century, food riots diminished in importance, except when riots and strikes were conducted side by side. The skilled craft workers—wool combers, framework knitters, keelmen, shipwrights, colliers—were the most militant, but generally they fought more for specific craft rights than for such broad rights as "liberty," though they often equated the two. They battled not only employers but competition from apprentices and the unskilled and they resisted technological change that threatened their status as "aristocrats of labor."

The ultimate test in the struggle for broad rights lay in the power of national collective action to protect and expand the rights of unskilled workers, women, children, and the poor. Despite Combination Acts passed at the end of the eighteenth century to discourage unionism, workers' organizations expanded during the early 1800s and gradually widened their scope, from the first craft unions of skilled workers to general trade unions, until, by 1833, Robert Owen, a manufacturer turned reformer, was planning to bring a massive proletarian movement into a Grand National Moral Union of the Productive Classes.

Most such organizations had short lives. Not only did they face government oppression and employer resistance; they differed among themselves over both social ends and political means. The fundamental strategic dispute was one that would bedevil labor movements everywhere—and not least in the United States—for the next century or so: whether to rely primarily on the assertion of labor's latent economic power, through trade union organization and work stoppages, or whether to devote its resources to political action, to working through or challenging traditional political structures.

In the vast pool of the working poor, women were near the bottom, initially so submerged and disorganized as to be virtually untouched by such debates over strategy. Only limited leadership for women's rights could emerge; rare radical intellectuals like Mary Wollstonecraft spoke from somewhat protected social positions that allowed them far greater freedom in the play of ideas than women who were chained to the carts they hauled in mines could ever possess. Indeed, it was not a woman but Thomas Spence who wrote a pamphlet entitled *The Rights of Infants; or, the Imprescriptable RIGHT of MOTHERS to such share of the Elements as is sufficient to enable them to suckle and bring up their Young.* But though men took the lead in organizing unions, strikes, and protests, even for those trades in which female workers were dominant, women came gradually to active participation in fights against wage cuts, brutal working conditions, and the introduction of new machines—and they were harassed, beaten, imprisoned right along with their male counterparts. And in some cases they struck out on their own: the first Female Reform Societies appeared in 1818 and 1819 in Manchester and other industrial cities, and in 1825 the Edinburgh Maidservants' Union Society was organized with the threat to strike for standardization of their working conditions.

The rising protest of the 1820s centered increasingly on reform of the suffrage—abolishing rotten boroughs that exaggerated the power of the squirearchy, giving cities more seats in Parliament, lowering money or property requirements for voting. By securing the right to vote and fair representation in government, some calculated, workers could effectively pursue broader rights. But the Reform Bill of 1832 was essentially a victory for the liberal bourgeoisie; little changed in the lives of the millions caught up in the throes of industrialization.

Still, in the early decades of the nineteenth century militant workers had helped to sharpen issues of social and economic rights that would dominate British politics for a century. And leaders rising up from the ranks of the workers were beginning to leave their imprint on public opinion and politics. Such leaders were vitally necessary, indeed indispensable—in a society dominated by the idea of property, by its owners and its defenders, there were few others who could address the true needs, the fundamental rights of the working and nonworking poor.

CHANGING RIGHTS:
PROPERTY AND HAPPINESS

AND WHAT did the vaunted birthright of Englishmen consist of? Mary Wollstonecraft asked in 1790. As the title of the groundbreaking book she published two years later—*A Vindication of the Rights of Women*—indicated, Wollstonecraft was primarily concerned with promoting the rights of her sex—especially educational equality—but she had a keen eye out for what right English *men*, in those early days of the Industrial Revolution, held in highest regard, even as a birthright. Her scornful answer: "Security of property!"—that was the whole definition of "English liberty."

Though the reactionary radicals of the nascent British working class might uphold a more generous conception of their birthrights, private property indeed became a central—in some respects the dominant—institution of Western society in the nineteenth century. The proliferation of factories, the spread of transportation systems controlled by entrepreneurs, the piling up of private investment, the pell-mell growth of cities with the construction of residential and commercial buildings, the transformation of once common land into private holdings—these and other forces were putting immense properties into the hands of individual capitalists. Even more potent were the ideas that lay behind—and were further propelled by—economic and social revolution. These ideas, endorsed by the bulk of the philosophical establishment, legitimated the virtually exclusive control by owners of their property and of those who labored on it.

Had the benevolent ideas of the eighteenth century's philosophers of happiness yielded so quickly, with so little protest, to the doctrines of the advancing Iron Age? Those men had written for a world still largely pastoral, but even so they were not prepared to concede to property ownership the sanction of divine or natural law. Francis Hutcheson had believed that "universal industry" was necessary for the support of mankind, and that "hopes of future wealth, ease, and pleasure to themselves" and their offspring motivated people to hard work, and he recognized that "these hopes are presented to men by securing to every one the fruit of his own labours, that he may enjoy them, or dispose of them as he pleases." Even the philosopher of happiness had to concede that the pleasures of property ownership had their utility.

But though Hutcheson justified inequalities in property and would not tolerate indolence—"slothful wretches are to be compelled to labour"—his property rights were by no means natural or absolute. Property and its rights must serve the public good, and "we are never to put in the ballance with the liberty or safety of a people, the gratifying the vain ambition, luxury, or avarice of a few." No person or society could "by mere occupation acquire such a right in a vast tract of land quite beyond their power to cultivate, as shall exclude others who may want work, or sustenance for their numerous hands." If Hutcheson had lived a century later, he might well have found occasion to apply a similar principle to mills and mines.

While Hutcheson grounded ownership morally in the common good, his close friend and onetime disciple David Hume held more severe criteria. Public utility was "the *sole* origin" of justice in property rights, he contended in his *Enquiry Concerning the Principles of Morals.* What "a man's art or industry" achieved ought to be secured to him and to his heirs, but there should be a rough equality in the distribution of both the necessities and the "comforts" of life. "Wherever we depart from this equality," he wrote, "we rob the poor of more satisfaction than we add to the rich." Yet Hume's emphasis on the "highly conducive, or indeed absolutely requisite" role of property rights in securing the stability of possession that underlies civil society, even while "particular hardships" might result, meant that, in Thomas Horne's summary, "justice was left with the sole task of protecting the status quo in property holdings."

IDEAS ARE WEAPONS, we are told. The linked ideas that happiness is desirable for its own sake, that the equal pleasures of any or all human beings are equally good, that no action is justified unless it can be shown to contribute to the greatest happiness—this battery of ideas might have appeared powerful enough to come to the aid of those millions of European laborers and their families experiencing unhappiness as the Industrial Revolution uprooted them from their rural existences and exposed them to endless pain, to shortened lives in mill and mine, and to the suppression of their most fundamental liberties by owners and overseers. But ideas, like weapons, are vulnerable to counterideas. If happiness was the most evocative and spacious idea of the eighteenth century, another compelling idea, property, became the arsenal of the nineteenth-century counterattack. It would prove an unequal contest.

Property rights had for many centuries made a powerful appeal to the minds of people of both high and low estate. Property ownership was seen as the rightful reward of those who had mixed the sweat of their brows with the soil. It was a natural right, a right not dependent on tradition or authority or the grace of king or pope. John Locke had helped elevate long-held notions of property rights to a high philosophical plane. A natural individual right to property, with each having the right to the fruits of his labor, was essential to his account of the origins of political society. He minced no words. "The great and *chief end*" of "Mens uniting into Commonwealths, and putting themselves under Government," he wrote in the *Second Treatise, "is the Preservation of their Property."*

There were, however, crucial ambiguities in Locke's treatment of property, particularly with respect to his conception of the extent of property rights. Did these rights pertain only to a man or woman's tangible personal property—food, land, goods, tools—or more broadly to one's "Life, Health, Liberty, or Possessions"? And how extensive could one individual's "Possessions" be without weakening his claim to them under his "Natural Right" to property?

Natural law for Locke required that people, "being all equal and independent," be kept safe from harm to their life, health, liberty, and possessions. But what if the issue became the right to restrict the holding or use by some of large possessions in order to protect others' life, health, and liberty or that of the community? Here Locke once again demonstrated his genius. "Locke's astonishing achievement," C. B. Macpherson writes, "was to base the property right on natural right and natural law, and then to remove all the natural law limits from the property right."

One moral justification for restricting property rights to small possessions, sanctioned both by tradition and by Locke's version of natural law, had been that surplus food might spoil before being consumed or that excess tracts of land might lie fallow, but Locke noted that the introduction of gold and silver, of a money economy, would prevent such waste. From this, he leaped to the conclusion that, "having by a tacit and voluntary consent found out a way, how a man may fairly possess more land than he himself can use the product of," men had "agreed to disproportionate and unequal Possession of the Earth." This "consent" to a money economy and inequalities, which, like the Social Contract, was nothing more than a convenient fiction, led ultimately to the elimination of *any* justification for natural law restrictions on the scale of possessions protected by property rights. And it led also to Locke's discovery of one's "natural right" to alienate his property in his own labor, since in a money economy he might sell that property for wages.

All this might appear to be an amazing intellectual hat trick, but Locke was not engaged in some philosophical conspiracy. His many-dimensional thought was responding to the busy world evolving around him. He opened up avenues of reflection and argument that would allow others to put his imprimatur on their own philosophical assumptions and economic and social biases. Rousseau was a striking example of such selective adoption. Although the natural rights theory of property had not taken as strong a root in France as in Britain, Rousseau saluted the "wise Locke" and accented the terminology of natural rights even while on other occasions directly attacking the whole doctrine, including property rights.

On such rights, indeed, Rousseau demonstrated philosophical volatility at its acme. In 1755, in his discourse on the origin of inequality, he waxed eloquent in denouncing the mythic man who had first enclosed a piece of ground and then yelled, *"This is mine."* From how many "crimes, wars, and murders" would mankind have been saved, Rousseau wrote, if someone had only warned people against this "imposter" and cried out the reminder that "the fruits of the earth belong to us all." But not long after, in an essay written for Diderot's *Encyclopédie*, "Political Economy," Rousseau called the right of property "the most sacred of all the rights of citizenship"—"even more important in some respects than liberty itself." And later, in his most noted work, *The Social Contract*, the French philosopher took a still different line. Property rights were no longer natural but man-made rights created under the Social Contract.

No wonder that a host of disparate groups—French liberals, German nationalists, European revolutionaries, English egalitarians—would cite Rousseau as gospel. And this same ambiguity made Rousseau a tempting target to enemies all along the philosophical and political spectrum. Edmund Burke, in his attacks on the excesses of the French Revolution, fixed the target on Rousseau's egalitarianism.

As Burke watched the aristocrats of France lose their most precious private possessions—including the most private of all, their heads—he cried out in horror and anger against the "monstrous fiction" of human equality. The alleged right to equality was not a product of natural right but an artifice that served only to "aggravate and embitter that real inequality, which it never can remove." Equal justice under law was a natural right, but an equal reward was not. In a partnership "all men have equal rights; but not to equal things," Burke wrote. "He that has but five shillings in the partnership, has as good a right to it, as he that has five hundred pounds has to his larger proportion." With such an example Burke revealed his willingness to accept flagrant inequality in rights since those with vast property possessed proportionately vast rights over it, including rights over those who merely labored on the property.

THE DOMINANT IDEA of property in the Industrial Revolution represented the triumph of what Macpherson has called Lockean "possessive individualism." Natural rights had become most importantly property rights, and property rights in turn had become the defense of great property holdings against the unpropertied. But what would happen when property confronted Hutcheson's potent criterion for moral action, "the greatest happiness for the greatest numbers"? This confrontation took place most significantly in the mind of Jeremy Bentham, who, a generation after Hutcheson's death, took up the Scot's mighty phrase and made it his own.

Echoing Hutcheson's creation of formulae, Bentham worked out a "felicific calculus" by which the value of a given amount of pleasure or pain could be calculated by measuring each of its elements for such qualities as duration, intensity, certainty, purity, and number of persons involved. Such calculations could be applied to a wide variety of public concerns, including the degrees of punishment of lawbreakers of various types, the kind of political system that would provide the greatest pleasure and smallest pain, and—not least—the relation between property and happiness.

Yet Bentham was far from conceding human beings the right to happiness—or the right to anything, for that matter. It was absurd, he wrote, to speak of natural and inalienable rights as though these might precede civil society or have meaning outside the terms of positive law. The error was in part, he found, linguistic, the conversion of an adjective ("this is right") into a noun ("a right") which was then, without regard to reason or practical consequences, endowed with characteristics of the eternal and absolute—a process he described as the raising of nonsense upon stilts.

And so Bentham's instinctive sympathy for the American Revolution against Britain was compromised by his contempt for Jefferson's handiwork in the Declaration of Independence. What consistency was there, he demanded, in the assertion, on the one hand, of inalienable rights to life, liberty, and the pursuit of happiness and, on the other, of the need for the government of men which must, through laws, qualify and restrict those rights? "If the right of pursuit of happiness is a right unalienable why (how) are thieves restrained from pursuing it by theft, murderers by murder, and rebels by rebellion?" The whole natural-rights doctrine, he wrote later in an assault on the French Declaration of Rights, was so much "*bawling* upon paper."

As he judged the happiness principle his greatest formulation, Bentham had every reason to keep it in the center of philosophical and political debate. Yet for over forty years after 1776 he shrank from using the phrase, until in 1820 he referred to it in new comments on the American Declaration of Independence. But happiness had become tightly bound in Bentham's thought with property ownership. The state's proper function was to enable the fullest expression of man's instinctive greed and desire for abundance. Individual happiness was related directly to individual wealth: "*Of two individuals, he who is the richer is the happier or has the greater chance of being so.*" And "what is the wealth of society, if not the sum of all individual wealth?" But Bentham would not for the sake of property and abundance bend his view that there were "no rights without law—no rights contrary to law—no rights anterior to the law." Property's high virtue was a creature—and also a condition—of law: "Property and law are born together and must die together."

But the law that controlled property was itself controlled by Parliament, consisting of a House of Commons elected by a small fraction of the adult population, and a House of Lords elected by no one, save, perhaps, the king. Parliament and Crown, representing the lesser number, could hardly be expected to respond to the claims to happiness of the "greatest numbers." For Bentham as a thinker the test was not votes but values. He contended that every code of laws designed to promote the ultimate end of happiness must include "the four most comprehensive particular and subordinate *ends*": "*Subsistence, abundance, security, and equality.*" Always collected in his thought, he listed these in order of importance, and it was significant that "equality" was at the end of the list, where Hobbes had likewise put it a century and a half earlier. "When security and equality are in conflict," Bentham wrote, "it will not do to hesitate a moment. Equality must yield."

Once again, in the battle of ideas, the heart had been cut out of a humane and generous conception, the happiness of the many, and a narrow notion of property and security substituted. No one saw this more keenly, or regretfully, than John Stuart Mill. An ardent Benthamite in his youth—indeed, he served as Bentham's secretary for a year and a half—Mill later concluded that his mentor's concept of human nature and psychological motivation was too pinched and mechanical. The master's elaborate felicific calculus, Mill came to believe, was wrong in principle since "motives are innumerable; there is nothing whatever which may not become an object of desire or of dislike by association." Mill's rejection of Bentham was also an act of filial intellectual rebellion, for his father, James Mill, had been philosophically and personally close to Bentham. Even more—and almost as proof of Mill's more complex view of human motives—he was much influenced, in rethinking his philosophical ideas, by his intellectual and romantic partnership with Harriet Taylor, a leading feminist writer.

Mill would modify Bentham's doctrine of pleasure and pain by taking a much richer, more spacious and explicit approach to the concept of happiness. "Happiness is not an abstract idea," he wrote, "but a concrete whole," and while he denied that the whole of happiness could be measured by a product of its parts, he examined these constituents, which, in his broader view, included not only all the ordinary pleasures but also elements of freedom, duty, morality, sympathy, even self-fulfillment. Against Bentham's—and his father's—narrow definition of self-interest as the raw pursuit of pleasure and avoidance of pain, John Stuart Mill found that self-interest, or individual happiness, might take many apparently contrary forms, as for instance when a mother chose to risk her own life to protect her child's.

This variegated and open-ended concept of happiness contained a potentially fertile and imposing theory of rights. "When we call anything a person's right," Mill wrote, "we mean that he has a valid claim on society to protect him in the possession of it, either by the force of law, or by that of education and opinion." Thus it was not enough that individuals be protected against others' interference with their rights; society—individuals in the mass—had a duty to help promote and secure the rights of each of its members. And in the balance against Bentham's emphasis on security, Mill placed liberty and autonomy—the right to the pursuit of individual happiness in all its dimensions.

But here Mill's thought reached a hurdle that it was never fully to overleap. Did the individual have not only a right to pursue happiness but a right to happiness itself, and if so how was it to be claimed against and secured by government and society? "The love of liberty and personal independence" was essential to happiness, and no one spoke more eloquently and forcefully of the meaning and value of freedom than Mill did in *On Liberty*. And though he recognized the claims of the "common good" he was far less willing than his utilitarian predecessors had been to sacrifice individual happiness to them. Indeed it was his caution toward the idea of the "common good" together with his exaltation of maximal individual autonomy that caused him to recoil from embracing a positive role for government in the promotion of individual happiness.

Mill's conception of freedom was essentially negative—freedom from interference or restraint—and in political economy laissez-faire "should be the general practice: every departure from it, unless required by some great good, is a certain evil." Among the exceptions to laissez-faire Mill allowed was the tempering of the worst consequences of the Industrial Revolution upon the working poor—relief was "an absolute right to be supported at the cost of other people"—but this ameliorative function of government was a far cry from a thick and binding societal commitment to individual self-fulfillment. Thus there was no "right to happiness" in the sense that government was obliged to serve and protect the personal happiness of its citizens; rather, to the degree that Mill recognized such a right, it was more on the order of a "moral" right, an expression of how men and women ought to live, both in their private pursuits of happiness and in their concern for the happiness of others—Christ's Golden Rule, Mill wrote, was "the ideal perfection of utilitarian morality."

Nevertheless, at a time when invocations of rights were increasingly limited to property rights and property rights were increasingly limited to the propertied, Mill broke with the conventional wisdom to embrace a broad and broadly distributed concept of the application of individual rights. While rejecting as sure paths to tyranny schemes designed to enforce equality of condition or to redistribute radically or communalize property, Mill insisted that each person had an equal right to the enjoyment of individual rights and that gross inequalities—whether grounded in law or wealth or social position or education—were destructive of human autonomy and ended in the subjection of the inferior to the superior. And so, among the "great goods" that might permit limitations upon laissez-faire, Mill included, besides poor relief, provisions for the schooling of children and the legal and economic liberation of women.

BUT EVEN as the debate over liberty and equality, property and happiness occupied center stage, a powerful challenge to its very terms was being mounted in Berlin by the Young Hegelians. Just as the main intellectual thrust of the master, G. W. F. Hegel, was ethical and spiritual in contrast to the materialism of utilitarianism and other doctrines, so Hegel and his followers attacked Western notions of rights as hopelessly individualistic, reductionist, and contractual, and instead emphasized the organic relations of human beings each to the other and to society as a whole, with rights serving less to protect the individual against the community than to secure his status within the networks of interdependence that sustain the community. Thus in an ideal family, relations among its members would be regulated not by invocations of rights, entitlements, or obligations but by a spirit of affection and generosity.

Karl Marx, trailing clouds of Hegelianism even as he rejected much of it, shared his mentor's disdain for individual rights but emphasized economic forces rather than ethical in the history of societies. Indeed, Marx meant to turn Hegel upside down by, in Jeremy Waldron's words, a "greater involvement with the messy business of man's natural life of labour, production, interaction with nature, industry and material consumption." To Hegel, power over property was essential to the exercise of man's free will, but Marx defined property quite simply as selfishness—the right to property was "the right to enjoy one's fortune and to dispose of it as one will; without regard for other men and independently of society. It is the right of self-interest." While property relations, or their intensifying distortion and inequity, served the purpose in capitalist society of creating the conditions for revolution, the advent of socialism would render private property merely an institution to be abolished.

If Marx turned Hegel upside down, he turned Mill's liberalism inside out. In every lofty liberal idea Marx perceived a malign essence. Liberalism? In fact a cloak for capitalism. Individualism? In fact atomism, isolation, *anomie.* Liberal democracy? In fact class rule. Reformism? In fact window dressing designed to distract the masses from fundamental social change.

It was over competing doctrines of the rights of men and women that socialism and reform liberalism were fighting. The "so-called *rights of man,*" Marx said, "are simply the rights of a *member of civil society,* that is, of egoistic man, of man separated from other men and from the community." Marx considered that he was more concerned with real human wants and needs than with those represented by such liberal—actually "bourgeois"—rights as liberty and property and even equality. In Marx's vision of a harmonious socialist society, the problem of individual rights—of rights in any form—would not exist; the members of his cooperative commonwealth would have no need to require such guarantees for the satisfaction of wants and needs to which they were entitled.

By the mid-nineteenth century the intellectual conflict over rights among Burkean and laissez-faire conservatives, Mill's liberals and socialists, was deepening. The contestants were not irreconcilable on all points. Even Marx granted, however grudgingly, that Mill should not be classed with "the herd of vulgar economic apologists," and he reminded liberalism's critics of the importance of those liberals "who have taken over the painful role of fighting for freedom step by step within the constitutional limits." Fighting for freedom—here was a struggle that all sides would undertake, each with its sharply distinct definition of freedom. In the ever quickening and broadening Industrial Revolution, which definition would prevail? Nowhere would the answer be more important, or the testing of property and happiness rights under capitalism be harsher, than in the burgeoning industrial nation across the Atlantic.

PROPERTY RIGHTS IN THE LAND OF EDEN

DURING THE EARLY 1800s machines, money, and men and women continued to make the long sea voyage from the Old World to the New. Immigration—probably about 50,000 souls in the decade of the 1790s—had more than doubled by the decade beginning in 1810. British financiers in particular were looking on American land, canals, and state bonds with rising avarice. But the most important import from the British Isles was technology and the men who invented or applied it. For a time hardly a major mill or shop in the United States did not boast a prized "English mechanic." Dutch glass workers, Italian silk reelers, and German sawyers also brought with them their specialized skills and tools.

Threatened by the repression and devastation sweeping Europe during the Napoleonic wars, many immigrants fled to the United States as a beacon of political or religious liberty; the Declaration of Independence, the revolution, and the Bill of Rights were evidence to them of Americans' commitment to liberty and equality. To others, America beckoned as an Eden where they could pursue their chosen paths to happiness as free individuals. Some, perhaps victims of the Industrial Revolution, had specific aims—lacking property, or having had and lost it, they hoped to gain a home and farm or shop of their own in the New World. Inevitably people holding such diverse values and goals would come into conflict with one another and with those who already held property, or were seeking it, in the United States.

While under the pressures of industrialization Europeans were moving on from the ideas of Locke and Hume, Montesquieu and Rousseau to those of Adam Smith and Bentham, Mill and Marx, the young republic across the Atlantic failed to produce homegrown intellectual leadership as Americans now underwent the painful process of economic and social revolution. A later generation had found no worthy successors to the galaxy of constitutional and political thinkers of the founding era—Jefferson and Madison, Paine and Hamilton, and the others—and continued to draw on their stock of ideas.

One member of that founding galaxy persisted well into the nineteenth century in puzzling out the tough issues. In the long years following his famous substitution of "happiness" for "property" in the trinity of the Declaration of Independence, Thomas Jefferson thought deeply about the meaning and implications of both these ideas, balancing them against each other and meditating on their relation to liberty and equality. Central to his thinking on these issues was the question of the distribution of land.

As minister to Louis XVI in 1785, horrified by the misery of France's poor, he had written to James Madison: "Whenever there is in any country, uncultivated lands and unemployed poor, it is clear that the laws of property have been so far extended as to violate natural right. The earth is given as a common stock for man to labour and live on." If land was appropriated to encourage industry, he went on, other employment should be provided to those "excluded from the appropriation." As few as possible should be "without a little portion of land." Everyone, he suggested, had a natural right of access to the common stock.

Even in his earlier, more radical phase, Jefferson did not deny property rights. On the contrary, he believed in them so strongly as facilitators both of republican virtue and of the individual pursuit of happiness that he wanted their widest practical distribution. The task was to eliminate "an aristocracy of wealth" and "make an opening for the aristocracy of virtue and talent" that was "essential to a well ordered republic." In Virginia, Jefferson had favored abolition of primogeniture, by which property was passed entirely to eldest sons, and of entail, which limited the rights of heirs to alienate inherited property. Even more, in early summer 1776, not long before he would replace "property" with "happiness" in his draft of the Declaration, he proposed that every person "of full age neither owning nor having owned" fifty acres of land "shall be entitled to an appropriation" of that amount to hold in "full and absolute dominion." And as Jefferson supported the right to vote for freeholders (males owning at least a quarter of an acre), his proposal would have considerably broadened democratic participation.

His friend Madison took a much more "balanced" approach to property, even in the heady revolutionary decades. "Give all power to property," he wrote, "and the indigent will be oppressed." Give all power to the poor, and the effect would be reversed. "Give a defensive share to each and each will be secure." His great fear was that the poor would combine to threaten the "rights of property & the public liberty"—two values Madison appeared to equate. He even resorted to one of the hoariest and most disingenuous arguments for restricting suffrage to the propertied—that the poor might become the "tools of opulence & ambition" and hence if they had the franchise vote against their own real interests.

The views of Alexander Hamilton on property were still more "realistic." And they certainly were blunt. As inequalities in property increased, he told the New York convention considering ratification of the Constitution in 1788, "the tendency of things will be to depart from the republican standard. This is the real disposition of human nature." He went on: "Look through the rich and the poor of the community; the learned and the ignorant. Where does virtue predominate?" The difference, he said, was not in the quantity but in the kinds of vices incident to the various classes, "and here the advantage of character belongs to the wealthy. Their vices are probably more favorable to the prosperity of the state, than those of the indigent; and partake less of moral depravity."

In the revolutionary and founding eras Hamilton was the kind of elitist a Virginia democrat would love to oppose. But as Jefferson passed through his active years as secretary of state, then as leader of the Republican opposition to the Federalists, and finally as president, his views of property lost some of their egalitarian tone.

Earlier he had declared it "self evident" that "*the earth belongs in usufruct to the living*"; thus "the dead have neither powers nor rights over it." In 1813 he reaffirmed as "universal law" that whatever belonged to all men equally and in common was "the property for the moment of him who occupies it," but when he gave up the occupation, "the property goes with it." Yet three years later he offered a vigorous defense of virtually unrestricted property rights: "To take from one, because it is thought that his own industry and that of his fathers has acquired too much" in order to spare others of less industry or skill was "to violate arbitrarily the first principle of association, 'the *guarantee* to everyone of a free exercise of his industry, and the fruits acquired by it.' " Only if the "overgrown wealth of an individual be deemed dangerous to the State" was it to be corrected by inheritance laws.

How account for Jefferson's shifts and ambiguities? He was living in a continually changing America, an America that under the impact of the Industrial Revolution was coming less and less to resemble his dream of a democracy of small landowners and becoming more and more "Hamiltonian." "Those who labour in the earth are the chosen people of God,"

Jefferson had written. "Cultivators of the earth are the most virtuous and independant citizens." Property in land and in labor Jefferson had invested with profound moral and political value. "Let our work-shops remain in Europe," he had urged. But the workshops had not remained abroad, and the rise of commerce and manufacture was beginning to transform, as it was doing in Europe, the very nature of property, with capital displacing land as its dominant form. Jefferson tried to accommodate himself to this change, but not without ambivalence or without reflections on "commercial avarice and corruption."

Another source of instability in Jefferson's ideas about property was his failure to bring ends into alignment with means. A foundation stone of his thought was the principle of severely limited government. Yet once unappropriated public lands had been exhausted, how were the fifty acres of his 1776 plan to be acquired and apportioned without strong governmental intervention? And, from the opposite view, how could weak government protect society—protect small landholders, the poor—against the great concentrations of wealth rising in the Industrial Revolution?

Jefferson's many-compartmentalized ideas were all the more evocative for their variety and adaptability. Still, it would perhaps have been better for the deepening and expansion of rights in the United States if the earlier, more egalitarian and idealistic Jefferson had prevailed more strongly, at least in the nation's consciousness, over the later, more "realistic," more Hamiltonian Jefferson. The less privileged Americans needed a leader who was both a national hero, as Jefferson indeed became, and an intellectual guide to the nature of rights and to their pursuit. It was difficult to follow a man who would come to be quoted by capitalists and communists, decentralists and nationalizers, slaveholders and abolitionists, with equal fervor—and a man who could be caricatured by Kurt Vonnegut as a "slave owner who was also one of the world's greatest theoreticians on the subject of human liberty." Neither a mere slaveholder nor a great theorist, Jefferson was intellectually most impressive when he followed his instincts and his bottomless compassion—when he went back to the needs and happiness of people, whether in the form of good beds in France or fifty acres in America.

In this one thing he never wavered, that the "right to property is founded in our natural wants," that property ownership's moral justification lay ultimately in its service to the pursuit of happiness. And in another sense Jefferson's ambiguities were perhaps a boon to oppressed Americans. Along with his magnificent moral leadership he left a political and policy gap that would have to be filled by the people themselves as they, with the help of new leaders, converted their wants and needs into new hopes, expectations, and demands on the polity.

Their task would be made more urgent by philosophy's falterings. No philosopher of rights worthy of the name emerged in the first half of the nineteenth century to take up the challenges left by Jefferson and sharpened by the Industrial Revolution. American political thought seemed perplexed by the uneasy meeting of old revolutionary traditions and ideals and new economic and social conditions. The situation was well reflected in the political writings of James Fenimore Cooper, whose radicalism in the Jacksonian cause sat awkwardly beside his contempt for the "tyranny" of "publick opinion" and his exaltation of property rights as a supreme value. "As property is the base of all civilization," he wrote in *The American Democrat,* "its existence and security are indispensable to social improvement." Where there was a "rigid equality of condition, as well as of rights, that condition must necessarily be one of a low scale of mediocrity." On the other hand, Cooper inveighed against commercial excesses and opposed suffrage restrictions on the poor. Then again, he accepted business oligarchs as bulwarks against the dangers of popular demagoguery.

When philosophy falters, praxis prospers. "Practical" thinkers and men and women of action take over. During the early decades of the nineteenth century in the United States, thought about the complex relationships among liberty, equality, and property was the province mainly of jurists, politicians, and other practitioners, as were the political and legal decisions that ensued. Equally—perhaps more passionately—concerned with these issues was a collection of leaders of workers, women, and African-Americans as well as a very different breed of thinker-activist, the utopians and communitarians. But in the struggle to seize the legal ground of property, the hardheaded men of business and law were the first to occupy the premises.

EQUAL RIGHTS: LAW AND POLITICS

ANYONE HAPPENING to enter the hearing room of the Supreme Court of the United States on a certain March day in 1818 would have beheld an arresting scene. Behind the bench the seven justices were following with rapt attention the speech of a commanding figure who, with his strong gestures and flashing eyes, appeared more the statesman and orator than a pleader at court. So he was, for this was Daniel Webster. And if the visitor had tarried for two or three hours he would have witnessed the dramatic finale—Webster crying out, "It is, sir, as I have said, a small college. And yet *there are those who love it*"—and the spectacle of Chief Justice John Marshall shedding helpless tears.

Such was the story taught to generations of American college students: that Dartmouth College had been incorporated by royal charter in 1769 as an independent institution; that its president, John Wheelock, son of the noted founder, Eleazar, had begun to flirt with New Hampshire Jeffersonians against the wishes of the board of trustees, who had then sacked him; that the Jeffersonians, after gaining control of the state legislature and governorship in 1816, had packed an expanded board with friendly trustees, changed the name to Dartmouth University, and made the new institution responsible to the state. Some of the old trustees hired Webster for an appeal to the Supreme Court on the grounds that the original charter was a grant of private property rights, that grants were contracts and hence the legislature had violated the contract clause of the federal Constitution.

A true story, but incomplete. Dartmouth as a private institution had been involved in its own kind of politics—the religious conflict of the time, notably between Congregationalists and Presbyterians. The action of the legislature reflected the Jeffersonian ground swell of popular hostility to "aristocratic" institutions much involved with the public interest but immune to public control. Dartmouth and other colleges had fallen under the tight oligarchical domination of interlocked elites, as witness the conferring of honorary degrees by Harvard and Princeton on two justices of the Supreme Court while the Court was considering the Dartmouth case.

Given Daniel Webster's legal and forensic skills, Marshall's tears, and the conservative complexion of the high court, the outcome seemed almost predetermined: in his opinion for the Court, Marshall held that Dartmouth was a private corporation, that its charter was a contract under the meaning of the federal Constitution, that the New Hampshire legislature had indeed violated the contract clause. While the justices as a whole were somewhat divided, the significant result, according to William Swindler, was that the contract clause became "at the least an unequivocal limitation upon the states and at the most could be an indefinitely expanding immunity for public and private agreements from all future impairments."

Dartmouth was the most striking and symbolic blow for the inviolability of private contracts and the protection of property rights. It was neither the first nor the most important legally. Almost ten years earlier, in *Fletcher* v. *Peck*, Marshall for the Court had upheld a Yazoo River land grant reeking with corruption which the Georgia legislature had repudiated. The Georgia repeal act, Marshall held, violated both the contract clause and natural law—presumably the natural law of property rights. Over his thirty-four-year tenure as Chief Justice, Marshall steadily built a legal foundation for his three crucial concepts: the supremacy of federal law over the states, the power of judicial review, and—the linchpin—the sanctity of property rights.

Marshall's principles formed one of the points of stability and continuity in a fluid environment. The United States in the 1820s was at once a static and a changing society—static in the continued domination of government by the old Jeffersonians, even during John Quincy Adams's presidency, but shifting economically, socially, and politically. The Jeffersonians were in fact running out of partisan and ideological steam, and Jefferson himself died on July 4, 1826. The Federalists had long since given up as a party; they awaited a radical opposition against which to mobilize. The frontier, ever westward-moving, nurtured in its wake a vast diversity of farmers, riverboatmen, speculators, lawyers, flour millers, road builders, distillers, printers, teachers. Back East the rich were growing richer, the less equal less equal. No wonder that political scientist Louis Hartz could more than a century later describe the American democrat of this era as a hybrid personality, the "man of the land, the factory, and the forge" who had "all the proletarian virtues that Marx was forever contrasting with the pettiness of the petit-bourgeois," but who was at the same time "an aggressive entrepreneur, buying 'on speculation,' combining 'some trade with agriculture,' making 'agriculture itself a trade.'"

Out of this heterogeneity arose a man, Andrew Jackson, who embraced much of it. So multisided was he that his first major biographer, James Parton, could marvel, only a decade or so after Jackson's death in 1846, at the conflicting images the man's complexity projected: he was seen as the most brilliant of generals and a military ignoramus, as an accomplished writer and an illiterate hardly able to spell, as a great statesman who never framed a law, as an honest man and a liar. In short: "A democratic autocrat. An urban savage. An atrocious saint."

As president, Jackson embodied the general public ambivalence toward property rights—favoring both property holders and the right of the state to regulate their use of it, without drawing a clear line between the two. But on one matter, at least, Jackson was consistent and unwavering—hostility toward paper money, corporate economic power, and the property rights of the bankers and other capitalists who had risen to economic dominance in Philadelphia, New York, Boston, and other financial centers. In his assault on Nicholas Biddle's Bank of the United States, long a target of popular hostility for its conservatism, its backing of "monopolists," and its identification with Eastern interests against those of other regions, Jackson personified the issue: the bank, he told Martin Van Buren, "is trying to kill me, *but I will kill it!*" But the President also generalized his attack. Vetoing its recharter, he made the bank the central issue of his successful 1832 campaign for reelection by accepting the challenge of the "rich and powerful" and appealing to the "humble members of society—the farmers, mechanics, and laborers—who have neither the time nor the means of securing like favors to themselves."

Just as the early Federalists had empowered and perpetuated their central doctrine by installing Marshall as Chief Justice, so Jackson did in 1836 with his choice of Marshall's successor, Roger Taney. Jackson had made his selection carefully. Taney as attorney general had carried the fight against the bank and could be relied on to make an issue of "equal rights for all." And in a decision of his first term on the bench, Taney rejected the pleas of the proprietors of a Charles River toll bridge that the Commonwealth of Massachusetts had unconstitutionally impaired their contract—their profits too—by chartering a competing and now toll-free bridge nearby. For *his* Court majority Taney opined that while the rights of property were "sacredly guarded, we must not forget, that the community also have rights, and that the happiness and well-being of every citizen depends on their faithful preservation."

So the issue once again was what rights, whose rights. And when it came to a people who were even more vulnerable and isolated than poor workers and farmers, the Jacksonians had a remarkably stunted vision. For decades before Jackson's presidency Native Americans had been forced from their lands and chased west. A vicious pattern had developed: bloody skirmishes broke out along the frontier, the federal government intervened and signed treaties with Indian delegations, state and local governments flouted the pacts, and conflict erupted again.

Like many frontiersmen, Jackson did not care for Native Americans. He considered them fickle, treacherous, murderous, unable to govern themselves. They were "subjects"—and you didn't make treaties with subjects. After calling in his inaugural address for a "just and liberal" policy toward Indians he started a systematic removal process, pushing Cherokees and Creeks out of their ancient lands. "My children," the President told his "subjects," "you have no right to stay, and you must go." They had no right to liberty or the pursuit of happiness—even to life, as countless died in further fighting and in such tragic treks westward as the Cherokees' Trail of Tears.

If Indians had no rights, neither did slaves, in the eyes of most Westerners and Southerners, of many Northerners, and of Andrew Jackson. The right that counted was the right to own slaves. Quick to passionate defenses of the rights of so many whites, Jackson appeared never to consider the moral dimension of slavery, nor would he allow that abolitionists might care morally about slaves. As for Taney, defender of "equal rights for all," he would before too long author an opinion that thrust the nation a giant step forward toward civil war with its holding that "the Constitution recognises the right of property of the master in a slave, and makes no distinction between that description of property and other property owned by a citizen." Members of "this unfortunate race"—including Dred Scott, the slave in the case at hand—were not and could not be American citizens, and to permit them to claim the rights of citizenship would infringe upon the legitimate property rights of their citizen-masters.

THE INDUSTRIAL REVOLUTION transforming Western societies in the 1800s had a similarly relentless impact on people's lives in the New World as in the Old. American factories proliferated, railroads, their iron rails spearing through the countryside, took over from canals and stage-coaches, mines deepened and widened, cities expanded. A relative hand-ful received huge profits from this revolution, others gained broader opportunities, the lots of still others improved—but vast armies of the poor, the working poor, immigrants, African-Americans, women, and children were worse off than before. In the spreading industrial jungles misery for the many rose in rough proportion to the explosion of big profits for the few.

In certain respects the situation of the working and nonworking poor in the New World was different from that of the poor in the Old. The American poor both competed with and joined hands with a rising tide of immigrants from Europe. And they might become emigrants them-selves, as land and other opportunities enticed them west. But few could truly escape the iron grip of industrialization, and these few—the poten-tial leaders—perceived from the British example in particular the dangers that faced the poor in America. Their view of the factory system, historian Edward Pessen noted, "was that drawn by Charles Dickens and Thomas Carlyle, by Friedrich Engels' *Condition of the English Working Classes,* and by the Parliamentary investigations of the Sadler Committee and Lord Shaftsbury," with "labor of all ages and both sexes . . . shamelessly overworked and underpaid under abysmal working conditions."

Even armed with these impressions, American workers and their lead-ers could improve only to a small degree on the fragmented responses of their comrades overseas to the ravages of industrialization; the indus-trial system was too powerful, and, by its own standards, too successful. But they could protest and strike—within limits—and seek to organize.

Workers in America, as they had in Britain, tended first to organize around specific needs and problems. The earliest unions were craft un-ions led by skilled workers struggling to achieve or preserve their special status in guild and shop. The first strikes, in the late 1780s and 1790s, were conducted by journeymen printers, carpenters, masons. The issues were immediate and local ones of pay, hours of work, working conditions. Often the associations faded away soon after the strike ended. Slowly labor organizations became more permanent and workers began to coordinate their tactics and goals with other workers, rallying in numbers to such symbolic and concrete crusades as that for the ten-hour day. By the 1830s, as industrialization quickened, hundreds of unions could claim altogether two or three hundred thousand members.

As labor organization broadened, so did its concerns and appeals. Many workers supported Andrew Jackson in his attacks on monopoly and privilege. Their leaders talked more and more of "equal rights" and even formed an Equal Rights Party. The *Working Man's Advocate* masthead proclaimed that all children were *"entitled to equal education; all adults to equal property, and all mankind to equal privileges."* Its editor wrote that all were "at birth entitled to equal means to pursue happiness," including "food, clothing, and shelter." Jacksonian labor leaders liked to evoke the glorious phrases of the Declaration of Independence. They were, according to Pessen, heirs of the Enlightenment, "ardent believers in natural laws and natural rights." Thomas Skidmore, for instance, answered the question "What are rights?" with: "the title which each of the inhabitants of the globe has to partake of and enjoy equally with his fellows, its fruits and its productions." The Jacksonians held "artificial social institutions" responsible for the plight of the poor—institutions that, in Pessen's words, frustrated "nature's benevolent designs for man. Happiness would result when society's institutions would be changed, enabling men to realize their natural rights."

The denial of what Jackson-era labor leaders devoutly believed were inalienable rights hit women workers harder than their male counterparts. Thousands of girls, recruited off farms in the Northeast, had led insular lives that had little prepared them either for the rigors of factory life or for asserting their right to organize, protest, or strike. The first recorded strike of women laborers—by Pawtucket weavers—did not occur until 1825. Working women faced not only the usual upper- and middle-class hostility to unionism of any kind but the additional stigma of "unladylike" behavior when they joined a protest meeting or picket line. Nevertheless—or perhaps in response to their special handicaps in the industrial world—some women by the 1830s and 1840s were vigorously demanding redress and claiming their rights.

The "factory girls" of Lowell were among the most militant. The huge Lowell mills thirty miles north of Boston had been planned as the largest and most efficient cotton factories in the nation. They had been planned too to avoid the squalor, vice, and illness that bred in English mill towns;

to this end, a heavy regime of paternalistic control was imposed on employees. The young women were packed into boardinghouses, two to a bed, fifteen or twenty to a room, under strict supervision. Every hour of their lives was clocked, monitored, regulated. They typically worked twelve hours a day, six days a week, with only three regular holidays a year.

Even so, the Lowell women somehow found time and energy to read books, stage theatricals, procure a piano, and publish the *Lowell Offering,* a remarkable though short-lived journal whose sprightly fiction, poetry, and essays for the most part praised the "pleasures of factory life." Visitors from afar came to behold and admire their virtuous cultural life. Charles Dickens toured the mills and left in amazement that tired workers could be so relentlessly bent on self-improvement. But many of the Lowell women did not deceive themselves. The rigor of the work, the occasional speedup and stretch-out, the stern discipline provoked rebellions over the "rights of female workers." By the mid-1840s militant female operatives were in full revolt, denouncing the *Lowell Offering* as the mouthpiece of the owners and putting out their own protest publications.

The Lowell rebels protested in the name of "Freedom—freedom for all!" Their sisters in Manchester, New Hampshire, demanded "Equal Rights and Equal privileges" with those "whom you give fat Dividends." Working women proclaimed that "Men, (and women too,) are beginning to realize the great truth which has been so oft sounded in their ears. 'All men are created free and equal.'" During a Pittsburgh strike they appealed to the Declaration of Independence and "inalienable rights." Wrote a striker: "The whole Factory Scheme, as at present in operation, is a libel on Humanity, and a disgrace to the Republic, and yet only so as an effect of the omission to establish the fundamental right essential to 'life, liberty, and the pursuit of happiness,' the Right of Rights, the right to use the earth to obtain the means of existence."

Demands for specific redress were no more successful than these appeals to broad rights. The reform women workers sought above all was the ten-hour day. In New England, Pennsylvania, and elsewhere they agitated for ten-hour laws, but after decades of struggle both in conjunction with workingmen and separately, by mid-century they had gained nothing in Massachusetts and only weak enactments in New Hampshire and Pennsylvania with clauses that permitted employers to coerce laborers into signing contracts to lengthen working hours. In Pennsylvania a fierce strike by women workers finally brought about a true ten-hour day—together with a sharp cut in wages.

Lacking the right to vote, women could bring little weight to bear in the legislative chambers. A Massachusetts Senate committee reported that while the legislature had the authority to pass a ten-hour law, it could not "deprive the citizen of his freedom of contract." Property rights remained intact.

The women workers' efforts that had waxed in the 1840s faded in the prosperity of the 1850s. The explosion of claims for their rights left little permanent mark on the nation. It did leave some brilliant rhetoric and stirring poetry. Be strong, be united, a "Ten Hour Woman" urged the "Mechanics of Fall River":

> Woman is upon your side,
>   Full armed for moral fight,
> For brother's aye, and sister's wrongs,
>   For God and human right.

A S W O R K E R S met roadblock after roadblock to what they viewed as moderate demands, leaders became more radicalized in their political strategy if not in their goals. The most obvious stratagem was to reject both of the existing major parties, and between 1828 and 1834 over sixty independent workers' political parties were organized. A common concern of these parties was public education for workers' children, not as "a grace and bounty or charity" but as "a matter of right and duty." They inveighed against compulsory enlistment in state militias, noting that the rich could easily pay the fines for nonparticipation. They opposed imprisonment for debt, chartered monopolies, competition from convict labor, and called for a "fair income or property tax" to replace existing poll taxes or taxes on staples.

But labor's third parties failed to break the political stranglehold of the American two-party system; often they accomplished little more in elections than to split the liberal vote and ensure the victory of the most conservative candidates. Potentially more effective was working within the major party most sympathetic to workers, in an effort to move it further toward labor's positions. In the mid-1830s in New York City, the Equal Rights movement erupted within the Jacksonian Democracy. More than a faction but less than a party, the Locofocos, as they came to be called, joined with regular Democrats in ventures against monopolies and "special privilege," but fought the regulars—especially the Tammanyites—when they appeared to be deserting the cause of labor. But working within the party system offered no easy route to power either, especially in the 1840s and 1850s as Whigs and conservative Democrats alternated in control of the presidency.

If some labor leaders rejected the party rivalry of Tweedledum and Tweedledee, "true radicals" rejected the whole political system; they would simply desert it. Such was the attitude, at least, of leaders of the scores of utopian communities that sprang up in settled, and often unsettled, parts of the United States. The prime example was New Harmony on the Wabash River in Indiana. Its founder, Robert Owen, the "boy wonder of English capitalism," had turned against the ugliness of British industrialism to come to a new world where he could establish a community free of the competitive scramble and gross inequality. His purpose, Owen said, was "to introduce an entire new State of society; to change it from the ignorant, selfish system to an enlightened social system, which shall gradually unite all interests into one." The aim would be to secure the "greatest amount of happiness" for Americans.

The New Harmony experiment, alas, disintegrated after little more than a year amid disillusion and conflict. Other communities also failed, including those established in the spirit of the French thinker Charles Fourier, a cosmologist who engaged in such delightful fantasies as the fornication of the planets. Like Owenism, Fourierism supposed that men and women living together in small communities could overcome their natural divisions, fulfill their most fundamental needs, and realize their most human instincts and passions. But this doctrine of "associationism," as Arthur Schlesinger, Jr., noted, "rarely talked about democracy, exhibited no interest in equality and attached small value to political liberty." Nor did it comprehend the essential role of conflict in the promotion of liberty and equality.

It was this scorn for conflict that most provoked the Marxists: the utopians "reject all political, and especially all revolutionary, action," Marx and Engels wrote in the *Communist Manifesto* in 1848; "they wish to attain their ends by peaceful means, and endeavour, by small experiments, necessarily doomed to failure, and by the force of example, to pave the way for the new social Gospel."

Yet as the utopians pursued their "small experiments" in the hinterlands, the Industrial Revolution continued its merciless work in mid-nineteenth-century America, breeding inequalities, pitting capitalists against laborers, arming the oppressed with an awareness of their deprivations, fertilizing the soil of conflict. And on the horizon loomed another irrepressible conflict, a quite different and ultimately far bloodier conflict, but one that also had the rights of the oppressed at its heart. In 1854, George Fitzhugh, a Virginia lawyer and writer, drew the two types of oppression into a single view. He maintained, and with a disturbing touch of plausibility, that conditions for the laboring poor in Northern cities had become so desperate that slaves on Southern plantations were on the whole more comfortable and better fed, and enjoyed more security and so peace of mind, than the industrial "slaves" of the North. And thus, he concluded, slave society was "the best form of society yet devised for the masses." At this point the debate over rights in America reached its nadir.

PART TWO

CHAPTER FOUR

CROSSING TO JERUSALEM

As Thomas Paine's *Common Sense* had emboldened American rebels to fight against British tyranny, so another impassioned pamphlet appearing half a century later urged enslaved Americans to revolt against those ex-rebels and their descendants who had themselves become tyrants. David Walker had been born a "free" black in Wilmington, North Carolina, in 1785 and moved to Boston in his thirties when he could no longer bear the slave society surrounding him. Self-taught, he sold used clothes for a living. Becoming active in the Massachusetts General Colored Association, founded in 1826 for moral and economic "uplift" and the abolition of slavery, he lectured and also served as Boston correspondent for *Freedom's Journal* in New York (later called *The Rights of All*), the first African-American newspaper. Walker's pamphlet, *Appeal to the Coloured Citizens of the World,* was published in 1829.

"Can our condition be any worse?" the revolutionary *Appeal* asked its readers. "Against all accusations which may or can be preferred against me, I appeal to Heaven for my motive in writing—who knows that my object is, if possible, to awaken in the breasts of my afflicted, degraded and slumbering brethren, a spirit of inquiry and investigation respecting our miseries and wretchedness in this *Republican Land of Liberty*!!!!!!" His tract spoke to both white and black. After quoting the heart of the Declaration of Independence he lambasted its hypocrisy. "Compare your own language above," he demanded of white readers, " . . . with your cruelties and murders inflicted by your cruel and unmerciful fathers and yourselves on our fathers and on us. . . . I ask you candidly, was your sufferings under Great Britain, one hundredth part as cruel and tyranical as you have rendered ours under you?"

Walker worried that his black brethren were too passive, too timid, and too quick to court favor with their "natural enemies" who have "for hundreds of years stolen our *rights*," thinking that "we are too servile to assert our rights as men." He looked for black people with "Moses' excellent disposition" to lead the battle. "Fear not the number and education of our *enemies*, against whom we shall have to contend for our lawful right; guaranteed to us by our Maker; for why should we be afraid, when God is, and will continue, (if we continue humble) to be on our side?"

In less than a year Walker printed three editions of his *Appeal* and distributed it widely, sending literary shock waves out from the "cradle of liberty." Blacks extolled it as "an inspired work," but panicky white Southerners damned the "diabolical Boston pamphlet" as utterly seditious. Southern mayors fired off angry protests to the mayor of Boston. Georgia, Louisiana, and North Carolina reacted by banning all such incendiary writings, with heavy penalties for violators, including death. Four black men in New Orleans were jailed for circulating Walker's pamphlet.

Even Northern whites who fought to abolish slavery did not approve of Walker's brash militance. In January 1831, William Lloyd Garrison founded *The Liberator* in Boston, for many years the leading organ of the abolitionist movement. Garrison, who helped create the American Anti-Slavery Society and led it for three decades, pulled few punches in his rhetorical pounding of slavery, offending many whites. But moral outrage had limits for him when it came to deeds such as Walker advocated. In his paper's second issue he declared that the *Appeal* "was too violent and irreverent in its 'spirit and tendency' and sought vengeance, which was the prerogative of the Lord." Walker was in no position to defend himself against this charge. He had been found dead outside his store several months prior, rumored to have been poisoned by slaveholders' agents.

David Walker had articulated the right of African-Americans to be free from slavery and degradation and had called for a revolution to seize it. Many slaves expressed this fundamental right in less literate forms and more covertly but with no less conviction. Through prayers, dreams, hushed talks, singing of spirituals, and in the letters of those who could write, black people communicated their assumption that they had "birthrights" as Americans and human beings. Even the great majority compulsorily illiterate (teaching slaves to read and write was generally forbidden) were not insulated from the pervasive language of rights inherited from the American Revolution. Many knew that the "unalienable rights" to life, liberty, and the pursuit of happiness were, in actuality, the rights of whites only, but they fervently believed these rights belonged to them as well. This faith was belied, however, by almost everything in their experience.

A black correspondent who signed his letter "Euthymus" pointed out these confusions and contradictions in Garrison's *Liberator*. Citing the 1776 Declaration's promise of rights, he remarked that "either the man of color was forgotten, or he was not recognized as a human being, or he is an exception to the universal rule, or his right is superseded by the paramount right of his master to hold him in servitude, and to work, scourge and sell him like a slave." The property rights of slaveholders reigned supreme, virtually abrogating the basic natural rights of those they claimed to own. Black minister Nathaniel Paul asserted that if he was in error about blacks having equal rights, it was Washington, Jefferson, and other founders whose sentiments "have caused me to stray." From Gabriel Prosser's thwarted slave rebellion of 1800 to the present day, the essential demand of black Americans has been for the nation to be true to its own stated ideals and promises—for all of its citizens.

Unlike Jefferson and his peers who gave lip service to the divine sanction of rights—religious skeptics that they were—African-Americans' certitude about their entitlements was embedded in their spirituality, which fused African traditions and Protestant evangelism. Akin to the hybrid Christianity they cultivated was their development of a distinct interpretation of rights (both natural and conferred by citizenship), in which religious authority, human and divine, stood at the center.

Through the tumults and traumas of the nineteenth century—before, during, and after the cataclysm of the Civil War—black Americans fashioned the language of rights into a formidable, multi-edged weapon in their mostly nonviolent battles for freedom. Rights had a resonance for black people not shared by those who took them for granted. "Blacks always believed in rights in some larger, mythologic sense—as a pantheon of possibility," explains legal scholar Patricia Williams. "We gave them life where there was none before; held onto them, put the hope of them into our wombs, mothered them . . . we nurtured rights and gave rights life."

WHICH ROAD TO FREEDOM?

AMBROSE HEADEN, a carpenter, grew up a slave in North Carolina and was later sold at auction to a new owner in Alabama. "During all my slave life I never lost sight of freedom," he recalled after the Civil War. "It was always on my heart; it came to me like a solemn thought, and often circumstances much stimulated the desire to be free and raised great expectation of it." The same theme was heard over and over. Thomas Likers: "I came to the conclusion that God never meant me for a slave ... No matter what privileges I had, I felt that I had not my rights as long as I was deprived of liberty." Harriet Jacobs escaped from slavery in the early 1840s and published a gripping autobiography. In a letter to a friend she proclaimed that God "gave me a soul that burned for freedom and a heart nerved with determination to suffer even unto death in pursuit of that liberty which without makes life an intolerable burden."

If enslaved men and women held such unwavering faith in their entitlement to life, liberty, even happiness, why did they revolt so rarely? To slaves, Southern society felt like a vast prison with many walls, every institution and resource at the slaveholders' command. Any uprising faced insurmountable odds, as had been shown by the crushing of rebellions led by Gabriel Prosser, Denmark Vesey, and Nat Turner. Far more widespread were less visible forms of resistance, such as work slowdowns, feigning illness or pregnancy, spoiling crops, breaking tools, theft, arson, and physical self-defense. Much resistance was expressed communally via spiritual channels, especially in praying and singing for "deliverance" in fields or woods or behind closed doors. "When de day's work was done," Alabaman Mingo White remembered, "de slaves would be found locked in deir cabins prayin' for de Lord to free dem like he did de chillen of Israel. . . . De slaves had a way of puttin' a wash pot in de door of de cabin to keep de sound in de house." If caught they were brutally whipped. "Dey don't allow a man to whip a horse like dey whipped us in dem days."

Since over half the states had prohibited slavery, as had Canada further north, increasingly slaves concluded that flight from bondage was the only feasible route to freedom.

How different was life for the free black people, "slaves without masters," who lived up North? By 1830 about 5 percent of the black population of three and a half million lived in the Northern states, mainly in the larger cities. Unschooled, or poorly taught in segregated schools, barred from many jobs and discriminated against in others, forced to sit apart in streetcars, steamships, and restaurants, in most states unable to vote, sit on juries, or even testify against whites—Northern blacks seemed to have few if any rights. That conditions were a notch or two above slavery was scant comfort. During the nation's first four decades pragmatic black leaders for the most part did not try to secure civil and political rights directly. Understanding that certain foundations had to come first, they built an array of institutions aimed at elevating the race, such as schools, mutual aid societies, and independent black churches, especially African Methodist Episcopal (AME). This work of self-organization, moral training, and economic self-sufficiency fostered racial pride and cohesion indispensable for further advances.

Then came the 1830s and 1840s, an era of deep social turmoil that included agitation by Workingmen's parties, strikes by women textile workers and others, temperance drives, and the birth of Transcendentalism. At the forefront was the crusade for the immediate and unconditional abolition of slavery that burst forth in Northern cities in the early 1830s. It was a biracial movement of women as well as men, but its leaders were mainly white male editors, lawyers, and ministers. Fueled, as was other social protest, by the long tradition of Protestant evangelism and its current "Great Awakening," and symbolized by Garrison's fiery and uncompromising rhetoric, abolitionism flourished as an intensely moralistic appeal to Americans, including slaveholders, to recognize slavery as a sin and to repent by peacefully destroying it. The movement employed a strategy of mass moral conversion that, until the 1840 schism, eschewed both electoral politics and violent resistance. Its weapon was words. Abolitionists "sought not merely social change," notes historian Lori Ginzberg, "but spiritual transformation, the moral regeneration of the world." This evangelical impulse "provided the framework in which radical social change was articulated in the antebellum period."

African-Americans, many of them ex-slaves, played central roles in abolitionist agitation while simultaneously organizing to uplift their communities and secure their own rights. From the start they had an uneasy relationship with white abolitionists. Hundreds of black activists participated in the local, state, and national antislavery societies springing up in the 1830s, some working as agents and lecturers, particularly those who had tasted slavery firsthand. Their visibility did not translate into power to make policy. Few served as officers, especially at the national level. They resented the exclusion but protested quietly for the good of the cause.

Northern blacks were concerned as much with their own oppression as with slavery; for them abolitionism was inseparable from a broader rights crusade. Not only did most of their white allies downplay any goals beyond minimal liberty but, assuming racial inequality as given, many did not believe that blacks should be accorded equal rights. Or they thought that civil and political rights were permissible but not "social" rights to integration. The interest of morally oriented white abolitionists in a spectrum of reforms, including women's rights and temperance, did not extend beyond abolition to other reforms that free blacks cared deeply about, such as voting rights. The white agitators assailed slavery as a moral evil but did not take seriously the positive steps required for African-Americans to be truly free.

The response of blacks, characteristic of their fractured cultural identity, was to move in two directions at once: to work within the white-led organizations and to create their own as a framework for independent action—the latter drawing criticism from whites for promoting separatism. The main vehicle of autonomous activism was the black convention. The first such gathering was held in September 1830, at the Bethel AME Church in Philadelphia, the nation's first black church. Its respected minister, Richard Allen, presided over an assembly of leaders from eight states. Like its successors, the meeting began its manifesto by paying homage to the truths of "that inestimable and invaluable instrument," the Declaration of Independence.

Black conventions met annually in Philadelphia or New York for the next several years. They dealt with emigration to Canada, repeal of "black laws" (repressive laws exclusively affecting blacks), creation of independent schools, and plans for economic uplift and self-sufficiency, never divorcing these from emancipation.

By the late 1830s the national parleys had become moribund, their vigor absorbed by state gatherings concerned mainly with legal rights and suffrage, reforms that called for state action. These assemblies in turn served as a "bridge" to the more confrontational national black conventions of the 1840s. Besides providing a forum to chart strategy and forge political unity, the national and state black conventions enhanced racial identity and served as training grounds for dozens of talented leaders such as William Wells Brown, Henry Highland Garnet, and John Mercer Langston.

ONE WHOSE LEADERSHIP matured in these spirited conventions was Frederick Douglass, the preeminent American rights advocate of the nineteenth century, who was born to bondage in Maryland in 1817. Douglass's intelligence and drive enabled him to learn to read and write as a young boy. Detesting slavery, he escaped at twenty-one after "hiring out" as a caulker at a Baltimore shipyard. Settling in New Bedford, Massachusetts, with his free black wife, Anna Murray, in 1838, Douglass began reading Garrison's *Liberator,* became a devoted follower, and three years later gave his first antislavery speech on Nantucket Island. Garrison and others were so awed by his eloquence that they persuaded him to join the cause as a paid lecturer.

He jumped in just after the movement had split in two. On one side, the Garrisonians insisted on moral suasion as the exclusive strategy, condemned churches that condoned slavery, attacked the Constitution as proslavery, promoted secession of the North, and linked abolition with other, nonracial reforms. The more pragmatic types who broke away to form a rival antislavery society focused single-mindedly on ending slavery and worked with mainstream Protestant churches and with electoral parties to achieve political leverage.

Black activists chose sides as well. For a decade Douglass remained faithful to the Garrisonian creed. His commanding presence, resonant voice, dramatic skills, gift for mimicry, photographic memory, and careful preparation made him one of the great orators of the age. He rode the lecture circuit with Garrison and others for several years, then took refuge in England when his safety seemed in jeopardy. After returning a celebrity in 1847, he founded his own newspaper, *The North Star*—to the Garrisonians' chagrin—and emerged as an independent force, working more closely with blacks than with whites. Eventually renouncing Garrisonian principles, he delved into electoral action and antislavery parties and stepped up his agitation for civil and political rights tied to racial uplift. As a leader of black people and of multi-issue reform, including women's rights, he reached his pinnacle of moral and political leadership in the 1850s.

"Douglass's influence derived largely from his uncanny ability to articulate his people's needs and aspirations," according to biographer Waldo Martin, Jr., "couching his people's struggle in the context of a quest for rights and privileges basic to American democracy." Expositions of "human rights" or "rights of man" were the bedrock of his lectures, writing, and organizing. In an early speech he asserted that "a large portion of the slaves *know* that they have a right to their liberty." Later he suggested that the right to liberty "entered into the very idea of man's creation. It was born with us; and no laws, constitutions, compacts, agreements, or combinations can ever abrogate or destroy it. . . . It is written on all the powers and faculties of the human soul."

Douglass's ambivalence toward the Constitution kept him from justifying rights on the basis of that document, even after he had decided that it was not, in its essentials at least, proslavery. Initially he had supported the Garrisonian position that the Constitution's counting of a slave as three-fifths of a person in determining the size of congressional districts, its fugitive slave clause protecting slaveholders' legal claims to their human property, and its provision to continue the slave trade for another two decades outweighed whatever positive features it contained, such as the added-on Bill of Rights. Instead Douglass appealed to the moral and political authority of the Declaration of Independence, which he deemed a higher charter. He believed that the chief obstacle to abolition and elevation was the power of an illegitimate right that conflicted with the Declaration's promise of life, liberty, and pursuit of happiness: "the right of property in man."

As he grew more independent of white leaders, Douglass expounded more and more forcefully the principle that black people had to fight for their own rights. In *The North Star* he asserted that the "main work must be commenced, carried on, and concluded by ourselves. . . . Our destiny, for good or for evil, for time and for eternity, is, by an all-wise God, committed to us; and that all the helps or hindrances with which we may meet on earth, can never release us from this high and heaven-imposed responsibility. . . . A man who will not labor to gain his rights, is a man who would not, if he had them, prize and defend them."

Here perhaps lay the kernel of his homegrown philosophy. Attaining rights was the precondition for integration into American society; but the seizing of civil, political, and economic rights was at the core of black people's responsibility to raise themselves as a group. The two paths were interwoven. Rights could not be fully realized until prejudice was diminished, which would not occur without exemplary black efforts at moral and economic uplift. Collective self-help was the crucial tool of liberation in all areas; in the realm of rights, not just the struggle to clothe them in law but, even more, to carry them out. Moreover, such organized autonomy and self-reliance were vital to remove slavery's psychological legacy of deference and dependence.

INDEPENDENT black activism in the North came into its own in persistent campaigns for suffrage, linked with efforts to desegregate schools and transportation and to change laws barring black testimony and juries. Prior to the Civil War black men could vote only in New England (except Connecticut); they could vote in New York if they owned property. Several states had taken the franchise away from them, leaving doubled resentment since it was extended to all white males during the same period. Black leaders knew that they would have to exercise some degree of political leverage in order to effect substantive changes, through swing voting if not officeholding.

Pennsylvania was an early suffrage battleground. Except in Philadelphia blacks could generally vote in the state until a constitutional convention disfranchised them in 1838. African-Americans organized a mammoth petition campaign, and a Philadelphia mass meeting issued an "Appeal of Forty Thousand Citizens": "We lay hold of the principles which Pennsylvania asserted in the hour which tried men's souls—which BENJAMIN FRANKLIN and his eight colleagues, in name of the commonwealth, pledged their lives, their fortunes, and their sacred honor to sustain: We take our stand upon that solemn declaration; that to protect inalienable rights 'governments are instituted among men, deriving their JUST POWERS from the CONSENT of the governed,' and proclaim that a government which tears away from us and our posterity the very power of CONSENT, is a tyrannical usurpation which we will never cease to oppose."

The white majority did not listen, ratifying the new charter by a wide margin. Adding insult to injury, a story circulated afterward about a white boy who stole a black boy's marbles with the taunt "You have no rights now." Blacks kept agitating for the vote through conventions and petition campaigns but did not reclaim it until Reconstruction.

In New York the suffrage battle aimed at abrogating the blacks-only property requirement. A dynamic young leader took the helm at a formative Albany convention in 1840. As a ten-year-old, Henry Highland Garnet had escaped from slavery with his parents. Schooled at the Oneida Institute in upstate New York, he became a pastor in Troy and a vigorous abolitionist. Even more than Douglass he stressed the need for his people to take liberation into their own hands. "*Ours* is the battle," he said, self-assertion "the great law of our being." A disciple of David Walker, he urged slaves to rebel: "Awake, awake; millions of voices are calling you!" Garnet exhorted them. "Let your motto be RESISTANCE! RESIST-ANCE! RESISTANCE!—No oppressed people have ever secured their liberty without resistance."

Garnet journeyed up and down the Empire State collecting suffrage petitions at countless local meetings, which he and a fellow organizer brought to the capital—only to be rebuffed by legislators too busy planning a bridge across the Hudson. Undaunted, state and local conventions grew in size and fervor, enhanced by active female participants, and churned out reams of resolutions and petitions, leading to a constitutional convention that dropped the property barrier—only to lose when the amendment was placed on the ballot. Fourteen more years of work produced another suffrage amendment that again was rejected by white voters.

Ohio had a large black population since it bordered on Kentucky and western Virginia and offered a safe haven for slaves who made it across the Ohio River. Not surprisingly, the state harbored the strongest movement for black rights west of New York. Stirring conventions debated a broad agenda of reforms with suffrage at the center. Another promising leader, John Mercer Langston, made his debut at the age of nineteen at the 1849 gathering. One of the earliest black graduates of Oberlin, the first college to admit nonwhites, Langston organized Ohio as methodically as Garnet had New York, becoming renowned as an abolitionist speaker; one associate called him "a walking and talking encyclopedia." In 1850 he and Douglass, touring together, barely escaped a vicious mob in Columbus. When not on the road, Langston practiced law in Oberlin, the first black lawyer in the West. Ohio blacks did secure the right to testify against whites in court, but suffrage remained out of reach. Only in Rhode Island were black efforts directly responsible for winning the vote. In most "free" states their rights were still held hostage by white prejudice.

Although for reasons of race and gender the vast majority of black people could not vote, many rights activists helped to form a series of new parties to challenge the proslavery two-party system of Democrats and Whigs. First was the Liberty Party of the 1840s, unequivocally abolitionist and prosuffrage; then came Free Soil, opposed to the *extension* of slavery; finally, "Conscience" Whigs, Free-Soilers, and antislavery Democrats founded the Republican Party after passage of the 1854 Kansas-Nebraska Act, which did not bar slavery in these territories and ignited a small civil war in Kansas. As changing circumstances improved electoral chances, each new party compromised on slavery more than its predecessor. Nevertheless black citizens (enfranchised or not) joined the moderate Republicans in sizable numbers during the late 1850s.

Although gaining political rights might have been a more effective long-run strategy, many individuals angered by mistreatment and exclusion took direct action to assert their rights in matters of everyday life, such as getting to work and going to school. Elizabeth Jennings was a young organist at a Congregational church in New York City. When she boarded a horse-drawn streetcar on her way to church one Sunday morning in 1854, the conductor ordered her into the next car, already full, "reserved for her people." She refused to budge. "He took hold of me and I took hold of the window sash," she reported to a mass meeting of supporters. "He pulled me until he broke my grasp. I took hold of his coat and held on to that." Conductor and driver then "seized hold of me by the arms and pulled and dragged me down on the bottom of the platform, so that my feet hung one way and my head the other, nearly on the ground. I screamed, 'Murder,' with all my voice." She climbed back on, and the conductor ordered the car forward until he found a police officer, who "thrust me out and then tauntingly told me to get redress if I could." Infuriated, she sued the streetcar company and with the aid of a young lawyer (and future president) named Chester Alan Arthur eventually won a damage claim from the state high court and an order for equal treatment. Her bold action sparked further agitating and litigating by women and men that succeeded in integrating the city's public transport.

Activists had been fighting Jim Crow accommodations for years. In the 1830s, the partly blind David Ruggles, an abolitionist, journalist, the first known black bookseller, and later a renowned specialist in water therapy (which apparently cured his own blindness), had been kicked off trains and steamboats in Massachusetts for sitting in whites-only sections. Ruggles's lawsuit against a railroad was dismissed by a judge who held stock in the company. Further protests and legislative lobbying halted this type of discrimination in the state. In the course of his organizing jaunts around New York, Henry Garnet often defied segregated railroad cars. Despite an amputated leg, "he generally hugged the seats," a report said, "and sometimes they would go with him as a whole or in part." He ended segregation on one line, but on another was badly beaten and thrown out.

Since equal educational opportunity was considered fundamental both to group uplift and to gaining rights, campaigns against school segregation were hard fought. Yet the black community was not united on this issue. An outspoken minority argued for separate schools to instill racial pride and identity and to offer more useful training in a less hostile setting. But few could ignore the abysmal quality of most black schools. Ohio conventions debated the question year after year, seeking the most appropriate means to educate the young. In Rochester, New York, where his daughter had to attend school in a cold church cellar, Douglass led a winning effort to desegregate public schools.

The most determined campaign took place in Boston, where years of protest and legal maneuvers, including a test case argued by white attorney Charles Sumner, compelled the legislature to ban segregated schools in 1855. At a victory celebration, leader William Nell announced that it was the women of color who deserved most credit for "equal school rights." "In the dark hours of our struggle," he said, "when betrayed by traitors within and beset by foes without . . . then did the women keep the flame alive." Elsewhere in the North schools and other public facilities generally stayed segregated.

As Douglass, Garnet, Langston, Jennings, Ruggles, and thousands of other black citizens made clear, campaigns for rights and desegregation reinforced efforts at moral and economic elevation, and vice versa, notwithstanding the latter's tendency toward separatism. Bridging these paths was the widely shared ethic that African-Americans had to assume the duty of their own liberation, encapsulated in the oft-proclaimed adage that if blacks "would be free, they must themselves strike the blow."

THEMSELVES STRIKE THE BLOW

DESPITE the torrent of organizing and institution-building by nominally free African-Americans, their conditions appeared to be worsening.

A momentous event in 1850 brought this home to them: congressional passage of a harsh Fugitive Slave Law, the linchpin of the "Compromise of 1850" aimed at forestalling disunion over slavery. Crafted by two elder statesmen, Whig senators Henry Clay of Kentucky and Daniel Webster of Massachusetts, the Compromise sought to balance sectional interests but favored the South—admitting California as a free state but allowing slavery in New Mexico, both seized in the recent Mexican War; abolishing the slave trade (though not slavery) in the nation's capital but enacting a statute giving slaveholders or their agents free rein to capture alleged escapees in the North.

What was new about the law on fugitives was its power of enforcement. The Constitution itself contained a vague fugitive clause that implicitly sanctioned the right to slave property, key evidence in the Garrisonian indictment that the charter upheld slavery. In 1793 Congress passed a law that lacked teeth regarding fugitive slaves. The 1850 statute stripped the accused fugitive of such basic rights as trial by jury and habeas corpus, paid judges a doubled fee for conviction, and required not only Northern authorities but all citizens to act as accomplices in slave-catching; it made aiding fugitives a serious crime. Slaves suffered most, but free blacks were hardly less vulnerable to legalized kidnapping. Battle lines were sharply drawn between the human right to life and liberty and the right to property in human beings—a conflict made more irrepressible since the monetary value of such "property" had been steadily rising due to the cotton gin, the collapse of the transatlantic slave trade, and the opening of slave country to the southwest. More than ever slaves were precious commodities.

Nothing showed better the wide gulf between the races than how each responded to "the Armistice of 1850." Most whites expressed relief, believing that the contentious slavery question had finally been settled. Blacks, who had remonstrated against the fugitive bill during the legislative debate, were outraged. It marked a turning point in the freedom struggle, a shift from protest to defiant resistance and to African-Americans taking center stage of the abolitionist movement. "Now blacks were major shapers of the policies and methods which after 1850 many white abolitionists accepted and made their own," conclude Jane and William Pease.

This change was dramatically symbolized by Douglass's abrupt turn away from Garrisonian doctrines. In an 1852 Rochester speech entitled "The Meaning of July Fourth for the Negro," he declared that "slavery has been nationalized in its most horrible and revolting form . . . The right of the hunter to his prey stands superior . . . to *all* rights in this republic, the rights of God included!" Earlier, in Boston, he had asserted that "no legislation can for one moment alienate man's right to his own body," and in Syracuse he counseled resistance, violent if necessary, shocking Garrisonians who clung to nonviolence as a matter of principle. He had once considered human life the highest value, he admitted, but "now thought Liberty of more value"; the slaveholder who denied another's liberty "has no right to live."

Through speeches, passionate debate at public meetings, petitions, editorials, and informal gatherings, a consensus emerged in the Northern black community that civil disobedience was the proper recourse. Summing up resolutions from meetings up and down the Atlantic seaboard, one editorial warned those who would execute the law "that the business of catching slaves, or kidnapping freemen, is an open warfare upon the rights and liberties of the black men of the North." Reverend J. W. Loguen, an escaped slave and Syracuse abolitionist leader, appealed to a mass meeting of whites and blacks to block the authorities from stealing him back to bondage. "The people of Syracuse and of the whole North," he exclaimed, "must meet this tyranny and crush it by force, or be crushed by it. This hellish enactment has precipitated the conclusion that white men must live in dishonorable submission, and colored men be slaves, or they must give their physical as well as intellectual powers to the defence of human rights. The time has come to change the tones of submission into tones of defiance—and to tell Mr. Fillmore and Mr. Webster, if they propose to execute this measure upon us, to send on their blood-hounds. . . . I received my freedom from Heaven, and with it came the command to defend my title to it."

Long before the new repression, free blacks had acted on their own against slavery by rescuing fugitives. In 1836, for instance, a group of black women "invaded" the Massachusetts Supreme Court and freed two women whose status was being decided; predictably the deed was scored by Garrison and the state antislavery society. Now such exploits proliferated, drew white support, and set the tone for the whole movement. Abolitionists discovered that one well-publicized rescue effort was worth a hundred speeches. Many were carried out by efficient black-run Vigilance Committees in several cities that formed a loose network. When Shadrach, a Boston coffeehouse waiter, was arrested in early 1851, an assemblage of blacks entered the court during his hearing and spirited him to freedom in Montreal. Juries refused to convict the perpetrators. Underlining federal determination to enforce the law, Secretary of State Webster condemned the episode as "an act of clear treason."

The bloodiest resistance occurred near Christiana in southeastern Pennsylvania. William Still of the Philadelphia Vigilance Committee alerted ex-slave William Parker, a local abolitionist, that slaveholders and

U.S. marshals from nearby Maryland had warrants to seize four fugitive slaves who had taken refuge in his house. When they broke in, a horn blew from upstairs and the invaders were surrounded by a group of blacks armed with rifles, clubs, axes, and corn-cutters. In a pitched battle the slave owner was killed, his son badly injured; Parker fled with the fugitives. Interpreting the skirmish as a virtual act of war, the Fillmore administration dispatched Marines to aid police as they scoured the countryside; innocent blacks were harassed and many were arrested. Thaddeus Stevens and other respected barristers defended those tried for treason. The jury acquitted them.

Here as elsewhere the government was stymied. It quietly retreated from its impossible mission. Slaveholders fumed at losing their valuable property and at what they felt were Washington's halfhearted efforts to protect their rights. In word and deed Northern blacks kept pressing their case that, as expressed by a convention of fugitive slaves in upstate New York, although slaves had been taught to respect rights to property, "no such rights belong to the slaveholder. His right to property is but the robber-right."

Despite the draconian fugitive law, most enslaved blacks who got to the North managed to avoid capture. Rescues were the visible arm of a larger operation to guide slaves out of the South, provide food, clothing, and safe shelter en route, and assist resettlement in free states and increasingly in Canada, beyond the reach of slave-catchers. Black and white abolitionists had abetted flight since before the nation's founding, but the "Underground Railroad" became highly organized as more and more slaves chose this strategy of freedom. Many left upon learning of imminent sale further south where treatment was worse—or after one more whipping, or rape, pushed them over the edge. It was not only fear of getting caught that made it such an agonizing decision. Many men, and some women, left their families behind, hoping to bring them out later. Both blacks and whites served as "station agents" offering shelter and support at stops along the way, but the "conductors" who guided the fugitives to safety were almost entirely black.

The most skillful and successful of conductors was Harriet Tubman, who in ten years reportedly led nineteen excursions that freed two to three hundred, including almost all of her big family. One of eleven children growing up on a Maryland plantation, she started household labor at age five and in her early teens was forced into field work. One day an overseer threw a weight at another slave Tubman was trying to protect but hit her instead, fracturing her skull and causing permanent injury that left her subject to sudden sleeping spells. From childhood she cultivated a deep spiritual faith and grew confident that she could speak with God. When her master died in 1849, answering her prayers, and with her family about to be sold, she decided to escape—though unable to persuade her husband or brothers to join her.

"I had reasoned dis out in my mind," she later recalled. "There was one of two things I had a *right* to, liberty, or death; if I could not have one, I would have de oder; for no man should take me alive; I should fight for my liberty as long as my strength lasted, and when de time came for me to go, de Lord would let dem take me." Heading off alone, guided by the North Star, she reached Philadelphia and worked as a hotel maid until she saved enough money to make her first expedition homeward. With each winter journey word of her missions spread more widely among slaves and slaveholders, the latter placing a huge bounty on her head. She became a legendary symbol of courageous resistance to slavery.

The enslaved had a special fealty to the Old Testament and had always identified with the "chillen of Israel" fleeing from Egyptian bondage. They called Tubman "Moses." Not just her exuberant sense of divine guidance but her down-to-earth leadership abilities made this name fit. Scouting paths through the nocturnal wilderness, recruiting helpers to rip down runaway-slave notices, scavenging for food and supplies, singing spirituals with secret messages, swimming across raging frigid rivers, she "accomplished her purpose with a coolness, foresight, patience, and wisdom," wrote an abolitionist editor. "She was unsurpassed in the logistics of escape," notes Benjamin Quarles, "in anticipating the needs of her fugitive flocks, whether for food or clothes, disguises or forged passes, train tickets or wagons."

Yet Tubman and other conductors could not have completed their missions without heroic station agents like David Ruggles (who harbored Frederick Douglass), Thomas Garrett, and William Still, and the railroad's far-flung infrastructure. And even without conductors, thousands resolved to implement their birthright to liberty by heading north. Frightened, famished, fatigued, and frostbitten, most eventually reached the promised land. A few shipped themselves in wooden boxes. Ellen Craft masqueraded as a well-heeled master, her husband as servant, and they lodged at the finest hotels.

Though only a tiny fraction of four million slaves rode the fabled railroad, its effect was to further divide the fractured nation by accelerating abolitionism and convincing slaveholders that their property rights were imperiled. Closing his thorough study of the subject, Wilbur Siebert judged that the Underground Railroad "was one of the greatest forces which brought on the Civil War, and thus destroyed slavery."

———

IN MARCH 1857 the Supreme Court tried to end the slavery impasse by judicial fiat. The principal protagonists personified the glaring social divide. Dred Scott was a slave hailing from Southampton County, Virginia (site of Nat Turner's rebellion in 1831), who was taken first to Missouri and then, by a new owner, to the free state of Illinois and the free territory of Wisconsin. Prevented from buying himself when he returned to Missouri, he sued for his freedom on the grounds that his slave status ended when he was transported to Illinois. Rebuffed by lower courts, antislavery lawyers eventually brought his case before the highest tribunal. Dominating the Supreme Court during this era was Chief Justice Roger Taney, conservative Southern Democrat and scion of an upper-class, slaveholding family of Maryland tobacco planters.

Taney's long-winded majority opinion, regarded as the Court's definitive judgment in a decision with two dissents, far transcended the life of one human being. The eighty-year-old jurist proclaimed that neither slaves nor free blacks—together "a subordinate and inferior class of beings"—were citizens; thus they were entitled to none of the rights and privileges of citizenship. Scott, therefore, had had no legal standing to bring suit in the first place.

In reasoning fraught with historical and legal errors Taney insisted that blacks were excluded not just from all rights guaranteed by the Constitution but from those set forth by the Declaration of 1776 as well. They had no rights even as *persons.* Referring to the representation and fugitive clauses of the Constitution, he stated that the "only two provisions which point to them and include them, treat them as property, and make it the duty of the Government to protect it." The state "had no right to interfere for any other purpose but that of protecting the rights of the owner."

Then, invoking the little-used power of judicial review—the half-century-old doctrine of his predecessor, John Marshall, that the Supreme Court could veto legislation—he judged that the congressional ban on slavery in the territories was unconstitutional because Congress had no authority to deprive citizens of property rights without due process. By thus striking down the 1820 Missouri Compromise, the Court for the first time nullified a major federal law. Here in the light of day stood the emperor stripped bare—the slavery-coddling Constitution that abolitionists had railed against for a generation, "with 'property' substituted for 'persons,' with free Negroes undifferentiated from slaves, with all antislavery 'interference' proscribed and proslavery interference required," in Don Fehrenbacher's summation.

The North's newspaper headlines blared the stark implications: SLAVERY ALONE NATIONAL—THE MISSOURI COMPROMISE UNCONSTITUTIONAL—NEGROES CANNOT BE CITIZENS—THE TRIUMPH OF

SLAVERY COMPLETE. For black people and white supporters it came as a crushing blow to their hopes and aspirations. One startling phrase from Taney's proclamation stuck in the collective craw of African-Americans: they had "no rights which the white man was bound to respect." These became household words in the black community, damned by literate and illiterate alike, most vigorously at "indignation meetings" multiplying throughout the North. These assemblies sizzled with the movement's rising militancy. Resolutions urged blacks to break their allegiance to a government "founded and administered in iniquity" and to repudiate it at every opportunity. While some leaders counseled sedition, and some mass emigration to Canada, Africa, or Haiti, others pressed for still greater efforts to claim their rights nonviolently.

Seeing "this judicial incarnation of wolfishness" as a blessing in disguise since it might bring the crisis to a head, Douglass tried to calm the fury of his fellows and utilize the decision as an organizing tool. "Happily for the whole human family," he instructed an antislavery audience in New York City, "their rights have been defined, declared, and decided in a court higher than the Supreme Court. . . . Your fathers have said that man's right to liberty is self-evident. There is no need of argument to make it clear. The voices of nature, of conscience, of reason, and of revelation, proclaim it as the right of all rights, the foundation of all trust, and of all responsibility." He waxed confident that this ruling "against God" could not stand, that Northern citizens would refuse to submit. It might be "one necessary link" in the chain of events that would finally shackle slavery.

DOUGLASS'S PROPHECY came to pass. The slavocracy was not placated for long by Taney's decree. The vindication of their constitutional rights emboldened Southern leaders to make more aggressive moves to defend their property and particular pursuit of happiness. In 1860 Illinois lawyer and politician Abraham Lincoln overwhelmed the divided Democrats to win the White House for the new Republican Party. Following South Carolina's lead, eleven Southern states seceded and dissolved the Union—an outcome advocated for years by many abolitionists who had wanted the North to divorce the South.

But now both sides prepared for war, as Lincoln refused to permit the nation to be sundered and the South was determined to divide it. Fighting began with the capture of Fort Sumter in Charleston Harbor by the just-formed Confederacy in April 1861. The well-led Southern army garnered early gains, then stalemate set in. All-out industrial mobilization and superior numbers eventually brought Northern victory. The most destructive war ever in the Americas left 600,000 dead.

As more and more slaves deserted plantations to cross Union lines, weakening the "peculiar institution" from within, as the war's manpower needs mounted, and with unceasing abolitionist agitation, Lincoln could no longer resist embracing the cause—if gingerly and out of military necessity. On New Year's Day 1863, midway through the ordeal, the President signed the Emancipation Proclamation commanding that three-quarters of the slave population, those residing in Confederate-held territory, would be "forever free." Excluded were those in border states within the Union or in the Union-occupied South—but it seemed likely that banning slavery in the Deep South would lead to its extinction.

Wherever they heard the news, black people celebrated. A huge assemblage at Boston's Tremont Temple waited for hours until word arrived near midnight. After hearty cheering a black minister led the crowd singing, "Sound the loud timbrel o'er Egypt's dark sea, Jehovah hath triumphed, his people are free." Many slaves, however, did not learn of their freedom for many months. The delayed freedom would inspire an African-American holiday called "Juneteenth," celebrating the day, June 19, 1865, when the last slaves were freed in Texas—when the right to liberty from bondage had been fully enforced, and not just officially proclaimed.

The war to save the Union became a war to free the slaves. Lincoln's order "transformed a war of armies into a conflict of societies," according to Eric Foner, "ensuring that Union victory would produce a social revolution within the South."

The Emancipation decree also authorized black enlistment. From the outset abolitionists had advocated creating a liberation army of blacks—they were "the key of the situation," said Douglass. Already some Northerners were in combat, and escaped slaves were building fortifications. Now the trickle became a flood. Nearly 200,000 black soldiers played a pivotal role in turning the tide against the South, impressing the nation with their valor and effectiveness. Douglass, Martin Delany, and other leaders converted their lecture tours into recruiting missions, or took command of black regiments. No soldier made a bigger contribution than Harriet Tubman, scout and spy for the Union army. In one operation along South Carolina's Combahee River, "General" Tubman masterminded the rescue of seven hundred slaves by black troops.

Combat revolutionized self-image. New pride and self-respect made old deference and submission no longer tolerable, prodding black veterans to claim their due. "Has not the man who conquers upon the field of battle, gained any rights?" implored ex-slave William Murphey at a postwar constitutional convention in Arkansas. "Have we gained none by the sacrifice of our brethren?" W. E. B. Du Bois suggested that nothing made black emancipation and citizenship rights possible "but the record of the Negro soldier as a fighter."

When troops, white or black, arrived to free them, many slaves had no doubt that God had answered their prayers. On April 3, 1865, an African-American regiment helped to liberate the Confederate capital of Richmond and, marching proudly to the cheers of fellow blacks, flung open the gates of the slave prison. The joyful prisoners led a big crowd chanting, "Slavery chain done broke at last! . . . Gonna praise God till I die." Next day President Lincoln toured Richmond and black residents surged around him, touching him, calling him their "Messiah." Ten days hence, on Good Friday, the nation endured his crucifixion.

A few months before Lincoln's assassination Republican majorities in Congress had approved the Thirteenth Amendment abolishing slavery throughout the land. By Christmas 1865 three-fourths of the states had ratified it. Slavery chain done broke at last.

In large part by their own toil and sacrifice over many years, black Americans had realized the right to be free—from slavery. Influential white abolitionists wanted to close up shop, with Garrison urging his antislavery society to disband. Would freedom mean more than this? Who would enforce it? What about equality, another promise of 1776? "Verily," wrote Douglass, "the work does not end with the abolition of slavery but only begins." Having reached the goal that for so long had been the core of their striving, African-Americans had an opportunity to push freedom further, perhaps even to shape it into a vehicle for pursuing happiness. "Instead of a predetermined category or static concept," Foner discovered, "'freedom' itself became a terrain of conflict, its substance open to different and sometimes contradictory interpretations." In their everyday lives and relationships, in fashioning new modes of labor, and in the formidable struggle to build a more just and democratic nation, blacks now took responsibility for implementing the rights they had won.

BOTTOM RAIL ON TOP

FOR THREE DAYS after learning they were free, black women and men at Wood's Crossing, Virginia, rejoiced with singing, "shoutin' an' carryin' on," Charlotte Brown remembered years later. Then on Sunday morning "we was all sittin' roun' restin' an' tryin' to think what freedom meant an' ev'ybody was quiet an' peaceful." Setting out on a long journey to define the meaning of freedom, the emancipated people of the South shared a common premise: they were entitled to more than liberty from bondage. What this larger scope of freedom might encompass they explored in the texture of their lives, centering on aspirations for autonomy and self-improvement. Seeking to be their own masters, "to belong to ourselves," they asserted rights to move about freely, to find work elsewhere, to control the pace of labor, to have more free time, to grow their own gardens, to choose new names, and to reunite families severed by slavery. For many freedom meant a right to dignity, self-worth, self-respect—and respect from whites. At the same time they felt entitled to raise themselves as individuals and as a community, insisting on the right to practice their own religion and establish their own churches and schools. Freed men and women sometimes refused to work on a plantation unless a school was provided for their children.

What about economic rights? Black people knew that even with some degree of autonomy, freedom would ring hollow without the right to a livelihood. A group meeting in Petersburg, Virginia, declared that "we do understand Freedom to mean" not "idleness and indolence" but "industry and the enjoyment of the legitimate fruits thereof; for he that works we believe has a right to eat." A man later recalled: "De slaves, where I lived, knowed after de war dat they had abundance of dat somethin' called freedom, what they could not eat, wear, and sleep in. Yes, sir, they soon found out dat freedom ain't nothin', 'less you is got somethin' to live on and a place to call home. Dis livin' on liberty is lak young folks livin' on love after they gits married. It just don't work." Another was more blunt: "We soon found out that freedom could make folks proud but it didn't make 'em rich."

The Southern planters' right to own slaves legally had been extinguished, but otherwise property rights were left untouched. Rarely did black families have a choice but to toil on land owned by a white. Aided by local authorities—who, for example, closed down temporary shelters and enforced laws making vagrancy a crime punishable by forced labor—planters moved quickly to rehabilitate slavery in all but name. They tried to impose a wage labor system but it did not take hold. Then, under pressure from laborers, they agreed to share a portion of the crop. A new battleground was the sharecropping contract signed after the harvest for the next year. The first autumn of peace, field workers generally were handed a bad deal, aggravated by postwar economic collapse and the plummeting price of cotton. With better organization landless laborers learned how to bargain, in some cases getting half the crop—and winning other demands such as no white overseers or even the right to choose their own.

Yet no matter how fair the written contract, many were defrauded when the time came for "settlement." Frequently they responded to blatant exploitation with slowdowns or strikes, or by leaving the plantation in a group exodus. Fragile as it was, field workers had begun to legitimize a right to collective bargaining. Yet this contractual labor system was merely a Southern variant of the "free labor ideology" of Northern capitalism whose formal equality masked the substantive inequality between employer and laborer.

Most former slaves understood that they would not be truly free until they owned their own land and secured the independence imagined to go with it—another heritage of republicanism. Many were convinced that they were *entitled* to this "foundation of freedom," that they had earned it or the government had promised it. When Congress set up the Freedmen's Bureau to oversee the social transition out of slavery, its mandate included redistribution of abandoned and confiscated lands. This never occurred on more than a small scale, partly due to the resistance of entrenched landowning elites and partly due to Washington's lack of commitment. Land reform would probably have required the expropriation of ex-rebels' plantations; such a step, quite just under the circumstances, was politically too risky for most white Republicans.

Expectations were raised by the freed people's own leaders as well—for instance, slaves rescued along the Combahee River who heard General Tubman sing to them that "Uncle Sam is rich enough to give you all a farm." Black families clung to this aspiration, "always the great motivating ideal," Du Bois thought. Eventually a small minority fulfilled the dream and then, if they were fortunate enough to keep their land, discovered that land alone was not enough; they needed tools, livestock, and above all credit. Most who stayed on the land over the next decades, however, eked out survival as tenant farmers or sharecroppers shackled by debt to landowner and merchant. Here collided not just personal rights and property rights, but two fundamentally different conceptions of the right to property. Was it a right belonging to a few, or, as Jefferson had envisioned, to the many? Moreover, was it the right simply to own property, or the right also to the resources needed to make that property fruitful?

African-Americans themselves were not united on the priority of getting land. Union Leagues and other grass-roots groups sprouted throughout the South. Some were the handiwork of local activists like Thomas Allen, preacher, shoemaker, tenant farmer; others were planted by such intrepid organizers as Methodist minister Henry Turner, whose whirlwind tours through Georgia reaped a bumper crop of Union Leagues, Republican committees, and African Methodist Episcopal churches. Freed people played a big part in these local groups. Although they discussed and demanded land, legal rights and suffrage were the groups' immediate practical goals.

As much as ever resolutions and petitions from the bottom appealed to rights sanctified by the Declaration of Independence. Blacks had read that document "until it had become part of their natures," observed Reverend J. M. Hood, a North Carolina leader. A Tuscaloosa, Alabama, group protested to the Freedmen's Bureau about various violations of their legal and civil rights, including contract fraud; "this is not the persuit of happiness," they concluded.

Complementing grass-roots organizing in rural areas were statewide conventions in the cities. Attended mostly by freeborn blacks, these gatherings did not respond to the clamor for land and said little about economic needs. But they addressed every other right of citizenship that blacks were denied, particularly the right to testify against whites who violated their rights. Activists in city and country risked their lives to create democracy. At a New Orleans convention seeking to democratize the state constitution, police and vigilantes slaughtered thirty-four blacks and three whites before federal troops intervened. Most antiblack violence was more covert.

It began to seem as if the South had won the war. Holding back change was the conservative administration of Lincoln's successor, Andrew Johnson of Tennessee, which rather quickly allowed the planter class to restore its dominion. New "black codes" restricted the liberties of the freed people, segregation laws were enacted for the first time, and unorganized field workers who tried to enforce their rights were treated harshly. Despite courageous efforts to shape the boundaries of their freedom, many blacks faced "de worse kind of slavery," as Jane Johnson put it. They needed power to protect their rights. Economic rights might be the foundation of autonomy and independence, but political rights were increasingly seen as the means of securing all their entitlements.

AFRICAN-AMERICANS were not the only ones debating the meaning of freedom. The Republican majority in Congress, particularly the cutting edge of "Radicals" led by two seasoned reformers, Massachusetts senator Charles Sumner and Pennsylvania representative Thaddeus Stevens, were charting a new definition of national citizenship. The first order of business was to establish equal rights before the law, specifically the right of blacks to protect contracts, sue and testify in court, and serve as jurors. Republican moderates pushed through Congress the Civil Rights Act of 1866, which declared that all persons born in the United States except Indians were citizens—thus overturning the Dred Scott ruling—and prohibited discrimination by law. It did not cover such extralegal matters as racial exclusion by custom. President Johnson vetoed it as an invasion of states' rights—the first in a string of actions that led to his impeachment and near-removal two years later. Congress overrode the veto.

Unrelenting Southern violence and Johnson's alleged betrayal of the Northern cause enabled the Republicans to win an expanded congressional majority in the first postwar elections. Sumner, Stevens, and their Radical Republican wing now had the power to overthrow the planter oligarchy and begin to build an interracial democracy in the South. Their instrument was the Reconstruction Act of 1867, which reimposed military control in the ex-Confederacy and enfranchised black males. To gain readmission to the Union, Southern states had to create new governments by means of constitutional conventions elected by, and establishing, manhood suffrage, and the constitutions had then to be approved by the broadened electorate.

Republicans set a further condition for every state returning to the fold: ratification of the Fourteenth Amendment guaranteeing equal rights under the law. The year before, Radicals had won congressional passage of this amendment, which would become the most widely applied and most contested provision of the entire Constitution. After months of heated debate over a few key phrases, laboriously revised, the Joint Committee on Reconstruction had produced an acceptable compromise. The new amendment first stated that all persons born or naturalized in the United States were citizens and then declared: "No State shall make or enforce any law which shall abridge the privileges or immunities of citizens of the United States; nor shall any State deprive any person of life, liberty, or property, without due process of law; nor deny to any person within its jurisdiction the equal protection of the laws." Another section reduced a state's representatives in Congress in proportion to the number of "male citizens" not permitted to vote.

Moving tortuously through state legislatures during the next two years, the amendment was condemned by Southern Democrats and President Johnson, and most ex-Confederate states at first rejected it. But it was pounced upon almost as hard from the left. A "fatal and total surrender," thundered abolitionist Wendell Phillips, since it did not mention voting rights and thus seemed to legitimize the denial of black suffrage. Feminists like Susan B. Anthony and Elizabeth Cady Stanton denounced it for embedding the word "male" in the Constitution and limiting representation on the basis of racial but not gender disfranchisement. Now that they were officially citizens, would the amendment guarantee women's legal rights? Could they be citizens without the rights of citizens? Black men were asking that question too.

For decades to come jurists, lawyers, and scholars would quarrel over the amendment's vague and ambiguous wording. The Supreme Court served as final arbiter. As it slowly transmuted abstract principles into judicial doctrines, the august body carried the amendment through an Alice in Wonderland of topsy-turvy incarnations. The politicians who framed it had little more than the short run in view. Their objectives were to codify African-American citizenship, to harness national power behind their legal rights, and to enshrine in the Constitution the nation's supremacy over the states. The amendment was less a judicial tool for the future than a "peace treaty . . . to secure the fruits of the North's victory," in legal historian William Nelson's opinion.

What was the nature of its murky ambiguity? Earlier drafts had spoken of political and civil rights, but the final version expunged any mention of rights in favor of "privileges and immunities," without defining what these consisted of. Federal power would be restricted to enforcing "due process" and "equal protection of the laws." A big question was whether it was intended to apply the federal Bill of Rights, whose explicit language limited its application to the national government, to the states—in an era when such basic rights were being trampled daily throughout the South. Even some Northern states did not have bills of rights.

Did the amendment *absolutely* protect personal rights like freedom of speech and religion, or require only that states enforce equally whatever rights already existed in statute? At least one of its chief architects, Representative John Bingham, intended it as a means of executing the amendments of 1791 throughout all levels of government. But the Supreme Court would generally interpret it to mean uniform, not absolute, protection. For many years the only rights upheld unequivocally were property rights of corporations (except when corporations battled legally with each other). The Court used the amendment far more often to protect or adjudicate corporate rights than to carry out its original mandate of enforcing black people's civil rights. In its actual implementation the Fourteenth Amendment reduced "equal rights" to a shadow of its rhetorical brilliance.

Clear and simple in contrast was the last in the trinity of Reconstruction amendments that barred Congress or any state from denying the right to vote on account of race. The harvest of three decades of persistent black organizing in the North and four years of postwar South-wide mobilization, Congress passed it after Republican war hero Ulysses S. Grant won the presidency in 1868.

The Fifteenth Amendment was a half measure, however, that fell short of the full guarantee of political rights sought by Radical Republicans and black activists. It did not prohibit property, literacy, or other restrictions that would affect blacks adversely (the prior amendment notwithstanding), provided no means of enforcement, and failed to ensure the right for blacks to hold office. Most troubling, it did not grant suffrage to women, forcing feminist leaders to oppose it and precipitating a final divorce of the women's rights crusade from abolitionism, closely allied for a generation.

These omissions did make it easier, however, for the Republicans to push it through the Northern states, the majority of which did not yet allow black men to vote. The amendment entered the Constitution in early 1870. Whatever its flaws, most male reformers hailed it as a long-overdue triumph for human rights and a crucial tool for more substantive democratic change. Abolitionists were so elated that they laid to rest the American Anti-Slavery Society.

BLACK MEN AND WOMEN already had been making history in the South, emboldened by the Reconstruction Act and the Northern military presence. Taking myriad forms, grass-roots activism reached its peak as the decade moved to a close, including strikes by longshoremen and other workers and direct action that desegregated streetcars in Charleston, New Orleans, and elsewhere. When three blacks refused to leave a whites-only car in Richmond, a throng of supporters backed them up, shouting, "Let's have our rights."

As the freed people faced the exhilarating task of building new state governments from the ground up, electoral organizing and party-building took off. In many localities the Republican Party rivaled the church as a unifying institution of the black community; in some places party and church were one. Itinerant black lecturers, often Baptist or Methodist preachers, barnstormed the countryside spreading the political gospel. Though not able to vote or hold office, many women of color played indispensable roles in the electoral insurgency. That black men deeply valued their hard-won political rights was shown by exceptionally high voter turnout.

Barring many ex-Confederates from participation still did not ensure fair representation for blacks in the state constitutional conventions. Only in South Carolina and Louisiana did they have a majority. The new charters guaranteed political and legal rights for black males and, for the first time, established public school systems throughout the South—generally leaving undecided whether these were to be segregated. A few incorporated bills of rights on the national model, borrowing language from the Declaration of 1776. Some explicitly proscribed racial discrimination. The spirited South Carolina convention debated and enacted the most far-reaching reforms. These included reorganizing the court system

RECONSTRUCTION AMENDMENTS

Amendment XIII

Section 1. Neither slavery nor involuntary servitude, except as a punishment for crime whereof the party shall have been duly convicted, shall exist within the United States, or any place subject to their jurisdiction.

Section 2. Congress shall have power to enforce this article by appropriate legislation.   *Ratified December 18, 1865*

Amendment XIV

Section 1. All persons born or naturalized in the United States, and subject to the jurisdiction thereof, are citizens of the United States and of the State wherein they reside. No State shall make or enforce any law which shall abridge the privileges or immunities of citizens of the United States; nor shall any State deprive any person of life, liberty, or property, without due process of law; nor deny to any person within its jurisdiction the equal protection of the laws.

Section 2. Representatives shall be apportioned among the several States according to their respective numbers, counting the whole number of persons in each State, excluding Indians not taxed. But when the right to vote at any election for the choice of electors for President and Vice President of the United States, Representatives in Congress, the Executive and Judicial officers of a State, or the members of the Legislature thereof, is denied to any of the male inhabitants of such State, being twenty-one years of age, and citizens of the United States, or in any way abridged, except for participation in rebellion, or other crime, the basis of representation therein shall be reduced in the proportion which the number of such male citizens shall bear to the whole number of male citizens twenty-one years of age in such State.

to eliminate racial bias, expanding married women's rights, and setting up a commission to distribute land to the landless. Though this convention was led by African-Americans who were freeborn, urban, and educated, most of its black delegates were former slaves, a sign of how profoundly the South's politics had changed.

With black men the great majority of its voters, the Republican Party wrested control of the new governments in a nonviolent electoral revolution. In only half the Southern states, however, did black politicians hold statewide positions, and in South Carolina alone did they make up a legislative majority. Sixteen Southern blacks served in Congress during

Section 3. No person shall be a Senator or Representative in Congress, or elector of President and Vice President, or hold any office, civil or military, under the United States, or under any State, who, having previously taken an oath, as a member of Congress, or as an officer of the United States, or as a member of any State legislature, or as an executive or judicial officer of any State, to support the Constitution of the United States, shall have engaged in insurrection or rebellion against the same, or given aid or comfort to the enemies thereof. But Congress may by a vote of two-thirds of each House, remove such disability.

Section 4. The validity of the public debt of the United States, authorized by law, including debts incurred for payment of pensions and bounties for services in suppressing insurrection or rebellion, shall not be questioned. But neither the United States nor any State shall assume or pay any debt or obligation incurred in aid of insurrection or rebellion against the United States, or any claim for the loss or emancipation of any slave; but all such debts, obligations and claims shall be held illegal and void.

Section 5. The Congress shall have power to enforce, by appropriate legislation, the provisions of this article.   *Ratified July 28, 1868*

Amendment XV

Section 1. The right of citizens of the United States to vote shall not be denied or abridged by the United States or by any State on account of race, color, or previous condition of servitude.

Section 2. The Congress shall have power to enforce this article by appropriate legislation.   *Ratified March 30, 1870*

the next decade, including three senators. More did not win high office in large part because blacks remained junior partners in the unwieldy Republican coalition run by whites immigrating from the North and native white "scalawags." With the black vote taken for granted, the priority was to reach out to whites. Reconstruction's most radical dimension was the abundance of black elected officials at the grass roots, particularly in the "black belt" plantation country.

The feel of democracy further raised the expectations of the landless that they would somehow get land. So confident were they that the new constitution would make them landowners that some South Carolina field workers refused to sign labor contracts. That state's land commission eventually did sell land on easy credit to about one-seventh of South Carolina's blacks. No other state tried to meet the pressing demand for economic rights, perhaps partly because that demand was not sufficiently organized. Still, divisive debates about confiscation and land reform threatened to disrupt the delicate Republican alliance. Aspirations for an economic revolution subsided only when political and civil rights were under siege and had to be defended at all costs.

Dislodged from political dominance, white conservatives launched a counterrevolution of violence spearheaded by a fast-growing vigilante group called the Ku Klux Klan, which recruited many lower-class whites. The unprecedented campaign of terror was aimed at suppressing black political expression as well as agrarian self-organization, and wreaked devastation in both domains. About one-tenth of the black delegates to constitutional conventions were attacked, several assassinated. The imperatives of survival unified the black citizenry in prodding Washington to act. Neither the Reconstruction Act nor state charters, least of all the Fifteenth Amendment, offered remedies for such subversion of democratic rights. In 1870 and 1871 Congress responded with the Enforcement Acts authorizing federal intervention, including the army, to protect black electoral activity. The Ku Klux Klan Act in particular "pushed Republicans to the outer limits of constitutional change," since it applied to "private" as well as public actions. Right-wing violence abated, which allowed breathing space for Republican organizing, but the formidable problem of enforcing black rights festered.

Then like dominoes the Republican regimes fell to the conservative "Redeemers," aided considerably by election fraud. Once in power they proceeded to extirpate black gains. Urgent appeals rained upon Washington. After the loss of Alabama in 1874, a black convention asked "whether our constitutional rights as citizens are to be a reality or a mockery, a protection and a boon or a danger and a curse; whether we are to be freemen in fact or only in name; and whether the late amendments to the Constitution are to be practically enforced or to become a nullity and stand only 'as dead letters on the statute-book' . . . The solemn question with us is, Shall we be compelled to repeat the history of the Israelites and go into exile from the land of our nativity and our homes, to seek new homes and fields of enterprise, beyond the reign and rule of Pharaoh?"

Black activists had always known that they had to take responsibility for making emancipation and citizenship "something more than a delusion and a mockery." But they had counted on a partnership with benevolent national power. During the 1870s the Republican elite determined that unleashing the rights of the propertied, North and South, was more essential to national progress than guaranteeing any entitlements to those on the bottom rail, least of all the right to hold property of their own. As the Republican Party lost control of the South it abandoned the bulwark of its Southern constituency, letting it fight alone against overwhelming odds.

IN THE Civil War's aftermath the decades-long struggle of Northern blacks to secure their own rights intensified, swept forward by Reconstruction and the refurbished Constitution. At the forefront was the National Equal Rights League, born at an 1864 national convention in Syracuse, drawing together most African-American leaders. Delegates set forth a detailed "Declaration of Wrongs" and a "Declaration of Rights," which included the often voiced complaint that "we are taxed, but denied the right of representation." The League's stated purpose was racial uplift—"to encourage sound morality, education, temperance, frugality, industry"—combined with recognition of black rights. Moreover, "no distinction on account of color or sex" would be permitted in the League. Elected to head the ambitious new organization, John Mercer Langston journeyed throughout North and South forming branches in almost every state. Besides campaigning for suffrage, Langston and associates lobbied Congress for the Reconstruction Act, the amendments, and other rights reforms, eloquently articulating their people's "grievances and wants."

The League gave loose coordination to a sunburst of local rights campaigns in which black churches, newspapers, and conventions took the lead. Petitions, protests, and litigation, backed up by reluctant federal authority, resulted in "astonishing advances in the political, civil, and social rights of Northern blacks," in Eric Foner's estimation. Jim Crow streetcars and railroads, long a favorite target of direct action, disappeared in many cities. Pennsylvania outlawed segregation in transport, New York in all public facilities. Other states followed in the 1880s. Most black children in the North now had access to separate public schools—if still inferior to white ones—and in some places schools were integrated.

Reform reached its zenith in 1875 with congressional passage of a new civil rights law Langston had pushed for half a decade. He had drafted it at the behest of Senator Sumner, who did not live to see it enacted. Stripped of a provision requiring integrated schools, the bill made most other racial exclusions illegal—private as well as public—but placed the burden on black citizens to sue for redress in federal court. This loophole did not keep the Supreme Court from nullifying it eight years later on the basis of the Fourteenth Amendment, insisting that "individual invasion of individual rights is not the subject-matter of the amendment," but only state action.

No more than in the South did strides in political and civil rights translate into overall economic improvement, especially in the cities, where black poverty worsened due to employer and union prejudice and the influx of Irish and other immigrants to compete for scarce jobs. Greater liberty was won in certain realms, but Northern black citizens could rue with their Southern compatriots that "this is not the persuit of happiness."

WHITHER THE PROMISED LAND?

RADICAL RECONSTRUCTION died slowly during the 1870s, finished off by the "Compromise of 1877," which resolved an electoral deadlock by allowing Republican Rutherford B. Hayes to assume the presidency in exchange for the withdrawal of the army from the states of the ex-Confederacy. The Southern freedom struggle scattered for cover but had too much at stake to surrender. Activists hung on as subalterns in the battered Republican Party; or formed new organizations to defend their diminishing public rights, such as the National Afro-American League; or joined forces with white agrarian radicals in the Greenback Party and Populism; or, in some cases, accommodated themselves to the rule of the paternalistic conservative elite. Thousands of black families emigrated West, notably in the "Great Exodus" to Kansas in 1879.

The multiple survival strategies pursued by Southern blacks reflected, and helped to shape, a transitional period of some flexibility in race relations, a "time of testing and uncertainty," in C. Vann Woodward's judgment, "quite different from the time of repression and rigid uniformity that was to come toward the end of the century." Exploitation of black workers did not lessen, few got land, schooling was segregated and grossly unequal, and the Redeemer regimes, backed up by the Supreme Court, discarded civil rights laws. On the other hand, black men kept on voting and even held office, and segregation of public facilities was not yet everywhere the rule. Invented in the antebellum North, Jim Crow still felt somewhat alien to a culture where black and white had interacted closely, though strictly on the latter's terms, since long before the nation's founding.

As the cotton-based Southern economy deteriorated, in part due to the war's battering of agriculture, the white population coalesced around the priority of perpetuating a black underclass. By the 1890s blacks in the New South "found themselves enmeshed in a seamless web of oppression, whose interwoven economic, political, and social strands all reinforced one another." State and local authorities instituted legal segregation with a vengeance, and black males were systematically removed from voting rolls. To avoid judicial combat with Washington, revised state constitutions mandated literacy tests and other qualifications that applied "equally" to all men and in fact also disfranchised many lower-class whites. The terror tactic of lynching—aimed at deterring blacks from asserting their rights—reached an all-time peak. One of the more visible forms of organized resistance during this era was the antilynching campaign led by journalist Ida B. Wells; earlier she had defied segregation on a Tennessee railroad and, after being forcibly removed, had won a lawsuit that was overturned by the state's high court.

Racism was rejuvenated in the North too, where "scientific" theories of black inferiority were legitimated by opinion-makers, even Progressive leaders like Theodore Roosevelt and Woodrow Wilson. The capstone of the arch of tyranny was the 1896 Supreme Court decision in *Plessy* v. *Ferguson,* a suit brought by Homer Plessy, arrested in New Orleans for sitting in a white railroad car. Challenging the new state law requiring segregated transportation, Plessy appealed to the Fourteenth Amendment's equal protection clause. But the justices turned that clause against him, upholding state-imposed segregation as long as it was "separate but equal." They used the alleged viability of separate schools as evidence for their judgment. Justice John Marshall Harlan, once a Kentucky slave owner, dissented, calling the "arbitrary separation of citizens" a "badge of servitude" and declaring that "our Constitution is color-blind."

Influential voices in the black community had advocated separate schools, churches, and other institutions for a long time. The crux of the issue was exclusion more than separation per se, as well as the reality that segregation decreed by the dominant caste could never be egalitarian in either material or psychological terms. Two years later, in *Williams* v. *Mississippi,* the high court put its stamp of approval on the literacy test and the poll tax, central mechanisms of disfranchisement.

At the dawn of the new century, in the face of staggering defeat, many African-Americans questioned the old methods that had not borne fruit. Searching for new options, some people revived the traditional strategy of autonomous uplift and institution-building but disentangled it from the struggle for citizenship rights. This school of activism found a re-markable leader in Booker T. Washington. Born a slave in Virginia, laboring in a salt furnace and as a janitor to get through school, he became famous as head of the Tuskegee Institute in Alabama, a black vocational school.

Washington argued forcefully for a grand trade-off—notably in a speech to the Atlanta Cotton Exposition in 1895, the same year that Frederick Douglass died, just short of eighty. Out of necessity, Washington said, blacks should accept segregation and disfranchisement in exchange for white support of their economic advancement through hard work and frugality. Here was the most prominent black leader of the age calling for an exclusive focus on economic and moral uplift. "It is important and right that all privileges of the law be ours," he stated, "but it is vastly more important that we be prepared for the exercise of these privileges."

In the fine print, did he mean exchanging political and civil rights for economic rights and middle-class status, an echo of Thomas Hobbes, or giving up public rights altogether for the "right" to be exploited somewhat less flagrantly in the economic realm of capital and labor? Before long other leaders, like young scholar William Edward Burghardt Du Bois, would challenge Washington's accommodationist position and move in the direction of a renewed crusade to reclaim stolen rights.

ASPIRATIONS for rights were the lifeblood of the nineteenth-century black freedom struggle. Black people grasped hold of entitlements and molded them into vehicles to bridge the gap between the republican ideals of the American creed and the reality of racial subjugation that, they said over and over, mocked those ideals. As they translated parchment prose into popular practice, inherited rights were redefined, expanded, and thickened into multidimensional moral and political forces that were both the outcome and the catalyst of intense social conflict. George Rudé's analysis of how lower-class movements fashioned new ideologies by mixing "derived" with "inherent" elements only begins to describe the mutual interaction of republican rights language with African-American values and sensibilities, above all the pervasive influence of spirituality in black political expression. The determination of blacks to realize rights ran up against both the limits of the Constitution and the ideological and political constraints of the dominant culture that made implementation of their rights very uncertain. Moreover, the specific rights themselves had intrinsic inadequacies.

Although shaped by the republican vision of the American Revolution, the black movement transcended the liberal natural rights tradition that comprised a major current of republicanism. Not taking citizenship as given but as a condition to be created through action, African-Americans expanded the rights of citizenship beyond "negative" natural liberties to encompass positive claims for social justice. First asserting rights to freedom from slavery and prejudice, goals harmonious with the Lockean liberalism of most white abolitionists, the logic of struggle led to more substantive demands for self-realization and collective self-determination and for the public resources to bring about these aims.

To a large extent the effort to convert these higher moral claims into enforceable reforms was frustrated. Positive freedom aimed above all at equality—of access if not of condition—a vital element of the American creed. After the Civil War the political system defined a conception of uniform national citizenship and citizen rights. Even with a solid Republican majority the compromises that emerged scrapped equality, especially in the economic sphere, in favor of narrow procedural notions of equal rights as merely "equal protection before the law."

For many years to come, Fourteenth Amendment jurisprudence reduced equality to the requirement that, regardless of how inegalitarian the content, laws must only be applied uniformly to meet constitutional standards—equal rights as strictly legalistic. This opened the door to the separate-but-equal doctrine, suffrage barriers such as literacy tests and poll taxes that also disfranchised poor whites (except those exempted by "grandfather clauses" and the like), and other violations of both liberty and equality. Post–Civil War constitutional reformation did not close the gap between ideals and everyday life; rather, a chasm widened between the substantive rights of citizenship envisioned by African-Americans and the strictly procedural guarantees that seemed to represent the limits of liberal reform.

A related obstacle to the fulfillment of rights was their compartmentalization: legal, civil, political, social, economic, and even subdivisions of these. Black leaders preferred to speak inclusively of citizen or human rights, but political realism compelled them to accept such invidious distinctions and to set strategic priorities accordingly. With some exceptions white politicians inhabited "a world of walls," in Michael Walzer's formulation, and as agents of galloping liberalism "preached and practiced the art of separation. They drew lines, marked off different realms," chiefly to insulate vested interests of class, race, and gender from popular challenge.

Facing irresistible pressure, Republicans "granted" legal and then political rights to black men, but had to be pushed still harder to legislate civil rights that portended "social equality" or integration. Most threatening to white Republicans, and thus out of bounds for the have-nots, was the redistribution of economic rights. The party's entrepreneurial free labor ideology, Foner notes, "simultaneously inspired efforts to guarantee civil and political equality—essential attributes of autonomous citizenship in a competitive society—and inhibited efforts to provide an economic underpinning for blacks' new freedom. Indeed, it suggested that once accorded equal rights, the freedmen would find their social level and assume responsibility for their own fate."

By failing to incorporate economic entitlements into its definition of citizenship, the Fourteenth Amendment perpetuated the Constitution's exclusion of economic justice from its purview, hurting poor blacks the most. The amendment constructed a thin framework for citizen rights that left the economic realm undisturbed—unless the needs of large corporations, later recognized as "citizens" by the Supreme Court, called for due process or equal protection. Nor did it address whether political equality was attainable without greater economic equity.

The biggest roadblock to the realization of rights was the government's lack of commitment, or political will, to enforce them. While Radical Reconstruction was in full swing, German philosopher Karl Marx reported on a much smaller and far less violent civil war in France during which the Parisian working class controlled the capital. An exemplary feature of the short-lived proletarian regime, according to Marx, was the "working parliament" that both enacted laws and enforced them—unlike "bourgeois democracy," whose separation of powers divorced the two functions, to the detriment of the downtrodden. Black workers across the Atlantic direly needed such unified power. Not only did they have to organize for decades to gain formal rights on paper, but with only a toehold in the superstructures of the state they had to take responsibility for implementing those rights, often by mobilizing black communities to insist on compliance.

Even if ultimately unsuccessful, in the course of conflict black people stretched the scope of rights they felt entitled to and linked their claims with parallel efforts to build autonomous institutions and lift up the black community. African-Americans experienced rights both as individual possessions and as resources held in common. Many felt a moral duty to secure them not just on an individual basis but for their people as a collective entity. For these citizens, rights had a markedly different texture than for other Americans who, in Tocqueville's words, "were born equal instead of becoming so."

CHAPTER FIVE

BONDS OF WOMANHOOD

BOSTON, FEBRUARY 1838.

"God strengthen you, my sister," antislavery activist Maria Chapman said quietly to Angelina Grimké, with a reassuring smile, as they strode through an unfriendly crowd into the Massachusetts Statehouse. Trembling and feeling faint, Grimké stood at the podium of the legislative hall, the first woman to speak before an American legislature. Emboldened by her supporters and with God's arm "to lean upon," the serious young woman in gray Quaker dress and white kerchief let go of her fear.

She told the lawmakers that she represented twenty thousand Massachusetts women who had signed petitions against slavery. "I stand before you as a southerner," she announced, "exiled from the land of my birth, by the sound of the lash, and the piteous cry of the slave. I stand before you as a repentant slaveholder. I stand before you as a moral being, endowed with precious and inalienable rights, which are correlative with solemn duties and high responsibilities; and as a moral being I feel that I owe it to the suffering slave, and to the deluded master, to my country and the world, to do all that I can to overturn a system of complicated crimes, built upon the broken hearts and prostrate bodies of my countrymen in chains, and cemented by the blood and sweat and tears of my sisters in bonds.

"Are we aliens," she asked, "because we are women? Are we bereft of citizenship because we are mothers, wives and daughters of a mighty people? Have women *no* country—*no* interests staked in public weal—no liabilities in common peril—no partnership in a nation's guilt and shame? ... I hold, Mr. Chairman, that American women have to do with this subject, not only because it is moral and religious, but because it is *political,* inasmuch as we are citizens of this republic and as such our honor, happiness and well-being are bound up in its politics, government and laws.''

The dramatic speech climaxed a grueling, six-month lecture tour through northern New England during which Grimké and her older sister Sarah spoke and passed petitions at eighty-eight meetings in almost as many communities and toward the end of which Angelina came down with typhoid fever. The two had grown up in Charleston, South Carolina, Sarah the sixth and Angelina the youngest of fourteen children in a rich and prominent slaveholding family. Besides running a large plantation, their Cambridge University–educated father served as chief justice of the South Carolina Supreme Court. Both sisters hated the slave system that engulfed their childhood—Sarah never to forget a slave whipping she witnessed at age four—and they fled the South several years apart to settle in Philadelphia. They also left behind their straitlaced Episcopal upbringing to convert to the Quaker faith, which did not condone slavery and allowed women a more equal role.

After they joined the new Philadelphia Female Anti-Slavery Society, William Lloyd Garrison published in his *Liberator* a letter from Angelina attacking slavery, which made her name in abolitionist circles. Persuaded to become the national antislavery society's first women lecturers, the sisters drew large crowds, partly because of their gender but also because they were the only Southern white women publicly to extol abolition. They assailed not only slavery but prejudice, and advocated direct action against Northern segregation. And they portrayed with special force the brutalization of black women under slavery.

The mere fact of the Grimké sisters' speaking in public, a forbidden realm for women—and particularly to mixed male and female audiences—aroused a storm of protest in press and pulpit. The Congregational ministers of Massachusetts issued a Pastoral Letter decrying their "blasphemous" activities. "We are placed very unexpectedly in a very trying situation, in the forefront of an entirely new contest," Angelina wrote to her mentor Theodore Weld, "a contest for the *rights* of *woman* as a moral, intelligent and responsible being. . . . We ask no favors for ourselves, but *claim* rights for our *sex.*" Responding to his disapproval, she wrote a week later that "*the time* to assert a right is *the* time when *that* right is denied. *We must establish this right* for if we do not, it will be impossible for *us* to go *on with the work of Emancipation.* . . . If we surrender the right to speak to the public this year," she insisted, "we must surrender the right to petition next year and the right to *write* the year after and so on. What *then* can *woman* do for the slave when she is herself under the feet of man and shamed into *silence?*"

The controversy grew more heated as it spread through the abolitionist community. The two sisters' determination to keep speaking out for women's right to free speech was one of the factors that precipitated the split in the antislavery ranks, since the Garrisonians supported women's rights, to a degree at least, whereas the "political" abolitionists did not.

Angelina penned tracts opposing slavery, notably one addressed to white women of the South. But the controversy over women's role impelled Sarah to produce the first thoroughgoing treatise on female emancipation by an American woman: *Letters on the Equality of the Sexes and the Condition of Woman.* She dissected the familiar doctrine that the Bible decreed female inferiority (parallel arguments, of course, were used to justify slavery), grounding her entire case for equality in a contrary interpretation of Scripture. Her wide-ranging manifesto attacked marriage laws and the lack of legal rights, called for equal education and equal pay, asked women to forgo fashion, frivolity, and favors from men, and likened white women's fetters to those of slaves, particularly enslaved women. She urged women to participate fully in reform, but not to corrupt their moral purity by engaging directly in electoral politics. She stressed that "WHATSOEVER IT IS MORALLY RIGHT FOR A MAN TO DO, IT IS MORALLY RIGHT FOR A WOMAN TO DO." Throughout her discussion of the equal "human rights" of women and men she did not separate those rights from duties and responsibilities: "*All rights* spring out of the *moral* nature: they are both the root and the offspring of *responsibilities.*"

Three months after her pioneering speech to Massachusetts lawmakers, Angelina Grimké wedded the abolitionist Theodore Weld; their vows abjured woman's subordination in marriage. Two days later she gave her last public talk for many years at the women's antislavery convention in Philadelphia. While she spoke, imperturbable, a racist mob smashed windows all about her. The next day the mob burned to the ground this newly built hall that had been dedicated to reform.

The Grimkés had resolved not to let Angelina's marriage interfere with their calling, but in fact it silenced their public voices. Living with her married sister, sharing in child-rearing, Sarah bore with her the inequalities of the marriage institution she continued to theorize about. Her later writings on women's oppression were not published in her lifetime.

With the Grimké sisters and others like Maria Stewart blazing the trail of female participation, women played vital roles in abolitionism, particularly in organizing huge petition campaigns to statehouses and Congress. Excluded from membership in male societies (prior to 1840), they formed their own. Free women of color participated on a fairly equal basis in some of these groups but more often created independent societies. Besides the right and experience of speaking in public, these white and black women gained organizing and strategizing skills and self-confidence. Resentment about the subordination they faced was sharpened by the pervasive rhetoric of equal rights. Thus the female abolitionists reworked republican imagery about the tyranny of slaveholders, especially the abuse of slave women's bodies, into condemnations of men's tyranny over "free" women.

In the charged atmosphere of reform female activists, mostly white, conceptualized their rights as women and saw how these were violated by social norms and structures and by their own fathers, husbands, and co-workers in the cause. Historian Ellen DuBois suggests that "women's discontent with their position was as much cause as effect of their involvement with the antislavery movement. What American women learned from abolitionism was less that they were oppressed than what to do with that perception, how to turn it into a political movement."

Although these women had to break free of the dominance of male clergy to begin to assert their rights, the seedbed of their self-liberation was the spiritual renaissance of the age—from Protestant evangelism to "perfectionism"—without which neither abolitionism nor associated reform efforts like temperance would ever have grown so strong. Many of the white female rebels had tasted a measure of equality as Quakers. As much as male and female African-Americans, but in different idioms, they justified their claims on the basis of biblical authority and spiritual intuition. Grimké scholar Elizabeth Ann Bartlett comments that while "for the Enlightenment the governing principle of human rights was a natural law discoverable only through our senses and our reason," for Sarah Grimké and her ilk this rights principle was "inextricably bound to the notion of a Creator" and must find its ultimate justification "in the divine revelation of scripture." This spiritual commitment underpinned other, more secular motivations propelling women to realize their rights.

THE ARISTOCRACY OF SEX

DURING the tumultuous generation from the 1830s until the Civil War, the spiritual impulses that animated female activists reinforced the prevailing ideology that defined white Protestant women as repositories of moral virtue whose responsibility for the moral regeneration of society was greater than that of men. Indeed, it was the alleged immorality and sinfulness of men—as drinkers, sexual predators, politicians, slaveholders—that motivated many female crusaders. The identity of white women as vessels of virtue, as moral and spiritual role models, made them indispensable to the Garrisonian abolitionism driven by messianic passion to cleanse the nation of sin. Even if they were seen but not heard, even if their own rights were suppressed in the process, women served abolitionism and other moral crusades as exemplary agents of redemption. Moral suasion, notes historian Lori Ginzberg, "the chosen means for those who sought nothing less than the transformation of the public soul, conformed both to women's supposed qualities and to the nature of their access to those in power."

Although during the antebellum period the pervasive notion of the separate woman's sphere drew a sharp boundary between moral action rooted in home, family, and Christian virtue and the male domain of public politics, female activists in practice stretched the meaning of politics to encompass their various grass-roots campaigns and benevolent services. But starting in the late 1840s and 1850s, as Ginzberg discovered, when the party politics that women condemned as corrupt was becoming more prominent and it seemed that the great issues of the age such as slavery and temperance could be resolved only through the electoral system, middle-class women began to feel acutely their political disfranchisement. If moral regeneration was no longer the primary route to social change, if party politics, including the creation of third parties, was eclipsing the strategy of moral suasion, women would have to secure formal political rights in order to continue to play a central role in social reform—particularly in those areas, such as marriage and property rights, that impinged on their own lives.

In midsummer 1848, as the United States military was vanquishing Mexico and seizing about half of its territory—which opened a huge southwestern enclave to the expansion of slavery—five middle-class women sat around a mahogany tea table in rural upstate New York, absorbed in matters closer to home. Elizabeth Cady Stanton poured out "the torrent of my long-accumulating discontent, with such vehemence and indignation that I stirred myself, as well as the rest of the party, to do and dare anything. . . . I could not see what to do or where to begin—my only thought was a public meeting for protest and discussion." They decided to call a convention on women's rights—one week later—in the village of Seneca Falls, where Stanton had recently moved from Boston with her family.

She had grown up not far from Albany, her father a well-known lawyer and state high court justice. As a young girl she had often heard him offer consolation to married women left propertyless and penniless when abandoned by their husbands. After graduating from Emma Willard's pathbreaking Female Seminary in Troy and studying law with her father, in 1840 she married a Boston antislavery leader, Henry B. Stanton; it was he who had suggested that the Grimké sisters speak to the Bay State's legislature.

Shortly after their wedding—in which she omitted from her vows the word "obey"—she accompanied Henry to the World Anti-Slavery Conference in London. The schism in the American movement between Garrisonian and "political" abolitionists, with the latter not in favor of women's rights, led to a refusal by the majority to seat female delegates. One highly respected American delegate forced to sit in the balcony was Lucretia Mott of Philadelphia, Quaker minister and founder of the first women's antislavery society, where she had been a mentor to the Grimkés. Stanton struck up a close friendship with Mott, twenty years her senior. Roaming London together, they turned their anger into a vision of organizing a convention for the rights of women. But this dream had to be deferred, as Mott continued her antislavery work and Stanton became absorbed in bearing and raising children. Eight years later, Mott sat with her at the tea table as they fleshed out their dream.

The five women spread the word through the local paper and their personal grapevines. Arriving at Wesleyan Methodist Chapel on July 19, they found an unexpectedly large turnout of wagons and carriages from the countryside—and locked doors. A Stanton nephew clambered through a window to let people in. Though feeling as intimidated as if they "had been suddenly asked to construct a steam engine," according to a later report, the conveners had drafted a "Declaration of Sentiments and Resolutions"—indispensable to any reform convention. The first half, altering a few key phrases, reproduced passages from the Declaration of Independence as a manifesto for women. This reflected their need, as DuBois puts it, "to borrow political legitimacy from the American Revolution," but showed even more the hold of republican ideas on their political thinking as on the spirit of the age.

The Seneca Falls Declaration asserted that "all men and women are created equal," endowed with the same inalienable rights. "The history of mankind is a history of repeated injuries and usurpations on the part of man toward woman, having in direct object the establishment of an absolute tyranny over her." To prove this, letting "facts be submitted to a candid world," it enumerated a long list of injustices, including lack of citizenship rights and suffrage, married women ("civilly dead") devoid of property rights and subjugated by husbands, denial of educational opportunity, and not least that man "has monopolized nearly all the profitable employments, and from those she is permitted to follow, she receives but a scanty remuneration." It then demanded that women "have immediate admission to all the rights and privileges which belong to them as citizens of the United States." The declaration called for more such conventions and abolition-style agitation, heralding the birth of a new movement for rights.

After spirited discussion the gathering, two-thirds women, overwhelmingly approved the manifesto, along with resolutions written by Stanton. Only one of these aroused heated opposition, a breathtaking claim that "it is the duty of the women of this country to secure to themselves their sacred right to the elective franchise." Mott had tried to persuade Stanton to leave it out, apparently believing that it would divert or discredit efforts to attain more vital economic rights, such as married women's property rights. Others objected because it augured involvement in the sordid world of "politics." Though many considered it beyond the pale, the demand passed narrowly after Frederick Douglass spoke on its behalf. The real radicalism of the suffrage demand was its frontal challenge to women's powerlessness in relation to men, particularly as embedded in the law. It was a statement that women could neither fulfill their moral responsibilities nor live decent and humane lives merely as moral agents; they had the right and responsibility of participation in the world of political power that had heretofore excluded them.

The women's convention movement did not catch fire immediately, but when assemblies for rights mushroomed in the early 1850s the controversial call for suffrage was strongly espoused by participants, even though many still considered nonpolitical rights more central. The first national convention, held in Worcester, Massachusetts, in the autumn of 1850, drew women from seven states and launched a petition campaign for the vote. Unable to attend because of child-care duties, Stanton was appointed organizer for upstate New York.

Agitation spread westward. During a clamorous Akron meeting in May 1851 the opposition steadily gained ground, taking full advantage of the "open platform" custom at reform conventions that allowed anyone to speak. One man of God after another clobbered women's rights with the Bible. When all seemed lost, the chair, Frances Gage, recognized "a tall, gaunt black woman, in a gray dress and white turban, surmounted by an uncouth sun-bonnet," who strode solemnly to the front. For thirty years this woman had been a slave in New York, until the state banned slavery in 1827. Caught up in mystical offshoots of Protestant revivalism, she believed God had instructed her to take the name Sojourner Truth and to preach abolition and temperance. For several years she had lectured widely, unconstrained by illiteracy, embellishing her talks with gospel singing. She rode the circuit alone or with luminaries like Douglass. Sojourner Truth fully embraced women's emancipation and gave it equal billing with abolition, linking the two with her magnetic presence and graphic word pictures.

Though some of the Akron women did not want her to speak and men taunted her, she would not be held back. Her deep voice stilling the crowd, she met each allegation in turn, starting with female weakness and privilege. "Dat man ober dar say dat women needs to be helped into carriages, and lifted ober ditches, and to have de best place every whar. Nobody eber help me into carriages, or ober mud puddles, or gives me any best place"—her voice climbed to a thunderous pitch—"and ar'n't I a woman? Look at me! Look at my arm! I have plowed, and planted, and gathered into barns, and no man could head me—and ar'n't I a woman? I could work as much and eat as much as a man (when I could get it), and bear de lash as well—and ar'n't I a woman? I have borne thirteen chilern and seen 'em mos' all sold off into slavery, and when I cried out with a mother's grief, none but Jesus heard—and ar'n't I a woman?"

The audience roared with applause as she drove home her message that not all women had the status and privilege of white females, and that for this reason black women needed their rights at least as much if not more. Gage recalled that she had never "seen anything like the magical influence that subdued the mobbish spirit of the day and turned the jibes and sneers of an excited crowd into notes of respect and admiration."

Although women seized upon suffrage as both legitimate and necessary, it still seemed impractical in the 1850s. Of more immediate concern for middle-class white women were issues affecting their everyday lives, chiefly temperance and the lack of legal rights. In American jurisprudence, inherited from British common law, marriage embodied the concept of "femme couvert"; legally defined, the married couple were "one person, and that person the husband." Englishman William Blackstone's influential *Commentaries* stated that "the very being or legal existence of the woman is suspended during the marriage, or at least is incorporated and consolidated into that of the husband."

In the first half of the nineteenth century married women could not own or inherit property, control their earnings, sue in court, or have custody of children after divorce. Wives were not only propertyless but, worse, considered the property of their husbands, whose unlimited rights of sexual access and physical "punishment" were legally unassailable. It was not hard to see a close parallel between the legal nonexistence of white women, including their legal ownership by husbands, and that of slaves. Women too were denied the right to control the use of their own bodies, the right to personal autonomy and bodily integrity. "Man in his lust has regulated long enough this whole question of sexual intercourse," Stanton wrote to a new friend named Susan B. Anthony. Women's rights, she felt, "turns on the pivot of the marriage relation." Middle-class women were not only relegated to a narrowing, separate woman's sphere of domestic duties, a division of labor imposed by men, but within their own sphere they had few rights and decreasing autonomy.

During the 1840s activists had prodded several states, including New York, to pass laws permitting married women to inherit real property. But these laws did not mean much to those women, particularly working women, who had no property to inherit. In 1854, encouraged by Stanton, thirty-four-year-old Susan B. Anthony conducted a grass-roots petition campaign to broaden the New York law to cover earnings and child custody. This intrepid organizer was born in Adams, Massachusetts, in the state's mountainous northwest corner, where her Quaker father had built an early cotton mill. At six her family moved to northern New York, where her father took charge of a bigger factory; they prospered until the Panic of 1837 forced him out of business. Anthony became a teacher, one of few professions open to women, served as a school headmistress, then managed the family farm near Rochester. Influenced by her reform-conscious parents, who had attended the Seneca Falls gathering along with one of her sisters, she gravitated into the orbit of social reform.

After Anthony emerged as a leader of women's temperance in New York State, Stanton convinced her that legal rights and woman suffrage mattered more. With captains mobilized in every county, Anthony's innovative 1854 campaign collected thousands of signatures, which were handed in to the legislature at the climax of a women's rights convention in Albany. Neither the long rolls of petitions nor a riveting address by Stanton to the legislature swayed the male lawmakers. More determined than ever, Anthony returned to the hustings alone the next winter, fighting her way through merciless snowstorms to search out women and get more names. Her perseverance resulted five years later in a liberalized property law encompassing both inheritance and personal income, a model for the nation. This reform transcended strictly middle-class interests: legal entitlement to one's income helped working-class women more than those better off who generally did not have to work. In Massachusetts another indefatigable crusader, Mary Upton Ferrin, journeyed on foot several hundred miles with a petition, spurred other women to join her, and garnered a similar reform.

No aspect of the budding rights movement proved more fruitful than the extraordinary partnership of Stanton and Anthony, a political marriage and loving friendship that endured, not without conflict, for half a century. It was said that "I forged the thunderbolts and she fired them," Stanton later recalled. "She supplied the facts and statistics, I the philosophy and rhetoric, and, together, we have made arguments that have stood unshaken through the storms of long years." With her legal training, Stanton would serve as the movement's grand theorist and propagandist, while Anthony was its organizing genius and "propulsive force." As a mother of seven children Stanton could rarely travel until they were older. The two leaders thus turned her Seneca Falls home into a command post, Anthony often helping with household chores to free her friend to think and write, then setting off with renewed vigor to rally her sisters behind the cause.

Suffrage was the centerpiece of a multi-issue women's rights agenda. Burdened by family duties and resentful of her husband's freedom, Stanton was determined to make the marriage institution more egalitarian. She stirred a tempest at the 1860 rights convention when she argued passionately for a reform even more inflammatory than suffrage had been—a woman's right to divorce and to remarry, based on a redefinition of marriage as merely a civil contract voidable like any other. Many women denounced her resolution, especially Antoinette Brown Blackwell, the country's first ordained female minister. Garrison and Wendell Phillips sought to cut off debate, the latter so vexed that he tried to strike the discussion from the record. The issue was subdued for the time being but would reemerge in the 1870s.

By the eve of the Civil War, the idea of women's rights, at least in the abstract, had won a good deal of recognition. But pressed to their conclusion, note Mari Jo and Paul Buhle, "the rights of woman as an individual challenged the legal sanctity of the family, threatened to reform it drastically or destroy it. In part because 'personal' issues of marriage and morality could not be resolved, suffrage returned to the spotlight after the property rights agitation had faded."

BY AND LARGE women's rights activists halted work on female freedom, as a direct focus, during the War between the States. Thousands of Northern women threw themselves into the war effort as nurses and relief workers, mostly in the ubiquitous Sanitary Commission, a precursor of the Red Cross. When Senator Charles Sumner asked for grass-roots support to goad Congress into passing the Thirteenth Amendment, Stanton and Anthony formed a national women's organization that collected several hundred thousand signatures very quickly. Sumner and other Republicans credited their campaign with speeding the amendment's passage. Indirectly, the medical, relief, and political labors of these mostly white women contributed to a momentous step forward for women's rights—the emancipation of several million females from chattel slavery, along with males.

The Civil War transformed the landscape of reform. When abolitionists and Radical Republicans made black male suffrage the pivot of Reconstruction politics, women believed the constitutional door could be pushed open wider to encompass female suffrage—as Stanton put it, availing "ourselves of the strong arm and blue uniform of the black soldier to walk in by his side." How could women who had proven their patriotism be excluded from the gospel of equal rights when its moment seemed to have arrived? If others would gain protection and advancement with the ballot, why not women? Stanton, Anthony, Mott, Lucy Stone, and other leaders founded the American Equal Rights Association (AERA) to press for a universal suffrage that would not make distinctions of either race or sex but would "bury the black man and the woman in the citizen." They believed that women and black men both should be granted suffrage on the basis of their common citizenship and humanity.

But their abolitionist allies made it clear that "this is the negro's hour." Woman suffrage had to wait its turn lest it alienate support for black male suffrage. They argued that black men should be given the vote not primarily on the basis of citizenship rights per se, but for survival, protection, and advancement in a hostile South. Anthony and Stanton saw the handwriting on the wall when the Fourteenth Amendment, which dealt only indirectly with voting, inscribed the word "male" into the Constitution, putting women's rights in limbo. They felt they had no recourse but to agitate against its ratification.

Political skirmishes in 1867 half a continent apart convinced suffrage leaders that neither Republicans nor abolitionists were on their side. When a constitutional convention in New York offered an opening, Anthony fired up another grass-roots campaign, journeying up and down the state, as she put it, "like the flying of the shuttle in the loom of the weaver." Then she and Stanton lobbied delegates on behalf of a universal suffrage amendment and spoke to the suffrage committee headed by Horace Greeley, influential editor of the New York *Tribune*. Just before Greeley delivered his committee's rebuff of their proposed amendment, Stanton had someone announce that among their bundles of petitions was one signed by *Mrs.* Horace Greeley. Infuriated, the editor never forgave Stanton and Anthony and told the former that "no word of praise shall ever again be awarded you in the *Tribune*" and—the ultimate revenge—"If your name is ever necessarily mentioned, it shall be as Mrs. Henry B. Stanton." The delegates adopted suffrage for black males but not for women, and Greeley kept his promise.

In the frontier state of Kansas, voters faced two suffrage measures on the November ballot: one for black men promoted by the governing Republicans, the other including women—and opposed by the party. Week after week Stanton and Anthony crisscrossed the endless prairies on separate circuits, speaking wherever they could find people, often in log cabins, barns, and half-built schoolhouses, enduring hardships that ranged from inedible food to voracious bedbugs. The wedge between black and female suffrage did not help either cause; the white male electorate said no to both.

The fight over the Fifteenth Amendment made the break irreparable between uncompromising woman suffragists and the mainstream of Reconstruction reform. Many activist women, perhaps a majority, accepted the Radical Republican plea that if they joined forces on black male suffrage first, female suffrage would come next. The Stanton-Anthony wing, however, saw Reconstruction as a rare era of constitutional reform that might not recur for generations. "The few who had the prescience to see the long years of apathy that always follow a great conflict," Stanton wrote, "strained every nerve to settle the broad question of suffrage on its true basis while the people were still awake to its importance." They must act before the reform climate cooled.

On organizing jaunts through the East and Midwest and in their free-wheeling, broad-gauged journal called *The Revolution,* Stanton and Anthony condemned the amendment not only for leaving women out but because they had concluded it "would intensify sexual inequality," according to Ellen DuBois, giving "constitutional authority to men's claims that they were women's social and political superiors." The upshot of legitimizing female inferiority, Stanton warned, would be an even more entrenched "aristocracy of sex": all men, white and black, would have their rights, but all women would remain without. Rather than advance freedom and democracy, as its proponents promised, Stanton and Anthony claimed that the amendment would diminish them.

Moreover, along with Sojourner Truth they hammered away at what they considered the hypocritical disregard of half the black population. "If I have to answer for the deeds done in my body just as much as a man," Truth told the 1867 AERA convention, "I have a right to have just as much as a man. There is a great stir about colored men getting their rights, but not a word about the colored women; and if colored men get their rights, and not colored women theirs, you see the colored men will be masters over the women, and it will be just as bad as it was before." Despite apparent sensitivity to the plight of their black sisters, Stanton and other white suffragists made overtly racist attacks on the expansion of suffrage for black men only, voicing outrage that illiterate ex-slaves would secure political rights while educated middle-class women would not, at times even playing upon white women's sexual fears. This was a calculated effort to win the latter's support but it also reflected their frustration and resentment.

An attempt by Anthony and Stanton to reunify the ranks of reform resulted in a final rupture. Soft-pedaling their opposition to the Fifteenth

Amendment just passed by Congress, they called an AERA convention in May 1869 to launch a crusade for another federal amendment that would enfranchise all women. But Stephen Foster, Frederick Douglass, and other abolitionist leaders took the podium to denounce Stanton and Anthony for their racism. Douglass berated his erstwhile allies for deserting the great cause of black freedom.

"With us," he declared, "the matter is a question of life and death. . . . When women, because they are women, are hunted down through the cities of New York and New Orleans; when they are dragged from their houses and hung upon lamp-posts; when their children are torn from their arms, and their brains dashed out upon the pavement; when they are objects of insult and outrage at every turn; when they are in danger of having their homes burnt down over their heads; when their children are not allowed to enter schools; then they will have an urgency to obtain the ballot equal to our own." Loud clapping greeted his words.

"Is that not all true about black women?" asked a woman from the floor.

Yes, Douglass responded, "it is true of the black woman, but not because she is a woman, but because she is black."

Lucy Stone tried to mediate. "We are lost," she said, "if we turn away from the middle principle and argue for one class." She urged delegates to consider that "the Ku-Kluxes here in the North in the shape of men, take away the children from the mother, and separate them as completely as if done on the block of the auctioneer." Still she resigned herself to the seemingly inevitable: "I will be thankful in my soul," she lamented, "if *any* body can get out of the terrible pit."

Two days of tumultuous debate led to a stalemate, and the AERA's collapse. But female delegates meeting on their own, leavened by angry newcomers from the Midwest, decided spontaneously to create a national organization run by women to push for a sixteenth amendment. DuBois believes that this was the pivotal moment in "the transitional phase of suffragism between its prewar dependence on abolitionism and its emergence as an autonomous feminist movement."

The National Woman Suffrage Association (NWSA) did not have a clear field. Later in the year Stone and New England women still loyal to abolitionist priorities formed a rival group, the American Woman Suffrage Association (AWSA). They held that jettisoning Republican support would mean giving up all future leverage for women's rights. Differences in politics and strategy led to a convenient division of labor: NWSA, hopeful that national power could be harnessed behind women's rights, concentrated on Washington while the AWSA worked at the state level. The cautious and more hierarchical AWSA focused strictly on the vote, whereas the more militant and loosely organized group headed by Stanton and Anthony initially made that demand the foundation of a larger structure of rights reforms. At first, NWSA activists sought reconciliation with the breakaway group, but the latter kept its distance. The two would go separate ways for two decades.

At the final AERA convention Anthony had urged that the "question of precedence has no place on an equal rights platform," a stand she and her activist sisterhood had clung to for years. Yet historical circumstances and inequalities of power now forced many women to choose priorities, to compartmentalize rights they had assumed were indivisible and interdependent. They discovered that fights for rights and the rights themselves could be sources of division as well as unity—divisiveness exploited by enemies but engendered by "friends." Giving up coalition-building aimed at universal reform, which the Republicans had already forsaken for economic as well as political reasons, NWSA leaders resolved to mobilize an independent force of women, grounded in self-reliance and autonomous action. They would not ask for rights but assert them; and, for as long as it took, sustain enough grass-roots power to compel the male aristocracy to legislate a true democracy. They would then try to use the ballot to secure a wide array of personal, marital, civil, and economic rights. Black activists had pursued a similar course until they eventually won Northern white support for political rights during Reconstruction.

To some extent, however, the two wings of the postwar women's movement traveled the same road. Both left behind the universal suffrage strategy of the late 1860s, which stressed women's common humanity with men, in favor of an approach that played up gender differences. Reviving the antebellum identification of women with moral virtue, they argued that women must have the vote in order to carry out their moral duty to purify the corrupt public world dominated by men. This approach helped women to recognize their commonality as a separate group and infused new energy into the suffrage battle; but as DuBois concludes, the emphasis on difference "steered the women's rights movement away from its egalitarian origins," which meant that it "would ultimately become more compatible with conservative ideas about social hierarchy."

THE NEW DEPARTURE

IN THE EARLY 1870s activists in both camps of the women's rights movement looked back on its first quarter century with mixed feelings.

They had made considerable improvements in the legal status of married women, particularly in regard to property rights; though with husbands still assuming proprietorship over *them,* wives did not yet have rights to their own persons. Since the 1820s women had progressed the most in educational rights, as pioneers like Frances Wright, Prudence Crandall, and Emma Willard fought for equal education and shepherded girls' schools through storms of hostility. The movement had touched on a wide spectrum of issues affecting women's lives, but during Reconstruction it centered on suffrage. The larger crusade to emancipate slaves that had catalyzed the struggle for women's rights had also helped to fracture it. Stymied in their attempts to revise the Constitution, leaders explored new avenues of change.

For a time the NWSA embraced a creative strategy called the "new departure" that combined direct action with legal redress. It was originated by Missouri suffrage leader Virginia Minor and her attorney husband, who urged women to act on the assumption that the right of suffrage, implied in the fine print of the Reconstruction amendments, was theirs for the taking. Intending to force the Supreme Court to rule on the issue, Virginia Minor sued a St. Louis registrar for not letting her vote.

The new strategy caught the public's eye when flamboyant Victoria Woodhull testified before the House Judiciary Committee in January 1871. An aspiring Wall Street broker associated with financier Cornelius Vanderbilt, a devotee of spiritualism and advocate of free love, the thirty-two-year-old Woodhull argued with trembling but resolute voice that women did not need a separate amendment because the Fourteenth and Fifteenth amendments already guaranteed their right to vote on the basis of equal citizenship. The committee rebuffed her plea for a law affirming this right, but Woodhull was warmly welcomed into the NWSA and headlined its conventions. An overnight movement celebrity, she persuaded suffrage notables including Stanton to help her launch a multi-issue Equal Rights Party in 1872 with herself as its presidential nominee and Frederick Douglass as running mate; Douglass, an active Republican, was neither consulted nor interested. She saw the campaign as an opportunity for millions of women to assert their right to vote through direct action, but it sputtered and stalled.

Woodhull's openly expressed views on the right of sexual self-determination alienated many activists, as her ideas went far beyond equalizing marriage and controlling births. "I have an *inalienable, constitutional,* and *natural* right to love whom I may," she insisted, " . . . and with *that* right neither *you* nor any *law* you can frame have any right to interfere." Not even movement activists could stomach easily what seemed in the Victorian age a shocking interpretation, and expansion, of individual rights.

Because she was uncompromising and had little sense of propriety, her political star crashed as rapidly as it had risen.

To test what they considered to be their implicit right to vote, over a hundred women in scattered localities attempted to cast ballots in the 1872 presidential election—many wishing to vote Republican since that party had put a small women's rights "splinter" in its platform. "Well, I have been and gone and done it!!" Anthony jubilantly reported from Rochester. She and fifteen other women, including three Anthony sisters, had convinced election officials to take their ballots. Quite a few women had tried to vote during Reconstruction—in 1870 black women had voted in South Carolina and in Massachusetts the elderly Grimké sisters and forty others had braved a snowstorm to do so—but now women engaged in conscious acts of civil disobedience, hoping that a legal test case such as Minor's would lead to a favorable ruling by the Supreme Court.

Arrested, Anthony was charged with violating the federal Enforcement Act that had been aimed at guaranteeing black voting rights in the South. She mounted a local campaign to educate the public—and prospective jurors. "We throw to the winds the old dogma that government can give rights," she proclaimed in a speech setting forth the new constitutional argument for suffrage. The Declaration of Independence and the national and state constitutions "propose to *protect* the people in the exercise of their God-given rights. Not one of them pretends to bestow rights. . . . Here is no shadow of government authority over rights, or exclusion of any class from their full and equal enjoyment." Her conclusion was clear: the only way for women to claim their citizenship rights was to exercise them actively.

Fearing that the well-tutored jury would acquit, the Republican federal judge ordered it to find her guilty. Anthony had the last word with a cogent lecture prior to sentencing in which she lambasted the court's injustice—oblivious to the judge's repeated commands to stop. He fined her one hundred dollars, but she announced that "I shall never pay a dollar of your unjust penalty." He threatened to imprison her but backed down, knowing that if he let her stay free she could not bring her case to the Supreme Court.

The highest court settled the matter, from a judicial standpoint, in its 1874 ruling in *Minor* v. *Happersett*—but not as Virginia Minor had hoped. The justices unanimously rejected Minor's claim that suffrage was a right inherent in national citizenship. Furthermore, the ruling indicated that voting was not subject to the Fourteenth Amendment's equal protection clause, the Constitution's major enforcement mechanism, and in narrowly interpreting the Fifteenth Amendment set the stage for the Court to whittle down the voting rights of black males and others.

With suffrage blocked by both Congress and the courts, creative direct action carried on. In 1876 the nation celebrated the centennial of the Declaration of Independence with a lavish Philadelphia exposition of American industrial and technological progress. A women's group put together an impressive exhibit on female contributions to national development. Denied space, they built their own pavilion that included, as part of a display of steam-powered machinery run by women, a printing press that cranked out a women's rights newspaper. NWSA activists used the occasion to spotlight the continuing exclusion of women from the Declaration's promises, and to show that, in Alma Lutz's words, "the only suitable commemoration of the founding of the Republic was conferring equal rights on its unfranchised citizens—women."

Anthony joined with Stanton and Lucretia Mott, now eighty-three, to draft a new "Declaration of Rights for Women" to present publicly during the official observance on the Fourth of July. Not only did the centennial commission turn down this "slight request"; it permitted only a handful of women to attend the Independence Hall ceremony. Furious, Stanton and Mott boycotted the affair, but Anthony and four others did not let protocol get in the way. They sat patiently through the reading of the hallowed manifesto of 1776, then marched up to the chair, Senate president pro tem Thomas Ferry, a suffrage backer, and handed him their own parchment scroll as he paled and bowed.

As the women left Independence Hall they scattered copies of the scroll among the startled guests. Anthony then climbed atop an empty bandstand, and as Matilda Joslyn Gage shielded her with an umbrella from the broiling sun, recited their declaration to a large crowd milling in Independence Square. For violating "fundamental principles of our government" it arraigned male rulers with several "articles of impeachment," stressing denial of legal rights, judicial injustice, taxation without representation, and the despotism, more absolute than monarchy, of manhood suffrage. "It was the boast of the founders of the republic, that the rights for which they contended were the rights of human nature. If these rights are ignored in the case of one-half the people, the nation is surely preparing for its downfall. . . . at the close of a hundred years, as the hour-hand of the great clock that marks the centuries points to 1876, we declare our faith in the principles of self-government; our full equality with man in natural rights; that woman was made first for her own happiness, with the absolute right to herself—to all the opportunities and advantages life affords for her complete development."

Lacking the power to redefine the existing Constitution, the nub of the "new departure," NWSA activists reluctantly shifted to the goal of a woman suffrage amendment, its wording taken from the Fifteenth

Amendment with sex in place of race. Prepared for a long battle, NWSA fired up its boilers for a new nationwide crusade. A California senator introduced the amendment in Congress, Stanton and other women testified at hearings with customary eloquence, and both houses formed woman suffrage committees that reported out the measure almost every year for two decades, only to have it die regularly on the floor.

Riding the rails from coast to coast to mobilize support in prairie towns, in frontier cities, and throughout the Far West, Anthony and Stanton discovered a budding movement in the nation's heartland. Across the racial and socioeconomic spectrum, women were awakening to injustice and taking action, often in small ways, to assert their rights. Letters to Anthony showed that not only educated, middle-class, white women were drawn to the cause. Jane Sobers of Philadelphia wrote that "i feel proud that we have some noble woman to help unnBar the Prison Doors for the Poor Down trodden honst hard working woman of this countery. i have Suffered inJustice from the Law of this my native city. wronged and Robbed of what Did by Rights Belong to me."

Alzina Rathbun from Iowa informed Anthony that "I am so thankful there is so many capable to do something strike your best blows go to all their great conventions let them know you mean freedom if we never get it keep them stirred up that is some satisfaction if nothing more all this scribbling does not amount to much of course but I have give you my mind on the subject now you can laugh over my composition it will do that much good any way you will find my name in the list from Shellsburg Iowa was not able to write when I put it there poor show for a town of 600 inhabitants we had to work hard to get that many."

On behalf of the "Down Trodden Colored Sisters of Virginia," Live Pryor complained that the white men "who rule us with a rod of iron, and show themselves on every occasion the same Crule Task Master, as ever, have introduce on the Statute books right to wipp woman." And Mrs. L. M. R. Pool of Ohio wrote that "I always come to the same conclusion, namely that our rotten marriage institution is the main obstacle in the way of womans freedom, and just as long as our girls are taught to barter the use of their bodys for a living, must woman remain the degraded thing she is. Of course the Ballot is the great lever to lift her into self esteem and independence."

SUCH LINKING of personal and political rights resounded from hundreds of podiums as Stanton spent most of each year during the 1870s lecturing on the countrywide lyceum circuit. Too busy to crystallize her thinking in a formal treatise, in the course of producing an endless stream of speeches, articles, and manifestos she evolved a farsighted philosophy of rights for women.

Firmly grounded in the natural rights tradition so prominent in both the Seneca Falls statement and its 1876 reformulation, Stanton's philosophy stretched the paradigm of individual rights to its furthest limits. Unlike many later suffragists, she did not champion the vote as an end in itself but as "the vestibule of woman's emancipation," an instrumental end to secure other pressing rights—to one's person, to self-ownership and self-development, above all to sexual and reproductive self-determination. She advocated divorce reform, "voluntary motherhood" (birth control) based on the right to refuse intercourse, and the equal partnership of husband and wife in marriage. Her concept of "self sovereignty" did not call for abolition of the separate spheres, but it demanded that republican principles underpinning the public realm be carried over into the private.

"Conservatism cries out we are going to destroy the family," Stanton said. "Timid reformers answer, the political equality of woman will not change it. They are both wrong. It will entirely revolutionize it. When woman is man's equal the marriage relation cannot stand on the basis it is to day. . . . This same law of equality that has revolutionized the state and the church is now knocking at the door of our homes," leading toward a "purer, higher, holier" condition of marriage and family.

Like black leaders of the same epoch, she stressed the interconnectedness of rights and objected to their compartmentalization by gender, race, class, function, or realm. She never relinquished her Reconstruction-rooted conviction that national power was responsible for enforcing equal rights in all domains, public and private. Yet she bemoaned the alarming use of this new power "to oppress the citizens of the several States in their most sacred rights." She had no illusions about the limitations of the Constitution. "The numerous demands by the people for national protection in many rights not specified by the constitution," she noted, "prove that the people have outgrown the compact that satisfied the fathers."

In two important respects Stanton's political theory transcended the natural rights tradition of liberal individualism. During the nineteenth century suffragists self-consciously employed the term "woman" to signify their conception of the female sex as a unitary group or collectivity experiencing shared oppression and common needs. Taking a further step, Stanton argued that women constituted an actual *class*, frequently comparing them to slaves in order to underline their class identity. "All history shows that one class never did legislate with justice for another," she observed, "and all philosophy shows they never can. . . . It is folly to say that women are not a class, so long as there is any difference in the code of laws for men and women, any discrimination in the customs of society, giving advantages to men over women."

Accordingly, women had entitlements both as a class and as individuals. Because of the specific character of their subjugation, deriving from sex roles and reproductive capacities, they not only had to realize traditional rights to free speech, the vote, and so forth, but also had to fashion new rights reflecting their common reality, rights of sexual choice and of divorce and remarriage being fundamental. Twentieth-century feminists would go beyond such rights of negative liberty from male dominance to conceptualize positive rights to the social resources, such as contraception, legal abortion, and child care, that might enable them to stand on equal footing with men.

In a dialectical duel with her theory of woman as a sex class was Stanton's richly textured vision of woman's individuality, which matured as she aged. At its heart lay a woman's right to autonomy, to independence from men, along with the corresponding duty of self-reliance. Committed to integrating theory with practice, she exemplified these values more and more in her own life after raising her children and living separately (though not divorced) from her husband.

Stanton set forth this vision most poignantly in a farewell speech on her resignation at seventy-six as president of the recently reunified suffrage organization in January 1892. She began with the premise that women's infinite diversity of character overshadowed the biological and cultural attributes women shared with each other, the attributes that made them a class. The irreducible justification for a woman's claim to equal rights in the fullest sense, "her birthright to self-sovereignty," was "the solitude and personal responsibility of her own individual life."

Because women "must make the voyage of life alone," they must "know something of the laws of navigation. To guide our own craft, we must be captain, pilot, engineer; with chart and compass to stand at the wheel; to watch the winds and waves, and know when to take in the sail, and to read the signs in the firmament over all. . . . The great lesson that nature seems to teach us at all ages is self-dependence, self-protection, self-support." In such a heartless world, she believed, no one could be denied entitlements to those skills and powers requisite for survival. If untrammeled self-development could also lead to happiness, so much the better. A question she left unanswered, however, was whether women's condition was such that, like the "rugged individuals" of the other gender, they had no choice but to be alone, personally and emotionally if not in a literal sense.

As with her contemporary John Stuart Mill in England, Stanton had trouble disentangling her emancipatory vision of individuality from the negative connotations of liberal individualism. Did independence from male control necessarily mean separateness, atomization, competitiveness? "Feminism uses the individualist stance against men because men inhibit women's self and collective development," notes political theorist Zillah Eisenstein; "it need not extend this vision to premise women's isolation from one another." Though ambiguous in her thinking, Stanton realized, in Eisenstein's words, that "for women to develop their capacities as individuals, they need connection to other women." Women had to identify and mobilize as a collectivity, and draw on a sisterhood of support, in order to allow each to actualize her distinct individuality. Although inconceivable apart from prior claims to life and liberty, this higher right to individuality, and the complexities of its implementation and protection, dwelt in an uncharted region of human rights.

STANTON'S THEORY of woman as a class having a collective right to individuality, free of sex-role constraints, would be revived almost a century later in the vocabulary of "women's liberation." In the post–Civil War decades her radical views, which tied rights to personal responsibility, were drowned out by conservative values glorifying women's moral duties at the expense of their rights. Across the spectrum, social commitment to individual rights fell to a low ebb as scholars, opinion-makers, and business leaders consecrated the new deity of large-scale organization with its unheard-of power to transform society. Human beings were increasingly regarded as members of social aggregates, particularly of classes, races, and nations, more than as individuals. With conservative thinkers like Yale sociologist William Graham Sumner leading the charge, the new language of Social Darwinism—which held competition and strife to be necessary for positive social evolution—threatened to overwhelm the hardy old language of rights, whose "natural" basis and egalitarianism were disparaged by Sumner and his ilk. Property rights for owners of capital, anointed as society's "fittest," were secured and expanded by the colossal Industrial Revolution afoot that trampled on human rights promised by the political revolution of the previous century. As the unleashing of corporate capitalism ushered in a robust new propertied class, many of the educated women belonging to it felt that their touted moral virtue obligated them to nurse the social wounds that the latest revolution left in its wake.

Thus a cornucopia of women's organizations arose to deal with pressing social problems such as poverty and alcohol abuse, many of them, like the Young Women's Christian Association, aiding females directly. For the most part these groups did not advocate suffrage, or they carefully framed their support so as not to scare away members or money. Meanwhile, both suffrage organizations distanced themselves from the once widely held view of the vote as an instrument of progressive social change. To gain broader support the debate narrowed to whether suffrage represented an innocuous moral good with no agenda or a means to defend "Christian values" and woman's traditional roles. Those in the latter camp clutched tightly the banner of common womanhood—not as the emblem of a class in revolt, but as the elixir of social harmony. In any event, with the two suffrage associations growing more alike, the woman's movement succumbed to the orthodoxies of the age. The suffrage demand itself "was losing its radical associations," Ginzberg notes, "as more conservative women became convinced of the value of the vote in their own work."

The largest and most influential women's reform organization promoted these conservative tendencies while it used them to push suffrage and other entitlements in through the back door. The Woman's Christian Temperance Union (WCTU) was founded in 1874 in the aftermath of the remarkable "woman's crusade," when praying and singing bands of women had shut down thousands of saloons in the Midwest. Strongest in that region, the WCTU drew its membership mainly from among native-born, Protestant, middle-class women. Focusing on abuse of alcohol, the organization's deeper aim was to protect the vulnerable woman's sphere from the predations of men (especially male violence) and the dislocations of rapid industrialization. Under the imaginative leadership of Frances Willard, a suffragist, the WCTU carried out its "Do Everything Policy" to move toward her goal of the full emancipation of women. In addition to crusading for temperance and laws regulating liquor, the WCTU's "white ribbon army" lobbied for heavier rape penalties, agitated to raise the "age of consent," pushed for female police and prison reform, and set up day-care centers and mothers' support groups.

As Willard educated members about the importance of voting as a weapon to curb drinking and safeguard the family, the WCTU's franchise department turned into an organizing whirlwind, starting with petition campaigns for the "home protection ballot" to give women the power to vote locally on liquor control, a foot in the door. By the 1880s and 1890s the majority of suffrage activists in the Midwest and Far West were WCTU members. Suffragists outside the temperance movement came to rely on far-flung WCTU chapters to win converts they could not reach, though some suffrage leaders repudiated the organization for its strait-laced morality.

The WCTU proved that, according to DuBois, "support for the suffrage could be made compatible with relatively conventional ideas about the role of women and that it was therefore possible to create a much larger and broader woman suffrage movement." Fruitful cooperation with Willard and her cadres persuaded Anthony that the NWSA should strive to unify all reform-minded women behind suffrage, even if widen-

ing the constituency meant narrowing the focus. To launch such a grand
coalition, a lofty "universal sisterhood," NWSA leaders organized a
weeklong extravaganza in Washington, the first International Council of
Women. The call announced that "Literary Clubs, Art Unions, Temperance Unions, Labor Leagues, Missionary, Peace and Moral Purity Societies, Charitable, Professional, Educational and Industrial Associations
will thus be offered equal opportunity with Suffrage Societies to be represented in what should be the ablest and most imposing body of women
ever assembled."

Delegates arrived in March 1888 from fifty-three American organizations and eight foreign countries including India. The purpose was not
only to lay the groundwork for unity but, in commemorating the fortieth
anniversary of Seneca Falls, to take stock of progress. Besides a host of
female luminaries speaking from a platform awash in flowers and ever-
green, delegates heard from elderly black leaders Frederick Douglass and
Robert Purvis. Purvis had firmly backed the women's cause because, he
once said, he did not care to have rights his daughters could not share;
half a century before he had voted against excluding women from the
London antislavery conference attended by Stanton and Mott. A catalyst
of continuing efforts to consolidate women's activism, the assembly paid
a price for its harmony—omitting suffrage from the council's goals.

The Washington gala also brought together leaders of the two rival
suffrage organizations for the first time in two decades. As NWSA retreated from its broad-gauged agenda, differences had diminished.
Younger suffragists clamored for reconciliation. In 1890, after prolonged
negotiations mediated by Alice Stone Blackwell, daughter of Lucy Stone,
the groups merged into a single organization called the National American Woman Suffrage Association (NAWSA). Yet greater solidarity among
white middle-class women seemed to intensify class and racial divisions.
Spurning economic issues by and large, suffragists antagonized working-
class women with nativist attacks on immigrant men, whom they accused
of misusing the privilege of voting to keep women from exercising it. And
eager to make suffrage respectable in the eyes of Southern whites, they
alienated African-American women by failing to condemn and sometimes
condoning racism.

In practice reunification meant that for twenty-five years AWSA's state-
by-state approach would prevail over the federal amendment route,
which faded from view after 1896. The results of the myriad state campaigns mocked the prodigious energy expended. From 1870 to 1910
nearly five hundred grass-roots campaigns placed only seventeen refer-
enda on the ballot in eleven states, mostly in the West; with Populist
support, Colorado and Idaho eked out the sole victories. In some states

such as California the liquor interests triumphed by cranking up the male electorate's fear of prohibition.

The imperatives of party politics also fostered defeats. In 1890 NAWSA targeted the new state of South Dakota after both the Populist Farmers' Alliance and the Knights of Labor promised support; but when these groups formed the state People's Party the fledgling party backed off. Riding for months across drought-stricken plains under a scorching sun, wagon wheels sinking into the powdery soil, the seventy-year-old Anthony and a platoon of agitators spoke to hundreds of meetings organized by freshly sprouted women's clubs. But victory eluded them. In Kansas four years later, People's Party legislators placed suffrage on the ballot; the Populist convention endorsed the measure after passionate speeches by Anthony, Carrie Chapman Catt, and Populist leader Annie Diggs. But the Republicans opposed it—even Republican suffragists who put party before principle—and the male electorate once again voted it down.

The setbacks in the hinterland reinforced inertia at the national level. The unified but dwindling suffrage forces proved no match for the hardening alliance of big business, white supremacy, and Victorian moralism cemented by the McKinley Republicans' rout of Democrats and Populists in 1896. Driven into abeyance along with the beleaguered agrarian and labor movements, the suffrage crusade awaited rebirth in the new century as yet another generation of American women prepared to carry on the struggle.

DEMOCRACY SHOULD BEGIN AT HOME

AT THE TURN of the century, fifty years after the founding of the women's rights movement, suffrage remained out of reach except in a clump of four Western states and in numerous municipalities and school districts. Ironically women were making greater progress in areas more on the periphery of organized campaigns. Though divorce laws remained inequitable, women had secured rights to property and income in many states. In a nation that sanctified education, middle-class women continued to advance in educational opportunity, particularly with such new women's colleges as Smith, Vassar, and Bryn Mawr, and expanding co-education. The biggest change—bittersweet fruit of the Industrial Revolution—proved to be the accelerating influx of women into the labor force earning low wages as domestics, salesclerks, factory workers, and office secretaries, the last a new field for women. Although most movement activists concentrated on the vote, some were concerned more with securing economic rights now that the industrial juggernaut had produced a pressing demand for female labor. If women had a right to economic "self-support," independent of male providers, what would it take to realize it?

The most influential and systematic arguments for the economic independence of women poured from the pen of Charlotte Perkins Gilman, particularly in her pioneering work *Women and Economics,* published in 1898. In her autobiography she recalled writing it: "the smooth, swift, easy flow . . . the splendid joy" of distilling ideas long in ferment. One day, after writing four thousand words in four hours, "I went and ran, just raced along the country road, for sheer triumph."

Grandniece of a famous sibling trio of reformers—Harriet Beecher Stowe, Catharine Beecher, and Henry Ward Beecher—Gilman grew up in poverty after her father deserted the family. When her first marriage and childbirth caused severe depression, she separated from her husband and moved to California, where—finding meaningful work the best therapy—she earned her livelihood in the 1890s lecturing and writing on current political issues and was active in suffrage circles. Her intellectual explorations were shaped by Social Darwinism, particularly sociologist Lester Ward's progressive interpretation that argued for rational control of social evolution, and by the non-Marxist socialist ideas of novelist Edward Bellamy and the British Fabians. The international success of *Women and Economics,* translated into seven languages, marked Gilman as the movement's preeminent theorist during the early twentieth century, the "Marx and Veblen" of an emerging politics later called feminism. In a sense she took up where Stanton had left off, no less visionary but more focused on the economic dimensions of women's rights.

Anchored in evolutionary theory but turning Social Darwinism to different ends, *Women and Economics* located the origins of female subjugation in dependence on males for subsistence going back to prehistoric times. Because the exchange of sex for food and shelter had become crucial for sheer survival, women's sexual attributes were overdeveloped, Gilman said, at the expense of "rational" qualities more useful to social progress. Lopsided femininity had reached its apogee in Victorian images of female docility and selflessness and what she labeled the cult of "matriolatry" (worship of motherhood). The only means of uncoupling the "sexuo-economic relation" by which men dominated women was for the latter to gain economic self-sufficiency.

As Gilman saw it, the fundamental right to such autonomy did not derive from the Declaration of Independence, from the legacy of republicanism, or from God, but from a scientific understanding of dynamic natural processes; from "principles of development, of growth, of change," as Carl Degler interprets her thinking, "not static, God-given rights that inhere in the laws of the universe. In short, for all her talk about, and belief in laws, she was no exponent of the eighteenth-century idea of natural law. Those static defenses of equality she abandoned in the face of the triumph of Darwinian evolutionary thought." But unlike conservative Social Darwinists, she saw that the line had blurred between necessity and freedom. Women had to act for themselves to achieve economic emancipation. They were no longer powerless pawns of natural evolution but could help to steer it.

Gilman perceived that women's economic independence required sweeping structural reforms to remove the gender-specific barriers to full citizenship. Since the patriarchal family kept women subordinate it must be refashioned to meet their needs. To free women to pursue vocations outside the home the domestic duties of cooking, housekeeping, and child-rearing would be performed by well-paid female specialists.

"There is no cause for alarm," Gilman reassured the reader. "We are not going to lose our homes nor our families, nor any of the sweetness and happiness that go with them." But the private kitchen and nursery had become obsolete. "The cook-stove will follow the loom and wheel, the wool-carder and shears." The human race, she believed, was "not well nourished by making the process of feeding it a sex-function. The selection and preparation of food should be in the hands of trained experts" in communal kitchens serving multiple families eating together in common dining rooms. While women worked, their children would be cared for by professionals in neighborhood day nurseries. "The educative department of maternity is not a personal function," she remarked, but "is in its very nature a social function."

With these structural foundations in place, the economic self-determination of women would foster egalitarian relationships between male and female, and otherwise advance the public good. "We shall have far happier marriages, happier homes, happier women and happier men," she declared in 1903, "when both sexes realize that they are human and that humanity has far wider duties and desires than those of the domestic relations."

Gilman's vision of liberation from domesticity struck a chord among many middle-class women but had less relevance for those of the lower classes, white and black. These women had to work regardless of family obligations and could not dream of paying for help; indeed, many were themselves low-paid servants in other women's homes. Far from promoting independence, wage labor reproduced economic dependence in a harsher, more impersonal context. Decades would pass before Gilman's remedies would appear less elitist and less utopian, only when pressures from working women began to legitimize the use of public funds and resources to implement their common right to child care and to meet related needs.

MARCH 3, 1 9 1 3. When President-elect Woodrow Wilson's train pulled into Washington's Union Station the day before his inauguration, he was surprised not to be welcomed by adoring crowds and brass bands. "Where are the people?" asked a disgruntled aide. The people were out on Pennsylvania Avenue, half a million of them, watching a spectacular parade of several thousand suffragists that included twenty-six floats, ten bands, and five cavalry squadrons. Marching to the White House, the suffragists were announcing to the nation and its new president that the movement had come back with new power. Police did little to keep the crowds from pressing against the calm, resolute marchers. Hecklers assaulted them. Secretary of War Henry Stimson had to send in cavalry troops to restore order. After a congressional investigation the police superintendent was fired.

During the decade after 1896, as many female reformers in the Progressive era turned to causes such as working women's welfare, including lobbying for hours limitations and other protective laws, the suffrage crusade had lost its momentum. No new states had been won and the federal amendment seemed dead. Then a resurgence of grass-roots activism, from coast to coast, led to a string of victories. Deftly organized coalitions with Progressives and labor brought suffrage to Washington (1910) and California (1911); in the latter state campaigners had for the first time used automobiles and electric signs. Arizona, Kansas, and Oregon followed in 1912, and women secured partial suffrage in Illinois. Several factors accounted for the change: the climate of reform respectability brought by Progressivism, in which Jane Addams, Florence Kelley, Lillian Wald, and many other women played central roles; an influx of self-assured and committed young women, fresh out of college; the multiplication of local suffrage clubs; and the replacement of scattergun agitation by well-crafted electoral organization down to the precinct level. A major catalyst as well was the expansion of the female labor force and of union activism by wage-earning women, particularly in the Women's Trade Union League.

Creative new leadership molded these ingredients into a mass movement of suffragism that mobilized legions of women (and men) over the next decade. Harriot Stanton Blatch, daughter of Elizabeth Cady Stanton, had married an Englishman and lived near London for twenty years. Returning to the United States in 1902, she focused on building a suffrage alliance of working-class and professional women. In 1910 she founded the Women's Political Union, based in New York State; it organized big parades and outdoor meetings and sent squads of women to orate on soapboxes, all of which defied feminine respectability. Unlike most suffrage groups, it recruited many wage-earning women.

Some of the new leaders were inspired by the militant "suffragettes" in England, led by Emmeline Pankhurst and her daughters Christabel and Sylvia, who in turn had been influenced by the prior generation of American activists. The suffragettes engaged in direct action against Parliament that occasionally included rock-throwing and window-breaking. Two young Americans who had tasted British militance firsthand would have a decisive impact on rejuvenating the American movement. Vassar-educated Lucy Burns, a graduate student in Germany, and Alice Paul, Quaker, Swarthmore graduate, social worker, and sociologist (Ph.D. from the University of Pennsylvania), worked for suffrage in London and took part in civil disobedience. They joined forces back in the United States determined to transplant British strategy and tactics to their homeland, aiming solely at the Constitution. Paul persuaded NAWSA to let her take over its Washington-based Congressional Committee and organize the March 1913 pre-inaugural parade. Not ready to shift to a federal amendment strategy, however, and feeling upstaged by Paul's charisma, drive, and organizational acumen, NAWSA leaders insisted soon after the big parade that Paul, Burns, and the newly formed Congressional Union (CU) go their own way.

Paul and Burns sought to apply British parliamentary methods to a very different political context. In those states where women could vote, mainly in the West, the CU (renamed the National Woman's Party) campaigned against Democrats—even those who backed suffrage—in a wholesale effort to change party policy. The heart of the strategy was to compel the equivocating President Wilson to put his weight behind the amendment. During the 1914 campaign NAWSA leaders condemned the indiscriminate pillorying of Democrats by the NWP as a misuse of the American political system and a violation of the venerable suffragist tradition of nonpartisanship. Paul and her supporters countered that they had not abandoned independent political action but had perfected it.

Their underlying argument, however, was that the time had long passed for asking—begging—for rights by means of endless petitions and other "ladylike" behavior. Blatch told Wilson point-blank that "I have worked all my life for suffrage, and I am determined that I will never again stand in the street corners of a great city appealing to every Tom, Dick, and Harry for the right of self-government." The NWP judged that in order to win full political rights women would have to wield power directly, both inside and outside of the electoral arena. In states where they were enfranchised women could hold a balance of power and swing elections, especially the upcoming presidential contest. In the nation's capital Paul's forces would soon confront the President head-on.

The NWP's assertive politics, along with growing disquiet within NAWSA, prodded that organization's leaders to shake off their lethargy and shift into high gear. They brought back to the helm ex-president Carrie Chapman Catt, who had been honing her leadership skills for many years. Raised on a farm on the Iowa frontier, in her twenties she had been a high school principal and superintendent of schools, then a journalist, until she threw herself into suffrage, directing state campaigns and leading the international suffrage alliance. Anthony had chosen Catt to succeed her as NAWSA chief in 1900, but she left the post after four years. Then as leader of the New York campaign she had demonstrated the power of systematic organization, which she now planned to implement nationwide.

First she mobilized female battalions at the 1916 party conventions to push strong suffrage planks. Several thousand women holding banners and umbrellas marched through Chicago in a ferocious rainstorm, accompanied by two dozen bands, a Scottish bagpiper, two fife and drum corps, and a pair of elephants wearing rubber blankets, "swinging their trunks sadly" as they stumbled through the mud. The drenched multitude surged inside the GOP convention hall just as an antisuffragist was telling the Resolutions Committee that "women do not want the vote." In St. Louis the Democrats were greeted by a "Golden Lane" of women with yellow parasols, some of whom packed the galleries while the delegates debated their rights. "The sight of them had a most unnerving effect on the delegations," the *New York Times* reported. "The women with the rollcall blanks suggested the knitting women of the Reign of Terror" in the French Revolution. For the first time the parties endorsed woman suffrage—but through state action, not federal.

At an emergency NAWSA gathering in September, during which President Wilson addressed the "living petition" of delegates and offered ambiguous backing, Catt met privately with state suffrage leaders to present her "winning plan." In a "crowded stuffy room" in the basement of a Washington hotel, she persuaded them that all efforts had to be aimed at the amendment, but that stepped-up state campaigns would be the major means to pressure Congress—each state victory adding congressional support—and to prepare for the ratification struggle. It was not a choice between national and state strategies, she explained, but "we must do both and do them together."

Like a general in battle, she cast her pointer across a map of the nation, handing out detailed assignments to each NAWSA affiliate. In order to take the enemy by surprise, she required that each state leader sign a "solemn compact" to keep the plan secret. When all had made the pledge, recalled Massachusetts organizer Maud Wood Park, "I felt like Moses on the mountain top after the Promised Land had been shown to him and he knew the long years of wandering in the Wilderness were soon to end." Catt wrote later that after "the biggest week's work" of her life, "a great army in perfect discipline moved forward to its goal."

The troops did not waste any time. Two months hence, female voters in Western states were credited with Wilson's reelection—despite concerted efforts by the NWP to defeat him. In 1917 women finally won suffrage in New York, fifty years after Anthony and Stanton's skirmish with Horace Greeley. Within two years women could vote in half the states; their electoral clout was accelerating.

But the pace of change was still too slow for the NWP. Aware of the gulf between the moral recognition of a right and its implementation, the NWP had no illusions that Wilson's rhetorical flourishes would translate into a commitment to drive the amendment through a recalcitrant Congress. In January 1917, after Wilson waffled once more at a White House conclave with three hundred suffragists, NWP leaders decided to up the ante and adopt a picketing tactic used well by Harriot Stanton Blatch at the Albany statehouse. For over a year, small groups of "silent sentinels" in rotating shifts stood guard at the White House gates, brandishing banners of purple, white, and gold whose wording demanded that the President act.

When the nation entered World War I in April, the relentless moral witness turned into a serious political threat and tested the government's commitment to free speech and peaceful assembly. Both NAWSA and the NWP sought to make national suffrage a war measure so that it would not be put off again. While the former group embraced the war effort and cast suffrage as a reward for women's patriotic service, the latter (many of whose members opposed the war) set forth its own nonviolent "war policy," leader Doris Stevens recounted later, "based on the military doctrine of concentrating all one's forces on the enemy's weakest point," in this case "the inconsistency between a crusade for world democracy and the denial of democracy at home."

The banners women held at the White House threw back at the President his own ringing phrases about democratic ideals and "making the world safe for democracy." One quoted from Wilson's war message: "We shall fight . . . for the right of those who submit to authority to have a voice in their own governments." Picketers endured increasingly hostile denunciation from press and politicians. In June, after the stationary sentinels greeted visiting Russian diplomats with a banner blaring that "America is not a democracy," police began to arrest them on the spurious charge of obstructing traffic.

When a brief stay in jail did not deter further protests, the judge slapped the next group with sixty-day terms in the federal workhouse at Occoquan, Virginia. A few of these upstanding women were wives or relatives of influential Democrats, including one who had just dined with the Wilsons in the White House. Among notables attending their trial—where they made impassioned defenses of their right to protest for liberty—was Dudley Field Malone, a longtime friend and campaign organizer for Wilson who served in the administration. On the afternoon of the trial he collared the President to protest the jailings and tender his resignation. The prisoners reluctantly accepted a presidential pardon. With redoubled fervor they resumed their posts at the White House. As summer drifted into fall the picketers faced escalating assaults whipped up by war fever, especially from servicemen. And someone fired a bullet into their Lafayette Park headquarters.

As women continued to be carted off to jail they were replaced by an inexhaustible supply of fresh recruits. When the convicts were not cowed by hefty sentences or by Occoquan's normal hardships—including rancid, wormy food and rats as bedmates—the warden resorted to scare tactics and physical abuse. As it was wartime, Lucy Burns and others protested their mistreatment by demanding the rights of political prisoners. They believed, Stevens recalled, "that a determined, organized effort to make clear to a wider public the political nature of the offense would intensify the Administration's embarrassment and so accelerate their final surrender." Just before she was removed to solitary confinement, Burns crafted a manifesto on a "forlorn piece of paper" passed from one inmate to another "through holes in the wall surrounding leaden pipes, until a finished document had been perfected and signed by all" and smuggled out to the press.

Their demands ignored by the warden, the suffragists refused to eat. Put in isolation cells, they were painfully force-fed three times daily for three weeks. Tubes pushed down their throats caused them to vomit. The authorities had already sought to make an example of ringleader Alice Paul by giving her a seven-month sentence. When the dreaded force-feeding did not break her will they took her to the psychiatric ward of the Washington jail, boarding up the cell door and window to keep her in darkness. Interrogated by the head psychiatrist of the capital's insane asylum, who had been expected to commit her on grounds of paranoia and a persecution complex, Paul won him over with a lecture on suffrage. The hunger strike did not let up until, confronting a public outcry, the administration freed all prisoners in late November. It was a prudent move since, with the verdicts on appeal, higher courts would likely have ruled that the government had violated the defendants' First Amendment rights.

By now many Democratic politicians had concluded that the amendment's passage would be a lesser evil than more civil disobedience and hunger strikes by respectable middle-class women that hurt American credibility on its new global stage. It would certainly be preferable to granting political-prisoner status to peaceful picketers. Moreover, England, Canada, and other allied nations had just enfranchised female citizens. Wilson began touting the "Susan B. Anthony Amendment" as a high-priority war measure.

The amendment finally landed on the House floor in early January 1918. Wilson's last-minute lobbying made a difference as the House passed it without a vote to spare. The diehard opposition of the liquor industry, big corporations, political machines, and Southern racists, all rallying around the "magic touchstone" of states' rights, made for a tougher fight in the Senate. In late September, with the war in Europe roaring to a finish, Wilson took the unprecedented step of addressing the Senate on the bill's behalf. Asserting that the war could not have been waged without women's essential contributions, he asked the senators: "Shall we admit them only to a partnership of suffering and sacrifice and toil and not to a partnership of privilege and right?" The amendment still fell two votes short.

In the six months following the November armistice, the NAWSA and NWP bandwagons pulled out all the stops. In June 1919 they secured victory in the Senate. NAWSA's reenergized state organizations, cooperating with NWP activists, rolled over remaining opposition to achieve ratification on August 26, 1920, after a last dramatic battle in Tennessee. The Constitution no longer stood in the way of universal suffrage. Although the world war had sped things up, the constitutional guarantee of woman suffrage might have taken another generation had it not been for the acrimonious alliance between Catt's army of congressional district organizers and Paul's nonviolent guerrillas with their headline-grabbing confrontation tactics. Neither could have done the job alone.

AFTER seven decades of "pauseless campaign," in Catt's words, women had won the right to vote—or rather, its formal implementation as the law of the land. What would it mean? Questions that had been submerged during the final stage rose to the surface. Was it an end in itself, or merely a means to actualize further rights and more substantive change? Would it function, as some had hoped, to buttress the status quo, or even turn back the clock? By the onset of the Great Depression it had become evident that female suffrage would not make a measurable difference in terms of social reform, public policy, or purifying the political process. Activists did not forge a feminist voting bloc toward either left or right. No "gender gap" appeared, at least not for many years.

Starting about 1910 the revivified suffrage movement had built a broad single-issue coalition of elite, professional, and working-class women, along with male supporters, that for the first time generated mass support. Soon after the Nineteenth Amendment's ratification the fragile supercoalition was torn apart by antagonistic interests that had been kept under wraps. "Women with widely divergent views laid aside their differences to work together," explains historian Sherna Gluck, "and though this détente may have been necessary for the success of achieving woman's suffrage, it carried within it the seeds of the destruction of the women's movement. Because suffrage had become the goal, there was little to hold the movement together after the goal was achieved. Feminists who had a deeper understanding of women's position in society suspended their analysis while they worked for the immediate goal of suffrage. Consequently, they had developed no long-range program."

Most debilitating were differences that arose between middle-class professional women and working-class wage earners. Decades of conflict would ensue between the NWP's push for a new Equal Rights Amendment aimed at barring all legal inequities (first introduced in 1923) and advocates for working women who feared that hard-won protective legislation would be nullified by the ERA.

Stanton, Anthony, Mott, and others in the movement's founding generation had fought for suffrage as the cutting edge of a larger constellation of rights reforms encompassing property, employment, legal standing, divorce, sexuality, and even reproduction. Many of the early activists shared an assumption that although this body of rights spread across diverse realms, they were interdependent and mutually reinforcing. Through Reconstruction, Anthony had spoken out against giving some rights precedence over others, but in the last quarter of the century, pushed and pulled by the conservatizing tides of the age, she led the movement toward a fateful narrowing of its vision and goals, which reached its extreme single-issue focus after her death in 1906.

NINETEENTH AMENDMENT

The right of citizens of the United States to vote shall not be denied or abridged by the United States or by any State on account of sex.

Congress shall have power to enforce this article by appropriate legislation. *Ratified August 26, 1920*

"A great many people who wanted the vote didn't want anything else," recalled Miriam Allen deFord, a soapbox orator for the Women's Political Union, "so when they got the vote they were satisfied"—and turned back to private concerns. Many middle-class women might have thought that the franchise was the only important right they did not yet have. Alice Paul warned that "because of a great victory, women will believe that their whole struggle for independence is ended. They still have far to go."

The conclusion is hard to escape that the hollowing of women's rights to only the most glaring manifestation of female oppression not only inhibited campaigns for other rights—including those protecting personal autonomy such as reproductive rights and those needed most by working-class women and women of color—but resulted in little concrete change in most women's lives. Moreover, it led to the collapse of the woman's movement as a collective force, though small subdivisions shifted to new single issues such as the ERA, birth control, social welfare, consumer protection, and world peace. Of course, this outcome cannot be separated from the larger breakdown of Progressive politics after World War I. Women had mobilized as a class to win the franchise, but they did not sustain this fleeting unity to exercise their potential power on behalf of other claims that would benefit women collectively, at home and at work. Little solidarity remained to resist the centrifugal forces of liberal individualism pushing them away from their common womanhood toward a private pursuit of happiness. This was a far cry from the ethic of individuality extolled by Stanton.

Among radical critics who pointed out the limitations of suffrage was Russian-born anarchist Emma Goldman, longtime champion of workers' rights, feminism, free love, and birth control. A woman can give suffrage "no new quality, nor can she receive anything from it that will enhance her own quality," Goldman argued. "Her development, her freedom, her independence, must come from and through herself. First, by asserting herself as a personality, and not as a sex commodity. Second, by refusing the right to anyone over her body; by refusing to bear children, unless she wants them; by refusing to be a servant to God, the State, society, the husband, the family . . . by freeing herself from the fear of public opinion and public condemnation. Only that, and not the ballot, will set woman free, will make her a force hitherto unknown in the world." Only that, said Goldman, would lead to the fulfillment of "the right to self-expression, everybody's right to beautiful, radiant things."

This formidable agenda of liberation, which echoed the language of Stanton and other movement pioneers, would be reclaimed by a new wave of feminists later in the century.

CHAPTER SIX

RIGHTS TO BREAD
AND ROSES

IN JULY 1877, one year after the nation cheered the centennial of the American Revolution with a glittering display of industrial ingenuity in Philadelphia—where Susan B. Anthony and cohorts had announced their Declaration of Rights for Women—hundreds of thousands of railroad, mine, and mill workers mounted a revolt that spread to a quarter of the states before it was crushed by military force. It erupted at the height of the country's first full-scale depression, with millions jobless and organized labor in disarray. Believing that, as one proclamation put it, "every man willing to perform a use to society is entitled to a living," these workers rebelled against slashed wages and deteriorating labor conditions.

When another in a spiral of wage cuts hit the Baltimore & Ohio Railroad in mid-July, train workers outside Baltimore and in West Virginia launched a strike that within a day halted all freight traffic on the B&O line. Local police and state militias proved no match for the strikers, who were backed up by their communities, and the governor of West Virginia appealed to President Rutherford Hayes for federal troops. They were willing to sacrifice their lives, Maryland strikers declared in a manifesto, "not for the company, but for our rights. . . . Let the clashing of arms be heard; let the fiery elements be poured out if they think it right, but in heed of our right and in defence of our families, we shall conquer or we shall die."

The Pennsylvania Railroad, the nation's largest corporation, triggered greater upheaval when it abruptly reduced its work force by doubling up trains with fewer locomotives. Brakemen and conductors, then firemen and engineers, shut down the main rail yard in the coal and iron center of Pittsburgh, paralyzing freight traffic but letting passenger and mail trains run. Called in by the governor, the Philadelphia-based militia arrived by train. They assaulted the gathered crowd with bayonets and started shooting, killing at least twenty. Incensed, the railroad workers and residents fought back and forced the militia to retreat into the roundhouse, which they set on fire. The hated militia fled for their lives, and the spreading fire gutted a hundred locomotives and two thousand freight cars. The governor wired President Hayes that the revolt had "assumed the character of a general insurrection."

Workers on other railroads carried the action to cities throughout the Midwest, where aggrieved factory hands joined in and organized virtual general strikes in Buffalo, Toledo, Louisville, Chicago, and, with most success, St. Louis. After a week of heady victories, the chain reaction of revolt reached as far as Texas. Setting an ominous precedent, federal troops were sent to Indiana and Missouri to quell the disorders that some were calling the "Second American Revolution." Hayes wrote in his diary that "the strikes have been put down by *force.*" Over a hundred participants were slain.

Though defeated, the Great Strike brought in its wake a long wave of organizing for workers' rights. Labor leader Samuel Gompers remembered it as "the tocsin that sounded a ringing message of hope to us all." In particular it energized the Knights of Labor and other efforts to build national labor federations.

It was not surprising that the 1877 revolt centered on the railroads— the biggest, most powerful, and most unrestrained of the capitalist juggernauts to emerge after the Civil War. Fueled by federal subsidies and by vast land grants amounting to an area larger than Texas, these corporations had laid eighty thousand miles of track by 1877 (compared to twenty-two hundred in 1850) and monopolized the transport of people and goods. "Entire regions lay in their grip," notes historian Philip Foner, as well as government at all levels. The railroad empires set the tone for other giant enterprises that took control of coal, oil, iron, steel, and other staples of industrialization.

In the 1830s Tocqueville had warned Americans of the rise of an "industrial aristocracy" that would impoverish and brutalize "the men it uses." Labor leaders and activists after the Civil War saw alarming parallels between the "money kings" and "robber barons" they faced and the British tyrants fought by political rebels a century before. The new lords of capital were not only flagrantly denying their employees rights to life, liberty, and happiness, these men and women concluded, but they were even assaulting the Constitution. Reformers were most alarmed when the Supreme Court, a bastion of former corporation lawyers, utilized the

Fifth and Fourteenth amendments to make the property rights of corpo-
rations-as-citizens nearly invulnerable. It became clear that workers
would not be allowed to organize for their rights if this infringed upon
capitalists' freedom of contract and right of due process, nor would states
be permitted to regulate corporations in the public interest.

Many workers, particularly skilled craftsmen, felt a moral responsibility
to redeem and restore the republic to its egalitarian principles, labor
historian David Montgomery points out. The founders' dreams had been
stymied, the *National Labor Tribune* commented in 1874, and working
people "suddenly find capital as rigid as an absolute monarchy." Two
years later the journal asked: "Shall we let the gold barons of the nineteenth century put iron collars of ownership around our necks as did the
feudal barons with their serfs?" As the National Labor Union had done
earlier, the Workingmen's Party of Illinois in July 1876 proclaimed a
new version of the Declaration of Independence explicitly challenging
the exploitative wage-labor system as a violation of natural rights and
democracy.

By the first centennial labor reformers had a clear perception of the
nature of workers' rights. The preamble to the constitution of the Knights
of Labor, the foremost labor organization of the late 1870s and 1880s,
set forth as the Knights' mission to "secure to the toilers a proper share
of the wealth that they create; more of the leisure that rightfully belongs
to them . . . in a word, all those rights and privileges necessary to make
them capable of enjoying, appreciating, defending, and perpetuating the
blessings of good government." An 1884 correspondent to the prolabor
John Swinton's Paper did not waste any words: "Life implies the right to
the means of living," wrote J. O. Woods, "and all have a natural right
thereto."

Labor leaders did not consider their aspirations revolutionary or even
radical. The real revolutionaries, some thought, were the money kings
striving to produce an English-style dependent proletariat whose condition would ruin the American republic and its bedrock principle of independent citizenship. As Ira Steward, leader of the eight-hour movement,
and others pointed out, a dependent wage slave could not be an equal
citizen.

The rights workers affirmed were grounded not only in the natural
rights legacy of the American Revolution but also in an older work ethic,
transplanted from precapitalist Europe, that stressed the inherent dignity
of craft work and the need for mutuality and solidarity. Workers claimed
certain entitlements on the basis of their production of useful goods, the
most fundamental being the right to subsistence. They perceived their
rights as belonging simultaneously to the "producer-as-citizen" and to

the "citizen-as-producer." Weavers, carpenters, coopers, bricklayers, iron molders, printers, machinists, and other skilled workers did not need Adam Smith, David Ricardo, or Karl Marx to teach them about the labor theory of value, which, though heretofore a "mere strand of individualist Jeffersonian thought," explains historian Leon Fink, was shaped into "a moral pillar of the collective claims of the laboring classes."

To survive and to preserve self-worth amid the wrenching changes of the new capitalist order, workers would assert rights both as means—rights to organize and strike—and as substantive ends requisite for a decent life. The pivot of these efforts in the late nineteenth century was the long crusade for the right to an eight-hour day—from conceptualization to recognition to implementation.

FIGHTING FOR TIME

THE "first fruit of the American Civil War was the eight hours' agitation," Karl Marx wrote in *Capital* in 1867, "which ran from the Atlantic to the Pacific, from New England to California, with the seven-league boots of the locomotive." A new life had emerged from slavery's death, he conjectured; until this point the growth of the labor movement had been hobbled by the fact that "labour in a white skin cannot emancipate itself where it is branded in a black skin."

Marx understood that the limitation of the workday was a fundamental reform in relations between labor and capital and a first step toward complete social overhaul. He demonstrated that underlying the liberal contract myth of workers freely selling their labor power was the hard truth that they were forced to sell it, and on the buyer's terms; worse, that their wages, in reality, were paid only for the first few hours of the day, the rest of their labor creating "surplus value" for the capitalist. Thus Marx argued that any reduction in hours directly squeezed profits, which explained why it was so fiercely opposed.

Furthermore, although Marx derided abstract "bourgeois" rights to life, liberty, and property that always seemed to deify property alone, he saw indications that a "normal working day" was a universal right slowly being recognized. He quoted a British factory inspector's comment that capitalist opposition "must succumb before the broad principle of the rights of labour . . . There is a time when the master's right in his workman's labour ceases, and his time becomes his own." Marx exhorted workers to join together as a class and to compel passage of laws to protect them "from selling themselves and their families into slavery and death by voluntary contract with capital. In the place of the pompous catalogue of the 'inalienable rights of man' there steps the modest Magna Carta of the legally limited working day."

In the United States as in Britain, workers had been fighting to cut the workday since the late eighteenth century, when clocks first were used to regiment it and artificial lighting—"lighting up"—allowed work time to creep into the early evening and predawn hours. Some suggest that the American labor movement was born in this cause; no doubt the call for reduced hours was the most persistent and best-articulated workers' demand of the nineteenth century.

In Boston, Philadelphia, and New York a movement for a ten-hour day arose among carpenters, caulkers, painters, millwrights, bakers, and other skilled craftsmen during the 1820s. Boston journeymen issued a "Ten-Hour Circular" in 1835 claiming "the rights of American Free-man" as their revolutionary inheritance, coupled with "duties to perform as American Citizens"; the circular helped to spark ten-hour strikes in Boston and other Eastern cities. But after a surge of strikes in the 1840s and early 1850s by both craftsmen and factory workers, particularly women in textile mills, the drive for ten hours stalled.

The cataclysmic Civil War, which swept away slavery while sweeping forward black rights and, to a lesser extent, the rights of women, revitalized the crusade for a shorter workday. Having saved the Union through sacrifice in battle and in war production, and fired up by the overheated patriotic rhetoric of liberty and equal rights, Northern workers pushed beyond the old ten-hour goal, which was still unrealized by many, if not most. They now felt entitled to "eight hours for work, eight hours for rest, eight hours for recreation," a new rallying cry that expressed deeply held values and aspirations, according to historian David Roediger.

Certain continuities linked the prewar and postwar hours struggles, Roediger notes: solidarity among diverse groups of workers; combining trade union with legislative strategies; and organizing around workers' control of work and life. Moreover, the most widely expressed motive and purpose of reducing hours was to create time—"citizenship time"—for self-improvement and education that could make workers fully participating citizens. The eight-hour day would thus enhance democracy and facilitate the assertion of other rights, political and social. It gave the worker a "clearer conception of his rights" and more ability to secure them, as Samuel Gompers later contended.

In fighting for less, not more, workers were claiming a higher quality of life. Indeed, a minister told an Independence Day labor rally that shorter hours were "a part of the Declaration of Independence, 'the pursuit of happiness.' "

The leader of the early eight-hour movement and its chief philosopher was Ira Steward, a homegrown, self-taught socialist, some of whose ideas resembled those of Marx. In 1851, as a twenty-year-old machinist, he had been fired for eight-hour agitating. After several years of antislavery activism—reportedly fighting alongside John Brown in Kansas—he won passage of the first eight-hour resolution in 1863 at a machinists' union convention in Boston. Following the war he founded Boston's Eight-Hour League, which spawned a network of such pressure groups around the country.

Steward's influential pamphlets sought to prove, as one title stated, "A Reduction of Hours an Increase of Wages." Reducing hours would not only spread jobs and cut unemployment. More important, he theorized, increased leisure "will create motives . . . for the common people to ask for more wages [and] that where all demand more wages, the demand cannot be resisted." His thinking ran against the grain of conventional wisdom: not harder and longer toil, but increased consumption and pleasure engendered by more free time—in short, rising expectations—would activate workers' sense of entitlement to higher pay, as well as expand productivity. Like Marx, Steward believed that workers' rights would remain abstract without the power to enforce them, power derived in large part from workers' resolve to satisfy new wants and needs generated by greater control of their time.

As with black rights, enforcement was the crux of the problem. Steward and the Eight-Hour Leagues joined with local and national trade unions in 1866 to form the National Labor Union, whose program centered on legislating the eight-hour day. The NLU founding statement justified the demand by declaring that "the success of our republican institutions must depend on the virtue, the intelligence and the independence of the working classes." Within a year several states passed such laws, including industrial Illinois and New York, and in 1868 Congress enacted an eight-hour law for federal employees.

The new laws had fatal flaws, however. Most barred interference with the employer's freedom of contract. Moreover, enforcement provisions were lacking. Indeed, unlike Reconstruction-era black leaders, many white labor leaders did not push for administrative or judicial enforcement since, under the spell of laissez-faire doctrines, they did not conceive of it as a governmental responsibility.

In response to these legal failures a new labor alliance led by Steward-ites, socialists from Workingmen's Associations, and immigrant trade unionists decided to bypass the "political" route and directly implement the eight-hour right through education, agitation, and strikes. A grass-roots strike offensive culminated in 1872 and 1873 with walkouts in many cities. A hundred thousand workers, mainly from building trades, struck successfully in New York City, while in the "Sawdust Wars" of Pennsylvania, Florida, and Michigan, white and black sawmill workers fought a losing battle against rough mill owners. Most gains proved temporary.

When the depression of the 1870s set in, eight-hour militance faded as joblessness emptied union ranks and trade unions shifted their energies to resisting wage cuts. By the 1880s most workers still toiled at least ten hours a day. Employers who had long spurned the ten-hour standard now clung to it as a rigid natural law. Nevertheless, the expectation and aspiration for fewer hours had become so widely shared among the working class that the collective demand grew weightier.

S T E A D I L Y gathering strength after the crushing of the 1877 revolt, the labor movement resurged more powerfully than ever in the mid-1880s, the eight-hour day its galvanizing goal. With legislative reform still a dead end, the craft-based Federation of Organized Trades and Labor Unions (FOTLU) launched a campaign to make May 1, 1886, the deadline for employers to comply with the eight-hour demand, to be enforced by a "universal strike." FOTLU believed that mass organization "would prove vastly more effective than the enactment of a thousand laws depending for enforcement upon the pleasure of aspiring politicians or syncophantic department officials."

Although the leader of the Knights of Labor, Terence Powderly, privately denounced the impending strike and tried to stop it, the idea caught fire among Knights "local assemblies" and sparked hundreds of new locals. The first truly national labor organization, the Knights of Labor had grown up from the grass roots, originating in Philadelphia in 1869. From birth the order had dedicated itself to labor solidarity, regardless of nationality, race, gender, job, or skill. It actively recruited less skilled industrial workers, especially immigrants, though its base and leadership were Anglo-Saxon craft workers. The union proved to be the "outstanding vehicle of Negro-White unity in the eighteen eighties and early nineties," North and South, even with black members usually in segregated locals. Women workers, sometimes in "ladies' locals," made up a tenth of the membership. Besides the strikes and consumer boycotts that were their best-known tactics, Knights locals also set up producer cooperatives and organized labor-led electoral coalitions in dozens of cities. Animated by republican ideals, the Knights sought "to regenerate American life and institutions through a radical activation of citizenship," according to Leon Fink.

On May Day 1886, at least a third of a million workers, skilled or less skilled, native-born and immigrant, rallied and struck across the country, spearheaded by the Knights. Jubilant singing accompanied their marching:

> We want to feel the sunshine;
> we want to smell the flowers;
> We're sure that God has willed it.
> And we mean to have eight hours.
> We're summoning our forces from
> shipyard, shop and mill;
> Eight hours for work, eight hours
> for rest, eight hours for what we will.

Chicago, the movement's main artery, verged on a general strike. But a terrible event in that hotbed of labor unrest gravely damaged the eight-hour cause. On May 4, a few thousand working people gathered peacefully in Chicago's Haymarket Square to hear anarchist speakers condemn a lethal police attack at the McCormick Reaper factory. Just as the last orator was concluding, a police battalion moved in to disperse the crowd. Someone threw a bomb at the cops, who opened fire. Several police and protesters were killed, dozens injured. Eight anarchists were wrongfully convicted of murder and, despite an international outcry, four were eventually hanged. Though not directly related to it, the Haymarket affair cast disrepute upon the eight-hour mobilization and badly undermined it. Still, as many as two hundred thousand workers secured a shorter workday, and the struggle for time continued to make gains, though with less drama and visibility.

The collapse of the "great upheaval" of 1886 led to the Knights' rapid decline. FOTLU reorganized as the American Federation of Labor, headed by British immigrant Samuel Gompers of the Cigarmakers' Union. Dedicated to the proposition that trade unions had to achieve shorter hours and other goals independent of the state, which was seen as labor's enemy—Gompers adamantly opposed eight-hour laws—the AFL tried to revive the eight-hour drive. But the new effort was stymied by the AFL's craft-consciousness and growing conservatism. Unlike the Knights or FOTLU, it had little interest in forging the class-wide mobilization needed to actualize the right to leisure. Determined to keep the craft unions free of immigrants, people of color, and women, the AFL leadership not only turned its back on the less skilled but also failed to organize female workers, who had played a vital role in past struggles and were highly motivated to fight for fewer hours.

Yet under the spur of sporadic strikes, working hours continued gradually to decrease. When the century turned the terms of debate altered, and unlikely allies entered the fray. New techniques of "scientific management" promoted by Frederick Winslow Taylor showed that fewer hours could garner *greater* productivity if working time was managed more rigorously. Influential Progressive thinkers and politicians such as Theodore Roosevelt popularized an ethic of play, especially athletics and physical fitness, in the belief that purposeful leisure during off-hours enhanced workplace efficiency. Such considerations persuaded a small number of employers—Henry Ford most prominently—to institute eight-hour days.

Less enlightened capitalists, however, marshaled their forces to resist this reform, particularly the National Association of Manufacturers, which represented medium-sized, more competitive firms. In 1905, the Supreme Court in *Lochner* v. *New York* fortified the NAM's position when it nullified a ten-hour law bakery workers had won in New York State. The ruling declared that the "general right to make a contract in relation to his business is part of the liberty of the individual protected by the Fourteenth Amendment." Such laws restricting hours "are mere meddlesome interferences with the rights of the individual," worker and boss alike.

Insisting that the right of free contract "was of such fundamental stature that no government could infringe it," in William Nelson's words, *Lochner* reflected the expansive interpretation of the Fourteenth Amendment's due process and equal protection clauses with respect to property rights that had shaped the Court's jurisprudence for more than a generation. This blow to labor was partly offset three years later in *Muller* v. *Oregon,* shrewdly argued by attorney Louis Brandeis, in which the Court upheld laws limiting women's hours of work. But the Supreme Court generally challenged such hours regulations until the New Deal of the 1930s.

A resurgence of strikes in the century's second decade, combined with wartime federal labor policies, made the World War I era "the decisive period in the battle for the eight-hour day," according to David Montgomery. It became a central demand of the postwar strike wave of 1919, especially in coal, steel, textiles, and clothing. Although the number of eight-hour factory workers quadrupled during this period, by 1930 over half the labor force still toiled longer hours. In other industrialized nations, parallel struggles already had established eight hours as the norm.

Americans finally secured the legal right to an eight-hour day as an outcome of the New Deal's aggressive response to the Great Depression; no one could dispute that fewer hours meant more jobs. In 1933 the National Recovery Administration mandated maximum hours for most industries. Then in 1938 Congress passed the Fair Labor Standards Act, which, despite gaping exemptions such as farm and domestic labor, made the eight-hour day and five-day week the law of the land.

By the time the American worker won this right, however, its advocates had stopped talking about how workers, and society, might profit from the liberated time. Arguments about the need for "citizenship time," for education and political participation, had gone out of favor. The right to leisure had become an end in itself, no longer a means to higher ends. Finally granted a choice, some employees would opt to work longer, especially to earn overtime pay. Many would cram their leisure with conspicuous consumption and "trivial pursuits." Certainly the right to free time implied a corollary right: the freedom to pursue one's happiness according to individual wants and desires. But with increasing prosperity and other changes, the ethic of rights as implying responsibility, to one-self and to society, seemed to have diminished. Instead of funding empty lives, perhaps the treasury of free time could have been spent more wisely on real self-fulfillment and the betterment of society.

SOLIDARITY FOREVER

IN THE LATE nineteenth century, wage workers along with impover-ished farmers sought to resist the consolidation of corporate capitalism; they believed that it violated their rights as well as the values the nation stood for. During the 1890s, in fact, workers and farmers began to coa-lesce around common goals, their budding alliance disrupted by the defeat of the Populist crusade. Since both groups were imbued with republican principles of equal rights and democracy—government of, by, and for the people—what galled them almost as much as specific griev-ances was the big corporations' harnessing of the state to ride roughshod over the "producing classes." While Populist farmers clamored against "class legislation" that denied them credit and land, industrial and mine workers grew alarmed at the state's increasing use of raw military and judicial power to stifle direct action.

From the 1890s until the 1930s, wage earners persevered in an uphill battle to defend their right to organize—particularly its constitutive rights of free speech, free press, and peaceful assembly ostensibly guar-anteed by the First Amendment. Not that these political freedoms had ever been secure, or taken for granted; but as capitalism solidified its grip they were more vulnerable than ever. During these decades labor activists stretched the Bill of Rights to apply not just to individuals alone but to purposeful collective action. They were going beyond narrowly individualistic rights to define, assert, and legitimize a further right to associate and combine. With organization the watchword of the age, the producing classes realized that they must organize as effectively as the corporate trusts.

Two momentous conflicts in the 1890s epitomized the collusion between corporations and the state to suppress unionization. Scottish immigrant Andrew Carnegie's grand ambition to monopolize steel faced a major obstacle—the Amalgamated Association of Iron and Steel Workers, a potent AFL-affiliated craft union. Nowhere was the union stronger than at Carnegie's Homestead Works near Pittsburgh. To remove this obstacle, Carnegie ordered Homestead manager Henry Frick to refuse to sign a new union contract in 1892.

When the Association protested, Frick shut out its members. Unexpectedly, the noncraft workers who constituted most of the Homestead work force voted in a mass meeting to strike with the Association. Closing down the entire factory, Frick hired several hundred Pinkertons—armed guards frequently deployed against labor unrest—who stealthily sailed up the Monongahela River one night in two barges. Union sentries, tipped off, were patrolling the river in a paddle-wheel steamboat. An organized force of workers—fortified with rifles, dynamite, two brass cannons, and Fourth of July firecrackers—repulsed the invaders.

Finally the Pennsylvania governor summoned the state militia, who marched in and enabled strikebreakers to reopen the steel works. "Pennsylvanians can hardly appreciate the actual communism of these people," the militia commander reported. "They believe the works are theirs quite as much as Carnegie's." The strikers held out for four months, but in the end Carnegie succeeded in ousting the weakened Association from the steel industry, and he kept steel union-free for many years.

Unionism suffered an even more devastating defeat in 1894, in the throes of another deep depression, when corporate leaders launched a full-scale offensive against organized labor. The year before, a young Hoosier from Terre Haute, Eugene Victor Debs, had founded the American Railway Union (ARU), aimed at organizing all railroad workers regardless of skill. His prior experience as a leader of the Brotherhood of Locomotive Firemen had taught him that railroad employees could win their rights only if they created an industry-wide federation—an industrial union. A surprising victory in a strike against James J. Hill's Great Northern Railroad sparked astonishing growth; within a year of its birth, with 425 locals and 150,000 members, the ARU had emerged as the nation's largest union.

Workers at the Pullman Palace Car Company outside Chicago joined the ARU hoping that the new federation might help them restore wage cuts as well as improve deplorable conditions in their authoritarian company town—once touted as a model community. When in late spring 1894 the company refused to negotiate and fired the delegates bearing grievances, the employees struck—and with ARU assistance engineered an effective coast-to-coast boycott of Pullman sleeping cars by those who tended them. Yet the railroad owners proved to be better organized than their foes. Seizing the opportunity to crush industrial unionism before it spread, the industry's General Managers Association won full cooperation from President Grover Cleveland and his zealous attorney general, Richard Olney. For many years a railroad lawyer and director, Olney acted as "supreme strategist" in marshaling state power against the ARU.

More damaging than the deployment of the army in Chicago, where more than a dozen people were killed, was a sweeping federal court injunction that barred ARU activism, even internal communications. It abrogated the right not only to strike but to associate in any form. Drawing upon the 1890 Sherman Act, designed to break up trusts, the court order treated the ARU as the equivalent of a trust and declared it an illegal combination in restraint of interstate commerce. After Debs and other union leaders disobeyed the order they were jailed for several months, and the nation's first industrial union screeched to a halt. The industry blacklisted ARU members; many never worked on the railroads again.

With plenty of time for reflection in his Illinois prison cell, Debs realized that strikes and boycotts were no longer productive tactics in the face of injunctions and bayonets. Nor were industrial unions any match for the corporate-dominated state with its monopoly of violence. He could see but one solution: the broad class of citizen producers must organize in the electoral arena to win political power and throw out the plutocrats. After the demise of Populism, Debs helped to create the Socialist Party, which he came to personify as its legendary orator. He ran for president five times on the Socialist ticket, twice getting nearly a million votes, the second time while incarcerated for opposing World War I.

Many labor activists kept their faith in direct action. And some, like Mother Jones, tried mixing direct action with electoral politics. Mine workers in Appalachia and in the West spearheaded a revival of unionizing, particularly those battling cruel conditions in Pennsylvania and West Virginia coal mines. Their most famous organizer, the "Miners' Angel," was Irish-born socialist Mother Jones. Her husband and children had died long before in a yellow fever epidemic; later her dressmaking shop had burned in the great Chicago fire of 1871. In a life dedicated to uplifting workers, this fiery speaker and agitator was said to have taken part in almost every momentous labor struggle going back to the uprising of 1877.

Jones was in her seventies when 200,000 Appalachian coal miners struck for safer work and shorter hours in 1902. Out on bail for violating a federal injunction in West Virginia—"for calling a mass meeting there I was put behind the bars"—she spoke to a United Mine Workers convention in Indianapolis that was debating whether to back the West Virginia strikers. While urging support, Jones also called for an electoral offensive to deal with the denial of miners' rights.

"There is before you one question, my friends," she exhorted the delegates, "and you must keep that question before your eyes this fall when you send representatives to the legislative halls. Your instructions to these representatives must be: 'Down forever with government by injunction in the American nation.' This generation may sleep its slumber quietly, not feeling its mighty duty and responsibility, and may quietly surrender their liberties."

"Be true to the teachings of your forefathers," Mother Jones insisted, "who fought and bled and raised the old flag that we might always shout for liberty."

S H O U T I N G L O U D E S T for liberty during the next two decades were members of a new, militant labor organization called the Industrial Workers of the World (IWW), nicknamed the Wobblies. In June 1905 in Chicago, Mother Jones sat among two hundred trade unionists and socialists as "Big Bill" Haywood, charismatic leader of the Western Federation of Miners, pounded a piece of wood as a gavel to open what he called "the Continental Congress of the working-class." They were assembled, he said, "to confederate the workers of this country into a working-class movement that shall have for its purpose the emancipation of the working class from the slave bondage of capitalism."

The constitution of the IWW proclaimed its mission. "The working class and the employing class have nothing in common. . . . Between these two classes a struggle must go on until the workers of the world organize as a class, take possession of the earth and the machinery of production, and abolish the wage system." By organizing One Big Union of industrial workers that eventually would replace the bosses and manage all production, "we are forming the structure of the new society within the shell of the old."

IWW leaders had read widely, their thinking shaped by Marx, Edward Bellamy, Henry George, European anarchists and syndicalists, and particularly Charles Darwin, whose theory of evolution was reinterpreted to augur a final victory of workers over capitalists. But the Wobbly philosophy, a homegrown anarcho-syndicalism, was firmly grounded in the members' own experience of class conflict and reflected a Jeffersonian allegiance to the producers of wealth. In contrast to the AFL, led by "labor lieutenants of capitalism" in the Wobblies' view, the IWW welcomed all workers to its ranks, including women, blacks, Chinese, and Mexicans. It advocated strikes for higher wages, better conditions, and the eight-hour day but spurned bargaining contracts, which it saw as "no more binding than the title deed to a negro slave is just." Their inflammatory language notwithstanding, IWW leaders counseled "passive resistance" and considered violence a last resort.

With locals spanning the continent from Skowhegan, Maine, to Seattle, the IWW organized workers abandoned by the labor establishment, especially timber cutters, "hobo harvesters," and other seasonal labor in the West, and textile workers and longshoremen in the East. To recruit scattered migratory workers in Western states, Wobblies held street meetings in cities where the workers congregated during the winter. When the authorities banned these meetings and arrested the soapbox orators, Wobblies waged "free speech fights" in dozens of cities to secure their right to organize.

The most fruitful of such fights erupted in Spokane, Washington, heart of the "Inland Empire" region rich in ore, agriculture, and lumber, industries that were dependent on itinerant labor. When a thriving IWW local conducted street-corner meetings in early 1909, one speaker after another was jailed for violating a brand-new ordinance. Cells were crammed with agitators who refused to work on the rock pile and instead held jailhouse meetings, made speeches, and sang Wobbly songs day and night. The conflict calmed with the coming of summer, but when laborers returned to Spokane in the fall, the IWW called for reinforcements from all over the country.

"On to Spokane!" headlined the IWW journal *Solidarity*, "where the organized Capitalists are trying to steal from the unorganized workers, basic rights that the working class has won by long centuries of struggles.

"The fundamental principles of Free Speech, Free Press and Free Assemblage are at stake. Already in this benighted city these three so-called 'rights' are merely dreams of the future or recollections of the past . . . Even the right to organize—the very breath of life to the working class—is being denied the workers in Spokane. . . . Revolutionary men and women of the great working class, we need you in Spokane." One of hundreds of Wobblies heeding the summons was Elizabeth Gurley Flynn, nineteen and pregnant, fresh from arrest in a Montana free speech fight. Daughter of radical Irish immigrants, Flynn had already gained notoriety in New York and other cities as a magnetic orator. Charged with criminal conspiracy in Spokane along with other leaders, she testified that she based her speeches on the Bill of Rights. An appeals jury overturned her conviction even though she was depicted as "one of the most dangerous of the IWWs," who "makes all the trouble" and "puts fight into the men."

The men did not get off so lightly. Four hundred were jailed for up to six months—one for reciting the Declaration of Independence. Twenty-five or thirty were squeezed into each tight, steaming cell, surviving on bread and water. Routinely beaten, many were hospitalized and many left with lasting wounds and missing teeth. Yet Wobblies kept filling the jails. The city fathers finally negotiated an agreement with a Wobbly committee in March 1910. Hailed as the "Treaty of Spokane," it permitted IWW organizers to speak in public places and to publish their newspaper.

The Spokane victory invigorated kindred crusades for political freedom. In Fresno, California, migrant farm and construction workers hunted for jobs in the fertile, federally irrigated San Joaquin Valley. When the state's strongest IWW local (which had organized Mexican laborers) held peaceful street meetings in 1910, the grower-controlled city hall put dozens of speakers in jail, where they were sprayed with fire hoses and otherwise physically abused. Mobs assaulted Wobbly gatherings and burned down their camp outside town. As in Spokane, help poured into Fresno from all points, some arriving on the "box car special." After several months of combat the city knuckled under and recognized the union's right to agitate.

In some places the IWW lost its battle for First Amendment rights, notably in San Diego—"the hardest one in which we have been involved," one veteran reported. During the winter and spring of 1912, local authorities not only brutalized prisoners but used vigilante violence to keep Wobbly forces from invading the city. They then pressured the attorney general in Washington to conduct a conspiracy investigation.

"To hell with your courts, I know what justice is," Wobbly Jack Whyte exclaimed to a San Diego judge before being sentenced for illegal speech. "You have become blind and deaf to the rights of man to pursue life and happiness, and you have crushed those rights so that the sacred right of property shall be preserved."

Even when the IWW succeeded in its short-run goals, the free speech fights did not contribute much to organizing workers on the job. Yet Roger Baldwin, founder of the American Civil Liberties Union, believed that the Wobblies wrote a chapter in the history of American liberty on a par with abolitionists and suffragists. The IWW's "direct action of open conflict," Baldwin contended, proved far more effective "than all the legal maneuvers in the courts to get rights that no government willingly grants. Power wins rights—the power of determination, backed by willingness to suffer jail or violence."

———

WHILE free speech fights were erupting in the West, the IWW was winning converts among low-paid immigrant workers in the East, notably in the vast woolen mills of Lawrence, Massachusetts. Many workers in these mills were from southern and eastern Europe and over half were women and children. In January 1912, a Massachusetts law reduced weekly hours for women and children from fifty-six to fifty-four. When mill owners cut workers' pay proportionately, they ignited long-smoldering grievances.

Polish women abandoned their looms and walked out, followed by Italians, as a strike by more than 30,000 shut down the mills. When two popular Italian Wobblies were imprisoned on a false murder charge, Big Bill Haywood, IWW editor and organizer William Trautmann, and Elizabeth Gurley Flynn took over strike leadership. Flynn had been agitating in Lawrence for several months already, urging workers "to weave the shroud of capitalism." During one of the colorful musical parades to drum up publicity and community support, young women carried a banner with words that immortalized their sense of entitlement: "We want bread and roses too."

The banner inspired a poem by a sympathetic observer, James Oppenheim, about the women strikers' aspirations for a better life:

> As we come marching, marching in the beauty of the day,
> A million darkened kitchens, a thousand mill lofts gray,
> Are touched with all the radiance that a sudden sun discloses,
> For the people hear us singing: "Bread and roses! Bread and
>   roses!"

> As we come marching, marching, we battle too for men,
> For they are women's children, and we mother them again.
> Our lives shall not be sweated from birth until life closes;
> Hearts starve as well as bodies; give us bread, but give us roses!

> As we come marching, marching, unnumbered women dead
> Go crying through our singing their ancient cry for bread.
> Small art and love and beauty their drudging spirits knew.
> Yes, it is bread we fight for—but we fight for roses, too!

> As we come marching, marching, we bring the greater days.
> The rising of the women means the rising of the race.
> No more the drudge and idler—ten that toil where one reposes,
> But a sharing of life's glories: Bread and roses! Bread and roses!

To fashion solidarity among women and men of two dozen nationalities, a barrier that had defeated many such ventures, Wobbly organizers not only conducted separate meetings in every language but had delegates from each nationality serve on the strike and relief committees. These committees created an efficient system to help tens of thousands survive the winter—but something more had to be done. Leaders decided to send hundreds of the ill-clad, ill-fed children to New York and other cities, where immigrant families were eager to take them in. When the first trainload of children arrived at Grand Central Station, they were royally welcomed by thousands of cheering supporters. But as the mill owners could not tolerate the unfavorable publicity brought by the "Children's Crusade," Lawrence officials soon forbade the departures. As two hundred youngsters were about to board a Philadelphia-bound train, a phalanx of police surrounded them.

"Children were clubbed and torn away from their parents," Flynn recalled, "and a wild scene of brutal disorder took place. Thirty-five frantic women and children were arrested, thrown screaming and fighting into patrol wagons. They were beaten into submission and taken to the police station," which was besieged by strikers. The repression backfired, however, as the nation's eyes fastened on Lawrence and leading opinion-makers denounced the mill owners.

After two months of mounting pressure capped by a congressional investigation, the owners caved in and agreed to the workers' demands. A breathtaking victory for the moment, it could not prevent, and may have hastened, the closing of Lawrence and other New England mills over the next two decades as the textile industry took refuge in the nonunion South.

The following year, 1913, Wobblies tried to replicate the Lawrence triumph in Paterson, New Jersey, the nation's silk capital. Impoverished workers laboring sixty-hour weeks—again mostly immigrants and in large part women and children—launched a strike against long hours and a sudden speedup that doubled the number of looms per operator. Haywood and Flynn assisted a strong core of local Wobblies who formed a multinational, multilingual strike committee: six hundred delegates representing half as many silk shops. It was so egalitarian that when reporters asked who the leaders were they were told: "We are all leaders." Indeed, Flynn remembered that "our plan of battle was very often nullified by the democratic administration of the strike committee." But the owners adamantly refused to talk and retaliated against nonviolent tactics with mass arrests, beatings, and the killing of two workers.

With hunger gnawing at morale and strike funds hitting bottom, leaders gambled on a wild idea to draw dollars and publicity to the waning revolt. In June 1913, three thousand strikers marched thirty miles to New York City, where, turning life into art, they reenacted the strike story—replete with police clubbings and killings, a mass funeral, and orations by Haywood and Flynn—before a full house at Madison Square Garden. For weeks the workers had rehearsed the pageant, directed by young journalist John Reed and a cadre of left-wing bohemian artists from Greenwich Village. The one-night stand did not make money, however, and in using up scarce time and resources might have made matters worse.

The wearied ranks of labor finally split apart. Accepting company terms, skilled English-speaking workers returned to work on a shop-by-shop basis, and the less skilled immigrant majority soon followed.

Failing to take hold in the industrial Northeast, the IWW redoubled its efforts on more familiar terrain. Moving beyond street-corner rabble-rousing, it successfully organized farm workers on the West Coast and in the Midwestern granary, iron and coal miners in Minnesota's Mesabi range, and lumberjacks in the Northwest. On the eve of the American entrance into World War I, with membership and dues multiplying and a newly centralized structure under Haywood's command, Wobbly leaders reveled in their romantic vision of One Big Union. The booming economy and labor shortage brought by war mobilization fueled the IWW resurgence—but the war also created the opportunity for a fierce judicial attack on the union, in the name of patriotism, that soon left it mortally wounded.

LABOR'S EMERGING BILL OF RIGHTS

"WHAT'S ALL THIS that's in the papers about the open shop?" the fictional barfly Mr. Hennessey asked the well-informed Chicago saloon-keeper.

"'Tis like this, Hinnissey," said Mr. Dooley. "Suppose wan av these freeborn citizens is workin' in an open shop f'r th' princely wage av wan large iron dollar a day av tin hour. Along comes anither son-av-gun and he sez t' th' boss, 'Oi think Oi could handle th' job nicely f'r ninety cints.' 'Sure,' sez th' boss, and th' wan dollar man gets out into th' crool woruld t' exercise hiz inalienable roights as a freeborn American citizen an' scab on some other poor devil. An' so it goes on, Hinnissey. An' who gits th' benefit? Thrue, it saves th' boss money, but he don't care no more f'r money thin he does f'r his right eye. It's all principle wid him. He hates t' see men robbed av their independence. They must have their indipindence, regardless av anything else."

"But," said Mr. Hennessey, "those open-shop min ye menshun say they are f'r unions iv properly conducted."

"Shure," said Mr. Dooley, "iv properly conducted. An' there we are: An' how would they have thim conducted? No strikes, no rules, no contracts, no scales, hardly iny wages, an' dam few mimbers."

S E E K I N G to organize the lowest strata of the working class, particularly recent immigrants, the IWW embodied an alternative to the "pure and simple" trade unionism of the dominant American Federation of Labor. Membership in AFL-affiliated craft unions tripled in the first decade of the twentieth century, and trade agreements—precursors of collective bargaining contracts—were negotiated with employers in several industries, such as coal, railroads, printing, and building trades. Guided by Samuel Gompers and his philosophy of "voluntarism," AFL unions fought doggedly for the right to organize, to strike, and to establish the "union shop" with mandatory membership and exclusive jurisdiction. Committed to autonomous working-class organization, while downplaying traditional republican ideals, the AFL insisted on freedom from employer *and* state interference. Government could not be trusted, at least not yet, to protect fairly the rights of workers and unions.

Around the turn of the century, when the "corporate reconstruction of American capitalism," to use historian Martin Sklar's phrase, came into full swing, the managerial class battled hard to roll back the rights of labor and to solidify its own. On one front, the National Association of Manufacturers campaigned for the antiunion "open shop." On another front, a volley of Supreme Court decisions showed that the corporations' sway over the high tribunal had not abated. In the 1908 Danbury Hatters' case (*Loewe* v. *Lawlor*), the justices invoked the Sherman Act to outlaw secondary boycotts in labor disputes. The same year they struck down, as violations of due process and equal protection, state and federal laws that banned employer discrimination against union members; in so doing they affirmed the legality of "yellow-dog contracts" that forbade workers to join unions.

In a subsequent decision, Justice Mahlon Pitney encapsulated the Court's attitude toward equal rights between labor and capital. As it was self-evident that "unless all things are held in common, some persons must have more property than others," Pitney claimed that "it is from the nature of things impossible to uphold freedom of contract and the right of private property without at the same time recognizing as legitimate those inequalities of fortune that are the necessary result of the exercise of those rights."

In the face of these legal setbacks, Gompers retreated from his antipolitical stance and mobilized AFL forces in the electoral arena for specific remedies, particularly against judicial injunctions, over 1,800 of which were served against unions in the half century after 1880. An alliance with the Wilson administration and the Democratic Congress, both of which the AFL had helped elect, produced significant labor reform laws, especially the Clayton Antitrust Act, which, by implication, legalized trade unions. It stated that "the labor of a human being is not a commodity or article of commerce"—that is, not property subject to property laws; and that "nothing contained in the anti-trust laws shall be construed to forbid the existence and operation" of unions.

President Wilson attested that with the Clayton Act "justice has been done to the laborer. His labor is no longer to be regarded as . . . an inanimate object of commerce disconnected with the fortunes and happiness of a human being." Gompers took such hyperbole a step further, hailing the measure as "labor's Magna Carta." Although, as Harold Livesay suggests, the Clayton Act drew a line between human rights and property rights, the Supreme Court later ruled that the act exempted the mere existence of unions from antitrust laws but not necessarily their activities; injunctions and yellow-dog contracts could still be used if unions appeared to be restraining trade. Like so much of American rights reform, this advance in official moral recognition did not translate into meaningful implementation.

Nevertheless, the full-employment economy of the World War I era that gave the Wobblies a boost uplifted the whole labor movement. During the war AFL chiefs rubbed elbows with corporate executives on the National War Labor Board, which encouraged collective bargaining and other labor rights. In the war's aftermath "levels of strike participation soared far above those of any other period thus far," in David Montgomery's estimation, involving nearly a quarter of the industrial labor force. Notable was the nationwide steel strike of 1919.

Postwar repression followed by recession reversed some of organized labor's gains, though the long march toward actualizing workers' rights did not halt. Corporate capital reconsolidated itself and then delivered unprecedented prosperity to the middle and upper classes during the 1920s. Unions declined sharply during this decade, and in a few industries were challenged by company-sponsored employee representation plans. The Republican regimes backed off from the Wilson administration's cooperation with the AFL. But amid the social upheaval of the 1930s, the collapsing house of labor would rebuild and reach new heights—finally attaining full legalization of workers' long-sought rights.

Even before the Depression, and without specific legislation, the union shop had become widely accepted as a right of organized labor. Employers were fighting a losing battle for juridical and public support of the right to an "open shop," a worker's freedom to stay out of a union, or not be governed by it, if in a minority. "All unions sooner or later stress 'shop rights,' " according to labor historian Selig Perlman, "which, to the workingman at the bench, are identical with 'liberty' itself—since, thanks to them, he has no need to kowtow to foreman or boss, as the price of holding his job."

Yet the ability to organize the unorganized mattered most. Workers won the statutory right to organize in 1932, as the Depression bottomed out, when Congress passed the Norris–La Guardia Act. Upholding the right to engage in "concerted activities for the purpose of collective bargaining," such as strikes and boycotts, and virtually barring the injunction in labor disputes, the new law also refuted the myth of the free and equal contract between individual worker and employer. It proclaimed that the former "is commonly helpless to exercise actual liberty of contract and to protect his freedom of labor, and thereby to obtain acceptable terms and conditions of employment. . . . It is necessary that he have full freedom of association."

I N *Nation-Building and Citizenship*, sociologist Reinhard Bendix argues that in the industrial democracies, formal constitutional rights have promoted legal and political equality while fostering social and economic inequality. If society is substantially unequal to begin with, by class, race, and gender, then "equal" legal rights—particularly rights of property, due process, and equal protection—have tended to benefit the haves at the expense of the have-nots. This has been true even of First Amendment–type entitlements when, due to structural advantages, certain groups have been capable of a privileged use of them.

Why has this occurred? In the first place, to extrapolate from Bendix's analysis, members of disadvantaged groups typically have not had access, as discrete, ostensibly independent individuals, to the resources needed to implement constitutional rights; for the advantaged this has been a given. Second, formal equality has embedded in both law and custom the mythology that "free contracts" between unequal parties have been somehow egalitarian in substance as well as form, when in fact they have disguised, and legitimized, the resulting inequality; consider employment, landlord-tenant, or traditional marriage contracts.

Third, the prevalence of formally equal individual rights has provided stronger parties with the moral authority or justification to delegitimate and even to proscribe efforts by oppressed groups to mobilize collectively to alter their unequal social status—for example, outlawing trade unions or utilizing antitrust law to forbid strikes and boycotts. "One of the earliest results of the legislative protection of freedom of contract," Bendix notes, was "the legislative prohibition of trade unions," especially in

Europe. Collective movements had a hard time gaining legitimacy in the United States, as Leon Fink suggests, a nation that "offered legal sanction only to individual rights."

The European and American working classes had to contend for supplementary, supra-individual rights of association and combination in order to actualize their formal individual rights and to advance socioeconomic equality. Women and people of color in the United States, who had been denied even formal rights, claimed the right to associate both to gain the rights of citizenship that others possessed at least on paper and to enforce these citizen rights.

In their freedom struggles, in ways distinctive to their own social situations, African-Americans, women, and wage workers (these groups overlapping) transcended the purely individualistic character of "natural" rights and, through action, defined and exercised entitlements as jointly individual and collective. They discovered that for historically oppressed castes, the rights of the individual could not be realized on an individual basis but had to be secured through the collective or communal assertion of rights.

For many years American workers and their unions struggled for the right to organize, which became officially recognized both in the Norris–La Guardia Act and in Section 7 of the 1935 National Labor Relations Act (using identical language) as the right "to engage in concerted activities for . . . mutual aid or protection." This broad entitlement, subsequently upheld by the Supreme Court, encompassed actions such as picketing, strikes, boycotts, and other forms of collective free speech and assembly. Organized groups or communities had achieved rights that previously had been allowed, if at all, only to individuals acting alone, whose expression of these rights was far less efficacious than collective action.

Historian and activist Staughton Lynd considers the right to engage in concerted activity as the quintessential "communal right." Neither a narrowly individual nor a merely collective right, a communal right is "derived from the actual character of working-class solidarity and accordingly a right that foreshadows a society in which group life and individual self-realization mutually reinforce each other." Workers who had no rights as individuals that an employer was bound to respect had to join together and act in concert—philosopher Hannah Arendt's conception of power. The right to concerted activity, to a community of action, might occasionally interfere with nonessential personal rights, such as the right not to join a union or to cross a picket line, but for the most part it has amplified individual rights and massed the power to enforce them, actualizing to varying degrees the labor ethic of solidarity that "an injury to one is an injury to all." Lynd submits that the communal rights crafted by the labor movement differ significantly from the traditional interpretation of rights as individual property—the assumption that individuals "*possess* rights in the same way that they possess more tangible kinds of property." This view, he believes, takes as given "that the supply of rights is finite," that rights are a scarce commodity, and that "the assertion of one person's right is likely to impinge on and diminish the rights of others." Communal rights, in contrast, do not usually present a conflict between the well-being of one and of others, but rather enhance the rights and welfare of the whole group, if not of the larger society.

But how inclusive is the group? And what if one group is pitted against another? If by the mid-1930s the labor movement had largely realized the right to act in concert and related communal rights, a question arises as to the scope and boundaries of the communities whose rights these were. Many unionists sought to rise above intraclass divisions and aspired to rights that would be held in common by all workers—including the less skilled, immigrants, people of color, and women. Although not always practiced, this was the goal of the Knights of Labor and the IWW; in fact, Wobblies opposed bargaining agreements partly to preserve their freedom to strike in support of workers elsewhere.

Yet the AFL craft unions that dominated organized labor until the 1930s did not generally share this commitment. They frequently saw one union's gain as another's loss and were dedicated to taking care of their own. Far too often the hard-won right to associate and combine turned into a right to exclude others from a particular union or from benefits attained. Even when organized by industry rather than craft, as in the Congress of Industrial Organizations, more privileged groups of workers—encouraged by union leaders—tended to exercise their communal rights in ways that sometimes jeopardized less fortunate groups and exacerbated the fragmentation and stratification of the working class into separate, self-seeking interest groups.

Despite noble rhetoric, many unions have wielded group rights to serve particularistic ends, each organized entity acting as an individual writ large, fending for itself in the capitalist marketplace like any other "self-sufficient monad" of liberal individualism. Rights exercised in this way were hardly based on the connectedness or mutuality of individual groups, but on their separation. In effect, the groups were asserting a *right* to such separation or independence—in Marx's words, "the rights of the limited individual who is limited to himself."

Once secured, the exercise of union rights might have been parochial and self-protective in many instances, but the achievement of the right to organize and combine, followed by the legalization of collective bargaining, represented irreversible advances that not only would raise the living standards and quality of life of the working class as a whole but also prepared the soil for freedom struggles by other disadvantaged groups and by wage earners not yet unionized. Even if it was belied in practice, many labor activists held aloft a vision of universal rights, anchored in human solidarity, that might have been their most potent legacy to future generations.

Whatever the intentions of the men who framed the First Amendment, activist workers along with women and people of color had interpreted it in action as a guarantee of the right of persons, groups, and entire social classes—of "We the People"—to redress grievances, "establish Justice," and "promote the general Welfare."

PART THREE

CHAPTER SEVEN

THE RECONSTRUCTION
OF RIGHTS

BETWEEN 1876 AND 1891 Americans celebrated a series of centennials—of the Declaration of Independence in 1876, the Constitution in 1887, George Washington's inaugural in 1889, the Bill of Rights in 1891. The tone of these celebrations ranged from the jubilant to the merely complacent.

Philadelphia's Centennial Exhibition in 1876 was organized as a dazzling display of American technological progress. At the center of its fourteen-acre Machinery Hall stood the Corliss engine, forty feet high and weighing seven hundred tons, which like a great pulsing heart powered eight thousand other devices, from gigantic printing presses to sewing machines, scattered around the building.

Opening the Exhibition on July 4, President Grant invited Americans, in words that would find an echo in the mouths of countless orators over the course of the centennial celebrations, to feel satisfaction "with the attainments made by our own people during the past one hundred years." The Exhibition, Grant said, would show what the United States had done "in the direction of rivalling older and more advanced nations in law, medicine and theology, in science, literature, philosophy and the arts."

And indeed there seemed to be much cause for pride. The nation was expanding industrially and financially, threatening Britain's hegemony in iron and steel and much else. The young and vulnerable republic born a century earlier in revolutionary warfare and reconsecrated not long past in blood was now a developing democracy. While women were still denied the vote, as they were in most Western nations, male ex-slaves had been formally granted the ballot, and most suffrage restrictions had been lifted from the poor and unpropertied. The Reconstruction amendments and laws had been drafted with good intentions—they were meant to provide freedmen and women with opportunities for liberty and even a measure of equality.

Boasts of economic and political progress were joined in centennial oratory with claims of educational and intellectual advances. In "little red schoolhouses" North and now South, the great eighteenth-century dream of educational opportunity for all was assumed to be in the process of realization. American intellectuals of the late nineteenth century—while not yet "rivalling" their counterparts on the Continent—continued the New World tradition of assimilating Old World influences and then striking out on their own, and to a degree and with a prevision that appears remarkable, they were beginning to grapple with many of the philosophical questions and practical alternatives that Americans would face in the late twentieth century.

And the thinkers—both European and American—who made the problems of modern industrial society their study shone a light on the turbulence, the unexamined assumptions and unfulfilled promises that lay beneath the smooth surface of orators' platitudes. From John Stuart Mill, Americans might learn much about the duties and dilemmas involved in widening the dimensions of liberty and happiness. French philosopher Auguste Comte had laid the basis for a science of sociology that would seek to describe precisely the organic development of societies and that Comte hoped might, in Clarence Karier's words, "one day bring order out of the chaotic social conditions which were so much a part of his post-revolutionary society"—and this new approach would also have implications for post–Civil War Americans. Karl Marx was offering a dissection of capitalism and an egalitarian social vision that would grip the minds of Americans aware of the increasingly stratified society around them. Meanwhile Herbert Spencer and his apostles were proposing tough-minded theories of limited government and economic individualism.

American thinkers, even while absorbing such theories, were less and less dependent on their intellectual umbilical cords to the Old World. Psychologist G. Stanley Hall was presenting in embryonic form the problem of an "escape from freedom" that would come to the fore again in post–World War II America. Lester Frank Ward, a brilliant sociologist as famous then as he was forgotten a century later, frontally attacked Spencer's theories and called for humane, positive government to advance a program of collective freedom, thus anticipating central issues of the New Deal era. John Dewey would soon take on some of the most challenging questions of human personality and behavior and their implications for social organization and education in a democracy.

Americans, in the one hundredth birth year of their nation, were face to face, whether they acknowledged it or not, with some of the millennia-old problems and potentials of birthrights. As the United States expanded in population and industry, and headed toward great-power status, were they equipped, intellectually and politically, also to expand liberty and democracy and happiness, just as centennial orators vowed?

THE SHEPHERD AND THE WOLF

THE WORDS that might have fallen most easily, whether with passion or complacency, from the lips of centennial orators were those concerning the First Amendment liberties of the Bill of Rights. Rights to freedoms of speech and conscience, free assembly, and free press were virtually taken for granted by those who enjoyed them, and few seemed willing or able to recognize the many dimensions and ambiguities of liberty on which John Stuart Mill, in his 1859 book *On Liberty,* had dwelt. In a country approaching civil war, Mill's tract had little influence on popular attitudes or on the thought even of elites.

During that war, indeed, Abraham Lincoln noted that "the world has never had a good definition of the word liberty, and the American people, just now, are much in want of one. We all declare for liberty; but in using the same *word* we do not mean the same *thing.* " In this April 1864 address at the Sanitary Fair in Baltimore, Lincoln offered a homely example. "The shepherd drives the wolf from the sheep's throat, for which the sheep thanks the shepherd as a *liberator,* while the wolf denounces him for the same act as the destroyer of liberty." But even Lincoln was simplistic, or perhaps merely two-dimensional. The sheep—at least in the absence of the wolf—might denounce the *shepherd* for tyrannically herding *them* about.

How could the American idea of civil liberty have remained so undefined decades after the Bill of Rights? Between the Alien and Sedition Acts in the late 1790s and the Civil War there was neither intensive nor extensive national debate over the internal tensions and practical applications of First Amendment civil liberties. Historians differ over the reasons for this particular "dog that did not bark in the night." In 1833, Chief Justice Marshall had ruled in *Barron* v. *Baltimore* that the Bill of Rights limited the actions only of the federal government and not of the states, thus making those who claimed that their rights had been violated by state or local governments dependent on appeals to state constitutions, state judges, and local juries. The decisions of state courts could not be appealed to the federal judiciary. Perhaps this ruling discouraged debate

200 / A PEOPLE'S CHARTER

over key issues of First Amendment rights in states that lacked constitutional guarantees as sweeping as those in the federal Bill of Rights and
lacked also a nationally oriented press.

In urban centers conflicts erupted that reached fundamental issues of
civil liberties. Nativists hostile to immigrants and suspicious of Masonic
and Catholic "secret societies" sought to force immigrants to conform to
what they saw as American standards of openness and freedom in speech,
belief, and behavior. Immigrants often had a different idea of American
freedom: that they would be free to behave as they chose, according to
their own customs. But this was a "debate" conducted most dramatically
with the guns and torches of marauding nativists amid the raw fear of
beleaguered immigrants.

The United States was still largely a rural society, however, and doubtless most important in dampening widespread confrontations over the
meanings of civil liberty was the existence of "parochial tolerance" in
the small towns and villages of early-nineteenth-century America. When
the historian surveyed the early United States, John P. Roche observed,
"he notes an enormous diversity of opinion," which represented less a
toleration of heterodox views among the population at large, Roche
concluded, than tolerance of others' opinions within a variety of separated and relatively homogeneous communities, "each with its own canons of orthodoxy." The "average white Protestant American," Roche
noted, could go "through life with complete freedom and reciprocated
by bestowing on other white Protestant Americans the blessings of liberty." And so socialists built their New Harmonys in more or less splendid isolation while Shakers practiced their austere faith in well-ordered
worlds apart. Mormons could distance themselves from the larger national community that persecuted them by settling in the West, and
practice tolerance toward one another—if not always toward the non-
believer living in their mountain lands.

Thus the conflict over freedoms and over the rights to them tended
to be minimized both within these communities and between them.
What might alter this state of affairs? One answer was the rise of a great
and divisive issue to compel national debate, and that is what happened
in the strife over the denial of all rights to African-Americans. Another
spur to debate might be a nationwide threat to a crucial liberty so dramatic that the issue could not be avoided. Still another might be the
hypertrophy of one liberty threatening the subordination of other
rights, enough to challenge the old political and constitutional balance
among freedoms. Both these latter two conditions would arise and
would rouse fervent national debate during the second half of the nineteenth century.

T w o   w e e k s   before the Sanitary Fair address in which he contrasted the liberty of the sheep and of the wolf, Abraham Lincoln had used another plain metaphor in a letter to a Kentucky editor: "By general law," the President wrote, "life *and* limb must be protected; yet often a limb must be amputated to save a life; but a life is never wisely given to save a limb." Lincoln had good reason to make this point: his war administration's repeated violations of constitutional rights had created an uproar even throughout the North and provoked a rebuke by the Chief Justice of the United States. And the President was writing early in 1864, an election year.

To understand Lincoln's wartime violations of rights it is necessary to recognize the gravity of the crisis he faced on entering the White House in March 1861. South Carolina had seceded six weeks after his election, and by February six other states in the lower South fell in line. Throughout the North uncertainty, disarray, and conflict prevailed. As Don E. Fehrenbacher has summarized the new president's situation: "Many Northern Democrats insisted that the federal government had no constitutional authority to use force against the seceding states; some abolitionists and Republicans favored peaceable separation as a policy of good riddance to slavery; and it was obvious that any military movement against the Confederacy would set off another round of secession activity in the still uncommitted upper South." The outbreak of hostilities at Fort Sumter in mid-April brought Virginia, Arkansas, Tennessee, and North Carolina over to the Confederacy in the next five weeks. The border states—especially Maryland—seethed with pro-Southern political intrigue, mob violence, and secessionist propaganda. For a time it seemed that Washington might be cut off from the North.

In this crisis Lincoln acted with a bewildering combination of prerogative and prudence. He did not even convene Congress until four months after his inauguration. In the meantime he expanded the armed forces beyond the limits set by law, raised and spent funds for war-making, pledged the national credit for huge sums, blockaded Southern ports, all without congressional sanction. The President calmly asserted that the war power was vested in him constitutionally as commander in chief and that as president he possessed legal resources Congress lacked.

Both Northern and Southern leaders defended their cause and actions in the language of rights rather than of powers. Instead of claiming only a constitutional justification for secession, Southerners "were virtually appealing to the court of world opinion on the basis of fundamental rights," wrote historian James G. Randall; "for whatever motives would justify secession would also justify an appeal to the right of revolution."

202 / A PEOPLE'S CHARTER

At the same time, according to Randall, the war power as interpreted by Lincoln encompassed a host of "rights" belonging to a president, by which he might act against the rights of citizens—to proclaim martial law; to arrest persons without warrant; to seize private property for war purposes; to suppress newspapers. A president's war-making prerogative extended even to proclaiming the freedom of slaves owned by rebels— though Lincoln took this step only after two years of secession.

It was the suspension of the ancient writ of habeas corpus that most shocked even friends of the administration. This right, after all, had been written into the body of the Constitution in 1787, in its very first article, and over the centuries had withstood countless assaults in Britain and America. Lincoln's suspension was no mere formality or warning; ultimately hundreds and probably thousands of persons were arrested and held indefinitely. When John Merryman, a Baltimore secessionist arrested by the military, petitioned Chief Justice Roger Taney (sitting as a circuit judge) for a writ of habeas corpus, Taney granted it. But the military commander ignored the order, whereupon Taney cited him for contempt and drew up an opinion condemning military violations of constitutional rights. Lincoln would not yield, arguing that it was his supreme duty to preserve the nation on whose survival the life of the whole Constitution rested.

The President was equally adamant in his construction of his power in the case of former Ohio congressman and "Peace Democrat" Clement L. Vallandigham, arrested by a military commission for making an antiwar speech. The Supreme Court refused to review the military's decision. Ohio Democrats retaliated by nominating Vallandigham for governor, thus projecting the case into the political arena. A delegation of Ohio Democratic leaders, after meeting with Lincoln in the White House, drafted an appeal to the President on the constitutional issue. If a man believed that war could not serve to restore the Union but rather endangered both Constitution and Union, did he not have the right "to appeal to the judgment of the people, for a change of policy, by the constitutional remedy of the ballot box?" Lincoln answered in effect no; even free speech uttered directly in an electoral struggle would, he implied, have to yield if it was used to encourage desertion, noncompliance with conscription, and violent resistance to the war.

At the same time Lincoln displayed considerable flexibility and even magnanimity toward persons who had or might have fallen afoul of his wide justifications of his power. He changed Vallandigham's sentence from imprisonment to banishment behind Confederate lines. He sympathized with the rights of the conscientious objector and released many political prisoners. The arrests his administration authorized he defended as preventive rather than vindictive. He tried to target the real sources of sedition and treason. "Must I shoot a simple-minded soldier boy who deserts," he demanded, "while I must not touch a hair of a wiley agitator who induces him to desert?"

Lincoln's occasional forbearance and forgiveness were not enough, however, to assuage his critics. Not only Democrats attacked him for his "usurpations"—"War does not suspend the rights of men," declared New York governor Horatio Seymour—but a Republican senator from Lincoln's own Illinois condemned arrests outside the war zone as the very essence of despotism. For three years there was little the President's opponents could do except protest, but 1864 brought them the opportunity to vote him out of office, and Lincoln could not but be mindful that John Adams had been ousted in 1800 partly because of his suppression of liberties in the undeclared naval war with France. During the campaign, his foes attacked Lincoln with redoubled fury as a power-mad tyrant. The Democrats for their part nominated General George B. McClellan, apparently more willing to trust their liberties to a military man who had, in James Randall and Richard Current's words, "shown some signs of a Napoleonic complex" than to the civilian in the White House.

Ultimately Lincoln rested his defense of his wartime leadership on the Constitution itself and on the paradox that in order to preserve the national charter whole, parts of it had—for the duration—to be sacrificed. Are "all the laws, *but one,*" he had asked in 1861, "to go unexecuted, and the government itself go to pieces, lest that one be violated?" With his answer three years later that a limb must sometimes be amputated to save a life, but a life is never wisely given to save a limb, Lincoln struck to the heart of the matter. While defending the revolutionary values of life, liberty, and happiness the President knew that in that supreme hierarchy, life—the life of the nation—must come first, or the others could never be secured. But this left liberty in a secondary position, and as for happiness—its pursuit could hardly be invoked as millions suffered and died on the endless battlefields, and millions of others were left bereft at home.

In the half century that followed the Civil War many Americans felt reasonably secure about their First Amendment liberties. Their own freedoms of speech, of conscience, of assembly—so far as they chose to exercise them—were not perceptibly abridged. They could boast that not since John Adams had the federal government passed a sedition law. The curbing of individual liberties in the Civil War had, at least in the North, come by and large to be viewed through Lincoln's eyes as the inevitable and even necessary result of an especially dire internal conflict.

But large numbers of the underclass, millions of other Americans, could not take their liberties for granted in these decades. "Freed" Southern men and women after Reconstruction's collapse lay beyond the reach of the Bill of Rights, as did Northern and Western industrial workers, such as members of the IWW, who were subjected to legal harassment and blacklisting, false imprisonment and mob violence. Immigrants were vulnerable to repressive or restrictive actions by national, state, and local governments. By the turn of the century, the federal government was exercising its deportation power—a power amply sustained by the Supreme Court—against an ever-growing group of alien outcasts: "prostitutes, procurers, lunatics, idiots, paupers, persons likely to become a public charge, professional beggars, individuals suffering from a loathsome or dangerous contagious disease, polygamists, epileptics, persons convicted of felony, crime, or misdemeanor involving moral turpitude, and Chinese and Japanese." In vain Justice David J. Brewer protested against one of the first Supreme Court deportation decisions; deportation, he wrote in 1893, forcibly removing people from their homes and families and friends, their businesses and property, and sending them off to a distant land, was punishment, "and that oftentimes most severe and cruel." The Haymarket affair and a series of violent acts by isolated anarchists made any alien who was, or was suspected of being, an anarchist a particular target of federal fear and hostility. After several unsuccessful attempts, Congress in 1903 passed a bill specifically to exclude, deport, and deny naturalization to alien anarchists.

Few in pulpit or press came to the defense of the vulnerable. No more than before the Civil War was there a national debate over First Amendment freedoms—their definition, reach, application, priorities. As in economic, social, and other spheres of American life, a vast silence of incomprehension insulated the "haves"—those who took *their* liberties for granted—from the "have-nots."

A NEW great challenge to American complacency came in 1917–18 with another war, this one "the war to end war." On the eve of America's entry into World War I, President Woodrow Wilson predicted, in a perhaps apocryphal comment to a journalist: "Once lead this people into war and they'll forget there ever was such a thing as tolerance." This hardly seemed likely. Fighting Europeans now rather than one another, surely Americans would turn their hatred outward. And if they fought an alliance whose sons and daughters had come to the United States by the millions, surely these immigrants had become adequately assimilated—had become "American" enough—to ensure that their civil liberties would be respected. But Wilson turned out to be right. While Americans

fought and died abroad, the war induced an orgy of witch-hunting, persecution, and mob violence at home. An Oklahoma mob tarred and feath-
ered a former minister for allegedly speaking out against Liberty bonds.
An Arkansas mob beat a black Baptist preacher and he was kept in jail
for over three months for alleged treasonable utterances that later were
held to be unproved by a grand jury. A Nebraska mob broke into a school,
removed all "German" books, including Bibles in German, and burned
them. In Illinois a man suspected of being a spy was dragged into the
street by several hundred fellow townsmen, wrapped in the flag, and
murdered. People were beaten, horsewhipped, driven out of town for
expressing mild reservations about the war.

   Not only did local authorities repeatedly fail to protect the victims; they
often joined in the intolerance and the persecution. Pittsburgh banned
Beethoven's music for the duration. Cleveland denied aliens licenses to
do business within the city limits. Columbus compelled schoolteachers to
paste blank sheets over "The Watch on the Rhine" and "The Lorelei"
in music books. Numerous local ordinances criminalized speech or actions viewed as threats to the war effort. Local governments also authorized private vigilante groups—the Boy Spies of America, the Sedition
Slammers, the Terrible Threateners—to take the law into their own
hands. Eleven states enacted sedition laws penalizing "disloyal" speech
or action; four passed criminal syndicalism laws directed at the IWW with
its compound threat of labor radicalism and opposition to a "business
man's war."

   It had long been constitutional wisdom, or at least folklore, that if
liberty was threatened locally, the federal government would stand above
parochial intolerance to protect it. "Extend the sphere," James Madison
had written in *The Federalist,* No. 10, "and you take in a greater variety of
parties and interests; you make it less probable that a majority of the
whole will have a common motive to invade the rights of other citizens."
This fine Madisonian principle did not hold in World War I. On the
contrary, Wilson himself seemed to forget that there was ever such a
thing as tolerance. Since 1914, the President had encouraged and exploited American doubts about involvement in Europe's war, presenting
neutrality as the noblest path; and in 1916 he had won reelection on the
slogan "He kept us out of war!" Now that he was leading an unprepared
people into war, Wilson faced the formidable task of marshaling popular
support for a crusade to make the world "safe for democracy." To control
public opinion, not only did he create a massive propaganda machine to
whip up anti-German feeling but his administration and the Congress led
the charge against dissent, with no effective resistance from the Supreme
Court.

On April 6, 1917, Wilson signed a joint congressional resolution declaring a state of war with Germany. The same day he announced regulations restricting the movements of enemy aliens, forbidding them to publish any attack on the government, and empowering federal officials to make summary arrests for national security reasons. He drew the authority for this proclamation from the hoary Alien Enemies Act of 1798. The next day he established a federal loyalty-security program and secretly ordered department heads to sack any employee deemed a loyalty risk "by reason of his conduct, sympathies, or utterances."

Over the next two months Congress framed an Espionage Act amid passionate debate. A senator introduced a proposal defining the whole United States as "a part of the zone of operations conducted by the enemy" and declaring that anyone who published anything endangering the operations of American forces could be tried as a spy by a military tribunal and executed. It was partly in an attempt to head off such hysterical measures that Wilson had acted through proclamation, and he insisted privately that Congress's espionage law would not in any way "be used as a shield against criticism." Yet when Congress debated a proposal to give him broad censorship authority, Wilson contended in a letter to a key House leader printed in *The New York Times* that this censorship power was "absolutely necessary to the public safety." Only by a House vote of 184–144 was the provision defeated.

Passage of the Espionage Act appeared to intensify rather than temper the drive toward regulation and repression. In October 1917 Congress approved a Trading-with-the-Enemy Act that allowed the president to censor international communications and that granted to the postmaster general what Paul L. Murphy described as "almost absolute censorship powers over the American foreign-language press." Then in 1918, as the war in Europe approached its climax, Congress took up the task of sedition legislation. Wilson's attorney general, Thomas Gregory, complained that the Espionage Act had left the national government able to move effectively only against organized propaganda, not against disloyal remarks by individuals. Others contended that the intolerance and violence sweeping the country might abate if federal law would deal decisively with disloyalty.

Members of Congress were sore pressed. Several senators feared that the proposed sedition bill would crush free speech in the United States. When Senator Joseph France of Maryland sought to add a provision stating that nothing in the act "shall be construed as limiting the liberty or impairing the right of any individual to publish or speak what is true, with good motives, and for justifiable ends," Gregory replied that "some of the most dangerous types of propaganda were either made from good motives, or else their traitorous motives were not provable." France's proviso was voted down, despite his warning that the Western world had seen "no such repressive a criminal statute since the dark ages."

The sedition measure that emerged in May 1918 from the impassioned debate was chilling in its terms, criminalizing a vast, vague range of expression and affording the government luxuriant means with which to lash back at its critics. The act struck not only at those who attempted to stir up insubordination or mutiny in the military but at anyone who would "willfully utter, print, write, or publish any disloyal, profane, scurrilous, or abusive language about the form of government of the United States, or the Constitution of the United States," or language that would bring the government, the Constitution, the military, or even the *uniform* of the military "into contempt, scorn, contumely or disrepute." Violators faced up to twenty years' imprisonment. Once again Americans possessed alien and sedition acts, and, since the new Sedition Act was incorporated into the Espionage Act as an amendment, now in a single brutal package.

By this time censorship was well entrenched. Postmaster General Albert S. Burleson exercised broad control over material circulated by mail. Having abused the great patronage powers at his disposal to rid his department of black employees in the South, the former Texas congressman turned now to banning mail that in his judgment constituted "wilful obstruction" to the war's progress. Before he was finished he suppressed an issue of *The Nation,* evidently for denouncing a "slacker roundup" in New York City; censored a Catholic journal for reprinting Jefferson's view that Ireland should be a republic; excluded from the mails Thorstein Veblen's *Imperial Germany and the Industrial Revolution,* apparently because it criticized both the British ally and the German enemy too harshly—at the same time that the administration's propaganda arm was extolling the book's usefulness in the cause. Against a dozen or so radical or socialist journals, Burleson simply swung the broadax and banished them from the mails.

Nowhere was the power and determination of the federal government to crush dissent more nakedly demonstrated than in the wartime campaign against an old antagonist, the IWW. Shortly after the United States entered the war, army troops advanced on Wobbly strongholds in the mining and lumber regions of the West to repress labor conflicts that might hamper war production. In September 1917, after an intensive investigation failed to substantiate allegations that the Wobblies were paid German agents, the Justice Department swept down on Wobbly offices and private homes from Chicago to Spokane and seized every document its agents could find—including the love letters of a Wobbly editor. From the several tons of "evidence" collected in the raids, the government constructed charges that the IWW was a criminal conspiracy to obstruct the war effort, and federal indictments were brought in Chicago and other cities. Each of the 113 Wobblies in the dock—Big Bill Haywood among them—when the Chicago trial opened in April 1918, faced over one hundred separate charges. The government did not intend—nor did it have the evidence—to try to prove the guilt of individual Wobblies on each count. Instead, for a month and a half prosecutors took turns lecturing the jury on the subversive and atheistic nature of Wobbly doctrine and reading from the captured documents. The defense, on the other hand, adopted the venerable course of putting its accuser—capitalism, in this case—on trial, and a succession of Wobblies took the stand to testify to their experiences in the struggle against the exploitation of man by man.

The outcome was a foregone conclusion. At the end of the four-month trial, the jury needed less than an hour to return with guilty verdicts on all of the 10,000 charges. Stiff prison terms were handed out to most of the defendants, with Haywood and two others receiving the maximum of twenty years. The government obtained similar results against some seventy Wobblies in trials in Sacramento and Wichita, while in Omaha, where sixty-four Wobblies languished in jail for a year and a half, all charges against them were dropped six months after the war's end. The Wobblies, Wilson had written to Gregory when the trials were in preparation, "certainly are worthy of being suppressed." But for how long? "Suppressed" during the war by the full force of federal and state power, the IWW was dealt a blow from which it would never recover.

PERHAPS in the long history of oppression the greatest defense of individual liberty was the right of appeal to the judiciary. The founders, reflecting and strengthening that tradition, had built judicial independence into the Constitution, as had the framers of state constitutions. The concept was simple: elected legislatures and politically appointed officials might bend to blasts of popular hysteria, intolerance, and repression, but judges and juries would stand firm. Usually chosen for life, separated from the passions raging in the political arenas, judges would approach the most heated issues independently and with disinterest and be answerable only to the principles of justice. Drawn from the people, juries would reflect popular distaste for governmental threats to individual liberty. As a further, if perhaps unintended, safeguard, cases typically wound their way slowly up through the layers of the judiciary and arrived at the ultimate court of appeals, the Supreme Court, only after popular passions had cooled. Indeed, the first Espionage Act case was not argued before the Supreme Court until January 1919, two months after the Armistice.

That case, *Schenck* v. *United States,* featured the "general secretary of the

Socialist party," charged with printing leaflets to be mailed to men await-
ing conscription that encouraged resistance to the draft. Claiming that
the Conscription Act violated the Constitution, one leaflet exposed "a
most infamous and insidious conspiracy to abridge and destroy the sacred and cherished rights of a free people." If *"you do not assert and support
your rights,"* it urged, the rights of all citizens would be jeopardized. It was
a case made in heaven for the Supreme Court to assert its independence,
but a unanimously patriotic Court in March 1919 decided against Charles
Schenck.

Oliver Wendell Holmes's opinion for the Court defended the government's action but at the same time opened a window for the less repressive treatment of speech in other cases. "The most stringent protection
of free speech," he noted, "would not protect a man in falsely shouting
fire in a theatre and causing a panic." The question in every case "is
whether the words used are used in such circumstances and are of such
a nature as to create a clear and present danger that they will bring about
the substantive evils that Congress has a right to prevent. It is a question
of proximity and degree."

A week later Holmes again spoke for a unanimous Court in another
First Amendment case, *Debs* v. *United States.* Eugene V. Debs had a far
greater renown than Schenck. Long a hero of the left, he had received
nearly 900,000 votes for president in 1912. A speech on economics that
included a condemnation of the war to Ohio Socialists in June 1918 had
led to his conviction for attempting to provoke insubordination in the
army and to incite resistance to the draft, with a sentence of ten years in
prison, even though, as Zechariah Chafee, Jr., would later point out, Debs
neither addressed soldiers nor urged the audience to resist the draft. The
high court upheld the conviction, with Holmes devoting most of his brief
opinion to a close reading of Debs's address in order to isolate those
passages that might have constituted "indirect though not necessarily
ineffective" encouragement to obstruct recruitment.

Twice Holmes had put his lofty liberal reputation behind the Court's
suppression of free speech, but in private he was equivocal. He regretted
having to deliver such opinions, he wrote his friend Harold J. Laski, the
British political scientist, "and (*between ourselves*) that the Government
pressed them to a hearing. Of course I know that donkeys and knaves
would represent us as concurring in the condemnation of Debs because
he was a dangerous agitator." So far as he was concerned, Holmes went
on, Debs could "split his guts" without interference. But Holmes "could
not doubt about the law." However, he added, the "federal judges seem
to me (again between ourselves) to have got hysterical about the war."
And he hoped that President Wilson might "do some pardoning."

The "donkeys and knaves" turned out to be some of Holmes's acquaintances. Liberal jurist Learned Hand and University of Chicago professor Ernst Freund deplored the *Debs* decision, the latter publicly. Chafee, according to Paul Murphy, "took Holmes to task for his position so vigorously and persuasively" in a *Harvard Law Review* essay "that Holmes, now smarting from liberal charges of his insensitivity in the civil liberties area, agreed to allow Harold Laski to arrange a meeting with Chafee at tea. Holmes emerged from this discussion convinced that the First Amendment established a national policy favoring a search for truth, while balancing social interests and individual interests."

Abrams v. *United States,* decided in November 1919, gave Holmes an opportunity to express this newfound sensitivity. The year before, Jacob Abrams and his colleagues had dropped leaflets from a loft window in New York denouncing Wilson for sending troops to Siberia to protect Allied interests against the new Bolshevik regime that had withdrawn from the anti-German coalition. One read:

"The Russian Revolution cries: Workers of the World! Awake! Rise! . . .

"Yes! friends, there is only one enemy of the workers of the world and that is CAPITALISM."

Another leaflet, targeted at factory workers and calling for a general strike, proclaimed that they were producing bullets and bayonets "to murder not only the Germans, but also your dearest, best, who are in Russia and are fighting for freedom."

Justice John Clarke, writing for the Court majority and quoting copiously from the leaflets, found that the "plain purpose of their propaganda was to excite, at the supreme crisis of the war, disaffection, sedition, riots, and, as they hoped, revolution, in this country for the purpose of embarrassing and if possible defeating the military plans of the Government in Europe." Dissenting, with Louis Brandeis, Holmes wrote his noblest words:

> . . . when men have realized that time has upset many fighting faiths, they may come to believe even more than they believe the very foundations of their own conduct that the ultimate good desired is better reached by free trade in ideas—that the best test of truth is the power of the thought to get itself accepted in the competition of the market, and that truth is the only ground upon which their wishes safely can be carried out. That at any rate is the theory of our Constitution. It is an experiment, as all life is an experiment.

SOMETHING QUITE REMARKABLE had occurred during the war against Germany. The United States took on a new enemy—the Bolshevik regime that had seized power in Russia in November 1917—without formally declaring war, and the Supreme Court majority applied the same tests to the loyalty of Americans opposed to this small undeclared war as to that of those opposed to the big declared one, arguing, as the *Abrams* decision did, that opposition to one necessarily hindered the national effort in the other. Curious as this procedure was constitutionally, the Court and the administration were following—and also feeding—the antiradical attitudes of the public as a whole, as earlier both had yielded to and fueled popular hostility against anything that hinted at opposition to the war against Germany. Indeed, many Americans were far more zealous in their fury against Bolshevism than they had been in their antipathy to Prussianism.

Logically there would appear to have been little to fear from the new Soviet government. The Russians were still exhausted from their vast human and material losses during the world war; soon they were exhausting one another even more terribly in a savage civil war. But the feeling against Marxism and its revolutionary kindred had never been logical. The Bolshevik coup seemed to touch ultrasensitive cells in the American psyche. Long before November 1917 many had taken in the lessons of press and politicians that socialists were really anarchists, godless despoilers of property, bloodthirsty would-be tyrants. Now, aroused by the Bolshevik takeover, some Americans, including some high officials, erupted in fear, hatred, and repression, exacerbated by a series of bombings, often of obscure origin, and scattered clashes between war veterans and militant pacifists and leftists.

Such was the background of the Red Scare that reached a climax a year after the war's end. In an atmosphere of terror, the Department of Justice, under Wilson's new attorney general, A. Mitchell Palmer, compiled an index of 200,000 alleged radicals—a file that, in Samuel Walker's words, "included virtually everyone who had ever criticized the government"— and initiated a series of raids on the headquarters of radical groups across the country. The worst of these, on January 2, 1920, targeted suspected radicals in thirty-three cities. Federal agents invaded offices without proper warrants, seized papers and destroyed property, and, again without warrants, arrested over four thousand people. "Anyone who looked vaguely 'foreign,' " wrote Walker, "was likely to be arrested." Many of the victims of the raids were detained for months—sometimes in solitary confinement—and hundreds were deported after hearings that observed few of the niceties of due process. "There is no time to waste," editorialized the Washington *Post,* "on hairsplitting over infringement of liberty."

The ordeal of two Italian immigrant anarchists, Nicola Sacco and Bartolomeo Vanzetti, arrested in Boston for the April 1920 murders of a shoe factory paymaster and security guard, came to symbolize the hysteria and abuses of the Red Scare. The presumption of guilt hung heavily over their trial. The judge, who had supported a weak prosecution case with efforts to prejudice the jury, boasted to a friend after Sacco and Vanzetti were convicted, "Did you see what I did with those anarchist bastards?" The two were sentenced to death, and after long years of appeals, and despite public campaigns for clemency or a new trial, they were finally executed in 1927. Vanzetti, who like Sacco had protested his innocence to the end, believed that there was redemption in their sufferings: "Never in our full life can we hope to do such work for tolerance, for justice, for man's understanding of man, as we now do by an accident."

It was idle during or after the Red Scare to ask whether the government was holding the line against repression; once again, as during the war with Germany, the government *was* the repression. So of course were Congress to some degree, several state governments, and numerous private patriotic societies. Palmer had moved against his targets only after the Senate resolved unanimously that he be ordered to explain his inaction. At the height of the Red Scare the House of Representatives twice refused to seat the twice-elected Victor Berger, editor of the socialist Milwaukee *Leader* and fiery opponent of the war; Berger had earlier lost his paper's second-class mailing privileges and he had been convicted in November 1918 of giving aid and comfort to the enemy, receiving a twenty-year sentence. The administration, the House, the judiciary—no governmental institution came to the defense of Berger's freedom of speech until 1921, when the Supreme Court reversed his conviction, his district again elected him to Congress, and the House finally seated him.

The case of the "Socialist Five"—as they might be called today—was no less egregious. In spring 1920, the New York Assembly expelled five duly elected members of the Socialist Party, a legal organization, solely on the grounds of their allegedly revolutionary and unpatriotic views. The exclusion aroused a storm, with liberal and conservative leaders joining in denunciations of this denial of the rights to free speech and assembly and of the rights of voters to choose their own representatives. But when the Socialist Five were reelected by their constituents, they were excluded again.

If neither the national nor state governments, neither executive nor legislative nor judicial branches, stood up for the Bill of Rights, what organization could be depended on to do so? One that could and would was the National Civil Liberties Bureau, founded in the war year of 1917 by Roger Baldwin and reorganized in early 1920 as the American Civil Liberties Union. A Harvard man and a Unitarian, pacifist, and social worker radicalized by the Wilson administration's assault on civil liberties, Baldwin presided genially over the NCLB's motley collection of middle-class civil libertarians, socialists, pacifists, unionists, and led the NCLB in militant resistance to conscription, censorship, and Espionage Act prosecutions. As the war neared its end in the fall of 1918 he notified his draft board that he opposed conscription, knowing this would land him in jail. And so it did—a fate, however, that Baldwin found quite bearable thanks to his jailer, an Irishman who liked "draft dodgers" because they would not participate in "Britain's war."

Urged to pardon Baldwin, Wilson heard from the Justice Department that wiretaps on Baldwin's phone had exposed his "opposition to the course of the government in the war" and also that he was "not leading a moral life." The President refused to grant the pardon. Baldwin and the NCLB found little more sympathetic support outside government. A July 4, 1917, *New York Times* editorial entitled "Jails Are Waiting for Them" explained that while free speech was "well worth fighting for," in wartime "good citizens willingly submit" to measures "essential to the national existence." The NCLB the *Times* dismissed as a "little group of malcontents" who were "noisy out of all proportion to their numbers."

The great majority of Americans stood aside from the battle over civil liberties in wartime and in the immediate postwar years. The struggle was dominated by government officials, press barons, small-town editors, articulate patriotic societies, all massed against politically ineffective dissenters. Yet ultimately, in a republic with representative institutions, the battle would turn on the attitudes of a concerned public. And on an educated public. It was significant that in 1921 the New York legislature approved measures for the suppression of sedition in the state's public schools. One bill compelled the expulsion of any teacher who advocated any "form of government other than the government of the United States or of this state."

The measures were a sharp reminder—the schools too were key battle sectors in the struggle for individual liberty and human rights in America.

EDUCATION: A BIRTHRIGHT?

AMERICAN LEADERS, whether in times of peace or war, appeared on the whole to be far more effective in proclaiming rights than in establishing them. Spelling out the people's rights in constitutions and at conventions, in homespun phrases and overblown rhetoric, had been the duty and delight of countless statesmen and orators. Presidents and other high priests of American politics and culture declaimed about equality in the

United States even while the Industrial Revolution continued to form an ever more stratified class and caste system, pressing down millions of African-Americans, European and Asian immigrants, and native white poor. Propagandists relentlessly denounced "Prussian," "Bolshevik," and other foreign despotisms even while the First Amendment liberties of many were crushed at home.

To these gaps between rhetoric and reality there was always one significant, though never adequate, exception—the right to a decent education. This right appeared nowhere in the federal Constitution or in the Bill of Rights. In the century after independence more and more state constitutions provided for education, most of them encouraged education and affirmed the necessity for it, and several of them mentioned it in their bills or declarations of rights. But only one nineteenth-century constitution—North Carolina's, after the Civil War—explicitly asserted a "right to the privilege of education" and the state's duty to "guard and maintain that right."

Yet Americans throughout the widening republic were increasingly bent on securing that right. In the late eighteenth century, when common schools were not common, voices were raised in behalf of education as a fundamental need. "Education should not be left to the caprice or negligence of parents, to chance, or confined to the children of wealthy citizens," a Delaware librarian and editor wrote in 1791. "Are ye aware, legislators, that in making knowledge necessary to the subsistence of your subjects, ye are in duty bound to secure to them the means of acquiring it? Else what is the bond of society but a rope of sand, incapable of supporting its own weight?" Deprived of education, the "subject" would become "a victim to his natural wants or to cruel and inexorable laws"— he would starve or be hanged.

A transforming school system, Americans of the revolutionary era believed, was necessary to vanquish prerevolutionary, antirepublican attitudes and conduct and to create a responsible citizenry. George Washington in his Farewell Address urged that, to the extent government gave force to public opinion, that opinion must be enlightened. "In our American republics," Noah Webster wrote, "where government is in the hands of the people, knowledge should be universally diffused by means of public schools," and he even concocted a "Federal Catechism" to indoctrinate schoolchildren with republican ideas.

Thomas Jefferson had long been preaching the need for a comprehensive school system for Virginia and the other states: his 1779 bill "for the More General Diffusion of Knowledge" provided for each local district in Virginia to set up at public expense a three-year primary school, open to "all the free children"—that is, all white children—of both sexes. The ablest scholars—boys only, however—might go on to a higher three-year county school, also free of charge. While Jefferson's plan remained unfulfilled for years, the strong lead he took on the matter served as a beacon for the state and local leaders of following generations who created large, decentralized school systems under state control.

Jefferson had been far more explicit about the details of his plan than decided as to its fundamental purpose. At times he conceived of education as mainly of practical use, at other times as having far broader import. "The main objects of all science" were "the freedom and happiness of man," he wrote to his friend General Kosciusko. For another friend he noted "the important truths": "that knoledge is power, that knoledge is safety, and that knoledge is happiness." Elsewhere he spoke of education as essential to the realization of democracy or freedom, egalitarianism or social reform.

He summarized some of his aims in an 1818 report on plans for the University of Virginia. Primary education should give "every citizen" the skills and basic knowledge that would enable him to transact his own business, to think about ideas and improve his morals and faculties, to understand his duties to neighbors and country, and to "know his rights; to exercise with order and justice those he retains; to choose with discretion the fiduciary of those he delegates; and to notice their conduct with diligence, with candor, and judgment."

This variety, even diffusion, of purpose characterized the diverse plans and hopes of education activists early in the nineteenth century as they began to establish, with a minimum of oratory and a maximum of effort and effect, public schools across the country. These early decades were times of innovation: of tax-supported primary schools for both sexes, of free secondary schools (limited for the most part to boys until after the Civil War), of the first women's high school, Emma Willard's Private Female Seminary, founded in 1821 in Troy, New York. Schooling for children as young as four was initiated in Boston in 1816 and included in the city's public school system two years later. Kindergartens, the innovation of a German educational theorist, Friedrich Froebel, were introduced just after mid-century. By 1870 over half of boys and girls five to seventeen years old attended elementary and secondary schools; by the early 1900s three-quarters were enrolled.

During the first decades of expansion, the public school was seen variously as forging national unity, inculcating patriotism, cultivating good citizenship, developing future leaders. In part these emphases were carryovers from the desperate need felt during the founding period to establish, strengthen, perpetuate, and defend the young republic. But they came to be allied with a somewhat different emphasis—the establishment of social controls over the population, pursued for diverse purposes by both conservatives and liberal reformers. Conservative means and ends ranged from requiring school attendance to supervising teaching methods to the integration of immigrants into the national culture to ensuring that conservative—usually business—views were advanced in textbooks and in the classroom.

Liberal reformers saw education as a means of elevating the morals of children, or instilling certain republican—later, liberal—values. Never would "wisdom preside in the halls of legislation," Horace Mann preached, until common schools created a "more far-seeing intelligence and a purer morality than has ever existed among communities of men." Neither educational party thought of its efforts and ultimate purpose as anything less than benign: the creation of a stable, orderly society with a capable population that shared a cluster of essential political and social values.

NEAR THE TURN of the nineteenth century these concepts of the purpose of education were becoming more specialized and hence even more varied. To business interests public schools were places for teaching youngsters to work hard, respect property, and sharpen skills that would be useful in the commercial and industrial world. Jane Addams noted astutely: "The business man has, of course, not said to himself: 'I will have the public school train office boys and clerks for me, so that I may have them cheap,' but he has thought, and sometimes said, 'Teach the children to write legibly, and to figure accurately and quickly; to acquire habits of punctuality and order; to be prompt to obey, and not question why; and you will fit them to make their way in the world as I have made mine!'"

Among more liberal educational theorists, the counterpart to this was "social engineering" or "corporatist liberalism," training children not for life in the jungles of capitalism but for clean social efficiency. Reacting against capitalism's waste and cruelty, the social engineers held that schools should mold students to the specified needs of a society that would tend to higher and higher levels of organization and whose smooth operation therefore required the subordination of individual difference to clockwork collective effort. "Draw up your specifications for man," proclaimed one such engineer-visionary, "and if you will give me control of the environment and time enough, I will clothe your dreams in flesh and blood." The care of sheep and chickens, he went on, had been "carried to the highest degree of perfection that intelligent planning can attain." Why then should "the education of a child, the choice of his employment," be left to the "ancient haphazard plan"?

Nor would the reformers of the Progressive movement leave children's educational development to custom or chance. Like the engineers, but with less emphasis on efficiency and more on ameliorating barbarous social conditions, their concerns were directed toward the total environment in which both children and adults lived and learned. To some Progressives, this meant setting up settlement houses, such as Jane Addams's renowned Hull House in Chicago, that might pull the poor up out of city squalor and bring them closer to middle-class living and educational standards and—more important—to middle-class attitudes. A generation or two later, in the 1920s, Progressive reformers were contending against the individualist emphasis in public schools and urging that the stake of the whole nation in education be honored. A Yale professor of education, George S. Counts, wrote that society was making an investment in public education, "not bestowing gifts" on individuals. Counts and others went further, holding that schools must act as a progressive corrective to conservative social institutions. But at the core of his argument was the simple proposition that education was not an "individual right."

Such social reorganizers or renewers melded with more radical reformers whose doctrines were in part an intellectual inheritance from the Jeffersonian and Jacksonian emphasis on education as a way to equality of opportunity. But they were even more emphatic that universal education might serve, as Horace Mann grandly put it, as the "great equalizer" of human conditions. This was a key argument for free, tax-supported schools, if indeed the schools were great equalizers. But were they? Could they be? Some contended—not always with disapproval—that public education froze the existing class system, even fortified it. To social engineers, for instance, who looked to fix youths to narrow vocational tracks, economic and social mobility was an unnecessary source of instability and inefficiency in the well-ordered society. A Reconstruction-era editorial in a North Carolina newspaper endorsed education for newly freed African-Americans, but only so that they might learn their place in a white-dominated society; education would check their desires for "elevation and equality," serving as a "powerful agent" for the perpetuation of racial separation and black inferiority: "The farther the negroes advanced in education, the more fully would they understand and appreciate the difference of caste and social position existing between themselves and the whites, and the more fully would they become impressed with the necessity of laboring earnestly."

While the percentage of African-American children enrolled in public schools more than tripled, to almost one-third, in the thirty years from 1870 to 1900, these figures were far below those of whites, nor did they address the quality of the education those black students received. In the segregated schools of Mississippi in 1907, $5.02 was spent to educate each white child, $1.10 for each black child; in some Mississippi counties, as much as $38 went to the schooling of a white child, while as little as $0.27 was spent on his black counterpart.

Those African-Americans who enjoyed what a conservative white Virginian called the "luxury" of an education and who proceeded beyond the barest literacy were most commonly shunted into restrictive programs of manual or, later, industrial training. As conducted by such rare educational leaders as General Samuel Chapman Armstrong, founder of the Hampton Institute in Virginia after the Civil War, or Booker T. Washington, a graduate of Hampton and founder in 1881 of Alabama's Tuskegee Institute, a "practical education" might, as Armstrong held, be "a force that promoted fidelity, honesty, accuracy, persistence, and intelligence" and, as Washington hoped, an African-American who had proven himself, "through his skill, intelligence and character, of such undeniable value to the community in which he lived," would not be denied his place in the American meritocracy.

But Washington's critics were quick to point out the reality that underlay his dreams of racial justice through mass manual education. The emphasis on industry, honesty, and thrift put African-Americans in the position of having to earn their rights by convincing whites of their moral worthiness to hold them, and Washington's opposition, as W. E. B. Du Bois wrote, to "the higher training and ambition of our brighter minds" would condemn African-Americans to perpetual inferiority and servility in manual or industrial labor. And so, despite Washington's genius and his individual successes, it was and remained: education did not build bridges of opportunity and acceptance from black to white America, but instead deepened the chasm between the two enclaves.

Although by the latter part of the nineteenth century white women were attending school at rates comparable to those of white men, they found that there was less strength in numbers than in conventions and expectations. As the education of women expanded, housekeeping became a science, with a specialized course of instruction. It was women's "natural" vocation, and its study became the female equivalent of manual or industrial training for boys. The home economics movement, spurred by the writings of Catharine Beecher, who saw domestic science as a noble occupation for "surplus" women who might otherwise be drawn into the sweltering darkness of factories, gathered momentum in the late nineteenth century and by the 1920s few were the female high school students who had not taken at least one home economics course, and one-fifth of all such students were enrolled in nothing else.

In competition with homemaking for the aspirations of women students were curricula in industrial training and commercial education. The former, as John L. Rury pointed out, amounted to little more than home economics on the factory scale: women were taught to cook commercially or to stitch and sew on industrial machines. Commercial education was a growing field in the late nineteenth and early twentieth centuries, preparing both girls and boys for the booming white-collar labor market, but here again the lines of gender were sharply drawn. A 1917 survey of high school principals indicated that men were to be trained to manage and women to be managed. Women, it was thought, did not want upward-moving careers in business, but only a "respectable" secretarial or clerical stopgap before marriage.

Education for national unity or a responsible citizenry, for social efficiency or control or moral uplift, for racial amelioration or the creation of a trained and effective work force—in all the diverse concepts one approach was missing. This was emphasis on children themselves. Most of the educators or reformers, of course, assumed that their great national or social purposes necessarily met the needs of the child, or at least of the child who would become an adult. They assumed that they were speaking for the child—what other purpose did schooling have?

HORACE MANN liked to dwell on the vital need for students' free speech and free thought. It was his desire, wrote historian Merle Curti, "to develop in children a love of truth more powerful than devotion to dogma, fortified by his own belief in freedom of religious opinion." Indeed, Mann orated that treason against free speech was worse even than treason against government. But he also insisted that schoolchildren learn that it was wrong to use rebellion to change "laws and rulers"— revolutionary forefathers to the contrary notwithstanding—and he was incensed when a normal school head he had appointed took his students to an abolitionist meeting.

Even under so ardent a reformer as Horace Mann, then, education had the character of an enlightened despotism, with students obliged to cram high-minded ideals about freedom that their teachers had the paternalistic liberty to violate in classroom practice. The freedom of children to learn had advanced little in the nineteenth century. But already, late in that century, creative minds were developing ideas to expand and enrich this freedom.

The American who most transformed prevailing notions was John Dewey. At the dawn of the new century, drawing on both his theoretical work and his headship of the University of Chicago's Laboratory School, Dewey published two books, *The School and Society* and *The Child and the*

Curriculum, filled with fresh psychological and philosophical insights. While child-centered, his views managed at the same time to be family- and community-oriented. "What the best and wisest parent wants for his own child," he wrote in *The School and Society,* "that must the community want for all of its children."

In his theory of education Dewey began with the needs and concerns of the growing child and it was here too, Dewey held, that the practice of education must begin. Thus in the early grades classes were to be designed to respond to children's curiosity, their need for conversation, their instinct for construction and art. Dewey had been much influenced by Francis W. Parker, superintendent of schools in Quincy, Massachusetts, who had abandoned the set curriculum to allow youngsters to learn to read from materials devised by the teachers rather than from old texts, to approach arithmetic through objects rather than by rules, to begin geography by taking trips through the countryside. The students went on to more conventional studies only after this free regimen of observing, handling, and comprehending. Dewey was moved to call Parker the father of progressive education.

Dewey followed other ventures in experimental education with enthusiastic interest. Marietta Pierce Johnson's Organic School at Fairhope, Alabama, founded in 1907, did away with achievement groupings, extrinsic standards or incentives, and other impositions on children, in order to encourage initiative and spontaneity. After visiting the school Dewey was unrestrained in his approval: Johnson's program, he wrote, demonstrated that it was possible for children to live "natural lives" in school, to "progress bodily, mentally, and morally in school without factitious pressure, rewards, examinations, grades, or promotions," while also using such "conventional tools of learning" as books.

Caroline Pratt's Play School in Greenwich Village also impressed Dewey. Pratt liked to relate her "conversion experience," which came when she was watching a friend's six-year-old build a miniature railroad system with blocks, toys, paper boxes, and any other materials within reach. As the child directed his little trains and "as I listened to the unceasing accompaniment of happy noises in realistic imitation of train whistles and bells and automobile horns—it seemed to me that this child had discovered an activity more satisfying to him than anything I had ever seen offered to children." Her method at the Play School, which opened in 1914, was to take children on outings to parks, zoos, stores, and other city sites, and then encourage them to describe what they had seen, in paint or with boxes, blocks, toys. She treated her small students as artists who clarified their ideas or experiences by exploring means of expressing them.

Shortly after World War I the Progressive Education Association was established, and principles were agreed to: that pupils should have the freedom to develop naturally, to be self-governing; that free interest should be the motive force of all work, nurtured by contact with the wider world; that teachers should act as guides, not as taskmasters; that school and home should cooperate to meet the needs of children.

Members of the association were also supposed to take leadership in converting private and public schools to these principles. This was a heroic assignment. Not only did progressive education require a revolution in the idea of children's place and their developmental needs in school and society, but as it began slowly to catch on during the 1920s, inevitably it attracted enthusiasts, overenthusiasts, and even charlatans. When creative self-expression in children's art came to be taken up as a fad, wrote Lawrence Cremin, "it elicited not only first-rate art, but every manner of shoddiness and self-deception as well. In too many classrooms license began to pass for liberty, planlessness for spontaneity, recalcitrance for individuality, obfuscation for art, and chaos for education—all justified in the rhetoric of expressionism." It not only aroused the humor of caricaturists, but opened progressive education to angry political attack, one of many plump targets it offered to defenders of the old educational order.

No progressive educator was more concerned about the potential for abuse in the ideas of the movement than Dewey himself. He had not believed that children should be left in school purely to their own devices, but rather that close and encouraging guidance by the teacher was needed at every turn. The moral development of children was necessary along with their physical and intellectual advance, and such development was impossible without teachers who acted as leadership role models. This in turn raised an acute question: how many teachers could supply such leadership?

The lot of American schoolteachers had never been easy. The burden of teaching had increasingly been borne by women, tens of thousands of them in public schools large and small. They worked long hours for small pay and often still smaller status, and their promotion to higher, administrative positions was usually cut off by the domination of those positions by men. Women teachers, conditioned by their own experiences and by their society's low expectations of women at work, directed even their abler female students into dead-end domestic, commercial, and industrial jobs. And the texts they had to assign typically reinforced stereotypes of women's inferior position at home and at work.

The freedom of teachers to teach and to choose their teaching methods improved somewhat through the nineteenth century as a result of higher appropriations for schools, which lifted teachers' salaries, reduced their work load, and encouraged improvements in their training; and of the gradual shift from ungraded to graded schools that opened the door to teacher specialization and, in Howard K. Beale's judgment, removed "one of the worst limitations upon choice of method."

Still, progressive education put high and multidimensional demands upon even those teachers bold enough to adopt Dewey and willing to offer nonauthoritarian classroom leadership. By the years of World War I, some 200,000 one-teacher schools remained in the United States, attended by some five million students. Engaging with the minds and hearts of children, as progressive education required, was in most of these schools virtually impossible. How could one teacher, coping with a small crowd ranging in age from five to fifteen, be expected to spend time with each individual student, lovingly "developing" her or him? Most public school teachers contented themselves with occasional, often indiscriminate helpings of Dewey's ideas or shunned them entirely, either because they themselves held conventional attitudes or because they felt themselves under the watchful eyes of conservative community interests—whether parents or school boards, businessmen or self-appointed guardians of orthodoxy.

By the 1920s, then, tens of millions of Americans over the decades had secured for children the right to a free education by paying taxes for schools and teachers. But the extent and quality of that right to education were still in doubt.

It was inevitable that, on such a cardinal subject and for such a massive effort as public school education, the various means and ends promoted by theorists and practitioners and other interests of the nineteenth and early twentieth centuries would compete for policy, programs, and funding. The problem was that they competed in a kind of political and intellectual free market. There was little lasting sense of priority, as the stocks of educational philosophies rose and fell. Immensely complicating the picture was the political system through which education was carried on. States assumed responsibility for public education, but they in effect delegated the making and execution of educational policy to thousands of school districts, even apart from independent private and parochial schools. So localized was the system and the attitudes supporting it that for most of the nation's history even state control was feared. Federal control was beyond the pale, aside from the establishment in 1802 of the U.S. Military Academy at West Point, which after all was set up under President Jefferson, and the 1862 Morrill Act, providing grants of land to states to encourage the establishment of agricultural colleges.

Many local initiatives, some of them vigorously reformist and egalitarian, blazed up and either shortly died or survived precariously but without broadening their influence beyond their narrow communities. Progressive education, with its impressive intellectual support and passionate devotees, had the potential, perhaps, of provoking a thoroughgoing educational revolution, but it was strong and pure only in isolated pockets, and to the extent that its ideas and practices were more generally diffused, their selective and inept application often brought only discredit and redoubled resistance to the movement. On the whole, the educational system was, in Fred Burke's apt phrase, "functionally liberal and structurally conservative."

The system indeed was founded on a remarkable paradox. At a time when Americans were increasingly alarmed by the rise of socialist ideology abroad and at home, they were running a public school system that was pure socialism—public ownership of facilities and governmental hiring, paying, and firing of employees. Not only this, but mothers and fathers were obliged by law to force their children into the jaws of this socialist Moloch seven or eight hours a day, where they would be under the supervision of state employees using state-selected textbooks. To be sure, this was benign and masked socialism, often taking the form of an overworked schoolmarm and a one-room village school, but even so public tolerance for it depended in no small measure precisely on the system's fragmentation—on the continued assertion of local control, on the continued absence of a national educational program.

Thus, not only was a true "Education Bill of Rights" never framed, but there was never a national debate over educational policy, or the machinery to carry out such a policy if one had been arrived at by some kind of consensus or majority vote. Instead, there was a congeries of concepts, interests, and demands, all filtered through a fragmented system. In that jumble educational freedom for children almost always ranked low. A century after the Jeffersonian "education era," the nation's schools as a whole were earning poor marks—and no group awarded those grades with more certain knowledge and greater sorrow than the educators themselves.

ROOT, HOG, OR DIE?

THE DISPUTE over progressive education in the 1920s mirrored a wider political and intellectual conflict over individual versus collective rights, a conflict with deep roots in American history. Against the British and among themselves Americans of the eighteenth century had fought for individual liberty, individualism, individual rights. Increasingly, before the Civil War, the right to individual liberty was interpreted and applied as the protection of property rights against public claims, and those trade unionists, socialists, and others who advocated much broader economic and social rights had little political influence in the world of burgeoning private enterprise.

The struggle against slavery, the great collective effort of the Civil War and Reconstruction, appeared to indicate the potential power of mass public action for the achievement and broadening of rights. But the Fourteenth Amendment's potential "revolution in federalism" that might have nationalized the rights of citizens and put them under the active protection of the federal government was crushed beneath a counterrevolution that buttressed the liberties of corporations. The failure of Reconstruction to lift Southern blacks out of serfdom and the failure of the Fourteenth Amendment to strengthen the power of the nation to act on behalf of the general welfare foreshadowed an era of unrestrained personal entrepreneurship.

That era also marked the domination in political and social thought of classical liberalism, construed narrowly as unbridled individualism. The presiding genius of this ideology was Edwin L. Godkin; the preeminent organ was *The Nation,* which he edited. "To Govern Well," the journal proclaimed, "Govern Little." The government, Godkin elaborated in 1873, "must get out of the 'protective' business and the 'subsidy' business and the 'improvement' and the 'development' business." The individualist ethic was effort, ambition, enterprise. It was in this same era that schoolchildren read in their McGuffey readers:

> . . . If you find your task is hard,
> Try, Try Again;
> Time will bring you your reward,
> Try, Try Again;
> All that other folks can do,
> Why, with patience, should not you. . . .

The shift from the spacious individualism of Jefferson and of John Stuart Mill to Godkin's free market liberalism found an analogy in the two Sumners, both "liberals" though otherwise unrelated. Boston's Senator Charles Sumner, pompous and self-righteous though he was, could redeem himself with a fiery five-hour oration on "The Equal Rights of All"—"By the same title that we claim Liberty do we claim Equality also. . . . One is the complement of the other." Yale philosopher William Graham Sumner, a fervent disciple of British Social Darwinist Herbert

Spencer, preached an untempered economic individualism, mincing no words: "strong" and "weak" were simply terms for the industrious and the idle, the frugal and the extravagant. Millionaires were the successful products of natural selection. If we tampered with selection to ameliorate natural inequalities, the survival of the fittest would become the survival of the unfittest. A Yale student spoke up in class:

"Professor, don't you believe in any government aid to industries?"

"No! it's root, hog, or die."

"Yes, but hasn't the hog got a right to root?"

"There are no rights. The world owes nobody a living."

There are no rights—no birthrights for the infant, no education rights for the growing child, no rights for the needy and wanting. Neither were there rights, according to this philosophy, for financial or industrial corporations.

Such a philosophy of naked individualism was too "classical," too brutal and simple to survive in pure form in late-nineteenth-century America. Frequent comparisons to the contrary, the American economy was not in the end a jungle. Few of Sumner's legions of followers in the business class were, for the sake of principle, eager to renounce the rights of corporations established by John Marshall's Supreme Court. Indeed, they noisily pressed on government their claims to tariffs, subsidies, freedom from regulation—above all their inalienable right to acquire and hold property and to exploit it as they saw fit. Other Americans, packed into cities or scratching to survive on farms in the West, laid other claims to rights grounded in economic or social concerns, including free or cheap land, railroad regulation, poor relief, curbs on sweatshops, regulation of hours and conditions of work.

Under such pressures classical liberal individualism split into several doctrines with separate constituencies. Social Darwinism was one branch. Another held to the old laissez-faire philosophy, symbolized by Adam Smith's hidden hand: that government intervention or regulation was unnatural and harmful except when it protected "liberty"—that is, liberty of contract and the right of property. Business-oriented constituencies found their interests best served by a dilution of "pure" laissez-faire and claimed much more positive "rights" from government—tariffs, subsidies, and the like.

From the overarching doctrine of classical liberalism another group split off, the liberal reformers who looked to government to soften the worst excesses of industrial society, to help the poor, protect the weak, and regulate business—though without undermining the capitalist structure. Rhetorically, at least, these reformers stood for the right of the "little fellow" to the opportunity of climbing the economic ladder, of the small businessman to compete on equal terms with large corporations, of the small-town banker to stand up to great aggregations of wealth. A poignantly nostalgic aroma clung to this doctrine. As manifested in Woodrow Wilson's New Freedom, William Diamond wrote, it was designed "to restore the American economy to a Golden Age of competitive capitalism: an age in which every man had been his own employer or could hope to become one."

A central source of controversy among the dissenters from classical liberalism was property rights. The stakes were high. As corporations proliferated, expanded, and consolidated in the turn-of-the-century decades, as capital became the crucial element in production, property rights were established as the very precondition of market activity. They now not only embraced physical things but extended to what John R. Commons called the "powers of acquisition," a near-infinity of "acquiring, holding, enlarging and selling" of those things, and extended still further to the most distant reaches of acquisitional transactions, such as labor-capital agreements and disputes.

No American in the late nineteenth century attacked the inflation of property rights more searchingly than journalist and reformer Henry George. In his book *Progress and Poverty,* published in 1879, George contended that the right of property ownership as exercised in the United States contradicted the foundation stone of the Lockean natural rights theory by which it claimed justification: the right of the laborer to the fruits of his labor. "As a man belongs to himself," wrote George, "so his labor when put in concrete form belongs to him." George would allow land ownership to the degree that it was based strictly in the owner's labor; his real targets were those who claimed title to more land than they themselves could work and whose land either lay fallow or was worked by hired laborers or renters. In the latter case, the landlord "receives without producing" while the laborers "produce without receiving. The one is unjustly enriched; the others are robbed." This "fundamental wrong," George maintained, was the source of all modern evils—"vice and misery, poverty and pauperism"—and to right it, he had a no less totalistic solution—the "single tax" on all rents or land values of private property, essentially a confiscatory tax that would force unproductive owners to sell their land to those who would make it productive and force landlords to lower their rents or sell out. The tax, by opening more land to more people for exploitation, would bring nearer the realization of the "equal right of all men to the use of land," a right "proclaimed by the fact of their existence."

Although George's almost obsessed campaign for single taxation was a failure, his analysis of capitalist property relations, striking at their very root, had an audience numbered in the millions and deeply influenced later generations of radicals and reformers. And by his insistence that the "unalienable rights" of Jefferson's Declaration were but empty phrases so long as the right of the laborer to the product of his labor was denied, he raised economic rights to the level of the political and civil rights of the American tradition.

Equally opposed to the bloated property rights claims of capitalism was another best-selling author of the 1880s, Edward Bellamy, and like George he sought a redistribution of wealth and the abolition of poverty, but his analysis was quite different. He looked not to the individual laborer for the production of wealth, but to the collective labor of the nation, and thus the rights both to the means of that production—the property—and to the fruits of that labor belonged to the community as a whole, whose government guaranteed each member his or her share of the product. Popularized through a futuristic novel, *Looking Backward: 2000–1887*, Bellamy's call was for a benign cooperative order, based on a strong sense of communal solidarity and a vision of a wholly just and indeed ethical society.

BELLAMY was in the vanguard of yet another split-off from classical liberalism, the forward-looking and transformational doctrines of "collectivism" or "corporatism." Collectivists stressed to varying degrees the need for an active, interventionist government to define the national purpose; direct and harmonize social and economic interests behind that purpose; and invite a positive role for business—especially large corporations—which would work less for selfish profit and more for the collective good. Collectivists valued individuals less for their individuality than for their potential social function. Like the educational social engineers, they saw people as malleable, defined by their social environment, and capable of being educated and trained away from selfishness and competitiveness toward sharing and altruism. Society was not an anarchy of grains in a sandpile but an organic amalgam of groups—workers, bosses, consumers, and many others—that could be harmonized in the best interests of the whole nation under energetic and farsighted leadership.

These views had direct implications for the nature and role of rights. To the extent that assertions of property rights led to conflict, inequities, disorder, and inefficiency there could be no absolute property rights; rather they had to yield to the national purpose. But other individual rights must be curbed as well, for true individualism was to be measured not by one's freedom from restraints but by the success with which one functioned in harmony with others for the good of all. Instead of individual rights collectivists offered what might be termed collective or national rights—the right above all of the people as a whole to determine and execute the national purpose, with the corresponding duty of individuals to fulfill their designated roles. By serving all, by operating as a unit of society, one served oneself and earned the right to such benefits as national defense and social security. For some collectivists this implied not only equality of opportunity and equality before the law but substantive equality, for people would not yield their individual rights to the collective right of the nation unless all believed they would share equally in the fruits of cooperation.

The intellectual leader of the collectivist school was Herbert Croly, author of *The Promise of American Life* and editor of *The New Republic* during and after World War I. A disciple of Comte, Croly looms still as one of the few American thinkers to repudiate most of the Jeffersonian heritage. For Croly rights were neither natural nor inalienable; rather they were "functions in a democratic political organism and must be justified by their actual or presumable functional adequacy." The promise of American life, he believed, lay in national rights, in a national purpose achieved through strong central government, business consolidation, trade union amalgamation, an elite leadership of broad-minded managers, engineers, and other experts, an order in which the average citizen was, apart from his service to the national purpose, to be relatively passive.

Many were excited by such iconoclasm. President Theodore Roosevelt, who had embraced progressive and collectivist ideas during his second term in office, warmly praised Croly's *Promise* and drew his slogan "the new nationalism" from the book. Some businessmen liked Croly's emphasis on a strong national state that would support and rationalize private enterprise, even if this entailed extensive regulation and even control. Intellectuals admired his proposals for a transforming government, his repudiation of classical liberal individualism. Walter Lippmann, for instance, seconded his mentor's dismissal of inalienable rights in favor of functionality. "It is a question of good use and bad use, wise use and foolish use."

John Dewey too shared many of Croly's ideas: he approved some forms of collective and group action that encompassed the whole society and promoted the rational organization of industry and labor. But he shunned Croly's elitist bias and maintained a faith in individual rights. In acknowledging the economic changes transforming the nation, Dewey contended that freedom should mean the right to equal opportunity and individual advancement based on talent and discipline, the right of workers individually to engage in meaningful labor and collectively to share in managerial decisions. The individual would achieve freedom and self-fulfillment, would possess and exercise rights, not in sterile isolation but as a member of the collectivity. Dewey excluded property rights from his collective economy; the private ownership of production not only encouraged selfishness and waste but had reduced most Americans to empty lives of drudgery under the control of owners and managers. Instead, the right of workers to participate in management would entail what William B. Scott has described as "a type of cooperative property right."

Many came to share the collectivist vision less through theory than by the American experience in World War I, which became a vast experiment in collectivist national action. A suddenly powerful central government marshaled hundreds of thousands of men and women, directed and supervised industry, organized and managed resources, demanded the subordination of "selfish" individualism to the single national purpose—victory. Those who participated in this extraordinary mobilization of the broadest national power found the experience a heady and unforgettable one.

Yet it ought also to have been a sobering experience, an illustration of the difficulties and dangers of a collective national enterprise. Businessmen and technocrats dominated the economic arms of the war machine, effectively excluding labor from its rightful share of power in the harmony of interests, and, as later congressional hearings would dramatize, armament manufacturers profited fabulously from their "selflessness." And to ensure unquestioning obedience to its version of the national purpose, Wilson's government conducted a mindless and demagogic propaganda campaign and swung its heavy hand against dissenters, while roaming vigilantes enforced their own brand of individual deference to the collective will.

THE YEARS between the end of the Civil War and the end of World War I witnessed increasing reformist and collectivist challenges to the emphasis on property rights as the foundation of individual liberty. If classical liberalism was in retreat on some fronts, however, it survived and thrived in one powerful bastion—the Supreme Court. Appointments to the Court by a string of conservative Republican presidents and by an almost equally conservative Democrat, Grover Cleveland, had produced a bench dominated by true believers and fellow travelers of an ideology centered on almost boundless laissez-faire and all but absolute property rights, a group John Roche has described as "dedicated to the proposition that entrepreneurial rights were a mundane manifestation of natural law."

It was by the work of these men that the Fourteenth Amendment, intended by its framers to provide federal protection to the rights not only of the freed slaves but of all citizens, became an instrument to assure virtually unrestricted entrepreneurial liberty. Through the clauses of that amendment, post–Civil War courts extended a series of simple propositions: that contracts and a widening array of economic activity were forms of property, that states could not deprive any "person" of such property "without due process of law," and that, as Chief Justice Morrison Waite confirmed in 1886, corporations were among such "persons" whose rights the federal government must protect.

This extension of the Fourteenth Amendment had its roots in a body of powerful dissenting opinions whose arguments would eventually be adopted by a majority of justices. The Court was not asked to rule on the Fourteenth Amendment until 1873, when a group of New Orleans butchers complained that the Louisiana legislature had deprived them of property—their livelihoods—without regard to due process or equal protection by granting a citywide monopoly on slaughtering to a new corporation. In a cautious reading of the amendment's grant of federal power over state action, the Court majority refused to reverse the legislature, adding the equally narrow view that the amendment's equal protection clause applied only to "discrimination against the negroes as a class, or on account of their race." But in a thundering dissent, Stephen Field contended that only strong assertions of national power would fulfill the amendment's purpose "to give practical effect to the declaration of 1776 of inalienable rights," and there was no "more sacred right of citizenship than the right to pursue unmolested a lawful employment." An equally influential dissent was filed by Joseph Bradley. "Rights to life, liberty, and the pursuit of happiness," he wrote, "are equivalent to rights of life, liberty, and property." Deprived by an "arbitrary and unjust" law of their calling—"a man's property and right"—the butchers deserved relief under an amendment whose purpose had been to "provide National security against violation by the States of the fundamental rights of the citizen."

Through much of the 1870s, a majority of the Court remained reluctant to extend its Fourteenth Amendment powers against state "interference" in corporate activity. But Field, Bradley and others kept up a drumbeat of dissent. When the Court in 1877 denied that "reasonable" state regulation of business "affected with a public interest" abridged property rights, Field retorted that this mild holding "practically destroys all the guarantees of the Constitution and of the common law." In the 1880s, as a new wave of conservatives arrived on the bench, Field's demands for broad and searching judicial review of state regulatory acts became Court dogma, and the virtual reduction of the Fourteenth Amendment to its due process clause and of that clause to a defense of property rights became entrenched. In 1890, Samuel Blatchford intoned for the Court that Minnesota's regulation of rail rates had deprived the offended company "of the lawful use of its property, and thus, in substance and effect, of the property itself, without due process of law."

Truly destroyed were the lofty aims of the Fourteenth Amendment's framers. Of the decisions between 1890 and 1910 in which the Supreme Court applied the amendment, 19 addressed the rights of its first concern, African-Americans; 288 addressed the rights of corporations. The Court tended to equate "liberty of contract" with the "general welfare" and used it to check labor actions and union organization and the modest efforts of states to improve working conditions. The mind of the Court was perhaps best revealed in Rufus Peckham's majority opinion in *Lochner.* Not content with striking down the maximum-hours bill for bakers in the name of "the liberty of the individual protected by the Fourteenth Amendment," he went on: "It is impossible for us to shut our eyes to the fact that many of the laws of this character, while passed under what is claimed to be the police power for the purpose of protecting the public health or welfare, are, in reality, passed from other motives." The men of the Supreme Court, Roche noted, were also dedicated to the proposition "that those who would lay profane hands on corporate prerogatives were the harbingers of socialistic serfdom."

The Court was rarely unanimous, nor did it in every case hearken to the plaints of businessmen. But few of those justices most eager to exert the ultimate federal power in defense of the rights of corporate property would extend that same power on behalf of the civil liberties of Americans. One who would attempt to recover the lost potential of the Fourteenth Amendment and adapt it to twentieth-century economic and social demands was Louis Brandeis. Appointed to the bench by Wilson in 1916, this "perpetual dissenter" again and again challenged Court conservatives over a central issue of civil liberty.

That issue was rights of property versus rights of people. Brandeis had a clear order of priorities. Things that were "fundamental," he said, included "Right to Speech. Right to Education. Right to choice of profession. Right to locomotion." Property rights? "There may be some aspects of property that are fundamental," but for him these did not include the right to be free of all legislative limitations. Again and again Brandeis challenged his fellow justices: Why should property rights be favored over other rights? Why should they not be adapted to changing economic conditions? Why was laissez-faire good in business while bad in free speech? Why should government regulate speech if it did not regulate business?

The Court majority was unmoved. They had contrary priorities and they had the votes.

THOUGH often paired in dissent, Brandeis and Oliver Wendell Holmes held markedly different views of First Amendment rights and approached free speech from different directions. To a degree Holmes clung to the classical liberal approach: as he had written in his *Abrams* dissent, ideas should compete for support in the marketplace of opinion, with the best ideas, or at least the strongest, winning out in good Social Darwinist fashion. The government—including the judiciary—had no business favoring one idea over another. And he applied this to economic doctrines as well. As early as 1905, in his *Lochner* dissent, he wrote that "a constitution is not intended to embody a particular economic theory, whether of paternalism . . . or of *laissez faire.*"

Brandeis too believed in a marketplace of ideas, and in experimentation, holding, however, that such experimentation should be purposeful and directed, grounded in a wide array of sociological data, and he also believed that the Court should make allowances for such reasonable ventures in reform. He angrily chastised his colleagues when they used the due process clause of the Fourteenth Amendment to block any social experiment that might tamper with corporate property rights.

Holmes, despite his respect for Brandeis, criticized social reformers who hoped that "wholesale social regeneration" could be produced by "tinkering with the institution of property." The notion that "with socialized property we should have women free and a piano for everybody seems to me an empty humbug." Long ago, he said, he had decided he was not God. "When a state came in here and wanted to build a slaughter house, I looked at the Constitution and if I couldn't find anything in there that said a state couldn't build a slaughter house I said to myself, if they want to build a slaughter house, God-dammit, let them build it."

Of all the justices through these decades, Holmes, despite his application of the marketplace metaphor to ideas, stood closest to the collectivist offshoot from classical liberalism. A wounded veteran of the great struggle to save the Union, he thought in terms of national community, nationhood, even nationalism. Within the nation the struggle of ideas and interests and sections could take place, protected by the Bill of Rights. Holmes shared the collectivist impatience with the concept of natural rights. The fundamental right to life was sacrificed in war or with capital punishment. The right to property was neither divinely given nor eternal but a convention of civil society and therefore in no way absolute. To talk of a right as moral was a fallacy—at best it was a substanceless prediction of legal action against violators. Similarly, Holmes would not accept a gentle reminder from his British friend Sir Frederick Pollock on the natural law underpinnings of ethical codes: "If you deny that any principles of conduct at all are common to and admitted by all men who try to behave reasonably—well, I don't see how you can have any ethics or any ethical background for law." Holmes replied that ethics was a body of "imperfect social generalizations expressed in terms of emotion." Even so, Holmes would defend the specific principles given living form in the constitution of a specific nation and shaped by that nation's experiences. All his life, he wrote Harold Laski, he had "sneered at the natural rights of man" and "at times I have thought that the bills of rights in Constitutions were overworked," but "they embody principles that men have died for."

There came to the Supreme Court in the mid-1920s a case that allowed Holmes to strike a blow for both of his great priorities, the Bill of Rights and the idea of nationhood. Benjamin Gitlow, a Communist pamphleteer, had been convicted under a New York criminal anarchy act for publishing a tedious manifesto calling for "mass struggle," "mass strikes," "mass action" toward "the final act of conquest of power," when "the dictatorship of the proletariat" would be established. Once again the Court majority sustained a conviction that denied the right to such speech, this time on the ground that Gitlow's words had not been meant academically but constituted "the language of direct incitement."

"Every idea is an incitement," Holmes replied in dissenting for Brandeis and himself. "Eloquence may set fire to reason," but Gitlow's "redundant discourse" posed no clear and present danger of starting a conflagration, and ultimately, if such views as those expressed in Gitlow's manifesto won wide acceptance, "the only meaning of free speech is that they should be given their chance and have their way."

Holmes's powerful and influential dissent aside, *Gitlow*'s historical importance lay in finally undoing John Marshall's handiwork, ninety years before, in *Barron* v. *Baltimore* and in acknowledging for the first time that the federal power implied in the Fourteenth Amendment might be applied to defend Bill of Rights freedoms against abridgment by the states. *Gitlow* confirmed that the nation, through the federal government, might set national standards in regulating and protecting free speech. The Court—unanimously now, for on this essential point Holmes and Brandeis joined the majority—held almost casually that for present purposes "we may and do assume that freedom of speech and of the press—which are protected by the First Amendment from abridgment by Congress— are among the fundamental personal rights and 'liberties' protected by the due process clause of the Fourteenth Amendment from impairment by the States." A pair of earlier cases had moved the Court toward this position, but, as Max Lerner noted, with *Gitlow* "jurisdiction of the Supreme Court to review state freedom of speech cases was first deliberately announced."

The ultimate significance of *Gitlow* was that it opened the way for a

Court majority—one more tolerant and less fearful of dissenting speech than that which had upheld Benjamin Gitlow's conviction—to apply a liberal national standard to First Amendment rights and so wipe clean what Zechariah Chafee called the American "checkerboard" with respect to those rights. It would end a situation in which, depending on the whims and passions of state legislators and the vagaries of state constitutions, speech that would in one state be merely the free exercise of a fundamental right might across the state line be condemned as an act of sedition, punishable by, say, five to ten years' hard labor in a state penitentiary.

In the meantime, Gitlow himself profited little by *Gitlow*. He had already served three years of his five-to-ten-year hard-labor sentence at Sing Sing when the Court majority upheld his conviction. He was ultimately pardoned by Governor Al Smith. As to the importance of the case that bore his name, Gitlow confessed later that he had been too consumed by "factional squabbles" within the Communist Party to give the matter any thought. So bitter was this infighting, Gitlow suggested, that the Court's decision to deny him his First Amendment rights had come as glad news to his left-wing rivals.

In the accounts of most cases like *Gitlow* the ultimate fate of the person involved is relegated to a footnote if mentioned at all. But for the Gitlows of the world their fates were not footnotes but their futures. After the great trials were held, the noble affirmations made by distinguished attorneys, the fine sentiments uttered in decisions and dissents—men and women went to jail. Gitlow had a five-to-ten-year sentence, Big Bill Haywood and Victor Berger got twenty years, Eugene Debs ten. Even amiable Roger Baldwin was incarcerated. Perhaps some of these convicts would have preferred not-guilty verdicts to fine speeches.

It came to be alleged, indeed, that the eminent civil libertarians who defended First Amendment rights in court, in the press, or on public platforms acted less from concern for the plight of persecuted individuals or even from a larger vision of the public weal than from a narrow and ultimately self-serving conception of liberty, that they were "more successful in preserving their own rights than in extending them to oppressed minorities," or in challenging a system that "equated freedom with property and security." "I want my crowd to fight fair," Zechariah Chafee had declared, but prefaced it with the assurance that "I believe in property and I believe in the making of money." Despite his radical leanings, Roger Baldwin insisted that civil libertarians were "not asking to change the system, only asking that the system would work fairly." After an exhaustive study of "distinguished dissenters" from the Red Scare, historian Anthony Gengarelly concluded that when those who were most dedicated to the realization of personal freedom and equal justice appeared so impervious to the need for fundamental change, "one is tempted to ask what 'rights' really mean in American society."

B Y T H E L A T E 1 8 0 0 S, oratory about the nation's pursuit of liberty and equality, justice and happiness rarely touched on a widening chasm in the Land of Opportunity between two concepts of rights. One was embodied in a vast and growing system of public education. The system had huge defects—confused goals, inadequate resources, rigid curricula, discrimination against females, African-Americans, and the poor. But every school day several hundred thousand teachers, most of them women, dealt face to face with more than ten million children, some in one-room schools, others in large bureaucratic institutions.

These teachers too had their inadequacies. Low-paid, overworked, sometimes themselves undereducated, they often had to cope with large classes and poor facilities. But we know from hundreds of accounts that many of these "schoolmarms" discerned the needs of their charges, encouraged their hopes and expectations, bolstered their self-esteem, helped them to grasp opportunities, and inspired them to higher effort and self-realization. Along with parents they too were nurturers.

Across the chasm, in sharp contrast with such nurturing, another system of education also was rapidly growing, one that was sometimes called "the school of hard knocks." This learning took place not in classrooms but in offices, shops, banks, factories. The teachers were not schoolmarms but successful men of commerce and finance and industry who served, wittingly or not, as articulate role models. Day after day by word and example they taught the supreme virtues of making one's way, of rugged and selfish individualism, aggressive competition, of earning money and accumulating property. Some even couched their views in grand doctrines, while others put the choices of life more starkly—to root, hog, or die.

The two systems overlapped of course. Individualism and competitive striving were preached in the public schools—not least in McGuffey readers—and enlightened corporate leaders preached business ethics and higher values. But side by side the two educational systems posed a fundamental question for Americans. If mothers and fathers provided nurture from birth and schoolteachers continued this process in various forms through primary school and into secondary school, should nurturing then stop? Must birthrights to material and social and psychological security abruptly cease on receiving a grammar school or high school diploma? If physical nurturing was necessary after birth, and if psychological and material support from families and social support from friends were necessary in the growing adolescent years, why should not a measure of *economic* security at least be provided as young men and women entered business, industrial, educational, professional, and other marketplaces?

What kind of economic system would be required to fulfill such economic rights? These questions became increasingly acute as Americans passed through eras of prosperity and depression.

CHAPTER EIGHT

NEW DEAL—NEW RIGHTS?

FALL 1929 ushered in a decade that would see a transformation in most Americans' conceptions of rights. Yet rarely have a great nation's leaders been so ill prepared to confront the intellectual and political challenges that lay ahead of them.

At the start of the decade now dying—the 1920s, years of enormous corporate growth and consolidation—President Warren Harding had asserted that "business has a right to pursue its normal, legitimate, and righteous way unimpeded." Calvin Coolidge, who once had said that "property rights and personal rights are the same thing," as Harding's vice president explained that along with the "solemn assurance of freedom and equality" in the American way "goes the guarantee of the right of the individual to possess, enjoy, and control the dollar which he earns." A vice president of the National Association of Manufacturers said that "history shows that the prime motive of capitalism—namely, *selfishness,*—merely reflects the conviction, *inborn in every living creature, that it is his natural right to keep, own and control whatever he himself has made, saved, thought out, bought or fought for."* Emphasis most decidedly the NAM's.

The creative, iconoclastic minds of the 1920s had not penetrated the idea world of the nation's political and economic leadership—or the consciousness of the mass public—even when those thinkers were in visible positions of power. Thus Justice Brandeis delivered a series of dissents on the balance both of the rights claimed by corporations against rights claimed by individuals and of these rights against the collective rights that protected and promoted the well-being of the people as a whole. "All rights," he wrote in a dissent to a 1921 Court decision that permitted corporations to obtain injunctions against secondary boycotts, "are derived from the purposes of the society in which they exist; above all rights rises duty to the community." In another dissent later in the decade he voiced his fear that "the rapidly growing aggregation of capital through corporations constitutes an insidious menace to the liberty of the citizen"; that "because of the guidance and control necessarily exercised by great corporations upon those engaged in business, individual initiative is being impaired and creative power will be lessened." Again and again in his dissents Brandeis put the fullest panoply of the citizen's liberties—personal, civil, political, economic—in a preferred position against those of corporations.

If Brandeis ever hoped he could persuade his hidebound brethren on the Court, that hope died. While working on a dissent he told his law clerk, Dean Acheson, that his sole purpose was to educate the country. "We may be able to fill the people with shame, after the passion cools," Brandeis went on, "by preserving some of it on the record. The only hope is the people; you cannot educate the Court." But how could he educate the people, remote from his voice, when he could not influence fellow justices who were obliged to hear him in conference and on the bench?

A more influential voice was one that expressed a better-balanced view of corporations, individuals, and their rights than those of Harding or Coolidge. This was Herbert Hoover's. In turn a mining engineer in China and elsewhere, a speculator in oil, top wartime relief administrator, and secretary of commerce, he was a man of parts who drew thoughtfully on his varied experiences. There appeared to be several Hoovers: Christian capitalist, technocratic organization man, Quaker near-pacifist, and even Jeffersonian agrarian. Perhaps this explained his rejection of the simplicities and shibboleths of the propagandists of capital—but it also accounted for some of the ambivalences in his political philosophy. He wanted the broad individual rights of classical liberalism along with economic cooperation; a strongly purposive nation but with limited governmental intervention in the economic and social spheres; both efficiency and voluntarism, harmony and competition, altruism and self-interest.

Hoover's effort in the 1920s to synthesize these mixed purposes produced what he called "American individualism." True American individualism was not the "every man for himself" doctrine of "rampant" laissez-faire. Hoover had seen the costs of "rugged individualism" in America and around the world: twelve-hour workdays, child labor, wretched education, mass poverty. His brand of individualism was different, taking its strength from inventiveness, creativity, from a fruitful interplay of cooperation and competition, and above all from "equality of opportunity."

It was on this last that Hoover wrote most eloquently. For a "better, brighter, broader individualism" he argued that *"we shall safeguard to every individual an equality of opportunity to take that position in the community to which his intelligence, character, ability, and ambition entitle him."* All the runners would have an equal place at the starting line, he promised in his first campaign for the presidency in 1928. But he was vague on the specifics. Just where was this starting line? Who would guarantee an equal place on it for all? Who chose the judges? What was the reward, the trophy? And who owned the track?

LEFT, RIGHT, AND CENTER

PRESIDENT HERBERT HOOVER entered the climactic campaign of 1932 with a far firmer grasp of the key issues of individual rights than his adversary had. But the Depression that had come with a crash in the first year of his administration had exposed his utter inability to adapt his high ideals to the task of relieving the desperate needs of the people. Franklin Roosevelt's immersion in the rural politics of New York as a state senator, then in the politics of the Wilson administration as an assistant secretary of the navy, followed by three years as New York's governor during the deepening Depression, had left him with a fine understanding of people's wants and hopes, and with strong views about the crucial role of government action. But he thought more in terms of people's immediate, practical needs than of their fundamental, enduring rights. In these terms, the two presidential candidates were opposites.

Roosevelt's only major invocation of rights came late in the campaign, in an address to the Commonwealth Club in San Francisco. Referring to the Declaration of Independence as a "contract" between the rulers and the ruled, the candidate maintained that under that contract "every man has a right to life; and this means that he has also a right to make a comfortable living." Government owed to everyone a portion of the nation's plenty "sufficient for his needs, through his own work." Then:

"Every man has a right to his own property; which means a right to be assured, to the fullest extent attainable, in the safety of his savings. By no other means can men carry the burdens of those parts of life which, in the nature of things, afford no chance of labor; childhood, sickness, old age. In all thought of property, this right is paramount; all other property rights must yield to it." With his flair for oratorical legerdemain, Roosevelt had evoked an expansive concept of rights and made property above all a matter of personal security and the right to it, but then he narrowed this right to the safety of savings. Of course, by 1932 millions of voters had no savings—and FDR did not need to remind his audience who was responsible for *that*. Roosevelt then turned to the "final term" of the "high contract"—liberty and the pursuit of happiness, which he defined as "the right to read, to think, to speak, to choose and live a mode of life," but he added that the individual had to assume the "accompanying responsibility."

What "old" rights would the victorious candidate's New Deal seek to revivify? What "new" rights, if any, would it seek to extend? FDR's bracing inaugural rhetoric gave little hint. Restoration of the "ancient truths," the freshly sworn-in president said, would be measured by the application of "social values more noble than mere monetary profit." Happiness lay not in the mere possession of property but in the "joy of achievement, in the thrill of creative effort." Confidence had languished, "for it thrives only on honesty, on honor, on the sacredness of obligations, on faithful protection, on unselfish performance." This moralistic grab bag suggested that the new president had not yet shaped a coherent doctrine of rights.

Having told the inaugural crowd that the people called for more than "changes in ethics," that they called "for action, and action now," Roosevelt galvanized the nation during the next "Hundred Days" by issuing a series of emergency executive orders, meanwhile pushing "must" legislation through a complaisant Congress. These measures comprised no grand scheme to transform "social values" but rather reflected his campaign remark that the country "demands bold, persistent experimentation. It is common sense to take a method and try it: If it fails, admit it frankly and try another. But above all, try something."

The momentum of events—and the Roosevelt administration's reaction to them—shaped the agenda of rights. While FDR had taken an advanced position on a number of issues, the cut of his presidential campaign had been toward the great center, toward balance. The shifting lines of his campaign rhetoric were driven in part of course by politics—he spoke in different voices to different audiences, to extend his reach to a variety of constituencies—but they also reflected his sense that the nation's fabric had been torn by the economic catastrophe and that it could be restored not by narrow appeals to interest but by what, alluding to Jefferson, and with echoes of Hoover's own cooperative vision, he had called a "concert of action, based on a fair and just concert of interests." And he had also drawn on Theodore Roosevelt in describing a "national community of interest."

It was indeed a Teddy Roosevelt brand of nationalism that his distant cousin appeared to adopt as president a quarter century later. Partisanship was suspended, at least rhetorically, as FDR appealed for Republican support from the country and in House and Senate. And in a nation long dedicated to the theory and practice of checks and balances among branches of government, the President also brought about a virtual partnership of legislature and executive, with himself as the dominating partner. He defended his course in a May 1933 radio speech, at the height of the Hundred Days. Prompt action had been vital, he told his audience, to "our national security." But he reassured listeners that there had been no actual surrender of power. "Congress still retained its constitutional authority, and no one has the slightest desire to change the balance of these powers."

The crisis-driven thrust toward unity—between parties, within government, between government and "interests," among interests, among the people as a whole—had potentially broader implications. Sociologist Robert MacIver suggested in a 1934 essay that it marked a national reaction against "the exploitative character of the individualistic order." Referring to the collectivist experiment of World War I—much in the minds of Roosevelt's planners—Walter Lippmann warned that such a national mobilization could not be so easily sustained or controlled in peacetime. But New Deal planners pointed to the economic chaos they saw as both cause and consequence of the Depression as justification of their effort and were hopeful that political and institutional integration—especially between president and Congress—would provide planning with a firm, wide, and continuing governmental foundation. FDR himself had referred to the need for a national economic plan on occasion in the campaign year of 1932—remarks which were, in Otis Graham's words, "invariably vague about details and hedged by qualifications." Others had stronger ideas, though few planning advocates could agree on just what planning meant or what it entailed, except of course that it was to be in the American grain—cooperative, flexible, democratic—not the dreaded Bolshevik type, with its coercive centralized direction and control.

The New Deal's early nationalism was most authentically realized in the NIRA and NRA—the National Industrial Recovery Act, enacted in June 1933, and the agency it brought into being, the National Recovery Administration. This program, the centerpiece of a huge multisided package, was the institutional expression of Roosevelt's "concert of interests," giving FDR the role of representing the whole nation rather than any group or party, acting as "president of all the people." The NIRA had something for everyone—at least everyone of importance. Industry was to draw up codes that would create a more orderly production, pricing, and selling structure, and thus receive some relief from antitrust regulations. Labor was to have higher wages and shorter hours under these codes; in Section 7(a) of the NIRA workers won a broad authority to organize. The unemployed received, in a separate title of the bill, $3 billion for a vast public works program. Even the consumer was granted some protection, at least theoretically.

Over this distribution and redistribution of loaves and fishes FDR presided confidently, adroitly, eloquently. To a Wisconsin audience in 1934, he quoted a Nebraska congressman's lyrical praise of a New Deal that sought to "cement our society, rich and poor, manual worker and brain worker, into a voluntary brotherhood of freemen, standing together, striving together, for the common good of all." To a convention of bankers he described government as "essentially the outward expression of the unity and leadership of all groups," while his task as president was to "find among many discordant elements the unity of purpose that is best for the Nation as a whole."

THE NEW DEAL's early emphasis on a national "unity of purpose" was not new. Hoover and the "corporatists" of the 1920s had urged it, albeit with far different emphases, especially as to the relative roles of government and business. Still earlier, it had been vigorously propounded by such collectivists as Herbert Croly, and taken up in Theodore Roosevelt's "new nationalism." The great "Bull Moose" champion himself had little opportunity to test the theory with practice, but Woodrow Wilson did—as had Lincoln—under the pressures of war. FDR's answer to such doubters as Lippmann was simple: the emergency the country faced was as severe as war itself.

With his usual skill Roosevelt had well articulated the arguments for the new nationalism—national recovery, security, and unity, at the expense, if necessary, of individual or corporate self-interest, group or sectional claims, greedy lobbies, even the opposition party. He did not make clear—he saw no reason to make clear—how the experiment in nationalism might impinge on rights. The idea of an overarching "national right," or of national rights, which reached back to the collectivist era and made paramount the welfare of the people as a whole, was assumed, not pondered. There was little time for pondering, in the rush and sweep of events.

It was inevitable, though, that Americans would start assessing and reasserting their rights as the economy showed signs of recovery. Improvement in their own living conditions only sharpened their concerns. The old local, regional, economic, social, and other interests that had been allayed by the Depression now were boiling up again. Capital was becoming more cocky, labor more rebellious, farmers more demanding.

What then would become of national rights? The longer the nationalist experiment went on, the more they came to seem a somewhat empty ideal. They did little to clarify the pursuit of values such as liberty and equality, security and happiness, the priorities and standards to be established among competing values, and—least of all—the ways in which fulfillment of those values could be tested.

Given its theoretical weaknesses and practical difficulties and the rising counterpressures, it was not surprising that the New Deal experiment in national rights began to disintegrate during the second year of the Roosevelt administration. Once the center of hope, now the NRA was the focus of crisis and disillusionment. Once hailed from both right and left, now it was attacked by both. Big business complained that the whole economy, including its own affairs, was being "regimented"; small business that the NRA was fostering monopoly and price-cutting at the expense of the "little man"; labor that the NRA's weak enforcement and corporate bias had cheated it of the full impact of the organizing rights recognized by Section 7(a); consumers that they were being gouged. The orchestrated harmony of the concert of interests gave way to a cacophony of protest.

Soon business was assaulting not merely the NRA but the whole New Deal—its budget-busting outlays, its endless regulations administered by callow "professors," its "collectivistic," "socialistic," and even "communistic" tendencies. Roosevelt was now a "dictator," fascist or Communist or somewhere in between. Some of this protest was an expression of "rational greed": in various ways the New Deal did curb business profit-taking and investment practices; and the increasingly heavy spending of the administration raised the portent of steeper corporate taxes. Psychologically the New Deal also threatened businessmen's sense of efficacy, power, and self-esteem. FDR had exploded one of the most enduring American myths, an observant Frenchman noted: he had disassociated the concept of wealth from the concept of virtue.

Was there no reason for this revolt by the right aside from naked economic self-interest or damaged self-esteem? For Herbert Hoover, the root issue, as he told Stanford's graduating class in 1935, was security. This was more than economic security; it could not be purchased through the sacrifice of freedom to "power-seeking, job-holding bureaucracies," with "their tyrannies and their interferences." The first security was freedom itself, the "freedom of men to worship, to think, to speak, to direct their energies, to develop their own talents and to be rewarded for their effort." Freedom, he went on, "is a spiritual need and a spiritual right of man. We can get security in food, shelter, education, leisure, music, books, and what not, in some jails. But we don't get freedom." The former president added that the only way really to help the "underprivileged and unemployed" was through the "creative impulses of liberty."

Hoover's fellow conservatives had already sounded the tocsin of "liberty," which they translated as individual rights against government, and which might be translated further as, above all, the unrestricted right to property. What had come to gall these conservatives as much as anything was that a lot of bureaucrats were sitting in Washington offices dreaming up codes and regulations and tax laws that would tell businessmen how they might or might not run *their* factories, *their* mills, *their* banks, *their* shops or slaughterhouses—in short, how they might or might not dispose of *their* property—as though their hold on that property—their right to it—had no other basis save the sufferance of the government. And so, even before Hoover spoke, conservatives had set up an organization to proclaim and protect their kind of liberty, calling it the American Liberty League. The purpose, a spokesman said, was "to teach the necessity of respect for the rights of persons and property," and to "foster the right to work, earn, save and acquire property," and preeminently "to preserve the ownership and lawful use of property when acquired."

THE LEFT was as quick as the right to turn on the New Deal, and the NRA was one of the first targets of its wrath as well. Radicals insisted that they would not be taken in by presidential appeals to people's needs and rights. "The radical has always reason to be wary when Mr. Roosevelt (and his minions) begins to talk the language of radicalism," said John T. Flynn, still in his own radical stage. "It is under cover of such talk that he always moves another step or two to the right." Section 7(a), which was supposed to have given labor "wide 'liberties,' " turned out to be an empty and fraudulent gesture, he went on, while under the NRA employers were "consolidated into cohesive, single units, acting as a unit, and presenting an unbroken front to any hostile force."

The left indeed was in disarray. The American Communist Party's initial reaction to the surge in labor activism inspired by Section 7(a) was bewilderment. Even in the apparently favorable conditions of the Depression, the party had so far performed disappointingly; from 1930 to 1934 its membership had quadrupled, but merely to 26,000 card-holders. And under 7(a)'s spur, workers were pouring into the industrial unions of the "fascist" AFL or into independent unions, while the party's own Trade Union Unity League recorded only modest—and transient—growth. The party's leaders were hard put to avoid acknowledging that the "industrial slavery act," as they called the NRA, might have provoked the revival of unionism and the rash of strikes that accompanied it. Grudgingly, organizational secretary Jack Stachel allowed that "the Roosevelt program is not a one-sided question from the point of view of results upon the masses." Soon enough, though, the Communists recovered their one-sidedness and resumed their attacks on the White House as "the central headquarters of the advance of fascism," where FDR served as agent for the "hidden dictatorship" of the Liberty League.

Socialist Party leader Norman Thomas was no less divided in his responses to the early New Deal, but his appraisal reflected a close and fair evaluation of what Roosevelt's programs were accomplishing—and what they were not. Thomas had polled nearly a million votes in the 1932 presidential race, but he would readily concede, as the Communists would not, that FDR was to be preferred over Hoover. Without the New Deal, he wrote, "no one knows what stage of disintegration we should have reached." Indeed, socialists might "emulate the President's vigor in getting things done." The New Deal, he noted, more nearly resembled the Socialist Party platform than the Democratic Party's. On the other hand, Thomas was annoyed when conservatives called the New Deal "socialistic." It might be admired as "an immensely bold attempt to stabilize capitalism," but in socialist terms it was "hopelessly inadequate." Instead of FDR's "grand adventure in opportunism," Thomas himself would have launched a "direct attack on the all-important question of the redistribution of national income."

Roosevelt could understand and respect Thomas's principled reservations, for he had been intermittently debating him and his cohorts for years, and some of his best friends were socialists of various hues. Less understandable, and far more menacing, were other voices, strange new voices, somewhere out there on the left.

One of these was the strident call of Southern Populism. Huey Long was born into the Protestant, small-farm, poor-white culture of northern Louisiana; from the poverty he had seen as a child and then as a door-to-door salesman, and his contempt, driven by native pugnacity and ambition, for the old guard of politics and business, had emerged a politician with a direct and flamboyant pitch to the poor. Long built one of the strongest state political organizations in the country and as governor had created a virtual dictatorship in Louisiana, a fiefdom he continued to rule from his Senate post in Washington.

Long's strength lay in specific promises and speedy action—but above all in his antiestablishment, soak-the-rich rhetoric. "Every Man a King," he proclaimed. As governor he had brought people direct help in the form of free textbooks for schoolchildren, upgraded health services, better roads and bridges. With his egalitarian record, his hammerlock on his Louisiana base, his noisy conspicuousness in the Senate, and his national network of Share-Our-Wealth clubs, Long was in a fine position to build a broad following with castigations of New Deal subservience to corporate power at the expense of the poor.

A quite different voice from the left was that of Father Charles Coughlin, but it ended up on the same pitch of social justice. A Detroit priest sickened by the poverty and social chaos of the city even before the Depression, Coughlin from the pulpit denounced unbridled capitalism and the American plutocracy, along with Communism, socialism, divorce, birth control, and Prohibition. Turning to his natural medium, radio, by 1934 he had a weekly audience estimated by some at over ten million. He announced plans to form a new association, the National Union for Social Justice, as an "articulate, organized lobby of the people." A devoted follower and indeed political acolyte of FDR in the 1932 campaign and early in his administration, Coughlin soon added the New Deal to his ever-expanding list of hate objects, denouncing it as a "broken down Colossus," with "its left leg standing on ancient Capitalism and its right mired in the red mud of communism"—an ironic epitaph to the President's early effort to appeal for consensus to both right and left.

Long's and Coughlin's movements were not the only popular forces turning against the New Deal midway through Roosevelt's first term. There was Dr. Francis Townsend of California, an aged and impecunious physician, whose promotion of a scheme for monthly federal pensions appealed so effectively to the desperate needs of the elderly that he enrolled at least two million people in several thousand "Townsend clubs" across the nation. There were farm associations, veterans' groups, Progressives in the "old Northwest," consumer groups, all aroused to ever-greater protest as the New Deal seemed to falter in fulfilling the expectations it had aroused.

The protest movements were dissimilar in membership, grievances, and style, but one idea united them—the people's right to social justice, above all the erasure of the economic inequalities bred by American capitalism. Often they did not define their ideas of equality clearly and would not have agreed among themselves about precisely what it meant and how to achieve it, obsessed as they were with their separate needs and demands. The potential of these movements—that they would somehow suspend their differences and come together in a crusade for social justice—though it was felt and feared in Washington by Roosevelt's political associates and influenced the course of the administration, was never effectively realized.

And while these movements and their outspoken leaders were seizing much of the national spotlight, the most dynamic force of all for economic justice was mobilizing in the industrial heartlands of America.

LABOR'S MAGNA CARTA?

THE NORRIS–LA GUARDIA ACT, signed reluctantly by Herbert Hoover in his last year in office, ought to have been cause for rejoicing in the ranks of labor. Beyond limiting the use of injunctions and effectively outlawing yellow-dog contracts, the measure for the first time made a worker's "full freedom of association, self-organization, and designation of representatives of his own choosing" to bargain collectively with management a matter of national policy. But Norris–La Guardia was, in Irving Bernstein's words, "a lone bright star in an otherwise dark sky." For one thing, those ranks of labor had been thinned by the Depression. Unemployment had climbed from 4 million at the beginning of 1930 to 10 million late in 1931, and by March 1933 had reached 15 million. Union membership, which had already dropped from an all-time high of over 5 million in 1920 to barely 3.5 million in 1929, suffered further losses by 1933 of a half million workers.

Though the labor movement had retained enough energy and muscle to help its legislative allies win passage of Norris–La Guardia, its friends in the executive branch were exceedingly few. A Republican administration that resisted any and every proposal of federal relief for the unemployed until circumstances or politics forced its hand could scarcely be expected to enforce workers' newly acknowledged rights to organize and bargain collectively, especially when no provision in the act obliged it to do so. And workers, preoccupied with simple day-to-day survival, were in no position to press their claims. Thus, as the Depression hit a new bottom in the terrible winter of 1933, the rights pronounced in the Norris–La Guardia Act remained little more than the whispers of a promise.

The redemption of that promise and the transformation of the rights of labor had their beginnings in the heady days of the early New Deal. The first stirrings of recovery, the reemployment of hundreds of thousands of workers, Roosevelt's exuberant leadership and his administration's concern for the plight of labor, the atmosphere of reform and innovation, all created the milieu in which workers regained strength enough to claim their rights. The triggering event was the NIRA's Section 7(a). "Employees shall have the right to organize and bargain collectively," it read in part, "through representatives of their own choosing, and shall be free from the interference, restraint, or coercion of employers of labor, or their agents, in the designation of such representatives."

Hardly a call to revolutionary action, and, indeed, little different from the language of Norris–La Guardia, this plain statement was now received by labor as an invitation to overrun or bypass the old management-dominated company unions and organize the great mass-production industries that over the decades had largely defied unionization. The workers flooding into the big industrial unions of the American Federation of Labor—John L. Lewis's United Mine Workers, Sidney Hillman's Amalgamated Clothing Workers, David Dubinsky's International Ladies' Garment Workers' Union, the United Textile Workers of America—threatened the primacy of the craft brotherhoods that had dominated the AFL since its founding. And inexorably as labor came to feel its strength, a wave of strikes swept the country.

Labor leaders needed not only bare legalization of their right to organize, which Norris–La Guardia had given them before 7(a), but legitimation. "The United States Government Has Said LABOR MUST ORGANIZE," trumpeted an AFL handbill in Kentucky. "PRESIDENT ROOSEVELT WANTS YOU TO JOIN THE UNION," proclaimed posters that Lewis's men plastered by the thousands throughout mining country. In Alabama miners hymned:

> In nineteen hundred an' thirty-three,
> When Mr. Roosevelt took his seat,
> He said to President John L. Lewis,
> "In union we must be."

Was Roosevelt really urging workers to organize? There was "more drama than truth" in the union claims, Secretary of Labor Frances Perkins wrote later. Workers were moving ahead too fast and aggressively for a president who was still trying, in 1933 and 1934, to tack back and forth between labor and capital. But perhaps FDR understood—or intuited—that the New Deal was unleashing forces that would carry it beyond its early goals. Perhaps he understood that as he offered great hope to the hopeless, as he aroused the expectations of those who had expected little, those hopes and expectations would be transformed into feelings of entitlement and then into demands that would turn back on the government as well as on employers.

Counterattacked by those employers, pressured by Lewis and Long, Coughlin and other movement leaders, Roosevelt was on the verge of a broad shift to the left by 1935, and when in the late spring of that year the Supreme Court unanimously struck down the NIRA in *Schechter* v. *United States,* the decision found FDR in a fighting mood. New Dealers joined with labor leaders in a determination to salvage the one component of the NIRA that had had a deep and positive impact, Section 7(a).

It would prove to be a hard salvaging operation. The labor relations board set up to police 7(a) had shown itself strong enough to antagonize both union and business leaders, weak enough to be vulnerable to attack from all sides. It was not the board but the workers 7(a) emboldened that had made the provision effective. Even before the NIRA was invalidated Senator Robert Wagner of New York and other Democrats and representatives of the old board and of the AFL were drafting measures for a more powerful, more independent labor relations board, and after *Schechter* came down, they pushed ahead on ways finally and truly to guarantee the worker's right to choose a union and labor's right to organize, bargain collectively, and strike.

The main problem was not the fierce opposition of business leaders— that was expected—but the strange vacillations in the White House. Historians and biographers have long puzzled over Roosevelt's persistent wariness on this issue, despite his anger at the *Schechter* decision and other Court rebukes and even when the leftward turn that would lead to the "Second Hundred Days" had brought him to firm commitments to such reforms as social security, the regulation of utility holding companies, and a more equitable tax structure. It was only in part because the NRA's labor relations board had caused him endless headaches, or that some union excesses had aroused in him almost as much indignation as those of big industrialists, or that he was still trying to preserve some harmony in the concert of interests.

A deeper explanation has been well expressed by Arthur Schlesinger, Jr.: "Reared in the somewhat paternalistic traditions of prewar progressivism and of the social work ethos, Roosevelt thought instinctively in terms of government's doing things for working people rather than of giving the unions power to win workers their own victories." FDR's approach to leadership reflected this instinct. His way of getting things done was to win a position of power in government and use that power and the platform and trappings it gave him to inspire, persuade, and manipulate other power holders to follow his direction. He had less grasp of—or at least less confidence in—the capacity of grass-roots leaders to work out their own strategies and build their own futures. So did some of his advisers. Brain truster Rexford Tugwell saw labor as always in opposition, "resisting progress." Frances Perkins complained that labor never had ideas of its own, but rather depended on middle-class reformers.

All the credit for the Wagner Act belonged to Wagner himself, Perkins wrote later. The New York senator conducted hearings on the National Labor Relations Act, as Wagner's bill was formally titled, lobbied for it on Capitol Hill and at the White House, and forced FDR's hand to the point where the President finally threw his support behind the measure. But it was the struggles and sacrifices of millions of workers reaching back at least a century that had set the agenda and the terms of debate. From what other source would Wagner have drawn the meaning and purpose of his bill? For, while expressed in the dry language of statutes, here were *their* demands, *their* needs—citing the "inequality of bargaining power between employees who do not possess full freedom of association or actual liberty of contract, and employers who are organized in the corporate or other forms of ownership association," the National Labor Relations Act declared: "Employees shall have the right to self-organization, to form, join, or assist labor organizations, to bargain collectively through representatives of their own choosing, and to engage in concerted activities, for the purpose of collective bargaining or other mutual aid or protection." And not the least of labor's contributions to the Wagner bill was its political muscle, at growing strength in 1935. The threat that workers at the grass roots in every state and district might be mobilized against recalcitrant legislators helped the Wagner Act breeze through Senate and House.

The President, who endorsed the bill publicly only after the Senate had acted, issued a cautious statement of approval upon signing it. Only after invoking values of order and stability did he add that the measure sought to guarantee, "for every worker within its scope, that freedom of choice and action which is justly his." Congress had taken a bolder stand in bringing rights and principles to the forefront, and so would the courts.

Two years later, when the Supreme Court upheld the constitutionality of the National Labor Relations Act, the decision was viewed as a clever move to undermine FDR's proposal to smother the Court's conservative majority by "packing" the bench with new liberal justices—and doubtless it was. But in his opinion Chief Justice Charles Evans Hughes rose to the higher ground of rights. Citing the statute's safeguard of workers' right to organize and choose their representatives, Hughes went on: "That is a fundamental right. Employees have as clear a right to organize and select their representatives for lawful purposes as the respondent"—Jones & Laughlin Steel—"has to organize its business and select its own officers and agents."

SOME HAILED the National Labor Relations Act as "labor's bill of rights." It might more truly have been said that workers had secured their First Amendment liberties. In just about the same number of words, one passage in the Wagner Act—"full freedom of association, self-organization, and designation of representatives of their own choosing" in order to demand better terms from employers—evoked the liberating phrases of the First Amendment about freedom of assembly and the right to petition government for the redress of grievances. Far more important was another similarity. Both the First Amendment and the Wagner Act described rights in the briefest, flattest, and most general terms. This terseness opened the way in each case to a potentially enormous expansion of rights; it also made imperative further definitions of the rights acknowledged and made inevitable intense conflict over those definitions.

The interpretation of rights in labor's arena would prove as intellectually challenging and politically vexing as had been the struggle to define rights in the broad fields of the First Amendment. One of the toughest questions centered on the new National Labor Relations Board's power to certify employee "units" as agents for collective bargaining with employers and whether these units would be designated by craft, by plant, by industry, or in some other manner. This question had bedeviled the NRA's labor relations board, which paradoxically was protected to some degree by its limited powers of decision and enforcement; now, especially with the rising conflict within the AFL between craft and industrial unions, it loomed even more ominously over a stronger act and a more authoritative board.

Behind such politically divisive questions was a philosophical foundation stone of the Wagner Act—its provisions for unprecedented federal intervention into the affairs of unions and the relationships between unions and employers. After all, if the NLRB was empowered to decide how workers were to be represented in collective bargaining, it would inevitably shape or perhaps even dictate the structures and policies of unionism. Under the AFL's historic philosophy and strategy of Gompersism, government regulation or interference was rejected, not least because local, state, and national government had in the past so often violated workers' rights. But now federal protection of the right to organize and bargain collectively appeared so beneficial to the AFL that it could not let pass this bounteous cup. Or would it prove a poisoned chalice, revealing the feds' new powers to curb the rights of labor as well as protect them?

Most employers, on the other hand, did not even debate these issues. They were categorically, passionately against the act. It was a "vicious" piece of legislation that would destroy "the fine spirit of cooperation between employers and employees" that company-sponsored employee-representation plans had nurtured, complained industrialist Ernest T. Weir. The act "would out-STALIN Stalin, out-SOVIET the Russian Soviets," declared the Associated Industries of Oklahoma, adding that it was the "most amazingly vicious and daring attack upon industry and the liberty of individual conduct in the history of American government!"

The question of the Wagner Act's provisions for federal intervention and their implications for the labor movement would have been arresting enough even in placid times. But the act was passed in the midst of a period of conflict. Leaders of American industry and finance had already declared war on the New Deal. The Republican Party was mobilizing its constituencies for an all-out attack on the Roosevelt Democracy in the forthcoming 1936 congressional and presidential battles. No less fierce was the struggle for predominance between craft and industrial unions, and fiercest of all was the battle between capital and labor.

Feeling during these years was further inflamed on all sides by the findings of the La Follette Civil Liberties Committee. Set up to investigate "violations of the rights of free speech and assembly and undue interference with the right of labor to organize and bargain collectively," and chaired by Robert M. La Follette, Jr., son of the great Wisconsin Progressive, the committee held extensive hearings between 1936 and 1940. Ample testimony and documentation was received about infringements of workers' rights, and their airing by the committee made many a headline. Republic Steel was found to have stockpiled an arsenal that compared favorably with that of the Chicago police department—552 revolvers, 245 shotguns, 143 gas guns, 4,033 gas projectiles, 2,707 gas grenades—for use against striking workers or, as a Republic vice president blandly explained to the committee, "to repel an invasion." The private police forces of Republic and other corporations harassed union activists and prospective members with intrusive surveillance, threats and break-ins, and the destruction of union literature; and company spies and provocateurs were hired to destroy unions from within.

"You have no liberties at all," an anonymous worker at a General Motors plant in Saginaw, Michigan, told La Follette. "You couldn't belong to a union and breathe it to a soul. That soul would probably be a spy." Of the thirteen members of the executive board of the Flint auto workers' local in 1934, at least three were spies, including the chairman of the organizing committee, and within two years membership in the local dropped from 26,000 to 120. Companies also whipped up community sentiment against strikers in the name of peace, law and order, and anti-Communism, creating ostensibly independent "citizens' committees," whose actual objectives, according to a rabbi who had briefly belonged to one in Johnstown, Pennsylvania, were "first, to get as many men back to work as possible, and to get them back as soon as possible. Second, to break the strike. Third, to break the union."

Such abuses of labor's rights dramatized a crucial issue of the federal role under the Wagner Act—how extensively and in what ways might the government intervene to protect the rights of workers while keeping in some balance the liberties traditionally claimed by employers? For their part, employers demanded to know why La Follette was not investigating coercive acts by unions or individual workers against management.

But even this controversy paled in comparison with the uproar over union representation. The new NLRB was making policy and case decisions on this issue amid the crack-up of the AFL as its industrial unions finally broke away to form the Committee for Industrial Organization under the leadership of John Lewis, provoking a conflict that had the savage bitterness of a civil war. Cases poured into the board from both sides raising the toughest legal—and political—questions. What comprised the proper bargaining unit? How should the NLRB arbiter the claims of a craft and an industrial union to the same unit? Should small unions of craft workers be "submerged" for representation and election purposes in a huge industrial union of semiskilled and unskilled workers? And tied to these questions were those introduced by the NLRB's role as intermediary between employers and employees. What were the implications of the NLRB's avowed "neutrality" between capital and labor? Did labor need more than neutrality to achieve fair bargaining power?

One of the policies adopted by the board illustrated its thicket of problems and the dimensions of its authority. This was the NLRB's principle of majority rule in worker elections held to resolve rival representational claims. The board considered that by introducing "traditional political forms of representation" into its procedures, the bargaining agents chosen in this way would have firmer legitimacy in the eyes of employers and the public. But, as Christopher Tomlins noted, the NLRB's insistence on majority rule meant that "claims based on anything other than majority rule—tradition, custom, and so forth—received no imprimatur and thus imposed no obligation on the employer to recognize the claimant union." And since it was the board that in each case defined the composition of the collective bargaining unit and so, in effect, of its majority, the NLRB assumed for itself "determinative power over the structure of labor representation."

Perhaps few AFL or CIO leaders understood the long-run risks of the power the government had taken upon itself for influencing the hitherto private arena of union activity and decision. But they understood the immediate practicalities of power well enough to wage a bitter struggle for influence within the NLRB. The board was showered with cries of bias at virtually every step it took. And bias was inevitable, for whatever its intentions, the government could never be a truly neutral arbiter, particularly in a conflict as sharply drawn as that between the AFL and the CIO. Nor, in conflicts within labor or between labor and capital put to the government for mediation, could it be assumed that the interests of the government and the interests of labor would be the same.

Bringing the affairs of labor into what Tomlins called the "regulatory ambit of the administrative state" meant for workers that their right to organize and create collective bargaining procedures now had governmental support. "The right was to be exercised, however, subject to the state's determination of how the public interest might best be served in the resolution of industrial controversies." What if the federal government, representing the broadest public, decided that its "national purpose"—of, say, order and harmony—obliged it to assert its "national rights" against the more partial interests and rights of union members?

It was these questions about the projection of the federal government through the NLRB into the domains of labor and capital, and their answers, under the broad recognition of the right to organize and bargain collectively, that affected the daily lives and liberties of employees and employers alike—and sparked sharp legal and even physical clashes between CIO and AFL adherents and between the forces of capital and the ranks of labor.

THE UPSURGE of unionism in the days of Section 7(a) and of the transmutation of 7(a) into the Wagner Act had been dominated by the "big men" of labor—William Green and his craft union associates in the AFL, Lewis and Hillman and Dubinsky for the industrial unions. But, as happens in the heat and turmoil of revolutions, those at the top felt the control of the forces of change slip from their grasp, as younger union leaders, spurred in turn by their grass-roots constituencies in auto, steel, rubber, and other plants, increasingly took matters into their own more militant hands. Almost spontaneously—though there were precedents in Europe and India—grass-roots leaders developed a new tactic—the sit-down strike. During 1937, 400,000 workers conducted almost 500 sit-downs in major and lesser industries to secure their rights to organize and bargain collectively, and in the process transformed, at least for a time, the industrial world they lived in.

A simple device, and a most effective one, or so it appeared. Workers merely sat down amid their assembly lines—perhaps on the auto cushions they were supposed to be installing. With a "quickie" sit-down—a warning shot across the bows of management—strikers resumed work after a few minutes. If it lasted longer, perhaps days or weeks, workers set up camp among the machines, while their families and friends sent in food and blankets. No need to organize pickets or worry about scabs. Management, fearing bloodshed and damage to property, would hesitate to drive them out.

Sitting down gave strikers the intoxicating sense that they were personally, physically, protecting their rights. They were fighting on their own

turf, in their own workplace, ensconced among their own tools and comrades. In the past, they had besieged employers' citadels from the outside, on picket lines; now they held those citadels. Before, they had been
repulsed legally or even with force because employers had held possession of property; now workers held the property. For a brief heady moment, they had turned property rights upside down. "We had not asked
for it," said Bob Travis, a leader of a General Motors sit-down. "But when
pressed to the issue, we had to answer blow with blow to convince General Motors of our rights under the law." Some of the sit-downers sang:

> When they tie the can to a Union man
>   Sit down! Sit down!
> When they give 'im the sack, they'll take him back
>   Sit down! Sit down!
> When the speed up comes, just twiddle your thumbs
>   Sit down! Sit down!
> When the boss won't talk, don't take a walk
>   Sit down! Sit down!

Propelled by such tremendous momentum from labor's grass roots,
the CIO scored notable organizing victories in the automobile industry
and in Big Steel. Sit-downs against GM erupted in Flint early in 1937 and
kindled similar actions in Toledo, Detroit, and other cities. After the
company won an expulsion order from a friendly judge in Flint and cut
off food and heat in the plants, strikers beat back encroaching police with
a barrage of bottles and brickbats. The strikers stood—or sat—fast, with
the key material and moral support from outside of the Women's Auxil-
iary and the Women's Emergency Brigade, while John Lewis loudly
pressed his demand for exclusive representation of the auto workers.

Its production reduced to a driblet and under pressure from Roosevelt
and Perkins to settle, GM suddenly capitulated, granting recognition to
the Auto Workers as bargaining agent for union members and promising
not to negotiate with any other union for six months. The country's—
indeed, the world's—largest and richest manufacturing corporation had
been obliged to acknowledge that it was not above the law of Wagner.

Big Steel was next. Lewis had established the Steel Workers Organizing Committee under his lieutenant Philip Murray, whose warmth and
compassion concealed a fierce commitment to industrial democracy that
reached out to ethnic and black workers. Murray's strategy was to turn
U.S. Steel's myriad "kept" company unions into militant locals under
SWOC control. By January 1937 he could claim over 100,000 members,
including numerous activists who instigated sit-down strikes throughout

the company. Soon U.S. Steel chief Myron Taylor and Lewis conducted a series of secret negotiations in Washington, producing what has been called the most important single agreement in the history of the labor movement: not only recognition of SWOC as collective bargaining agent for its members but a grant of the forty-hour week with time and a half for overtime.

Other organizing victories followed, but the great momentum of the mid-1930s soon faltered. The 1937–38 recession once again demonstrated that in the United States labor's organizing and negotiating power depended heavily on high or at least rising employment. Labor influence on Capitol Hill weakened as New Deal defeats in 1938 left the Republican–Southern Democratic coalition with a tightened grip on congressional committees and procedures. Antiunion and Red-baiting legislators exploited the war between the AFL and CIO and made the more militant CIO their particular target. A House committee chaired by the reactionary Virginia Democrat Howard W. Smith divided and virtually paralyzed the NLRB in a hunt for pro-CIO bias and Communist influence. The House Un-American Activities Committee under Martin Dies, Texas Democrat, publicized alleged ties between the CIO and the Communist Party. AFL leaders did not hesitate to feed the congressional frenzy against their rivals, as a *New York Times* headline over a report on Dies Committee hearings indicated: "Communists Rule the CIO, Frey of the AFL Testifies: He names 248 Reds."

Out on the labor battlefronts the counterattack on the industrial unionism of the CIO intensified. The National Association of Manufacturers distributed two million copies of a pamphlet that pictured Lewis brandishing a picket sign with the words "JOIN THE CIO AND BUILD A SOVIET AMERICA." Murray's SWOC tackled Little Steel and ran into smaller companies with ruggedly independent owners and managers, led by Tom Girdler of Republic, whose bitter resistance to unionization found an effective strategy, the Mohawk Valley Formula: Brand union leaders as extremists. Arouse the community by threatening to shut down the plant. Mobilize an antiunion army of police, vigilantes, and special deputies. Set up a puppet group of "loyal" employees to stage a noisy back-to-work campaign. Resume production as far as possible, announce that the plant is in full operation, and condemn any remaining stay-aways as violators of the "right to work."

By the beginning of the 1940s, just before unionism renewed its growth in the wake of expanded defense spending and industrial reemployment, a balance sheet of gains for labor and its rights offered a mixed verdict. Organizing drives since 1933 had tripled—to almost 8.5 million by 1941—the numbers of workers in the ranks of unionism, but those ranks had fractured, apparently irreparably, in the war between the AFL and CIO. Many workers had won the right of majority rule in choosing their representatives, but in an era of conflict between and within unions, the rights of dissident workers were insecure. "In industries where intense factional strife developed, such as coal mining and ladies garments," Milton Derber concluded, "tolerance of dissenting views within unions probably declined." Labor had won the right in some industries to due process and equal protection in the handling of grievances—for instance, employers were now obliged to show cause for disciplining or firing their employees—and had secured in some agreements the right to a minimum wage.

In 1938, with the passage of the Fair Labor Standards Act, the minimum wage became national law. The act also brought to a climax the labor movement's long fight for time, mandating a maximum workweek of forty hours, with time and a half for overtime. But the act did not extend these rights to farm workers, domestics, or professionals, and millions of those excluded, especially in the South, were black.

Nor did black workers enjoy fairly the advances won by labor in industry. The racism of many white unionists—especially within the AFL's craft brotherhoods—and fears of competition from cheap black labor made it difficult for African-Americans to find industrial employment except as strikebreakers or in the diminishing number of nonunionized factories. A clause in the Wagner Act to ban racial discrimination in unions was struck at the insistence of the AFL, and black leaders, much to their chagrin, found themselves in tacit alliance with right-wing and corporate opponents of the bill. But for black workers, the closed shop meant the "white shop." "If labor organizations were to get a footing," explained a Cleveland steelworker, "the colored would lose out." That was why "we have to fight against the labor organizations."

The emergence of the CIO improved black prospects somewhat, as it sought aggressively to organize a variety of mass-production industries where black workers were heavily employed. The CIO also reached out to another caste of workers the AFL had virtually ignored—women. Several of the CIO's founding unions represented industries dominated by working women, and similar industries were key targets of CIO organizing drives. Thousands of women at the grass roots participated in labor's wars, whether on their own behalf or in "auxiliaries" that supported male strikers. By 1940, 800,000 women were unionized, a sevenfold increase over 1934. Even so, union membership did not mean equality with men. As Philip S. Foner noted, most CIO contracts with management "froze the existing pattern of discrimination in industry." Seniority rules, relegation to the least desirable jobs, unequal pay for equal work, together with their scanty representation in the CIO hierarchy, combined to deny working women the full benefits of unionization.

With labor's gains, then, there was always a price. Union leaders had indeed secured a place at the table of national power, but once there they were expected to behave "responsibly" and submit to what was later described as the "orderly institutionalization of conflict." The piling up of administrative laws and judicial decisions based in the Wagner Act and other legislation, while guaranteeing labor's freedom of action in some directions, curtailed, directly or not, its freedom to act in many others. In the NLRB labor possessed a sharpened wedge to drive into the hitherto closed counsels of capital, but that wedge no less forcefully opened its own affairs to public scrutiny and governmental interference. Thus after a century's bitter, ardent struggle labor had demanded and obtained recognition of its rights from the newly responsive national government, but at the same time had bound itself by a thousand strings of dependence to that government.

TOWARD AN

ECONOMIC BILL OF RIGHTS

WHILE THE NEW DEAL was being both supported and pressured by labor, both utilized and derided by the left, American conservatism was mobilizing its full strength against the administration, with the Liberty League as vanguard. At the core of the League's ideology lay a narrow conception of liberty, a liberty that, with its aspects of individual self-reliance, of self-seeking ambition and effort, possessed a strong Social Darwinian cast. Life was a "root, hog, or die" competition, just as William Graham Sumner had preached. Many of the League's leaders, among them three du Pont brothers, were heirs to great wealth and had never had to root, but they might contend that their forebears had. Theirs was the kind of individualism, often brutal and selfish, that Herbert Hoover had rejected, and it was significant that the ex-president, in his California exile, kept his distance from the League.

Even to some members of the League, however, individualism of this stripe appeared a slender foundation on which to mount an attack on New Dealism and radicalism. Stripped of its philosophical finery, their naked individualism cut a poor figure alongside the more generous, compassionate, fraternal visions of the 1930s. Moreover, it sounded hollowly on the lips of men who ran huge corporate empires that closely regulated the lives of tens of thousands of employees, both white- and blue-collar. And so the League also talked in terms of rights.

But what kind of rights? Here again the bareness of its ends was proven. The more that League publicists spoke out, the more it became clear that rights to them meant property rights, that it all came down to holdings: the great purpose of individual liberty was the free acquisition and use of property, and that free acquisition and use was to be protected against government and other interference by property rights. Indeed, the founders of the League had thought at first of calling their organization the "Committee for the Integrity of Property," or "Association Asserting the Rights of Property," or simply "National Property League," before they concluded that "Liberty" had more political sex appeal.

If at heart the League grounded liberty in property rights, it automatically excluded from its concern the vast numbers of Americans who had little property or none. Some liberals seized on this chink in the League's ideological armor. Arthur Garfield Hays, general counsel of the American Civil Liberties Union, sent the League nine questions asking how far it was prepared to go in protecting the civil liberties of liberals and radicals. There appeared few names among League members, Hays wrote, "who have been conspicuous in fighting for the rights of individuals, particularly workers." The League did not deign to reply.

The League in any event was far more intent on wielding the polemical and political bludgeon against specific aspects of the New Deal than philosophizing abstractly about rights. A sizable staff churned out scores of pamphlets, distributed by the hundreds of thousands across the country, with titles like "Constitutional Heresy," "Americanism at the Crossroads," "Professors and the New Deal," "The New Inquisition," "You Owe Thirty-One Billion Dollars." For all the League's single-mindedness, some of these pamphlets managed to present serious arguments that won wide influence, especially in regard to the alleged unconstitutionality of some New Deal measures.

This kind of challenge brought out all the wiliness of the President, who had kept his eye on the Liberty League from its birth. When Jouett Shouse, the League's paid head, came to the White House as a courtesy to present its program, Roosevelt turned on his charm. "I can subscribe to that one hundred per cent and so can you," he said after listening intently to the platform. "I think it is fine." He even rang for his press secretary and told him to put out a statement that the President approved "most heartily" of the association's aims and purposes. But little more than a week later FDR was telling reporters that the League was like an organization founded to "uphold two of the Ten Commandments." While clamoring for the protection of private property it had nothing to say about helping the jobless and others in need, in the spirit of the commandment "Thou shalt love thy neighbor as thyself." The League, he concluded, was putting "too much stress on property rights, too little on human rights."

To the League, after FDR's seduction of Shouse, these remarks were a declaration of war. "All the big guns have started shooting," Roosevelt wrote happily to a friend. During 1935, as FDR embarked on his Second Hundred Days of liberal measures, the League redoubled its attacks on the administration. Having failed to elect anti–New Deal congressmen in the 1934 elections, the League and its conservative allies now pinned their hopes on 1936.

Roosevelt took the offensive in his State of the Union address to Congress early in January of that year. Before an exuberant chamber dominated by Democrats he castigated the "money-changers" who sought "the restoration of their selfish power." He went on: "They steal the livery of great national constitutional ideals to serve discredited special interests. As guardians and trustees for great groups of individual stockholders they wrongfully seek to carry the property and the interests entrusted to them into the arena of partisan politics. They . . . engage in vast propaganda to spread fear and discord among the people—they would 'gang up' against the people's liberties."

Anticipating such a presidential onslaught, the League had planned a mammoth dinner three weeks later at Washington's Mayflower Hotel to unleash its secret counterweapon—none other than Al Smith, erstwhile liberal governor of New York and Democratic presidential candidate, but now out of power, out of sorts, and out of patience with his onetime political protégé, who, he felt, was betraying the Jeffersonian ideals of the Democracy. Interest in the dinner ran so high that the Mayflower had to place tables in its main corridor to handle the overflow crowd of 2,000; 4,000 others were turned away.

Decked out in white tie and tails, Al did not disappoint his audience, which included a dozen du Ponts, a galaxy of other industrialists and financiers, and scores of dissident Democrats. He began sorrowfully. "It is not easy, it hurts me to criticize a Democratic Administration." But the New Deal, abandoning the Democratic Party platform of 1932, had set class against class and replaced government by law with government by bureaucracy and representative democracy with socialism. Smith had never been more sardonically humorous. "The young brain-trusters caught the Socialists in swimming and they ran away with their clothes." Then he came to his peroration, to the roars of the crowd:

"There can be only one capital, Washington or Moscow. There can be only the clear, pure, fresh air of free America, or the foul breath of communistic Russia. There can be only one flag, the Stars and Stripes, or the flag of the godless Union of the Soviets. There can be only one national anthem, The Star-Spangled Banner or the Internationale."

He leaned into the microphones and, "twisting his mouth in a snarling expression," warned that at the Democratic convention that summer he and his friends would "either take on the mantle of hypocrisy or we can take a walk, and we will probably do the latter."

THE LIBERTY LEAGUE battled with the New Deal through the summer and fall months of 1936, until the eve of the election. Al Smith did take a walk, but he failed to bring many Democrats over to the Republican candidate, Alf Landon. The campaign came to a raucous climax at New York's Madison Square Garden where Roosevelt declaimed that "government by organized money" was just as dangerous as "government by organized mob." His voice hardening, he went on: "Never before in all our history have these forces been so united against one candidate as they stand today. They are unanimous in their *hate* for *me—and I welcome their hatred.*"

The showdown that the Liberty League had pressed on the New Deal ended in a victory of historic dimensions for Roosevelt on election day. Yet it had been the League and its allies, far more than the divided Republican Party, that had converted the campaign into a national, if somewhat ambiguous, debate over the dimensions of liberty, the rights of people and property, and the implications of federal social and welfare policies. Had the League lost the electoral struggle but secured a place for its conception of rights in the enduring ideological battle?

The answer to this question was still uncertain following the election, because neither the Roosevelt New Dealers nor the Liberty League and GOP conservatives had clearly defined the issues. Once again American political leaders had shown a penchant for uttering general principles and values and at the same time making expedient day-to-day proposals and policies, with little linkage between the principled and the pragmatic. Thus both sides called for less or more governmental intervention in the society depending on how their own political or economic interests were affected, and regardless of the long-term impact of less or more intervention on people's rights and on the nation's strength and security.

Still a conspicuous exception to this tendency was Herbert Hoover. More than any other leader he gave the impression, as changes sweeping much of the world brought to power dictators in Europe and Asia and elsewhere, of a thinker earnestly puzzling through the nature of liberty and how to nurture it. "Who may define Liberty?" he had asked in his 1934 book, *The Challenge to Liberty.* "It is far more than Independence of a nation. It is not a catalogue of political 'rights.' " He then offered a catalogue of rights: "Liberty is a thing of the spirit—to be free to worship, to think, to hold opinions, and to speak without fear—free to challenge wrong and oppression with surety of justice. Liberty conceives that the mind and spirit of men can be free only if the individual is free to choose his own calling, to develop his talents, to win and to keep a home sacred from intrusion, to rear children in ordered security. It holds he must be free to earn, to spend, to save, to accumulate property that may give protection in old age and to loved ones."

Notable in this definition of liberty was its consistency with Hoover's earlier treatment in *American Individualism,* published over a decade before, in which he had urged that all must be given "an equality of opportunity" to thrive in freedom. Notable too was his contention in 1934 that liberty required an economic foundation: "these intellectual and spiritual freedoms cannot thrive except where there are also these economic freedoms." But, as before, Hoover was long and eloquent on broad concepts and short, virtually silent, on specifics, particularly those policies that might promote "equality" at the starting line and make the race itself open and equitable for all.

Making policy was precisely what Roosevelt was doing during his second term, as he offered a host of detailed proposals to Congress. As before, he acted to meet immediate needs without explaining his actions in terms of a coherent conceptual framework. The nation witnessed the curious spectacle of a president offering content without context and a former president offering context without content.

As FDR's conflict with the domestic opposition intensified during the late 1930s, however, and as Hitler challenged more and more aggressively the whole Western ideology of freedom and equality, the President began saving in his speech file ideas for what began to take shape in his mind as an economic bill of rights—ideas gathered from personal advisers, administration officials, newspapers, religious leaders. In July 1940, when Western Europe had fallen to the Nazis and as Roosevelt was contemplating a campaign for a third term, a reporter—primed perhaps to do so—asked him to spell out his goals for a postwar world. Thoughtfully the President itemized them: freedom of information, of religion, and of self-expression, and freedom from fear. Wasn't there another freedom, a reporter asked—freedom from want? Yes, he had forgotten it, FDR said.

Early in January 1941, two months after he secured his third term by beating Wendell Willkie, Roosevelt warned Congress that, with German domination of Europe and Japanese belligerence in the Pacific, American security had never been so seriously threatened, and, drawing on the words of Benjamin Franklin, he warned also against appeasement: "Those, who would give up essential liberty to purchase a little temporary safety, deserve neither liberty nor safety." Then he issued a presidential call for a world order founded upon the Four Freedoms:

"The first is freedom of speech and expression—everywhere in the world.

"The second is freedom of every person to worship God in his own way—everywhere in the world.

"The third is freedom from want—which, translated into world terms, means economic understandings which will secure to every nation a healthy peacetime life for its inhabitants—everywhere in the world.

"The fourth is freedom from fear—which, translated into world terms, means a world-wide reduction of armaments to such a point and in such a thorough fashion that no nation will be in a position to commit an act of physical aggression against any neighbor—anywhere in the world."

This was no vision of a distant millennium, the President added, but a "world attainable in our own time and generation."

In this address FDR offered some details, but as the nation headed toward war he did not wish to emphasize issues that might prove divisive at home. By January 1944, however, with the defeat of the Axis becoming more and more a matter of time, he was ready to present Congress and the nation with a full statement of both the old and his new Bill of Rights. After referring, as he had before, in his 1937 inaugural address, to the "one-third or one-fifth or one-tenth" of the nation "ill-fed, ill-clothed, ill-housed, and insecure," he went on with great deliberation and with heavy emphasis on certain words and phrases:

"This Republic had its beginning, and grew to its present strength, under the protection of certain *inalienable political* rights—among them the right of free speech, free press, free worship, trial by jury, freedom from unreasonable searches and seizures. *They* were our rights to life and liberty.

"As our Nation has grown in size and stature, however—as our industrial economy expanded—these political rights proved inadequate to assure us *equality in the pursuit of happiness.*

"We have come to a clear realization of the fact that *true* individual freedom can't exist without economic security and independence. 'Necessitous men are *not free* men.' People who are hungry—people who are out of a job—are the stuff of which dictatorships are made.

"In our day these economic truths have *become accepted as self-evident.* We have accepted, so to speak, a *second Bill of Rights* under which a new basis of security and prosperity can be established for all—regardless of station, race, or creed.

"Among these are:

"The right to a useful and remunerative *job* in the industries or shops or farms or mines of the Nation;

"The right to earn enough to provide adequate *food* and *clothing and recreation;*

"The right of farmers to raise and sell their products at a return which will give them and their family a decent living;

"The right of every *businessman,* large and small, to trade in an atmosphere of freedom from unfair competition and *domination* by *monopolies* at home or abroad;

"The right of *every family* to a decent *home;*

"The right to adequate *medical* care and the opportunity to *achieve* and *enjoy* good health;

"The right to adequate protection from the *economic* fears of old *age* and *sickness* and *accident* and *unemployment;*

"And finally, the right to a *good education.*"

In fifteen minutes Franklin Roosevelt had coupled the expansion of traditional civil liberties and protections to eight explicit social and economic freedoms. In these few minutes he had set the economic and social agenda for the Democratic Party and for American liberalism for at least the next half century.

ROOSEVELT'S eloquence and his prowess at the polls—even apart from the undeniable popular appeal of most New Deal programs—put Hoover and other moderate conservatives on the defensive during the 1930s. Even so, most on the right did not modify the simplistic argument American conservatives had been making for well over a century—the more government, the less liberty. They did, however, develop more specific ways of applying this argument to the effects of New Deal programs on people's personal lives and freedom of action. There were of course some hysterical charges—most extremely, that social security numbers would be hung around citizens' necks or even tattooed on their arms. But most conservatives—in Congress, in the newspapers, over the radio—simply kept up a steady drumbeat of criticism of every failure, every intemperate statement, every example of overreaching committed by New Dealers and their agencies.

The New Dealers' response to criticism on the issue of the relationship between government and liberty was only somewhat more original. On occasion they admitted to excesses that impaired people's liberty of action but they maintained that on the whole the impact of government's growth was marginal, even trivial, such as having to fill out more forms or wait in more lines. What conservatives called freedom, they insisted, was actually "antisocial license," the kind of liberty an automobile driver takes in running through a red light. "No civilized community ever existed without restraints," argued Joseph P. Kennedy, a businessman himself. It was wrong, said a New Deal assistant attorney general, to view economic restrictions as "interferences with personal freedom in its essential or spiritual sense." Restrictions in the economic realm were far less important than abridgments of religious freedom or freedom of speech. Besides, if the people disliked the restrictions, they could vote the government out. This argument, as James Holt has noted, "left unresolved the problems of individual and minority rights," since even " 'free and honest elections' did not preclude the possibility of tyranny by the majority."

Indeed, in one respect New Deal opponents did modernize their credo, contending that the Roosevelt administration had played havoc with the constitutional system of checks and balances—by creating an all-powerful presidency, fostering a supine Congress, undermining states' rights, ignoring due process—and hence raised the specter of individual rights crushed by majority tyranny exercised through government. The decisive rebuttal to this criticism came from the system itself—the President had been allowed to take emergency measures but courts ultimately checked his agencies; Congress did yield power at first but later reclaimed it—in some cases, with a vengeance; the Supreme Court invalidated key New Deal measures before "switching" in 1937; and states' rights were fiercely guarded by the Republican-Southern Democratic coalition on Capitol Hill.

So the New Dealers clung to their essential argument during the 1930s—not only that benign government intervention into economic and social areas was compatible with the maintenance of First Amendment liberties but that the expansion of economic and social freedoms, such as the right of workers to organize, even enhanced those liberties. The New Deal, they ultimately contended, was fighting for all the Four Freedoms, which were mutually enhancing. Yet New Dealers also advanced a different but related right—one that had deeper and more difficult implications—and on this issue the conservatives made a far stronger case.

The issue was the right to security. During 1934, as FDR was reviewing his first year in office and planning 1935 legislation, he returned more explicitly to a theme that had long concerned him—"security for the individual and for the family," in the form of good housing, a decent livelihood, protection against the "misfortunes which cannot be wholly eliminated in this man-made world of ours." Soon he was extending the concept to proper land use, "social insurance," employment security on the railroads. In 1935 he reiterated that his "first and continuing task" was "the security of the men, women and children of the Nation." In 1936, during his reelection campaign, he again and again made security a central theme.

Roosevelt's suggestion of a right to security opened up a huge and ill-defined area of promises on the part of the administration, and potential demands on the part of the public. It raised a host of questions—the nature of security, security for or against whom or what, and above all, in the ongoing clash of values and ends, what weight a right to security had in the scales against First Amendment and other rights. At the end of a fireside chat in 1934 FDR said: "I am not for a return to that definition of liberty under which for many years a free people were being gradually regimented into the service of the privileged few. I prefer and I am sure you prefer that broader definition of liberty under which we are moving forward to greater freedom, to greater security for the average man than he has ever known before in the history of America."

What did the President mean? Was he merely putting human needs before such narrow liberties as corporate property rights? Or was he suggesting that if a choice had to be made between traditional Bill of Rights liberties and economic and social rights, the provision of security to men and women devastated and demoralized by the Depression, he would choose the latter?

What responsible conservatives feared was that Roosevelt would make the wrong choices. The issue of security seemed to arouse their own worst fears, and they quickly converted FDR's idea of it into a cloak for statism, for the violation of individual rights, the invasion of personal privacy. They pointed to Germans, Italians, and Russians as having surrendered freedom in order to gain economic security—and ended up with neither. They pictured Americans as becoming overly dependent on paternalistic government, robbed of ambition and motivation, lazy beneficiaries of the expanding welfare state.

The passage of the Social Security Act in 1935 reflected both the political momentum of the New Deal and some of its intellectual strengths and ambiguities. The measure won powerful support in Congress and among the public, and it was the capstone of the Second Hundred Days of progressive legislation. While FDR, who was captivated by the proposals for "cradle-to-grave" economic and social insurance popular at the time in Europe as well as the United States, wanted a well-rounded program, he was also wary of trying to do too much at once. The bill dealt with several key areas of need: old age, unemployment, dependent children, public health. It was attacked on the left as far short of universal and comprehensive coverage, too dependent on the states for the definition of rights, and insufficiently redistributionist, and on the right as paternalistic and anti-individualistic.

Accustomed to being raked from both sides, the President was satisfied with the program as a good beginning. But the bill left open major questions about whether social security was merely a dole to meet practical needs of people or a fundamental right in an economic bill of rights.

During his second term Roosevelt downplayed security as a central right. Perhaps he feared that the "regimentation" charge, raised to a pitch by his conservative opponents in the 1936 election, would prove to be a more and more formidable argument as the New Deal expanded. Perhaps he saw that Americans preferred to think in terms of sets of orderly rights, rooted in tradition but also changing, and of priorities among these rights, rather than in terms of a seductive, never-ending, and possibly dangerous search for security.

When Roosevelt explicitly shifted roles from "Dr. New Deal" to "Dr. Win-the-War," some liberals feared that the hard-won economic rights of labor and farmers and others would be lost. But just as he had prepared for war during the New Deal, so he continued to fight for economic freedoms during the war. He was able to enact pieces of his great economic agenda because Congress passed his bills as bipartisan war measures. That agenda would have hard going under his successors in the absence of war consensus, as the checks and balances that Madison and others had built into the Constitution to protect individuals against governmental oppression were used by conservatives to block the realization of economic rights for lower-income Americans. Those conservatives, echoing the Liberty League, would protest that FDR's wartime measures, just as much as his New Deal programs, threatened individual security, especially property rights.

Roosevelt flatly disagreed, of course. But, looking abroad, he realized that personal security rights in the form of economic and social services, as well as rights to individual liberty including property, would grow less and less relevant—that the crucial need would soon become the common security of all, indeed the very survival of the nation.

CHAPTER NINE

HOT WAR, COLD WAR:
RIGHTS BESIEGED

AS FRANKLIN ROOSEVELT continued to talk about security during the late 1930s, he did so increasingly in a new context and with a significantly different meaning. The mounting Nazi menace was casting a shadow over the security of nations large and small. By April 1939 the Germans had completed their dismemberment of Czechoslovakia and were setting their sights on Poland. Benito Mussolini had sent troops to take Albania as a springboard for future operations against Yugoslavia and Greece. Like other Western democratic leaders, Roosevelt had stood by—sometimes taking two steps forward to condemn, then a step or two back or sidewise in helpless acquiescence—while the dictators advanced from target to target. The security of his nation and other threatened nations had now become his central preoccupation.

That same April, FDR fell victim to the cunning of Adolf Hitler. In a telegram, the President appealed personally to Hitler to assuage the fears of "hundreds of millions" who lived under constant danger of war. As "a friendly intermediary," he asked the Führer to give assurances that his army would not attack "the following independent nations," and he listed thirty-one countries within striking distance of the Wehrmacht. Embarrassing though such a public challenge to his plans was, Hitler saw an opening and pounced on it. First he demanded of the weaker cited nations whether they felt threatened by Germany; one by one they meekly declared they did not. Only Romania had the temerity to answer sharply that the "Reich Government were themselves in a position to know whether a threat might arise." Then Hitler called together the puppets of his Reichstag, and with their hoarse roars as backing, he gave a world-wide radio audience a stunning two-hour display of sarcasm and irony, brazen lies and hypocrisy. After comparing Germany's treatment by the victors at Versailles in 1919 to the "degradations" that white Americans had "inflicted on the chieftains of the Sioux tribes," Hitler read out the nations from FDR's list and reported their negative replies. The Reichstag rocked with laughter when the Führer went on to add a "solemn declaration" that rumors of Nazi plans to invade North or South America were "rank frauds and gross untruths," fruits of "a stupid imagination." And then he brought his performance to a close with a straight-faced appeal to the values "for which we are all concerned, namely, the justice, well-being, progress and peace of the whole community."

The President, scoffed isolationists in the United States, had been administered a deserved put-down for his meddling. Certainly he had received a lesson in international demagoguery. And within a year all the world received a series of lessons in sudden, naked, and unprovoked aggression, as Hitler's armies swept first through Poland, then, after a six-month "Sitzkrieg," into Scandinavia, through the Low Countries, and in June 1940 overran the north of France. Already, in his annual message to Congress in January 1940, FDR's tone had hardened. "What we face," he told the legislators, "is a set of world-wide forces of disintegration— vicious, ruthless, destructive of all the moral, religious and political standards which mankind, after centuries of struggle, has come to cherish most." Against this threat, Roosevelt said, the "most valuable asset" was national unity; unity was "the fundamental safeguard of all democracy" and essential to the "permanent security of America."

So the President's new priority in the new situation of world conflict was crystal clear—national security through national unity. While he continued to insist on the close link between national security and individual security, he was shifting with amazing dexterity and few backward looks from the champion of individual security to the defender of national security. Perhaps it was not wholly coincidental that only six months after FDR's speech, Felix Frankfurter, appointed to the Supreme Court the year before and speaking for the majority in the *Gobitis* case brought by a family of Jehovah's Witnesses, held that schoolchildren could be compelled to salute the flag even though their religious convictions prohibited the honoring of a secular symbol. "National unity is the basis of national security," Frankfurter declared.

The summons to national unity was the oldest, most persuasive call a leader could make to his people in times of danger. It invoked folk memories of peasants deserting their huts and flocking into walled towns and castles in the face of invading hordes. The ruler's first duty was the protection of his people, the maintenance of order, the safeguarding of the right to *life*.

But did the imperative of national unity mean the submergence or suppression of intellectual diversity, factional differences, unpopular thought and expression? Did it mean the submergence or suppression of minority rights, individual rights to freedom of speech and religion, of individual or group claims to social and economic security? Did it mean that assertions of individuality must be considered acts of selfishness, reflections of a lack of patriotism?

The exercise of the collective right to national security, in short, raised the most serious questions of the status of individual and minority rights, and by no means for the first time. There was little indication as the world crisis deepened, however, that much thought was being given in the White House to rights in wartime. Rather the Roosevelt administration would feel its way, in time-honored fashion.

"ARMS IN THE DEFENSE OF LIBERTY"

ON DECEMBER 15, 1941—one week after Pearl Harbor—President Roosevelt delivered a radio address commemorating the 150th anniversary of the ratification of the Bill of Rights.

"Free Americans," he began. "No date in the long history of freedom means more to liberty-loving men in all liberty-loving countries than the fifteenth day of December, 1791. On that day, 150 years ago, a new Nation, through an elected Congress, adopted a declaration of human rights which has influenced the thinking of all mankind from one end of the world to the other. . . .

"There is not a country, large or small, on this continent and in this world which has not felt the influence of that document, directly or indirectly. . . . "

Abruptly the President shifted to the menace to American liberties from the Axis, which, he said, was challenging Jefferson's "rights to life, liberty, and the pursuit of happiness" and challenging the individual's right "to a soul of his own, or a mind of his own, or a tongue of his own, or a trade of his own; or even to live where he pleases or to marry the woman he loves." Roosevelt concluded: "We covenant with each other before all the world, that having taken up arms in the defense of liberty, we will not lay them down before liberty is once again secure in the world we live in. For that security we pray; for that security we act—now and evermore."

With all three Axis powers having declared war on the United States in the past week, it was inevitable that on this anniversary of the Bill of Rights, the President would emphasize the threat to Americans from abroad and seal the renewed covenant with a prayer for their security. But he did not address threats to individual freedom from within a democracy at war. Lincoln's parable of the shepherd and his flock seemed as apt as ever. If the shepherd was intent on driving off the wolf, would the sheep's liberty be sacrificed for the sake of the collective security of the flock?

The shepherd had long been on guard. In August 1936 Roosevelt had met with J. Edgar Hoover, director of the Federal Bureau of Investigation, and secretly ordered him to monitor suspected fascist and Communist subversive activities. With the outbreak of war in Europe, and even more with the fall of France, the American public was treated to lurid stories from across the Atlantic of Nazi infiltrators who had weakened Hitler's targets from within and of the "fifth columnists" who had risen in aid of invading troops. Roosevelt gave Hoover more and more authority to investigate individuals and organizations; by 1940 the FBI, with its hundreds of agents, had become the central agency for combatting domestic subversion.

Nonetheless, while the President worked closely with the director, they had different agendas. Not unaware of Communist activity in the United States, FDR was far more concerned about the fascist threat. Hoover, though willing to investigate Axis infiltration, was relentlessly, then and ever after, fixated on the Red menace.

So was much of the public. Helping to fuel its fears was the House of Representatives Special Committee on Un-American Activities, chaired by Martin Dies. With scant regard for the constitutional rights of its targets, the committee named hundreds of persons it claimed were Communists or (far less often) Nazis, and used its power to harass New Dealers, radicals, and other leftists, as well as such "Communist-infested" New Deal agencies as the WPA arts project.

Much as he detested Dies and his whole publicity-seeking operation, Roosevelt was reluctant to battle him openly. Instead, late in November 1940, he invited Dies to the Oval Office and administered a scolding mixed with honeyed words. The President exhorted Dies not to pursue individuals or organizations when evidence of subversive activities was lacking; Dies should take care to protect the rights of the innocent. According to a White House transcript—Roosevelt was careful to have a stenographer present—the dialogue continued:

"I have in mind a man I know who works in an arsenal," FDR said; "he is a nice little man of 55. He has been a theoretical Socialist, he has been a theoretical Communist; he would not hurt—he would not kill a fly. He is the most inoffensive little man I know of. He would no more raise his hand against the Government of the United States—the most loyal person I know in this country. Now, I would not fire him. Why? Because I would trust him with my last dollar."

"But," said Dies, "if his record has been that of an agitator—"

Roosevelt interrupted: "That's a very different thing." The Communist Party, he went on, had polled no more than a few hundred thousand votes in 1936. "Now, I would not bar from patriotic defense efforts every one of those people who have voted for a Communist in 1936 or 1937-8-9 or 40. Neither would you."

"I would be suspicious of them," Dies replied.

"Oh, I would check them—absolutely," FDR said, but the mere fact that they had voted Communist did not mean they were disloyal.

It was a rare glimpse of an exchange at the highest level between a dedicated pragmatist and an anti-Communist ideologue. FDR as usual was mediating among factions and interests, balancing pressures, and manipulating rival leaders; his grants of authority to the FBI had also had the purpose of taking the sting out of Dies's charges against the administration. But operating in an increasingly charged atmosphere where fears of Communists and fears of fascists were blurring—especially after Hitler's August 1939 nonaggression pact with Stalin—Roosevelt's freedom for opportunistic action was becoming more and more limited. And expediency had its price.

It was during the rapprochement between Berlin and Moscow, indeed, that Congress put into law the "most drastic restrictions on freedom of speech ever enacted in the United States during peace," in the judgment of Zechariah Chafee, Jr. An alien registration bill introduced in 1939 by Congressman Howard Smith—the same Virginia Democrat who had investigated the National Labor Relations Board with such zeal—had been amended to include a separate sedition measure that would make it a crime to "advocate, abet, advise, or teach the duty, necessity, desirability, or propriety" of overthrowing the government by force or violence, or to encourage "insubordination, disloyalty, mutiny, or refusal of duty" in the armed forces. When Congress passed the Smith Act in June 1940, Roosevelt refused to veto the bill, maintaining that its advocacy restrictions could "hardly be considered to constitute an improper encroachment on civil liberties in the light of present world conditions."

So once again was posed the ancient American dilemma, harking back to the Alien and Sedition laws of the late 1790s and to their World War I successors—how to balance individual civil liberties against the collective right to national security, now in another time of crisis, although—and this was almost as disturbing to some civil libertarians as the substance of the Smith Act—it had become law at a time when the United States was not yet at war. The question would be the manner of applying the act—and Roosevelt soon made clear what he had had in prospect when he approved it.

During his battles with domestic isolationists while war raged in Europe and the White House maneuvered to send aid to anti-Nazi forces, FDR was particularly incensed by denunciations of himself, of Eleanor Roosevelt, of the preparedness effort, and of the "Jew Deal" by an assortment of men and women he viewed simply as fascists. After Pearl Harbor, in the spring of 1942, with the Germans deep into Russia and the Japanese moving from conquest to conquest in the Pacific, the President made no effort to conceal his avid desire to bring his foes—whom he now considered seditionists—to book. Francis Biddle, his attorney general, noted that FDR was not much interested in abstractions about the right to criticize the government in wartime—he wanted the "anti-war talk" stopped.

Week after week at cabinet meetings, when it came Biddle's turn to report, Roosevelt with tightened face demanded, "When are you going to indict the seditionists?" It was the only time, Biddle remembered later, that the President had pressured him for a decision. In midsummer 1942, twenty-six "native Fascists" were charged with conspiracy to violate the 1917 Espionage Act and the sedition provisions of the Smith Act, specifically those of the latter that outlawed efforts to subvert the morale of the armed forces.

Granted that those indicted included some of the most odious bigots and racists in the country—people like William Dudley Pelley, founder of the Silver Shirts Legion of America, who advocated registering "all persons of Hebrew blood or extraction under penalty of confiscation of their goods"; Frank W. Clark of the National Liberty Party, who went even further by pledging that when the "masses wake up," all Jews would "be buried here"—killed, he proposed, with good American baseball bats; and Elizabeth Dilling, publisher of *The Red Network,* which listed some of the nation's leading liberals as "reds" or, in the case of former Chief Justice Charles Evans Hughes, "pink." Oliver Wendell Holmes had defended "freedom for the thought we hate," and these "native Fascists" were touching the outer limits of hateful thought and doing so in accents akin to those of the Nazi enemy.

Still, as constitutional scholar Edward S. Corwin of Princeton argued a few years later, it was by no means evident that the defendants had conspired with one another or with the Germans to impair military loyalty or morale; it appeared they had acted, and not in concert, for the more general purpose of poisoning the well of public opinion. "That any federal court," Corwin wrote, "should have consented to try anybody under an indictment so utterly lacking in specifications touching the *when,* the *where,* and the *how* of the *essential charge* against him—in this instance the charge of conspiracy—is really amazing."

As it turned out, the trial of the "seditionists," when at last it began almost two years after the original indictments, was a fiasco. Nearly forty attorneys, representing the final roundup of twenty-seven men and two women, made the court into a bedlam as they jumped to their feet in relays or in unison to shout every conceivable objection; the judge fined the obstreperous lawyers again and again without regaining control of his courtroom; the proceedings ended with a mistrial in December 1944 on the death of the exhausted judge. With the war in Europe nearing its close, the government gave up.

HISTORICALLY, Americans most vulnerable to the denial of their rights in peacetime also fare the worst in war. Rallying cries of "one united nation," of "common sacrifice," of "we're all in it," seem not to extend to those marked in some way by "difference," as though they are not part of the common weal. Among the most threatened have been "enemy aliens," presumed to heed the cries, not of the American government, but of their national regimes. The Smith Act required the registration and fingerprinting of the three and a half million aliens living in the country—a process that the President believed necessary to tighten security by extending immigration controls but that caused a stir of alarm among those concerned with the uses government might make of such information. In signing the bill FDR had reassured critics that most aliens were loyal and would not be harassed. Indeed, Roosevelt and Biddle expected that the law would discourage state and local government measures against aliens and damp vigilantism and demands for deportation. Still, the President's decision to move the Immigration and Naturalization Service out of the Labor Department to Justice brought aliens that much closer to the police power and to the FBI.

The rights of conscientious objection were taken into account by a provision of the 1940 Selective Service Act that exempted from duty as a combatant anyone who "by reason of religious training and belief, is conscientiously opposed to participation in war in any form." Persons gaining CO status from local draft boards could be assigned noncombatant duties, or if they refused military service of any kind, "work of national importance under civilian direction." But what did "religious training and belief" mean? Could opposition to war as an ethical choice, an act of conscience without reference to theology, qualify? Early rulings by officials and courts interpreted the provision liberally, but in March

1942, the director of the Selective Service System, Lewis B. Hershey, sharply narrowed the grounds with his declaration that religious belief "contemplates recognition of some source of all existence, which, whatever the type of conception, is Divine because it is the Source of all things." This, combined with the "wildly disparate standards" of local draft boards, contributed to confusion and ill feeling on the part of both objectors and the public.

Some 25,000 objectors chose noncombatant roles in the military, while another 12,000 who refused all military service were sent to civilian camps, where they built roads, cleared trails, dug irrigation ditches, worked in mental hospitals. They were paid nothing for this menial work which in some cases appeared to contribute to the war effort. To Norman Thomas, "for the government to require unrequited service smacks of slavery to the state and is a bad precedent in these times." Even so, COs in past wars had suffered persecution or imprisonment, and the relative comfort of their "enslavement" weighed on the consciences of objectors. "Precisely because the system, for all its shortcomings, conferred privileges upon conscientious objectors," notes Richard Polenberg, "it diluted the purity of their witness against war." Several thousand men— many of them Jehovah's Witnesses—avoided this conflict of conscience by refusing to register for the draft or persisting in their objection when draft boards denied them CO status and then sitting out the war in jail.

African-Americans had never been dealt fully into the New Deal and had gained little from the expansion of rights in the 1930s. Roosevelt's deference to Southern power in Congress and in the electoral college and black political and economic weakness had denied them a distinct and effective voice in the harmony of interests. By the spring of 1941, however, pressed by black leaders, some union heads, and—not least—Eleanor Roosevelt, and aware of the potential contribution of black labor to the defense effort, the President was considering the abolition of discrimination in defense agencies and industries by executive order. When A. Philip Randolph, president of the Brotherhood of Sleeping Car Porters, Walter White of the National Association for the Advancement of Colored People, and other black leaders insisted on an antidiscrimination program with teeth, Roosevelt hesitated. The sharpness of black demands inflamed not only his political sensitivities but also the paternalism that streaked his compassion for African-Americans.

And when Randolph threatened a march on Washington, FDR appealed to him through his wife. She feared, Eleanor Roosevelt wrote Randolph, that the march would "set back the progress which is being made, in the Army at least, towards better opportunities and less segregation." It might harden opposition in Congress and outside. Still flatly

opposed to the march, the President deployed every weapon in his arsenal of charm and importunity to discourage it.

In vain—the black leaders would not budge. Only at the last minute,
when negotiations had produced the draft of an executive order, did they
cancel the march. But the order issued by Roosevelt in June 1941 proved
little more than a statement of policy. Defense contracts were to include
provisions against discrimination; government agencies that oversaw vocational and training programs for the defense effort were instructed to
ensure that their procedures were nondiscriminatory. A Committee on
Fair Employment Practices was established to enforce the order, but
without any real policing power or significant funds and without much
personal backing from FDR, it promptly fell victim to foes and foot-
draggers in government and industry. Training and jobs were caught in
a vicious circle that the executive order did not begin to break: employers
turned African-Americans away on the grounds that they lacked training;
training classes would not have them because of an alleged lack of jobs.

Paradoxically, many blacks were better off materially in the army. By
the spring of 1942 about 10 percent of Selective Service registrants were
black; several hundred black aviation cadets would soon be in training;
and over three hundred black officers—including three colonels—shared
in the command of five black combat units. Thousands of African-
American soldiers were receiving better food, shelter, and health care
than they had known in civilian life. But the army was still segregated and
would remain substantially so for the duration, except when black troops
served under white officers, and, apart from messmen, the navy was
virtually lily white. And no black serviceman could ignore what was going
on back home:

"I am a corporal in the U.S. Army," one wrote to the commander in
chief. "I am a Negro with an American heart, and have been doing my
duties as an American soldier. I consider myself as one of the best. I have
never had a punishment. I have been awarded the 'Good Conduct Medal,'
good driving medal, and sharpshooting with a 30–30 rifle and carbine,
and a key man with a 50 calibre machine gun.

"I was sent some papers from the states a few days ago. And I read
where colored people in my home, New Iberia, La., were being beaten
up and chased out of town." One was his sister's husband. "They are
being beaten up because they succeeded in getting a welding school
for the colored, so they could build the tanks and ships we need so
badly. . . .

"I thought we were fighting to make this world a better place to live
in." He was giving the cause all he had, and would die for it if necessary,
"but I think my people should be protected. . . ."

F E W I N T H E D A Y S before Pearl Harbor would have guessed that any substantial group of Americans were more vulnerable to the cruelties of discrimination than blacks. But they would have guessed wrong, not anticipating the impact of war on the lives of another people of "difference," Japanese-Americans. Especially in the Far West, where they were concentrated, they were among the poorer and least organized Americans. Race bias and abuse had shadowed them since their first arrival in the United States. Hence they were in no position to protect themselves against the fears and furies of their fellow Americans when the Japanese military struck at the base in Hawaii and extended its attack throughout the Pacific.

The story has long been told—usually in tones of chagrin or penitence—of what Edward Corwin would describe as "the most drastic invasion of the rights of citizens of the United States by their own government." The events of early 1942 took on a remorseless quality: a few weeks of relative calm as the government detained German, Italian, and Japanese aliens alike on a selective basis and hearing boards were established to decide which would be released and which interned, while the press cautioned that the excesses of the last war should not be repeated; then a shift in the climate of opinion, especially in California, as the apparent threat of a Japanese attack on the coast bred wild rumors of its imminence, of lights flashed as signals to offshore planes and ships, of strange and unaccountable noises in the darkness, and all the other delusions that accompanied the onset of hysteria; finally long-smoldering feelings against Japanese-Americans burst into flames of hatred, now unresisted by politicians or press, or by a military that had at first held evacuation unnecessary but yielded to passions on the coast and to unrelenting pressure in Washington from Western congressional delegations.

Over a hundred thousand "persons of Japanese ancestry," two-thirds of them American citizens, were routed out of their homes, tagged like checked parcels, and dispatched to assembly centers, where they were kept for months in converted stockyards or fairgrounds ringed by guards and searchlights. Loaded onto trains, they were shipped, with blinds drawn, to camps located in remote deserts and flatlands, where families lived in crowded barracks and old and young alike used communal showers and toilets. Comprising a new class of money-poor—a class that was a direct creation of the government—they dug irrigation canals or grew vegetables or cleared sagebrush for $8 to $16 a month.

Eventually Americans would learn that in the eyes of decision-makers at the time there had been little military justification for such drastic action, and in retrospect none whatever. In Hawaii, where after Pearl

Harbor an American government imposed martial law for the first time since the Civil War and where the danger of renewed Japanese attacks was far more real, several hundred Japanese-Americans were detained, several thousand more were questioned by loyalty boards, and aliens among them were asked to move if they lived near military bases. But the Japanese-American population of 160,000—a third of the territory's total—was otherwise unmolested; there were no calls for mass evacuation. At the heart of the West Coast relocation was pure racial feeling. In a governmental system whose elaborate checks and balances were designed to safeguard individual and group liberties, how could this have happened? What persons, what institutions, had failed in the breach?

Did the President, who only a few months earlier had rededicated the nation to the defense of the Bill of Rights, stand as a bulwark against this wholesale violation of it? Untypically, FDR played a relatively passive role. He allowed the military to develop an evacuation plan and, presented with an executive order authorizing the action, he signed it without formal cabinet discussion or, evidently, White House staff consideration. He supplemented this order with others, and "personally directed" that the termination of the program "be delayed until after the presidential election of 1944." Roosevelt had no illusions about what he was doing and bandied no euphemisms about "wartime communities"; he was among the first to call them concentration camps. Once again he was putting national security, or at least the politics of national security, far ahead of individual liberty.

The Justice Department? Attorney General Biddle was a stalwart civil libertarian and had reservations about the evacuation. Somewhat troubled by FDR's disregard for the implications of the program—he summarized the President's attitude as "What must be done to defend the country must be done"—but much impressed by War Secretary Henry Stimson's support for it as an unfortunate military necessity, Biddle did not try to enlist Interior Secretary Harold Ickes or other high officials who might have been willing to press alternatives on Roosevelt.

Congress? Not only the West Coast delegations but a host of other senators and representatives pressed the administration to act, and complained of delays. The congressional authorization—coming a month after Roosevelt's order and when the military had all but completed its plans to implement it—passed both chambers without a roll call. Debate in the House was so brief as to occupy less than one page of the *Congressional Record.* When a Republican congressman expressed dismay that the "rights of citizens" were receiving such short shrift, he was reminded of the "extremely urgent" situation and he subsided. After-the-fact approval in an atmosphere of unreason, without debate, in herdlike unanimity—Congress for the moment offered little contrast to Hitler's Reichstag.

The press? Outside left-wing newspapers, editors and commentators lined up behind the administration. Walter Lippmann, so concerned about liberty against government back in his anti–New Deal days, declared the entire Pacific coast a combat zone and brushed off objections to evacuation with the argument that "nobody's constitutional rights include the right to do business on a battlefield"—a well-turned phrase that shed absolutely no light on the issue. Citing Lippmann's view, columnist Westbrook Pegler demanded that every Japanese in California be put under guard, "and to hell with habeas corpus until the danger is over."

Civil libertarians? A few tried to stem the immense tide. While its national board cautiously affirmed the legality of the President's order, the American Civil Liberties Union opposed the racism its execution reflected, as well as many specific aspects of its implementation, and supported its victims in the courts. The League for Industrial Democracy, California units of the ACLU and of the American Friends Service Committee, and a range of religious leaders took stands against evacuation and its brutalities. But the protests were scattered and too moderate in tone to compete with the roar of approval from across the country.

The Supreme Court? This great final barrier against governmental usurpation had failed before to protect the rights and liberties of Americans, particularly in wartime, and now it failed again. Unwilling to confront the broadest implications of its holdings on the presidential war power, the Court chose to act on the narrower aspects of the cases it reviewed. When Gordon Hirabayashi was arrested for failing to report to undergo exclusion and for violating a military curfew, the high court ducked the issue of the exclusion's constitutionality and dealt only with the second matter, sustaining the curfew. When Fred Korematsu likewise disobeyed an exclusion order, the Court this time upheld the legitimacy of the order before it but simply ignored the wider issue of forced detention in relocation centers.

Three justices—Robert Jackson, Frank Murphy, and Owen Roberts—dissented in *Korematsu*, with Roberts denouncing exclusion as "a clear violation of Constitutional rights" and Jackson writing that the Court was distorting the Constitution "to approve all that the military may deem expedient." But the majority took the path of least resistance, deferring to what Chief Justice Harlan Fiske Stone had called in his *Hirabayashi* opinion "the war-making branches of the Government," which themselves had taken the path of least resistance, as Stone admitted, in displacing an entire population when the "number and strength" of its "disloyal members . . . could not be precisely and quickly ascertained."

Silent enim leges inter arma: Laws are silent in war. During World War II some laws like the draft act and the order for Japanese-American reloca- tion spoke very loudly—they practically shouted—while the great body of legislation built up over the years to guard individual liberty was quiet, even silent. As one looks back—and it was apparent to some at the time—a striking aspect of the violations of the Bill of Rights was how gratuitous they so often were, how often they missed their mark, the real enemy. That enemy, the Axis, had launched the deadliest assault on human rights the world had ever known. That assault required full atten- tion, but often the laws and the prosecutions were turned against the most harmless and helpless elements at home—Japanese-Americans, African-Americans, draft resisters. The one sustained effort against an internal "enemy"—the so-called seditionists—was wrong in principle and an absurdity in outcome. As World War II demonstrated once again, in times of crisis the rights of the vulnerable were too easily bent or broken by the iron law of "military necessity."

THE PURSUIT OF NATIONAL SECURITY

DURING WORLD WAR II, and for some years after, many observers maintained that Americans and their government, having learned from their failures in World War I, on the whole protected individual liberty far more successfully than in the earlier effort to make the world safe for democracy. A favorite example was press censorship. Relying heavily on self-censorship, especially in the area of military secrets such as ship departures and troop movements, the Roosevelt administration banned few publications outright. A half century later the Japanese-American internment was criticized as universally as earlier it had been almost unanimously acclaimed, but relocation was considered an aberration, the product of irresistible racial forces.

But by then, the Roosevelt government's trespasses on rights had come to be viewed far less benignly, even apart from the relocation episode. Historians had made discoveries that cast a light on official policies and actions even more disturbing—because more insidious and for prece- dents they set—than the excesses of World War I. A central set of revela- tions concerned the mutually supportive relationship of FDR and FBI director Hoover. As the source of Hoover's expanding power, Roosevelt was cultivated carefully, fed savory morsels of political and personal information the Bureau collected. Many of these were unsolicited, but the President asked for reports on the activities of his foreign policy critics, especially the isolationists opposing his interventionist maneuvers.

Not long after he dropped isolationist Joseph Kennedy as ambassador to Britain, FDR told Hoover that it was a "pious idea to put one of your men at Palm Beach," where Kennedy owned a home. Roosevelt and the FBI later extended the campaign to Kennedy's son. When Ensign John Kennedy had an affair with Inga Arvad, a newspaperwoman suspected of pro-Nazi attitudes and connections, the FBI wiretapped her apartment, photocopied her papers, and bugged two of her weekend trysts with Kennedy. Even after the Bureau uncovered no evidence of espionage and ended the investigation Roosevelt asked that it be reopened and Arvad "specially watched." In July 1940 FDR, concerned that his predecessor might obtain information to use against him in the presidential campaign, suggested that the FBI look into rumors that Herbert Hoover was in contact with the French politician Pierre Laval; the Bureau found nothing. The next year Roosevelt had the FBI try to break up an embarrassing affair between his cousin Kermit and a masseuse. At times, then, FDR used the Bureau as his personal investigative agency—blurring the line, historian Richard M. Fried wrote, "between national security and his own political well-being"—and this served as a precedent for his successors.

Despite his Missourian distrust of the FBI, Harry Truman continued FDR's practice of using—and being used by—the Bureau and its chief. Hoover sent a steady stream of intelligence to the White House, ranging from such spectacular and breathlessly reported discoveries as the Communist Party's "plans" to "stir up among the rank and file of the workers of the country a feeling of revolt" against Truman's labor policies to such mundane items as an old Roosevelt aide's telephone talk—but including information about real or suspected political foes. In 1948, when Truman faced a threat to his tenure in office both from some liberals and laborites hoping to draft Dwight Eisenhower for the Democratic nomination and from a left-wing third-party bid, Hoover demonstrated an extraordinary capacity to penetrate the private conversations of those the President suspected of plotting against him. He provided a wealth of details on organizations too, among them the Federation of Atomic Scientists, the National Council of Arts, Sciences, and Professions, the NAACP, and the National Lawyers Guild.

Republican president Dwight Eisenhower, despite his careful image of high-minded abstention from partisan politics, was no less enmeshed with the Bureau than his Democratic predecessors had been, nor any less willing to use it for political advantage. On one matter, indeed, Eisenhower made a concession the Truman administration had not been willing to make—explicit permission to install a wiretap even when that involved "a trespass under existing law," in short, a break-in. Of course, the FBI had been doing just this for many years, with varying shades of approval—or at least no outright ban—from two administrations, but

Hoover, when conducting activities that touched the borders of, or plunged forthrightly into, illegality, was always eager to obtain formal authorization from his superiors and so insulate himself from repercussions should those activities become a public issue. In this case, capitalizing on what historian Athan Theoharis called the "ignorance and anticommunism" of the new administration, the Bureau won from Eisenhower's Justice Department a "less restrictive" interpretation of the Fourth Amendment, the holding that a break-in to plant a microphone was not an illegal search and seizure, and a little later Hoover also gained approval for the "broadened" use of wiretaps.

During the Eisenhower years the FBI continued to gather "political intelligence," reporting on the political and social contacts of such notables as Supreme Court justice William Douglas, financier and politico Bernard Baruch, and even a deputy assistant to Eisenhower himself. Hoover sent over to the White House files on Norman Thomas, Linus Pauling, Bertrand Russell, and ten others who were suing to stop nuclear testing. The Bureau advised the administration on the activities of the growing civil rights movement, which to the FBI mind was little more than another Communist front. With fine impartiality, but with equal disdain for the rights of political militants, Hoover also transmitted findings on the right-wing demagogue Gerald L. K. Smith and his Christian Nationalist Crusade and on the "scurrilous attacks" of the John Birch Society on Eisenhower and other government officials.

Eleanor Roosevelt's eminence as former First Lady did not preserve her from the FBI's unwanted attentions. Reports were duly filed, for instance, on her plans to hold a reception for the head of a civil rights organization. She could hardly have been surprised; she had not been protected against the Bureau even during her husband's tenure. Early in 1942 the FBI had broken into the offices of the American Youth Congress and photocopied her lengthy correspondence with AYC leaders. Later that year FBI officials reported that "Eleanor Roosevelt Clubs" had formed to encourage black maids in the South to demand better terms of work under the slogan of "A White Woman in the Kitchen by Christmas." The clubs proved to be mere phantoms, the inspirations not of Eleanor Roosevelt but of the fevered imaginations of Southern segregationists.

During these war and postwar years the FBI expanded in size and scope. The number of microphones installed by the Bureau doubled between 1953 and 1955. And by late 1954, the FBI had over 26,000 individuals listed in its "Security Index"—all of whom were to be "detained" in the event of a "national emergency." As late as 1959, the FBI's New York field office alone had more than four hundred agents assigned to "Communism," while only four were detailed to investigate organized crime. The agency had penetrated deeply into the media and thus into the popular mind by exploiting its famous encounters with criminals and constructing an image of infallibility, of utter uprightness in its own ranks and unceasing vigilance against the machinations of the other side—in short, the quintessence of "Americanism."

While the FBI itself operated in almost total secrecy, it had lines into virtually every major institution of American public life. The Bureau's relations with Congress and its committees were complex, but immensely profitable, as it shared or traded intelligence with members, all the while stuffing its files with information—from the rankest sexual gossip to serious, if largely unsupported, allegations—on the activities of legislators. Every year at appropriations time, Congress handed Hoover enlarged budgets and new grants of authority.

American leaders, Democratic or Republican, understood there must be limits to the reach of a federal bureau of investigation. They feared the independent power base Hoover was building within the Justice Department. But it was so easy—so politically safe, so easy to rationalize in terms of the national security—to deal with Hoover, to make little concessions and trade-offs, to turn a blind eye, to be pragmatic. It was not so easy to comprehend that the FBI was but the spearhead of a much larger structure of national security attitudes, laws, institutions—and with the spear aimed often at the innocent as well as the guilty.

H O W E V E R G R A V E the violations of rights during World War II, the violators could point to one towering fact—the dire threat to national security, and hence to the individual security that hung on national security, from Nazi and Japanese aggression. That threat was not illusory or manufactured or, usually, much exaggerated.

Granting the peril, civil libertarians might have expected that after the war Americans would reclaim the fullness of their traditional liberties under the Bill of Rights. Any such expectations soon were crushed. The years following World War II brought the most comprehensive assaults on liberty the nation had witnessed since the late 1790s. The postwar era would come to be called the Age of McCarthy. Not only did this label overstate the role of one man, Republican senator Joseph McCarthy of Wisconsin; it obscured the fact that for five years after the German surrender McCarthy himself had no part in "McCarthyism," that other notables started the charge for national security at all costs, including the sacrifice of Bill of Rights liberties, and that a leader of those activists was the president of the United States, Harry S Truman.

In the Cold War atmosphere that quickly enveloped Washington after

World War II, Truman was first off the mark in fortifying the internal front of the national security crusade against the erstwhile partner-in-arms, the Soviet Union. He was just completing his second year in office when, on March 21, 1947, he ordered the investigation for "disloyalty" of all government employees and all applicants for federal jobs. The criteria for a judgment of "disloyalty" under his executive order included such obvious threats as sabotage, treason, and the like, but also such vague standards as acting "so as to serve the interests of another government in preference to" American interests, and "membership in, affiliation with or sympathetic association with any foreign or domestic organization" designated by the attorney general as "totalitarian, fascist, communist, or subversive." With Japan and Germany in ruins, no one could mistake the identity of "another government."

Soon loyalty boards in the State Department and other agencies were busily investigating thousands of federal employees, with the eager help of the FBI. Given the looseness of the "disloyalty" criteria and the temper of the times, abuse of individual rights was inevitable despite Truman's stated desire to protect innocent employees. Freedom of association appeared to be in direct danger, for within one year of the executive order the attorney general's list contained over 150 "subversive" organizations, more than two-thirds of which were labeled "Communist" or "Communist-front." Loyalty investigations produced predictable absurdities; employees were asked their opinions of marriage or religion or race relations or the House Committee on Un-American Activities. One was asked if he read *The New Republic* or books about the Soviet government, another what he thought of "female chastity."

For the employees involved, such questions were more a source of alarm than of mirth. Not only did these interrogations trespass on employees' freedoms of opinion, speech, and association, not only did the employees themselves bear the effective burden of proving affirmatively something so nebulous as their "loyalty," but they appeared before the inquisitors stripped of the most basic procedural safeguards. Rarely did they receive a full accounting of the allegations laid against them, rarely were they told the source of those allegations—whether office gossip or a malicious neighbor or someone who had once heard something about someone from someone else and had reported it to the FBI—and still more rarely—indeed never—were they permitted to confront their accusers. Often they were not even given the names of the suspect individuals and groups with whom they had allegedly associated. In the absence of anything that would enable employees to answer the charges against them, they were invited, as one investigator said, to "think back over your own career and perhaps in your own mind delve into some of the factors that have gone into your career which you think might have been subject to question and see what they are and see whether you'd like to explain or make any statement with regard to any of them."

Despite procedures so hostile to employees' rights, the results of the loyalty program in unearthing "subversives" were minuscule. Three years after Truman's order, the chairman of the Loyalty Review Board, a stalwart Republican named Seth Richardson, testified that his board, which had jurisdiction over the departmental boards, had approved 182 dismissals in all executive departments but had reinstated 124 other employees whom departmental boards had wrongly judged disloyal or suspect. His testimony indicated that after 10,000 full field investigations the FBI had discovered not a single case of espionage in any federal department and that the loyalty program's "unfitness tests"—standards of suitability for government work that went beyond loyalty to alcoholism, homosexuality, and other personal behaviors that might create a "security risk"—had produced adverse conclusions on less than one twentieth of 1 percent of federal jobholders.

These meager findings did not disturb or surprise some supporters of the loyalty program in the Truman administration. The program's main purpose, they insisted, had been to deflect Congress from taking actions much more dangerous to First Amendment rights. How successful was this effort to take the wind out of congressional sails?

While Congress for a time allowed the White House to carry the heaviest load in ferreting out the disloyal, its members played the anti-Communist angle for all its political worth and congressional committees presented pageants of repentance and accusation. The House Committee on Un-American Activities, after a brief wartime eclipse and the loss of Chairman Dies to retirement in 1944, retook center stage with spectacular forays into Hollywood, where HUAC's cast of "friendly" witnesses included Gary Cooper, Walt Disney, veteran character actor Adolphe Menjou, Ronald Reagan, and the mother of Ginger Rogers. HUAC's relentless scrutiny of Hollywood's performers and products for traces of Communist influence led to the creation of an industry blacklist that would make it impossible for hundreds of actors, directors, and writers, among them sixty or seventy of HUAC's "unfriendly" witnesses, to find work in films. HUAC served also as a public confessional for a very different cast—ex-Communists, whose penitence involved painting the dimensions of their old party's threat to internal security in the most lurid colors and naming all those with whom they had associated in their previous lives; and each name, before denial or rebuttal could be made, was duly entered into HUAC's thickening ledger and printed on the front pages of newspapers.

Truman's loyalty program merely fed the atmosphere of fear and suspicion, and when it failed to produce satisfying results, Congress picked up the reins of repression. A series of events beginning in the fall of 1949 gave legislators their head. In September came the shocking news that the Soviets had detonated their first atomic bomb, ending the United States' nuclear monopoly years before the American public had expected and raising to a certainty suspicions that Soviet agents had stolen the bomb's "secrets." Late in January of the following year Alger Hiss was convicted of perjury. Hiss, a New Dealer who had served in Roosevelt's Agriculture and State departments, had been accused in 1948 by one of HUAC's ex-Communists, Whittaker Chambers, of passing State Department documents to the Soviets a decade before, and Hiss's denial of the allegations had led to the perjury indictment. To many congressional Republicans, the Hiss case was final proof that the New Deal—to which, they would not fail to note, the incumbent administration was heir—had been little more than a Communist front.

A week after Hiss's conviction, newspapers bannered reports that a German-born scientist, Klaus Fuchs, had confessed to spying for the Soviets while working on the American atomic bomb project at Los Alamos. Over the next six months, nine Americans were arrested as members of the "Fuchs spy ring," including Ethel and Julius Rosenberg, who would become the first civilians executed by the United States for espionage. The week after Fuchs's confession was announced, a hitherto obscure senator from Wisconsin stood up before a Lincoln Day crowd in Wheeling, West Virginia, and declared he had hard evidence—"here in my hand"—that 205 known Communists were working in Truman's State Department, triggering a tumult of denials, countercharges, and fresh accusations.

One last event, and that the most dramatic, followed in June 1950—Soviet-backed North Korea's sudden invasion of American-backed South Korea. In the Cold War's trembling mobile of world politics this was the one inexcusable act—an outright assault across national borders. It was immediately assumed to have been instigated, or at least encouraged, or at the very least tolerated, by Moscow. Sending a hurricane of fear, anger, and recrimination across America, the attack quickly sucked Congress into its vortex. As legislators tumbled over one another in their haste to propose anti-Communist measures, Truman himself labeled the atmosphere of repression he had helped to create as the worst since John Adams's time.

The lead gladiator in the stepped-up Cold War, "internal security" division, was a senator not from Wisconsin but from Nevada and not a Republican but a Democrat. First elected on FDR's coattails in 1932, Pat

McCarran was now chairman of the Senate Judiciary Committee. Early in August 1950, as American and allied troops retreated to a beachhead at the foot of the Korean peninsula, McCarran introduced an omnibus Internal Security Act that combined several earlier proposals to provide for the registration of Communist and "Communist-front" organizations, to bar Communists from national defense jobs, and to prohibit anyone who had ever belonged to a totalitarian organization from entering the United States.

It was a drastic set of measures that ought to have led to a grand debate and confrontation in Congress between liberals—Democratic and Republican both—who might argue that national security at the expense of the Bill of Rights was an empty husk, and conservatives from both parties who would put national security alone at the top of their priorities. Neither debate nor confrontation ensued. The House shouted the bill through; the Senate endorsed it 70–7.

Harry Truman, in one of his finest moments, vetoed the bill with a ringing message. His grounds were in part practical: the measure would actually damage the national security, by requiring the government to publish a list of secret defense installations and by wasting the resources of federal investigators trying to enforce its "unworkable registration provisions." But it was in the bill's threat to freedom of speech that Truman found "a clear and present danger." By putting the government "in the thought control business," the act would "make a mockery of the Bill of Rights and of our claims to stand for freedom in the world." "Our free system" was the bulwark of defense against "Communist aggression," and that cause must fail if Americans "destroy all that we seek to preserve, if we sacrifice the liberties of our citizens in a misguided attempt to achieve national security."

Even this presidential appeal to freedom of speech, the most sacred of First Amendment rights—sacred not least, one might think, to the politicians who invoked and exploited it at every opportunity—failed to move members of Congress. A mere 48 representatives voted to sustain the veto, while 286 voted to override it; only 10 senators voted to sustain, against 57 to override. Almost a third of the members of each chamber ducked the whole issue by simply not voting.

Truman had taken his stand on principle, but perhaps the most revealing behavior of the entire episode had been that of a number of his fellow liberals in Congress when the McCarran bill first arrived on the Senate floor. Looking to slow and deflect the rush toward "internal security," less from solicitude for the rights of Communists than from fears that the registration provision would be used to cripple or destroy liberal and civil rights organizations and labor unions, several Democratic senators—

most notably Hubert Humphrey, Estes Kefauver, Paul Douglas, Herbert Lehman, and William Benton—had suggested an emergency detention bill to replace McCarran's measure. Their proposal, which Humphrey argued was much tougher than McCarran's "cream-puff special," empowered the attorney general during presidentially declared emergencies to detain persons he had "reason to believe" might act subversively. It would, Humphrey boasted, enable the government "to act with speed and certainty" when there was "a real menace to our internal security."

The McCarran forces had had little trouble with this ploy. They simply had tossed the liberals' "tough" internment provision into the original bill and passed the whole thing, "cream puffs" and all.

WAS THERE any way out of this bipartisan preoccupation with national security, this bipartisan indifference to individual rights? The only hope, said some as the Truman administration staggered to a close in 1952, was the election of a Republican president who would turn the GOP from the irresponsibilities of the party outside the tent trying to pound and slash its way in—with power it would display the responsibility and self-restraint of the insider. Walter Lippmann feared that if the party was frustrated in a sixth consecutive presidential election, it would fall into the hands of its "most irreconcilable and ruthless factions," who would further divide and embitter the country. An Eisenhower administration offered "the prospect of a united nation." This turned out to be a miscalculation about the new Republican president, who was disgusted by his party's anti-Communist hysteria but did not know how to cope with it. It was even more a miscalculation about the Republicans in Congress, who in 1952 gained narrow control of both houses by riding in on Eisenhower's coattails.

For Eisenhower, the formidable problem was the existence not of one Republican Party but of two. The presidential Republicans behind Ike were heirs to the party's internationalist tradition, and in the Cold War they had rallied bipartisan support behind Truman's foreign policies and soft-pedaled their attacks on the administration's "internal security" failings. The congressional Republicans, led by Senator Robert A. Taft of Ohio—who had been beaten by Eisenhower in a savage struggle for the presidential nomination—tended historically to be isolationist toward Western Europe, interventionist toward the Pacific and Far East, and above all intensely hostile toward the Soviet Union, its empire, and the Communism it backed. This was Lippmann's "irreconcilable and ruthless faction." They had led the charge against Truman's "coddling" of Communists, milking the issue for every partisan advantage, and now, with the memory of Taft's defeat still fresh, they looked to Eisenhower to "get tough" with the Reds. And Eisenhower could not ignore them. With the change of majorities in both houses a band of "irreconcilables" had come to power as chairmen of key committees and subcommittees. Among them was the senator from Wisconsin, Joe McCarthy, suddenly catapulted to the chair of the Permanent Subcommittee on Investigations of the Government Operations Committee.

McCarthy was already so notorious by the early months of 1953 that his saga was sharply etched on the public mind, and his continued depredations in the Eisenhower years only deepened his dark legend: how he had risen from a minor Wisconsin judgeship to beat out the celebrated Robert M. La Follette, Jr., for the Republican senatorial nomination in 1946; how he had languished in the sonorous upper chamber until he latched almost by chance on to the "Red" issue at Wheeling; how, when his charges had been disproved, he kept his foes off balance with a battery of further allegations; and how now, as the Senate investigator in chief, he dared take on any target he wished, from Ike's White House itself—party loyalty be damned—to an obscure officer in an army unit.

That obscure army officer—in fact a dentist, allegedly "pink"—did not remain obscure for long after McCarthy had fastened on him, and neither did many of the senator's other targets: Owen Lattimore, pilloried by McCarthy as "the top Russian espionage agent in this country," in fact an expert on Asia who had been remarkably insightful in his advice to the government on the situation in China and the strengths of Mao Zedong's Communist insurgents, a classic case of killing the messenger; Dorothy Kenyon, who as a liberal activist had worked during the New Deal era with leftists of all varieties, including Communists, now denounced by McCarthy as an "extremely bad security risk" who ought, the senator blustered, to be fired by the State Department (which did not, as McCarthy failed to notice, employ her) within the hour; Charles Bohlen, Eisenhower's nominee for ambassador to the Soviet Union, tainted by his association with the foreign policies of Roosevelt and Truman.

McCarthy's abuses of governmental processes, procedural rights, civil liberties, and civility were as reckless as the charges he made. He distorted or invented evidence to support his accusations. He solicited perjury from "friendly" witnesses and tore mercilessly into "unfriendly" ones, reducing them to tears or stunned silence with his brutal interrogations and tirades (to a witness he had accused of espionage, he bellowed, "Do you feel that you should be walking the streets of this country free, or that you should have the same fate as the Rosenbergs?"), and if they dared decline to answer his questions by claiming their right against self-incrimination, he stigmatized them as "Fifth Amendment Communists." He called on government employees to supply him with classified materials on the grounds that "there is no loyalty to a superior officer which can tower above and beyond their loyalty to their country."

Even worse, McCarthy was not alone. Others shared the probe lime-light—and his contempt for rights and the facts. Republican senator William Jenner, who had once labeled General George Marshall, orga-nizer of America's military victory in World War II, a "front man for traitors," had taken over McCarran's Internal Security Subcommittee and was "investigating" Communism in education. And of course it was HUAC that had pioneered many of the techniques brought to perfection by McCarthy. As one of its chairmen, J. Parnell Thomas, had informed the lawyer for an uncooperative witness: "The rights you have are the rights given you by this Committee. We will determine what rights you have and what rights you have not got before the Committee," a position well captured in the conclusion drawn by a committee member who had since been called to higher things, Richard Nixon, from the testimony of a witness who had refused to testify: "It is pretty clear, I think, that you are not using the defense of the Fifth Amendment because you are inno-cent." HUAC was still in business in the early 1950s, and for long after-ward, returning again and again to the ever-fertile fields of Hollywood. And outside the halls of Congress, but with myriad strings crossing into it, there was—always—J. Edgar Hoover and his FBI. Investigation was a growth industry.

McCarthy & Co. were operating in an atmosphere of fear that made audacity, mendacity, and unaccountability enormously effective tactics in the absence of firm and resolute opposition. For a time Eisenhower had clung to the hope that McCarthy would prove a "team player," suscepti-ble to guidance from the administration, but though the emptiness of this illusion became apparent swiftly enough, still the general in the White House would not challenge McCarthy directly; he was reduced to protest-ing that "I just will not —I *refuse*—to get into the gutter with that guy." Nor did his foreign policies reduce the fears of dangers abroad on which McCarthyism battened. While the protracted conflict in Korea kept the country in a kind of semimobilization, Eisenhower vowed also to protect the Chinese regime on Taiwan against aggression by the Communists in Beijing. Washington contemplated intervention, possibly even atomic, on the side of the colonial French against nationalists in Indochina. And Secretary of State John Foster Dulles, author of a strategy for "liberating" Soviet satellites in Eastern Europe, announced the capacity of the Ameri-can nuclear arsenal to apply "massive retaliatory power" instantly against the Soviets "by means and at places of our choosing." This would, he explained, provide "permanent security."

With hysteria in the saddle and the range of debate narrowed, freedom to speak out faltered, political opposition dwindled, and incidents multiplied. An Oklahoma librarian was fired for subscribing to *The Nation* and *The New Republic*. American Legionnaires in Illinois warned that Girl Scouts were being poisoned by subversive doctrines. Once again books took the worst beating; they were indiscriminately banished, banned, and burned. On a much-publicized European junket, McCarthy aide Roy Cohn and his friend G. David Schine rummaged the shelves of the State Department's overseas libraries in a hunt for books of subversive influence. The most egregiously senseless act was that of Dulles's State Department itself, which admitted burning an issue of the scholarly and staid *Annals* of the American Academy of Political and Social Science. Because it advocated Communism? No, because it dealt with the dangerous subject of "one world government and one-world citizenship."

Once again the cardinal issue was less the willingness to exploit or yield to fear, to perpetrate dangerous or stupid deeds or acquiesce in their perpetration, than the willingness and capacity to resist the prevailing temper, and once again the record was mixed at best, deplorable at worst. As civil libertarian Joseph Rauh, a hero of the resistance, put it: opposing McCarthyism was a "mighty, mighty lonesome business."

Consider the stand of businessmen who for years had been belaboring the federal government for its growth in size and reach, for its intrusions into such spheres of individual autonomy as property rights. Somehow government did not seem so dangerous when it bestirred itself merely to abridge individuals' First Amendment rights. For a time during and after World War II, corporate America had come to imagine that it was possible after all to do business with the Soviets—*Fortune* summarized a September 1945 poll of executives by writing, "Russia's best friend is the businessman"—but the abrupt emergence of the Cold War quashed these dreams, and the old instinct to demonize Communism and Communists reasserted itself. And, as at the same time a massive strike wave swept industry, so again rose the old cries of Communist domination of unions. Businessmen liked to compare their hard line on labor with Truman's stand against Stalin. Chamber of Commerce officials included a few fanatics. One contended during the strike wave that to avoid becoming a Soviet satellite "we will have to set up some firing squads . . . and liquidate the Reds." Another called for a preventive "war of aggression" against the Soviet Union, which "would win for us a proud and popular title; we would become the first aggressors for peace."

As a whole the church was no bulwark against Cold War hysteria. Thoroughly enjoying the first-listed of First Amendment rights, religious leaders were not always eager to extend the same measure of liberty to those accused of disloyalty and treason. Too many saw in Communism the hand of the Antichrist and cared as little as McCarthy for the truth of allegations, even when these were leveled against fellow ministers.

Others did speak up, to chide or to lament, but it took an attempt to tar the entire clergy of an entire faith with the Communist label for those voices to join and rise in a shout. In 1953, in collaboration with Eisenhower's White House, a rabbi, monsignor, and Presbyterian minister, together representing the National Conference of Christians and Jews, lambasted McCarthy aide J. B. Matthews's claim that "the largest single group supporting the Communist apparatus in the United States today is composed of Protestant clergymen."

The explosion of indignation over that preposterous statement—not only from religious leaders and the White House but from McCarthy's Senate colleagues and millions of believers of all faiths across the country—played a part in the reversal of the senator's fortunes, helping to start him downhill politically.

Would the educational establishments do any better? Not the public schools. Under state and community control, they were extraordinarily vulnerable to pressures from patriotic anti-Communist organizations. Nationally the American Legion and the Conference of American Small Business Organizations, under such slogans as the Legion's "Your Child is Their Target," examined and deplored "left-wing texts." Richard Fried notes that often "anti-subversion crusades meshed with less frenzied yet deep worry about the cost of progressive education's 'fads and frills' and about the rise of 'life-adjustment' courses at the expense of the 'three R's.'" For some school systems this kind of attack was an old story. Since the first Red Scare after World War I, New York City schoolteachers had lain under the vigilant eyes of the Red hunters. Then in 1949 school authorities conducted further purges of "subversive" teachers that lasted through the 1950s; it was estimated that by the end of that decade some three hundred New York City schoolteachers had been fired or forced to resign.

The capacity of educators to stand up to the Red hunters would test the leaders of the great private universities and prestigious state institutions that had big constituencies of alumni and friends. The fundamental question was simple—should Communists be allowed to teach students at the college level? By one measure the academy appeared divided. In the late 1940s and throughout the 1950s the American Association of University Professors took the position that there was "nothing in the nature of the teaching profession which requires the automatic exclusion of Communists." The 1949 convention of the National Education Association, on the other hand, adopted, by a vote of 2,995–5, a report holding that a Communist Party member was "unfit to discharge the duties of a teacher in this country."

Neither group actually hired or fired professors but those who did had no doubts about the matter. "Card-holding members of the Communist

Party," said President James Bryant Conant of Harvard, "are out of bounds as members of the teaching profession." And President Charles Seymour of Yale said: "There will be no witch-hunts at Yale, because there will be no witches. We do not intend to hire Communists."

An epic confrontation took place at the University of Washington, which cooperated with a state un-American activities committee by bringing charges against six tenured professors, three of whom had refused to testify to the committee about their political activities and three who had acknowledged past Communist Party membership but declined to talk about the activities of others. Two of the three professors who had refused testimony to the state committee admitted before the university's Tenure and Academic Freedom Committee that they still belonged to the Communist Party but contended that their membership had not contaminated their teaching of medieval literature or philosophy; the third denied party membership. After taking 4,000 pages of testimony the tenure committee unanimously proposed that the university drop its charges against all six. But the university's president and trustees overruled the committee, sacking the three "Fifth Amendment Communists" and putting the three admitted ex-Communists on probation.

And so it went at other institutions. Confrontations were not as numerous as they might have been because the message became clear: to profess Communist beliefs or party membership meant losing one's job. The most remarkable aspect of the controversy was the relative lack of controversy. It came to be assumed—it came to be conventional wisdom—that an honest Communist could not be a good teacher. Few asked the basic questions: How much influence did Communist teachers actually have on their students—any more than non-Communist teachers, whose impact was usually minimal? And if such teachers came to their Communist views not from coercion but on the basis of their own study and experience, should they not introduce their beliefs into the academic discourse? Would it not indeed be better for that discourse if professors openly declared their beliefs and subjected them to rebuttals in the classroom and outside? And if Communist teachers in the give-and-take of academic life discovered the falsity of their beliefs, should they not be free to turn away from those beliefs and their party, as thousands of Communists had done inside and outside the academy?

CENTERS OF INTOLERANCE

DECADES AFTERWARD, historians and social scientists were still analyzing the impact on American rights of the intense Red Fear of the late forties and early fifties. They had passed beyond the stage of simply blaming individuals or institutions for their failures to resist the tensions and hysteria of the time. Blaming was too easy; it had become well established that a host of political, media, academic, and business leaders and institutions had, in various ways and to varying degrees, succumbed. Rather students of the period were exploring larger questions—questions that might throw light both on the Red Fear's fundamental causes and on the possible fate of rights during future "fears" of whatever character.

In broader historical perspective the outburst of anti-Communism after World War II was seen as yet another sector—but the most costly one—of the long cold war between the United States and the Soviet Union. After breaking out virtually at the birth of Bolshevik power in 1917, hostilities had waxed and waned with the rush of events—rising to a pitch after World War I, subsiding a bit as American businessmen invested money in Russia during the 1920s, falling off further when Franklin Roosevelt recognized the Soviet Union in 1933, and even further during the Popular Front years of the later 1930s, only to be rekindled with the 1939 Nazi-Soviet pact, then yielding to Soviet-American partnership after Hitler's assault on Russia in 1941. Only the relationship's volatility did not change; even as Soviet and American troops shook hands over a prostrate Germany in the spring of 1945, the embers of cold war were glowing in the ashes of Europe's devastated capitals.

Abetted abroad by Communist conquests in Eastern Europe and China and the North Korean invasion of the south, a "great fear," as David Caute called it, descended on the American people. Its ostensible object was the Soviet threat but it turned to what was nearer at hand, to what could be touched by the actions of the hatred bred by fear—those who were thought to be doing Moscow's work at home: the American Communist Party, its "fellow travelers," and, indiscriminately, radicals of various hues. Almost half the states took repressive action against Communists: banning them from public employment, banning them from politics, banning them outright, or requiring them to register with the government.

Repression worked. There could be "little doubt," James L. Gibson wrote in 1988, "as to the effectiveness of this anti-Communist legislation. Not only were the Communist Party U.S.A. and other Communist parties essentially eradicated, but so too were a wide variety of non-Communists." The Eisenhower administration had brought a new rigor to the federal loyalty program, weakening its already slack safeguards of employees' rights and lengthening the roster of causes for dismissal, while myriad similar programs—in state and local government, in industry and education—probed the private lives and beliefs of American citizens. It was estimated that by 1957 over 13 million Americans in public and private employment had had to "prove" their loyalty, whether by swearing an oath or completing a statement or by surviving an investigation, and at least 10,000 persons had been denied security clearances or sacked outright. Wild charges of Communism destroyed the good names and careers and even—for there were cases of suicide—the lives not only of government workers but of teachers, writers, unionists, ministers, political activists, scientists. If a "silent generation" emerged from the Red Fear, it was testimony to the pervasive impact, both direct and indirect, of the political repression of that period.

The question about the era most discussed by historians and social scientists, at the time and more recently, has been the broad location of the fear and intolerance that lay behind the repression. Was the main source the leaders of American opinion and policy, or the mass public? Both of these entities were defined vaguely—the former as the established political, intellectual, and economic leadership at the national, state, and local levels, often called the "elites," and the latter as tens of millions of more or less "average" persons.

During the Red Fear itself, in the 1940s and 1950s, many among the nation's intellectual elite contended that the repression of hated political minorities stemmed chiefly from the intolerances of the mass public. This public was characterized psychologically as insecure in its social and economic status, resentful of the elites, fearful of conspiracies, combining, in Richard Hofstadter's description, "enormous hostility to authority" with the "massive overcompensation" of an "extravagant submissiveness to strong power." Sociologically it was classified variously as rural, as lower-middle-class, as small-town, evangelical Protestant, big-city Catholic, as ethnic. Politically it was portrayed as an amalgam of conservative Republicans, rural Populists, disenchanted Democrats.

Such, members of the intellectual elite alleged, comprised the mass base, the political and social constituencies, of McCarranism and McCarthyism, of the FBI and HUAC. These people were seen by the intellectual elite not as passive applauders of repression; rather they made their own voices clear, they were politically active, they exercised their intolerance aggressively and in ways large and small against both political minorities and the tolerant elites. In 1930 Ortega y Gasset had sought to rally Europeans against the threat of the "revolt of the masses." But now these "masses" wielded great power because they had Communism as a simple, totalistic explanation for all they loathed and feared, and used their opposition to it as a political vehicle.

In recent years this account of masses brimming with intolerance has undergone considerable revision. Some scholars have concluded that, in James Gibson's words, "elites, not masses, were responsible for the repression of the era." New studies cast doubt on the extent and depth of mass intolerance and on the salience to the public of Communism as an issue. It was the leaders, political and otherwise, who were intensely fearful and intolerant of Communist ideas, the leaders who would circumscribe free expression, the leaders—including liberal intellectuals and politicians—who made compromise after compromise with McCarthyism.

Revisionism went further to contend that the elites had created, even if not fully realizing the consequences, the atmosphere of the Fear by painting the American-Soviet conflict as a series of moral absolutes— good and evil, freedom and slavery, totalitarianism and democracy; by whipping up public support for an aggressively anti-Soviet foreign policy with rhetoric suggesting that the final battle between these absolutes was at hand; and by taking the first measures against domestic Communists. By setting up loyalty programs and the like, moreover, elites legitimated anti-Communist repression and the idea that national security had strong precedence over individual rights. Richard Pells contended that intellectuals who described the intolerance of the masses overlooked the fact that "postwar liberals had functioned as modern Dr. Frankensteins." Only later did they "begin to feel horrified by the monster they had created," and then discovered the fault, not in themselves, but in their monster.

That the American elites could not be relied on to protect "freedom for the thought we hate" was an ominous conclusion. As worrisome was the conclusion that the mass public could not be counted on to tolerate unpopular minorities but rather had to be monitored by "responsible" elites, because this was the electorate that would choose future leaderships. Some recent scholarship, however, has suggested that neither "elites" nor "masses" were or are especially prone to tolerance—"that the potential for intolerance exists among all citizens, and is likely to be activated if their interests are threatened sufficiently," in the words of a trio of political scientists. "There is no particular group that can be trusted to protect the rights of other groups." Americans, they concluded, "are generally intolerant of extremist groups on the left and the right." This, as the authors admitted, was not news. But it raised the most frightening prospect of all—that virtually no one could be depended on to tolerate dissidence or to refrain from the suppression of dissidents, to defend Bill of Rights liberties in times of trial.

IT WAS the supreme tragedy of the era that the intellectual leadership should have been no more immune than political and business and other elites to the Red Fear's grip. Politicians must court voters and business-men their customers, attorneys and other professionals their clients, cler-ics their parishioners. Intellectuals, often occupying relatively protected positions, are supposed—most suppose it for themselves—to rise above self-interest and self-protectiveness to take a more reflective, informed and balanced, longer view of threatening ideas and groups. This the postwar intellectual leadership as a whole failed to do.

It was the supreme irony of the era that the intellectual elite and the mass public regarded each other with mutual suspicion and mispercep-tion. The public as a whole judged that intellectuals as a class were "soft on Communism," subversive, even traitorous, when in fact the most influential intellectuals were articulately anti-Communist and helped form and lead an American consensus against "Reds" and all their works. Elites looked out into the country and saw an intolerant, chauvinistic, belligerent, and repressive mass, when in fact that mass embraced these qualities to no greater degree, though perhaps without such smoothened edges, than the intellectual leadership.

The attitude of elite toward mass reflected intellectual presuppositions that were crucial during the Red Fear and could affect Americans' rights in a future era of perceived tension and crisis. The Fear came to its height during the early 1950s, paradoxically a self-styled era of compromise, pragmatism, and accommodation. In social life it was labeled the Age of Conformity; in the intellectual world it marked the End of Ideology, the Revolt against Absolutism. Dwight Eisenhower's election and his gener-ally transactional and soothing performance as president in domestic policy-making were expressions of the temper of those years.

The intellectual rulers who had proclaimed an end to ideology never-theless—for ideology, too, abhors a vacuum—had one, whatever they chose to call it—an ideology that envisioned the calm, nonpartisan, con-sensual adjustment and balancing of differences and claims among eco-nomic and social groups, an "empirical" strategy, wrote Daniel Bell, that would specify "*where* one wants to go, *how* to get there, the costs of the enterprise, and some realization of, and justification for the determina-tion of *who* is to pay." This consensus ideology was even more notable for what it disdained—social and political instability, clear-cut conflict between groups and parties, "extremist" movements of the right or left, an emphasis on such general, indeterminate, and hence potentially divi-sive ideals as liberty, justice, and equality, and the open-ended commit-ment of means to such ends. Give up "living dangerously in the exciting land of either-or," Arthur Schlesinger, Jr., urged Americans, and instead "enter the unromantic realm of more-or-less." Planting themselves squarely in the intellectual and political middle ground—or redefining that middle, that "vital center," in Schlesinger's phrase, so that they might monopolize it—the consensus ideologists looked on the ideological left and right as equally menacing to their values of stability, pluralism, cooperation, compromise, and incremental progress.

Consensus politics and thought had an indirect but significant impact on the struggle over rights in the United States. The intellectual and political liberals who at the very least might have been counted on to defend the Bill of Rights and its protections of individual rights—even for Communists—instead became caught in currents that led to an extremism of the center: fearful of being labeled radical, afraid, as Robert Bendiner was, that the "repressive spirit" would "get out of hand," they adopted a defensive, compromising position at the start and then erected an ideology that justified their compromises as expressions of a supreme political value; while bemoaning scapegoating by the right, they castigated scapegoats of their own in "extremist" movements; while attacking mass conformity, they made an even more rigid conformity the unspoken cornerstone of their consensual society; and finally by redefining tolerance to extend only to those willing to play within the limits of pluralist consensus, to "legitimate dissenting groups," by drawing lines all around the great center to distinguish "tolerable" from "intolerable" exercises of civil liberties and rights, they legitimated the exclusion of the "extremists" from the protections of the Bill of Rights.

All of this diminished the rights of radicals and reactionaries alike.

CONSENSUS IDEOLOGY not only led many intellectuals and politicians down the seductive but dangerous path of compromise on the rights of "extremists." It also led them to misperceive the nature of conflict itself, both within the United States and outside.

The most serious example of their misconceptions—at least in its implications for the rights of Americans—was their evaluation of the Communist threat to both American national security and individual liberty, a threat they judged to be clear and present, and posed not only by the Soviet Union's military power but by the American Communist Party working from within. While consensus ideologists belittled the significance of conflict within the pluralist "vital center," their extremism of the center brought many of them to describe the conflict against Communism in black-and-white terms and to exaggerate grossly both the external and the internal threat.

Soviet behavior in the Cold War was in part a reaction—an overreaction, perhaps—to the perceived American menace, especially the growing American nuclear arsenal. Churchill had once memorably described Soviet foreign policy intentions as "a riddle wrapped in a mystery inside an enigma," but in fact Moscow was following an ancient Russian pattern.

As a result of centuries of invasions Russians were "rationally obsessive" about controlling nations on their borders. Their Marxist-Leninist doctrines led them to indulge in messianic rhetoric about global revolution and in the support of Communist parties around the world, but they would invariably and often brutally put their own national interests ahead of ideology and the aspirations of those parties. And where possible, they would, in good Machiavellian fashion, seize targets of opportunity, but almost never at the risk of worldwide conflagration.

The American Communist Party was far less a serious threat to the national security or to the freedoms of Americans. The party, always small in number—at its peak in the years immediately following World War II, it had perhaps 74,000 members, including a sizable proportion of FBI informers—and racked by internal divisions, now and then gained footholds in a wide scattering of unions and other organizations and through "Communist fronts," but its domination was rarely long-lived and usually ended in factional fighting. The party never threatened to break out of these enclaves into broader influence, nor did it ever find a place in the American structure of political power. Its strict obedience to the ever-changing line sent down by Kremlin bureaucrats without regard for American conditions or attitudes destroyed the party's credibility even—or perhaps especially—among sympathetic leftists. But neither was the party a nest of Soviet spies; as David Caute has emphasized: *"There is no documentation in the public record of a direct connection between the American Communist Party and espionage during the entire postwar period."* When its external and internal foes had finished with it, the party was a burntout shell buried half underground and housing a few handfuls of embittered fanatics.

The unreasoning fear of domestic Communism fanned by the intellectual elite, by politicians and press, reached the nation's highest court, which also held that the dangers of internal subversion were both clear and present. Since Holmes had first announced the "clear and present" doctrine in his 1919 *Schenck* ruling, the Court had not only adopted it but gradually set stricter standards for the clarity and imminence, as well as the magnitude, of danger that justified suppression of speech. Now, so that the armies of anti-Communism might have their tools of choice, the Court under Chief Justice Fred M. Vinson reversed that long progress.

Of all the judicial spectaculars of the Red Fear era, none posed so clear or so present a danger to the First Amendment as the case of eleven leaders of the American Communist Party. The eleven, among them the general secretary, Eugene Dennis, were indicted in 1948 under the Smith Act, not for conspiring to overthrow the government but for conspiring to organize "a society, group, and assembly of persons"—the party—that would advocate violent revolution. Such a general charge—no overt act had to be demonstrated—took the government a long step toward what even Congress had so far refused to do: illegalize the party by defining it and its advocacy as a conspiracy and subject all its members to Smith Act prosecution.

When the Smith Act's subversive advocacy law had first been used, early in World War II against the Trotskyist Socialist Workers Party, the Stalinized Communists had approved; the American people, wrote the *Daily Worker,* demanded "the destruction of the Fifth Column in this country." Now, themselves charged as fifth columnists, the defendants protested that they had done "no more than project an idea for discussion, for consideration, for thinking, in the market place of ideas, which is precisely what the First Amendment says you can do." To no avail. At the end of the rancorous nine-month trial, Judge Harold Medina instructed jurors that "I find as a matter of law that there is a sufficient danger of a substantive evil that the Congress has a right to prevent to justify the application of the statute under the First Amendment." With Medina taking the trial's central issue—the alleged danger posed by the party's advocacy—out of the jury's hands, convictions were duly returned.

On appeal to Learned Hand, that venerable civil libertarian dealt another blow to Holmes's old doctrine by setting it a new standard: "whether the gravity of the 'evil,' discounted by its improbability, justifies such invasion of free speech as is necessary to avoid the danger." The danger no longer need be imminent—it need only be not "improbable"—and with North Korea striking south the day after Hand heard the appeal, he had no difficulty discerning a probable threat in the party's program.

The Supreme Court approved Hand's new test. The national security was heavy in Fred Vinson's mind when, writing in June 1951 for a 6–2 majority, he described the party as a "highly organized conspiracy, with rigidly disciplined members subject to call when the leaders, these petitioners, felt that the time had come for action." Considering the "touch-and-go nature of our relations with countries with whom the petitioners were in the very least ideologically attuned," the government could not wait until "the *putsch* is about to be executed." William O. Douglas, dissenting with Hugo Black, noted that no evidence of seditious activity had been advanced at trial, and he scorned Vinson's portrait of the eleven at the head of a monstrous conspiracy: "in America they are miserable merchants of unwanted ideas." The party had lost out in the marketplace of ideas, free speech itself had defeated it, and free speech "should not be sacrificed on anything less than plain and objective proof of danger that the evil advocated is imminent."

Having upheld the deployment of the Smith Act against Communists, the Vinson Court went on to give constitutional blessings to other instruments of repression. In a series of decisions, the Court—with regular dissents from Black and Douglas—defended loyalty oaths for state political candidates; approved a federal loyalty board's dismissal of a woman who had not been given the names of her accusers, as well as New York's firings of "subversive" public school teachers; sanctioned the harassment of witnesses by congressional committees and the deportation of aliens who belonged—or who had *ever* belonged—to a "subversive" organization. In 1952, the Court ordered the deportation of an Italian-American who had come to the United States in 1920, joined the Communist Party in 1923, and quit it in 1929. Under the cloak of "judicial restraint," the Court deferred again and again to the judgment of the executive and legislature when it came to "national security"—so eager was its deference that, as one critic observed, "the McCarthy-McCarran era could scarcely roll the repression along fast enough to keep pace with the Vinson Court's approval of it."

Not until the mid-1950s, until the domestic hysteria had subsided and Joe McCarthy had faded from the scene, until world tensions had eased and Eisenhower was sitting down with Soviet leaders at a summit in Geneva, did an equilibrium between individual rights and the claims of national security begin to be restored. The appointment as Vinson's successor of Earl Warren, who had come to regret his enthusiasm as California's governor in 1942 for the Japanese-American relocation, and the arrival on the Court of William J. Brennan, Jr., added two stout defenders of civil liberties to the Black-Douglas camp. Then, like a movie reeling backward, the Warren Court started to undo the handiwork of the Vinson Court, case by case. The Court struck at the power of congressional committees to "inquire into private affairs unrelated to a valid legislative purpose" and at the tarring of those who claimed their rights against self-incrimination as "Fifth Amendment Communists." It insisted that subjects of security investigations be supplied with the evidence against them, limited the McCarran Act's security provisions to federal employees who had access to classified information, and blocked the practice of professional associations of denying membership to Communists or alleged Communists.

And on June 17, 1957—"Red Monday," right-wing critics called it—the Warren Court delivered stunning blows to several of the principal levers of the machinery of repression. The Court ordered the reinstatement of John Stewart Service, a China hand who had survived seven separate State Department loyalty investigations but whom John Foster Dulles had fired anyway as a scapegoat for the "loss" of China. The Court also condemned the "hunting licenses" congressional committees had assumed for themselves—"There is no congressional power to expose for the sake of exposure"—and asserted that the Bill of Rights applied to congressional investigations as to any other governmental action. In another case, the Court leashed New Hampshire investigators who had harassed a left-wing editor invited to lecture at the state university.

And in *Yates,* the Court at last effectively destroyed the Smith Act as a tool against Communists. In a careful holding by John Harlan, it drew a sharp line between "advocacy of forcible overthrow as an abstract doctrine and advocacy of action to that end" and argued that doctrinal advocacy, "even though uttered with the hope that it may ultimately lead to violent revolution, is too remote from concrete action" to justify suppression. Thus *Yates* placed a far higher standard of proof on prosecutors than *Dennis* had done, and in its wake some seventy Smith Act convictions were overturned or referred back to lower courts and dismissed, and eighteen pending prosecutions were dropped.

Although *Yates* did not itself return Holmes's clear and present doctrine to its earlier fullness, although Hugo Black, in a concurrence, insisted that the Smith Act should be simply declared unconstitutional, and although the Warren Court's vindication of rights was slowed by congressional diehards who threatened to clip the Court's jurisdiction, its decisions in the later 1950s marked the passing of the Red Fear. Those decisions also began to redeem Black's hope, expressed in his *Dennis* dissent at the start of the decade, that "in calmer times, when present pressures, passions and fears subside, this or some later Court will restore the First Amendment liberties to the high preferred place where they belong in a free society."

PART FOUR

CHAPTER TEN

EVERYBODY SING FREEDOM

DECEMBER 1, 1955. Jo Ann Robinson, an English professor at the black Alabama State College in Montgomery, had been waiting six years for this day, ever since a white bus driver had cruelly abused her for absentmindedly sitting in the forward, white section of a city bus. She had just received word that forty-two-year-old Rosa Parks, a highly respected civil rights activist, had been arrested that evening for violating the bus segregation laws.

Eager to get home after a long day of tailoring in the pre-Christmas rush at a Montgomery department store, Parks had climbed into a bus at Court Square, once a center of slave auctions and site of the Confederacy's first capitol. She sat in a seat between the "white only" section and the rear seats reserved for "colored." A white man boarded the crowded bus and the driver—by chance the same man who, a decade before, had ejected Parks for refusing to enter through the back door—commanded her and three other black passengers to stand so the white man could sit alone. She did not move, believing that she had not broken the law by sitting in the unreserved middle section. The driver stopped the bus and called the police, who arrested her and took her to jail.

Parks, a longtime officer of the Montgomery NAACP, had not planned her quiet protest but was ready for it when—like Elizabeth Jennings, Ida B. Wells, and other black women before her—she could accept injustice no longer. She recalled later that she had "a life history of being rebellious against being mistreated because of my color." The time had come "when I had been pushed as far as I could stand to be pushed. . . . I had decided that I would have to know once and for all what rights I had as a human being and a citizen."

Parks was bailed out by E. D. Nixon, an older activist who had been president of the local and state NAACP, worked as a Pullman porter on the train to Chicago, and served as a regional officer of the Brotherhood of Sleeping Car Porters founded by A. Philip Randolph. Considered the "most militant man in town," he had been the backbone of civil rights activity in Montgomery, working closely with Parks for years. For Nixon, his friend's arrest had the makings of an ideal test case on the constitutionality of the bus segregation law that inflicted daily humiliation on much of Montgomery's black populace. Robinson convinced him over the phone that night that the legal route had to be reinforced by something more dramatic: the boycott that had been discussed for months by the Women's Political Council, the black counterpart of the white-only League of Women Voters. Under Robinson's leadership, this activist group of professional women had been lobbying city hall to improve the bus situation, without success.

Around midnight, Robinson hastily typed a leaflet that urged all black citizens to refuse to ride the buses on Monday, December 5, the day of Parks's trial. She drove to the college and with the help of a colleague and two trusted students stayed up all night mimeographing, cutting, and bundling 50,000 copies. After carefully mapping out distribution routes, the next day between classes and into the evening she and her students drove all over town, delivering bundles to schools, businesses, stores, factories, taverns, beauty parlors, and barbershops. Knowing that the boycott had to have the support of Montgomery's black ministers, Nixon called each one. They announced it at Sunday services.

Monday morning, scarcely any black riders got on the city buses. Thousands rode cabs offering cut rates, hitched rides, or walked, while buses rolled by almost empty. Awed by the unexpected success, the women leaders and the ministers assembled in the late afternoon to plan a mass meeting to decide whether to continue the boycott. They formed the Montgomery Improvement Association (MIA) and elected as president Dr. Martin Luther King, Jr., the twenty-six-year-old pastor of the middle-class Dexter Avenue Baptist Church. Resident of Montgomery for only a year, King was the son and grandson of prominent Atlanta Baptist ministers; a great-grandfather had been a Georgia slave preacher. After graduating from Atlanta's Morehouse College and Crozer Seminary near Philadelphia, King had earned his Ph.D. in systematic theology at Boston University, where he studied every major Western philosopher and was deeply influenced by a spectrum of theologies from the Social Gospel of Walter Rauschenbusch to Reinhold Niebuhr's Christian realism. Yet he never strayed from his firm grounding in black Baptist culture and tradition.

That evening the big Holt Street Baptist Church overflowed long before starting time, and 5,000 stood outside in the cold, listening through loudspeakers. After people sang "Onward Christian Soldiers," prayed, and heard a scripture reading, King gave a stirring speech, punctuated by thunderous applause. They had gathered, he declared, because "we are determined to apply our citizenship to the fullness of its meaning . . . because of our deep-seated belief that democracy transformed from thin paper to thick action is the greatest form of government on earth."

"The great glory of American democracy," King went on, "is the right to protest for right. . . . When the history books are written in the future somebody will have to say, 'There lived a race of people . . . who had the moral courage to stand up for their rights. And thereby they injected a new meaning into the veins of history and of civilization.' " Another young preacher, Ralph Abernathy, read the boycott resolutions calling for fairer treatment, and with great cheering several thousand stood up to affirm that they would not ride the buses until the demands were met.

When the city prohibited fare-cutting by black cabdrivers, the MIA constructed a highly efficient car pool system—a full-scale transportation network—which made the boycott sustainable for a long period. The brigade of volunteer drivers included ministers, laborers, teachers, students, and homemakers. Autos, pickup trucks, and a fleet of shiny new church-bought station wagons collected riders at forty-eight dispatch points and returned them after work. Their spirits sustained by frequent mass meetings rotated among churches, where King and other ministers gave rousing pep talks, the boycotters persevered month after month. After being tutored in Gandhian nonviolence by veteran activists Bayard Rustin and Glenn Smiley of the Fellowship of Reconciliation, King taught his followers about the moral and redemptive power of Gandhi's *satyagraha,* or "truth force."

While King quickly took charge—his strong leadership celebrated by the white and black media alike—the women activists who had started the boycott performed the multitude of vital day-to-day tasks that kept it running. "We really were the ones who carried out the actions," remembered Women's Political Council leader and MIA officer Erna Dungee Allen, "the power behind the throne."

At first the MIA sought merely to humanize bus segregation without changing the law. But when in negotiations the city commissioners resisted any improvement, and after King's and Nixon's homes were bombed, the MIA filed a federal lawsuit with the help of the NAACP challenging the constitutionality of bus segregation. The city responded by indicting King and ninety others for violating a little-known Alabama antiboycott law aimed at union organizing. Three months later, in early

June, the Montgomery federal court struck down the city and state bus segregation laws; but Jim Crow held on while the city appealed, and the boycott continued apace. Finally in November 1956 the Supreme Court upheld the June decision. When the Court's order was implemented just before Christmas, 8,000 men and women, gathered in two churches, gleefully voted to end the boycott, the longest and most significant protest campaign by African-Americans thus far. Despite more bombings and shootings by white extremists, Montgomery's bus system no longer treated blacks as an inferior caste. The yearlong protest sparked boycotts in Birmingham, Tallahassee, and other cities and led to bus desegregation in about twenty communities.

At the height of the Montgomery protest, King testified on behalf of a strong civil rights plank at the 1956 Democratic National Convention in Chicago and made a compelling plea for the government to enforce racial equality. "We, the Negro citizens of Montgomery," he began, "wish to stress the urgent need for strong federal action," the question of civil rights being "one of the supreme moral issues of our time."

Detailing the suppression of black voting, economic reprisals, and the "tragic reign of bombings, beating and mob rule," King noted that many basic freedoms were denied in the name of states' rights. But states' rights "are only valid as they serve to protect larger human rights," which are prior and more fundamental. "Whenever human rights are trampled over by States' Rights, the federal government is obligated to intervene," since it has a "basic responsibility to guarantee to all of its citizens the rights and privileges of full citizenship."

"If democracy is to live," King concluded, "segregation must die."

FREEDOM NOW!

DURING THE FIRST HALF of the twentieth century the oppressive conditions of African-Americans had changed little. Through much of the rural South, and in cities too, white elites succeeded in preserving the psychological, social, and economic rudiments of slavery, even with the decline of Southern agriculture and the plantation system. Black people who asserted their rights, or violated the strict canons of Jim Crow justice, faced summary brutality. Hundreds of innocent blacks were lynched, or "legally" executed in travesties of due process. Although protests did not cease after the consolidation of white supremacy, they were sporadic and often invisible beyond the locality.

The mechanization of cotton-growing and its diminishing importance, combined with the lure of industrial employment, particularly during wartime, brought a massive migration of black people to the big cities. As noted by Frances Fox Piven and Richard Cloward, an impoverished rural peasantry turned into a slightly less poor urban proletariat in both North and South. In many cities lower-class whites resisted the newcomers with assaults and rioting.

The spread of antiblack violence prompted the founding of the Niagara Movement by W. E. B. Du Bois, Ida B. Wells, Mary Church Terrell, and other activists, who then joined with white liberals to form the National Association for the Advancement of Colored People in 1909. Under the leadership of Du Bois, James Weldon Johnson, and Walter White, the NAACP rejected Booker T. Washington's "accommodationist" advocacy of moral and economic uplift in lieu of integration or legal entitlements. Guided by special counsel Thurgood Marshall, a Howard Law graduate, the organization mobilized legal resources during the 1930s and 1940s to argue test cases in federal courts that contested segregation and denial of voting rights and won Supreme Court decisions banning the Southern "white primary" election (which excluded black voters), restrictive covenants in home sales, and separate but demonstrably inferior law and graduate schools.

The NAACP lawyers' spectacular triumph came in May 1954 with the unanimous Supreme Court ruling in five cases consolidated as *Brown* v. *Board of Education of Topeka, Kansas,* which built on the NAACP's prior legal inroads against segregation. The decision nullified the 1896 *Plessy* v. *Ferguson* "separate-but-equal" doctrine by declaring that state-imposed segregated public education violated the Fourteenth Amendment's equal protection clause. Chief Justice Earl Warren's opinion held that, even with equal facilities and resources, to separate children "from others of similar age and qualifications solely because of their race generates a feeling of inferiority as to their status in the community that may affect their hearts and minds in a way unlikely ever to be undone." Thus separate schools were "inherently unequal." By implication, *Brown* seemed to invalidate all racial segregation, providing the judicial and moral justification for further challenges.

The ruling would not have been unanimous, however, and might not even have won a majority, had not Warren's opinion left wide open the matter of how and when to implement the constitutional principle it asserted. The Court waited a full year to promulgate an order that, making allowances for the issue's "considerable complexity"—that is, racial sensitivity—permitted lower courts and school boards to enforce desegregation "with all deliberate speed." Nor did the *Brown* ruling go beyond the quantitative objective of racial balance to define qualitative standards for "equal education." Once again, the federal judiciary had exposed the often vast chasm between rights formally guaranteed and rights actualized. Accordingly, during the 1950s and 1960s school integration moved at a glacial pace, hindered not only by the lack of national enforcement power but by the "massive resistance" of Southern politicians allied with the rapidly proliferating White Citizens' Councils. Their legal maneuvers, economic retaliation, and outright defiance were supplemented by the terrorism of the resurgent Ku Klux Klan.

The NAACP legal strategy of utilizing the Fourteenth and Fifteenth amendments to win rights might have been limited in terms of implementation and in the breadth and depth of the specific rights sought, but it nonetheless set the constitutional and moral compass within which the emerging black freedom movement would pursue its agenda. *Brown* emboldened Southern activists to expand and intensify their fight against American apartheid.

BY THE 1950s, a number of factors had joined to generate a quantum leap in the aspirations and sense of entitlement of African-Americans. Hundreds of thousands of veterans returned from World War II and Korea, having fought for freedom and democracy abroad, with new self-esteem, new expectations, and less willingness to tolerate the racial status quo. These attitudes were shared by other black men and women who had labored in the nation's war plants. In the postwar era black Americans were energized by the liberation of African and Asian peoples from colonial domination; around the globe white supremacy seemed to be collapsing. In Southern cities an increasingly independent and assertive black middle class—its growth partly a legacy of segregation—began to challenge the Jim Crow system, as Jo Ann Robinson and the Women's Political Council did in Montgomery. In the wake of the Supreme Court's outlawing of the white primary election, urban blacks organized voter registration campaigns. Even the scourge of McCarthyism could not smother the resurgence of black activism.

The central institution of black life did not initiate the new activist spirit but quickly signed on. The black church, "born in protest," had played a pivotal role in antebellum slave resistance and abolitionism and in Reconstruction political mobilization. But after Reconstruction most church leaders came to believe they had no alternative but to accommodate themselves to white supremacy, some becoming power brokers between white elites and the black community. Then in the 1950s a new generation of young ministers began to reclaim the older tradition of resistance. Their churches offered invaluable resources—charismatic leaders insulated from white manipulation; a large, highly organized constituency; a communications network; an independent financial base; relatively safe meeting places; and the "common church culture," grounded in a rich heritage of empowering prayers, oratory, and spirituals. Thus throughout the course of the freedom movement the black church—Baptist and African Methodist Episcopal (AME)—would constitute its driving force and institutional core, at once spiritual, moral, cultural, political, and organizational.

The Montgomery bus boycott, whose collective leadership was both lay and clergy, transformed one of these preachers into the most acclaimed black leader since Booker T. Washington and the preeminent national symbol of black advancement. A trio of Martin Luther King's advisers in New York, Bayard Rustin, Ella Baker, and radical white lawyer Stanley Levison, persuaded him to utilize the Montgomery victory, and his new fame, to fuse into a South-wide federation the church-based movements that had arisen in several cities. As sociologist Aldon Morris notes, the strength of the new Southern Christian Leadership Conference (SCLC) was its ability to unify local black leaders "by bringing them directly into leadership positions while simultaneously organizing the black masses"; the mass base of the church was built into the SCLC structure. Although King, not yet thirty, dominated SCLC from the outset, his leadership style nurtured a remarkable cadre of second-level leaders, astute and courageous organizers such as Fred Shuttlesworth, C. T. Vivian, James Bevel, Dorothy Cotton, and Andrew Young, most of whom were also men of the cloth.

Yet the clergy-led federation floundered for a while in charting a strategy for the cause. SCLC launched a voter registration campaign, "Crusade for Citizenship," with disappointing results, and it created a community of activists from isolated Southern cities. But by the end of the decade it seemed to have lost its bearings.

On Monday afternoon, February 1, 1960, four well-dressed young men, first-year students at the mainly black North Carolina A&T College in Greensboro, bought some school supplies at Woolworth's, then sat down at the store lunch counter and ordered coffee. "I'm sorry," the waitress said, "we don't serve you here." Ignoring the manager's pleas and the arrival of police, the four refused to leave until the store, now crowded with onlookers, closed early. They had planned their protest the night before, after weeks of dorm bull sessions about the injustice of segregation and the power of Gandhian nonviolent resistance. Soon more than 90 percent of the area's black college students were sitting in, picketing, or boycotting segregated eating places.

News of the sudden protest flashed across the South. Similar "sit-ins" had been tried in Nashville, led by Reverend James Lawson, Jr., and elsewhere, but the idea now spread "like a fever." By February's end sit-ins had occurred in thirty cities in seven states and by April they pervaded the South. The young women and men stayed calm and resolute when food and ketchup were flung at them, when they were jabbed with lighted cigarettes, and when they were beaten up. Police intervened only to take them to jail. As historian Clayborne Carson observes, never again in the decade would such a high proportion of college students, black or white, engage in protest. Hundreds of lunch counters and restaurants were opened to black citizens.

SCLC director Ella Baker, then fifty-six, saw the sit-in movement as a momentous development but knew it would not endure without a structure to coordinate the local groups. Defiance of racial oppression had been a tradition in her family. When Baker was a child her grandmother, for whom she was named, told her stories of slave revolts and of how she had been whipped for refusing to marry the man chosen by her owner; she wed instead a rebellious slave who became a Baptist preacher and was an important role model for his granddaughter. Baker had been organizing for thirty years—setting up black consumer cooperatives during the Depression, recruiting NAACP members throughout the South, serving as NAACP director of branches, and then heading its New York office before helping to found SCLC.

On Easter weekend 1960 she convened a conference of sit-in leaders from over fifty black Southern colleges at Shaw University in Raleigh, North Carolina, where as a student in the 1920s she had been class valedictorian. Baker believed that, rather than be co-opted into forming a youth wing of SCLC, the students needed an autonomous organization "with the right to direct their own affairs and even make their own mistakes." The young activists set up a loosely structured Student Nonviolent Coordinating Committee (SNCC) and adopted a statement of purpose that affirmed its commitment both to ending racial domination and to a Christian-based nonviolent philosophy.

Inspired by Baker, who had grown so critical of SCLC's rigid, preacher-dominated hierarchy that she resigned, SNCC embodied an alternative style of participatory "group-centered leadership." Opposed to the centrality of charismatic leaders who were best at organizing the media, SNCC activists lived out the idea that real change came through the empowerment of people at the grass roots. They understood that to overcome racial subjugation, especially in the rural South, black people would have to rely on themselves, not outside leaders, to claim their rights.

SNCC's reputation for fearless militancy derived from the "freedom rides" of 1961 to desegregate bus terminals in the heart of the Deep

South, a campaign initiated by the Congress of Racial Equality. CORE, an offshoot of the pacifist Fellowship of Reconciliation, had been founded by James Farmer, Bayard Rustin, and others and had pioneered the use of nonviolent direct action in an effort to integrate Chicago restaurants in the early 1940s. As the Warren Court had just declared segregated terminals unconstitutional, Farmer now hoped that "putting the movement on wheels" would force federal intervention to execute the law.

In May 1961 thirteen black and white activists left Washington on two buses, headed for New Orleans. Outside of Anniston, Alabama, one bus was forced off the road and firebombed; the choking riders barely escaped the inferno. Eight men burst into the second bus and assaulted the passengers, nearly killing a retired white professor. The Ku Klux Klan ambushed the freedom riders on their arrival at the Birmingham station; white pacifist Jim Peck underwent hours of surgery for head wounds.

CORE decided to declare victory and go home, but Diane Nash and other SNCC members resolved to complete the journey. After intercession by Robert Kennedy, the new attorney general, a SNCC group rode a bus from Birmingham to Montgomery, protected by police cars and helicopters. But when the bus drew into the Montgomery terminal the police had gone; the riders were greeted by a mob that beat them mercilessly, maiming one young man.

The next night King spoke in support of the freedom riders at a mass meeting in Ralph Abernathy's church. Nash and Farmer insisted that King reject a request from Kennedy for a "cooling-off period." Tell the Attorney General, Farmer instructed King, "that we have been cooling off for 350 years." Hundreds of white rioters besieged the church, throwing rocks through its stained-glass windows, while those inside steeled themselves with spirited singing. The mob was about to break down the doors when a battalion of U.S. marshals sent by Kennedy dispersed it with tear gas. National Guard troops belatedly reinforced the outnumbered marshals.

Three days hence two busloads of freedom riders, National Guardsmen, and reporters departed for Jackson, Mississippi, escorted by legions of police in cars and aircraft. As the result of a deal between Kennedy and Mississippi officials ostensibly to avoid violence, the riders were arrested upon entering the Jackson terminal. They served two months at the tough Parchman state penitentiary, where defiant singing of freedom songs got them through. Over the summer of 1961 hundreds more activists flocked to the Jackson terminal and joined their peers in prison. Prodded by the Attorney General, the Interstate Commerce Commission enforced the Supreme Court ruling by banning segregation in interstate terminals. The freedom rides not only led to the integration of transportation facilities, Carson notes, but also "contributed to the development of a self-consciously radical southern student movement prepared to direct its militancy toward other concerns."

In fall 1961 SNCC organizers launched a campaign to abolish Jim Crow in Albany, a city in rural southwestern Georgia. They recruited local students, especially from the NAACP Youth Council, and catalyzed a broad coalition of black residents. When the campaign sagged and local leaders invited King to help revive it, his jailing sparked huge turnouts and national publicity. But SNCC workers resented King's cautious approach and willingness to "settle for half a loaf"; they accused SCLC of taking over the Albany movement. Civil disobedience continued into the spring and summer of 1962, coupled with boycotts of white stores and segregated buses, but Albany's shrewd police chief, Laurie Pritchett, and uncompromising city commissioners maneuvered deftly to exploit the movement's divisions and held fast to segregation.

SCLC applied lessons from the Albany defeat the next year in an all-out campaign of direct action in Birmingham, the industrial capital of the South and reputedly the most segregated city in the country. The spring 1963 campaign would focus on a single target; pursue a definite strategy with careful planning; remain unified, under the control of SCLC; and profit from the recklessness of a police chief who, unlike Albany's Pritchett, would not hesitate to use brutal tactics and thereby expose the ugliness of racism. The immediate goal: to desegregate lunch counters and hiring at the downtown department stores. The strategy: marches and store boycotts, aimed to split the business elite from the city officials.

SCLC leaders sought a morale-lifting victory that would "set the pace" for the South and spur the federal government to enact sweeping civil rights legislation. "If we can crack Birmingham," King said, "I am convinced we can crack the South."

Workshops trained thousands in nonviolent combat. Nightly mass meetings were rocked by spirited speeches and the freedom songs that King called "the soul of the movement." It would be hard to exaggerate the cultural power generated by the fervent singing at church meetings, on the streets, and in jail cells, which had made the black freedom struggle a "singing movement." The songs people sang were often slave spirituals with lyrics freshly crafted to fit the moment, or songs refurbished from labor battles. The movement's anthem, "We Shall Overcome," came from both traditions. Bernice Johnson Reagon, an Albany State College student activist, daughter of a Baptist preacher, and soon one of SNCC's traveling Freedom Singers, said that after singing "the differences among us would not be as great. Somehow, making a song required an expression of that which was common to us all." Singing was the unifying language of protest, the vital tool to build solidarity, sustain morale, instill courage, and deepen commitment.

"Get on board, children, children," the Freedom Singers sang. "Let's fight for human rights."

On Good Friday, King, Ralph Abernathy, and fifty others defied a state injunction barring protests obtained by police commissioner Eugene "Bull" Connor. Kneeling in prayer, they were thrown into paddy wagons and jailed. King was held in solitary, a dark cell with no mattress or blanket, until President Kennedy intervened. He spent his days behind bars scribbling a long letter in the margins of a newspaper and on scraps of paper, challenging a statement in a Birmingham daily by moderate white Alabama clergy that condemned his tactics and timing. "Letter from Birmingham Jail," widely published, offered the most cogent defense of the right and indeed duty of civil disobedience since the famous essay by Henry David Thoreau that King had read years before.

"I submit that an individual who breaks a law that conscience tells him is unjust," King wrote, "and who willingly accepts the penalty of imprisonment in order to arouse the conscience of the community over its injustice, is in reality expressing the highest respect for law."

When King and Abernathy were set free, the crusade took off. While the boycott disrupted downtown business, wave after wave of protesters—including over a thousand eager, well-trained children—were mauled by police dogs and hurled against walls and to the pavement by ferocious cannonades of water blasting from fire hoses. But Connor's harsh tactics defeated him as vivid television coverage shocked much of the American public into support of the protesters' cause. Pressured by President Kennedy and fearing economic calamity, Birmingham's business elite agreed to most demands, despite resistance from a divided city hall. SCLC won a crucial if largely symbolic victory in this American Johannesburg.

The electrifying Birmingham drama ignited or energized indigenous movements in hundreds of cities across the South. Campaigns in places like Danville, Virginia, Orangeburg, South Carolina, and Jackson, Mississippi, did not get the national media attention that King had orchestrated in Birmingham. But they were often as skillfully organized, particularly the NAACP-backed local efforts to integrate public schools.

The pace of school desegregation was slower than even the cautious Supreme Court had intended. Tactics of delay and evasion proved so effective that by 1963 only about 1 percent of Southern black children attended mixed schools; much more progress had been made in border states, however, than further south. Washington intervened to enforce desegregation only as a last resort, when unyielding governors flouted federal mandates. President Eisenhower, who privately wished that the Court had upheld *Plessy*'s separate-but-equal doctrine in the *Brown* case, reluctantly sent a thousand paratroopers to Little Rock, Arkansas, in 1957 after a white mob, emboldened by Governor Orval Faubus's defiance of a court order, tried to bar nine black students from entering Central High School. In fall 1962 John Kennedy had deployed the army and National Guard to enforce admission of James Meredith to the all-white University of Mississippi. Two days of street battles between troops and a few thousand whites had left two dead and hundreds injured before Governor Ross Barnett finally relented. Then, just after the Birmingham victory, Alabama's new governor, George Wallace, had stood "in the schoolhouse door" of the state university to block Vivian Malone and James Hood from enrolling. He stepped aside at the last minute, yielding to federal marshals.

For months prior to Birmingham, labor leader A. Philip Randolph and his longtime protégé Bayard Rustin had been planning a march on Washington to focus attention on black joblessness and poverty. King and other mainstream leaders, including Roy Wilkins of the NAACP and the National Urban League's Whitney Young, formed a coalition with liberal white clergy and labor unions to mount the march, with Rustin in charge. The leaders decided to downplay economic issues, however, in order to concentrate on pushing for passage of the civil rights bill that Birmingham had put on President Kennedy's front burner. On August 28, 1963, a quarter of a million people gathered in Washington, including many poor blacks bused by SNCC from the Deep South, and marched to the Lincoln Memorial. After singing by Odetta, Joan Baez, and Peter, Paul and Mary, and speeches by civil rights notables, Martin Luther King, Jr., stood beneath the brooding stone face of Abraham Lincoln and lifted the sea of people to a pinnacle of jubilation and hope with his stirring dream of racial justice.

DURING the last months of his life, John Kennedy had been edging away from his conservative caution on the issue of black freedom—particularly from his reluctance to propose civil rights legislation that might offend Southern congressional oligarchs, such as Virginia's Howard Smith, who dominated key congressional committees. First Kennedy toughened his rhetoric. At the peak of the Birmingham upheaval he told a Nashville audience: "No one can gainsay the fact that the determination to secure these rights is in the highest traditions of American freedom."

On the day that George Wallace courted arrest at the University of Alabama, JFK addressed the nation on television. We are confronted with a moral issue, he declared, that "is as old as the scriptures and is as clear as the American Constitution. . . . We preach freedom around the world, and we mean it, and we cherish our freedom here at home, but are we to say to the world, and much more importantly, to each other that this is a land of the free except for the Negroes; that we have no second-class citizens except Negroes; that we have no class or caste system, no ghettoes, no master race except with respect to Negroes?

"Now the time has come for this Nation to fulfill its promise. The events in Birmingham and elsewhere have so increased the cries for equality that no city or State or legislative body can prudently choose to ignore them."

With this acknowledgment that he was responding to mass demands, Kennedy sent a civil rights bill to Capitol Hill that, in spite of serious limitations, represented the first substantive rights legislation since the civil rights act drafted by John Mercer Langston at the close of Reconstruction. The bill was not enacted until after Kennedy's assassination in November 1963. The machinery of Congress was so cumbersome, if not antidemocratic, that passage required an all-out lobbying campaign by the Leadership Conference on Civil Rights, a grand interracial coalition in which liberal churches played a decisive role. "Washington has not seen such a gigantic and well-organized lobby," rued Georgia senator Richard Russell, "since the legislative days of Volstead and the Prohibition amendment."

Moreover, it took the genius for cajolery of Kennedy's successor, Lyndon Johnson, combined with the tenacity of Hubert Humphrey and other liberals, to win over GOP leader Everett Dirksen and enough Republican senators to muster a two-thirds majority to end the Southern filibuster. The Senate then followed the House in overwhelmingly approving the omnibus measure, which LBJ signed on July 2, 1964. The bill and its passage were the fruit of the cumulative political force generated by the nonviolent protests throughout the South.

The 1964 Civil Rights Act established a national policy prohibiting racial segregation and discrimination. It outlawed discrimination in public accommodations and public schools, authorizing the attorney general to bring suit against offenders, and it banned discrimination in employment on the basis of either race or sex. The new law was not as strong as activists had wanted but better than Kennedy's original proposal. In C. Vann Woodward's words, "Jim Crow as a legal entity was dead."

The test would be its effect on racism and on altering race relations, South and North. The major difficulty, as always, was enforcement, which depended on a committed attorney general with ample political will. The law provided exclusively judicial remedies largely inaccessible to ordinary citizens without legal resources. Nevertheless, widespread fear of prosecution did compel the desegregation of most public facilities in the South, although not much changed with segregated housing and jobs. School integration did not advance markedly until the federal bureaucracy swung into action in the late 1960s.

While most black leaders applauded the law, some were troubled by its inadequacies, particularly its irrelevance to the majority of those African-Americans who lived outside the South. Since it did not affect "most types of *de facto* civil rights problems," a CORE analysis pointed out, "the ghetto minorities in the urban North are ignored."

It was condemned for this reason by Malcolm X, the most popular leader of lower-class urban blacks. Son of a Baptist preacher who had organized for Marcus Garvey's Universal Negro Improvement Association, Malcolm was a high school dropout, educated in the ghettoes of Roxbury and Harlem, who had once made his way as a drug dealer and pimp. While in prison he had converted to the separatist Nation of Islam, founded by Elijah Muhammad, and after his release became an extraordinary speaker and organizer for the fast-growing sect. When the Civil Rights Act passed he had just broken free of the Nation of Islam to begin developing an internationalist strategy for black liberation based on building alliances with Third World countries. He intended to "expand the civil-rights struggle to a higher level—to the level of human rights," encompassing economic and social entitlements, and as a first step to put American racism on trial at the United Nations. Malcolm criticized the 1964 law as "only a valve, a vent, that was designed to enable us to let off our frustrations. . . . " It was not designed "to solve our problems" but to "lessen the explosion."

Malcolm's efforts to move beyond narrowly defined civil rights and to internationalize the black struggle were cut short by his assassination on February 21, 1965, as he presented his new program at Harlem's Audubon Ballroom.

IS THIS AMERICA?

THE OMISSION of voting rights protection from the 1964 law perpetuated the old syndrome of compartmentalization that had plagued nineteenth-century rights activism. No more than their forebears did later black leaders want to divide rights, but the mainstream leadership acquiesced for reasons of expediency. While Malcolm X was calling for a more comprehensive focus on broad human rights, King and his coalition partners deferred economic entitlements and even put civil before political rights. During Reconstruction the priority had been reversed: black men secured their voting rights, igniting a short-lived political revolution in the South, while civil rights and integrated facilities were denied by a white consensus. This bifurcation made it easier for Southern elites gradually to eliminate black suffrage, the Fifteenth Amendment notwithstanding. In the 1940s and 1950s blacks began reasserting their right to vote in larger numbers, but by 1960 the arsenal of literacy tests, poll taxes, intimidation, economic pressure, and violent retaliation was still intact, keeping black registration down to abysmal levels—lowest in Alabama (13 percent) and Mississippi (5 percent).

Unlike desegregation, universal suffrage did not threaten an abrupt change in customary race relations and was difficult for white leaders to oppose publicly. Yet whites and blacks keenly understood the potential leverage of political rights in realizing such social and economic rights as might eventually transform the South; ruling groups thus employed every available weapon against black enfranchisement. This partly explains why SCLC's voter registration campaigns made little headway in the late 1950s and early 1960s, despite the creative efforts of Ella Baker, citizenship education leaders Septima Clark and Dorothy Cotton, and many at the grass roots.

The dramatic struggle for civil rights-as-desegregation had an unexpected effect on the suffrage drive: it prodded the Kennedy administration early on to take steps, behind the scenes, to promote the right to vote. Back in mid-June 1961, while young freedom riders were singing their way through tough times at Parchman state pen, Attorney General Kennedy met in his office with the Freedom Ride Coordinating Committee, which was angling for stronger federal support. Instead, Kennedy proposed that they drop direct-action tactics and concentrate on voter registration. To sweeten the pot, he would help arrange foundation money, tax and even draft exemption. Considering this a bribe, SNCC activist Charles Sherrod jumped to his feet. "You are a public official, sir," he angrily lectured the nation's chief law enforcement officer. "It's not your responsibility . . . to tell us how to honor our constitutional rights. It's your job to protect us when we do." Kennedy did not back off. Later that summer his staff collaborated with rights leaders to set up the foundation-funded Voter Education Project, which would channel money to grass-roots registration efforts.

Thus powerful Washington actors were trying to push the movement to choose voting rights over civil rights, though they argued that the former would lead, in a less disruptive and more rational fashion, to the latter. SNCC agonized about whether this was an opportunity for a real breakthrough—or a trap. Some members urged further civil disobedience to end segregation. Others argued that racial domination would not be overthrown until blacks had electoral power. Wary of co-optation, the first camp felt suspicious of a registration strategy plugged by the Kennedy administration, whose political interests would be well served by an expanded black electorate.

Ella Baker broke the logjam during a SNCC conference at the Highlander Folk School in Appalachian Tennessee, an important movement meeting place. She proposed that SNCC have two branches, one for desegregation direct action and the other for voter registration. The latter strategy soon eclipsed the former as SNCC discovered that no action was riskier and more militant than organizing blacks to vote in Mississippi, the kingpin of Southern white supremacy—and of white terrorism.

Amzie Moore, a local NAACP leader, persuaded SNCC to start a voter registration program in Mississippi. In late summer 1961 Bob Moses, architect of the new campaign, moved to McComb, a small city in southern Mississippi, where he set up the first of a string of registration "schools." In his mid-twenties, Moses had grown up in Harlem and, after attending Hamilton College, had been a Harvard graduate student in philosophy, drawn to Camus and existentialism. While a high school teacher in New York he had organized with Bayard Rustin and then, inspired by the lunch counter sit-ins, arrived at SNCC's makeshift Atlanta office. Moses would become a legend in SNCC not only for his courage but for his genius at motivating participation and leadership in other people, particularly impoverished rural blacks.

Moses and his small cadre were beaten and arrested when they accompanied prospective black voters seeking to register at the county courthouse. Herbert Lee, a farmer and father of nine and supporter of SNCC's work, was gunned down by a state legislator, who was never prosecuted. When Moses and fellow organizers marched to protest the murder, they were jailed for two months. They left McComb in December and fanned out into the flat, fertile Mississippi Delta region in the northwest, recruiting local activists. SNCC people were shot at in their cars, and mobs invaded their offices. Risk and repression became a way of life.

Success in turning out disfranchised voters for an unofficial, movement-sponsored state election in fall 1963 convinced SNCC and its partners in the Council of Federated Organizations (COFO) that black citizens could build an electoral vehicle independent of the segregated state Democratic Party. As its immediate goal the Mississippi Freedom Democratic Party (MFDP), founded in early 1964, prepared to challenge the all-white state party for official seating at the August Democratic National Convention.

At the same time, COFO launched the Mississippi Summer Project that brought a thousand Northern college students, predominantly white, to join an intensive registration crusade parallel to the MFDP effort. COFO calculated that if white students were beaten or killed, it would grab national attention and might lead to federal protection of voting rights; black victims of Mississippi's reign of terror—several dozen dead in the first half of the decade—had been largely ignored. Just as the student army began to arrive after exhaustive training, a trio of Freedom Summer organizers, James Chaney, black, Michael Schwerner and Andrew Goodman, white, were lynched by the Ku Klux Klan, their bodies mutilated and buried in an earthen dam. Despite sensational media coverage, Robert Kennedy—the champion of voter registration—claimed the Justice Department had no authority to intervene, except for the ineffectual FBI, whose Southern agents seemed reluctant to offend local police.

Over the summer more black people were killed for aspiring to be citizens, and dozens of church headquarters were burned or bombed. Unable to make significant gains, the general voter registration work gave way to the building of the MFDP. "Have you freedom-registered?" organizers asked—in churches, on backwoods roads, on cabin porches, and riding plantation buses with cotton pickers long before sunup. MFDP conventions in each county chose delegates to the state convention in Jackson. "People straight out of tarpaper shacks," participant Sally Belfrage reported, "many illiterate, some wearing a (borrowed) suit for the first time, disenfranchised for three generations, without a living memory of political power, yet caught on with some extraordinary inner sense to how the process worked, down to its smallest nuance and finagle." Ella Baker gave a passionate keynote address to the Jackson gathering, many of whose delegates were black women—the most popular being forty-six-year-old SNCC organizer Fannie Lou Hamer. Just two years before, she had been fired as a sharecropper for trying to register. Sixty-eight men and women were chosen to fight for party recognition at the national convention in Atlantic City.

With nine state delegations lined up behind them and armed with a solid legal brief drafted by Democratic power broker Joseph Rauh, counsel for the United Auto Workers, the MFDP delegates felt confident they would be seated, especially since their rivals refused to pledge loyalty to the national ticket. At a live televised hearing, poor black Mississippians testified vividly about what happened when they sought the right to vote. In gripping cadences Hamer told of being brutally beaten in jail "'til my hands was as navy blue as anything you ever seen." She concluded that "all of this is on account we want to register, to become first-class citizens, and if the Freedom Democratic Party is not seated now, I question America. Is this America," she asked, "the land of the free and the home of the brave?"

The nationwide TV audience did not see the end of Hamer's testimony because President Johnson abruptly preempted it with an impromptu press conference. LBJ opposed seating the MFDP lest he lose white Southerners in November. But the ex-sharecropper had so stirred up the public that Johnson had to offer a small compromise: two at-large seats for the delegation heads and a promise of nondiscrimination in the future. The MFDP would have accepted "any honorable compromise" but Johnson's offer felt like a slap in the face; and the nondiscrimination pledge meant little without a guarantee of black voting rights.

Resisting eloquent cajolery by King, Rustin, and other luminaries who feared funding cutoffs by liberal backers, the MFDP delegates instead followed Hamer's lead—"We didn't come all this way for no two seats!" she exclaimed—and voted down the proposal. The battle was lost when their supporters on the Credentials Committee caved in to White House arm-twisting. The MFDP's last hurrah was a televised sit-in in the vacated seats of the all-white delegation, who had walked out to protest the compromise offer. MFDP activists returned to the Southern battlefield disillusioned and angry. They had learned that, before seeking alliances with whites, they had to get political power of their own.

SEVERAL MONTHS LATER, veteran community activists Amelia Boynton and Frederick Reese of the Selma, Alabama, Voters League asked King and SCLC to undertake a voting rights campaign in their city of 30,000. For over two years a SNCC team had been organizing ward meetings and registration marches, without much success. Of 15,000 eligible black voters in the county, only 300 were registered.

King came to Selma in January 1965, just after being awarded the Nobel Peace Prize in Norway. Leading a march to the county courthouse, he was jailed along with hundreds of others by Sheriff Jim Clark. Three thousand were arrested that week as the protest escalated. Two weeks later, black people marching peacefully in the nearby town of Marion were savagely attacked by state troopers, and twenty-six-year-old Jimmie Lee Jackson was shot point-blank as he tried to shield his mother and grandfather, both badly beaten. When he died several days later, local blacks decided to march on the state capital, an idea embraced by SCLC leaders.

On Sunday, March 7, defying a ban by Governor Wallace, SCLC's Hosea Williams and SNCC's John Lewis led several hundred out of Brown AME Chapel, heading for Montgomery, forty-five miles away. When they crossed the Edmund Pettus Bridge, named for Selma's own

Confederate general, the marchers were stopped by a phalanx of gas-masked state troopers, who with little warning lunged at them, smashing heads and lobbing tear gas grenades. The troopers and Sheriff Clark's mounted posse chased and trampled the marchers all the way back to the church headquarters, madly flailing whips, clubs, and cattle prods. Many were injured. As had happened in Birmingham, the graphic televised brutality won over much of the American public to the nonviolent demonstrators and their cause. Protests against "Bloody Sunday," demanding federal action, erupted nationwide, including a SNCC sit-in at the attorney general's office and a White House vigil.

Two days later, reinforced by dozens of prominent Northern clergy, King led another march across the Pettus Bridge but turned his followers around after crossing it; he had made an agreement with Washington to go no further. Bloody Sunday and its aftermath, not least the murder of Boston Unitarian minister James Reeb, persuaded President Johnson to push a voting rights bill with provisions for federal registrars and a ban on literacy tests. He and Robert Kennedy's successor as attorney general, Nicholas Katzenbach, quickly crafted a congressional coalition to enact it.

In mid-March Selma activists huddled around TV sets to watch Johnson plead for the bill before a joint session of Congress. "At times history and fate meet in a single time in a single place," he said, "to shape a turning point in man's unending search for freedom. So it was at Lexington and Concord. So it was a century ago at Appomattox. So it was last week in Selma, Alabama." SCLC leaders were watching at the home of Jimmie Lee Jackson's family. When Johnson promised the nation that "we shall overcome," a subdued Martin King cried while his colleagues cheered.

Presidential support did not dampen the determination to reach Montgomery. After careful logistical preparation, hundreds of marchers set off across the now-famous bridge, guarded closely by a far more numerous force of National Guard and army troops sent in by the commander-in-chief. For five days the rain-soaked, "mudcaked pilgrims" trekked onward, past half-collapsed shacks, rickety Baptist churches, and a dilapidated black school.

Their numbers multiplied as they marched into Montgomery and filled the long avenue leading to the statehouse, with its Confederate flag still flying. Finally at their destination, they held a rally below Governor Wallace's window. "How long?" King asked, standing near the bronze star where Confederate president Jefferson Davis had been inaugurated, and looking down Dexter Avenue at the church he had pastored. "Not long," he answered, repeating the litany over and over as more and more voices joined in. "How long?" he concluded. "Not long, because mine eyes have seen the glory of the coming of the Lord; tramping out the vintage where the grapes of wrath are stored. . . . His truth is marching on!"

One of those listening was Viola Liuzzo, a white volunteer from Detroit who had labored to make the march a success. That night, as she drove her green Oldsmobile back to Montgomery to ferry another carload of protesters home, she was murdered by four Klansmen, one an FBI informer.

After weeks of legislative wrangling, a surprisingly strong voting rights bill passed Congress. Prior to the Selma campaign Johnson had had no intention of pushing for a voting measure soon, believing that the dust had to settle first from the 1964 law. SCLC's three-month Selma crusade, the culmination of the entire Southern movement but especially of voting rights efforts, not only turned the administration around but sped up the legislative process, toughened the bill, and won over the wavering. New York Democrat Emanuel Celler, head of the House judiciary subcommittee that shaped it, acknowledged that the "climate of public opinion throughout the nation has so changed because of the Alabama outrages, as to make assured passage of this solid bill—a bill that would have been inconceivable a year ago." It had been a long, tortuous road since black suffrage campaigns had begun in the North a century and a quarter past.

The implementation of the 1965 Voting Rights Act in the eleven covered Southern states, in particular the use or threatened use of federal registrars, brought a big jump in black registration. From 1967 on, a growing majority of those eligible were registered. The numbers of Southern black officeholders increased substantially in absolute terms but did not rise proportionately with the black electorate. Nearly all were local positions; by 1990 only one Southern black had been elected to statewide office. A handful, including Barbara Jordan, Andrew Young, and John Lewis, were elected to the lower house of Congress. Clearly, the right to vote has not actualized a right to representation.

What accounts for the limited electoral success so far? First, the Voting Rights Act has seldom been strictly enforced. The extent and vigor of enforcement reflected the ebb and flow of the freedom movement; when the movement's political clout diminished, so did the law's enforcement. Some black citizens have not registered or voted due to lingering fear of physical or economic reprisal. And through evasion of the law, registration obstacles, removal of blacks from voting rolls, at-large elections, gerrymandered districts, and judicial harassment of black politicians, white elites have continued to subvert the exercise of black political rights.

Despite these problems, in a long-term perspective Southern black voters have steadily gained political influence, regionally and nationally. For example, they enabled Jimmy Carter to win the presidency in 1976. They were the backbone of the constituencies that built the Rainbow Coalition in the 1980s and made Jesse Jackson the first credible black presidential candidate. When combined, the Southern and Northern black electorates have enormous potential as the central dynamic of new political coalitions, particularly if joined by other people of color.

THE GOVERNMENT'S VIOLATION of its constitutional obligation to enforce rights laws has a long history. For two hundred years organized citizens have prevailed upon legislators, presidents, and the judiciary to recognize and promise fundamental entitlements and have amended or redefined the Constitution when feasible. Sometimes rights movements have gone further and assumed the responsibility for enforcement abdicated by civil authority. During Reconstruction Southern black activists mounted an adroit organizing campaign to implement rights to suffrage and representation, including defending against assaults by the Ku Klux Klan and other white supremacists. Decades later their great-grandchildren's generation was still organizing to carry out the Fourteenth and Fifteenth amendments. One of the more memorable efforts, for example, was the freedom riders' direct enforcement of the Supreme Court ban on segregation in interstate transportation.

Significantly, the black movement abandoned its enforcement mission, by and large, after enactment of the Civil Rights and Voting Rights acts, apparently expecting that the government, then run by liberal Democrats, would do its job. In fact this mission was needed as much as ever. Historically rights advocates in all areas have responded well to the need to implement, through enacting new laws or by direct action, constitutional provisions and judicial rulings that have lacked enforcement mechanisms. Where they seem to have gone astray is in trusting that the government would enforce adequately its statutes and executive orders. Creating or reforming laws was only half the battle. Given larger social forces and constraints, the additional responsibility of enforcement had to be shared by grass-roots activists in creative tension with the state, particularly to ensure that rights laws were implemented as intended by those who fought for them.

ECONOMIC JUSTICE

IN AN INSTRUCTIVE PARALLEL with the nineteenth-century black movement, especially during Reconstruction, the later freedom movement did not make economic needs and aspirations a high priority. At first glance the abundance of movement rhetoric about black poverty and joblessness and the obligatory demands for economic betterment seem to belie this. But if one looks at deeds not words, and to the deployment of movement resources, it is clear that economic rights were slighted— until it was probably too late to make a real difference.

The chief reason was that the Southern movement remained tied to the constitutional framework charted by Reconstruction leaders and taken up by the NAACP in the next century. The overarching aim was finally to implement the unfulfilled promises of the Fourteenth and Fifteenth amendments. Although a majority of African-Americans still lived in or near poverty, most leaders held that securing constitutional rights had to be the foundation and precondition for economic advances.

Moreover, partly because the Constitution did not speak to economic justice, and thus did not provide any authority or guidance in this domain, movement strategists did not know how to tackle entrenched economic inequality. In the 1930s, black activists had been able to ride the New Deal bandwagon and take advantage of a national concern with unemployment and economic deprivation; black unionists and leftists, often aided by the Communist Party, found the climate more conducive to the organization of urban blacks around economic rights. Indeed, W. E. B. Du Bois resigned from NAACP leadership during the 1930s in part because he had challenged NAACP orthodoxy by advocating economic strategies, such as building cooperatives, along with civil rights efforts. In the ostensibly prosperous 1950s and 1960s poverty—black and white—faded from majority view. Yet while focusing on desegregation and voting, local activists in many Southern communities organized around economic needs as best they could, for example by setting up producer and consumer cooperatives. Particularly if poor themselves, they experienced the inseparability of racism and poverty and did not have the luxury of placing one ahead of the other.

To a lesser extent, movement organizations incorporated economic goals into their civil rights work. A secondary demand of the Montgomery bus boycott was the hiring of black bus drivers. The Birmingham campaign pressured department stores to hire black clerks. SNCC workers in rural communities assisted co-ops and economic development projects. Increasingly, CORE chapters in Northern cities turned to direct action against housing and job discrimination.

On the national level, black leaders offered legislative proposals for economic uplift. In mid-1963 Whitney Young, head of the moderate National Urban League, argued that the "discrimination gap" caused by "more than three centuries of abuse, humiliation, segregation, and bias has burdened the Negro with a handicap that will not automatically slip from his shoulders as discriminatory laws and practices are abandoned." To equalize opportunity, to enable blacks to begin the social race at the same starting line, Young called for "an immediate, dramatic, and tangible domestic Marshall Plan" (referring to the U.S.-financed rebuilding of Western Europe after the devastation of World War II). The heart of his proposal was a "special effort"—which he distinguished from special privileges—of massive compensatory action, over ten years, by government, business, and foundations to generate employment, to improve education, housing, and health, and to "reverse economic and social deterioration of urban families and communities." Both Young's sweeping proposal and Martin Luther King's more general "Bill of Rights for the Disadvantaged" drew precedent from the generous compensatory program of postwar veterans' benefits; and both would have included not only blacks but all of the poor or disadvantaged.

At the same time, socialists Bayard Rustin and A. Philip Randolph, who had wanted the 1963 Washington march to stress economic goals, insisted that black people could not move forward without attacking the economic roots of racism. They put their faith in a grand coalition of blacks with organized labor, liberal Democrats, and clergy—a more progressive version of the old New Deal alliance, with African-Americans in a more prominent position. In a widely read 1965 *Commentary* article, Rustin suggested that the movement would not be victorious without "radical programs for full employment, abolition of slums, the reconstruction of our educational system, new definitions of work and leisure. Adding up the cost of such programs, we can only conclude that we are talking about a refashioning of our political economy." He noted that "preferential treatment" alone would not help the hard-core unemployed.

None of these economic strategies bore fruit. Congress did not take them seriously, nor did leaders mobilize the grass-roots armies behind economic entitlement reforms.

One consequence of the black movement's relative inattention to economics was its secondary role in motivating and shaping the government's antipoverty effort. Most scholars looking at the "war on poverty" concur that, in contrast to the civil rights and voting rights acts, it was not a response to movement pressures. They credit President Kennedy for initiating it, his concern kindled by Michael Harrington's vivid investigation of poverty, *The Other America;* President Johnson for enlarging it and winning congressional approval; and social scientists for making the case for state intervention. Yet though the movement exerted little overt influence, it had a decisive indirect effect: first of all, by producing a favorable moral and political environment; also, as in the mid-nineteenth century, by popularizing notions of entitlements and the expectations that activate them, now stretched to encompass economic wants and needs; finally, by inducing both presidents to offer economic remedies, more palatable to Southern Democrats, as a move to head off touchier rights laws.

Very likely the antipoverty campaign would have been more effective had rights leaders been centrally involved in it. The long-term end of preventing poverty was more ambitious than the New Deal's goals had been, but its means were paltry in comparison. The philosophy behind it was the old American ideal of expanding opportunity, while "rehabilitating" the poor. The various programs, delivering services rather than cash to the inner-city and rural poor, aimed at helping them to help themselves rise out of poverty. "They tried to open up doors, not set down floors," writes historian James Patterson, "to offer a hand up, not a handout." The programs "never seriously considered giving poor people what many of them needed most: jobs and income maintenance." Among the critics was the National Association of Social Workers, which contended that antipoverty measures should "assure income as a matter of right."

The war on poverty's main weapon was the decentralized Community Action Program (CAP), which marshaled legal, educational, social work, and health resources to give poor people more options. A controversial feature was the requirement that CAPs be "developed, conducted and administered with the maximum feasible participation of residents." But just as the phrase "all deliberate speed" had marred the *Brown* desegregation order, so the qualifier "feasible" encouraged noncompliance with this mandate. In the few cities such as Syracuse where poor people actually helped run the program, federal, state, and local authorities cut funding; nowhere was "involvement of the poor" converted into real power, or into structural change.

By the late 1960s the Vietnam War had drained so much funding from the war on poverty, inadequate to begin with, that a respected scholar branded it a "charade." In his thorough study of Community Action Programs social psychologist Kenneth Clark judged that they "have so far not resulted in any observable changes in the predicament of the poor."

The most damning indictment of the poverty war came from the poor themselves. The programs' failure, combined with explosive expectations raised by the rhetoric promoting them—the widening gap between promise and performance—helped to ignite a more literal war on poverty by ghetto dwellers. Usually provoked by police misconduct, violent black uprisings escalated in number and intensity from one summer to the next starting in 1963; well over a hundred people were killed, mostly by the police and military. The first large-scale "riot" erupted in August 1965 in the Los Angeles ghetto of Watts, where many buildings were burned down. Two summers later the revolts climaxed in Newark and Detroit. In the latter city thousands of National Guard and army paratroopers moved in with heavy firepower, thirty-three blacks were killed, and a vast area was gutted by raging fires. Flying over the Detroit battleground, Michigan governor George Romney testified later that "it looked like the city had been bombed . . . with entire blocks in flames."

The Johnson administration subsequently refused to heed its own investigative commission's warning that "our nation is moving toward two societies, one black, one white—separate and unequal." Possibly the "unprecedented levels of funding and performance" the Kerner Commission called for would have been more available if not for the other war ten thousand miles away.

STARTING IN 1966, King and other movement leaders were compelled to raise "economic justice" to the top of their agendas. Shaken by the urban rebellions, King acknowledged that he bore a degree of responsibility; he too had not delivered on all his promises. The Watts uprising helped persuade him to take the nonviolent struggle to the Northern war zones. In early 1966 SCLC launched a campaign in Chicago to try to prove that militant nonviolence could work in the ghetto. To symbolize his commitment King moved with his family into a dingy tenement in one of the Windy City's worst slums. Aimed mainly at eradicating slum conditions and integrating neighborhoods, the SCLC's marches and rallies led to a "half a loaf" compromise agreement with Mayor Richard Daley. SCLC also organized "Operation Breadbasket," a national clergy-led effort to force corporations to hire inner-city blacks and support black businesses, using the threat of consumer boycotts to win agreements. But the program proved more beneficial to black entrepreneurs, by and large, than to the unemployed.

During this tumultuous period of ghetto warfare and mounting Vietnam protest, King not only spoke out strongly against the Asian war that was robbing the antipoverty program and killing young men of color in cruelly disproportionate numbers, but denounced the capitalist system and became, more openly, a democratic socialist. Moving beyond his liberal individualist outlook oriented to individual rights and self-advancement, he came to understand that economic deprivation was rooted in class as much as race and that racism, poverty, and militarism were interlocked. He called for a radical redistribution of wealth and power, starting with a guaranteed income for all citizens, the lever for which would be an interracial alliance of the poor and oppressed. His ultimate goal now was "a reconstruction of the entire society, a revolution of values," and the creation of a "socially-conscious democracy which reconciles the truths of individualism and collectivism."

In late summer 1967, when King did not know where to go after the nation's worst civil disorders since the Civil War, an idea conveyed by Marian Wright, an NAACP poverty lawyer in Mississippi, lifted his sagging spirits: bring poor people to Washington to demand meaningful aid. Overruling objections of impracticality from other SCLC leaders, King envisioned "waves of the nation's poor and disinherited" engaging in mass civil disobedience—shutting down the capital if necessary—refusing to leave "until some definite and positive action is taken to provide jobs and income for the poor." He intended to stage a springtime drama as riveting as the urban riots, a "last, desperate demand," he declared, "for the nation to respond to nonviolence."

During the winter of 1968 King and SCLC organizers barnstormed the country recruiting soldiers for the poor people's army. In March, however, King could not turn down a plea to help a strike of black garbage workers in Memphis that seemed headed for defeat. After a week of speaking and marching for a cause that vividly symbolized the inseparability of racial and class oppression, and that won in the end, King was shot dead on a Memphis motel balcony on April 4. In response, enraged black youth rioted in a hundred cities, the most widespread disorder of the decade.

King's death knocked the wind out of the Poor People's Campaign, which already was running aground. The army of the poor descended on Washington in mid-May and put up a tent shantytown of canvas and plywood. Soon heavy rains conspired with human disorganization to make inhospitable the flooded, muddy "Resurrection City" and it had to be abandoned. The poor, who always seemed to lose, had been routed once again.

OTHER ACTIVISTS embarked on a different strategy to end poverty in the world's wealthiest nation. In fall 1965, social work scholar Richard Cloward and political scientist Frances Fox Piven circulated a working paper among civil rights and antipoverty organizers later published in *The Nation*. Responding to the black movement's search for new directions, they proposed organizing a mass movement of welfare recipients, who were mainly women. Given that for every existing recipient, another was eligible, several million of the poor could be recruited to the welfare rolls. And given that welfare agencies typically refused to grant clients the full benefits to which they were entitled, Cloward and Piven pointed to a huge untapped potential for expanded payments. If these were the immediate objectives, their longer-term goal was to disrupt the welfare system and foster such a grave bureaucratic, fiscal, and electoral crisis that Washington would be compelled to guarantee an unconditional, livable income for all citizens.

Without any leadership the urban poor already had been sweeping into welfare centers in much larger numbers, which resulted in a near-quadrupling of clients during the 1960s. The freedom movement had taught poor people that they had rights as citizens, even economic rights, while at the same time activists and antipoverty lawyers were inducing bureaucrats to loosen eligibility requirements. "Accompanying the rise in expectations," Patterson observes, "was a broadened, if unforeseen, definition of the rights of citizenship" to include economic and social needs, a redefinition explained partly by improvements in education and mass communication. Simultaneously the idea of economic rights had begun to take hold in academic and policy circles. Liberal economist Robert Theobald argued for the poor's "entitlements," stating that "we all need to adopt the concept of an absolute constitutional right to an income" from the federal government sufficient to enable every citizen to live with dignity. Thirteen hundred economists petitioned Congress for a national system of income guarantees and supplements.

Many activists dismissed the Cloward-Piven strategy, either because they did not think the welfare poor could be organized or because they felt that economic solutions required the creation of jobs, not the perpetuation of dependence. One experienced organizer, however, took hold of these ideas as the answer to his political frustration. George Wiley, great-grandson of slaves, had grown up in Rhode Island, conquered one racial barrier after another, including becoming the first black to earn a Ph.D. in chemistry from Cornell, and in the early 1960s had blossomed as a prominent research chemist at Syracuse University. But civil rights activism inexorably took over his life, as he worked first as a local CORE leader, then with James Farmer as CORE's associate director. He came to realize that neither CORE nor any other existing rights group was prepared to build the grass-roots movement of poor people he dreamed of.

"A lot of us who have come out of the civil rights movement have been quite frustrated," Wiley reflected, "about finding significant handles for bringing about some substantial change in the living conditions of people in the northern ghettoes. . . . For millions—particularly people who can't work, the aged or female heads of households—just encouraging them to assert their rights is a very attractive thing. . . . The potential here is enormous for getting the people involved in demanding rights as human beings from a system that doesn't treat them as human beings."

As a first step, in June 1966 Wiley's new Poverty/Rights Action Center coordinated protests for specific "welfare rights" in twenty-five cities. Marching 150 miles from Cleveland to Ohio's state capital to present grievances to the governor, several hundred welfare women sang:

> We feed our children bread and beans
> While rich folks ride in limousines.
> After all, we're human beings,
> Marching down Columbus Road.

Responding to such expressions of need, Wiley created the National Welfare Rights Organization to represent the lowest stratum of the American citizenry—impoverished urban women of color. Not merely an extension of the civil rights movement, welfare rights was a distinct "social protest of women who were poor," historian Guida West discovered. NWRO was led jointly by Wiley and a national board of dynamic, nononsense black welfare mothers including chair Johnnie Tillmon from Los Angeles; the shared leadership was animated by creative tension. Calling for concrete reforms grounded in principles of adequate income, dignity, justice, and democracy, NWRO set forth its goal: "Jobs or income now! Decent jobs with adequate wages for those who can work; adequate income for those who can not work."

Local groups multiplied in 1967 and 1968. With the help of resources from the national office such as "how-to" welfare rights handbooks, they carried out the "street strategy" of creative direct action. Most effective were "basic need" campaigns to secure special grants for winter clothing, furniture, and school lunches. NWRO organizing spread throughout the country, even among poor whites in Appalachia and the South, but it proved most successful in New York and Massachusetts. In New York City, the *Times* reported that demonstrators were invading and camping out en masse in welfare centers, breaking down administrative procedures, wreaking havoc on "the mountains of paperwork," and throwing welfare services into "a state of crisis and near-chaos." More often than not they won their demands.

In Washington, Wiley skillfully lobbied Congress and the welfare bureaucrats for reform. He and Columbia University law professor Edward Sparer fashioned a legal strategy using antipoverty lawyers and class-action suits that liberalized policies and led to several Supreme Court decisions that nullified provisions denying recipients certain procedural rights. But as the explosion of welfare clients and funding reached crisis proportions—linked by the media to urban riots—a public backlash set in. The Democratic Congress enacted punitive restrictions, many states cut welfare benefits, New York and Massachusetts abolished special grant programs, and the Nixon era's more conservative Supreme Court, led by Chief Justice Warren Burger, limited welfare clients' right to privacy. Eventually the attack on the welfare poor, combined with NWRO's internal divisions and its shift from direct action to lobbying, brought about its collapse in the early 1970s. Yet in the long run, the movement's success in expanding access, obtaining fairer treatment, and educating the public helped to solidify the legitimacy of welfare entitlements and to give greater dignity and self-respect to those who claimed them.

R E V E R E N D A N D R E W Y O U N G, SCLC's executive director during the 1960s, later credited welfare rights organizing with pushing the civil rights movement toward economic goals. Why did he think it took so long? "Religion was the language the South understood," Young explained, "and there was an almost calculated avoidance of any economic questions. . . . In SCLC we were working with college students, with independent business people. The civil rights movement, up until 1968, anyway, was really a middle-class movement. There were middle-class goals, middle-class aspirations, middle-class membership, and even though a lot of poor people went to jail . . . it was still essentially a middle-class operation."

Just as black Reconstruction activists had discovered that venturing beyond the bounds of the Constitution—its boundaries contentious enough already—to demand land from the Freedmen's Bureau was as politically hazardous as it was urgently needed, so activists a century later found that the struggle to expand citizenship rights to encompass economic aspirations faced insurmountable opposition and complexity. Given the odds against success, they should not be judged harshly for failing to make more headway.

Over the next quarter century the class stratification of black and white condemned by Martin Luther King intensified; even more did class cleavage widen within the black population. In the mid-1980s the National Urban League concluded that, in Derrick Bell's words, "in virtually every area of life that counts, black people made strong progress in the 1960s, peaked in the 1970s, and have been sliding back ever since." The "progress" was very uneven. A minority of upwardly mobile African-Americans were able to take advantage of legally established individual rights and affirmative action policies to rise into the middle class, or rise further within it. But the majority declined in well-being, many, if not most, falling into deepening urban poverty. At least half of all black children were growing up ill fed, ill clad, ill housed, and certainly ill schooled. The plight of the urban underclass was probably never worse than in the

1990s, with everyday life dominated by drug wars and drug addiction, with joblessness, teenage births, fatherless families, and violent crime steadily increasing.

To end poverty and to "guarantee the right to a decent life to all Americans," as NWRO leader Beulah Sanders put it, the implementation of economic rights would have required going beyond incremental gains facilitated by economic growth—the traditional liberal approach—to actual redistribution of the American economic pie. But democratic redistribution of wealth by the government has remained a taboo in American political culture, especially in eras of economic downturn.

STILL, the structural constraints of the "system" have not been all that has stood in the way of achieving economic and social rights. Movement leaders often accepted the inevitability of such constraints when in fact more options and leeway were available. In most rights campaigns, leaders had a fairly comprehensive vision of what their followers were entitled to, but at some point they decided, or reluctantly agreed, to divide rights claims into categories (legal, civil, political, social, economic), to set priorities among them, and to choose short-term political expediency over longer-term linkages of rights that would likely bring less immediate payoff. Though they frequently assumed that winning rights near at hand would lead to securing others, rarely did gaining one type of right automatically open the door to the claiming of another more remote or elusive. More radical factions sometimes tried to broaden the focus, particularly to integrate political with economic and social demands, but the mainstream leaders normally chose a less risky course. This politics of compartmentalization and deferral has entailed major social costs.

The tendency to compartmentalize rights claims resulted from several interconnected factors: the sway of liberal ideology that separated politics from society and the economy; the fragmentation of the political system with its divided powers and checks and balances; the government's openness to assimilating reform if gradual and piecemeal; the pull of American pragmatism; and the strategic priority of social movements to maximize the constituency of support by reducing goals to the lowest common denominator. Activists' lifelong conditioning to the limits of the political realm was continually reaffirmed by the experience of politics as "the art of the possible" with its incentives and rewards for playing by the rules. A vicious circle revolved: the more that reformers, over time, accepted apparent political limits in order to make incremental progress, the less pressure was put on the state to carry out substantive reform that pushed beyond those limits. And the more impoverished was the historical achievement of real reform, the more utopian seemed the activists who still sought it.

PLURAL BUT EQUAL

IF NAVIGATING the troubled extraconstitutional waters of economic rights proved daunting, more tempestuous still was the long striving of African-Americans for the right to political and cultural self-determination as a people, a right recognized in international covenants.

The aspiration of black Americans for independent nationhood as a response to oppression probably originated before the American Revolution. From early in the nineteenth century until emancipation, this growing sentiment found expression in a number of ambitious plans for blacks to establish a new nation in Africa or the Caribbean. Some of these schemes were backed by whites with racist motives and condemned by black people. Others were serious strategies of liberation, such as the visionary project of physician and writer Martin Delany for the settlement of American blacks in East Africa.

Lack of practical success and the abolition of slavery put a damper on the emigration strategy, though it was resurrected briefly after World War I by Jamaican-born leader Marcus Garvey and his Universal Negro Improvement Association. From the 1930s until the 1960s the chief proselytizer of black nationhood was Elijah Muhammad, whose separatist Nation of Islam won thousands of converts from the black underclass. One of these converts, Malcolm X, turned black nationalism into an overtly political movement while placing it in the global context of racial oppression.

Black nationalism has been "an ever-present but usually latent (or unarticulated) tendency," Robert Allen points out, "particularly among blacks who find themselves on the lower rungs of the socioeconomic ladder." Allen notes that the yearning for national identity, for peoplehood, has always found expression in black culture, especially through music. At its core the nationalist impulse remained "a belief that Black people in this country make up a cultural nation," according to Maulana Ron Karenga.

When in the mid-1960s the Southern-based freedom movement turned into a wider campaign for black liberation, nationalist sentiment gained greater visibility than ever before. Three related developments accounted for this: victorious national liberation struggles in Africa, Asia, and Latin America, and the influence of their theorists; growing adherence to the idea of "domestic colonialism"—that is, that African-Americans comprised a fragmented, internal colony; and the emergence from the South of the language of Black Power.

As a concept and slogan Black Power originated in SNCC's efforts, after passage of the 1965 Voting Rights Act, to build independent black political structures in Alabama, Mississippi, and Georgia. The mass media made it famous in the summer of 1966 when cries of "Black Power!" drowned out the old chant of "Freedom Now" during a Mississippi rights march led jointly by King, SNCC's Stokely Carmichael, and Floyd McKissick of CORE. King tried to persuade Carmichael and McKissick that while he agreed with the concept, the slogan lent itself to inflammatory images that would damage the movement. Moderate black leaders and white allies publicly repudiated Black Power. But as SNCC and CORE shifted their center of gravity to Northern ghettos, the new rallying cry rapidly replaced civil rights as the unifying theme of black liberation.

In practice Black Power had multiple meanings that ranged across the spectrum from insurrectionary violence to black capitalism. In the most basic sense, inspired by Malcolm X, it meant racial pride and identity— the celebration of "blackness," of black culture and consciousness. More tangibly it expressed democratic aspirations for collective self-determination, for the political, cultural, and economic control of black communities by blacks, including the election of black officials and the development of black-owned businesses.

While Black Power advocates supported civil rights and desegregation as necessary first steps, they opposed the broader, more complicated goal of social integration, as generally understood. Carmichael rejected integration as a "one-way street" if carried out on white terms, with newfound black identity drowned in a sea of white values; it was "meaningful only to a small chosen class" within the black population. He distinguished between the assimilation of fortunate individuals into the white mainstream, which would weaken group cohesiveness, and a more egalitarian integration of the African-American community. "The racial and cultural personality of the black community must be preserved," Carmichael wrote in 1966, "and the community must win its freedom while preserving its cultural integrity." In any event, large-scale integration-as-assimilation did not seem realistic given economic and demographic barriers and white racism.

Black Power implied separatism, but disagreements arose about how far to go in that direction, and whether coalitions with whites were acceptable on black terms. Some followed Malcolm X in seeing separatism more as a strategy than as an end. Two conflicting strands of black nationalism vied for Malcolm's mantle. Political nationalists, such as the Black Panthers, stressed the interdependence of racial and class oppression and sought alliances with white radicals. More fundamentally separatist were cultural nationalists, the best known being Karenga and poet and playwright Amiri Baraka (LeRoi Jones), who focused on reclaiming African culture and tradition and insisted that cultural revolution must precede political change. Both strands were deeply affected by Frantz Fanon's study of the Algerian war of independence, in which he contended that for a colonized people to liberate itself, violence was not only a strategic but a psychological need. Yet the violence associated with some Black Power groups was mainly rhetorical and stylistic; overt violence rarely went beyond armed self-defense, ostensibly a constitutional right guaranteed by the Second Amendment.

Through tight discipline and artful use of media the Oakland-based Black Panther Party, which opened chapters nationwide, emerged as the most renowned expression of Black Power, although the latter assumed many less dramatic forms. The Panthers' ten-point platform espoused community control, full employment, freedom for all black prisoners, and "our major political objective, a United Nations–supervised plebiscite to be held throughout the black colony . . . for the purpose of determining the will of black people as to their national destiny." Committed to enforcing laws that protected black rights, they gained notoriety for "patrolling the police" and informing black people of their legal rights when facing arrest. The Panthers' brash militance so threatened white authorities that local police teamed up with the FBI to extinguish the party, which had spread to dozens of cities. Reminiscent of attacks on radicals' civil liberties during the World War I era, the campaign of official repression included unconstitutional FBI covert operations; it resulted in the killing, imprisonment, or self-exile of many leaders and the party's eventual demise.

If the Southern movement's historic accomplishment was the abolition of legalized segregation, Black Power's major legacy was its stimulation of black electoral politics in many cities and, most of all, its regeneration of black identity and culture. Among its enduring contributions were the hard-won black studies programs in many colleges and universities and a flowering of African-American art, literature, music, drama, and film. New generations of black youth still face galling social obstacles, especially those from lower-class families, but the recovery of their common heritage and identity has produced an upwelling of self-esteem, self-respect, and collective self-confidence that are critical tools of empowerment in the ongoing struggle for black freedom.

Black Power's yet unfulfilled struggle for the right to collective self-determination—for the right, in Carmichael's words, "to create our own terms to define ourselves and our relationship to the society"—can be seen as an expansion of the language of rights to encompass the goal of raising the black community as a whole to a position of equality with other groups. The realization of this communal right, as Malcolm X recognized, would be the prerequisite for a genuinely pluralist nation in which African-Americans would have equal power to determine the nature and future of the society. Neither separate and unequal nor integrated and unequal, but rather the democratic ideal of *plural but equal,* Harold Cruse suggests, remains the underlying purpose of black liberation.

CHAPTER ELEVEN

RIGHTS TO LIBERATION: WOMEN AT THE CUTTING EDGE

SOMETIMES nothing fails like success. When organized feminism demobilized after ratification of the Nineteenth Amendment in 1920, activist women lost the sense of solidarity that they had experienced during the suffrage crusade—their shared identity as an oppressed group. Rather than redirect their formidable grass-roots power toward broader feminist goals, most suffragists exited the public stage to pursue self-fulfillment as private citizens. Some turned their attention to other single-issue causes such as birth control, child welfare, or the Equal Rights Amendment. Then the Great Depression struck, making clear the dependence of individual freedom on economic rights and how little of the latter had been achieved, for either sex. Husbands lost their jobs, and wives were excluded from many positions, even as schoolteachers, that men might want. Married or single, employed or unemployed, women earned money as best they could.

A very different national crisis furthered the economic rights of women, as a side effect, when female labor became indispensable in the home-front mobilization for World War II. When men went overseas, more than six million women joined the work force, many in highly skilled jobs in war plants; the government even subsidized some day-care centers. But when the soldiers came home, women for the most part resumed their second-class citizenship. Public hostility to women working and discriminatory policies, combined with "veterans' preferences, protective labor restrictions, rising birth rates, suburban living patterns, and the absence of childcare," in feminist scholar Deborah Rhode's summary, "helped oust women from the labor force or relegate them to traditionally female, low-paid occupations."

Betty Friedan's 1963 best-seller, *The Feminine Mystique,* examined the severe cost of the retreat to domesticity paid by those middle-class women who traded career aspirations for full-time housewifery. She explained that after the war, educators, social scientists, mass media, corporate advertising, and Freudian theories of female sexuality had persuaded educated women that their only source of fulfillment was home, family, and sex. "The core of the problem for women today," she wrote, was "a problem of identity—a stunting or evasion of growth that is perpetuated by the feminine mystique. . . . Our culture does not permit women to accept or gratify their basic need to grow and fulfill their potentialities as human beings."

But Friedan's solution to "the problem that has no name," for women to work outside the home, was already being tried—not only by working-class women and women of color who always had to work but by growing numbers of white middle-class wives. By 1960, two-fifths of American women were employed, compared to less than a quarter in 1920. They sought jobs not so much to escape domestic drudgery but from economic need. One breadwinner was less and less able to earn a decent family income, particularly amid the soaring expectations of the "affluent society." Whether as factory workers, secretaries, service employees, or professionals, women faced discrimination at every turn, in hiring, promotion, layoffs, pay, benefits, and, less openly, through "sexual harassment"—a term that feminists would later invent and introduce into law. As the result of occupational segregation and sex-stereotyping of jobs, females earned an average of sixty cents for every dollar men earned.

During the 1960s, as the black movement was gaining victories against both social and psychological oppression, more and more women, including women of color, grew aware that not only were they denied their rights in the public sphere of education and employment but they were treated as a subordinate caste at home. Moreover, they came to realize that their inequality in the public world *derived* from inequality in their personal lives, from the sexual division of labor in the family. Something had to give. Once it was widely perceived, this debilitating double bind motivated a far-reaching revolt that led to a reconstruction of women's roles, responsibilities, and rights.

ARE EQUAL RIGHTS ENOUGH?

THE FIRST SMALL STEPS toward realizing women's rights, after four decades of drift, were taken by the Kennedy administration, prodded by a coalition of working women's advocates headquartered in the Women's Bureau of the Department of Labor. Assistant Labor Secretary Esther Peterson, a former AFL-CIO lobbyist, persuaded President Kennedy to create a national commission on the status of women, chaired by Eleanor Roosevelt, a revered role model for many professional women and a feminist in deed if not in word. The commission's fact-finding report, released two weeks before Kennedy's assassination, documented pervasive discrimination, particularly in employment. The remedies it proposed were mild, however, and it opposed the Equal Rights Amendment championed by a hard core of feminists for decades. Nevertheless, the commission publicized and legitimized women's issues and solidified an underground activist network in Washington bureaucracies. The formation of state women's commissions spread this "seething underground of women" to the hinterland.

Lobbying by the Washington women's network helped win passage of the 1963 Equal Pay Act, the first federal law that explicitly addressed women's rights. But equal pay for the same work would make little difference in a labor force segregated by gender. Something had to be done about the exclusion of women from higher-paying and higher-status occupations. An unexpected opportunity arose with the 1964 civil rights bill, whose Title VII dealt with employment discrimination. Black leaders and their congressional allies had not wanted to hurt the bill's chances by going beyond outlawing racial discrimination; some prominent women leaders concurred. Sex discrimination was not mentioned once in hearings.

Representative Martha Griffiths, Michigan Democrat, intended to offer an amendment adding "sex" to Title VII coverage, but Virginia's Howard Smith, conservative czar of the House Rules Committee, beat her to it. Smith's hope was that his ploy would either sink the whole bill or ensure that black men would not be favored for jobs over white women. Since he had the votes, Griffiths let him offer it, prompting guffaws and ridicule in what was dubbed "Ladies Day in the House." But the amendment passed and survived through the bill's final passage.

Not only did many lawmakers consider inclusion of gender a joke. The first director of the Equal Employment Opportunity Commission (EEOC), which was set up by Title VII to promote compliance, called it a "fluke . . . conceived out of wedlock." The EEOC's scornful attitude coupled with its complete lack of enforcement power meant that little action was taken on thousands of complaints filed by working women, white, black, and Latina. Men of color did not fare much better given the agency's inadequacies.

Although women activists saw the EEOC as window dressing, they sensed its potential as a lever of change and sought to make it more effective. In June 1966, a cadre of feminist insiders tried to have the third national conference of state women's commissions pass a resolution demanding that the EEOC carry out its mandate. The resolution, ruled out of order, did not even reach the floor. Stunned that so modest a proposal would be blocked, its proponents turned to Betty Friedan, there gathering material for her next book. She had already been approached by feminists, and even by frustrated EEOC commissioners, urging her to start a movement for women modeled on the black movement, or at least an organization like the NAACP to push for legal reforms. They knew that no real change would come without pressure from below. Not long before, black attorney, legal scholar, and poet Pauli Murray had shocked a staid convention of women's clubs by asserting that Title VII would never be enforced "unless women march on Washington like the blacks."

When at the national conference Friedan, Murray, and Dorothy Haener of the United Auto Workers had first broached the idea of a feminist pressure group, the proponents of the resolution had been lukewarm. The silencing of their resolution turned them into firebrands. During the last plenary session two dozen women from government, state commissions, and unions—including black EEOC commissioner Aileen Hernandez, who would soon resign from the agency in protest—gathered hastily to make plans. Friedan later wondered "if Esther Peterson and the other Women's Bureau officials and Cabinet members who talked down to us at lunch knew that those two front tables, so rudely, agitatedly whispering to one another and passing around notes written on paper napkins, were under their very noses organizing NOW, the National Organization for Women, the first and major structure of the modern women's movement."

Although the impetus for its birth was the need to enforce Title VII in regard to gender discrimination, from its founding convention in October 1966 NOW aimed at a wide-ranging agenda of reform. "We, men and women," its statement of purpose declared, "believe that the time has come for a new movement toward true equality for all women in America, and toward a fully equal partnership of the sexes, as part of the worldwide revolution of human rights now taking place within and beyond our national borders. . . . The time has come to confront, with concrete action, the conditions that now prevent women from enjoying the equality of opportunity and freedom of choice which is their right as individual Americans, and as human beings. . . . We do not accept the traditional assumption that a woman has to choose between marriage and motherhood, on the one hand, and serious participation in industry or the professions."

NOW's leaders and membership were mainly middle-class professional women. Focused on Washington lobbying, it made up for its lack of a mass base by expert use of the media. As state and local chapters grew, NOW activists set up task forces on a host of issues such as discrimination, marriage and divorce laws, child care, media images of women, and the "masculine mystique."

NOW fairly quickly achieved legislative, judicial, and administrative remedies, though battles for enforcement often took years. The first victory came when the organization impelled President Johnson to issue Executive Order 11375 banning sexual discrimination in institutions with federal contracts—especially in higher education—and in the government. As the self-appointed watchdog of the EEOC, NOW successfully filed suit against the agency's sanctioning of sex-segregated "help wanted" ads in newspapers. Its first direct action was to dump piles of newspapers at EEOC offices. Several months later NOW protested at the White House on Mother's Day, demanding "Rights, Not Roses" and ceremonially throwing aprons on the ground by the White House gate where suffragists had once been arrested.

Title VII enforcement victories included ending the airlines' involuntary retirement of flight attendants when they married or turned thirty-two and a historic settlement with AT&T, which the EEOC had singled out as the "largest oppressor of women workers," that included back pay and wage increases to compensate for past discrimination. NOW lobbied hard for the 1972 EEOC reform that strengthened the agency's enforcement powers and expanded its scope, converting Title VII into a "magna carta for female workers," according to political scientist Donald Robinson. By the early 1970s, he contends, the EEOC was "responding alertly to the feminist movement and the need for the definition of rights and the legitimation of demands. Under intense pressure, the commission was taking advanced positions on sex discrimination, and to a remarkable extent its interpretations were being supported by the courts." NOW not only took responsibility for enforcing Title VII in a pathbreaking fashion; it also spearheaded congressional passage of the Equal Rights Amendment, a law banning discrimination in all schools that received federal funds, and other important women's rights measures.

NOW did not achieve these gains without dissension and division. When it ratified a "Bill of Rights for Women" to press on candidates and parties in 1968, labor delegates threatened to bolt because their unions opposed the ERA, fearing it might nullify hard-earned protective laws for working women. And a group of more conservative members walked out in protest of NOW's support for reproductive rights and the repeal of abortion laws, the first time that "the right of every woman to control her own reproductive life" was formally proclaimed by a women's organization.

A vivid linkage across time between the old suffrage crusade and the new movement was the Women's Strike for Equality in August 1970, commemorating the fiftieth anniversary of the Nineteenth Amendment's ratification. Sensing that something more dramatic than lobbying and litigation was needed, NOW president Friedan conceived the "strike" as a way to channel the burgeoning movement toward concrete objectives, such as abortion on demand, publicly funded child care, and equal opportunity in jobs and schooling.

Locking arms with Judge Dorothy Kenyon, an eighty-two-year-old suffrage veteran, and with a young jean-clad radical, Friedan led a mammoth march of women down New York's Fifth Avenue. Defying orders to stay on the sidewalk, they took over the street, holding banners high and calling out, "Come join us, sisters," to women waving from skyscraper windows. Women marched for rights in many other cities that day. It was the first nationwide mobilization of women since the suffrage era; and for the first time the new crusade was covered seriously by the media. NOW was suddenly famous, and its membership swelled.

NOW and allied groups had remarkable success winning legislative and legal reforms at the national level. In half a dozen years they gained official commitments to personal, civil, and economic rights that had taken the black movement much more time and strife, though they built upon that movement's momentum and triumphs. "A federal policy of equal opportunity, if not total equality, was clearly emerging in piecemeal fashion," political scientist and activist Jo Freeman noted in 1975.

Though the EEOC did not adequately enforce Title VII, it was the first in a series of policy tools, including affirmative action, that substantially improved educational opportunity and the hiring and promotion of women in many areas. But while work opportunities expanded, the overall "earnings gap" narrowed only a few percentage points over the next two decades. Since equal pay for the same work did not help much, feminists would later campaign, unsuccessfully by and large, for equal pay for jobs of "comparable worth." Moreover, the gains in education and employment disproportionately favored white middle-class women.

Like the black movement, feminism proved least effective in uplifting women economically as a group. Some did advance, but what came to be called the "feminization of poverty" forced many others downhill in the 1970s and 1980s, particularly women of color and women raising children without partners. Feminists failed to remedy the structural subordination of women in the economy and the generally low status of female workers. Nor did they alleviate the economic vulnerability inherent in traditional modes of motherhood, or the financial perils of divorce and single parenting. According to Ellen Boneparth, "while women's roles as workers have received increasing governmental attention over the last two decades, their roles as mothers, as childbearers and childrearers, have either been ignored or misrepresented in the public policy arena."

With a new body of law to empower them, why didn't women make more progress in realizing economic and social rights as means of overcoming gender oppression? Lax enforcement, of course, was a big reason, but significant also was the philosophy underlying sex discrimination laws. Like the larger civil rights legislation they were associated with, laws prohibiting gender discrimination were authorized by the equal protection clause of the Fourteenth Amendment. This clause reflected the Aristotelian principle of equality as *sameness:* treating equally those with the same attributes, status, or condition, treating unequally those who were different. Once the Supreme Court overturned *Plessy* v. *Ferguson* in 1954, this sameness principle no longer legally impeded the equality aspirations of blacks and other racial minorities, since whatever physical or cultural differences existed were no longer considered legally relevant. But the fact that biological differences between the sexes were so inflated and distorted by the dominant culture meant that, as a general rule, the law treated women equally only to the extent, or only in those aspects, that they were similar to men.

Thus the hidden premise of sex discrimination law, remarks feminist legal theorist Catharine MacKinnon, was that under the sameness standard, "women are measured according to our correspondence with man. . . . Under the difference standard, we are measured according to our lack of correspondence. . . . Masculinity, or maleness, is the referent for both." A case in point: even without popular pressure, the government legislated equal pay for the same work, but a strong movement was not able to secure equal pay for different but comparable work. Most consequential was the fact that working mothers (and mothers-to-be) suffered far more pervasive discrimination than women who, because they did not have children, were more "equal" to men.

Deborah Rhode argues that women will not enjoy full legal equality until lawmakers and judges stop focusing narrowly on gender differences (chiefly women's ability to bear children)—which frequently results in invidious differential treatment—and look instead at "the difference difference makes," the disadvantages that legally and culturally defined differences have produced. This would mean, for example, that the state would not permit corporate "fetal protection" policies that banned women from working with harmful materials; instead, companies would be required to show equal concern for male workers' health and reproductive competence and to eliminate dangerous conditions for everyone, including the surrounding community.

Probably the only way to attain both equal access to jobs and equal treatment at work would be to restructure the job market, jobs, and the workplace to take into account women's special needs and thus special entitlements, including child care, flexible schedules, and parental leave. As these entitlements are implemented and legitimized for women, they might increasingly be extended to men. This in turn might catalyze a larger transformation of work norms and work culture—making them as much female-centered as male-centered—to help free both men and women from traditional sex-role constraints, and in particular encourage men to take more responsibility for parenting.

NOW INITIATED the "second wave" of feminist activism, but what made it a mass movement were thousands of younger women, many of them veterans of the black freedom struggle and the New Left. Just as the nineteenth-century woman's movement had emerged from white and black women's involvement in the abolitionist crusade—and from awareness of their second-class status within it—so radical feminism originated in women's experience of subordination in the peace and freedom movements of the 1960s. White women felt the discrepancy between principles and practice more sharply than black women, however, since the latter experienced the freedom movement as affirming their rights (as black people if not as women), whereas the former felt that their rights were being ignored, more so in the New Left than in civil rights groups like SNCC.

Starting in 1967 radical feminist collectives mushroomed quickly as the impulse of revolt spread through networks of disaffected New Left women. These activists resolved to apply their organizing skills to make a movement of their own. Because it was seen as the key to liberation, the pursuit of self-understanding and self-empowerment became the central mission of the "younger branch" of feminism. The vehicle for this pursuit was the "consciousness-raising group"—at once a recruitment tool, a process for shaping ideas and commitment, and a miniature egalitarian community. Radical feminists demanded not equality of sex roles, which they compared with the Jim Crow doctrine of separate but equal, but their elimination. They were not satisfied with improvements in jobs and schooling that felt like tokenism. Rather they dug to what they saw as the root of the problem: the subjugation of women in relationships with men and in domestic roles, which put severe limits on opportunities outside the home and could be little affected, they thought, by public policies. What they scornfully called "careerism"—Friedan's remedy— did not challenge the sexual division of labor and seemed an option for only a minority of women.

This perspective struck chords in a multitude of young, mainly white, middle-class women who became convinced that, like men, they had the right to define themselves as they chose and to shape their own destinies. "For most American women," historian Sara Evans has suggested, "only a movement that addressed the oppression at the core of their identity could have generated the massive response that in fact occurred." Radical feminists concentrated on sex-role and sexuality issues and sought to empower women to take control of their bodies, not only by campaigning for reproductive rights but by initiating and leading a crusade against rape and all other violence against women. This crusade resulted in a proliferation of rape crisis centers and shelters for battered women. One of their most visible and enduring accomplishments, particularly of lesbian feminists, was the creation of an autonomous women's culture, a rich movement culture akin to that of the black struggle, pouring out feminist poetry, prose, music, art, and theory.

Younger branch feminists fashioned a political language very different from that of the "older branch" in NOW, Women's Equity Action League, and National Women's Political Caucus (NWPC). Not only did they replace "women's rights" with "women's liberation," but they developed a thoroughgoing critique of the women's rights paradigm, disparaging it as liberal, individualistic, legalistic, and incapable of addressing the heart of female oppression. While radicals did not reject rights, they held that NOW's emphasis on them as the remedy for oppression was woefully incomplete, treating merely the "superficial symptoms of sexism," in Shulamith Firestone's words. Moreover, the older branch so compartmentalized rights that those most pressing to radicals, rights to control of one's body, did not receive equal attention with legal and economic entitlements.

NOW and NWPC feminists were criticized for perpetuating the old liberal dichotomy between the public and private realms, waging battles for equality chiefly in the public world of education, employment, and government. Because they defined politics as government-related activity, older branch activists were reluctant to recognize women's oppression in family and domestic roles as legitimately political. Theorist Zillah Eisenstein has written that the "liberal equation between public power and politics excludes the family from political analysis." Evans has contended that Friedan's critique of housewifery recommended only that women, like men, be permitted—freed from constraint—to act fully in both realms, never seriously questioning the functional division in the home that made this difficult. While backing away from radical calls to abolish the nuclear family, liberal feminists avoided the question of how it might be reformed to enable women to actualize all their rights, both inside and outside the home. Nevertheless movement pressures eventually expanded the liberal framework to encompass family and body issues.

The older branch believed that, like other disadvantaged groups, once granted civil and economic rights women would assume "full participation in the mainstream of American society." Radicals, on the contrary, were convinced that the struggle for liberation would require not just legal reforms but fundamental social transformation. In their view, not only did women constitute an oppressed caste or class, as did African-Americans, but the male-female division was the "primary class system" underlying all other human divisions. "Male supremacy is the oldest, most basic form of domination," the Redstockings Manifesto proclaimed. What women were up against was not simply an inheritance of discriminatory laws and practices open to amelioration, but an all-pervasive system of institutionalized social hierarchy or "patriarchy." To eradicate the patriarchal system, radicals believed, women needed more than individual rights within it. They needed power against it as a class, a collective force.

Yet even when the lines between younger and older feminists were most sharply drawn, some like radical Jo Freeman thought the differences not that great. As the two branches of the broadening movement increasingly converged and cross-fertilized during the 1970s, in part because NOW et al. took the radicals' concerns more seriously and focused more on women's right to control their bodies, feminists in both camps found that, as a movement editorial put it in late 1971, "they have a great deal more in common than was originally thought." The edges blurred between women's rights and liberation.

NOTHING so well embodied all that the younger branch criticized about the women's rights perspective than the ERA and the ten-year campaign to ratify it. Passed overwhelmingly by Congress in 1972, its brief text declared: "Equality of rights under the law shall not be denied or abridged by the United States or by any State on account of sex," and that Congress would have the power to enforce this mandate.

In 1923 Alice Paul's National Woman's Party had introduced an Equal Rights Amendment in Congress as the logical next step after suffrage. For years it faced insurmountable opposition from Florence Kelley's National Consumers League and other progressive groups, labor unions, and many ex-suffragists, who had fought to obtain protective legislation for female workers (such as maximum hours and limits on weight lifted), which they thought the ERA would jeopardize by forbidding special treatment. Title VII of the 1964 Civil Rights Act turned the tide for the ERA effort since it led to the invalidation of protective laws by the EEOC

and the courts (they were judged to be discriminatory because they restricted female opportunity), or to the extension of such laws to men.
When NOW and other feminist groups showed that protective laws had
hurt women more than helped—by keeping them out of certain jobs or
making it easier for employers to exclude them altogether—even the
AFL-CIO, the ERA's most powerful foe, came around.

Less than a week after Congress passed the ERA six states had ratified
it. Within a year two dozen others did so, with only a handful to go.
Several of the early votes were unanimous; rarely was there much debate.

Just when it looked like a sure thing, a cannily organized opposition
spread quickly through unratified states of the South and Midwest.
Grounded in the grass roots, its commanding general was Phyllis
Schlafly, a lawyer, longtime right-wing activist, and seasoned speaker who
had written a laudatory book on Barry Goldwater and another one calling
for a strong military. Despite an enviable public career, she promoted
herself as a simple housewife and mother of six. Distributing tracts like
"The Right to Be a Woman" and claiming that the ERA would "wipe out
a wife's right to support," legalize rape, put mothers in combat, and
require unisex public toilets (all in fact false), Schlafly won over legions
of housewives and GOP legislators.

Fanning women's fears worked better than appealing to their aspirations, and the pro-ERA momentum stalled. No state ratified it after 1977,
and the amendment died, three states short of the required thirty-eight,
when a three-year extension ran out in 1982. For both sides, according
to Rhode, the ERA had become "a stand-in for more fundamental concerns and a battleground for symbolic politics. . . . Once family and
feminism were fixed as the symbolic poles of debate, many women could
be expected to rally around the symbol by which they had ordered their
own priorities."

The ERA campaign failed for strategic and organizational reasons and
because of inherent limitations of the amendment itself that reflected old
problems of constitutional interpretation and reform. With a sure grasp
of the moral and cultural differences dividing American women, the
anti-ERA forces mobilized their constituents far more effectively than did
their opponents around the politicizing of personal issues—even though
feminism was centered on the principle, which it expressed very differently, that the personal was political. Nor did proponents persuade the
public of the overriding national urgency of the ERA, that a serious social
problem existed that could be remedied only by constitutional change;
this, according to legal scholar Mary Frances Berry, historically has been
a prerequisite for amending the Constitution. Moreover, amendments
with a concrete focus, such as citizenship, suffrage, or liquor prohibition,

were more conducive to marshaling broad support than was an abstract and open-ended one.

The ERA's abstract nature and indeterminate language might have been its own worst enemy. Political scientist Jane Mansbridge discovered that equal rights for women as a general principle was widely supported by the public, which explained why the ERA won so many easy early victories. But because the amendment avoided specific provisions and said nothing about what or how much would change, opponents had a field day making distorted claims about its impact, which eroded support. The growing opposition had legitimate fears, Mansbridge has suggested, that the Supreme Court would implement the ERA in ways that would threaten women's traditional roles. The Court had a deserved reputation for applying egalitarian principles in unpredictable, inconsistent, and even contradictory fashion, particularly the Fourteenth Amendment and its derivatives. What havoc might it wreak with the ERA?

The ERA might have won more adherents, and more fervent feminist backing, if its provisions had attached equal rights principles to specific mandates for reform, such as equal pay for comparable worth or entitlement to child care, rather than leaving definition and enforcement to the courts and Congress. By divorcing the recognition of formal rights from their substantive implementation, the ERA perpetuated liberalism's propensity to hollow out fundamental reform and reduce it to procedural rights and open-ended process.

Some analysts of the ERA campaign have concluded that although proponents did not win, neither did they lose. More "a catalyst than a source of change," the ratification struggle educated and activated millions of women on both sides and taught political skills and lessons. The heated debate itself prodded courts and legislatures to take stronger action against gender discrimination. And even more than had the 1920 woman suffrage amendment, an ERA victory might have fostered the illusion that, implanted in the Constitution, women's rights had been realized and the long battle won. Instead, defeat lifted the consciousness of many women about the tenuous status of their rights and how much work lay ahead.

TO OWN THE FLESH WE STAND IN

IF IN THIS COUNTRY the suppression of black people's rights became the overarching moral conflict of the nineteenth century and again in the mid-twentieth, historians may well look back upon the fierce battle over reproductive rights as the paramount moral struggle of the last third of this century. No cataclysmic civil war was fought over it, but an untold number of small wars, in legislative halls, on the street, inside homes, psychically scarred the nation. Both sides in the conflict deployed the language of rights, highlighting the predominance of this discourse in American political culture: forces championing the right of the unborn fetus to life versus those upholding a woman's right to choose whether or not to bear a child. As the debate escalated over two decades, the apparent simplicity of each side's claims masked thorny complications. If a fetus had an inalienable right to life, when did that life begin—at conception, at "viability" outside the womb, at some point in between? If a woman had the right of choice, was it absolute? Was it as fundamental as rights guaranteed by the First Amendment? Was it merely a right of privacy, or a right to full control of her body and reproduction, an entitlement to sexual freedom and sexual equality?

Although until recent decades most did not think of it as a "right," for centuries women around the world had made the hard decision to end pregnancy, out of personal or family need. Until the late nineteenth century abortions were commonly performed by midwives and by female healers using risky and unreliable herbal medicines and folk remedies. Otherwise, pregnant women sought help from female relatives or friends, or literally took matters into their own hands. For several decades after independence the United States had no laws regulating abortion. A tolerant common-law tradition inherited from England did not treat abortion as a crime until after "quickening," four to six months into pregnancy, when a woman first felt fetal movement.

This laissez-faire attitude changed rapidly in the second half of the nineteenth century with the professionalization of male-dominated medicine, the founding of the American Medical Association, and an all-out campaign by physicians to outlaw abortion—unless approved and conducted by a "regular" doctor. Historian James Mohr and sociologist Kristin Luker have shown that the ulterior purpose of the physicians' crusade was to eliminate competition from unlicensed medical practitioners and to enhance their own status and control. What Luker has called the first "right to life" movement, led by elite physicians, claimed both that abortion was murder and that doctors could make exceptions to save the mother's life. Proselytizing the public and lobbying legislatures, the doctors obtained abortion bans in virtually every state by 1900.

The medical establishment's expropriation of abortion shielded it from public controversy until the early 1960s, when physicians and other professionals realized that abortion laws were too restrictive in some cases, as when the fetus, due to the carrier's illness or use of sleeping pills, was deformed. By the late 1960s efforts by activists in medicine and social work had persuaded lawmakers to liberalize abortion laws in a third of the states. But the abortion decision was still ultimately the right of the physician, usually male. Then after a decade of intense national focus on black civil rights, the new feminist movement burst forth and turned the debate upside down, insisting that abortion was every woman's fundamental right, that the decision was hers alone, and that abortion laws must be repealed, not reformed.

"When we talk about women's rights," one feminist explained, "we can get all the rights in the world—the right to vote, the right to go to school—and none of them means a doggone thing if we don't own the flesh we stand in, if we can't control what happens to us, if the whole course of our lives can be changed by somebody else that can get us pregnant by accident, or by deceit, or by force." Without the right to elective abortion "we'd have about as many rights as the cow in the pasture that's taken to the bull once a year. You could give her all those rights, too, but they wouldn't mean anything; if you can't control your own body you can't control your future."

Moreover, women would never overcome job discrimination as long as unwanted pregnancy could disrupt their work lives, as long as employers treated them as mothers or potential mothers rather than as autonomous individuals.

Though some feminists initially did not consider abortion a vital issue, in 1969 NOW leaders and others founded the National Association for the Repeal of Abortion Laws (NARAL, later the National Abortion Rights Action League), which by redefining abortion as a personal right, Faye Ginsburg notes, built a broad coalition that included more conservative women in church groups and the YWCA. When legislative repeal campaigns were stymied, NARAL shifted to a judicial strategy, challenging the constitutionality of restrictive abortion statutes. By 1971 seventy test cases were inching forward in more than twenty states.

While the older branch strategy emulated the NAACP's legalistic attack on segregation, radical feminists mobilized for abortion rights through consciousness-raising groups and direct action. In their first public protest, Redstockings members disrupted a February 1969 New York legislative hearing on abortion law reform. After testimony by a retired judge, Kathie Sarachild stood up in the audience and shouted, "All right, now let's hear from some real experts—the women." As the lawmakers stared dumbstruck, a dozen angry women stood and lectured the male officialdom. "Why are 14 men and only one woman on your list of speakers," one inquired, "and she a nun?" Unable to pacify the protesters, the committee escaped the din into a closed executive session.

A month later Redstockings organized its own hearing or "speak-out" on abortion, partly to "confront the spurious personal-political distinction," as Redstocking Barbara Mehrhof put it later, the notion that abortion was strictly a private problem. Twelve women testified in graphic terms about their own dangerous or demeaning abortion experiences to an audience of three hundred at a Greenwich Village church. Radicals engaged in civil disobedience as well by referring women to safe but illegal abortion clinics.

Although radical feminists deprecated rights talk in most areas, they embraced the demand for rights in the realm of reproduction and sexuality—but such rights in *their* terms, as they expanded and deepened their meaning. Emphasizing empowerment more than mere choice, radicals placed reproductive rights within the larger fabric of "control of our bodies"—the right to bodily integrity—the unifying theme of the younger branch that stretched beyond abortion to encompass opposition to forced sterilization of poor, mainly nonwhite women and especially to rape and other violence against women. As historian Alice Echols has pointed out, unlike the older branch the radicals always saw abortion as closely tied to sexuality and as foundational to sexual freedom and equality. Radicals also envisioned reproductive rights through the filter of class and race. Whereas NOW's 1968 "Bill of Rights for Women" demanded simply repeal of abortion laws, the younger branch insisted that abortion be freely available for all who needed it.

Finally, refusing to compartmentalize women's entitlements, radical feminists explicitly linked compulsory childbearing to the blockage of other rights. "Without the full capacity to limit her own reproduction," contended abortion rights leader Lucinda Cisler, "a woman's other 'freedoms' are tantalizing mockeries that cannot be exercised. With it, the others cannot long be denied, since the chief rationale for denial disappears."

The crescendo of agitation and litigation culminated in a monumental triumph for feminist forces in January 1973. In a ruling with two dissents the Supreme Court struck down all state abortion laws (including recently liberalized ones). Justice Harry Blackmun's majority opinion declared that any restrictions on abortion during the first trimester violated a constitutional right to privacy; that abortion could be regulated in the second trimester only to protect a woman's well-being (such as requiring adequate medical services for the procedure); and that abortion would be permitted in the final three months only if a woman's health or survival was deemed at stake. The trimester demarcations, which Blackmun admitted were "arbitrary" in an internal memo to fellow justices, were intended as a compromise between a woman's right to end a pregnancy and the state interest (and that of the medical establishment) in regulating both the abortion process and, in the third trimester, the *potential* life of the fetus. Although *Roe* v. *Wade* (and its companion case *Doe* v. *Bolton*) did not recognize an unconditional right to abortion, it came unexpectedly close, since most abortions occurred in the first three months.

The decision followed recent Court precedents—particularly the 1965 *Griswold* v. *Connecticut* ruling that voided a state ban on contraceptive use—that seemed to grant women a partial constitutional right of control over childbearing. Rather than ground the abortion right in equality claims or the Fourteenth Amendment's equal protection clause—the justification for the 1954 *Brown* decision and other antidiscrimination rulings—*Roe* v. *Wade* followed *Griswold* in recognizing a constitutional right to privacy implicit in the ambiguous due process clause of the same amendment with its "concept of personal liberty and restrictions upon state action." Given the Supreme Court's tendency to sidetrack substantive equality with procedural liberty, this finding was predictable, since an equal-protection-based ruling presumably would have mandated not merely a limited right of choice but equal access to abortion, enforceable by government—that is, requiring public funding.

The most controversial aspect of the historic decision, however, was its refusal to grant constitutional personhood to the fetus and thus to assert any constitutional protection for its alleged right to life. This more than anything stirred up the howling storm that quickly gathered force.

THE CATHOLIC CHURCH hierarchy had tried to block abortion reform ever since states began liberalizing their statutes in the late 1960s. The church had doctrinally opposed abortion for a century: an 1869 papal encyclical declared it a sin. *Roe* v. *Wade* awakened deep alarm among millions of lay Catholics and other socially conservative citizens who had taken it as gospel that a fetus was a human life. Catholic bishops created the National Right to Life Committee (NRLC) to mobilize the faithful and others behind legislative restrictions and a Human Life Amendment to the Constitution declaring the fetus a person and outlawing most abortions.

Although the NRLC became increasingly independent and secular, the Catholic Church remained the driving force of the emerging "right to life" movement, providing, in the words of Connie Paige, the "organizational infrastructure, the communications network, the logistical support, the resources, the ideology and the people, as well as a ready-made nationwide political machine." Its institutional and spiritual role paralleled that of the Protestant black church in relation to the Southern freedom movement. The majority of activists were Catholic women, mainly homemakers. Though there were prominent women leaders, most were men.

From the mid-1970s on, the movement tried to mobilize single-issue voting blocs to elect a "pro-life" Congress and lobbied successfully for state and federal restrictions such as parental and spousal consent and prohibitions on public funding. In 1976 Congress passed an appropriations amendment to cut off Medicaid funds for abortion; its author, Irish Catholic Republican Henry Hyde of Illinois, once introduced himself to an NRLC convention as "a 626-month-old fetus." Challenged by a Planned Parenthood class action suit, the Hyde Amendment was declared unconstitutional by a New York federal judge. Subsequently the Supreme Court decided that states did not have to pay for "nontherapeutic" abortions and in June 1980 upheld the Hyde Amendment. Perpetuating a familiar judicial pattern, the high court had ruled in *Roe* that women had an absolute right to an early abortion, then later blocked the right's implementation for those who could not pay: poor women, largely non-white, and many teenagers. This contradiction demonstrated the flimsiness of an abortion right premised narrowly on an individualistic right to privacy.

As the right-to-life movement reached its peak, a rising political juggernaut latched on to it. Ever since Barry Goldwater's crushing defeat by Lyndon Johnson in 1964, right-wing Republicans had been methodically organizing to win power, spearheaded by a cadre of true-believing young conservatives who dubbed themselves the New Right. Though their main goals were liberating "free enterprise," revamping the military, and rehabilitating interventionism abroad, they realized that votes could best be gained by exploiting "personal" issues like abortion—giving a right-wing cast, as had anti-ERA forces, to the personal politics that had animated the New Left and feminism. New Right architects won over the right-to-life leaders with their political know-how, computerized mailing lists, and money, then brought in the "electronic ministry" of fundamentalist preachers like Jerry Falwell and millions of "born again" followers—resulting in an unlikely alliance of Catholics and evangelical Protestants. Arm in arm with these powerful allies the New Right deployed the abortion issue as the forward line of a "pro-family" offensive that, in the guise of restoring traditional Christian morality, was actually a full-scale assault on sexual self-determination and women's autonomy, a virtual counterrevolution against feminist gains of the past decade.

Although the abortion conflict was caught up in bigger goals, broader worldviews, and deeper emotional and spiritual needs, the majority of abortion opponents passionately believed that the fetus was already a human life and thus had a God-given natural right, and a human right, to be born. New Right, fundamentalist, and right-to-life leaders might themselves have had hidden agendas for the pursuit of power, but their large following was sincere in its moral commitment. While most assumed that human life began at conception, probably only a minority believed that the fetus had an absolute right to life, that the pregnant woman's rights were always subordinate even if her survival (her right to life) was at stake, or in cases of rape or incest.

The more antiabortion activists held rigidly to the life-at-conception principle, however, the more vulnerable they were to attack, even on the moral ground that they thought they monopolized. In a thoroughgoing critique of the right-to-life perspective, utilizing physiological evidence as well as moral reasoning, feminist theologian Beverly Wildung Harrison challenged the notion that the potential life of an early fetus had the same moral status as a fetus nearer to birth. She contended that strong social support for first-trimester abortion was the best means of reducing later abortions, particularly those in the viability stage that many feminists personally felt ambivalent about. Indeed, the unwillingness of abortion rights advocates to speak publicly of their qualms about late-term abortions seemed a mirror image of their opponents' absolute claims about fetal life.

Along with much of the pro-choice camp, Harrison expressed concern about the quality of life facing a newborn infant, an issue generally minimized by the antiabortion leaders, who appeared to value life more highly before birth than after. The latter's lack of commitment to establishing the necessary social conditions for nurturing both child and mother would make the presumed fetal right to life very short-lived. In Harrison's view, it was the reproductive rights advocates who exemplified moral and social responsibility. "To celebrate the potentiality of a life we do not intend to care for concretely," she commented, " . . . signifies not moral maturity but childish moral irresponsibility."

Harrison suggested that "the quality of all our lives depends not on blindly embracing an automatic organic process but on the texture of concern and our very human, very moral readiness to provide for the children we choose to bring into the world." How to weigh the conflicting claims, not just of woman and fetus, but of the fetal right to life and the newborn's entitlement to a *decent* life, free of abuse and neglect? Harrison advocated a restructuring of society that would have the effect of decreasing abortions while enhancing women's life choices and control, particularly of procreation.

Feminists made abortion rights central not only because women's equality would be impossible without reproductive freedom—control of reproduction being the precondition for self-determination in other areas—but as a response to what they perceived as the veiled purpose of the right-to-life camp. Only on the surface, they claimed, did the fierce debate concern the rights of the fetus; more fundamentally, it was about the proper roles and responsibilities of women and "the place and meaning of motherhood," in Kristin Luker's words. Changes in technology, in the structure of work, and in women's values and aspirations "have opened up possibilities for women outside of the home undreamed of in the nineteenth century," according to Luker. For the first time they had the option to decide "how and when their family roles will fit into the larger context of their lives." Defying these trends, abortion opponents were declaring, "both practically and symbolically, that women's reproductive roles should be given social primacy." Abortion thus served as the moral battleground between those who sought to preserve the old sexual division of labor and those striving to transform it, a seemingly irreconcilable conflict between opposing values, beliefs, and social worlds.

Just when the antiabortion movement appeared to have taken over Washington, after the New Right's coalition had put Ronald Reagan in the White House in 1980, Planned Parenthood, NARAL, ACLU, and other pro-choice groups launched a counteroffensive with lobbying and demonstrations that impeded their opponents' legislative drive and the campaign for a constitutional amendment guaranteeing a fetal right to life. By the mid-1980s, after the ERA defeat, reproductive rights emerged as feminists' make-or-break issue.

Challenged by the growing pro-choice coalition, abandoned by President Reagan as he turned to economic restructuring and military buildup, set back by Congress and then by a 1983 Supreme Court decision that reaffirmed *Roe* in striking down a restrictive Akron abortion law, many right-to-life activists judged that conventional methods had failed. More and more of them turned to direct action against hundreds of independent abortion clinics. Though extremists engaged in bombing and sabotage, most of the new militants chose confrontation tactics— blocking clinic entrances and harassing women seeking abortions.

It seemed paradoxical, Faye Ginsburg has noted, that activists "who hope to overturn much of the social change of the 1960s consider the civil rights and antiwar movements as models for action." But harassing women and otherwise violating their personal rights betrayed the tradition of civil disobedience to which they claimed adherence. In 1990 the Supreme Court upheld an appeals court ruling that banned "Operation Rescue" members from blocking New York clinics; the appeals court had declared such action a breach of the 1871 Ku Klux Klan Act that was designed, after the Civil War, to prevent assaults on the rights of freed slaves.

Rarely did harassment stop women from actualizing their right to abortion. Sometimes it provoked them to raise their voices against the screams of "babykiller" and worse. As a young black woman made her way through a threatening blockade at the Atlanta Feminist Women's Health Center, a blond white man yelled that Dr. King would "turn over in his grave" at what she was doing. She lifted her head, stared at him with tears in her eyes, and said firmly: "You're a white boy, and you don't give a damn about me. . . . You even know less about Martin Luther King or being Black. What you have to say to me means nothin', not a damn thing." She walked inside, leaving him speechless.

Pro-life militancy did not noticeably affect the long-standing majority support of Americans—even among Catholics—for conditional abortion rights. But the cause found a powerful benefactor in the new Supreme Court. Reagan's four appointees, including the first female justice, Sandra Day O'Connor, tilted the high bench sharply to the right; antipathy to abortion apparently had become a tacit requirement for nomination to the federal judiciary. In July 1989 the polarized Court in *Webster* v. *Reproductive Health Services* narrowly sustained most of a 1986 Missouri law that barred the use of public facilities or employees for abortion services and that ordered physicians to test for fetal viability at five months. Although because of the reservations of O'Connor, who held the swing vote, the majority did not reverse *Roe,* the *Webster* ruling opened the door to more state restrictions. Critics of the decision feared that, as columnist Ellen Goodman wrote, "slowly, in the post-Webster world, law by law, without ever 'overturning *Roe,*' abortion could remain legal and become impossible." By preserving intact an increasingly abstract right to first-trimester abortions, while inviting states to deny the means for many women to secure this entitlement, the decision reflected once again the Court's historic tendency to affirm formal rights while at the same time legitimizing the class, racial, and sexual barriers to their realization.

As with other pivotal rulings such as *Roe* and *Brown* v. *Board of Education,* the role of *Webster* in energizing activism proved as significant as its actual legal effect. In the next year, as state legislators scurried to propose abortion restrictions, few of which were enacted, the pro-choice forces mounted a nationwide campaign of direct action, lobbying, and electoral organizing, capped by a huge Washington march in November 1989. Feminists finally seemed to be translating the amorphous pro-choice majority into activist commitment—and votes. Many of the new protesters and precinct walkers were young women who had always taken their reproductive rights for granted. In response Operation Rescue stepped up its blockades, while Catholic bishops, alarmed by rising pro-choice feeling within their fold, hired public relations experts, fired up a multi-million-dollar ad campaign, and threatened pro-choice politicians with excommunication. As the Supreme Court further whittled down *Roe* in the early 1990s, and seemed prepared to overturn it altogether, abortion remained a critical political issue. Some feminists started a new "underground railroad" to enable women to get an abortion elsewhere if it was prohibited where they lived; others were teaching women how to do their own.

Activists on both sides wondered what the future would hold. It seemed likely that technological advances would transform the tumultuous debate—and possibly end it. On the one hand, new reproductive technologies were likely to make the fetus "viable" earlier, which, as Justice O'Connor argued in the 1983 Akron case, might roll back *Roe*'s third-trimester demarcation and thus jeopardize the entire decision; of course, much depended on the definition of fetal viability. On the other hand, the French-developed "abortion pill," RU-486, permitted women to terminate a pregnancy independently within the first two months. More refined oral abortifacients would probably extend this time period. Other advances such as *in vitro* fertilization, sperm and egg donation, frozen embryos, artificial uteruses, genetic screening, and fetal surgery could, in effect, endow women (and men) who would otherwise be infertile with a "right" to procreate, or to bear healthy children free from birth defects or deformation. The latter might also be seen as a child's right to natal health and well-being.

Yet even if startling breakthroughs empowered women to stop early pregnancies with ease, controversy would continue over the morality of late-term abortions. And with advances in the transferability of both sperm and fertilized eggs, strife over reproductive rights moved into new domains, such as the maternal rights of women who contracted to bear a child for another party, the legality or constitutionality of such contracts, and the ethics, as some saw it, of buying and selling babies. Surrogate parenthood meant "the loss of rights for women," claimed feminist health activist Becky Sarah, "loss of the basic right to our kids." Would the rise of what Jennifer Terry has called "prenatal surveillance technologies" give women "more choices and control over their reproduction," or, in light of social crises like AIDS and drug abuse, permit only those women to bear children who are judged "fit" to reproduce—leading toward a "new eugenics" of population control?

Legal historian Eva Rubin has suggested that a "whole new jurisprudence may be needed" to grapple with the impact of reproductive technology on women's rights, "which cannot be made dependent on the latest developments in bioengineering." Still, despite setbacks and new obstacles, over the long run women did seem to be gaining more control over their procreative power, with technology as both ally and adversary.

This did not mean, however, that they had much influence in shaping the new technologies or in setting the priorities for research and development, which remained largely in white male hands. But with more and more women becoming scientists and physicians, this too might change.

It would not have been a just outcome, however, and ultimately might have been self-defeating, if women finally secured the unconditional legal right to abortion without also actualizing rights, for *all* women, to a wide range of social supports in order to make meaningful the right to procreative choice. This would go beyond full public funding for abortions to include equal access to high-quality sex education, contraception, prenatal care, health services, nutrition, child care, and housing—so that women have the right to become parents along with the right *not* to. Many women of color have been reluctant to embrace the pro-choice cause because of its thin focus on legalizing abortion and neglect of a thicker fabric of reproductive rights.

A major drawback of the liberal feminist pro-choice crusade has been its inability to transcend its middle-class, individualist premises. All the rhetoric about rights to "privacy" and "choice," sometimes portrayed as if ends in themselves, has perpetuated an assumption that the abortion decision is solely an individual matter or "private choice." Claiming that something is private, noted Beverly Wildung Harrison, "has come to mean that it is 'unrelated to social reality,' or that it affects an individual alone and should not be a shared reality. . . . Our liberal political rhetoric is saturated with such antisocial implications."

In fact the abortion right is simultaneously individual and social. Although a person's right to bodily integrity ought to be no less inviolable than one's individual right to life and liberty, and is constitutive of these, reproductive rights cannot be abstracted or divorced from the social context and conditions within which a woman tries to exercise them. As in the full attainment of other rights, freedom from constraint, the touchstone of liberal values, is essential but insufficient. To achieve these rights Harrison and Rosalind Petchesky have called, like radical feminists before them, for a sweeping transformation of the conditions of reproduction. The tragedy of the pro-choice movement, Petchesky has suggested, was that a majority of Americans believed in an abstract reproductive choice but were not convinced that deep-seated social change was needed to make it universal. "Until privacy or autonomy is redefined in reference to social justice provisions that can give it substance for the poorest women, it will remain not only a class-biased and racist concept but an antifeminist one, insofar as it is premised on a denial of social responsibility to improve the conditions of women as a group."

Such a commitment to reproductive rights broadly defined would transcend the liberal feminist goal of equal rights that used men as the standard—impossible, of course, in the area of reproduction. In organizing mainly around abortion and employment rights, mainstream feminists fell into the same process of compartmentalization that hurt their forebears in feminism's "first wave." The political narrowness of the pro-choice movement seemed a throwback to woman suffragism, as the multifaceted goal of reproductive rights, entailing body rights as well, was reduced to the right to choose an abortion whether or not funds or services were available.

A larger vision of reproductive rights would encompass not only the negative right to be free from compulsory childbearing, rape, and domestic violence, but the positive entitlement to all the resources necessary to be a mother *and* a self-determining human being—whether one is married or a single parent. It was women, not fetuses, whose personhood demanded full recognition by the Constitution, the state, society, and by women themselves. Such a liberation agenda would not play into the old trade-off of motherhood and personhood but would insist that society be restructured so that each would nourish, not deplete, the other, so that the two would no longer be warring within many women's souls.

THE EXPANDING UNIVERSE OF RIGHTS

FOR A TIME, everything seemed possible. The revolts of African-Americans and women helped to inspire a virtual chain reaction of rights claims by other oppressed groups. Black and feminist activists along with Vietnam War protesters generated ideas, imagery, strategies, tactics, legal springboards, and above all confidence that fired the imagination and will of Latinos, American Indians, Asian-Americans, gay and lesbian people, the disabled, and the elderly. None of these populations would have acted, however, had they not been "ready from within," to borrow a phrase of black leader Septima Clark.

In 1962 a young Chicano named Cesar Chavez drove his old car 15,000 miles all around California's vast Central Valley. He talked to hundreds of farm workers in hot, dusty fields and in house meetings and asked them to write on cards the wages they felt entitled to. Chavez had grown up laboring in the fields and had later been a top-notch organizer with Saul Alinsky's community organizing network. His grueling, three-month journey led to the creation of the first strong union of farm workers in the United States, composed largely of Mexican and Filipino immigrants. After several years of nonviolent strikes, marches, and a nationwide boycott, the United Farm Workers won contracts with California's grape industry in 1970, then switched to an even steeper battle with lettuce growers. The UFW appeared to have clinched victory with passage of California's Agricultural Labor Relations Act in 1975 (farm workers had been excluded from the Wagner Act), but the ALRA's lack of enforcement by Reagan-era Republicans forced the union to resume strikes and boycotts in the 1980s.

Although the UFW aimed at economic rights—the right to a union, to a decent wage, to health and safety—it traced the footsteps of the Wobblies and other labor vanguards in strengthening the crucial rights of collective free speech that would allow its message to be heard and have an impact. Longtime UFW general counsel Jerome Cohen recalled that the farm workers "created a lot of first amendment law during their struggle," with union lawyers carving out "legal niches" in which First Amendment rights could be vigorously exercised; for example, by winning the right to use bullhorns in the fields, overturning restraining orders that barred pickets, and requiring California judges to give notice and hold hearings when such orders were requested.

During the late 1960s, Chicano student activists started a "Chicano Power" movement in California cities that, like its model of black liberation, drew strength from revitalized group identity and rejected assimilation into the dominant "Anglo" culture. It fought for Chicano studies programs and formed a political party called La Raza Unida. Meanwhile, in New York and Chicago, Puerto Ricans struggled for their own rights as citizens and for their homeland's right to self-determination.

Though far from what it would take to overcome the poverty they experienced, the country's worst, some strides were made by dozens of American Indian "nations" toward actualizing tribal rights to land and resources promised in nineteenth-century treaties that had been systematically violated by the United States government. After decades of brutal military conquest, resulting in the confinement of several hundred Indian tribes to reservations, Washington shifted to a policy of forced assimilation late in the nineteenth century, spearheaded by the 1887 General Allotment Act that Theodore Roosevelt called "a mighty pulverizing engine to break up the tribal mass." The law encouraged individual Indians to own tribal property and opened reservations to non-Indian settlement and use.

Beginning in the late 1950s, however, many tribes skillfully utilized federal courts to enforce, if partially and piecemeal, certain legal obligations embedded in treaties and treaty substitutes. These court orders, which also bolstered tribal self-rule, reaffirmed the unique constitutional (or extraconstitutional) status of Indian tribes and the legitimacy of Indi-

ans' communal rights, which coexisted with the dominant system of individually based entitlements.

Indians would not have secured these legal victories without local
protests and land seizures that dramatized their grievances, most notably
a yearlong takeover of Alcatraz Island, the abandoned federal prison in
San Francisco Bay, and the American Indian Movement's spring 1973
occupation of the Oglala Sioux village of Wounded Knee, South Dakota,
site of the massacre in 1890 of unarmed Indians by U.S. cavalry. Rather
than heed AIM's demands to address the Sioux reservation's dire poverty, the government sent heavily armed FBI agents and federal marshals
to blockade Wounded Knee. After seventy days of hostile standoff, punctuated by gun battles in which two Indians were slain, the two sides
reached a settlement that Washington predictably disregarded. But the
second Wounded Knee emboldened Indians elsewhere to seize their
rights.

In contrast to American Indians whose communal rights had long been
promised, if only on musty paper, was the plight of people desiring
intimate relationships with others of the same sex. Gay men and lesbians
had been so saddled by society with shame and self-hatred that until the
late 1960s many did not think they *had* rights as openly gay persons.
Indeed, early "homophile" groups like the Mattachine Society and
Daughters of Bilitis did not seek rights but rather personal adjustment,
respectability, and assimilation—in part by downplaying or concealing
public homosexual identity.

Then, as unexpectedly as Rosa Parks's refusal to give up her seat in
Montgomery, a single event in June 1969 sparked a formidable new
movement for gay rights. When police raided the Stonewall Inn, a popular gay bar in Greenwich Village, the patrons responded not with fear as
before, but with fury, heaving cobblestones at the cops and for four days
fighting back violently. Formation of the Gay Liberation Front and related groups coincided with the revolt of lesbians within the feminist
movement who, refusing any longer to keep their sexual identity invisible, made it a political issue. Some lesbian activists crafted a separatist
politics of "lesbian-feminism" that condemned compulsory heterosexu-
ality as a "primary cornerstone of male supremacy."

The new liberation movement, which "talked optimistically about new
ideas like gay power and even gay revolution," according to journalist
Randy Shilts, encouraged gays and lesbians to "come out" publicly and
to seek human rights *as* homosexuals. Influenced by the black movement,
particularly Black Power, and by radical feminism, it cultivated pride and
dignity and the conviction that "gay is good," "gay is beautiful." Demanding deep-rooted change to eradicate what it called "heterosexism,"

particularly heterosexual domination and homosexual stigma, the movement aimed not only at civil rights and freedom from prejudice but also
at personal and social rights to familyhood, including legalization of
"domestic partnerships" and child custody, and the social legitimation of
homosexual values and culture.

Through the 1970s and 1980s activists organized marches, nationwide
"Gay Freedom Days," and electoral and lobbying campaigns to press
their claims. They made a historic breakthrough by electing openly gay
San Francisco supervisor Harvey Milk in 1977—and suffered a grievous
loss when he was assassinated a year later. Gays and lesbians made their
greatest advances in banning discrimination in employment and housing,
as scores of cities and counties along with Wisconsin, Massachusetts,
Connecticut, and Hawaii enacted antidiscrimination laws. Fewer gains
were made in family or sexual rights. Though half the states repealed laws
against consensual homosexual practices, in 1986 the Supreme Court in
Bowers v. *Hardwick* narrowly approved the right of states to pass such laws,
rejecting arguments that the constitutional right to privacy protected
homosexual conduct.

The greatest barrier to progress in the 1980s was the ghastly AIDS
epidemic, which Harry Britt, gay president of the San Francisco Board of
Supervisors, called "our Holocaust." Despite the devastation in lives and
suffering, which extended to heterosexuals and disproportionately affected people of color, the crisis galvanized extraordinary activism in gay
communities aimed at defining and realizing the rights of AIDS patients,
particularly to adequate health care and more effective treatments. These
efforts culminated in a 1987 march of several hundred thousand in Washington and the carpeting of the Capitol mall by a vast quilt sewn by
thousands to remember the names of the dead.

OVER TWO CENTURIES—the pace accelerating and the path widening especially since the 1960s—many groups of oppressed citizens waged
collective struggles for rights, in large part by marshaling group identity
and solidarity. Their circumstances, resources, readiness, and the nature
of opposing forces have varied as much as the actors themselves. Yet in
every case, building upon the precedents and advances of forerunners,
leaders and followers have conceptualized, articulated, shaped, and demanded the rights that they felt entitled to by God, nature, citizenship,
or their existence in the human family. Once these rights, or pieces of
them, were enacted into law or emplaced in the Constitution, citizens
sought to implement their new rights, to actualize them in their everyday
lives, not always with much success but enough, in many instances, to
motivate further rights aspirations. All along the way the meaning of

rights was redefined, expanded, and deepened through popular pressure in the crucible of conflict.

With few exceptions, however—such as sporadic enforcement of Indians' tribal rights, extensive implementation of physical access rights for the disabled, and workers' collective bargaining rights—the American political and legal system converted the diverse aspirations for communal rights into the ostensibly uniform legal rights of atomized individuals. Citizens' group or class connections, from the state's point of view, dissolved into a homogenized "melting pot." At first glance, such a sweeping assertion would seem to be contradicted by what might well have been the most intensive and sustained government effort to enforce rights in the nation's history—affirmative action policies. Was not affirmative action the quintessential example of state recognition and implementation of group rights? To the extent that these policies failed, moreover, didn't this experience illustrate the dangers of resorting to group-based rather than individual entitlements? Yet looking beneath surface appearances, it seemed evident that affirmative action was not an articulation of group or communal rights at all; it remained squarely within the traditional parameters of liberal individualism.

Although the term first appeared in the 1935 Wagner Act, affirmative action as federal policy was rooted in Title VII of the 1964 Civil Rights Act banning job discrimination, and in President Johnson's Executive Order 11246 in September 1965—a month after the Watts ghetto exploded—which required all federal contractors to make a priority of recruiting, hiring, and promoting racial minorities; women were added two years later as a result of feminist lobbying. In this first phase of "soft" affirmative action, Title VII's prohibition of preferential treatment such as racial quotas held sway, the EEOC had no enforcement powers, and compliance was pretty much voluntary. Nevertheless, CORE and SNCC continued to advocate preferential treatment for blacks as compensation for past injustice.

Growing pressure from the black movement, from ghetto rebellions, and from feminists pushed all three government branches to tighten antidiscrimination enforcement. With the black movement now demanding costly, collective economic remedies, even "reparations," federal bureaucrats engineered a less disruptive pressure valve. The EEOC was permitted to bring offenders to court, and a new Office of Federal Contract Compliance (OFCC) formulated detailed instructions for contractors, including universities, and where necessary set goals and timetables to reach approximate proportional representation of racial minorities and women in the workplace or classroom. This mandate later included the physically disabled.

The shift from "soft" into "hard" affirmative action was ratified by a unanimous 1971 Supreme Court ruling in *Griggs* v. *Duke Power Company* that interpreted Title VII to proscribe "not only overt discrimination but also practices which are fair in form, but discriminatory in operation. . . . Good intent or absence of discriminatory intent does not redeem employment procedures or testing mechanisms that operate as 'built-in headwinds' for minority groups and are unrelated to measuring job capability." Rather, the Court said, Congress aimed Title VII at "the *consequences* of employment practices, not simply the motivation." Critics such as Nathan Glazer and Charles Murray argued that the courts and enforcement agencies thus redefined equal opportunity from the simple principle of nondiscrimination against individuals into equality of representation, of result.

By the late 1970s an angry backlash set in. White male allegations of "reverse discrimination," even "reverse racism," were supported by neo-conservative scholars and the Reagan Revolution's policy-makers. The Supreme Court's 1978 *Bakke* decision—which, while approving less rigid affirmative action methods, invalidated an admissions quota for minorities at the University of California at Davis Medical School—opened the way to a spate of high court rulings a decade later that nearly reversed the *Griggs* decision and made it harder to seek legal redress for job discrimination or to preserve past gains. In his *Bakke* dissent, in a comment even more appropriate for the later decisions, Justice Thurgood Marshall argued that the Court had "come full circle": just as it had invalidated civil rights laws passed after the Civil War, a century later it was striking down rights reforms achieved during the nation's "second Reconstruction."

The 1990 Civil Rights Act, designed to overturn these rulings legislatively and to expand the rights of people facing discrimination—notably the right to sue not just for racial but also for sexual harassment—was passed overwhelmingly by Congress, then vetoed by President George Bush, who claimed rather spuriously that it would reimpose quotas. The lawmakers barely sustained the veto.

Although the extensiveness of past quotas was debatable, no one could dispute that affirmative action toughened during the 1970s and that in the process of implementation bureaucrats and judges altered the goal itself from equal treatment to roughly equal results. "It is this policy watershed," historian Hugh Davis Graham has concluded, "between classic liberalism's core command against discrimination on the one hand, and the new theory of compensatory justice on the other, that was crossed" as a result of movement pressures. It was a shift, he suggests, from "positive-sum" to "zero-sum" affirmative action, from antidiscrimination procedures that affected only the individual involved to mechanisms that purposely advantaged certain individuals at the direct expense of others. Where Graham and other interpreters, both liberal and conservative, erred was in assuming that somehow individual-based rights metamorphosed into group-based ones.

The later emphasis on results instead of intent did not have much to do with entitlements of specific groups as such. It marked a shift from mere procedural fairness toward implementation of a desired substantive policy outcome, signifying administrative and judicial recognition of continuing institutionalized discrimination—"institutional racism"—and the virtual irrelevance of good intentions in the context of governmental, corporate, or educational bureaucracies with lives and histories of their own. This represented an advance beyond liberalism's traditional allegiance to the "supremacy of the procedural principle," whose invisible hand, while avoiding substantive goals, would somehow still produce the common good; beyond the liberal view, as expressed by constitutional expert Alexander Bickel, that the highest morality "almost always is the morality of process." Graham has pointed out that when the courts ruled that "Congress's overarching substantive purpose (more jobs for minorities) was more compelling than its specific procedural prohibitions (no discrimination in a color-blind society), sympathetic legal scholars argued that the Warren-era judges were correcting a formalist bias of the late 19th century."

But the competitive individualism at the core of the process remained undisturbed, if not accentuated. *Groups* did not apply for jobs or seek admission to schools; *individuals* did. And whatever advantages persons of color or white women were given in the selection procedures, they still competed against other individuals. The right enforced here was the right, as Mary Ann Mason put it, to contest with white males in the marketplace "in keeping with the distinctly American ethic of 'rugged individualism.'" Furthermore, it was the right to compete individually not only with privileged white males but with other disadvantaged persons, including members of one's own racial or sexual group. How could one have a "group right" to compete against individuals in one's own group?

Moreover, the realization of these allegedly group-based rights has not benefited the entire group but only part of it. African-Americans as a people have not benefited very much from affirmative action policies; only the middle-class minority has. William Julius Wilson and other scholars have claimed that the exodus of successful middle-class blacks from the inner cities has actually worsened the condition of the black underclass. Far from unifying and equalizing blacks, Latinos, women, and other targeted populations, affirmative action has inadvertently helped to intensify class divisions within each group.

Yet, instead of perverting the right to equal opportunity, as Glazer and Murray have charged, hard affirmative action has epitomized it. Political theorist John H. Schaar has written that the "equal opportunity" doctrine—originating in the 1840s as a Whig slogan to deflect Jacksonian radicals' clamor for "leveling" equal rights—was "the product of a competitive and fragmented society, a divided society, a society in which individualism, in Tocqueville's sense of the word, is the reigning ethical principle." Extending the marketplace mentality to all spheres, equal opportunity in this sense treated "the whole of human relations as a contest in which each competes against all others for scarce goods," in which "one man's gain is usually another's loss." Schaar contended that "it is the perfect embodiment of the Liberal conception of reform. It breaks up solidaristic opposition to existing conditions of inequality by holding out to the ablest and most ambitious members of the disadvantaged groups the enticing prospect of rising from their lowly state into a more prosperous condition." While it has made some individuals more equal to others, in the larger context equal opportunity has produced increasing inequality.

Although these assertions might be overstated if applied to affirmative action, it nonetheless seems evident that while affirmative action has shifted the pattern of social inequalities, it has not substantially diminished, and may have even bolstered, the overall amount of inequality. Derrick Bell has suggested that affirmative action mechanisms "have flourished because they offer more benefit to the institutions that adopt them than they do to the minorities whom they're nominally intended to serve." Yet the conclusion to draw is not, as some critics have claimed, that people of color and white women, or American society as a whole, would have been better off without aggressive affirmative action programs; on balance, they clearly have done more good than harm. The point is to look closely at the inadequacies of affirmative action in order to learn how to do more to remove inequality, not less. If remedies based on principles of liberal individualism have proved incapable of pulling society away from entrenched class, race, and gender privilege, and in fact have tended to reinforce it, other strategies ought to be considered.

An alternative approach would encourage society to embrace the actualization of communal rights, rights that are simultaneously individual and shared with other citizens, especially rights to social resources. Expanding the original concept of "compensatory justice" sketched in the mid-1960s by black leaders such as Whitney Young, Jr., A. Philip Randolph, and Bayard Rustin, this strategy would call for a rethinking and comprehensive reordering of social priorities. It would aim not at individual solutions but at far-reaching collective ones: reconstruction of public education from the ground up, especially for the poor, to realize the right to a good education; innovative job training programs of a quality and relevance never tried; publicly subsidized work geared to the physical and spiritual rebuilding of American society; diverse and creative housing programs to solve homelessness; community-controlled national health care oriented to prevention as much as treatment. For women in particular, communal rights to compensatory justice would include free and safe abortions, universal child care, paid parental leaves, benefits and pensions for part-time work, a livable income, and commitment to comparable worth. Ultimately these programs would not only refashion the American political economy, but lead to "new definitions of work and leisure," as Rustin posited in 1965.

The implementation of communal rights would necessarily entail structural reforms that both hinged upon a major redistribution of social power and resources and propelled such redistribution—reform that was thus "non-reformist." Rather than a zero-sum game pitting individual against individual and group against group, communal rights would be inclusive not exclusive, motivated by and enhancing cooperation not competition, capable of expansion not driven by scarcity. Properly understood, communal rights would tend to transcend narrow individual or group interests and move toward the realization of universal entitlements for all citizens.

PART FIVE

CHAPTER TWELVE

THE CROSSFIRE OF RIGHTS

ADOLESCENTS WHO GAIN with adulthood the suffrage and a host of other rights enter a world of complex and competing freedoms. But one right is clear and there for the taking—absolute and untrammeled freedom of belief, thought, conscience. This right, so taken for granted in the United States today, has been, for many centuries and in many lands, violated by those in authority who cannot endure the idea that some might *think* differently from them, even when those thoughts give birth to no action. The most barbarous tortures have been inflicted in attempts to force heretics to recant. It is a measure of the power of ideas that such recantations have been thought necessary and that uncounted men and women have suffered and died for their beliefs.

In no area has the right of conscience been violated more brutally than religion. Jews and Christians martyred by Romans, Protestants martyred by Catholics and Catholics by Protestants in the religious wars of the Reformation and Counter Reformation, Protestants martyred by other Protestants, the terrible martyrdoms of Jews at the hands of Christians from the dawn of the Christian era to our own time—these horrors of hatred and intolerance are inescapable, they form a part of our fundamental education. Doubtless the framers of the Bill of Rights had had very much in mind the endless examples of persecutions that had occurred when the church was an extension of the state power, or the state power an extension of the church—they themselves had lived under a crown that was also head of a church, and knew colonies that had been governed by intolerant theocracies—for they wrote into the beginning of the First Amendment what would come to be called the "establishment" clause: "Congress shall make no law respecting an establishment of reli-

gion." And certainly they had had the long history of religious intolerance in mind—James Madison perhaps remembering the harassment of
Baptists in Virginia—when in the First Amendment's second clause they
barred Congress from "prohibiting the free exercise" of religion.

In returning to the original Bill of Rights for an appraisal of the modern
standing of liberty in the United States, we bring up to date the mixed
record in the application even of the First Amendment, our most precious
set of rights. Amid the never-ending crossfires of rights, as various groups
struggle to achieve their own liberties while ignoring or threatening the
rights of others, national, state, and local governments have lurched
forward, backward, sidewise, or run for cover. Thus there has been no
steady march toward a First Amendment Utopia but a series of skirmishes. If these skirmishes have in the end yielded significant victories for
civil liberties, the reason lies largely in the existence of a powerful national creed of liberty expressed in constitutional provisions that have
been at last given some teeth.

We begin as the First Amendment does, with freedom of religion. We
can measure much of the progress made in securing this right, but some
of it we cannot. For religious freedom is not merely a matter of legislative
enactments and judicial findings. It is also a matter of the mind and of
the heart, of individual feeling and integrity. Those familiar with the
history of the American people must acknowledge the enormous amount
of religious intolerance that has stained the record. But they would also
have to admit that the decline of intolerance has been remarkable. Those
who listened in to the conversations of even the best-educated and most
economically secure Americans earlier in this century can never forget
the veiled or open references, the snide remarks, the slightly embarrassed
but cutting references to people of different creeds. Such attitudes had
their effect on behavior. One of the authors has seen the records of a
college that in the early 1920s tendered a professorship to a distinguished
scholar, later discovered he was a Catholic, and revoked the offer. Jews,
Muslims, and members of other religious minorities could report similar
incidents. Not only have laws made this kind of discrimination difficult
today, but along with the laws have come crucial changes in attitudes.

FIRST AMENDMENT: THE FIXED STAR?

THE INTENT of the First Amendment's framers to protect religious
belief was noble—but it was not enough. The sources of that belief also
needed protection. In 1972, the Supreme Court was confronted by a

complex case involving the sources of belief when Amish parents asked relief from a Wisconsin law that compelled children to attend formal schools, whether public or private, to age sixteen. The Amish accepted that their children should obtain basic skills in formal schools, but argued that beyond the eighth grade they should have the informal schooling that would prepare them for life in the Amish community. The Court had to balance the state's interest in the early education of all children with the rights of the Amish under the First Amendment's "free exercise" clause, and in *Wisconsin* v. *Yoder* the Court sided with the Amish: compulsory attendance beyond eighth grade not only violated Amish belief but posed a "very real threat of undermining the Amish community and religious practice."

Other forms of free exercise received equally fine balancings of rights and interests. Polygamy was sanctioned by the Mormon church, but in 1878 the Court drew a line between belief and practice, holding that while Congress could not touch "mere opinion," it might "reach actions which were in violation of social duties or subversive of good order," and that believers could not be exempted from laws under which nonbelievers might be convicted and punished. If religious doctrines were held superior to public law, every citizen would "become a law unto himself."

A century later free exercise faced another test. When the Internal Revenue Service withdrew tax exemption from a South Carolina religious university that practiced racial discrimination, denying "admission to applicants engaged in an interracial marriage or known to advocate interracial marriage or dating," the Court ruled in 1983 that the government had a "fundamental, overriding interest in eradicating racial discrimination in education" and that this interest "substantially outweighs whatever burden denial of tax benefits places on petitioners' exercise of their religious beliefs."

If the state might prohibit a particular religious practice in the public interest, could it also—in the public interest—oblige believers to perform an action that violated a fundamental tenet of their creed? A pair of cases involving Jehovah's Witnesses aroused passionate conflict over this issue within the high court. To twelve-year-old Lillian Gobitis and her ten-year-old brother, William, a state law that required students to salute the American flag was a violation of the biblical injunction against the worship of false idols, and when they refused to salute, they were expelled from their school in Minersville, Pennsylvania. The year was 1940, when war raged in Europe. The Court sustained the expulsion by an 8–1 majority, with the opinion by Felix Frankfurter, who found in the flag a "binding tie of cohesive sentiment" and held that no "exceptional immunity" from "the subtle process of securing effective loyalty to the traditional ideals of democracy" need be granted to "dissidents." Harlan Stone disagreed, writing that "the very essence of liberty" was "the freedom of the individual from compulsion as to what he shall think and what he shall say, at least where the compulsion is to bear false witness to his religion."

Of course, it was exactly Frankfurter's "effective loyalty" that the Witnesses abjured, and his decision helped set off mob attacks on them in more than forty states. Many hundreds of children were expelled from schools. But three years later, in 1943, a new flag salute case reached the Court, this time from West Virginia, and now, in an extraordinary reversal, six of the nine justices came to defend the Witnesses' First Amendment rights. The decision became famous through Robert Jackson's noble utterance for the majority: "If there is any fixed star in our constitutional constellation, it is that no official, high or petty, can prescribe what shall be orthodox in politics, nationalism, religion, or other matters of opinion or force citizens to confess by word or act their faith therein."

Frankfurter, clinging to his former position, was equally eloquent in a long dissent. "One who belongs to the most vilified and persecuted minority in history is not likely to be insensible to the freedoms guaranteed by our Constitution," he began. Personally he supported Jackson's views. "But as judges we are neither Jew nor Gentile, neither Catholic nor agnostic." And as judges, he continued, it was not for them to decide how a state might or might not promote the high purpose of "good citizenship," only whether the means chosen were reasonable. In the case of a flag salute, they were. "One may have the right to practice one's religion and at the same time owe the duty of formal obedience to laws that run counter to one's belief."

Clearly the difficulties of balancing rights and interests with even so simple a pledge as the free exercise of religion could provoke impassioned disagreements and even violence. No less simple was the First Amendment clause prohibiting the establishment of religion, which was said to have erected a Jeffersonian "wall of separation" between church and state.

This "wall" was an attractive and powerful metaphor—but what did it mean? Was it impassable? Did it imply that the authorities could make no accommodations for religion, even if they were neutral with respect to particular faiths? Or considered another way, did not religious "constituencies" have an equal right to receive special protections or exemptions from government as enjoyed by such other constituencies as farmers, students, or the handicapped? In practice, the wall was not absolute—a nation founded "under God" would not be averse to promoting religion, so long as no faith in particular was favored and so long as that promotion did not go too far.

Again the delicate balancings were left to the Court, which in 1971 fashioned a threefold test of legislation that would not go too far in establishing religion: it must have a "secular legislative purpose"; in its principal effect it had neither to advance nor to inhibit religion; it must avoid "an excessive government entanglement with religion." Perhaps by design, these were vague tests, with the result that government was more "entangled" with religion than the establishment clause would seem to permit.

The Court's principle that the clause did not "require complete separation of church and state; it affirmatively mandates accommodation, not merely tolerance, of all religions, and forbids hostility toward any," led it to balance and weigh with sometimes strange results. A city could display a Nativity scene or a Hanukkah menorah on public property along with other holiday symbols if the message seemed on the whole more secular—for instance, commercial—than religious. Tax funds might be used to provide religious schools with textbooks, remedial services, meals, transportation to and from school, but could not be allotted to repair facilities at church-operated schools or pay teachers' salaries or provide equipment or counseling to students. Yet each of these separations or inseparations had its Court-certified logic. Thus routine busing to and from school had no religious element in itself, while transport for field trips could not be tax-funded because teachers might introduce religious content.

For all the fine distinctions—or perhaps because of them—and despite the fact that government's role in all areas of life had grown more pervasive and religious groups were more variegated than ever, "we have done better," according to political scientist Jack Peltason, "than almost any other nation in the world in removing religious disputes from politics and keeping religious tensions among us to a minimum." Still, questions arise as to whether religious groups are deprived of rights to public support that have been bestowed so generously on other constituencies. Even more, if such groups chose to demand more rights and exerted pressure on the courts through Congress and other political agencies, might conflict increase sharply?

IF RELIGIOUS FREEDOM was the first concern of the framers of the Bill of Rights, for most Americans in a later and more secular age freedom of speech lay at the heart of the First Amendment. For them this freedom was the true "fixed star" of people's rights. Yet even stalwart believers in free speech often forgot that it was Congress, and only Congress, that was explicitly forbidden by the framers to abridge that right. The national legislature was given no power to prevent other governments, state or local, or private entities, such as corporations or unions, from curbing it. And while a survey in the early 1980s indicated that virtually all Americans supported free speech "in principle," that support dwindled when citizens were asked whether they would grant it to this or that particular group holding unpopular or controversial positions. The foundations of free speech, in short, were fragile.

Some Americans also believed that the freedom of speech clause in the First Amendment had stood for two centuries as a sentinel over the rights of all. In fact, it was well over a century before the clause came to be an effective legal, instead of essentially a moral, force in safeguarding free speech. A Chief Justice of the United States observed that no "important case involving free speech was decided by this Court prior to *Schenck*" in 1919, and the burden of this first great decision was the Court's approval of federal abridgments of free speech. Before the 1920s, citizens had had to seek protection of their freedom of speech against state and local repression under state bills of rights, with mixed success in state and local courts. But suddenly there came before the high court three cases that would initiate a transformation in the reach of First Amendment free speech rights. Those who pressed this change upon the Court were not eminent jurists or statesmen or educators or ministers concerned about the ineffectiveness of the promise of the First Amendment, but three unsung victims of the Red Scare after World War I, two Communists and one Wobbly.

The first was Benjamin Gitlow, the Communist convicted under a New York criminal anarchy law for his pamphlet advocating "proletarian revolution." In appealing to the Court, Walter Pollak, an attorney for the American Civil Liberties Union, not only maintained that advocacy in itself was no crime and that the citizen's liberty to speak out was in the interests of the whole community, but took a bold step—he contended that free speech was among the rights to "life, liberty, and property" protected by the due process clause of the Fourteenth Amendment. The Fourteenth, Pollak argued, "incorporated" the First Amendment's free speech guarantee, giving the federal government the responsibility and power to enforce national standards in free speech by striking down repressive state and local laws that failed to meet those standards. The high court had previously held that the First Amendment was protection only against federal abuses. But though its decision in 1925 affirmed Gitlow's conviction and upheld the constitutionality of the New York law, the Court stated its new "assumption" that freedom of speech and press were "among the fundamental personal rights and 'liberties' protected by the due process clause of the Fourteenth Amendment from impairment by the States."

For the first time a clause of the First Amendment was nationalized against state power; now victims of state violations of their rights could appeal for relief to the federal judiciary. The Court, wrote Zechariah Chafee, Jr., had seized a "sharp sword with which to defend the ideals of Jefferson and Madison against local intolerance."

Even so, this assertion of national authority seemed for the moment to do little more than add federal imprimatur to New York's repression of Gitlow's free speech. In 1927 Pollak and other alert attorneys seized on another case coming before the Court that involved another Communist, Charlotte Anita Whitney, a Wellesley graduate and labor activist. Her conviction under California law was not for giving a fiery speech or handing out an incendiary pamphlet but simply for organizing a political party, as Jefferson and Madison had done more than a century earlier, and despite her claim that she had dissociated herself from the party's call for revolutionary violence. Once again the Court upheld a state's suppression of speech but Whitney scored a moral victory when Louis Brandeis declared in a concurring opinion that the American revolutionaries of 1776 "were not cowards. They did not fear political change. They did not exalt order at the cost of liberty." The remedy, Brandeis wrote, was not enforced silence but more speech.

So far the civil libertarians seemed to be losing all the individual battles even while gaining in the doctrinal war. But in the next case, decided the same day as Whitney's, they scored a free speech victory and also got the defendant sprung. Harold Fiske, an organizer for the Industrial Workers of the World, was indicted under a Kansas criminal syndicalism statute merely for possessing the preamble to the IWW constitution, even though that preamble did not advocate—or so much as mention—violence. The Court reaffirmed the Fourteenth Amendment's application to free speech and upheld Fiske's First Amendment rights in reversing his conviction. Chafee noted that with *Fiske* in 1927 "the Supreme Court for the first time made freedom of speech mean something."

Radicals like Fiske and Gitlow could never have fought their free speech battles on their own. They turned to organizations like the ACLU, to lawyers who often were "bourgeois," to principles of individual liberty that some of them scorned. The free speech attorneys, for their part, rarely agreed with their clients' ideas, but the "truth" of those ideas was irrelevant—the only issue was the right to express them. This approach eventually won out in the Supreme Court itself, which in 1963 would hold that the Constitution protected expression without regard to "the truth, popularity, or social utility of the ideas" offered. Indeed, the Court declared a decade later that under the First Amendment "there is no such thing as a false idea."

Agreed on this fundamental concept, civil libertarian attorneys often disagreed heatedly among themselves over tactics. The ACLU's founder, Roger Baldwin, saw the courts as essentially hostile to freedom of speech. He had witnessed and suffered himself too many outrages at their hands, including his conviction in the 1920s, under a 1796 law, for organizing a free speech march by striking New Jersey silk workers that police broke up when someone merely began to read the First Amendment. That his conviction was reversed by a higher New Jersey court in a decision calling for "the most liberal and comprehensive construction" of free speech guarantees did little to relieve his pessimism.

Pollak and his fellow attorney Morris Ernst, another shrewd and devoted civil libertarian, had more faith in the courts. Felix Frankfurter, a Harvard Law School professor and ACLU adviser before his elevation to the Supreme Court in 1939, held a third view—that the courts might yield an occasional victory to civil liberty but were not reliable or appropriate vehicles. What the courts gave, he warned, they could as easily take away. Better to work through state and national legislatures to build in democratic fashion a secure foundation for free speech.

While attorneys debated tactics, judges argued constitutional doctrine. Holmes's pronouncement in *Schenck*—that the question in every case was whether the speech created "a clear and present danger" of "substantive evils"—had won broad acceptance in the judiciary and was further refined by Brandeis in *Whitney:* "no danger flowing from speech can be deemed clear and present, unless the incidence" of "serious violence" or "serious injury to the state" was "so imminent that it may befall before there is opportunity for full discussion. . . . Only an emergency can justify repression." Brandeis's construction put the heaviest burden of proof on those who sought to restrict free speech.

Under the intellectual leadership of Hugo Black, William O. Douglas, and other FDR appointees, a faction of the Court, in the late New Deal and World War II years, adopted the doctrine of "preferred position," compelling judges to give free speech highest priority among constitutional issues. An attempt to interfere with free speech faced the *presumption* of unconstitutionality and could be vindicated only by the most compelling evidence of clear, present, and substantial danger. The reasoning behind this position was significant: Congress and other elected decision-makers might try all sorts of social and economic experiments, without undue restriction by an unelected judiciary. If an experiment turned out badly, it could be abandoned, with little harm done. But when political bodies interfered with freedom of speech and other First Amendment liberties, they threatened the very channels that would check or redress those interferences. In short, hands off the fundamental means of protecting free speech and other basic rights—free speech itself.

Critics such as Frankfurter had grave doubts about the preferred position doctrine. Free speech, they contended, must be balanced against such other constitutional claims as national security or the public interest in curbing pornography. The "balancers" were in turn attacked for defending free speech in the abstract while denying it in specific cases and for pitting a bloated conception of the "national interest" against the free speech rights of the individual. Still, for all the priority Black, Douglas, and the others gave to free speech—indeed Black and Douglas would convert that priority into a virtual absolute—Black himself would not extend the same preference to other forms of expression, to what the Court came to describe and increasingly protect as "speech-related conduct" or forms of "symbolic speech." Black was willing to uphold severe restrictions on picketing, demonstrations, and the use by protesters of public streets and buildings, and critics in turn charged him with an overly narrow definition of speech and its freedoms.

Balancing tilted a majority of justices toward the Red Fear after World War II, as national security, in cases like the *Dennis* prosecution of Communist Party leaders, was put heavily into the scales against individual rights. But in later years the Court under Earl Warren rehabilitated the preferred position doctrine and the strong presumption of the *un*constitutionality of legislation that threatened free speech. This did not mean that the Court abandoned balancing or invalidated all such legislation—far from it. Even William Brennan, who approached Black's absolutism, acknowledged that "there are governmental interests that may justify restraints on free speech." But Brennan also wrote that "delicate and vulnerable" First Amendment freedoms needed "breathing space to survive."

After the landmark decisions and dissents of the 1920s, the Court had developed more and more specific tests for a variety of potential abridgments of freedom of speech. The Court insisted on clarity and explicitness in legislation, defining as unacceptable in a 1939 decision any law that "either forbids or requires the doing of an act in terms so vague that men of common intelligence must necessarily guess at its meaning and differ as to its application." The Court watched for overbreadth—measures so broad they struck at protected as well as unprotected speech. It favored "the least drastic means"—laws directed at a problem without menacing First Amendment freedoms. And it was always more protective of the political speech that was "at the heart of the First Amendment's protection," while other speech was of "reduced constitutional value."

In applying such tests and balances the Supreme Court had finally to come down to a series of questions whose answers would guide its decisions in particular cases. In Peltason's words, such questions were:

"*What* was said? *Where* was it said? *How* was it said? What was the *intent* of the person who said it? *Which government* is attempting to regulate the speech"—a city council or a state legislature or Congress? "*How* is the government attempting to regulate the speech? By prior censorship? By punishment after the speech? *Why* is the government acting? To preserve the public peace? To prevent criticism of those in power?"

Inevitably, with such a variety of free speech doctrines, each nuanced by the temperaments of individual judges and by the ever-growing sheaf of precedents, and with such a battery of tests, each weighed one against another, against its own past applications, against claims of the larger "public interest"—in short, in the absence of a single, hard, all-purpose standard, the judiciary was left with great interpretive flexibility and broad powers in determining the nature and extent of the First Amendment's guarantee of freedom of speech.

SINCE ANCIENT TIMES the most dramatic confrontations over free expression have pitted the individual writer or artist against authority, political, religious, or intellectual. Plato paid an extraordinary compliment to poetry when he banished poets from his ideal Republic, so highly did he estimate the corruptive influence of their false songs of the gods on the morals of the youth of Athens. And not only poets but all artists were to be so "controlled," for "we would not have our guardians grow up amid images of moral deformity, as in some noxious pasture, and there browse and feed upon many a baneful herb and flower day by day, little by little, until they silently gather a festering mass of corruption in their own soul." Instead artists were to blow into youthful souls "a health-giving breeze from a purer region" that would "insensibly" fill them with the "beauty of reason."

A like fear that their flock would wander into "noxious pastures" moved the oligarchs of Puritan New England twenty centuries later to ordain that "on the Sabbath or Fasting Days" no woman should kiss her child; nor should women bake minced pies, or "play any instrument of music except the drum, the trumpet or the jew's harp." All thirteen colonies outlawed blasphemy and profanity; as early as 1712 Massachusetts illegalized such temptations to "moral deformity" as "composing, writing, printing, or publishing of any filthy, obscene, or profane song, pamphlet, libel, or mock sermon in imitation or mimicking of religious services."

Yet the men of enlightenment in the founding period did not find it necessary to encumber their national Bill of Rights with such proscriptions. At the same time, the First Amendment was not extended to the states, which passed laws dealing with obscenity. Mid-nineteenth-century developments—the Civil War, immigration, industrialization, the spread of literacy—brought social changes that produced liberating efforts and movements. Some were led by remarkable women: Fanny Bloomer, who campaigned for less confining female garments; Lucy Stone, urging that married women had the right to keep their own names; and Victoria Woodhull, flamboyant advocate of women's rights in general and of sexual freedom in particular.

From the stresses of this rapidly changing society arose another extraordinary figure, Anthony Comstock. Starting out as a store clerk and temperance crusader, peculiarly fascinated and repelled by the "sin" of masturbation, he undertook a personal campaign in New York and Connecticut against magazines and books that offended him. In the early 1870s he moved on to Washington, where he came to wield a singular combination of powers: as national head of the Society for the Suppression of Vice, in 1873 he successfully lobbied Congress for a stringent law that would ban all "indecent or immoral" publications—including those having to do with abortion—from the mails, and then got himself appointed the Post Office special agent charged with enforcing the measure.

After just a few months on the job Comstock could boast that under the new law he had seized 194,000 obscene pictures and photos, 134,000 pounds of books, 14,200 pounds of stereotype plates, 60,300 "rubber articles"—presumably contraceptives—and 31,150 boxes of "pills and powders"—presumably aphrodisiacs. He crusaded against Lady Godiva and Peeping Tom and confiscated over a hundred paintings by French classical masters. Nor was his reign of power brief; he remained head of the Suppression Society until his death in 1915, and its treasury waxed fat on his share of the fines levied against the offenders he hunted down in his Post Office job. And he enjoyed the ultimate, if dubious, distinction of lending his name to a new word—"Comstockery."

Comstock's personal triumph was a tragedy for the First Amendment. Publishers and editors cowered before him; by 1900 thirty states or more had antiobscenity statutes; and as usual the ultimate victims were not writers or peddlers of "filth" but the women who desperately needed information about contraception and abortion. In this atmosphere it was not surprising that in 1882 Walt Whitman's publisher withdrew a new edition of *Leaves of Grass* when the Boston district attorney, egged on by Comstock's society, threatened to prosecute the book as obscene. Perhaps a low point was reached when H. L. Mencken, who had already achieved some reputation as a scourge of Comstockery, met with Comstock's successor in 1922 to negotiate deletions in a novel by Mencken's friend Theodore Dreiser, *The "Genius,"* a book the Suppression Society had suppressed since 1916.

Perhaps a high point was reached a few years before the curb on *The "Genius"* when in 1913 there came before Judge Learned Hand a novel, *Hagar Revelly,* that had the compound audacity of presenting a shopgirl who had strayed from virtue into prostitution because of the low wages paid to working women. "I question," wrote Hand, "whether in the end men will regard that as obscene which is honestly relevant to the adequate expression of innocent ideas, and whether they will not believe that truth and beauty are too precious to society at large to be mutilated in the interests of those most likely to pervert them to base uses." He would not "reduce our treatment of sex to the standard of a child's library . . . "

Other jurists thought differently and decided differently. While in many cases twentieth-century courts upheld the First Amendment by dismissing charges of obscenity—most dramatically, overturning in 1933 the ban on the importation of James Joyce's *Ulysses;* allowing in 1959, thirty years after it was written, publication of D. H. Lawrence's *Lady Chatterley's Lover;* reversing in 1966 the suppression in Massachusetts of the eighteenth-century erotic novel *Fanny Hill*—it was clear that judges continued to wrestle with the question of what exactly obscenity was. Basic in law is the requirement that statutes should be clear and indictments laid out with precision. At one time jurists actually contended that precise charges were impossible in obscenity prosecutions because the court records themselves had to be protected against defilement by the particulars of a case. But the great problems facing judges were definitional and analytical. Hundreds of judgments were rendered, with little enduring agreement over standards.

Would the judiciary ever settle on a definition of obscenity? In 1957 the Supreme Court used two cases—*Roth* and *Alberts*—in an effort to fix standards, but far from putting the matter to rest, the decision merely raised new questions and provoked a new round of appeals, obliging the Court to issue "clarification" after "clarification." At last in 1973 a bare majority came together behind a landmark clarification in *Miller* v. *California,* which involved a publisher of pornography convicted of distributing unsolicited publications through the mail. Chief Justice Warren Burger refined the *Roth* and *Alberts* tests and their evolution since 1957 in holding that a work might be deemed legally obscene if the average person, applying contemporary standards of the community, would find that the work as a whole appealed to a "prurient" interest in sex, and if the work depicted in a patently offensive way sexual conduct contrary to local law or authority, and if the work as a whole lacked serious literary, artistic, political, or scientific value.

The vagueness of such concepts as "prurience," "patently offensive," "as a whole," and "serious" was compounded by the Court's enshrinement, carried over from *Roth* and *Alberts,* of the old concept of "community standards." How were such "standards" to be determined? How was a community's "average person" to be found? Was obscenity to be defined by the principle of the lowest common denominator? Or did it hang on aggressive prosecutors and their skills in swaying juries? *Miller* handed local bluenoses a broad mandate and opened the way to a Court-sanctioned "checkerboarding" of the country—much as had existed in the area of free speech before *Gitlow*—when a simple boundary between two communities and their "standards" might mean the difference between legality and illegality, between free expression and imprisonment.

A year after *Miller* the high court had to issue yet another clarification—the warning that it would be a serious misreading of that decision "to conclude that juries have unbridled discretion in determining what is 'patently offensive.' " As an example of "community standards" taken too far, the Court offered a hypothetical case in which the jury convicted a defendant for the depiction "of a woman with a bare midriff." But the justices would find that they had a lot more explaining than *that* to do.

THE PEOPLE'S RIGHT TO KNOW

THERE WAS always something dramatic—perhaps romantic too, and even poignant—about the lone speaker or writer standing against authority. Rather straightforward as well: a tavern orator bellowing against the government, a nonconforming minister leading a crowd to another church, a soapbox Demosthenes denouncing taxes, a young radical printing up and handing out a tract. It was a showdown between David and Goliath—though Goliath often won. Even when the protester worked with others—with a printer willing to risk a crackdown, or on a platform with other speakers—the adversaries were few and the conflict simple and visible.

It was this type of protest above all that the framers had had in mind when they drafted the Bill of Rights. In the two centuries since, the conflict had become immensely more complicated, the stage more crowded, the adversaries more varied and numerous, the stakes even higher. In the area of the freedom of the press, it was no longer simply journalist or pamphleteer against the local censor, but journalists against their own publishers in the press's dual role of public servant and profit-seeking corporation; journalists and publishers united against the threat of government censorship; journalists using the government (for instance, when unionized reporters appealed to a labor board) against their bosses; publishers using the government (the police, say) against picket-ing or protesting employees; the government using journalists (perhaps by selectively leaking information); and the government using publishers (against journalists who had displeased it). And now there were many stages—the plethora of newspapers, magazines, and book publishing houses, radio stations, television networks, local and cable television channels, all these often packaged with film and music divisions into huge media conglomerations.

And out there somewhere was the vast, variegated public, ignorant and informed, aroused and apathetic, organized, unorganized, and disorga-nized. Absolutely fundamental to maintaining the American constitu-tional experiment, to preserving the Bill of Rights, was the people's capacity to comprehend and discuss public affairs, to act on them, and fundamental to those capacities was the people's right to know. "The notion that human beings should be silenced," wrote Judith Schenck Koffler, "rather than free to pursue their own consciences; licensed rather than free to write something that rattles the catechism of the day; bound up by paternalistic laws rather than free to investigate everything under the sun—such a notion reduces human beings to a brutish condition," and she added the view of scholar Alexander Meiklejohn, that it was just this "mutilation of the thinking process" that the Constitution outlawed.

The idea of a people's right to know was entwined with the freedom of the press, each dependent on the other. The marriage, however, con-tained an inescapable source of tension. The right to know meant that the press must supply all the information the people needed to make knowl-edgeable judgments. "All the News That's Fit to Print," *The New York Times* proudly and daily proclaimed. But who was to judge this fitness? The press had its own notions of what the "news" was, and what was fit for publication and what was to be withheld either because it was judged irrelevant or because of certain "higher obligations" that superseded the obligation to inform the people.

Those "higher obligations" have included not reporting ship move-ments in time of war, suppressing the names of teenage felons, withhold-ing photographs of Franklin Roosevelt's paralyzed legs. Freedom of the press, John Merrill noted, "has always meant that editors had the free-dom *not* to let the people know." But every time they exercised this freedom, they were challenging the people's right to know, the very rationale of a free press.

Time and again the press withheld information in the very situations where the public would seem to have the greatest claim to knowledge, at least as measured by their immediate and ultimate stake in the decisions of their government—war-making. Usually officials did not need to insist on the dangers that publication of information about a military operation or diplomatic maneuver would pose to the national security; they could count on executives, editors, reporters to share their understanding of "national security" and its requirements. But sometimes officials tried to intimidate journalists by challenging their patriotism. "Whose side are you on?" Secretary of State Dean Rusk demanded of reporters quizzing him on American policy in Vietnam. "I'm on our side."

Perhaps the most dramatic and instructive example of press self-censorship in the name of national security came early in the Kennedy administration, when the CIA was recruiting and training an army of Cuban exiles to invade Cuba and overthrow Fidel Castro's Communist regime. The administration was desperate to keep the operation, especially the CIA's role, secret. Kennedy's aides were sworn to silence or simply kept in the dark. When the Miami *Herald*'s Washington reporter tracked down the recruiting efforts, CIA chief Allen Dulles persuaded his editors not to publish the story. When *The New Republic* planned to print an accurate account titled "Our Men in Miami," the President got the piece killed. When *The Nation* reported on a large CIA-sponsored invasion base in Guatemala, the rest of the press ignored the story. When *New York Times* correspondent Tad Szulc produced a long, detailed description of invasion plans, with a prediction of the action's "imminence," *Times* executives ordered that the story be watered and cut down and given a less prominent position on the front page. Even so, Kennedy exploded when he saw it, exclaiming, "Castro doesn't need agents over here. All he has to do is read our papers."

Nothing fails like failure. Two weeks after the invasion's collapse, Kennedy told editor Turner Catledge of the *Times*, "Maybe if you had printed more about the operation you would have saved us from a colossal mistake."

This case, and many others, made clear that the press suffered as much from self-censorship as from the overt use of governmental power. The stirring call from the White House about the urgent need to preserve an operation's secrecy, the fear of compromising national security, the fear of being blamed for alerting the enemy, for jeopardizing American lives—these might seem almost irresistible. But did not the press's sense of a "higher obligation" too often lead it to neglect a still higher one—the obligation to consider that, in a longer-run view of the interests of the nation, a president, his plans, his conception of the national security, might be mistaken?

And the government was secretive not only in times of crisis; it was secretive before and after crises, about large matters and small, about legitimate national security information and information whose publica-

tion would threaten only the political security of the incumbent administration; and its secrecy was codified and encased in a dense system of
classification. Following a long campaign in the press on behalf of the
people's right to know, Congress in 1966 required federal agencies to
provide both historical and current records to citizens on request, with
certain exceptions for genuine national security materials and trade secrets. "A historic turning point," trumpeted a society of journalists, that
would redefine relations between press and government. "If government
is to be truly of, by and for the people," wrote Attorney General Ramsey
Clark in a memo explaining the new law to the federal bureaucracy, "the
people must know in detail the activities of government. Nothing so
diminishes democracy as secrecy."

But Clark's audience was unmoved. A report by consumer advocate
Ralph Nader two years after the law became effective disclosed that agencies used delay, misclassification and reclassification, complex appeals
procedures, steep fee charges, and other devices of "bureaucratic ingenuity" to frustrate requests. Violations had come so regularly, Nader
reported, "that they seriously block citizen understanding and participation in government." The Freedom of Information Act was amended
in 1974 when a flood of revelations of governmental misconduct was
released by the collapse of the Vietnam War and the Nixon administration, but while the strengthened act eased access and helped produce
some notable reporting, it was only a matter of time before government
officials spun out and drew around themselves a new, tougher cloak of
secrecy.

IF THE PEOPLE'S RIGHT to know was rooted in their capacity to
acquire knowledge, that right would appear to have been enormously
enhanced with the rise of the mass press in the nineteenth century and
the electronic media in the twentieth. However tawdry, sensationalist,
and superficial was the "penny press" of the post–Civil War era, it
brought at least some news to the masses—including the half-literate
immigrant masses—and the print media enjoyed extensive if not full First
Amendment rights.

Those rights received the strong imprimatur of the Supreme Court in
the twentieth century. It was "no longer open to doubt," Chief Justice
Charles Evans Hughes wrote for the Court in its 1931 *Near* decision, "that
the liberty of the press and of speech is within the liberty safeguarded by
the due process clause of the 14th Amendment from invasion by state
action." In this first exercise of federal power against state and local
abridgments of press freedom, the Court ordered reopened Jay Near's
Saturday Press, a right-wing scandal sheet shut down by Minneapolis authorities after Near printed scathing allegations of corruption against a

host of local officials. The Court declared unconstitutional a "gag law" that permitted prior restraint of publications deemed "public nuisances"—such a law, wrote Hughes, was "the essence of censorship."

Exemption from prior restraint was a historic doctrine—Blackstone had put it at the core of press freedom—but the Court's ban on it was never absolute; as in other spheres of freedom, the press's exercise of its rights was to be balanced and weighed against other public interests, including the national security. The Nixon administration in 1971 made just such a claim when it sought and won in a federal appeals court an injunction to block *The New York Times* from publishing further installments of a classified Defense Department account and analysis of the Vietnam War—the first time in American history that the federal government had asked for prior restraint. In a matter of days, the case reached the Supreme Court, where the administration argued that continued publication would do "irreparable harm" to the American position in the ongoing war. "It will affect lives," said Solicitor General Erwin Griswold. "It will affect the process of the termination of the war."

The nine justices returned nine separate opinions, but six came together to agree that the administration had failed to overcome the "heavy presumption" of unconstitutionality confronting "any system of prior restraints of expression." Justice Potter Stewart noted that excessive national security claims might cloak "secrecy for its own sake" or for "self-protection or self-promotion"; the "only effective remedy," he wrote, was "an informed and critical public opinion which alone can here protect the values of democratic government," and it was in this "that a press that is alert, aware, and free most vitally serves the basic purpose of the First Amendment."

Chief Justice Hughes had tendered offended public officials one consolation in his *Near* judgment: if they could not suppress a journalistic "nuisance," they might sue it for libel, much as the colonial government had done two centuries before with critic John Peter Zenger. But in the 1960s the Supreme Court sharply narrowed this avenue of relief. In March 1960 *The New York Times* had run a paid advertisement soliciting funds for the black student sit-in movement and the legal defense of Martin Luther King, Jr., and describing a "wave of terror" directed at African-Americans by public officials in Montgomery, Alabama. Though the ad had named none of these officials, several, including city commissioner L. B. Sullivan, stood up and sued the *Times* for libel.

That the ad contained inaccuracies and exaggerations the newspaper acknowledged, but William Brennan's 1964 opinion for the Court held that a public official must meet the highest standard before a statement made against him could be judged libelous—he must prove that it had been made with " 'actual malice'—that is, with knowledge that it was false or with reckless disregard of whether it was false or not." Otherwise, Brennan wrote, "would-be critics of official conduct may be deterred from voicing their criticism." A free press reflected a free society's commitment to "uninhibited, robust, and wide-open" debate of public issues that "may well include vehement, caustic, and sometimes unpleasantly sharp attacks on government and public officials." Seven years later, in a decision extending the *Sullivan* standard to libel actions brought not only by public officials but by any private citizen who became "a subject of public or general interest," Brennan conceded that in its pursuit of "hot" news "the press has, on occasion, grossly abused the freedom it is given by the Constitution. . . . But from the earliest days of our history, this free society, dependent as it is for its survival upon a vigorous free press, has tolerated some abuse."

The rise of radio in the 1920s and television in the 1950s seemed to both government and the public to be quantum leaps into a vastly different form of expression, so much so that it was thought they required a different application of the First Amendment. As there were only a limited number of radio and television channels, these were deemed the property of the people as a whole, and it was a public responsibility to control their allocation and use. In short, government was to regulate these media. The days when anyone with a penny press and a few dollars could set up shop—as could his competitors—were over.

The power of the new media would remain in relatively few hands, subject to federal licensing. Accompanied by standards of use, licensing soon would involve government in the regulation of content—banning, for instance, "filthy language" from the airwaves, denying license renewals to stations that failed to serve the "public interest"—to an extent far beyond anything the print media had ever experienced. The Supreme Court concluded in 1978 that several decades of regulation had meant that, "of all the forms of communication, it is broadcasting that has received the most limited First Amendment protection."

Among the most significant of the regulatory standards was that of access. Since the early years of government regulation in the 1920s, the emphasis had been on the simple concept of fairness—that the public interest required "ample play for the free and fair competition of opposing views." In announcing the "fairness doctrine" in 1949, the Federal Communications Commission held it "evident that broadcast licensees have an affirmative duty generally to encourage and implement the broadcast of all sides of controversial public issues over their facilities."

Noble words—but how to define and apply them? As usual, the task was left to the judiciary. In its 1969 *Red Lion* decision upholding the constitutionality of the fairness doctrine and the right to free airtime for replies to personal attacks, a unanimous Supreme Court insisted that "the people as a whole retain their interest in free speech" in broadcast media and that it was "the right of the viewers and listeners, not the right of the broadcasters, which is paramount." Under the First Amendment, broadcast media were obliged to "preserve an uninhibited marketplace of ideas" and thus to recognize "the right of the public to receive suitable access to social, political, esthetic, moral, and other ideas."

Red Lion advanced the principle of a right to access by a wide variety of individuals, groups, interests, and institutions—in short, access by a broad public—to media, and thus the right of people to hear those diverse views, their right to know. Just as president and Congress and courts and public opinion had earlier moved from defending economic and social liberty against government to promoting such liberty through government, now the Supreme Court was taking an epochal step in moving beyond a purely negative interpretation of the First Amendment that would protect broadcast media against government intrusion to an insistence that those media themselves act to widen the impact of the First Amendment.

In upholding the fairness doctrine, the Court continued to distinguish the First Amendment standing of broadcast media from that of print. But its justification of the access principle in terms of "scarcity" (of frequencies and channels) and monopolization of the media (by a limited number of licensees) might, in an era of increasing consolidation and cross-ownership, be as readily applied to the print press and inspire similar claims to access on positive First Amendment grounds.

The Court's continued distinction between print and broadcast media might be explained by Lucas Powe's observation that "even in 1969 the Court still seemed perplexed by this newer and better means of communication," but it perhaps also indicated that the "newer" media, especially television, were perpetually renewing themselves, that the justices were operating not in a settled environment but in an environment of ceaseless change. The change was driven in part by technology—most of all, the emergence of the cable television industry expanded enormously the numbers of available channels and the potential for diversity, a potential recognized by Congress in 1984 when it sanctioned free public access to channels. The change was in part political—the impact of television and television news on governmental and political processes; the proliferation of articulate advocacy groups across the ideological spectrum, demanding direct access to the airwaves and favorable treatment in programming; the rise of fanatical, even violent groups spewing hate through the media and testing the public's tolerance. And the change was critical or philosophical or moral—a growing public dissatisfaction especially with television and its commercialization and trivialization, its apparent incapacity to educate and enlighten, its failure to recognize and respond to the people's right to know.

And always the dilemma—how much could and should the electronic media be regulated for the sake of the people's right to know, without jeopardizing fundamental First Amendment freedoms of speech and press?

COUNTERPART to the right to know was the "right" *not* to know—the "right" not to be exposed to "offensive" or "harmful" information, ideas, images. This "right" has always underlain censorship principles and practices. Plato expressed an authoritarian version of it—a central power would determine what would and would not be suitable for its people. In the United States the exercise of this "right" was usually local, through assertions of "community standards." Despite the frenetic efforts of its namesake, Comstockery had its severest, most immediate bite in the crusades of local prosecutors and judges, anti-vice societies, religious groups, and other zealots. The Supreme Court's *Miller* decision merely gave national sanction to what had become an American tradition—the vital role of community attitudes and pressures.

No form of art or entertainment was more persistently entangled in the thickets of "community standards" than film. From their earliest days the movies were bedeviled by censorship boards in states, cities, and towns across the country, each with its peculiar "community standards" and with the authority to exercise prior restraint—if a board refused to license a film, that film could not be displayed in area theaters. Sex was the great preoccupation of most boards, but many did not hesitate to use their power to control political content. Chief Justice Earl Warren, in a 1961 dissent to a decision upholding Chicago's censorship, detailed examples of political suppression: Chicago licensors barring newsreels of local police firing at labor pickets or a film portraying a black doctor's struggles against racism because "it could cause trouble," Memphis censors refusing a license to a film that treated the poverty of tenant farmers, a Maryland board deleting from a film the line "We, the workers of the world, will take care of that," an Ohio board condemning as "harmful" a film that represented the Nazi persecution of Jews.

Still, the film industry received little comfort from the Supreme Court. For over three decades—from 1915, when the Court dismissed film as mere "spectacle," to 1948, when it granted that moving pictures *might* be given the guarantees of the freedom of the press—films were deemed not worthy of the protections of the First Amendment. Where was Hollywood to turn? Its films were produced for the broadest national distribution—

for one thing, and not the least thing, that was where the money was—but a story with an actress playing a pregnant woman that might breeze through a New York board might be axed in Pennsylvania. Local censors might mutilate a film—and destroy its continuity and sense—or they might ban it outright, eliminating an entire market at a blow.

So Hollywood turned to self-censorship. In 1922, with censorship boards operating at full throttle, a rash of proposals in state legislatures for further censorship, the danger of federal investigation, pressure from their Wall Street financiers, as well as a series of sensational off-screen scandals, film company presidents formed the Motion Picture Producers and Distributors of America to police the industry. Appointed head was the respectable Will Hays, postmaster general, Presbyterian Church elder, and former Republican Party national chairman. Hays's charge from the industry was not so much to "purify" films as to persuade the public that he was doing so and that Hollywood was capable of self-control. He was largely successful in heading off the worst threats of censorship, so much so that, under cover of his public relations campaign, films in the 1920s grew racier than ever. By the end of the decade the censors were reacting. In the first six months of 1929, boards imposed an unprecedented number of cuts in films. Over half the American audience was watching films that had passed some form of censorship. And most ominously a movement for federal censorship—supported by press baron William Randolph Hearst—was gathering steam.

Hollywood tried to parry these threats with stepped-up public relations. Cross-pressured by the prospect of a Depression-driven decline in ticket sales, the industry knew that the antidote to falling attendance was heavy doses of sex and violence in films. But the censorship menace was too great, and in March 1930 producers adopted a "Production Code," an overt statement of self-censorship. "Though regarding motion pictures primarily as entertainment without any explicit purpose of teaching or propaganda," the producers acknowledged that movies could be "directly responsible for spiritual or moral progress, for higher types of social life, and for much correct thinking."

The Code then laid out detailed prescriptions in such areas as the cinematic portrayal of murder (not to be pictured in a way that would inspire imitation, no brutal killings, no justifications of revenge); of sex (the "sanctity of the institution of marriage and the home shall be upheld"); of scenes of passion (to stop short of "excessive and lustful kissing, lustful embraces, suggestive postures and gestures"). Outlawed altogether were displays of "sex perversion" (not even to be hinted at), miscegenation, sex hygiene, "actual child birth," or children's sex organs. Further provisions encompassed obscenity ("in word, gesture, reference, song, joke, or by suggestion''); profanity (banned were the words God, Lord, Jesus, Christ—''unless used reverently''—and hell, S.O.B., damn, Gawd); costumes, including the absence of costumes; the flag (only ''consistently respectful'' uses); and religion (no ridiculing any faith or ministers or rituals).

Anyone perusing the Code could understand how miraculous—albeit a miracle that was the fruit of endless negotiations between producers and the Production Code Administration—it had seemed in 1939 that Rhett Butler was able to say on screen to Scarlett O'Hara, ''Frankly, my dear, I don't give a damn'' (although the ''action of Scarlett belching'' in Scene 38 was banned). But ridiculous as many of its strictures appeared, there was nothing funny about the Code itself. On the one hand, it reflected the militantly moralistic attitudes and fears of white, middle-class, religious-minded Americans; on the other, it revealed the monumental hypocrisy of an industry that would subscribe to it while continuing to get away with whatever the traffic would bear.

Once the Code had served its immediate purpose of relieving censorship pressures, films grew more sordid as producers sought to recapture an audience ravaged by the Depression. Then the clamor for censorship was renewed, and in 1933 Hays concocted a ''New Deal'' for the industry—actually to *enforce* the Code, by way of a centralized Production Code Administration. ''We must put brassieres on Joan Blondell,'' was how one producer interpreted Hays's New Deal.

But this did not break the cyclic pattern in the extent and rigor of the Code's application. When the censorship brigades were relatively quiescent, Code administrators were more inclined to respect the ''artistic integrity'' and ''freedom of expression'' of producers, particularly if ticket sales were in a slough. But when the Catholic Legion of Decency and the like began again to clear their throats, out came the brassieres from studio vaults. To some in the Hollywood community, the publicity generated by battles over self-censorship and the hide-and-peep the Code encouraged compensated handsomely for abridgments of their right to more explicit self-expression. ''I believe in censorship,'' Mae West wisecracked. ''After all, I made a fortune out of it.''

With local censorship boards extending their reach to the political content of films and calls for further censorship in the 1930s, 1940s, and 1950s directed nearly as much to the ideology of movies—especially their ''leftist'' ideology—as to their sexuality, it was natural that the Production Code Administration would move to head off political ''controversies.'' Even during Depression days Code administrators carefully scrutinized films that portrayed poverty, prostitution, slums, and other social ills. Under the Code, producer Walter Wanger complained in the late 1930s, it was ''almost impossible to face and deal with the modern world.''

In the late 1950s and 1960s—a time of rapid change in cultural attitudes and behavior—the Production Code began to fall of its own overex-
tended weight. Some of the old "decency" crusaders lost their bite; the
Supreme Court was at last beginning to strike down film censorship
statutes and put the boards out of business; the public was in a more
experimental and tolerant mood; foreign films and even domestic ones
were finding ways to evade the Code. And in this new environment the
Code's absurdities were becoming even more glaring to producers and
directors. Stanley Kubrick, directing a film adaptation of Vladimir Nabokov's novel *Lolita,* told Nabokov that under the Code his nymphet might
be younger (and a wife) or older (and a concubine), but not both twelve
and unwed. And Code administrators for their part were terrified that
Lolita's producers *would* submit the film to them for approval: given its
subject, it could not possibly meet the Code's standards—to approve it
would destroy the Code—but to reject the film would expose them to a
devastating outburst of indignation and ridicule.

Jack Valenti, whose background was in Texas politics and Lyndon
Johnson's White House, was appointed president of the Motion Picture
Association in 1966 and emerged as a shrewd and conciliatory mediator,
as appropriate for these new times as the old politico Will Hays had been
for the 1920s. Under Valenti's leadership self-censorship took the form
in 1968 of a rating system that had two goals: to "encourage artistic
expression by expanding creative freedom" and to "ensure that the freedom which encourages the artist remains responsible and sensitive to the
standards of the larger society." The new system—with ratings ranging
from G for general audiences to X for no one under sixteen (later seventeen and eighteen) admitted—had three great virtues, at least for the
industry: it was vague, it was voluntary, and it won swift and broad public
acceptance.

Some wondered whether anything much had changed. "An air of monumental self-righteousness" survived in the new system, wrote Vincent
Canby in *The New York Times,* "a sense of patriarchal duty that is intolerable when it is manifested by attempts to shape the contents of a film."
Still, moviegoers found a remarkable loosening of the old restrictions,
hearing words and seeing scenes they could not have dreamed, a decade
earlier, to have encountered in a public place. Valenti sold the new system
effectively to interested parties on all sides, put it under a historian,
Richard Heffner, who had a broad perspective and a dedication to free
expression, and chose as raters not "psychologists, psychiatrists,
Ph.D.'s," as he proudly told a congressional committee, but "average
citizens" in the form of parents.

For a time passions lessened, the potentials for creative exploration in
film widened, exhibitors happily presented films across the whole ratings

spectrum, audiences came to theaters ready to be shocked and titillated, but not to burn the place down or call in the police. Yet those with memories of a previous era of convulsive self-censorship wondered how long the new era of benign self-censorship would last. In this sector of American life as others the only certainty was change—but to what?

TOWARD A
CULTURAL BILL OF RIGHTS?

AS LATE AS a half century ago a discussion of cultural rights could end here. It would have been enough to treat the rights of writers, artists, actors, and other performers in the United States by examining to what degree, and in what way, and with what effect government limited or crushed those rights. In that half century, however, the subject has become immensely broad and complicated. Today we must consider not only the rights of creative persons against government's hindrances but their rights to government's help. And we must consider not only the "opportunity rights" of individual writers and artists and performers but the opportunity rights of the people as a whole to benefit from the fruits of creative work.

These opportunity rights arose as controversial issues only in recent decades because for three centuries in the United States, and for far longer in Europe, organized cultural life was a virtual monopoly of the elites—the state and church and merchant patrons, the networks of blue bloods that set standards of taste and excellence, the cultural institutions that were the playgrounds of privilege. It was the cultural aristocracy that determined whether a writer or artist would gain access to the drawing rooms of patronage and sales, recognition and prestige. During these centuries, of course, poets versified even as they languished in garrets, artists painted and sculpted even while living on their families or the whims of patrons, actors performed at night and worked at odd jobs by day—and they did all this amid general public indifference. Workers formed unions to protect their rights, women fought together to gain the suffrage, farmers organized to press their grievances, but artists and writers—many of them isolated, poor, vulnerable—struggled as best they could to survive and create.

"I mean to work *very hard*—," wrote Samuel Taylor Coleridge to a friend when he was the author only of a slim and neglected volume of verse, "as Cook, Butler, Scullion, Shoe-cleaner, occasional Nurse,

Gardener, Hind, Pig-protector, Chaplain, Secretary, Poet, Reviewer, and omnium-botherum shilling-scavenger." Evidently all this was not enough; later two members of the Wedgwood pottery family supplied him with an annuity—which he promptly and regularly overdrew.

In the United States, not until the turn of the nineteenth century was there even a flutter of government interest in the arts: Congress considered proposals for a national office of the arts and President Theodore Roosevelt appointed a thirty-member Council of Fine Arts. State governments—Utah's was the first—established arts councils. Local groups set up community theater or music programs, neighborhood or settlement arts centers. Land-grant universities sponsored arts extension programs.

These efforts, innovative though many were, touched only marginally the countless artists who needed recognition or support. All this changed—almost overnight, it seemed later—not because artists and writers mobilized politically or in the streets, nor because government had suddenly awakened to the state of American culture. What happened was a depression, and the coming into power of an administration capable of recognizing that writers, artists, musicians, dancers, actors were among the millions in want. In its first two years of feverish activity, the Roosevelt administration gave limited emergency aid to over 3,000 artists; provided funds to the states for another 1,000 artists; retained artists to embellish federal buildings. But this was only the beginning: in 1935 FDR established the Federal Art, Music, Writers', and Theater projects under the Works Progress Administration.

Never before, wrote Edward Kamark, had arts in America seemed so to "surge with energy, with creative excitement," with such a sense of vital mission. WPA programs had a multiplier effect. In thousands of out-of-the-way places, "arts clubs, theatres, writing groups, choral societies, symphonies, and what have you, suddenly sprang into being—wondrous florescence, with infinitely rich promise."

At first the measures of WPA success were mainly quantitative—so many guidebooks written and printed, plays performed, canvases covered, dances danced, concerts offered. Later, when many of its alumni became renowned, it was plain that the WPA had nourished hundreds of significant talents. WPA officials, moreover, showed discrimination in choosing projects of importance that could not have found commercial or institutional funding—such as an Index of American Composers listing 5,300 works and oral histories of grass-roots leaders, local personalities, and "ordinary people" that would prove a treasure house of primary materials for historians.

The WPA and its good works were short-lived, eviscerated in the general counterattack against the New Deal by the conservative coalition in

Congress in the late 1930s. Though proposals were regularly made to renew government support for artists and writers, hopes languished during the war and with the advent of the Cold War. The issue became entangled in Cold War politics. Proponents of government aid often argued that it would elevate American prestige in the international struggle for hearts and minds by once again displaying America's "even greater superiority over the Communist way of life." Opponents would reply with reasoning they had earlier deployed against the WPA: that modern, especially nonrepresentational, art was one of the "avenues of propaganda" for Communists and their fellow travelers, who were "stabbing our glorious American art in the back with murderous intent."

Nevertheless, in the 1950s the Eisenhower administration put public support of the arts among "national goals." Eisenhower himself bucked the arts reactionaries in a statement on the Museum of Modern Art's twenty-fifth anniversary in 1954, when he asserted that "freedom of the arts" was a pillar of American liberty and that the public should have the "unimpaired opportunity" to "see, to understand, to profit from our artists' work." Controversy, he noted, was inevitable in an atmosphere of creative freedom; controversy could be "healthy."

The Kennedy and Johnson years brought the greatest outburst of federal cultural activity since the WPA. Kennedy's special consultant on the arts, August Heckscher, proposed the establishment of a national foundation to administer grants-in-aid. The government should support the arts not merely as a Cold War effort, Heckscher urged, but for the impact of culture on "the well-being, the happiness, and the personal fulfillment of the citizens of our democracy." Kennedy's effort to gain congressional backing for an arts foundation failed; a month after his assassination the Senate approved such a measure, as a kind of memorial tribute to his concern, but the House took no action.

It required the demonic energy and lobbying muscle of Lyndon Johnson's White House to push through a bill setting up the National Foundation on the Arts and the Humanities. Under this umbrella were established the National Endowment for the Arts and the National Endowment for the Humanities. In 1966, when the NEA began with an appropriation of $2.5 million and introduced programs in dance, education, literature, music, and theater, almost two thousand applications for aid were received.

During the late 1960s and the 1970s federal and state cultural activities burgeoned: architectural and environmental projects, Works of Art in Public Places, programs in dance touring, museum purchase, artists-in-schools, jazz, visual arts, craftsmen's fellowships, folk arts, filmmaking, television. NEA budgets grew to well over $100 million a year. Encouraged by the NEA's example and the lure of matching grants, corporate and individual support also swelled in these years.

Ronald Reagan entered the White House determined to replace the NEA with a privately funded public corporation. To head the Endowment, Reagan selected a former White House aide, Frank Hodsoll, who promptly made clear his belief that patronage of the arts should be primarily a private-sector and local effort. But by the 1980s federal, state, regional, and community arts programs had become so entrenched and had attracted such powerful constituencies that they could defy the ax. And a few months' close contact with the NEA's elite networks swung Hodsoll so far around that he asserted that if there were no arts endowment he would favor starting one. He went on to present some of the most cogent arguments for it, as summarized by Edward Arian: "to recognize the importance of the arts with prestige and advocacy at the highest level; to ensure support, as in the sciences, for new and experimental ventures that may be too risky to generate support privately; to foster 'a climate for the unpredictable to happen'; to provide some cushion for the 'most excellent' artistic institutions; to encourage the 'kaleidoscope' of American culture with support of folk arts, for example; and to give more people better access to the arts." Alas, noted Arian, Hodsoll, like his predecessors, failed to match rhetoric with money.

NOT AN IMPORTANT STEP was taken in these decades of expanding arts subsidies without prolonged and often sharp debate. Particularly when the NEA ran the reauthorization gantlet in Congress, it seemed as though it had again and again to justify its existence from scratch. Should the government be in this business at all? Why not leave culture to the free market? Or would this mean leaving it to the cultural aristocracy? But did not the elites dominate government cultural policy anyway through their political and social power and their control of the leading private institutions? And if the aim was to "democratize" the arts through government intervention, would this merely result in a tyranny of mediocrity? Or would "democratization" produce an explosion of quality, both through the energy of mass participation and by casting a broader net for individuals and groups of exceptional talent?

Advocates of public funding would contend that the nation was enjoying a "culture boom," even while culture itself was suffering financially, thus creating a curious combination of high demand and low yield; that public support was economically rational, promoting tourism and its related businesses; that in any case art should be exempted from the strict trials of the market, because public funding fostered equality of opportunity for both artists and their audiences and because the arts, like educa-

tion, contributed to the nation's welfare, even if not always in ways that
could be counted in dollars; that as a matter of world prestige the United
States must not be the only developed country that failed to fund the arts.
"Do we remember ancient Egypt by its lists of Pharaohs—or for its
Pyramids?" Senator Claiborne Pell demanded.

Funding opponents answered that those who wanted to enjoy the arts
ought to bear their full cost and that those who did not—"average taxpayers"—should not be expected to subsidize others on the grounds of some
intangible benefit to the public weal; that there were more pressing claims
to government attention and money than the arts, such as crime and
illiteracy; that poverty was a great stimulus to creativity, indeed that only
a hungry man felt compelled to show "what's in him."

The burning question over which the two sides joined was freedom—
whether public support would enhance the freedom of the artist and the
arts or stifle it. Some contended that the subsidized would be bound in
dependence more tightly and more insidiously to a government bureaucracy than they had ever been to private patrons. S. Dillon Ripley, secretary of the Smithsonian Institution and a supporter and indeed
beneficiary of public funding, warned museum heads that "with federal
funding come certain reciprocals: oversight, control, bureaucratic management, accountability and increased administrative and overhead responsibilities." Money begat power, he noted, "but the ultimate power
rests with the dispenser of the money."

Supporters of public funding maintained that it was precisely for this
reason that arts aid had to be democratized. Private patrons had attached
plenty of strings to the money they had doled out; at least governmental
controls would be visible and subject to democratic restraints and pressures. In any case, NEA backers argued, the Endowment had no agenda
to promote by issuing diktats to artists and arts institutions. Its role was
"not to shape national policy in the arts" but "to develop a national policy
of support for those fields."

These arguments tended, however, to evade or obscure a more fundamental issue—the rights of recognized and aspiring writers and artists
and performers to the fullest possible opportunity to practice their crafts
and to bring their work to the attention of peers and public. For many
creative persons such opportunity rights were more meaningful than the
often abstract and ideologized debates over government controls and
"artistic freedom"—their crucial need was to have the chance to do the
work and to get it published, performed, or exhibited, and then they
would worry about censorship or other restrictions. For many artists,
public funding offered the simple hope that this need might be satisfied.

The potential demand was staggering. It was estimated in 1969 that in
the United States there were 1,200 community orchestras, 30,000 ama-

teur theater groups, between 10 and 15 million amateur painters and millions more ceramists, weavers, lapidists, and other craftspeople. Government with its funding power could meet only a fraction of the needs of a fraction of these artists, but a fraction might amount to tens of thousands who would otherwise lack artistic opportunity.

For millions of others, the NEA raised hopes and expectations without satisfying them. But this was inevitable. Not only were the resources of government limited, but the level of government support—such as it was—depended on appropriations processes that turned far less on the specific needs of artists than on broader cultural and political considerations. That was the democratic process, and if artists didn't like it, they might fight it, and as they did so, they might point out that in other democracies the process somehow worked in such a way that per capita funding for artists was much greater than in the United States.

In the end, someone said, the biggest subsidizer of art has always been the individual writer or artist. Certainly that remained true in the United States toward the end of the twentieth century. The only fundamental right of artists, writers, and performers was their right to struggle for recognition, access, and funds in a culture that remained largely commercialized. Genius, wrote Oliver Goldsmith, "requires only subsistence and respect." In late-twentieth-century America both subsistence and respect were measured in terms of dollars.

IN THE DISTANT PAST, the arts public had consisted perhaps of a king and his court, a lord or cardinal and his retainers. More recently the arts public was seen as those who flocked to museums, galleries, concert halls, theaters, and the like. They numbered perhaps in the millions, but many tens of millions of others were not informed, motivated, or cash-rich enough to attend. The first of the expressed aims of the NEA was "to make the arts more widely available to millions of Americans," to expand the opportunity rights of the public to have access to the arts. One of the prime means it chose to fulfill this mission was to reduce the "cost of culture" through subsidies. There was "something intrinsically abhorrent," wrote economist Dick Netzer, "about a policy of making the cultural and artistic heritage of our civilization available to only, say, the richest 20 or 30 percent of the population."

Public funding had a marked impact on the cost of culture. In the early 1970s, around 13 percent of all tickets at the 166 leading nonprofit performing arts companies in the country, according to a Ford Foundation survey, were sold at reduced student rates. Altogether, it was estimated that perhaps some 40 percent of all attendance at the nation's arts performances was free or at reduced rates.

But further surveys of the same period disclosed that subsidized performances had done little to increase the involvement of low-income persons in cultural life. For example, people with incomes of $15,000 or higher attended live performing arts—ballet and modern dance, concerts and opera and theater—three times as often as those with incomes under $5,000.

This failure to reach a broader public—especially the huge low-income public—gave fresh arguments to those who opposed government funding in the first place. If such funding did not serve the egalitarian function of expanding the opportunities of low-income Americans, of "redistributing" cultural wealth, why not leave art wholly to the market and in the hands of private interests? In television, film, and other vast culture-distributing activities those interests had shown their capacity to reach virtually the entire public.

In answer to this more sophisticated brief against public support, advocates could point out that the market, whether economic or cultural, had its own serious shortcomings, especially in the realms of equity and egalitarianism. They might also make a powerful case that the NEA's failures reflected something far more fundamental and intractable—the doleful fact that the great majority of Americans, and especially of the poor, had not received a deep and wide exposure to the arts. They had not had teachers or other immediate role models who could relate art to their own potentials, they had not been encouraged to make art themselves or to respect its makers, they had not lived in homes where great art was studied and discussed but in homes flooded with the products of Hollywood.

But to other, "populist" critics the NEA was simply not trying very hard to take "art to the masses." The problem was less inadequate funding than spending priorities. These critics pointed to an "interlocking cultural elite" of NEA administrators and grants-selection panelists, boards and directors of major institutions, and corporate and private patrons. They pointed to the NEA's own report that in the 1970s "6.2 percent of the nation's arts organizations received 51.6 percent of the Endowment's dollars." A study of the NEA's budget at the outset of the Reagan administration, before further cuts were made, indicated that only 14 percent was allocated to "programs with mass constituencies"—such as artists in education, projects in rural or hard-pressed urban areas, folk arts.

Almost ignored by the NEA was the rising community arts movement. Community arts challenged elite shibboleths about what was "legitimate" art, its assumptions that "popular culture" was mere commercial entertainment and that arts "consumption" was a passive exercise in a formal setting. Community arts programs mushroomed in the 1950s and 1960s—by 1967 a national survey discovered 443 of them, mainly in rural areas and ghettos—and ranged from the creation of a half-mile-long mural in California that grew from a collaboration between trained artists and young gang members to a folk art program in Knoxville that encouraged the children of Appalachia to gather oral histories, produce plays about their lives, and learn such traditional arts as quilting, stitching, folk dancing. "The talent is in the community with the people," an observer of the Knoxville project noted, "and their discovery that they can be the creators of their own art is very exciting."

Such participatory exercises suggested that there was nothing inexorable in the division between the culturally rich and the culturally impoverished and nothing fanciful in the assertion of the United Nations Declaration of Human Rights that "Everyone has the right freely to participate in the cultural life of the community."

I N 1 9 8 9, a bolt of political lightning struck at the heart of the debate over cultural rights, briefly illuminating the arts landscape in all its bright and shadowy areas. The thunderclaps that followed reverberated through the halls of Congress, the bureaucratic maze of Washington, the media, the arts establishments and antiestablishments, and across the hinterland.

What set off the storm was one photograph—of a plastic crucifix dipped in a bath of urine, a work by Andres Serrano entitled "Piss Christ." Castigated by the Reverend Donald Wildmon and his American Family Association, the photo created a furor in Congress when politicians discovered the NEA had indirectly helped to fund Serrano's work. North Carolina Republican Jesse Helms labeled the artist a "jerk" on the Senate floor; his Republican colleague Alfonse D'Amato of New York ripped Serrano's catalogue to pieces. Over one hundred members of Congress joined to condemn the NEA's involvement and vowed to block any further public support of "blasphemous" or "pornographic" works. The House deleted the supposed amount of Serrano's support from its NEA appropriation.

By now the Serrano flap was joined to an even louder uproar, triggered when Washington's Corcoran Gallery canceled its installation of a traveling Robert Mapplethorpe retrospective that had among its 175 photographs a handful of his "homoerotic" or "sadomasochistic" images—including a portrait of two men in leather, one urinating in the other's mouth. This exhibit was also partially funded by an NEA grant. Sensitive to Washington pressures, the Corcoran explained that the cancellation was intended to lower temperatures while Congress was debating the NEA appropriation. But to no avail—the arts war hawks in Congress rolled out their heaviest rhetorical cannon. If someone "wanted to write nasty things on the men's room wall," the irrepressible Helms blustered, the taxpayers need "not provide the crayon." More surprising was some of the liberal response. "No artist has a First Amendment right to a government subsidy," declared *The New Republic*'s TRB. And Jules Feiffer caricatured an artist who boldly sounded off against society but ended with a pitch, "FUND ME." It would seem, commented *New Republic* theater critic Robert Brustein, "that federal subsidy completely changes the ground rules governing freedom of artistic expression."

Worse was to come. The Mapplethorpe retrospective moved on in spring 1990 to Cincinnati's Contemporary Arts Center, whose director, Dennis Barrie, was undeterred by the controversy in Washington. But Cincinnati was a daring venue: its antiobscenity laws were among the harshest in the country. On the exhibition's opening day, police drove out visitors and closed the museum for an hour and a half while they videotaped the show. A grand jury indicted Barrie and the museum for displaying Mapplethorpe's sadomasochistic photos and two portraits of children with their genitals exposed. It was thought to be the first time a museum had been prosecuted for the content of an exhibit. As for Barrie, he faced a year in jail. "Our intention," said his lawyer, "is to preserve the rights of the First Amendment and there will be no prior restraining."

The trial turned on the question of the "artistic value" of Mapplethorpe's works—the defense rallied an impressive array of museum directors and critics to affirm it, while the prosecution seemed intent on rousing the largely working-class jury to disgust at the images. But that jury acquitted the director and his museum. "Mapplethorpe was an important artist," Barrie said sadly. "It should never have been in court."

Despite this victory, the slow march toward cultural rights seemed almost overnight to have been reversed; now, at least in one city, police were swarming into an art museum—and proposing to jail a heretic. But it was not only one city. After a federal judge in Florida declared the highly profane album of a black rap group, 2 Live Crew, obscene under the *Miller* standard, the Broward County sheriff ordered the group's arrest for performing material from the album at a local concert and the arrest also of a record store owner for selling it. 2 Live Crew was acquitted while the store owner was convicted—an awkward outcome for those with faith in the consistency of "community standards."

And in Washington, congressmen who weren't looking to abolish the NEA altogether were attaching a slew of restrictions to its reauthorization bill. NEA chairman John Frohnmayer took the treacherous path of defending the agency by appeasing its worst enemies—imposing an oath on grant recipients to return their subsidies if their work was judged "obscene" and intervening in the grants-selection process to deny money to four artists whose work he feared would offend the Jesse Helmses.

It was clear that the large majority of Americans loathed the art most never saw but was described to them as pornographic or obscene, yet three times more adults in one poll asserted their own right to "determine what they may see and hear" than offered blanket approval to laws that barred "material that may be offensive to some segments of the community." It seemed clear too that the public was closely divided on the use of federal funds to support arts projects. But issues of rights could not be resolved by polls. However many Americans might be willing to see their intolerance of "offensive" art converted into repressive legislation, did that mean that they or their leaders should have their way?

From the widest perspective, the controversies over Serrano, Mapplethorpe, 2 Live Crew, and all the rest involved the relationship of artists with their society. It was not the function of art to reassure or flatter society, to reflect for it only its own best image of itself. Artists had the right—and also the responsibility—to challenge society, to question orthodoxies, to undermine complacency. Significant art would always directly or indirectly be political art, and as such it must, in Robert Hughes's words, always try "to alter its audience's perception of its own social rights, duties, and opportunities" and "to make the viewer think critically about social relations—including the language in which they come wrapped." A nation's art must inevitably tend toward the subversive. "Art is the mole," Hughes continued. "It works below the surface of social structures. Its effects come up long after it has been seen." It might not set crowds to marching—but it must set them to thinking.

And who could perform this task of art? Not corporations or government agencies or congressmen, but the individual artist, isolated and vulnerable though she or he might be. "Artists belong out front," wrote Charles Mee, Jr., " . . . out at the edge of society and beyond—where the pain is, where the raw nerves are, where the subtlest and most delicate and most easily overlooked things are." If artists were both the makers and the principal subsidizers of art, they must also be the principal defenders of their right to the freedom to make an art true to their vision.

RONALD REAGAN'S BILL OF RIGHTS

BY CEMENTING the Bill of Rights into the Constitution the framers underlined their intention that the first ten amendments endure as a solid, indestructible foundation for individual liberty, beyond the reach of fleeting intolerant majorities and would-be despots. But the framers also created a federal government that would respond to majorities that gained power in its three branches. With conflict built into the system, the Bill of Rights became a field for rival leaders seeking variously to maintain or modify, reduce or expand, sanctify or pervert people's rights. And the Bill of Rights was also caught in the crossfire of the never-ending guerrilla warfare among parties, movements, and pressure groups fighting to use it for their substantive ends and institutional needs.

Linking these struggles over time was the flux of generations along the span of American history. John Adams's suppression of First Amendment liberties followed by the Jeffersonian counterattack—Jacksonian expansion of voting and other political rights yielding to a Whig devotion to property rights—Lincoln's emancipation of slaves triggering Republican efforts to guarantee political and civil rights for the freed, in turn frustrated by generations of Southern white supremacists under the banner of states' rights—FDR's Four Freedoms and Economic Bill of Rights setting the agenda for the next three Democratic presidents, culminating in the 1960s, then giving way to reaction in the next four Republican presidencies.

These conflicts amounted to a series of experiments testing whether the values built into the Bill of Rights could endure repeated assault. We might give these experiments the names of presidents, as convenient handles, even while we recognize that popular forces and wide arrays of political leaders—legislators, judges, bureaucrats, movement activists at local and state and national levels—in fact determine the outcomes.

No more extensive and effective campaign against the Bill of Rights of liberal orthodoxy has been mounted in this century, save perhaps during the Red Fear, than by the Reagan initiatives of the 1980s, renewed by George Bush at the end of that decade. The Red Scare after World War I, the attacks on union activists in the 1930s and Vietnam protesters in the 1960s—these might have seemed more ominous in their day, and even for a time in retrospect. But as they lacked strong and stable support at the grass roots, they proved as volatile and short-lived historically as a summer storm. Reaganism was quite different. The conservative assault on the Bill of Rights was seated not in a spate of shifting emotions but in an ideology broad and deep enough to challenge the liberal rights consensus on all its fronts.

The Reaganites had plenty of exposed targets, many first thrown up in the social and political turmoil of the 1960s: disrespect for God and flag and parents—slack and permissive schools—liberal and left-wing bias among intellectual and cultural elites—liberal and left softness toward

Communism abroad, especially in the Third World—coddling of criminals—tolerance of pornography. While many liberals by the 1980s were
defensive, self-doubting, even guilt-ridden, the Reaganites were confident and aggressive. So abundant and vulnerable were their targets that
they had no need to mount a single grand counteroffensive but produced
a multitude of sorties on the different fronts. Only in retrospect did the
sheer breadth and force of the attack become evident.

RONALD REAGAN had grown up within the homogeneous world of
small-town Illinois, where it was easy to practice "parochial tolerance"
since there was little essential diversity of opinion among neighbors—a
kind of "freedom for the thought we appreciate." As governor of California he had been outspokenly hostile to radical and antiwar students and
their sympathizers. In the White House, and now offering a model to the
whole nation, he exhibited that parochial tolerance with a benevolently
paternalistic attitude toward "average" Americans and continued intolerance toward dissidents, especially those on the left who appeared to side
with Communists abroad. His administration quarantined "dangerous"
ideas by making extensive use of the 1952 McCarran-Walter Act to deny
visas to "undesirable" foreign visitors who might propagate them. As *The
Nation* commented, the Reagan administration's "faith in the miracle of
the free marketplace has never extended to the marketplace of ideas."
Reagan's own attitude emerged most pointedly in his admonition to
those who would exercise their First Amendment freedoms that they had
"the responsibility to be right." And for Reagan to be right was to bear
right.

Restraints imposed on intelligence agencies in the 1970s were relaxed
during his administration, as the FBI conducted a massive program of
"close surveillance of groups opposed to U.S. policies in Central America," in Donna Demac's words. Political "conspiracy" trials were resurrected, with such innovations as preventive detention, heavily guarded
courtrooms, anonymous juries, and bans on the use of a free speech
defense.

A particular target of the Reaganite assault on the First Amendment
was the people's right to know. After Jimmy Carter's effort to limit need-
less classification, the Reagan administration tightened up classification
and declassification standards. Indeed, the administration indulged in the
reclassification of documents that had long been declassified and had
even appeared in print. "Just because information has been published
doesn't mean it should no longer be classified," explained the head of the
National Security Agency. In a small but astonishing usurpation of power
the NSA ordered a research library at the Virginia Military Institute—the

kind of private institution that true conservatives might have held to be beyond the reach of federal power—to remove from its shelves declassified materials a scholar had already published in his unauthorized history of the NSA.

Most presidents and their staffs have become obsessed with blocking "leaks" after a few painful experiences with the publication of "unauthorized material"; in contrast the Reaganites moved preemptively. The administration imposed new restraints on contacts between bureaucrats and journalists and required prior review of officials' speeches and writings; insisted that all federal employees, past and present, with access to any classified information sign nondisclosure agreements; and ordered a wide use of lie detector tests. White House staff members had a taste of their own medicine when the President ordered them to take lie detector tests after the press disclosed plans for military action in Lebanon.

The Freedom of Information Act—that historic blow for the people's right to know—was less administered than abused in these years. By the start of the 1980s the act had enabled historians, journalists, and activists to unearth information on a plethora of remarkably important and varied episodes, often hitherto concealed by governmental cover-ups—radioactive fallout from bomb tests in Nevada, tank problems in the army, the use of federal funds to support NOW and other liberal organizations (the FOIA request made by a conservative group), Richard Nixon's directive to the IRS to investigate such liberal groups as the Americans for Democratic Action, CORE, and the National Council of Churches, as well as FBI surveillance of isolationists during the Roosevelt administration, of Martin Luther King, Jr., of politicians' sexual activities. In the administration's campaign to shroud governmental action—especially abuses of power—in secrecy, the FOIA was a particular irritant and, as a historian concluded in 1988, the Reaganites "consistently attempted to cripple it through legislative and executive initiatives."

The Reagan administration, said constitutional lawyer Floyd Abrams, acted "as if information were in the nature of a potentially disabling disease which must be feared, controlled and ultimately quarantined." At the same time that they combated leakers and suppressed information the Reaganites were also busy putting out disinformation of their own. The politer term was "news management." Here again the administration demonstrated its contempt for the press and for the people's right to know. "That surrogates of the public stuff is bullshit, it's total crap," said Reagan campaign press aide Lyn Nofziger. The only reason reporters used that argument was "because they want a story," he went on. "They talk about the public's right to know. I say, show me. Here's the Constitution, you show me anywhere in there about the public's right to know, that you have a right to answers to questions. . . . "

The Reaganites soon were conducting a program of news management that led one analyst to call the administration "the most skillful practitioner of executive branch public relations in American history." Reagan's White House carefully orchestrated events and "photo opportunities" as previous administrations had done; but to an unprecedented degree it succeeded in divesting policy packaging of policy content, and the press proved for the most part an unresisting conduit for the Reaganite fables.

It was a great irony: while through the 1980s the White House demonstrated unremitting hostility to the press, journalists in turn wavered between the gullible and the supine in their coverage of the administration and as a whole served its purposes perfectly. An author titled his intensive study of the press's surrender to Ronald Reagan simply *On Bended Knee.*

THE REAGANITE campaign against the First Amendment was reinforced from the grass roots, by private New Right organizations and by an amalgam of fundamentalists, right-wing evangelicals, and other religious conservatives that touted itself as the "moral majority." Millions of committed Christians stood aside from this "moral majority," or condemned it outright, but, as Donna Demac noted, "the movement has also received some measure of assistance from mainstream denominations" that shared its distress over the decline of "morality" in the United States. The Christian in the White House, whose 1980 race against "born-again" Baptist Jimmy Carter was solidly supported by the religious right, postured as the lead crusader for a conservative social agenda grounded in moralistic hostility to liberalism and its culture and in the resurrection of "traditional values." But in the end Reagan committed relatively few of his administration's deep resources to the cause.

No "excess" of the 1960s had outraged the "moral majority" more than the 1962 Supreme Court decision barring formal prayer in public schools. The decision served as a point issue in the religious right's broad assault on liberal culture, or what it called "secular humanism." The religious activists were nothing if not outspoken. "I hope I live to see the day," said the Reverend Jerry Falwell, "when, as in the early days of our country, we won't have any public schools. The churches will have taken them over again and Christians will be running them." He and his allies and followers demanded the return of school prayer, religious instruction, and the teaching of the biblically based creationist dogma of human origins in science classes along with, or—better yet—in place of, Darwin's theory of evolution.

The opposition to "secular humanism" focused on school textbooks. Tennessee parents sued their own school system for using a textbook series that, they claimed, taught not only "secular humanism" but "one worldism," disobedience to parents, and even witchcraft. The failure to offer alternative readings denied their children religious freedom. A lower court not only supported the parents' arguments but allowed students to refuse regular instruction that included exposure to excerpts from such works as *The Wizard of Oz* and *The Diary of Anne Frank*. An appeals court, however, held in 1987 that while students had the right to voice their religious convictions in the classroom, they had no right in a public school to be shielded from the diverse views expressed in textbooks or by other students.

Conservatives then tried a daring constitutional ploy, contending that the entire curriculum of the Mobile, Alabama, public school system violated the First Amendment's establishment clause because it promoted "secular humanism," which was itself, they asserted, a religion. The case came before federal judge Brevard Hand, who had encouraged the suit after his earlier finding in favor of school prayer had been struck down by the Supreme Court. The texts he now ruled "religious" included such statements as "People of all races and cultural backgrounds should be shown as having high ideals and goals" and "The foundation of integrity has to come from within a person." Once again Hand was rebuffed judicially, this time by a federal appeals court that shrewdly evaded the issue of whether "secular humanism" was a religion by finding simply that the plaintiffs had not proven that the use of the textbooks violated the establishment clause. Their use had been "purely secular."

The creationists had more—if short-lived—success in state legislatures. Arkansas and Louisiana lawmakers passed measures requiring that creationism be given equal time in science classes—only again to run into the judicial roadblock when the Supreme Court in 1987 invalidated the Louisiana bill, which had outlawed the teaching of evolution unless the "science" of creationism was taught as well. The Court ruled that the measure violated the establishment clause because "it seeks to employ the symbolic and financial support of government to achieve a religious purpose." This holding was called the "strongest blow yet to the creationist cause"—but few expected any relaxation in the efforts of religious conservatives to integrate church and state in the nation's public schools.

If it took some courage—or at least First Amendment commitment—for the largely Republican-appointed Supreme Court of the 1980s to stand up to the "moral majority," it took even more courage to reject the howls of the "patriots" in the flag-burning furor of 1990. In effect the Court was defying two overlapping constituencies—flag-wavers and moral majoritarians—for patriotism and Christianity had long been enmeshed in American symbols and attitudes. It was not God and country for nothing.

The flap over the flag brought out all the worst in American culture—the gratuitous burning of the flag in the first place, the hysterical reaction that converted a small, otherwise unnoticed incident into a dreadful assault on all that was holy in America, the orating and posturing on Capitol Hill, presidential demagoguery, and finally the quick and quickly aborted effort to protect the flag by amending the First Amendment. It also brought out the best in America—strong opposition from grass-roots organizations, some conservatives as well as liberals rejecting the flag-waving and the proposed amendment, and a decision to submit the issue to congressional action rather than to constitutional amendment. And it finally produced that most American of solutions—throwing the new act before the courts—and the Supreme Court on this occasion lived up to its heritage, scarred though it was, of putting the First Amendment first.

L o o k i n g a t the Bill of Rights, Ronald Reagan's eye appeared to slide over the First Amendment and fasten on the rights of defendants from the Fourth through the Eighth Amendment. Looking at the Bill of Rights, libertarians tended to dwell on the "Glorious First" and to glide through the rest of the articles. Both sets of rights, however, were sources of controversy for both sets of observers; the arguments over the rights of defendants were at least as fierce and continuous as those over the First. And no wonder—those defendants' rights related to such critical matters as searches and seizures, self-incrimination, double jeopardy, trial by jury, bail, and cruel and unusual punishment.

The pendulum swing of generations had brought the Supreme Court to its particular posture of the 1980s. The transformation in defendants' rights had had its origins a half century earlier, spurred by dreadful miscarriages of justice. On the eve of the Roosevelt era the Court had reversed the capital convictions by the Alabama courts of seven poor, illiterate black youths—the "Scottsboro boys"—who had been wrongfully accused of raping two white girls and tried in one day amid mob hysteria, without adequate counsel. Then the high court in 1936 overturned the Mississippi capital convictions of three African-Americans whose confessions had been extracted by torture.

The Supreme Court's shift toward strong Bill of Rights positions, under the leadership first of justices like Hugo Black and William Douglas and later of Chief Justice Earl Warren, did not take the form merely of modifications—even reversals—of specific precedents. Far more important, after *Gitlow,* the Court continued to "nationalize" provisions of the

Bill of Rights by recognizing their incorporation into the Fourteenth Amendment's due process clause, and thus extended federal protections against state and local abuses to a widening array of individual rights, including the rights of defendants. In the cases of the Scottsboro boys in 1932, defendants' rights were nationalized for the first time—the right to counsel in capital cases and, more generally, the right to a fair trial. Other incorporations followed, bringing federal guarantees to the right to a public trial and safeguards against unreasonable searches and seizures.

But it was not until the 1960s that the revolution in defendants' rights reached its peak. Between 1961 and 1969, the Warren Court moved to check police, prosecutorial, and judicial abuses in the states by incorporating Bill of Rights protections against cruel and unusual punishment, compulsory self-incrimination, and double jeopardy, as well as the rights to a speedy trial and to the confrontation with witnesses. The "exclusionary rule"—providing that evidence obtained in improper searches and seizures was inadmissible in court—was also applied to the states. These sweeping extensions of the rights of defendants provoked extraordinary conflict among the justices. After a Court majority ruled in 1964 that Winston Massiah, indicted for narcotics trafficking, had been denied Fifth and Sixth Amendment rights to counsel and against compulsory self-incrimination and reversed Massiah's conviction, Byron White complained from the bench that after this decision "the Massiahs can breathe much more easily," while "the public will again be the loser and law enforcement presented with another serious dilemma."

Tempers on the high bench rose even higher a month later with the decision in *Escobedo* v. *Illinois.* The year before, in *Gideon,* the Court had ruled that all defendants in felony cases had the right to counsel at the trial stage; *Massiah* set a new standard, holding that the right to counsel began with the accused's indictment. Now the majority in *Escobedo* created yet another standard, pushing back the stage at which a person might assert his right to counsel to the point when he was in custody as a prime suspect, when "the process shifts from investigatory to accusatory—when its focus is on the accused and its purpose is to elicit a confession." Such a rule, White sarcastically declared in dissent, was "wholly unworkable and impossible to administer unless police cars are equipped with public defenders."

But the height of conflict came in 1966 with *Miranda.* By a 5–4 vote, the Warren Court overturned the kidnapping and rape conviction of Ernesto Miranda, once again broadening the rights of defendants and setting firm guidelines for police conduct. Not only must a suspect in custody be informed of his right to counsel; he must be advised of his right against self-incrimination—his right to remain silent—and he must not be questioned unless he voluntarily waived these rights. This time it was John Marshall Harlan, his face flushed and his voice rising and falling with emotion, who denounced the ruling as "dangerous experimentation," offering a "balance in favor of the accused" at a time of rising crime.

White and Harlan were not alone. Although the Warren Court expanded defendants' rights gradually, case by case, and selectively—protections against excessive bail and fines were not nationalized—the cumulative changes were sweeping enough to fuel a furious debate over law enforcement. Amid the ghetto uprisings and political demonstrations and assassinations of the 1960s, conservatives complained that the Court, in its solicitude for criminals and their rights, had "handcuffed" the police. Richard Nixon made "law and order" the heart of his successful 1968 presidential campaign. Police and prosecutors, while adapting their procedures to meet the Court's guidelines and in the process becoming more responsible and professional, took up the cries of White and Harlan that the Court had made their jobs far more difficult, almost impossible. They were particularly bitter about the exclusionary rule, and they and their allies could point to "obviously guilty" defendants whose prosecutions had been frustrated or convictions overturned by this rule.

Ironically, while law enforcers were ultimately less incensed by *Miranda*—it had little effect on the numbers of voluntary confessions they obtained—*Miranda* was the case that in the public mind embodied the revolution in defendants' rights, and the decision itself was embodied in a small card used by police to warn suspects of their rights. Its words drawn directly from the *Miranda* opinion, the card shown the accused in Philadelphia police headquarters read:

WARNINGS TO BE GIVEN ACCUSED

We have a duty to explain to you and to warn you that you have the following legal rights:

A. You have a right to remain silent and do not have to say anything at all.

B. Anything you say can and will be used against you in Court.

C. You have a right to talk to a lawyer of your own choice before we ask you any questions, and also to have a lawyer here with you while we ask questions.

D. If you cannot afford to hire a lawyer, and you want one, we will see that you have a lawyer provided to you, before we ask you any questions.

E. If you are willing to give us a statement, you have a right to stop any time you wish.

A key difficulty for those who would defend the rights of criminals in the caustic debates was the criminals themselves. As Holmes had long ago said, they were not nice. Miranda's common-law wife testified that after the Court's decision and while he was serving a long sentence for another crime he had confessed to her his guilt in the case that had become historic—the kidnapping and rape of an eighteen-year-old girl. In a second trial, he was duly convicted of that crime. After nine years in prison, he was paroled, arrested again on gun and drug charges, let off because of Fourth Amendment violations, paroled again, returned to jail for violating parole, and soon released again. A year later he was murdered in a skid row bar in a fight over a card game.

But seemingly inhuman humans can have a redeeming social effect, however unwitting—Miranda's suspected murderer was read the Miranda warning upon arrest.

F R O M T H E L A T E 1 9 3 0 s through the 1960s conservative Republicans had watched bitterly and helplessly as FDR built up the "Roosevelt Court" and his successors made it seem almost permanent. Eisenhower's nomination of Earl Warren as Chief Justice struck the right wing as a catastrophe after Warren revealed strong liberal and libertarian leanings. But now—in the 1970s and 1980s—it was the conservatives' innings on the Court. This was fair and proper; as part of the great generational flux in American politics, liberal victories at the polls would be followed by conservative ones, and these victories in turn followed by conservative judicial appointments. As Mr. Dooley had said, the "supreme coort follows th' iliction returns," but just how quickly, and how fully, and with what effect, depended on accidents of personality as well as political decisions by the president and the Senate. Other presidents besides Eisenhower had chosen judges who on the bench departed almost completely from the president's philosophy.

The Reagan Republicans did not want any accidents. Indeed, rarely has an administration come into power so determined to reshape the judiciary, and if the result included the selection of some judicial mediocrities, at least they were dependable mediocrities. Soon, under the banners of "original intent," "judicial restraint," "law and order," and "rights for victims," the Reagan White House and Justice Department, backed up for a time by a Republican Senate, pressed for a virtual counterrevolution in the federal judiciary.

Judicial reality did not match Reaganite rhetoric. Just as liberals before them had discovered that a liberal judiciary was not enough, so the conservatives learned that many congressional, bureaucratic, regional, and interest-group forces intervened between the decisions of the courts and the ultimate impact in the streets and police stations. Still, the Reagan Court brought about notable shifts in favor of the police and against suspects, in favor of eavesdroppers and against the bugged, in favor of the expedited use of the death penalty and against the procedural rights of convicted murderers. And the judicial counterrevolution continued in George Bush's term in the White House.

"Scarcely any political question arises in the United States that is not resolved, sooner or later, into a judicial question," Alexis de Tocqueville wrote after his return from America. A century and a half later this was still the case. But in the complex checks and balances of the American constitutional system, and in the great generational shifts from left to right and back, political forces outside and within the judiciary remained crucial, whatever the findings and decrees from on high. And whatever the words of the Constitution, whatever the "original intent" of the framers, whatever the enduring power of the Bill of Rights and its extensions, whatever the appeal of the "Glorious First," the rights of Americans would remain caught in political and intellectual crossfires, not only between conservatives and liberals, Democrats and Republicans, but among legislators and jurists, presidents and protesters, street fighters and law professors, police officers and anarchists.

CHAPTER THIRTEEN

A GLOBAL BILL OF
HUMAN RIGHTS

S H O R T L Y   A F T E R its establishment following World War II, the United Nations Educational, Scientific, and Cultural Organization set up a group to explore the historical development and philosophy of the concept of human rights. In spring 1947, the UNESCO group, called the Committee on the Theoretical Bases of Human Rights, circulated to a global array of distinguished scholars, writers, and statesmen a series of questions on "the changes of intellectual and historical circumstances between the classical declarations of human rights" with roots in the eighteenth century and the "bill of rights made possible by the state of ideas and the economic potentials of the present." The purpose, the questionnaire stated, was to develop "a common formulation of the rights of man" which would inspire and guide all peoples, whatever their level of political and social development.

By the end of June, the committee began to sift replies from its far-flung correspondents, and these answers, far from yielding the hoped-for "common formulation," instead underscored the diversity of the idea of human rights. Thus Mahatma Gandhi, nearing the climax of his struggle against the British Raj, wrote briefly that he had learned from "my illiterate but wise mother that all rights to be deserved and preserved came from duty well done" and that even "the very right to live accrues to us only when we do the duty of citizenship to the world," while the German philosopher Kurt Riezler argued from the still-fresh experience of Hitlerism that the conditioning of rights by public duties made the individual prey to "any kind of totalitarian leader. He will enforce the duties while ignoring the rights." Aldous Huxley worried that the centralization of authority in socialist governments would, through ever-expanding means of coercion and control, extinguish individual liberty, but Boris Tchechko, a Soviet law professor, countered that eighteenth-century declarations of rights assumed that "the main purpose of liberty is to serve the ends of the bourgeoisie," while the "true liberty of the individual," secured in the Soviet Union by the Stalin Constitution of 1936, was "his right to work within the socialist organisation of the national economy." Amid such a conflict of concepts, Italian philosopher and historian Benedetto Croce advised that any effort to paper over these differences or to reconcile them with compromises would "prove either empty or arbitrary" and invite ridicule.

If Croce's warning were ignored and a consensus reached on an international declaration of human rights, how would such a document be implemented? What action might the international community take against a nation that violated its provisions? A look at history offered only more mixed counsel. For one thing, there was not much history. Over the centuries, of course, statesmen and clerics, soldiers and humanitarians had been roused to protest and action by reports of repression in distant places, but such concerns tended to be a bit specialized. "Protestant powers sought rights for Protestants in Catholic countries; but not for Jews or Jesuits," according to Evan Luard. "Christians sought freedom for Christians in China, or for Armenians in the Levant; but not for Muslims or Buddhists." Missionaries in Africa often opposed slavery but might campaign actively for abolition only after the enslaved had been safely converted to Christianity.

Increasingly slavery evoked wide concern in the West. During the nineteenth century most European states took unilateral action against the slave trade, and in 1890 sixteen nations joined in the Brussels Agreement to terminate the inhuman practice. Britain in particular also protested atrocities inflicted on subject peoples, for example, by the Turks in Bulgaria in 1876. Although in this case Britain was moved by moral concern to condemn its Turkish ally, it was not always so clear whether real humanitarianism or the pursuit of national interests motivated its government. British efforts to encourage independence for Spanish colonies in Latin America, Luard noted, reflected both support for the ideal of self-government and promotion of Britain's commercial and political interests.

The world struggle for human rights in the next century would rarely be free from the politics and economics of power. Woodrow Wilson's call during and after World War I for global democracy and the right of self-determination was attacked one day as a cloak for the advancement of American hegemony, the next as naïve utopianism.

So the UNESCO thinkers had neither illuminating historical experience nor coherent political theory as they tackled questions about international human rights. And these questions were the most demanding of moral judgment, the most intractable for political strategy and leadership:

Should—and could—international human rights be promoted by states without regard to their other national interests, or even at the expense of those interests? Should—and could—human rights be promoted globally without regard to the weakness and fragmentation of the international system, with its scores of sovereign states, its confusion of democracies and despotisms, its diverse levels of political, economic, and social development?

Were some human rights more "fundamental" than others—antecedent and necessary to other rights? And so should—and could—certain classes of rights—civil and political, say—have priority over others, such as social and economic? Or were human rights ultimately indivisible—they could not be advanced on one front unless they were simultaneously advanced on the others?

What human rights were global, or at least might be applied with global standards? Should—and could—human rights that evolved in the Western tradition be applied to Third World cultures, and vice versa?

THE ROOSEVELT LEGACY

ONCE AGAIN world war had been the testing time for ideas and values as well as for warriors and machines. On New Year's Day 1942 in Washington twenty-six nations, including the "Big Four" of the United States, the Soviet Union, Britain, and China, affirmed the principles of the Atlantic Charter. The human rights expressed in Roosevelt's Four Freedoms, drawn against Hitler's fanatical attacks on individual liberty, democracy, and social tolerance, provided the ideological ballast of the anti-Axis coalition, whatever its internal divisions. The United Nations Organization established in San Francisco after Germany's defeat would be looked to as an engine of global human rights as well as of international peace and security. Under its charter the UN would "reaffirm faith in fundamental human rights, in the dignity and worth of the human person, in the equal rights of men and women and of nations large and small." The UN's General Assembly was mandated to make recommendations for "the realization of human rights" and an economic and social council was organized. The council in turn created a Human Rights Commission and assigned it the task of preparing a declaration of human rights.

"We have good reason to expect the framing," new president Harry S Truman told the UN's founding conference in June 1945, "of an international bill of rights" that would be "as much a part of international life as our own Bill of Rights is a part of our Constitution."

Rhetoric was already outrunning reality. That same UN charter stated that nothing in it "shall authorize the United Nations to intervene in matters which are essentially within the domestic jurisdiction of any state or shall require the Members to submit such matters to settlement." In succeeding decades, Tom Farer wrote, "every rogue regime would seek shelter" behind this provision.

The story of the making of the UN's Universal Declaration of Human Rights is one of conflict and compromise—a laborious effort by a large number of men and a few women from around the world to cut and shape a document that both reflected and transcended a vast congeries of cultural attitudes, political interests, and ideologies. But two persons were central to it, a man and a woman who were also husband and wife, one dead and the other very much alive, one an American president, the other a former American First Lady, who would, quite rightly, come to be dubbed "First Lady of the World." They of course were Franklin Roosevelt and Eleanor Roosevelt.

In the uncertain years after the Nazi invasion of Poland, when the United States was an active supporter of Europe's beleaguered democracies, and then after the attack on Pearl Harbor in late 1941, FDR had been so preoccupied with military and diplomatic affairs that his human rights role has long been seen as that of the aloof promulgator of high-sounding ideals. Yet the President was closely involved, from its first stages, in the drafting of what would become the Atlantic Charter, whose value in his eyes lay not only in its usefulness as a propaganda weapon; it represented also a clear and true expression of war aims and an earnest of the rights to be enjoyed by captive peoples after the expulsion of the Germans and Japanese. But as Roosevelt was reluctant to enshrine detailed commitments that might cause divisiveness at home or among friends abroad, the Charter's drafting became a difficult political and diplomatic balancing act. Still, his tilt toward generality did not spare him controversy. Rumors spread from London that two of FDR's Four Freedoms—of religion and of speech and press—had been omitted from the Charter. Roosevelt cabled to his press secretary in London with unusual asperity that one of the rumormongers was "either senile or an ass."

The rumors proved true; the declaration agreed to by Roosevelt and British Prime Minister Winston Churchill in August 1941 during a conference on warships off Newfoundland contained no explicit reference to liberties of speech, press, or worship, acknowledging only the rights to the choice of form of government and to "freedom from fear and want." In a report to Congress after the summit, FDR was obliged to answer the Charter's critics, insisting that the absent liberties were "of necessity" implied in the declaration, as "a part of the whole freedom for which we strive." And in a public message to Churchill on the Charter's first anniversary, he emphasized the Anglo-American "faith in life, liberty, independence and religious freedom." The inclusion of "independence" might have been a quiet dig at his war partner, whose truculent assertions of British imperial rights had ensured the vagueness of the document's provisions for national self-determination.

From the war's earliest days, FDR's State Department had been laying plans for a postwar international organization, as well as for a global bill of rights that would serve as "an integral part of the new world order," and administration officials were already grappling with issues of definition and implementation that would later bedevil delegates to UN committees.

At the Dumbarton Oaks UN preparatory conference in September 1944, the American delegation presented proposals for the inclusion of human rights in the new organization's charter and, with flexibility and patience, overcame British and Soviet objections. When Secretary of State Edward Stettinius reported to FDR, he found the President pleased that the "extremely vital" human rights provision had been accepted. Roosevelt, Stettinius noted, seemed "rather surprised that the Soviets had yielded on this point"—a realistic hint of the work and the wrangles that lay ahead.

It was this work that Eleanor Roosevelt would carry on. She had had virtually no experience in diplomacy when her husband died in April 1945. She received a short course in international politics when late in that year President Truman put her on the delegation to the first session of the UN General Assembly in London. She had to learn to work with Republican members of the delegation, including John Foster Dulles, who had been foreign affairs adviser to Thomas Dewey in the 1944 presidential campaign against FDR and who at first appraised this fledgling diplomat as an intellectual lightweight. She had to endure carping from the likes of her husband's longtime antagonist, columnist Westbrook Pegler, who complained that she wasn't worth the $12,000 a year the government paid her. She had to cope with the maddeningly slow and obstructionist Soviet delegates. And she had to tussle with the issues themselves—most notably the searing question of the status and protection of refugees, one of the first and most pressing postwar human rights problems.

It was while serving this brief apprenticeship that Eleanor Roosevelt was appointed the American representative to the UN's Economic and Social Council and member of its Commission on Human Rights. Her debut on the commission in New York was typically unpretentious. Spurning a government limousine, she took the subway to a Bronx stop and then, dressed in her usual long gown and black stockings, she walked to the Hunter College library where makeshift quarters had been set up. In the initial order of business she was chosen by acclamation to head the commission.

Eleanor Roosevelt was the first to admit that none of this would have been possible had she not been the wife of Franklin Roosevelt. But if FDR had taken leadership of the human rights campaign during the first half of the 1940s, then, wrote historian M. Glen Johnson, "the second half of the decade was characterized by the leadership of Eleanor Roosevelt." It was a curious partnership of the living memory of Franklin Roosevelt and the activism of his widow. Even more curious was their reversal of roles. During her husband's presidency Eleanor Roosevelt had served as the house idealist, constantly pressing him—sometimes to his annoyance—to rise above brokerage to an elevated position on the great moral questions facing the nation and the world. He had sought always to bring her back to what was politically practical. Now his heritage embodied the ideals both had believed in, while Eleanor Roosevelt, struggling with the most complex issues amid the diverse pressures and interests of scores of nations, had to become the politician—the negotiator, the compromiser, sometimes even the Machiavellian.

TWO CENTRAL QUESTIONS faced and soon divided the commission as it set to work drafting an international declaration of rights. The first was only too familiar to Eleanor Roosevelt and all those who had lived through the bitter fight over the League of Nations: whether and how far the implementation of an international declaration might impinge on the national sovereignty of member states. The United States had remained out of the League largely from fears that the organization would intrude on American sovereignty, and even now, after a second world war, there was rising public and congressional opposition to a binding rights document. Southern congressmen in particular worried that the UN would become an ally of the nascent civil rights movement, and already the Soviets were demanding an investigation into the conditions of African-Americans. But the Soviets themselves were hotly opposed to any implementation provision that would "ignore the sovereign rights of democratic governments," and Roosevelt could silence Soviet insistence on an examination of American rights abuses by guilelessly declaring that the United States would welcome such an inquiry—if the Soviet Union also opened itself to inspection. It was largely by her efforts that a compromise was finally reached: two documents would be prepared, the first the declaration itself, a nonbinding statement of principle setting "a common standard of achievement," followed by an implementation covenant that would have the force of law on ratifying states.

The other question cut to the heart of the debate over the definition of human rights—and to the intensifying rivalry between two wartime allies now emerging as postwar superpowers. The American vision of an international declaration was, as a United States representative put it, "a carbon copy of the American Declaration of Independence and Bill of Rights," devoted to the individual's freedom from government. But the Soviets were determined to include an array of economic and social rights and "the less said about freedom of speech, the right to a fair trial, etc., the better." They also demanded that the declaration reflect the duties of citizens to the state and that the "universal" rights proclaimed be qualified by the phrase "corresponding to the laws of the State." Although Roosevelt was sympathetic to the inclusion of socioeconomic rights—they were, after all, among her husband's Four Freedoms—she was publicly bound by the American position opposing it.

While she lobbied the State Department to soften its opposition, in commission sessions she used all her skills to avert a breakdown over the issue. She patiently countered Soviet arguments and delaying tactics and urged delegates to shun "theoretical conjecture" and focus on the declaration's specific language. A "balance," she insisted, could be struck, and indeed, through her labors, it was—but in many ways it proved a Pyrrhic victory. The American government finally accepted the inclusion of socioeconomic rights in the declaration, but only because all enforcement powers had been stripped from it and placed in the separate covenant, which was now broken into two—one concerned with the implementation of civil and political rights, the other with socioeconomic rights—and if a state refused to ratify one or the other or both, there was nothing to hold it to the declaration's principles. Nor were the Soviets appeased by the enshrinement of socioeconomic rights. As the commission voted to adopt the declaration, they abstained and issued a minority report describing the draft as "weak and completely unacceptable."

Considering the depth of these disputes, it seemed a miracle that the commission had come up with a declaration at all. Eleanor Roosevelt's singular contribution was recognized when, after its debate on the declaration, the General Assembly accorded her a standing ovation. And when the Assembly voted on December 10, 1948, there was not a single negative vote. There were, however, eight abstentions: the Soviets again and several of their Eastern European satellites, in the curious company of South Africa and Saudi Arabia. On its passage, Roosevelt expressed the hope of many in the world: that the Universal Declaration would become the "international Magna Carta of mankind."

From the opening phrases of its preamble—"*Whereas* recognition of the inherent dignity and of the equal and inalienable rights of all members of the human family is the foundation of freedom, justice and peace in the world"—to the last of its thirty articles, the Declaration was terse yet comprehensive, eloquent yet explicit. Most of the provisions began with the word "Everyone," making for a stirring repetition.

The Universal Declaration seemed to overcome the diversity of human rights concepts by embodying them all: among the rights enumerated were those to life, liberty, and security of person, to freedom of movement within and from one's homeland, to property ownership, to freedom of thought, conscience, and religion, to political participation, as well as such social, economic, and cultural rights as the right to work and to equal pay for equal work, to union representation, to leisure and paid holidays, to adequate food, clothing, and housing, to medical care, to social security, to free participation in the cultural life of the community. Specific provisions acknowledged marital rights—including the equal rights of wife and husband—and the right of mothers and children to "special care and assistance," while elementary education was to be compulsory and free of charge and higher education generally available to all.

And there were proscriptions as well: "no one" should be held in servitude or slavery, or subjected to torture or cruel punishment or to arbitrary arrest or exile, and "no one" should be arbitrarily deprived of nationality or of property.

Now that the Declaration's principles had achieved international recognition, Eleanor Roosevelt devoted herself to the task of ensuring that they received international implementation. While she retained her seat in the American delegation to the UN, she turned much of her energy to winning congressional ratification of the two enforcement covenants. But opposition to binding the United States—especially on socioeconomic rights—had grown after the Declaration's passage. Constitutional and judicial objections were offered, but Cold War events—the 1948 Berlin blockade, the "loss" of China in 1949, the North Korean invasion of the south in 1950—brought in their wake a high conservative and nationalist tide that washed away any remaining chance of immediate ratification.

Still, when Eisenhower was elected in 1952, Roosevelt hoped to hold on to her UN position and keep the ratification fight alive from there. The President-elect, of course, had won his military glory under her husband's command, and he did not share the hostility to internationalism of his Republican right wing. But he was indebted to that right wing for his election, he would need its backing once in office, and he was not inclined to waste his political capital standing up for so tempting a target of right-wing hatred as the UN's internationalist rights agenda.

Nor would he stand up for the woman who had become the right wing's—and also, in a very different sense, the world's—symbol of that agenda. When, as a courtesy, she tendered her resignation to the President-elect, he accepted it quickly and coldly, with a few stiff phrases of gratitude. A few months later the new administration announced that it was washing its hands of the UN's human rights covenants.

MORAL IMPERATIVES AND
PRACTICAL NEEDS

"THE UNITED STATES is going backwards," wrote Eleanor Roosevelt when she learned of Eisenhower's abandonment of the UN covenants. It was, as David Forsythe noted thirty years later, a general retreat on human rights: beginning with the Eisenhower presidency, "U.S. human rights policy was collapsed into its anti-communist policy" and "the rhetoric of rights became the icing on the cake of anti-communism."

Two succeeding Democratic administrations did little to soften Eisenhower's coarse politicization of international human rights. In his inaugural address John Kennedy spoke of a new generation of Americans "unwilling to witness or permit the slow undoing of those human rights to which this nation has always been committed." Yet, despite his promotion of economic development in the Third World through such agencies as the Alliance for Progress and the Peace Corps, these programs and human rights itself remained for Kennedy primarily weapons in the Cold War arsenal. As the black freedom movement exposed to the world wholesale American violations of fundamental rights, Kennedy took the defensive. In an address to the UN General Assembly two months before his death, he frankly acknowledged American failures, while asserting that "we are working to right the wrongs of our own country," and then, arguing that "human rights are indivisible," Kennedy put the bombings of black churches in the South on a par with religious persecutions elsewhere in the world and maintained that the United States was by no means alone in falling short of "standards of fairness and justice." For all his action on civil rights at home Lyndon Johnson was too mired in Vietnam and too obsessed with the specter of countries falling like dominoes to Communism to do much more than talk about international human rights, and even then only as the "icing on the cake" of America's anti-Communist campaign in Indochina.

Yet the gaps between rhetoric and practice, as well as ambiguities and ambivalences about the role of the United States in the promotion of international human rights, were nothing new—they stretched far back into the American past. These uncertainties might be summarized in a handful of opposed terms: whether the United States should serve as a passive exemplar of freedom for other peoples to emulate or actively intervene to impose its values on them; whether the United States should denounce rights violations in other countries or concentrate on the ample failures at home; whether the United States should initiate boycott, blockade, or other sanction against a regime that oppresses or murders its people, or merely utter protests. So often had these conflicting counsels been debated, from a proposal to isolate Austria after its suppression of the Hungarian revolt in 1848 through Russian pogroms against Jews, Turkish massacres of Armenians, British repression of Irish, that they had been reduced to slogans: Idealism or pragmatism? Abdication or over-commitment? Optimism or realism? Moral posturing or low-key global bargaining?

Few scholar-statesmen expressed these choices and dilemmas more clearly in words, and confused and corrupted them more in practice, than Richard Nixon's assistant for national security affairs and later secretary of state, Henry Kissinger. In the campaign season of 1976, toward the end of his term as secretary, now serving Nixon's successor, Gerald Ford, Kissinger summarized thirty years of hard thought and experience in a closely reasoned, thickly textured address to the Synagogue Council of America. He laid out a series of choices and calibrations between "moral promise and practical needs," between aggressive posturing and quiet diplomacy. He summarized the "principles" that he claimed had guided the Ford administration: "Human rights are a legitimate international concern" and the United States would further that cause, using "all our influence to encourage humane conduct within and between nations" . . . but on the other hand would "be mindful of the limits of our reach" and of the "difference between public postures that satisfy our self-esteem and policies that bring positive results" . . . and of course would "never forget that the victims of our failures, of omission or commission, are human beings and thus the ultimate test of all we do."

All this would appear nicely weighted and balanced until one examined his words more closely and put them against his actions. For one thing, human rights was third on his list of "inescapable tasks," following maintenance of a "secure and just peace" and creation of a "cooperative and beneficial international order." And in office Kissinger was a practitioner of the most ruthless realpolitik, with the supreme goal of strengthening both American security and American power within a controlled and balanced global system. His preference for "quiet diplomacy" reflected not only an obsession with secrecy—the better to keep all the diplomatic threads in his own hands and to ward off "intrusions" from Congress and from his bureaucratic rivals within the administration—but also an unwillingness to draw public attention to repressive American allies or to hold them accountable for their rights abuses.

In the end human rights was not even a third priority for Kissinger. Human rights might have its occasional tactical uses in diplomacy or in a political campaign when the administration's opponents were condemning the "amorality" of its foreign policy. But oversensitivity to human rights reflected a certain lack of "toughness," or even "naïveté." Kissinger's aides were advised to avoid sounding "like a bleeding heart" if they wanted to influence him even on ostensibly moral issues, and when he learned that the ambassador to Chile had broached human rights abuses to the Pinochet dictatorship, whose brutalities were stirring outrage in Congress and the press, Kissinger snapped, "Tell Popper to cut out the political science lectures." Indeed, with Kissinger's emphasis on the stability and predictability of the international order— especially the stability and predictability of American allies—a military regime like Pinochet's had its virtues; as Arthur Schlesinger, Jr., wrote, a "policy aiming at the manipulation of the balance of power doubtless contained an inner bias in favor of governments that could deliver their nations without having to worry about political opposition or a free press."

The international campaign for human rights during the Kissinger years was led by such courageous Soviet dissidents as the physicist Andrei Sakharov and the writer Aleksandr Solzhenitsyn and equally bold rebels in other countries, and by members of Congress. Foreign oppositionists received little sympathy from the Kissinger regime. Ford's refusal, on the advice of Kissinger, to receive Solzhenitsyn after his expulsion from the Soviet Union seemed to reveal, in Schlesinger's words, a "moral vacuum at the center of American foreign policy."

Some members of Congress tried to fill that vacuum, becoming unacknowledged heroes of the human rights effort. Minnesota congressman Donald Fraser in 1973 launched hearings that helped lay the basis for a major legislative challenge to Kissinger's posture. His subcommittee's report condemned the State Department for embracing "governments which practice torture and unabashedly violate almost every human rights guarantee pronounced by the world community"; a stronger emphasis on human rights in foreign policy was "both morally imperative and practically necessary."

Other representatives and senators took up the campaign, and the Foreign Assistance Act of 1973 proposed "that the President should deny any economic or military assistance to the government of any foreign country which practices the internment or imprisonment of that country's citizens for political purposes." The next year, Congress added the recommendation that except in "extraordinary circumstances" the United States should reduce or end security assistance to governments that repeatedly engaged in "gross violations of internationally recognized human rights." Kissinger resisted such measures and, when they were enacted, dragged his heels in implementing them.

Congressional persistence, growing public distaste for Kissingerian realpolitik, and further outrages against dissidents abroad forced the Secretary to give at least a little more lip service to human rights during his last year or so in office. It was notable that the United States was present, and represented by President Ford in person, at the signing of the Helsinki "Final Act" on August 1, 1975. The Final Act was a "declaration of intentions" by its thirty-five signatories from Europe and North America to observe sovereign equality and the territorial integrity of states, to promote peaceful settlement of disputes, and the like—and it contained a provision that called on states to "respect human rights and fundamental freedoms" and to "promote and encourage the effective exercise of civil, political, economic, social, cultural and other rights" deriving from the "inherent dignity of the human person."

The Soviet government celebrated the long-wished-for formal recognition bestowed by the Final Act on its domination of Eastern Europe, but dissidents throughout the Communist bloc were galvanized by the human rights standards set at Helsinki and formed groups to monitor and publicize their governments' nonobservance of them. The West would continue to challenge the East on human rights at Final Act follow-up conferences in Belgrade and Madrid, but in the United States, Helsinki was for the short term merely a dynamic and tawdry campaign issue as the Republican right wing, led by Ronald Reagan, elevated Gerald Ford to the select company of Franklin Roosevelt in its demonology: Ford at Helsinki had completed the "sellout" of Eastern Europe that FDR had started at Yalta in 1945.

"OUR COMMITMENT to human rights must be absolute," Jimmy Carter told his inaugural audience in January 1977, "our laws fair, our national beauty preserved; the powerful must not persecute the weak, and human dignity must be enhanced." If some in the crowd saw this as a rather eclectic mix of values, they were doubtless reassured a bit later: "Our Nation can be strong abroad only if it is strong at home. And we know that the best way to enhance freedom in other lands is to demonstrate here that our democratic system is worthy of emulation. . . .

"The passion for freedom is on the rise," the new president went on, and the United States would join the international struggle not only for the protection of civil and political liberties but also, in the spirit of FDR, for economic and social progress: we "will fight our wars against poverty, ignorance, and injustice, for those are the enemies against which our forces can be honorably marshaled." To those at home wearied by the cynical pragmatism of the Kissinger era, to those abroad whose cries had gone unheard by the Nixon-Ford administration, the advent of Jimmy Carter, his commitment to human rights as a central value in international relations, came as a fresh and hopeful breeze. Four months later, before a University of Notre Dame audience, Carter renewed that commitment in even stronger terms: "We can no longer separate the traditional issues of war and peace from the new global questions of justice, equity, and human rights."

For a time, exploiting the momentum he had brought to Washington, Carter moved ahead energetically on human rights. The President, Secretary of State Cyrus Vance, UN Ambassador Andrew Young, and other administration officials proclaimed the high principles of the Universal Declaration, deployed American diplomatic and economic clout against oppressors, and even flew to human rights crisis areas to oppose repression.

But within a year or two the Carter human rights program lay in confusion, frustration, and apparent failure. Increasingly that program had been bedeviled by the question of how the promotion of human rights was to be reconciled with other diplomatic aims. The Nixon-Kissinger answer had been simple expediency: if there was no American strategic interest to be advanced in pressing human rights, it wasn't pressed. Carter did not seek such an easy way out. But despite his "absolute" pledge on human rights, inescapably he had other ends as well— reduction of nuclear and conventional arms through negotiations with the Soviets while maintaining American strength in dealings with them, regional conciliation in such areas as the Middle East, enlightened trade and energy policies—the pursuit of which required a multidimensional evaluation of the strategic positions and internal policies of other nations. Thus the President seemed to betray his own principles when he withheld or tempered criticism of the genocidal Pol Pot regime in Cambodia, which was the friend of China, the enemy of our enemy, the Soviet Union; or of the corrupt and repressive Ferdinand Marcos in the Philippines, where the United States had important military installations; or of the various right-wing tyrants throughout Latin America, most of whom had taken power with American support as reliable bulwarks against the spread of "Communism."

The Soviets posed the acid test of Carter's policies, and they did so very early in his administration. The President's moral stance on human rights encouraged Soviet dissidents and their American champions to put more pressure on both Moscow and Washington to end the persecution of dissidents and to allow Soviet Jews to emigrate. But when Carter within a month of his inauguration sent a personal pledge to Sakharov that he would actively promote human rights within the Soviet Union, he received what an adviser described as a "very sharp rebuff" in a letter from Communist Party general secretary Leonid Brezhnev, denouncing Sakharov as a self-proclaimed "enemy of the Soviet state," sneering at the "pseudo-humanitarian slogans" of Carter's human rights campaign, and warning the new American president not to try the patience of the Soviet leadership.

Carter would say in retrospect that his rights campaign had not damaged overall Soviet-American relations, but only caused tension that "prevented a more harmonious resolution of some of our other differences." One of those differences he overcame with the arms limitation treaty, SALT II, that he and Brezhnev signed in June 1979. But even if his campaign had caused more serious contention, he wrote, he would not have yielded to Soviet complaints, because the "respect for human rights is one of the most significant advantages" in the struggle for influence, and "we should use this good weapon as effectively as possible." But this was precisely Moscow's objection—that his rights policy was less an expression of American idealism and concern than a handy club with which to pound the Soviets and win leverage in the global competition for power.

Indeed, Carter's later description of rights as a "good weapon" reflected the extent to which he came to act as a transactional leader rather than as the transforming leader he had hoped to be. He thought in terms of balance, even within his own administration. The moderate, patient Vance was balanced by the President's assistant for national security affairs, Zbigniew Brzezinski, a prickly Polish-born anti-Soviet hard-liner who was wedded to old-fashioned realpolitik, so that the human rights component of his advice to Carter was closely attuned to the geostrategic needs of the moment.

Events pushed the President further from the early moralistic emphasis in his foreign policy toward traditional Cold War power politics. The Soviet occupation of Afghanistan in late December 1979 so shocked him that he retaliated with a flurry of punitive measures, canceling American participation in the Olympic Games in Moscow, limiting exports of grain to the Soviet Union, and postponing Senate action on SALT II. The taking of American hostages by a new and radically Islamic regime in Iran almost two months earlier had also jolted the administration.

By this time the balance between his advisers was tipped entirely in Brzezinski's favor and Carter's 1977 boast that Americans were "now free" of an "inordinate fear of communism" was forgotten. "Carter abandoned the philosophy of repentance and reform," wrote Gaddis Smith, and "under Brzezinski's daily tutelage and without substantial knowledge and experience of his own," swiftly adopted the rhetoric and policies of the militant cold warrior, "blaming the Soviet Union for almost everything that was going wrong, saying very little about human rights as an absolute principle of foreign policy, advocating higher defense budgets and the development of new nuclear weapons." In the spring of 1980, Cyrus Vance resigned.

Even for outsiders it is a daunting experience to witness what Herbert Spencer had described as the "murder of a beautiful theory by an ugly gang of facts." The facts Carter confronted—conflicts within his administration and with Congress, the competition of human rights with other ends, Soviet aggressiveness and repression, surprises like the hostage-taking—might have appeared to justify his stumbling retreat from human rights toward Cold War militancy. But these facts were not all hard, ineluctable, autonomous forces. How he dealt with them might change some of the facts themselves. And how he dealt with them, after the first year or two, was very much in the tradition of the brokers, the manipulators, the negotiators, the "foxes" in Herodotus's term, who had typically preceded him in the presidency.

Carter's failure was not that he compromised his "absolute" rights commitment; this was unavoidable. The problem was that, rather than link and integrate human rights with other ends in advance, he became reactive to events as others—mainly adversaries—did the linking for him. In the case of Iran, Carter followed the practice of his predecessors by muting public criticisms of the Shah's savage regime in deference to his importance as a strategic partner, but the President's global rights advocacy emboldened the regime's opponents. Only when it was far too late did the administration urge thorough political modernization on the Shah. The government that replaced him blamed the United States—not altogether unfairly—for thirty years of repression, while embarking on its own course of religiously inspired brutality. The result was a blow both to Carter's human rights campaign and to American strategic interests—an outcome that was, as one critic drily put it, "entirely unintended."

Complex though the domestic and global pressures and choices were, Carter's failure was more intellectual than political. His was a classic case of the "Tocquevillian void"—the breach noted a century and a half before by Alexis de Tocqueville between Americans' vast and general ideals and their shifting, day-to-day calculations, the two levels operating independently of each other rather than bound by a structure of ends-oriented means and means-oriented ends.

With his usual candor and introspection, Carter admitted later that "I did not fully grasp all the ramifications" of his human rights policies. Hence those policies and their execution gave the impression of inconsistency, confusion, cross-purposes, and by the end the hopes he had aroused retained little of their brightness. It was an unkind fate for a man who had been so willing to make a moral commitment.

C A U G H T between his initial unqualified pledge on human rights and his many compromises in specific situations, Carter was vulnerable to a challenger who could attack him on both flanks—as both an extremist and an appeaser. Republican nominee Ronald Reagan made the most of this opportunity in 1980. He and his conservative advisers claimed that Carter had made a general leftward tilt in applying his rights policy—"soft" toward the Soviet Union, Cuba, Vietnam, and other enemies and "hard" toward countries essential to American security. The Republican insurgents charged that the Carter administration's alleged pressure on the Nicaraguan dictator Anastasio Somoza and the Shah of Iran to end their rights abuses had brought down leaders friendly to the United States—Carter had "lost" the two allies, just as Truman a generation earlier had "lost" China to the Communists.

Like the Carter idealists four years back, the Reaganites approached office on a wave of euphoria, determined to sweep with a stiff broom. A group of conservative experts on Latin America advised the President-elect that the Carter emphasis on human rights must be "abandoned." The new—and short-lived—secretary of state, Alexander Haig, who had served apprenticeships under both Kissinger and Nixon, made this advice policy with his pronouncement that "international terrorism" would "take the place of human rights in our concern" on the grounds that terrorism was the "ultimate of abuses of human rights." Soon the administration was conducting a crusade against the "evil empire" of the Soviet Union, including two of its Latin American clients, Cuba and Nicaragua, while asking Congress to resume military support to four other Latin American regimes, including the military dictatorships in Argentina and Chile, cut off by the Carter administration because of flagrant rights violations. Junta generals and other tyrants, including South Korea's president, were welcomed to the White House. With these "friends," the administration made what critics described as only a "hypocritical show of interest" in their dismal human rights records.

But Congress did not echo the Reaganite contempt for human rights diplomacy. Even though the Senate was now under Republican control, its Foreign Relations Committee rejected, by a 13–1 vote, the President's first nominee for assistant secretary of state for human rights and humanitarian affairs, Ernest Lefever, a critic of congressional human rights initiatives, largely as a warning that Congress continued to take human rights seriously, even if the administration did not. Later in 1981 Senate and House committees specified that no military aid would go to El Salvador unless the President could certify that its regime was making progress toward meeting human rights standards.

Then in Reagan's second term, the ideologues in the White House began to confront their own brutal gang of facts. One of these was the appearance of Mikhail Gorbachev atop the Kremlin hierarchy, which seemed to portend a less confrontational relationship with the Soviets. But the most dramatic was a series of internal challenges—in Panama, the Philippines, South Korea, Chile, and elsewhere—to dictatorships the administration had supported. These challenges undermined Reaganite claims that private pressure on friendly leaders was more effective—both in curtailing rights abuses and in preserving the stability of allies—than public condemnation. "Quiet diplomacy," the Reaganites were now obliged to observe, had accomplished neither of these ends. Instead oppressed peoples were rising. Four years of "constructive engagement" with South Africa's apartheid regime collapsed in March 1985 when South African police fired on 4,000 demonstrators. The destabilization of allied governments also taught the administration that, as Tamar Jacoby wrote, in some cases "the promotion of human rights coincided with America's strategic interests." It was apparently on this consideration that Reagan finally agreed to distance himself from Ferdinand Marcos in the Philippines and encourage his flight into exile.

A quite different factor tempering White House zeal was the increasing institutionalization of human rights. Here again Congress had taken the lead. Since 1976, it had required the State Department to submit annual surveys of human rights conditions in all nations receiving American aid and held hearings to scrutinize the accuracy of these "report cards." Congressional resistance to repeated "certifications" of human rights progress in El Salvador and to Reagan's suggestion that the corrupt Salvadoran election of 1982 marked a fresh beginning finally convinced the administration to press the Salvadoran military to rein in its death squads and purge and punish guilty officers. On congressional initiative, a Bureau of Human Rights and Humanitarian Affairs had been established in 1975 in the State Department and it was enlarged and achieved influence in the Carter administration, under the leadership of veteran civil rights activist Patricia Derian, the first assistant secretary of state for human rights. But however policy might be defined from above, the fashioning of such a bureaucratic instrument had the effect of creating a focus for the efforts of human rights advocates from Capitol Hill and from "nongovernmental organizations."

These nongovernmental organizations, including the Human Rights Watch coalition, PEN, the Lawyers' Committee for Human Rights, as well as the American affiliate of Amnesty International and committees or chapters of such groups as the American Association for the Advancement of Science and the ACLU, had themselves become institutions. They monitored human rights conditions around the world and not only lobbied Congress but worked with it to draft legislation and oversee implementation. In the early 1980s, they managed to goad Reagan's first assistant secretary for human rights, Elliott Abrams, into a public argument. Abrams, militantly dedicated to broadcasting Communist rights violations and shrouding in silence those of repressive American allies, found himself boxed in and bedeviled by these activists whom he saw as determined to "restrain the American role in the world." When he resigned, his replacement was more moderate and conciliatory, in keeping with the less ideological approach to human rights and foreign policy of George Shultz, Haig's successor.

Another step toward the institutionalization of human rights concerns in foreign policy came with the creation in December 1983 of the National Endowment for Democracy to "foster the infrastructure of democracy" around the globe. A private corporation supplied with federal funds, the NED intersected with human rights efforts in its insistence that democratic institutions ultimately—and sometimes in the short run— were the most solid bulwarks of human rights. The NED was controversial from the start, less for its purpose than its practices—it was criticized for being packed with Reagan partisans, providing financial aid to right-wing political parties abroad, and papering over the administration's indifference to human rights abuses with dubious boasts of victories for democracy. As Aryeh Neier, executive director of Human Rights Watch, noted, the Reaganite "equation of human rights with electoral democracy has helped to deflect criticism on human rights grounds of a number of democratic governments," including those of El Salvador and Guatemala. Nevertheless, in the longer term, the NED offered an institutional base for the support of fledgling movements in the struggle to raise genuine democratic structures against oppressive regimes of both right and left.

Congressional and institutional pressures, events abroad forcing a recalculation of the place of human rights in American strategic interests, an American public that looked for its foreign policy to stand for something more than opposition to the dying threat of Communism, an image-conscious White House that wanted to appear to have human rights on its side—all these combined to create the irony that, in David Forsythe's words, "the second Reagan Administration seemed closer to the Carter Administration than to the first Reagan Administration." What had been for Carter a moral commitment the Reaganites begrudged as a practical necessity, but even they had had to acknowledge Carter's hope that "the expansion of human rights might be the wave of the future throughout the world.

"I wanted the United States to be on the crest of this movement," Carter had continued, yet as both his experience and Reagan's had shown, it was not the policies of American presidents but the desperate courage of countless rebels, oppositionists, dissidents, refuseniks, famous and obscure, resisting military juntas, corrupt oligarchies, and Communist dictatorships alike, that rode the crest and gave hope for the shaping of a true and effective international bill of rights.

THREE WORLDS OF RIGHTS

THREE MONTHS after Carter's inauguration, his secretary of state, Cyrus Vance, made a valiant attempt in a speech at the University of Georgia to summarize the new administration's definition of international human rights. First was "the right to be free from governmental violations of the integrity of the person," and he listed torture, inhuman treatment, arbitrary arrest, and similar abuses. Second was the "right to the fulfillment of such vital needs as food, shelter, health care, and education." These could be abridged by corruption that enriched a thin elite and "through indifference to the plight of the poor." Third came the classic Bill of Rights liberties, including freedoms of thought and speech, of religion and assembly.

While the speech blazed no trails in defining rights, it was notable in several respects: in its sweeping inclusion of civil and political and social and economic rights, in the placement of socioeconomic rights before Bill of Rights liberties, and above all in Vance's almost casual conclusion: "Our policy is to promote all these rights." This huge pledge reflected the new president's high purpose, but it also left the impression that all these rights might be realized without the need to establish priorities among them, or to sacrifice the pursuit of some of them if necessary. Yet by separating them into three categories—civil, political, socioeconomic—Vance also left the impression of a dichotomy, a tension, even an irreconcilability among them. Thus the inevitable choices would be made harder.

The divisions among civil, political, and socioeconomic rights, and especially between the civil and political and the socioeconomic, posed a series of intellectual challenges for Americans. The West in general and the United States in particular possessed a political and philosophical tradition of individualism that gave first priority to personal liberties in the eternal tension between individual and state—the American Bill of Rights was of course an enumeration of exclusively civil and political liberties. This tradition continued to dominate the constitutional and political assumptions of modern American leaders, as well as the thinking of European decision-makers—for example, the Council of Europe when it prepared the Convention on Human Rights in the early 1950s. In drawing up a "list of freedoms," the drafting committee's French rapporteur said, it seemed "preferable to limit the collective guarantee to those rights and essential freedoms which are practiced, after long usage and experience, in all the democratic countries." The Convention thus must "begin at the beginning" with civil and political rights—"others" could be added later.

But where was the "beginning"? What were the "others"? When was "later"? These were not givens but matters of policy, judgment, *choice.* Whatever their ideologies, whatever the strength of the individualist tradition, politicians and officials in London and Paris and Washington and other capitals had long been making day-to-day judgments and choices in both the civil-political and the socioeconomic arenas, passing social and economic measures relating to health, housing, education, employment, expediently and dexterously responding to felt needs and changing social and economic conditions, to interest-group and grass-roots pressures. The result varied from nation to nation—the United States, for instance, lagged far behind most Western European countries in such areas as child care and national health insurance—but it gave practical evidence that the advance of socioeconomic rights did not inevitably mean the diminishment of civil and political liberties.

In asserting the primacy of civil and political over socioeconomic rights, some Western thinkers would make three assumptions: that civil, political, and socioeconomic claims might all legitimately be considered rights, with the first two categories protecting the individual *against* government, while the last provided for the satisfaction of needs *through* government; but that civil and political rights were innately and inescapably more fundamental than socioeconomic, concerned with more basic human needs; and that "beginning" with civil-political rights did not impede pursuit of socioeconomic rights, but rather, as the historical record indicated, helped push socioeconomic rights to the forefront for debate and action.

Critics on both right and left disputed some or all of these assumptions. Maurice Cranston, an English moral philosopher, simply objected that socioeconomic rights weren't human rights at all. He contended that the classic civil and political rights to life and liberty met the three criteria by which human rights must be tested—they were universal, they were of paramount importance, and they could be effectively secured through simple legislation to restrain governmental power. Social and economic rights, by Cranston's reckoning, failed all three tests: They were not universal but applied only to certain classes of citizens—Cranston gave the example of the "right" to holidays with pay proclaimed in the UN's Universal Declaration, which, he held, was meaningful only to those who worked for pay. Their importance was of a "totally different moral dimension" from that of civil and political rights—thus the deprivation of holidays with pay or even of social security could not be compared to indefinite detention without trial or the denial of fundamental civil rights on the basis of racial distinctions. And the implementation of socioeconomic rights, for many millions in the world's poor countries, was impracticable, as guaranteeing social security or an adequate living standard required not merely the passage of laws but "great capital wealth"— and "if it is impossible for a thing to be done, it is absurd to claim it as a right." The affirmation of a "different logical category" of rights, argued Cranston, threatened "to bring the whole concept of human rights into disrepute," to push it "into the twilight world of utopian aspiration."

However inadequate Cranston's reasoning—such basic socioeconomic needs as food, housing, and medical care were undoubtedly "universal," at least arguably of "paramount importance," and their realization as rights might in many cases be more a matter of human choices and priorities than of possibilities and impossibilities—it suggested the deep conceptual differences within Western philosophical and political thought. It also indicated the kinds of rationalizations that Western political and intellectual elites might entertain—rationalizations that opponents could perhaps best overcome not by philosophical argumentation but by the mobilization of popular forces demanding the fulfillment of their rights to economic and social benefits.

THE DEBATE over civil-political and socioeconomic rights was not the province only of Western pundits and philosophers and policy-makers. In the ferocious ideological battles of the Cold War that dominated superpower relations from the middle 1940s to the late 1980s, the dispute was also injected into international power politics. As Eleanor Roosevelt's struggles with Soviet delegates over the inclusion of socio-economic rights in the UN's Declaration and other issues suggested, human rights had swiftly become a key weapon in the conflict between the First and Second Worlds. Each side tended to see the other's stand on rights as purely political and propagandistic and minimized its deep philosophical and doctrinal roots. But if much of the debate was sheer polemics, there was a hard core of serious intellectual dialectic.

For the Communist world, that core lay in Marxist writings, with their emphasis on economic forces as the primary cause in history. The modes and means of economic production gave birth to class divisions and defined political and governmental structures, which would inevitably serve the interests of the dominant class. Rights, Marx wrote, were likewise historically bound—they could "never be higher than the economic structure of society and the cultural development thereby determined"—and likewise they protected the interests of the dominant class. In capitalism, then, the "individualism" of the bourgeoisie—in particular its ownership of the means of production—was protected by civil-political rights, while the socioeconomic claims of the working classes were denied as inconsistent with private property rights.

A century after Marx, Soviet spokesmen were resonating to his ideas. In a revealing 1983 interview Georgi A. Arbatov, director of the Soviet Institute of United States and Canadian Studies and a sophisticated observer of American society, told a Dutch journalist that "communist ideology emphasizes collectivism," which meant "harmony between individual and collective interests, the latter being just as natural and necessary for individual freedom and development as the immediate interests of the individual," an emphasis that contrasted with the "extreme individualism typical" of Americans.

"Americans think that individualism helps them keep their freedom," the journalist interposed.

Without getting into definitions of freedom, Arbatov responded, he would merely say that "individualism has been a potent incentive in American history, but its balance sheet is getting heavier and heavier on the debit side. Americans are paying for their extreme individualism with widespread alienation; social atomization; increasing anarchic patterns in economic, social, and political organization; and escalation of antisocial behavior like crime, drug addiction, violence, and so forth."

Comparing the two social systems, would Arbatov conclude that the overall "cost-benefit balance" was in favor of socialism?

"The ultimate ideal of communism," Arbatov replied, "is the free and comprehensive development of the personality of each individual. This goal can be achieved only in a society organized for the common good rather than for private interest."

To bolster their argument that their society did foster this "free and comprehensive development," some Communists would point to the Soviet and other socialist constitutions that granted not only socioeconomic but also civil and political rights. The 1936 Soviet constitution, adopted in the early days of Stalin's Great Purge when millions of citizens were judicially or "extralegally" murdered or sent to die in labor camps, formally guaranteed basic "bourgeois rights": freedoms of speech, assembly, and press, the right to demonstrate, the inviolability of persons and their homes and correspondence, open and public trials and the independence of the judiciary, freedom of conscience and religious worship. And forty years later, at the peak of the Brezhnev campaign against dissidents, a new Soviet constitution reaffirmed the whole spectrum of socioeconomic and civil-political rights.

Western observers have long been mystified by the Soviet tradition of enshrining civil and political rights in their constitutions and denying them in practice. Given Marx's contempt for "bourgeois rights," that they were included at all was taken as testimony to the extent to which they had become universal standards. But many Westerners simply denied that any of the rights, civil, political, or socioeconomic, in Soviet constitutions were really rights. They noted what one Soviet academician described in 1980 as "the most important feature of the Soviet citizens' legal status"—"the organic unity between their rights and obligations," with the understanding that should the citizen fail to fulfill his obligations, the state had just cause to deny him his rights. By this "organic unity," the "right to work" was easily converted into the duty to work— the 1936 constitution had put it bluntly: "He who does not work, neither shall he eat." Soviet rights were further limited by "claw-back" clauses, providing that they must be exercised only "in conformity with the interests of the working people and for the purpose of strengthening the socialist system"—with both the "interests" and the "conformity" a matter of state judgment. In short, Soviets possessed "rights" not by their status as human beings or as citizens, but as conditional grants of the state.

Both the First and Second Worlds in fact apotheosized a vast array of "universal" rights, whether civil-political or socioeconomic, that governments in varying degrees had grossly or subtly violated in practice. Arbatov said that the two worlds were separated by "deep differences in values," but added that "every nation must make its choice and, having made it, should not complain about the consequences." Yet not only the choices but the way they were made differed. In the West the choice ultimately was made in a confusion of elections, party rivalries, interest-group competitions, and social movements, and further refined by a jumble of legislators, executives and bureaucrats, judges and activists. In the Communist nations the choice was made by the state.

During the late 1980s and early 1990s the Soviet people, sustained perhaps by their knowledge of rights set forth in their constitution, began to assert those human and democratic rights in a series of convulsions that rocked the Soviet state and the Communist Party that since 1917 had dominated it. State and party unraveled in the face of "cobblestone leaders" who rose from the streets and squares of ancient cities.

The West took immense satisfaction in the disintegration of an enemy ideology, its pretensions and power, and in the proclamations and pro-grams of rebels who often drew from Western history and practice. And through reports in the newly liberated Soviet media, it soon became clear that the state had fallen far short of fulfilling even the most basic social and economic rights of its citizens. Readers and viewers in the Soviet Union were treated to vivid accounts of homelessness, with estimates of the numbers of "vagrants" as high as 3 million, of a "universal" health-care system that served only 60 percent of the people's needs, of 16 million retirees who received pensions that were well below—in some cases less than half—the subsistence level. One Soviet economist even claimed that "class differences"—the disparity between rich and poor—were more severe in his country than in the United States and estimated that nearly 90 percent of all Soviets could be considered "poor."

But the complacency of Westerners was unjustified. Their societies too had failed to meet the needs of their homeless, their old and their ill, their desperately poor. The exiled Soviet dissident Andrei Amalrik bitterly opposed as "immoral" what Arbatov described as the Soviet choice—"A slave who has eaten his fill," Amalrik wrote in 1977, "retains the psychol-ogy of a slave"—but he was little more sympathetic to the Western liberal "choice" of civil and political rights, which "throws a man into the sea and says: Sink or swim." Human rights were inseparable, he argued; it was wrong to choose between them. Indeed, unless both classes of rights progressed "hand in hand, we shall live in a monstrous world."

W H I L E First and Second World superpowers clashed over the meanings of human rights, the Third World added fresh and urgent voices to the debate, voices from former colonies where the issue of rights confronted an intricate but dynamic interplay—of the civil-political rights legacy left by Western colonial powers, external and internal forces pressing for socioeconomic rights to meet dire economic conditions, and indigenous elements hostile to both First and Second World concepts of rights and fiercely protective of their own national, regional, and tribal traditions and beliefs and their own rights concepts.

As the Western powers pulled out of their colonial possessions during the middle decades of the twentieth century, liberal elements among both colonizers and colonized had high hopes for the realization of the civil and political rights that the departing masters were thought to have implanted. At last the "new nations," liberated from colonial rule, from the exploitation of and discrimination against native peoples, could secure and expand freedom and democracy, and achieve economic progress, in good Western style but through their own efforts. It soon became evident in many of the former colonies, however, that their Western masters had left only a veneer of democracy and that their abrupt withdrawal after decades or centuries of paternalism was an invitation to instability. Army officers seized power. Healthy party rivalry degenerated into multiparty fragmentation or one-party dictatorship. Democratic forms were continued in some places but without democratic substance. Western visitors were often startled but pleased to glimpse, in an Asian or African capital, bewigged and begowned lawyers presumably carrying on the great Western traditions of due process and equality before the law, though in fact the laws they administered and the political context in which they operated were often more authoritarian than democratic.

Many in the First and Second Worlds—in the "North"—would dispute the assumption that the adoption of civil-political rights in the "South" would lead to the expansion of such rights or to the advancement of socioeconomic rights. It was the old argument over dichotomies and priorities in human rights, applied now to the new nations. The debate most often took place in the vital and conflicted context of economic development. For instance, socialists, Communists, and other radicals in the North advanced the "full belly" thesis—the argument that only when the most basic economic needs were satisfied would civil and political rights become meaningful. Hence economic development must be the first priority.

For leaders of the new nations who respected the claims of both civil-political and socioeconomic rights, the question of priorities posed an agonizing practical choice—whether to satisfy the immediate needs of hungry constituents and so demonstrate to them that democracy "works" but at the risk of squandering resources necessary for long-term development, or whether to hold back on economic redistribution and relief and thus risk breeding a radical opposition that would condemn democracy as an unaffordable luxury, denounce civil-political rights as alien and colonialist, and demand stronger government—or simply one strong man.

To many in the South, especially in its poorest nations, there was only
an illusion of choice. "What freedom has our subsistence farmer?" demanded President Julius K. Nyerere of Tanzania. "He scratches a bare
living from the soil provided the rains do not fail; his children work at his
side without schooling, medical care, or even good feeding. Certainly he
has freedom to vote and to speak as he wishes. But these freedoms are
much less real to him than his freedom to be exploited." President
Kwame Nkrumah of Ghana, as if to answer him, wrote: "The economic
independence that should follow and maintain political independence
demands every effort from the people, a total mobilization of brain and
manpower resources. What other countries have taken three hundred
years or more to achieve, a once dependent territory must try to accomplish in a generation if it is to survive."

Nkrumah added a chilling note: "Even a system based on social justice
and a democratic constitution may need backing up, during the period
following independence, by emergency measures of a totalitarian kind."
Nkrumah, who had led his country's independence struggle but came
increasingly to "back up" his power with totalitarian methods, was in turn
overthrown by a military coup in 1966.

MUCH OF the North-South debate over human rights in the Third
World was dominated by First and Second World concepts and traditions, and some Third World leaders accepted these terms of debate,
even as they gave them their own twists. But others rejected all or many
of the institutions and assumptions of the First and Second Worlds.
Eddison Jonas Mudadirwa Zvobgo wrote that the replicas of Western
constitutional structures "bequeathed" by colonial powers to their erstwhile colonies "were not only alien, but were in fact obscene in an African
or Asian environment." Some Southern "traditionalists" threw out the
whole idea of rights as a Northern invention entirely unsuited to their
native cultures. Other traditionalists would agree that rights were a universal ideal but insisted that the specific content of rights was culture-
bound and evolved through particular customs and conditions, whether
African or American, Asian or European.

A central point united Third World traditionalists of both stripes—that
First World rights were based on excessively individualistic concepts of
human nature and human needs. Such individualism, and the competitiveness, selfishness, isolation, and alienation it generated, were at odds
with Third World patterns of community, family, tribal, and other forms
of group solidarity, with their inherent values of duty, obligation, belong-
ingness, and mutual aid and protection. To traditionalists who would
describe these values in the language of rights, rights then derived from
the person's group membership, and they were contingent on the ful-

fillment of social roles, with the resulting potential for both social cohesion and group coercion.

The values and customs celebrated by traditionalists weighed heavily on Third World women. Many were beyond the effective reach of civil or political or socioeconomic rights, and within the tribe or community or family that was the source of such rights as they enjoyed, they suffered more poverty than men, received less education, and were burdened with both productive and domestic labor. In sub-Saharan Africa, women were subject to such customs as child betrothal, bridewealth, polygyny, the "inheritance" of widows by the husband's relatives, and genital mutilation. Despite the proclamations of international organizations and the efforts of some African governments to bring women's rights into equality with men's, Rhoda Howard concluded that "in the culturally sacrosanct family, men retain a material, sexual, and moral dominance that many are unwilling to relinquish."

The Organization of African Unity, in its 1981 Banjul Charter, fused indigenous and Western rights concepts in what were described as "peoples' rights." The most significant of peoples' rights, the right of "all peoples" to economic development, strengthened Southern claims against the North for a fairer distribution of global wealth—it asserted a right to developmental assistance. But the right to development also encompassed the "right" of the people to be subject to Nkrumah's "total mobilization" by their surrogate, the state, for the mighty labor of nation-building. To assert this right, however, did not solve the problem of defining rights—rather it complicated it further. Must the exercise of the collective right to development diminish the individual's civil and political rights? Must the exercise of individual rights in a developmental context constitute, in the words of Senegalese jurist Kéba M'Baye, "an attack on public order"? The Banjul Charter itself surrounded individual rights with claw-back clauses—the right to liberty was qualified by "reasons and conditions laid down by law" and religious freedom was "subject to law and order." In many new nations of the South leaders used the slogan of peoples' rights to crack down on people's civil liberties and political rights.

For the First World it was déjà vu—the new nations were struggling through rights phases similar to the times of war and crisis when Western nations had put national survival before individual rights.

A significant difference, however, was that the wars which had provoked the worst abuses in Western societies were fought for a purpose that was relatively definite and clear, and when that specific purpose was accomplished, the claims of a "national right" faded as justification for the deprivation of individual rights. But the Third World's "war" for economic development lacked definition. How much economic progress was "enough" to permit the lifting of "emergency" measures? And who was to make that determination? Those leaders who, as Dunstan M. Wai noted, used the exigencies of development as "a mask—a convenient cover for a lust for power and wealth"? For the Third World's poorest nations, the prospect of even minimal economic development was so far distant that authoritarian rule in the name of peoples' rights might become what a group of jurists meeting in Dakar in 1967 described as "a permanent exceptional circumstance."

The human rights record in the Third World included such "worst cases" as the murderous tyrants Pol Pot of Cambodia, Idi Amin of Uganda, Emperor Bokassa I of the Central African Republic, Macias Nguema in Equatorial Guinea; it included holocausts of tribes by other tribes, the decimation or displacement of populations, invasions of other countries. Rarely did development and respect for human rights go hand in hand; many Third World countries exhibited the fragility of both. South Korea and Singapore approached Western levels of economic growth, but under repressive regimes. In 1986 the United States described the Ivory Coast's human rights record as "generally satisfactory," but the relative absence of overt repression reflected the effectiveness with which Félix Houphouët-Boigny, the nation's leader since independence, had "suspended public politics" and imposed personal authoritarian rule; and a late 1980s downturn in world prices of the country's principal exports, cocoa and coffee, "dealt an unparalleled blow to hopes for national development." Chile's Pinochet dictatorship waged a campaign of terror against its people, with mass arrests, torture, and indiscriminate murder, and meanwhile enriched a narrow elite, pauperized the peasantry and the urban lower classes, and produced a negative economic growth rate.

Pressures for economic development—often self-imposed, through frustrations, failures, unreasonable expectations—raised the stakes at the same time that they worsened the problems. Though a few Third World leaders rejected economic development in Western terms, most looked to the industrialization and wealth of the West for their example, and, as Nkrumah's comment indicated, they expected to accomplish in a generation or two what it had taken the West—and with the enormous advantage of its exploitation of these same countries as colonies or neo-colonies—centuries to achieve. For its part, the First World looked to the Third with similar expectations of rapid, Western-style development. Some in the First World advanced peoples' rights as justification for abuses, and many others were willing to overlook a measure of "temporary" repression as the price of progress, echoing the Banjul Charter's assumption that "the satisfaction of economic, social, and cultural rights is a guarantee for the enjoyment of civil and political rights." As usual, the causation was not so simple. Crimes were committed in the name of national development, as they had been, in both North and South, in the name of national security and survival.

And always there was the nagging question—what did the peoples of the Third World really want? Did they want above all to preserve and protect their tribal and regional and national cultures? Or economic progress even at the expense of those cultures? Or simply security and survival as nations so that they could follow their own paths without intervention by First, Second, or other Third World countries? Many Africans in particular answered simply: they wanted dignity, as individuals and as peoples and as nations. Dignity? To Western ears this appeared to be a minimal demand, overly conservative or at least static in implication. Was there not something more important—individual and collective opportunity? Economic, social, political, cultural opportunity, with all its dynamic prospects for growth, change, self-improvement, self-fulfillment? Or was this merely a First World bias?

CHAPTER FOURTEEN

TRANSFORMING RIGHTS

AT THE TURN of the 1990s Americans were transfixed by a global eruption that galvanized fighters for rights around the world. They watched as in country after country people took the opportunity for freedom into their own hands. The populace poured through the cobbled streets of ancient capitals, crowded with their banners into central squares, even lofted torn-up cobblestones at the palaces and fortresses of hated governments. From the people emerged cobblestone leaders, some of whom only months before had been in jail, their books or plays banned, their churches closed, their protesting voices stifled.

Americans could view these happenings with special pride. What helped to inspire the uprisings in China, Eastern Europe, the Soviet Union, and elsewhere were not only the "universal" principles of the UN's Declaration or the Helsinki Final Act but the values of the "American creed"—freedoms of speech, press, assembly, and religion enshrined for two centuries in the Bill of Rights. Even more, the revolutionaries were emboldened by the struggles of oppressed Americans for rights promised by the Declaration of Independence and the Constitution but long denied. Perhaps they understood from the American experience the paramount fact that rights were won far more by the struggles of the populace—of mechanicks and artisans, of blacks and women, of farmers, workers, street activists—than in grants from the powerful.

In Moscow and Warsaw, at huge rallies for democracy, cobblestone leaders and their aroused followers drew courage and counsel from the legacy of Martin Luther King, Jr., and the American black freedom movement. In Prague and Leipzig, even atop the crumbling Berlin Wall, people sang "We Shall Overcome," just as earlier those fighting words had emblazoned the banners and T-shirts of student protesters in Beijing's Tiananmen Square, and as they rang out across the black townships of South Africa.

It was clearer than ever—rights reigned as the common currency of political and social transformation around the world.

During these stirring months, another event also lifted the hearts and hopes of many people. At the UN World Summit for Children in the fall of 1990, global leaders gathered to address the needs of their most easily overlooked constituency, of those whose rights were most easily trampled—children. But at least at this New York convocation children were not voiceless.

"Everything is upside down in the world and maybe this conference will help bring peace in the world," said eleven-year-old Alice Kamai, of a Sierra Leone family.

"I would like all kids in the world to be happy," said thirteen-year-old Hussan Maki from the Sudan, after drawing pictures of a sad child and a happy child.

"We are the next mayors, Congressmen, presidents, and world leaders," said eleven-year-old Bonin Bough at a service at the nearby Cathedral of St. John the Divine.

"We are not inheriting the world from adults," he continued, "they are borrowing it from us."

The adults had come together at the summit in an atmosphere of urgency. "Each day, countless children around the world are exposed to dangers that hamper their growth and development," the UN Declaration on Children stated. "They suffer immensely as casualties of war and violence; as victims of racial discrimination, apartheid, aggression, foreign occupation and annexation; as refugees and displaced children, forced to abandon their homes and their roots; as disabled; or as victims of neglect, cruelty and exploitation.

"Each day, millions of children suffer from the scourges of poverty and economic crisis—from hunger and homelessness, from epidemics and illiteracy, from degradation of the environment. . . .

"Each day, 40,000 children die from malnutrition and disease, including acquired immunodeficiency syndrome (AIDS), from the lack of clean water and inadequate sanitation and from the effects of the drug problem. These are challenges that we, as political leaders, must meet." Some of these political leaders may have reflected that even as they joined for a three-hour session—or even while an American mother had her child in day care for the morning—perhaps 5,000 children would perish from malnutrition and disease around the globe.

The leaders at the children's summit made all the right speeches.

Simple survival was not enough, President George Bush declared, "for a child lacking in health or learning or denied the love of family and time for play." African leaders reported desperate famine conditions. President Václav Havel of Czechoslovakia, with the irony one might expect from a playwright, exclaimed, "How much evil has already been committed in the name of children!"—referring to tyrannies that professed to work for the sake of children and "for the false happiness of generations yet unborn in some false paradise"—but he went on to say that in the past year or two he had experienced the "beautiful revolt of children," for the Czech nonviolent rising against totalitarianism had been—"at least in its beginnings—a children's revolution."

Yet an air of pessimism also hung over the meeting. Would the lives of children actually be improved? delegates and others were asking. Would their rights be recognized? Would Thailand enforce its laws against child prostitution? Would India curtail child labor? Would Iran and Iraq withdraw child warriors from the battlefield? Some Americans were particularly skeptical of their own leadership. President Bush, they noted, had not yet signed the UN's 1989 Convention on the Rights of the Child. Opposition members of Congress complained that between pronouncements at the UN about the importance of education, Bush shuttled back and forth to Washington, where he was trying to cut aid for schools in budget negotiations.

Nor could Americans ignore one dismaying and embarrassing fact: that the United States, for all its power and wealth, compared poorly with other industrial nations in tending to the welfare of its children. According to a "report card" prepared in 1990 by the Children's Defense Fund, an advocacy group led by the visionary American champion of children's rights, Marian Wright Edelman, "by every measure, the U.S. performance is unsatisfactory." Seventy countries worldwide provided medical care and financial aid to all pregnant women; sixty-three provided family allowances to workers and their children. The United States provided neither. Eighteen nations had lower infant mortality rates than the American, and a black child born in inner-city Boston had less chance of living to its first birthday than a child born in Peru, Uruguay, or North Korea. Every year, 10,000 American children died because of poverty and as many were wounded by guns, 100,000 were homeless, and nearly 750,000 were abused or neglected.

"The mounting crisis of our children and our families is a rebuke to everything America professes to be," declared Edelman's report. The Children's Defense Fund called for "transforming action" in the faith that "what will heal our lost sense of community and national striving are our common hopes and dreams for our children."

CONTRACTING RIGHTS

TWO HUNDRED YEARS after the passage of the Bill of Rights it was evident that American society had not only failed many of its children, it had also failed to secure for millions of adults the rights enumerated in the Constitution and in laws of the United States or at least promised by the supreme American values of freedom—liberty, equality, justice. Some Americans had indeed reaped a cornucopia of rights bursting with plums for powerful interests. But others found in that cornucopia only wizened fruit and thistles.

Which Americans had failed to share in the bounty? Mostly those who had lacked the bounty to begin with—tens of millions of women, children, African-Americans, Latinos, nonunion and even unionized workers, the homeless, people living in impoverished physical and cultural environments. But how could this be, after the political and legislative victories of workers, women, blacks, the disabled, and others, in a land overflowing with milk and honey?

The answers become more clear if we recall the major campaigns for rights in American history and their aftermaths. African-Americans appeared to have won new rights with abolition and Reconstruction, only to see most of the few real gains—particularly black men's right to vote—slip away, as racists regained control of both Southern and national policy. After a century of struggle women won the suffrage, only to discover they had to wage another struggle over several decades before they would begin to achieve the actual progress that the vote was supposed to have brought in its wake. The campaign to improve the life-opportunities of children by abolishing child labor also took a century, marked with defeats in Congress, the state legislatures, and the courts, but its ultimate success only demonstrated that to keep children learning instead of working was by no means enough to ensure that their lives were not blighted.

The fate of rights measures and their implementation in the United States might be summarized as too little, too late, too short-lived.

Too little: Many of the measures passed to broaden the rights of Americans were fatally compromised in their very enactment. The Reconstruction amendments remain the most telling and tragic example. What the newly freed men and women needed so desperately was not merely their legal emancipation and the right to vote men received, but also land, jobs, schools, and they needed these not separately but together with emancipation and suffrage, in a mutually supportive and mutually enhancing complex of rights. As it happened, the failure to buttress constitutional grants of emancipation and male suffrage by securing the economic and social rights of former slaves, as well as suffrage for black women, disastrously undermined the ability of African-Americans to gather the economic and social power that would have helped them defend the constitutional grants themselves. Decades later many of Roosevelt's New Deal measures, especially during the late 1930s, were so badly compromised in their enactment or execution, or both, that they neither brought full recovery nor met fundamental needs, such as housing and health, and left hosts of Americans vulnerable to future economic upheavals.

Too late: Oppressed women, children, and people of color were not alone among Americans in gaining rights only after long struggles. Workers did not secure the right to organize and bargain collectively until the 1930s, and the right in federal law to shorter hours and a minimum wage was not won until 1938, and even then through a wages and hours act weakened by exclusions. Long after other industrial nations had legislated social security Americans were still dependent on private pensions and charity. If the Social Security Act had been passed in the 1920s rather than a decade later, millions of retired and unemployed Americans might have been less vulnerable to the economic and psychological havoc of the Great Depression. Those who argued that democracy—especially American democracy—was slow but "always got there in the end" forgot that the "end" came too late for whole generations of Americans—or it never came at all.

Too short-lived: Some rights enactments that appeared to be substantial in content, fully established in the nation's legislation or jurisprudence, well accepted by the public, turned out to be vulnerable and ephemeral. The Wagner Act of 1935 is still very much on the books, but its impact, following the heady days of the sit-downs, has been weakened, in part by later administrators of the act who were largely unsympathetic to it. The passage in 1947 of the Taft-Hartley Act, designed to tilt the balance back toward employers, could be seen as part of the normal counterattack by those who wanted to reassert employer rights. The real damage to the rights of workers has been done through a much more fundamental power shift that dramatically undercut labor's hand. Employers found that they might pick up and "move south," to the cheap—and unorganized—labor havens of the Deep South or Latin America or Asia, abandoning their plants, workers, communities, and union agreements. Or, more insidiously, employers filled the jobs of striking workers with "temporary"—that is, permanent—nonunion employees, without apparently violating the Wagner Act.

Largely lacking, even still in the 1990s, are such rights long accepted in other countries, as the right to a job, to free and adequate health care, to shelter and nourishment, to child care. Largely lacking too—as though they lie beyond the hopes of all but utopian dreamers or are utterly unrealistic in the American context—are visions and plans and programs that could reach to the very source of economic and political malaise and that may require a reconstruction of the social and political system.

Americans have long disagreed, of course, on the desirability of rights measures. On the whole American conservatives have opposed them, neither expecting nor really wanting them to be beneficial. On the whole liberals and many radicals have welcomed, even fought for, rights legislation, disagreeing with conservatives as to both its theoretical merit and its potential practical effect. But on one criterion both sides have tended to agree—the test of opportunity. Whether it was Herbert Hoover contending that all should have an equal place on the starting line, or women's rights leaders seeking to open up blocked-off career avenues for women, or supporters of desegregation or affirmative action, leaders of the right, left, or center have agreed broadly on the virtues of something they would call "equal opportunity."

But did equal opportunity mean real and effective opportunity? Was it enough that a family provide its children with food and clothing, that the state provide "equal" education, that employers provide a vague "fairness" in hiring? Or was the question less whether, for instance, children had the bare right to attend school, but whether they had been furnished with enough parental guidance and support, enough nurturing day care, enough nutrition and health care, enough exposure to books, music, and art, enough inspirational teachers and other motivational influences, enough psychological counseling if needed, to want schooling, to stick with it, to make the most of it as a springboard to further effort? Women have found that while suffrage might open one door of opportunity, in itself it would not assure the opening of another; even more crucial are women's educational opportunities, job availability, child care. Workers would want the opportunity not just to join the union of their choice, to earn a livable wage, and to be free from unsafe working conditions, but to engage in creative and self-fulfilling labor. The virtual reduction of "equal opportunity" to individualistic competition has been used to deny African-Americans as a group access to the substantive resources that might make that opportunity real.

The test, in short, is real opportunity, and the question becomes: why have not the national, state, and local governments been more effective in helping people—especially disadvantaged people with acute needs—to win that real opportunity in a country that has boasted of itself as the "land of opportunity"?

THIS QUESTION requires a close look at the institutional and political structures in which policy is made in the United States. Leaders of campaigns to expand rights and secure real opportunity inevitably encounter those structures, and the broader the rights demands, the more deeply entangled with institutions the reformers become. The checks and balances, established by the framers of the Constitution to thwart governmental interference with individual liberties, especially property rights, operate even more effectively to bar economic and social extensions of the Bill of Rights. It has been common for rights measures to pass in one chamber of Congress and be vetoed by the other, to pass the two houses and be vetoed by the president, to pass through both "political" branches and be vetoed by the judiciary, to become established in law and then be starved of funds and personnel, to be enforced halfheartedly, or only as a result of grass-roots pressure.

Rights activists face the same problem at the state and municipal levels, which have their own checks and balances and bureaucratic obstructions. Beyond this, the framers so craftily divided governmental power that Washington and the state capitals can pass the buck back and forth between one another. And state governments have the further excuse for evading responsibility, that much as they might wish to respond to demands for rights, they fear that other states will not respond—will not lift minimum wages or bar child labor or raise compensation requirements for injuries on the job—and hence that they will be put at a competitive disadvantage.

All this has been familiar to Americans since the government got under way in 1789—familiar even earlier to the founders, who planned it all—but the question is what to do about it. Perhaps nothing; the present system serves many interests with a stake in passive government. "If it ain't broke," the saying goes, "don't fix it." But the system poses enormous difficulties for rights activists and claimants, who typically seek from government comprehensive changes that threaten varieties of interests, many of them "vested" or rooted. For rights activists the system *is* broke and needs to be fixed.

One of the oldest dilemmas facing such activists has been whether and how to ally themselves with, or work through, one or both of the major parties. The huge ongoing constituencies of the parties, their power to frame and advertise platforms, and above all their direct control of the nominating process at every level of government—all these have made the parties tempting targets for co-optation. But rights reformers, through bitter experience, have learned that they themselves are more likely to be co-opted—their forces and resources used for party purposes, while their programs are swallowed up, suppressed, morselized or shoved aside, or ignored following party victory. They have been discouraged by the lack of democracy or representation in parties labeled "republican" and "democratic," the dominance of money, the tawdry aspects of party conventions and other conclaves.

Efforts to make state parties more participatory and representative have failed except in a handful of states such as Iowa and Massachusetts. Amid the reform spirit of the 1960s and 1970s the national Democratic Party opened its ranks to rights activists when it adopted a charter that provided for midterm national issues conferences to draw up interim party platforms without the distractions and high jinks of a presidential nominating contest. Women's rights and black rights activists and other "movement" representatives took part in the first of these conferences in 1978 and its 1982 successor, both turbulent but constructive affairs. That was the end of the issues conferences: the whole enterprise was called off in 1985 by the Democratic National Committee. Evidently the Washington establishment feared loss of control. The venture has not been resumed, even in later years when the party badly needed new blood, vigor, and ideas.

Yet if they shunned the major parties rights leaders and activists would cut themselves off from one of the key levers of power in the American political system. Or were there other ways to make that system more responsive to those millions of Americans still trying to realize their rights to political, economic, and social freedoms?

AN ALTERNATIVE was to restructure the government through major constitutional reformation. Rights leaders who favored this path argued as follows: The only hope for sweeping progress in the United States lay in the formation among rights claimants of wide electoral alliances that could gain control of the national government—the kind of thing that happened partly by plan and partly by chance when activists achieved some rights progress under Franklin Roosevelt and Lyndon Johnson. But the system of checks and balances in effect precluded majority rule at the national level, since minorities could exercise veto power through Senate or House or the courts. The most logical solution would be to make the choice the framers shunned: setting up a straight parliamentary system, like those in most democracies around the globe, that would operate on the basis of strict majority rule. Then if the rights alliance gained the support of a majority of voters, that support would be translated directly into majority rule through a single representative chamber of parliament, with no veto in the hands of the executive.

This structural reform has been proposed for more than a century, not only by liberals and radicals but also by conservatives seeking efficient, streamlined, and responsible government. The proposal has gotten nowhere with public or press or most politicians: it sounds too drastic, too "un-American," it is repugnant to the powerful national strain of Constitution worship and raises fears of majority tyranny and the suppression of minority rights. As an alternative some have urged adoption of mechanisms that would provide the essence of majority rule without raising the parliamentary bugaboo. To end staggered elections, which divide government and thwart popular majorities, presidents, senators, and representatives could be elected together on a "team ticket," all with four-year terms. To foster cohesion within the parties Congress might pass a law that would require all states to include a line or lever on federal election ballots enabling citizens to cast a straight vote for all of one party's candidates. The president might be given at least a limited power to dissolve Congress and call new elections, in the event of deadlock.

These proposals too have gotten nowhere. They too require "tampering" with the structures of the Constitution, and advocates of the parliamentary alternative contend that such moderate reform would not do the job while arousing as much opposition as their own recommendations.

Still, in a nation so given to economic and technological and social change throughout its history, the popular unwillingness to modernize the political system seems paradoxical. On closer scrutiny, this institutional conservatism appeared to rest in a concept of human nature that emphasized individuals' absorption in the pursuit of their own interests. This concept was not new; it could be traced back to the Greek Sophists. But it reached its full philosophical weight in the writings of Hobbes and Locke, and its full economic weight in laissez-faire—"jungle"—capitalism.

Politically this concept was reflected and reinforced in the static equilibrium of limited government and buttressed ideologically by the defense of individual liberty and property rights. The politicians and officials who emerged from this political culture, and who in turn reinforced it, were for the most part not leaders of vision and commitment but rather transactors, middlemen, who with great skill mediated among interests, brokered short-run compromises, fended off governmental regulation. They also articulated the rationale of the system, arguing that the sum of all individual interests equaled the public interest.

This kind of government, this kind of leadership, and the market society they have served, have not fostered—they have clearly impeded—the realization and expansion of rights through government in the United States, except for the property rights of some. Advances in rights have been achieved far more by grass-roots protesters, movement activists, and bold leaders—such as Martin Luther King, Jr., and his cadres, the

CIO militants of the 1930s, and two centuries of women pathfinders—than by even the most well-meaning political brokers of those days. Transactional leaders may be still less relevant in the years ahead, as the competition among rights claimants intensifies and as calls for new rights multiply—from the right of privacy to reproductive rights and sexual rights, to the right of personal fulfillment in every area of life, and even to the right to die.

Not merely changed institutions but a whole new way of thinking about leadership for rights and about rights themselves will be necessary for the successful pursuit of freedom and happiness.

NURTURING RIGHTS

TO THINK ABOUT RIGHTS in a wholly new way calls for rights claimants to make a leap of the imagination into a kind of intellectual shadowland. It means breaking out of the world of contractual rights in which Americans are so deeply immersed that they take it for granted, and plunging into a nascent world of nurturing rights. Currently some may live in that environment for a few years after birth and then largely abandon it for the familiar territory of impersonal contracts and fleeting personal contacts.

To make that leap into the world of nurturing rights, the best starting point is at the side of the newborn child, where—as was noted at the outset—rights begin. The birth of that infant establishes a claim to the right to survive and to grow, a right that must be assured first of all by the mother and other family members, who make up a "rights microcosm" of nurturing persons.

For centuries the family has been presented as a benign microcosmic model for the larger society. "The most ancient of all societies, and the only one that is natural, is the family," Rousseau wrote in 1762, and thus the family "may be called the first model of political societies," and "all, being born free and equal, alienate their liberty only for their own advantage." The family, wrote John Stuart Mill a century later, must be more than a school of obedience. "Justly constituted," it would be "the real school of the virtues of freedom," a "school of sympathy in equality, of living together in love, without power on one side or obedience on the other."

An ancient dream—and a dream often shattered on the rocks of social reality. The vast majority of American children, growing, going to school, taking jobs, enter a society far more patriarchal than nurturing or communitarian—a competitive, hierarchical society in which they will be treated generally as means to others' ends rather than as ends in themselves. The rights secured by justice, John Rawls argues, echoing Kant's central concern with human beings as ends in themselves, "are not subject to political bargaining or to the calculus of social interests." But it is precisely the bargaining among interests that dominates American political and social—and even intellectual—life.

Some feminists, notes Virginia Held, have urged that the right of women to enter freely and fairly into contractual relations in the broader society should be extended to their lives at home, with their mates and families. But other feminists have advocated the reverse process. "Instead of importing into the household principles derived from the marketplace," Held herself contends, "perhaps we should export to the wider society the relations suitable for mothering persons and children," so that relations in that wider society would be "characterized by more care and concern and openness and trust and human feeling than are the contractual bargains" in current political and economic life. Thus the household would replace the marketplace as a model for society.

Society as a caring, trusting "extended household"—would it also realize people's needs for personal and economic and social rights? Would it meet the test, in short, of real opportunity? This might be its supreme achievement. For the essence of the ideal nurturing family is not only caring and sharing but its willingness and capacity to open up opportunities for children to develop and pursue self-fulfillment, and to thwart the great enemies of the child's real opportunity, such as ill health, low motivation, emotional disability, damaged self-esteem. Could the potential of the nurturing family for fostering real opportunity be extended to the whole society?

TO PROPAGATE the ideal of nurturing parents, supportive families, caring households, and spread it to society at large—this has been the dream of visionaries for centuries. Utopian societies in the nineteenth century hoped to demonstrate that men and women might live in a spirit of communal equality, of loving solidarity, of mutual aid and protection. Religious communities sent out missionaries to preach Christian love and charity as well as hellfire and damnation. Populist farmers and others established economic cooperatives that incorporated family values of sharing and reciprocity on a larger scale.

Perhaps it would seem even more utopian today to expect that the ideal and the practices of the nurturing family could be extended to the broader society with more success than in the past. To achieve such an objective, rights activists and strategists would need first to identify and mobilize a huge coalition of Americans who would be devoted to the pursuit of nurturing rights for themselves and others. Next such a coalition must be ready either to form its own party or to convert an established party into a stronger rights force, and in either case to win elective offices. Yet the new coalition must be more than electoral if it expects to galvanize the commitment and moral passion needed to effect basic change; it must at the same time become a coalition of grass-roots activists and social movement groups involved in community organizing, direct action, and public education—a rich federation of diverse social forces. This broad rights coalition and its winning party must then be prepared to refashion governmental institutions, if necessary, in order to carry through rights legislation and implement it. And all these requisites would require something more—transforming leadership.

Does a "Great Majority" for the pursuit of rights lie out there for the mobilizing? One weakness of reform movements historically has been their certainty that their cause was so self-evidently just and noble that there must be a tremendous majority simply waiting to make it its own. Such a majority has rarely shown up at the polls on election day. Rights strategists would need to be realistic about potential support and the heavy task of mobilizing and extending it. They would have to understand too that most Americans think of rights not in terms of human, nurturing rights embedded in relationships and in an ethic of caring, but in terms of abstract Bill of Rights protections or individualistic and property-oriented economic rights.

Still, a Great Majority is there to be mobilized, in the homes and neighborhoods, schools and sanctuaries, streets and workplaces of the nation. It would include low-income workers, the inner-city and rural poor, activists in such human service professions as teaching and social work, peace activists, environmentalists. It would gather energy and staying power from millions of committed young people. Women of all ages—especially women of color—would be the common denominator and the unifying force in such a coalition and central to its leadership; women form the majority in most of these categories and constitute the great majority of those who are economically deprived or destitute. And women outnumber men in census tallies and voting rolls.

The numbers and the needs are there. Can they be mobilized? Success will turn largely on unity within and among the constituent groups, and unity in turn would depend on the capacity of such groups to rise above internal divisions and external rivalries to form the foundation of a rights majority. One of the striking aspects of these groups is how far they are fragmented into smaller, single-issue subgroups in many separate localities. Skillful negotiation would be needed to bring them together behind a program that transcended their differences, along with skillful arguments—most notably that their particular and separate goals have a far better chance of realization if they united in a Great Majority coalition to win political power.

To forge a majority that can win nationwide electoral power—this is the toughest endeavor of all. Indeed, the American system of checks and balances raises a series of hurdles that require activists to wage campaigns for president, senators, representatives, governors, and state legislators in staggered elections over an extended period. Forging a new majority would call for most of the traditional techniques of informing and registering would-be voters and getting them to the polls, but committed and savvy activists could do this with much more efficiency and spirit than is typically found in American elections today, especially if Congress finally passes an automatic and universal registration law, as proposed by Human SERVE and other organizations. The steadily falling numbers of voters indicate that the major parties do a poor job even by the criteria of conventional electioneering.

That decline in voting, so deplorable in itself, offers a special opportunity to a rights majority, for it can deploy its large array of troops on a smaller battlefield. Conventional politicians are particularly vulnerable in nominating contests, since primaries, even presidential primaries, attract exceptionally low turnouts. If a rights majority carefully marshaled supporters in crucial primary contests, it could secure a dominant role in the selection of nominees. Such an effort would call for big turnouts not only at the polls but at candidates' speeches and debates and at party conclaves, and for high-visibility rallies at key points in congressional, state, and presidential primary campaigns—in short, for directly confronting candidates with both the numbers and the determination of rights activists.

Standing above these tactical and organizational matters, for both the shorter and longer term, must be the moral and mobilizing power of the rights majority itself. Only an enduring and articulate commitment to overriding goals could carry a popular majority to continuing election victories. Only an abiding concern for the needs and aspirations and for the real opportunity of fellow Americans could sustain that commitment. Equally important would be the capacity to stand up against strong opposition, an opposition that should be regarded not as unfair or diabolical but rather as an opportunity to strengthen one's own ranks, to sharpen one's own commitment, and to pose for the American people policies and programs strikingly different from the consensus positions of the two major parties. Conflict has historically been the great engine of progressive politics in the United States; it could be a major weapon in the success of a Great Majority.

That success will turn ultimately on the capacity of a new majority to convert its principles into workable policies and programs. And that step will encounter perhaps the hardest obstacle—the intellectual and institutional resistance of the gridlocked political system to new initiatives and radical programs and to structural change. Systemic reform of the government would indeed require a great majority both quantitatively and qualitatively. Quantitatively, because sheer numbers in Congress and elsewhere would be essential to put through reforms when two-thirds majorities, for example, were required. Qualitatively because reformers would be so committed to rights purposes that they would adapt institutions to clear goals; they would restructure institutions to fit those objectives, in the process creating new centers of democratic power. In fashioning and implementing the necessary means to realize their ends, they would understand that just as ends should not be subordinated to means, neither should they unduly subordinate means to ends. Ends and means must be carefully matched since, as Gandhi stressed, means are ends-in-the-making.

FOR A GREAT MAJORITY to win power and put through a massive rights program will call for leadership of an extraordinary nature. Few contemporary American politicians could even begin to meet the tests of that kind of leadership. Today's standard practices of transactional leadership—the favor-swapping, the deal-making, the special-interest representation, all based on an ethic of calculated self-interest—are woefully inadequate, as two centuries of delay and deadlock have shown, to rise above brokerage and address the enduring wants, needs, and demands of millions of the less privileged.

Such large purposes call for a new generation of transforming leaders with the vision of a Thomas Jefferson or a Franklin Roosevelt, a Walter Reuther or a Martin Luther King, Jr.; and even more of an Elizabeth Cady Stanton, an Eleanor Roosevelt, an Ella Baker or Marian Wright Edelman. Far more important will be the leadership engendered at the grass roots. No fundamental advance in rights programs will be possible without the leadership of tens of thousands of activists, acting in the tradition of the agrarian rebels, the union militants, the black marchers and jailgoers who were the heart of the great radical and reform movements.

A Great Majority will depend heavily on the leadership of women, particularly women of color, who will face old hurdles and new. One of the oldest and highest is the assumption, "embedded in culture" and perpetuated by male scholars, in Sue Tolleson Rinehart's words, "that leadership would be exercised by physical males, and that the qualities of leadership are the qualities of masculinity." A related assumption is that if women do wish to lead, they must adopt traits of competitiveness, aggressiveness, person-to-person domination, on the model of former British Prime Minister Margaret Thatcher. Over the centuries femininity has been stereotyped as "dependent, submissive and conforming," in contrast to the masculine conception of leadership as command and control.

Ironically, it will be precisely these "feminine" qualities—better described as caring and sharing—that will be crucial to the leadership of a Great Majority. Feminist or nurturing leadership will draw its strength from the closeness of leaders to the evolving wants and needs of followers. The world of nurturing leadership and followership will not be hierarchical but mutually interactive, as leaders recognize the human wants of followers, legitimate them as needs, and begin to satisfy those needs. Followers, both fulfilled and emboldened as needs are met, will escalate their hopes and expectations; they will intensify their claims to entitlements and convert them into still higher demands on the leaders. Eventually, as leaders respond to followers' rising activism, they will in a sense become followers of their followers. Indeed the mutuality has been so deep in this spiral from wants to demands that the process is increasingly a reciprocal relation between leaders and followers in a dynamic interplay of forces, until leadership and followership are interwoven. Hierarchy and command yield to equality and mutuality.

Ultimately leadership means the exercise of power—the question is what kind of power, for the benefit of whom? A last intellectual barrier to feminist leadership is the contention that men know how to handle power—it is their daily currency—and women do not. Men's kind of power is defined in terms of certain resources—money, guns, status, connections. This definition of power, traditional in political science, is so inadequate as to be dangerously misleading. It is not these resources alone but whether and how activists and potential followers are motivated to make the best use of such resources as are available to them that is pivotal. This was one of the lessons of Vietnam—soldiers relatively poor in military resources but high in motivation and group support defeated soldiers armed with vast quantities of modern weapons but poorly motivated. Whether or not the traditional model of power will remain paramount in American politics and society will depend in part on the capacity of a Great Majority and its rights party to convert a collective desire for real opportunity into the motivational force behind dynamic social activism and the emergence of transformational leadership at all levels.

The prospects for success of a rights party are not high. The grip of tradition, intellectual rigidity, institutional gridlock, and transactional leadership is very strong. Even vitalizing our leadership, even mobilizing a new majority, even restructuring our institutions may not be enough.

We must ultimately make the most daring leap of all—to change ourselves, in our families and neighborhoods and communities.

EMPOWERING RIGHTS

FROM ROUSSEAU'S *Social Contract* to "second wave" feminist thinking of recent times, democratic theorists have faced the fact that people have to change themselves in order to make democracy work. Although the transformation of individuals and of institutions must reinforce each other, a critical mass of citizens with changed values, aspirations, and self-concepts would seem to be a precondition for building and sustaining an effective coalition for rights. Moreover, even if an electoral majority won sweeping legislative and constitutional reforms, little real social change would result if citizens were not motivated to actualize the new rights in their everyday lives.

American history abounds with precedent for rights creation from the bottom up. Over two centuries, millions of oppressed Americans defined and asserted basic entitlements long before these were officially recognized, and they transformed themselves in the process. The past generation has seen remarkable advances in the right to personal autonomy, particularly in areas of sexuality and "body rights." This right has been realized far more by individuals asserting it directly than by laws and court decisions that were, in fact, the consequence of people's changing conduct and expectations. For nurturing rights to achieve similar legitimacy in order to become the object of new national policies and programs, the informal practice of such rights would need to well up from the grass roots, prefiguring a nurturing society. A wide array of educational forums, organizing projects, community development efforts, and cooperative institutions would be needed to generate a base of common consciousness and commitment as catalyst for the large-scale implementation of nurturing rights by a restructured government. With transformation under way at the personal and community levels, the mobilization of a new majority would be less difficult to accomplish and more likely to translate new policies into real opportunity.

Thus the place to begin is with citizen education that would instill the nurturing rights ethic into the folkways and culture of the citizenry, a process of learning by doing in the spirit of John Dewey and Myles Horton.

Underlying nurturing rights is the assumption that rights are interwoven with responsibility. Unlike the liberal individualist paradigm that sees the individual as independent, unencumbered, and linked to others primarily by contract, nurturing rights are predicated upon people's interdependence and are constituted by social relationships. Feminists have taken the lead in showing that rights and an ethic of care are not contradictory. Carol Gilligan has illustrated how women have been socialized to perceive their claims to personhood as expressions of selfishness. But an underpinning of women's activism has been the opposite principle that asserting rights is a moral and social responsibility. Rather than dissolve "natural" bonds of family and community in order to promote individual claims, nurturing rights would involve a "morality of responsibility that knits such claims into a fabric of relationship, blurring the distinction between self and other through the representation of their interdependence." Self and other, individual and community, Gilligan suggests, would be experienced as "different but connected" not "separate and opposed." In some respects, as feminist practice has exemplified, individuality and community are less at odds than mutually reinforcing; the question becomes how to cultivate their cross-fertilization to bring out the best in each.

If nurturing rights are rooted in responsibility for oneself *and* for other people, not just in one's own circle but in the wider community, they are necessarily communal. While some communal rights, as Staughton Lynd stresses, involve means of political expression—the right to act in concert, for instance—the most vital are entitlements to social resources, such as universal child-care services, that aim to foster personal growth— physical, emotional, intellectual, cultural, spiritual. Thus nurturing rights would satisfy not only basic needs for nutrition, physical health, shelter, and a healthy environment, but such higher needs as education, cultural development, and emotional well-being, all of these in turn prerequisites to the fulfillment of everyone's right to individuality.

Moving beyond the liberal conception of rights as protections of due process and procedural fairness, nurturing rights are substantive, embodying explicit values and purposes. They would not jettison the liberal concern with process, however, but refashion it to serve directly these values and purposes. Substantive rights devoid of democratic process can be as deficient as procedural rights without concrete content. Animated by citizen responsibility and commitment, nurturing rights would combine substantive ends with modes of political participation and self-governance tailored to those ends. Socioeconomic entitlements would have democratic forms and mandates institutionally built in: for example, community-controlled health services, patient participation in federal AIDS policy-making, local planning councils for economic conversion of war industry, democratized welfare agencies. Such structures of grass-roots democracy would not be mere window dressing but empowered by law. The Johnson administration's war on poverty might have been more effective if its rhetoric of "maximum feasible participation" had been translated into real empowerment of poor people. Even if the implementation of nurturing rights required that revenue allocation and overall policy-making be somewhat centralized, the nature and delivery of services would have to be democratically determined in localities—and not, as with "revenue sharing," by unaccountable state and local bureaucracies. Democratic empowerment, through the integration of political and socioeconomic rights, would lie at the heart of nurturing rights.

TO EMPOWER THEMSELVES, people would need to alter both their identity as citizens and their conception of democracy. Citizenship, rather than merely an "outer frame" of duties such as voting, paying taxes, and obeying laws, would be experienced as "the core of our life," in Michael Walzer's formulation, which "assumes a closely knit body of citizens, its members committed to one another." Such an activist citizenship would express itself through the development of participatory democracy, an ideal crystallized in the 1962 "Port Huron Statement" of Students for a Democratic Society: "We would replace power rooted in possession, privilege, or circumstance by power and uniqueness rooted in love, reflectiveness, reason, and creativity. As a *social system* we seek the establishment of a democracy of individual participation, governed by two central aims: that the individual share in those social decisions determining the quality and direction of his life"; and that society be restructured to encourage both autonomy and common participation. Implicit in the SDS manifesto was the importance of combining movement-based grass-roots democracy with electoral politics, without compromising the former's principles, purposes, and passion.

Progress toward this ideal of democratic citizenship would not, however, replace a conformity of apathy with a conformity of activism, or substitute political duties for political rights. Participatory democracy would violate its own values if citizens did not have a right *not* to participate, or to participate differently or unconventionally. But perhaps as the experience of democracy came to mean more than hollow forms and smoke and mirrors, as it came to be a rewarding experience of fellowship and community and a means of enhancing self-esteem, self-confidence, and self-fulfillment, more and more people would rise to the challenge.

The new spirit of democratic citizenship would embrace an ongoing citizen responsibility not only to assert rights and strive to translate them into law but to engage actively in the further stages of implementation and enforcement. Reformers have proven more successful at legalizing rights than at actualizing them. Mobilizing diverse constituencies to push a comprehensive agenda of nurturing rights through a divided and sometimes deadlocked political system will not be easy. But no less formidable will be the continuing democratic process of deciding how the new entitlements, once enacted, should be put into effect.

Daunting dilemmas and differences will arise right away, threatening the endurance of the majority coalition. If, for whatever reasons, some rights had to be implemented before others, or for some groups ahead of others, how would these priorities be determined? How would various entitlements, especially economic ones, be fairly apportioned, given a national context of material and fiscal scarcity? If certain types of entitlement required a disproportionate share of resources, for an interim period at least, how would the groups having to make do with less be persuaded to cooperate, deferring what is due them? What if different rights seemed to clash, such as those to a decent livelihood and to a sustainable environment, or to free speech versus freedom from the discriminatory harassment of "hate speech"? Rights conflicts in the future will likely be less than in the past clear-cut clashes between "just" and "unjust" claims—as between the rights of slaves and of slaveholders—but will more tend to be conflicts between valid and even fundamental rights, each expressing cherished values and legitimate moral claims, which can be reconciled only through prudent and principled compromise.

Resolving such conflicts of rights will be a major purpose of the new, or renewed, institutions of participatory democracy that should foster the fullest possible debate and deliberation and ensure that all views are heard. Yet even the most appropriate structures to link ends and means would not succeed in reconciling serious differences without the commitment and perseverance of many citizens learning how to engage in constructive conflict. Transforming leadership will need to be cultivated at every level.

IS IT TOO LATE? Has the United States become so fragmented along crosscutting lines of class, race, ethnicity, gender, age, sexual orientation, culture, and education that it would be impossible to build a broad and powerful rights movement uniting diverse constituencies? Growing divisions, even within groups (such as African-Americans) previously more homogeneous, present the most fundamental obstacle to the creation of a new majority coalition. Is it pie-in-the-sky to imagine that social conflict can be waged constructively, without divisiveness, resentment, hostility, or violence, and within a larger context of solidarity? Here is the ultimate test of how far citizens can change their own values and attitudes.

As Audre Lorde, Charlotte Bunch, and other feminist thinkers have urged, citizens must learn to redefine and reclaim difference in order to bridge divisions. Throughout history, human differences have been distorted or misnamed in order to serve as tools of domination—racial distinction being the most odious example. Yet differences that to a large extent have been "socially constructed" can be reconstructed and turned into tools of empowerment. Speaking to women in particular, Lorde writes that "we must recognize differences among women who are our equals, neither inferior nor superior, and devise ways to use each others' difference to enrich our visions and our joint struggles. The future of our earth may depend upon the ability of all women to identify and develop new definitions of power and new patterns of relating across difference."

How can activist citizens, both women and men, recast differences as building blocks of authentic and lasting solidarity? Facing them honestly would help to overcome fears and prejudices and the perception of differences as more than they are. Moreover, seeing them clearly would enable diverse groups to understand not only their particular perspective in relation to others but the multiplicity of perspectives and the complex ways that these interact to constitute the social whole. If in the past, active citizenship and "civic virtue" were practiced mainly in homogeneous communities, the comprehension of multiple oppressions, needs, and aspirations might open the door to true citizenship in a heterogeneous, multicultural society. The more that differences are recognized and valued, the less difficulty citizens will have discovering and embracing what they have in common, and the more prepared they will be for trusting cooperation over the long haul.

In a sense activists "must strive to become 'one-woman coalitions,' " Bunch suggests, "capable of understanding and raising all issues of oppression and seeing our relationship to them—whites speaking about racism, heterosexuals about homophobia, the able-bodied about disabilities." The more that activists are able to gain a broadened, holistic view of social relationships—internalizing the ethic that "an injury to one is an injury to all"—the more personal wholeness they may come to feel as individuals. The surer their grasp of the multiplicity of social experience, the better equipped they will be to carry out a common program of nurturing rights that values equally the needs, expectations, and priorities of all groups.

A coalition for nurturing rights would thus diverge sharply from the traditional model that reflects the liberal individualist paradigm: coalitions motivated by narrow self-interest, entailing least common denominators, short-run goals, expedient compromise, and division—not difference—as the organizing principle. According to the old model, movements or pressure groups are "assumed to be competitive," Joshua

Cohen and Joel Rogers explain. Their coordination is "limited to select points of convergent interest" with no basis for "continuing coordination among fragmented groups." The guiding assumption is that no broader agreement is feasible and, ironically, that to pursue such agreement is itself divisive, threatening the fragile, superficial, and temporary "unity."

The concept of a coalition has to be redefined as an alliance or federation motivated by cooperation not competition, by common needs more than self-interest, and by respect for difference. "A true alliance is based upon some self-interest of each component group and a common interest into which they merge," Martin Luther King, Jr., wrote shortly before his death. "For an alliance to have permanence and loyal commitment from its various elements, each of them must have a goal from which it benefits and none must have an outlook in basic conflict with the others." As King associate Reverend James Lawson, Jr., has put it, each group's self-interest has to be "an enlightened self-interest within the context of the entire community." Tocqueville called this "self-interest rightly understood."

Perhaps women have begun to offer the answer. As the feminist movement has put diversity at the center, and as women of color have assumed more leadership, especially intellectual leadership, the formation of alliances—among women and with other rights forces—has become a growing priority. Theorists such as Lisa Albrecht, Rose Brewer, and Davida Alperin argue that alliances are essential to understand and confront the interconnectedness of political issues, particularly the simultaneous and interactive nature of various oppressions, by gender, race, class, and so forth. Unlike traditional coalitions, these alliances are intended to be "ongoing, long-term arrangements" for fundamental reform. Creating such alliances will mean learning how to make principled compromises, with people of diverse backgrounds, styles, and perspectives, that are in the long-run interest of all participants. This type of coalition activity "is not work done in your home," cautions singer-historian Bernice Johnson Reagon. "You shouldn't look for comfort." With feminists blazing the trail, alliance-building could be taken up as an intermediate objective by all progressive social movements, leading to a national federation of alliances that could exercise power both inside and outside political parties and the electoral system.

Forging movement alliances and fostering an activist citizenry would aim at the "structural renewal" of society, in Martin Buber's words, creating a more cooperative and nurturing society that would strive to fulfill pluralist ideals that have remained out of reach. The establishment of real pluralism is both more pressing and more possible (as well as more threatening to many whites) now that peoples of color, including many new immigrants from Latin America and Asia, are increasing their proportions at an unprecedented rate, and consequently their influence and power. Such pluralism would be more than the fruitful interaction of racial, ethnic, and other autonomous groups. The true measure of a pluralist society is the extent to which each group exercises equal political, economic, and cultural power. For power to be equalized, however, it would have to be democratized; for power to be democratized it would have to be transformed, replacing "power-over," power as control and manipulation, by "power-with," power widely shared, power as self-empowerment—above all, power as an enabling and energizing force, the capacity to nurture growth in human beings.

As power is transformed, democracy would take on new dimensions. It would mean not only the right of individuals to define their identities and determine their futures; and not only the right of groups and communities to preserve their autonomy and control their common life. Most important, it would mean the right of individuals and groups to participate fully in shaping the values, culture, priorities, and aims of the whole society.

At the dawn of the twentieth century, W. E. B. Du Bois cast light on the travail of African-Americans to hold on to their cultural roots while aspiring to make the nation better and happier for all. The black citizen did not seek to "Africanize America," Du Bois wrote in *The Souls of Black Folk*, "for America has too much to teach the world and Africa." Neither would this citizen "bleach his Negro soul in a flood of white Americanism, for he knows that Negro blood has a message for the world. He simply wishes to make it possible for a man to be both a Negro and an American, without being cursed and spit upon by his fellows, without having the doors of Opportunity closed roughly in his face."

The realization of equal participation in, and equal contribution to, the remaking of American society during its third century not only might create a nation of singular cultural and intellectual richness but might offer the best possibility for fulfilling the original American creed. Moreover, the growth of democracy might bolster the prospects for economic justice in an age of economic decline, while, to venture a utopian thought, gains in cultural wealth and in emotional and spiritual well-being might offset losses in material affluence—that is, for those who have enjoyed it. Still, it is likely to be an arduous journey forward, one that will call for new generations of Americans who have grown up in nurturing family, school, and community environments and will have learned since early childhood the value of personal empowerment.

Poet Langston Hughes, grandnephew of nineteenth-century black leader John Mercer Langston, voiced a bittersweet hope for the nation's

rebirth, and for the rebirth of the human rights whose promise lay at the
nation's core:

> O, let America be America again—
> The land that never has been yet. . . .
> O, yes,
> I say it plain,
> America never was America to me,
> And yet I swear this oath—
> America will be!

THE ENDLESS STRUGGLE

FROM NURTURING INFANTS to teaching youngsters to caring for needy adults, especially the elderly—from the battles for civil liberties and political rights to the forging of economic, social, and cultural bills of rights—from rights won from kings to contractual rights to nurturing rights—the struggle goes on. When and where will it end?

It will never end, in democratic societies. The struggle will continue as long as people's wants and needs grow, as long as the satisfaction of those needs leads to a demand for something more or different, whether in material or in cultural terms. It will continue as long as leaders and activists at all levels excite and respond to hopes and expectations, as long as followers greet those responses with higher hopes and expectations and with further demands on leaders. It will continue because people's strivings for self-fulfillment lie at the heart of the human condition.

Preserving old rights and seizing new ones will not come smoothly or harmoniously. Rising conflicts over rights may well overshadow past struggles in scope and intensity. Millions of Americans suffering deprivation and despair may finally declare and fight for their right to real opportunity, not merely formal or "equal" opportunity. Around the globe hundreds of millions of oppressed Chinese and South Asians, starving Africans, exploited Latin Americans will rise to demand their share of political and economic rights. Many will continue to assert the elementary right to emigrate as they confront the fortified border walls raised by their oppressors. Women worldwide who have borne and raised the children, done the cooking, collected the firewood, toted the water, and sown the crops with hand and stick will intensify their claims to a less burdensome existence, to the opportunity to cultivate their individuality. Stepped-up campaigns for these and other human rights will exacerbate conflicts within and among nations.

Nor will the conflicts involve simple divisions and clear-cut issues. In the United States, at least, it will not merely be a struggle between good guys and bad guys over rights, as in past battles between monopolists and the populace, police and workers, Ku Kluxers and black people. It will often be a struggle among a diversity of good guys with conflicting rights claims. Feminists seeking to censor pornography as a violation of women's civil rights will confront civil libertarians opposed to any infringement of the First Amendment at any time for any reason. Parents will continue to demand that their children be protected from the "explicit sex, violence, and satanic cultism" in rock music, and they will again confront defenders of free expression, as they did in the 1980s when the "Musical Majority" was rapidly organized by the ACLU. Such technological advances as computers and camcorders will generate ever sharper conflicts between people's right to information—their right to know—and their right to privacy. Women will differ among themselves over social and economic and political priorities and strategies, as will workers, people of color, community leaders and activists. Indeed, with affirmative action, people of color will face heightened competition not only among themselves but with less privileged whites.

Activists pursuing nurturing rights for all Americans will confront the most exacting challenges. They must take on the task of creating coalitions and generating efforts at empowerment on the grass-roots and community levels. In fashioning a Great Majority embracing men and women of all ages, creeds, colors, and ideologies, activists will have to cope with divisions among distinct constituencies. To build that majority they must regenerate the hopes and aspirations of Americans for significant social change.

How will rights speak to the aspirations of the nation's third century?

Life: Americans must reconceive this right not merely as the maintenance of national or personal security in the old, narrow, and negative senses, but as nurturing the material and spiritual lives and dreams of the whole people.

Liberty: Americans will need to guard the classic First Amendment and other constitutional rights against public and private power and at the same time press for freedom in a broader and deeper sense as the realization and expansion of economic and social rights through government.

The Pursuit of Happiness: What Jefferson had in mind when he placed

Happiness in the Declaration we will never know for sure, nor how he defined it. For the third century, the right to pursue happiness lies in real opportunity for individual self-fulfillment, the conditions for which can be created, paradoxically, only through collective leadership and action.

Epigraph: excerpted from an address, The Significance of Emancipation in the West Indies, delivered at Canandaigua, New York, August 3, 1857, in Douglass, *Papers,* John W. Blassingame, ed., series 1 (Yale University Press, 1979–   ), vol. 3, pp. 183–208, quoted at p. 204.

PROLOGUE

Moses and Exodus: Gaalyah Cornfeld, *Archaeology of the Bible: Book by Book* (Harper, 1976), esp. pp. 33–48; J. Severino Croatto, *Exodus: A Hermeneutics of Freedom,* Salvator Attanasio, trans. (Orbis, 1981); Lewis S. Feuer, *Ideology and the Ideologists* (Basil Blackwell, 1975), ch. 1; Paul Johnson, *A History of the Jews* (Harper, 1987), pp. 23–43; J. Maxwell Miller and John H. Hayes, *A History of Ancient Israel and Judah* (Westminster Press, 1986), esp. pp. 74–79; J. Coert Rylaarsdam, "Introduction: Exodus," in *The Interpreter's Bible* (Abingdon-Cokesbury Press, 1951–57), vol. 1, pp. 833–48; Daniel J. Silver, *Images of Moses* (Basic Books, 1982), esp. part 1; Michael Walzer, *Exodus and Revolution* (Basic Books, 1985); Aaron Wildavsky, *The Nursing Father: Moses as a Political Leader* (University of Alabama Press, 1984).

PAGE

4   [*"And it came to pass"*]: Exodus, 13:17–18, 21.

       [*"There remained"*]: Exodus, 14:28.

       [*"Fear ye not"*]: Exodus, 14:13–15.

       [*"Murmured against Moses"*]: Exodus, 15:24.

       [*"March toward a goal"*]: Walzer, p. 12.

5   [*"Grasped a liberating sense"*]: Croatto, p. 28.

       [*"Moral equality"*]: see Walzer, p. 84.

       [*"The covenant reflected"*]: *ibid.,* p. 80.

       [*"Only parallel of God's dealing"*]: quoted in *ibid.,* p. 4.

       [*Savonarola and Exodus*]: *ibid.,* p. 5.

6   [*"Radical contractualism"*]: *ibid.*

       [*"God's new Israel"*]: quoted in *ibid.,* p. 6.

       [*Franklin, Jefferson, and the Great Seal*]: *ibid.*

       [*"When Israel was in Egypt's land"*]: quoted in John Lovell, Jr., *Black Song:*

The Forge and the Flame (Macmillan, 1972; reprinted by Paragon House, 1986), p. 327.

1. THE BIRTH OF RIGHTS

13 [*"Unsteepled places"*]: see Thompson, *The Making of the English Working Class* (Victor Gollancz, 1963), p. 52.

DEFENDERS OF THE RIGHT

The Greeks: Aristotle, *Constitution of Athens and Related Texts,* Kurt von Fritz and Ernst Kapp, trans. (Hafner Press, 1974); Aristotle, *The Nicomachean Ethics,* Harris Rackham, trans. (Heinemann, 1926); Aristotle, *Politics,* Benjamin Jowett, trans. (Random House, 1943); M. I. Finley, *Democracy Ancient and Modern* (Rutgers University Press, 1973); Eric A. Havelock, *The Liberal Temper in Greek Politics* (Jonathan Cape, 1957); Donald Kagan, *The Great Dialogue: History of Greek Political Thought from Homer to Polybius* (Free Press, 1965); Plato, *Dialogues,* Benjamin Jowett, trans., 5 vols., 3rd ed. (Oxford University Press, 1924); George H. Sabine, *A History of Political Theory,* rev. ed. (Holt, 1950), part 1; R. K. Sinclair, *Democracy and Participation in Athens* (Cambridge University Press, 1988); Leo Strauss, *Natural Right and History* (University of Chicago Press, 1953), chs. 3–4; Sheldon S. Wolin, *Politics and Vision: Continuity and Innovation in Western Political Thought* (Little, Brown, 1960), ch. 2; Ellen Meiksins Wood and Neal Wood, *Class Ideology and Ancient Political Theory: Socrates, Plato, and Aristotle in Social Context* (Basil Blackwell, 1978).

The Romans: Cicero, *De Re Publica/De Legibus,* Clinton W. Keyes, trans. (Heinemann, 1928); F. R. Cowell, *Cicero and the Roman Republic* (Chanticleer Press, 1948); Sabine, ch. 9; Strauss, ch. 5; Wolin, ch. 3; Neal Wood, *Cicero's Social and Political Thought* (University of California Press, 1988).

Early Christian political thought: Augustine, *The City of God Against the Pagans,* George E. McCracken et al., eds., 7 vols. (Heinemann, 1957–72); Augustine, *Confessions,* William Watts, trans., 2 vols. (Heinemann, 1912); P. R. L. Brown, "Political Society," in R. A. Markus, ed., *Augustine* (Anchor, 1972), pp. 311–35; Herbert A. Deane, *The Political and Social Ideas of St. Augustine* (Columbia University Press, 1963); Sabine, ch. 10; Wolin, ch. 4.

The Middle Ages: Aquinas, *Selected Political Writings,* A. P. D'Entrèves, ed., J. G. Dawson, trans. (Basil Blackwell, 1959); Frederick Copleston, *Thomas Aquinas* (Search Press, 1976), esp. ch. 5; Jack Donnelly, "Natural Law and Natural Right in Aquinas' Political Thought," *Western Political Quarterly,* vol. 33, no. 4 (December 1980), pp. 520–35; D. J. O'Connor, *Aquinas and Natural Law* (Macmillan, 1967); Sabine, chs. 11–15; Walter Ullmann, *The Individual and Society in the Middle Ages* (Johns Hopkins Press, 1966).

The Reformation: W. D. J. Cargill Thompson, *The Political Thought of Martin Luther,* Philip Broadhead, ed. (Harvester Press, 1984); Norman Cohn, *The Pursuit of the Millennium* (Secker & Warburg, 1957), esp. chs. 11–12; Erik H. Erikson, *Young Man Luther* (Norton, 1962); Richard Friedenthal, *Luther,* John Nowell, trans. (Harcourt, 1970); Lewy, ch. 5; Martin Luther, *Reformation Writings,* Bertram Lee Wolff, trans., vol. 1 (Philosophical Library, 1953); Sabine, chs. 18–19; Wolin, chs. 5–6.

PAGE
14   [*Plato on democratic man*]: *Republic,* in Plato, *Dialogues,* vol. 3, p. 269.
15   [*"Beat or maltreat his slaves"*]: Sinclair, p. 28.
        [*"Eternal and unchangeable law"*]: Cicero, *De Re Publica,* p. 211.
17   [*"Noble Christian liberty"*]: Luther, *The Pagan Servitude of the Church: A First Inquiry,* in *Reformation Writings,* vol. 1, pp. 208–329, quoted at p. 224.
        [*"Hammered out on the roads"*]: Friedenthal, pp. 96–97.
18   [*"Outward peace"*]: quoted in Wolin, p. 161.
        [*Greek "liberals"*]: Havelock; Wood and Wood.

RIGHTS FOR ALL?

Enlightenment: Ernst Cassirer, *The Philosophy of the Enlightenment,* Fritz C. A. Koelln and James P. Pettegrove, trans. (Princeton University Press, 1968); Alfred Cobban, *In Search of Humanity: The Role of the Enlightenment in Modern History* (Jonathan Cape, 1960); Peter Gay, *The Enlightenment,* 2 vols. (Knopf, 1966–69); Kingsley Martin, *The Rise of French Liberal Thought,* J. P. Mayer, ed. (New York University Press, 1956); Roy Porter and Mikuláš Teich, eds., *The Enlightenment in National Context* (Cambridge University Press, 1981); Charles G. Stricklen, Jr., "The *Philosophe*'s Political Mission: The Creation of an Idea, 1750–1789," *Studies on Voltaire and the Eighteenth Century,* Theodore Besterman, ed., vol. 86 (1971), pp. 137–228.

Hobbes and Locke: Richard Ashcraft, *Revolutionary Politics & Locke's* Two Treatises of Government (Princeton University Press, 1986); Deborah Baumgold, *Hobbes's Political Theory* (Cambridge University Press, 1988), esp. ch. 2; Thomas Hobbes, *De Cive,* Howard Warrender, ed. (Clarendon Press, 1983); Hobbes, *The Elements of Law, Natural and Politic,* Ferdinand Tonnies, ed. (Barnes & Noble, 1969); Hobbes, *Leviathan,* Michael Oakeshott, ed. (Basil Blackwell, 1947); John Locke, *An Essay Concerning Human Understanding,* John W. Yolton, ed., 2 vols., rev. ed. (Dent, 1965); Locke, *Of Civil Government* (Dent, 1924); Locke, *Some Thoughts Concerning Education* (Cambridge University Press, 1880); C. B. Macpherson, "Natural Rights in Hobbes and Locke," in D. D. Raphael, ed., *Political Theory and the Rights of Man* (Indiana University Press, 1967), pp. 1–15; Macpherson, *The Political Theory of Possessive Individualism: Hobbes to Locke* (Clarendon Press, 1962); J. A. Passmore, "The Malleability of Man in Eighteenth-Century Thought," in Earl R. Wasserman, ed., *Aspects of the Eighteenth Century* (Johns Hopkins Press, 1965), pp. 21–46; Raymond Polin, "The Rights of Man in Hobbes and Locke," Sylvia Raphael, trans., in Raphael, pp. 16–26; Martin Seliger, *The Liberal Politics of John Locke* (Praeger, 1969); Seliger, "Locke's Theory of Revolutionary Action," *Western Political Quarterly,* vol. 16, no. 3 (September 1963), pp. 548–68; Strauss, ch. 5; Richard Tuck, *Natural Rights Theories: Their Origin and Development* (Cambridge University Press, 1979), esp. ch. 6; Howard Warrender, *The Political Philosophy of Hobbes: His Theory of Obligation* (Clarendon Press, 1957), esp. ch. 8; Wolin, chs. 8–9.

English Civil War: H. N. Brailsford, *The Levellers and the English Revolution,* Christopher Hill, ed. (Cresset Press, 1961); C. H. Firth, ed., *The Clarke Papers* (Camden Society, 1891), vol. 1; Maurice Goldsmith, "Levelling by Sword, Spade and Word: Radical Egalitarianism in the English Revolution," in Colin Jones et al., eds., *Politics and People in Revolutionary England* (Basil Blackwell, 1986), pp. 65–80; William Haller, ed., *Tracts on Liberty in the Puritan Revolution, 1638–1647,* 3 vols. (Columbia University Press, 1934); Haller and Godfrey Davies, eds., *The Leveller Tracts, 1647–1653* (Peter Smith, 1964); Christopher Hill, *The World Turned Upside Down: Radical Ideas during the English Revolution* (Penguin, 1975); Macpherson,

Possessive Individualism, esp. ch. 3; Sabine, chs. 24–25; Tuck, ch. 7; Austin Woolrych, "Putney Revisited: Political Debate in the New Model Army in 1647," in Jones et al., pp. 95–116; Perez Zagorin, *A History of Political Thought in the English Revolution* (Routledge & Kegan Paul, 1954).

PAGE

18   [*"Century of the Enlightenment"*]: Gay, vol. 2, p. 3.

19   [*"Lord and master"*]: modified from *Discourse on the Method,* in Descartes, *Philosophical Writings,* John Cottingham et al., trans. (Cambridge University Press, 1984–85), vol. 1, pp. 142–43.
      [*"Architect of his fortune"*]: quoted in Gay, vol. 2, p. 6.
      [*"Solitary, poor"*]: Hobbes, *Leviathan,* p. 82.

20   [*"Of all the Men"*]: Locke, *Concerning Education,* p. 1.

22   [*"First of all that fled"*]: Hobbes, "Considerations upon the Reputation, Loyalty, Manners, and Religion of Thomas Hobbes," in Hobbes, *The English Works,* William Molesworth, ed. (John Bohn, 1839–45), vol. 4, pp. 412–40, quoted at p. 414.
      [*Levellers as England's first left-wing party*]: Zagorin, p. 6.
      [*Excerpts from army debates*]: *Clarke Papers,* vol. 1, Wildman quoted at p. 260, Pettus at p. 300, Rainborow at p. 301, Sexby at pp. 322–23.

23   [*"Commoners by right"*]: Thomas Edwards, quoted in Sabine, p. 482.
      [*"Nott finde any thinge"*]: quoted in *Clarke Papers,* vol. 1, p. 304.
      [*"Thou shalt nott steale"*]: *ibid.,* p. 310.
      [*Pettus's reply to Ireton*]: *ibid.,* p. 312.
      [*"Cheif end"*]: *ibid.,* p. 320.
      [*"Qualifications to bee sett downe"*]: *ibid.,* pp. 363–67, quoted at p. 366.

24   [*Lilburne on "illegalitie" of proceedings against Charles*]: Lilburne, *The Legall Fundamentall Liberties of the People of England* (1649), in Haller and Davies, *Leveller Tracts,* pp. 398–449, quoted at p. 422.

LAWS OF FREEDOM AND HAPPINESS

Winstanley and the Diggers: Goldsmith; Hill, *World Turned Upside Down,* esp. ch. 7 passim; David W. Petegorsky, *Left-Wing Democracy in the English Civil War: A Study of the Social Philosophy of Gerrard Winstanley* (Victor Gollancz, 1940); Sabine, pp. 490–95; Gerrard Winstanley, *Works,* George H. Sabine, ed. (Cornell University Press, 1941); Zagorin, ch. 4.

Rousseau: Cassirer, pp. 258–74; Cobban, ch. 17; Stephen Ellenburg, *Rousseau's Political Philosophy: An Interpretation from Within* (Cornell University Press, 1976); Gay, vol. 2, pp. 529–52; Martin, ch. 8; Passmore; Kennedy F. Roche, *Rousseau: Stoic & Romantic* (Methuen, 1974), esp. ch. 10; Jean Jacques Rousseau, *Discourse on the Origins and Foundations of Inequality,* in Rousseau, *The First and Second Discourses,* Roger D. Masters, ed. and trans., Judith R. Masters, trans. (St. Martin's Press, 1964), pp. 101–228; Rousseau, *The Social Contract and Discourses,* G. D. H. Cole, trans. (E. P. Dutton, 1950); Sabine, ch. 28.

Scottish Enlightenment: David Daiches et al., eds., *A Hotbed of Genius: The Scottish Enlightenment, 1730–1790* (Edinburgh University Press, 1986); Daiches, *The Scottish Enlightenment* (Saltire Society, 1986); Francis Hutcheson, *An Essay on the Nature and Conduct of the Passions and Affections, with Illustrations on the Moral Sense,* 3rd ed. (1742; reprinted by Scholars' Facsimiles & Reprints, 1969); Hutcheson, *An Inquiry into the Original of Our Ideas of Beauty and Virtue,* 2nd ed. (1726); Hutcheson, *A System of Moral Philosophy,* 2 vols. (1755); James Moore, "The Two Systems of Francis Hutcheson: On the Origins of the Scottish Enlightenment," in M. A. Stewart, ed.,

Studies in the Philosophy of the Scottish Enlightenment (Clarendon Press, 1990), pp. 37–59; Nicholas Phillipson, "The Scottish Enlightenment," in Porter and Teich, pp. 19–40; William R. Scott, *Francis Hutcheson* (Cambridge University Press, 1900); Robert Shackleton, "The Greatest Happiness of the Greatest Number: The History of Bentham's Phrase," *Studies on Voltaire and the Eighteenth Century,* Theodore Besterman, ed., vol. 90 (1972), pp. 1461–82; W. L. Taylor, *Francis Hutcheson and David Hume as Predecessors of Adam Smith* (Duke University Press, 1965); Garry Wills, *Inventing America: Jefferson's Declaration of Independence* (Doubleday, 1978).

PAGE

24   [*"Give a reasoned elaboration"*]: Zagorin, p. 56.
25   [*"Most Lawes"*]: *A New-Yeers Gift for the Parliament and Armie* (1650), in Winstanley, *Works,* pp. 351–96, quoted at p. 388.
         [*"O you* A-dams*"*]: *The True Levellers Standard Advanced* (1649), in *ibid.,* pp. 245–66, quoted at p. 264.
         [*Winstanley anticipating Rousseau*]: see Sabine, p. 492.
         [*"Whoever refuses to obey"*]: Rousseau, *Social Contract,* p. 18.
         [*"Every man has naturally a right"*]: *ibid.,* p. 20.
         [*"Usurpations of the rich"*]: Rousseau, *Discourse on Inequality,* p. 157.
26   [*"At what is called"*]: Mr. Amyat, King's Chemist, quoted in David Daiches, "The Scottish Enlightenment," in Daiches et al., *Hotbed of Genius,* p. 1.
         [*Hutcheson as one of "fortune's favorites"*]: see Scott, p. 37.
27   [*"Many have been discouraged"*]: Hutcheson, *Nature and Conduct,* p. v.
         ["Our moral Sense"]: Hutcheson, *Inquiry into the Original,* pp. 177–78.
         [*Hutcheson's formulae*]: see *ibid.,* pp. 182–88, esp. pp. 185, 188.
         [*Shackleton on Hutcheson*]: Shackleton, p. 1467.
         [*"Desire the greatest happiness"*]: Hutcheson, *System of Moral Philosophy,* vol. 1, p. 10.

2 . THE NEW WORLD OF RIGHTS

European images of America: Henry Steele Commager, *The Empire of Reason* (Doubleday/Anchor, 1977), esp. chs. 3–5; Oscar Handlin, "The Significance of the Seventeenth Century," in Paul Goodman, ed., *Essays in American Colonial History* (Holt, Rinehart and Winston, 1967; reprinted by Books for Libraries Press, 1970), pp. 97–107; Hugh Honour, *The European Vision of America,* exhibition catalogue (Cleveland Museum of Art, 1975); Howard Mumford Jones, *O Strange New Land* (Viking, 1964), chs. 1–2.

Religion and liberty in colonial America: Jack P. Greene and William G. McLoughlin, *Preachers & Politicians* (American Antiquarian Society, 1977); Perry Miller, "The Contribution of the Protestant Churches to Religious Liberty in Colonial America," in Goodman, pp. 542–51; Miller and Thomas H. Johnson, "The Theory of the State and Society," in *ibid.,* pp. 137–51; Edmund S. Morgan, *The Puritan Dilemma: The Story of John Winthrop* (Little, Brown, 1958); J. R. Pole, *The Pursuit of Equality in American History* (University of California Press, 1978), ch. 3; Clinton Rossiter, *Seedtime of the Republic* (Harcourt, 1953), esp. chs. 2, 6–9.

PAGE

29   [*"Dragons, Droves of Devils"*]: quoted in Commager, *Empire,* p. 65.
30   [*"Just and equall laws"*]: Howard W. Preston, ed., *Documents Illustrative of American History, 1606–1863,* 6th ed. (Putnam, 1902), pp. 30–31, quoted at p. 30.

30   [*Puritan leader on dissenters*]: Nathaniel Ward, cited in Miller and Johnson,
         p. 141.
         [*"Divers dangerous opinions"*]: journal of John Winthrop, entry of July 8,
         1635, quoted in Rossiter, *Seedtime*, p. 182.

RIGHTS—CORNUCOPIA FOR SOME

Migration of European ideas to America: Bernard Bailyn, *The Ideological Origins of the American Revolution* (Belknap Press of Harvard University Press, 1967), ch. 2, and passim; Roland Bainton, "The Appeal to Reason and the American Constitution," in Conyers Read, ed., *The Constitution Reconsidered* (Columbia University Press, 1938), pp. 121–30; John Clive and Bernard Bailyn, "England's Cultural Provinces: Scotland and America," in Goodman, pp. 619–32; H. Trevor Colbourn, *The Lamp of Experience: Whig History and the Intellectual Origins of the American Revolution* (University of North Carolina Press, 1965); Commager, *Empire;* Paul Conkin, review of Garry Wills, *Inventing America: Jefferson's Declaration of Independence* (Doubleday, 1978), *American Historical Review*, vol. 84, no. 2 (April 1979), pp. 530–31; Ronald Hamowy, "Jefferson and the Scottish Enlightenment: A Critique of Garry Wills's *Inventing America,"* *William and Mary Quarterly*, 3rd series, vol. 36, no. 4 (October 1979), pp. 509–23; Richard L. Hillard, "Liberalism, Civic Humanism and the American Revolutionary Bills of Rights, 1775–1790," paper prepared for delivery at the 1988 annual meeting of the Organization of American Historians; Philip B. Kurland, "Magna Carta & Constitutionalism in the United States: 'The Noble Lie,' " in Samuel E. Thorne et al., *The Great Charter* (Pantheon, 1965), pp. 48–74 passim; Staughton Lynd, *Intellectual Origins of American Radicalism* (Pantheon, 1968), part 1; Kenneth S. Lynn, "Falsifying Jefferson" (review of Wills, *Inventing America*), *Commentary*, vol. 66, no. 10 (October 1978), pp. 66–71; Forrest McDonald, *Novus Ordo Seclorum: The Intellectual Origins of the Constitution* (University Press of Kansas, 1985); Pauline Maier, *From Resistance to Revolution: Colonial Radicals and the Development of American Opposition to Britain, 1765–1776* (Knopf, 1972), esp. ch. 2; Richard K. Matthews, *The Radical Politics of Thomas Jefferson: A Revisionist View* (University Press of Kansas, 1984), ch. 1; Henry F. May, *The Enlightenment in America* (Oxford University Press, 1976); J. R. Pole, review of Wills, *Inventing America, Journal of American Studies*, vol. 13, no. 2 (August 1979), pp. 271–74; Bernard Schwartz, *The Great Rights of Mankind: A History of the American Bill of Rights* (Oxford University Press, 1977), esp. ch. 1; Paul M. Spurlin, *The French Enlightenment in America* (University of Georgia Press, 1984); Morton White, *The Philosophy of the American Revolution* (Oxford University Press, 1978); Wills, *Inventing America;* Gordon S. Wood, *The Creation of the American Republic, 1776–1787* (University of North Carolina Press, 1969).

Rights and liberties in colonial America: James Alexander, *A Brief Narrative of the Case and Trial of John Peter Zenger, Printer of The New York Weekly Journal*, Stanley N. Katz, ed. (Belknap Press of Harvard University Press, 1963); Bailyn, *Ideological Origins*, esp. pp. 175–98; Bernard Bailyn, ed., *Pamphlets of the American Revolution, 1750–1776* (Belknap Press of Harvard University Press, 1965), vol. 1, esp. "General Introduction," chs. 4, 6–7; Leonard W. Levy, *Constitutional Opinions: Aspects of the Bill of Rights* (Oxford University Press, 1986), chs. 3–4; Levy, *Emergence of a Free Press* (Oxford University Press, 1985), chs. 1–6 passim; Lynd, *Intellectual Origins*, esp. ch. 2; McDonald, *Novus Ordo*, chs. 1–2 passim; Miller, "Contribution"; Miller and Johnson, "Theory of State and Society"; John P. Reid, *The Concept of Liberty in the Age of the American Revolution* (University of Chicago Press, 1988); Rossiter, *Seedtime*, parts 1–2 passim; Schwartz, *Great Rights*, ch. 2; Bernard Schwartz, ed.,

The Roots of the Bill of Rights (Chelsea House, 1980), vol. 1, part 2; Wood, *Creation,* esp. ch. 1.

Equality in theory and practice in colonial America: Sidney H. Aronson, *Status and Kinship in the Higher Civil Service* (Harvard University Press, 1964), ch. 3; Philip S. Foner, *Labor and the American Revolution* (Greenwood Press, 1976), ch. 1; Jack P. Greene and J. R. Pole, eds., *Colonial British America* (Johns Hopkins University Press, 1984), chs. 8–9; Staughton Lynd, *Class Conflict, Slavery, and the United States Constitution* (Bobbs-Merrill, 1967), esp. ch. 2 passim; McDonald, *Novus Ordo,* pp. 53–55; Jackson Turner Main, *The Social Structure of Revolutionary America* (Princeton University Press, 1965); Pole, *Pursuit of Equality,* chs. 1–4; Rossiter, *Seedtime,* pp. 19–21, and chs. 3–4 passim; Arthur M. Schlesinger, "The Aristocracy in Colonial America," in Goodman, pp. 524–41; Wood, *Creation,* pp. 70–75.

The disadvantaged and dispossessed in colonial America: Bailyn, *Ideological Origins,* pp. 232–46; Mary Sumner Benson, *Women in Eighteenth-Century America: A Study of Opinion and Social Usage* (Columbia University Press, 1935); Richard S. Dunn, "Servants and Slaves: The Recruitment and Employment of Labor," in Greene and Pole, pp. 157–94; Wilbur R. Jacobs, *Dispossessing the American Indian: Indians and Whites on the Colonial Frontier* (Scribner, 1972); Linda K. Kerber, *Women of the Republic: Intellect and Ideology in Revolutionary America* (University of North Carolina Press, 1980); Duncan J. MacLeod, *Slavery, Race and the American Revolution* (Cambridge University Press, 1974); Julie A. Matthaei, *An Economic History of Women in America* (Schocken, 1982), part 1; Herbert Moller, "Sex Composition and Correlated Culture Patterns of Colonial America," *William and Mary Quarterly,* 3rd series, vol. 2, no. 2 (April 1945), pp. 113–53; Francis Paul Prucha, *The Great Father: The United States Government and the American Indians* (University of Nebraska Press, 1984), vol. 1, pp. 5–33; Donald L. Robinson, *Slavery in the Structure of American Politics, 1765–1820* (Harcourt, 1971), chs. 1–3; Rossiter, *Seedtime,* pp. 90–92, 99–100.

Paine and Common Sense: Moncure Daniel Conway, *The Life of Thomas Paine,* 2 vols. (Putnam, 1892); Eric Foner, *Tom Paine and Revolutionary America* (Oxford University Press, 1976); Jack P. Greene, "Paine, America and the 'Modernization' of Political Consciousness," *Political Science Quarterly,* vol. 93, no. 1 (Spring 1978), pp. 73–92; Thomas Paine, *Writings,* Moncure Daniel Conway, ed., 4 vols. (Putnam, 1894–96).

Popular mobilization against Britain: Bailyn, *Pamphlets;* Edward Countryman, *A People in Revolution: The American Revolution and Political Society in New York, 1760–1790* (Johns Hopkins University Press, 1981); Philip Davidson, *Propaganda and the American Revolution, 1763–1783* (University of North Carolina Press, 1941); Foner, *Paine,* esp. chs. 2, 4; Foner, *Labor,* chs. 2–8; Ronald Hoffman, *A Spirit of Dissension: Economics, Politics, and the Revolution in Maryland* (Johns Hopkins University Press, 1973); Maier; Lee N. Newcomer, *The Embattled Farmers: A Massachusetts Countryside in the American Revolution* (King's Crown Press of Columbia University Press, 1953); Rossiter, *Seedtime,* part 3 passim; Richard A. Ryerson, *The Revolution Is Now Begun: The Radical Committees of Philadelphia, 1765–1776* (University of Pennsylvania Press, 1978); Schwartz, *Great Rights,* ch. 3.

Jefferson and the Declaration: Edward Dumbauld, *The Declaration of Independence and What It Means Today* (University of Oklahoma Press, 1950); Hamowy; David Hawke, *A Transaction of Free Men: The Birth and Course of the Declaration of Independence* (Scribner, 1964); Dumas Malone, *Jefferson and His Time* (Little, Brown, 1948–81), vol. 1, ch. 16; Ursula M. von Eckardt, *The Pursuit of Happiness in the Democratic Creed: An Analysis of Political Ethics* (Praeger, 1959); Wills, *Inventing America.*

PAGE

32   [*Burke on American Protestants*]: speech on conciliation with America, March 22, 1775, in Burke, *Works*, rev. ed. (Little, Brown, 1866–67), vol. 2, pp. 101–86, quoted at pp. 122, 123.

    [*"Bible as it was variously interpreted"*]: Appleby, "The American Heritage: The Heirs and the Disinherited," *Journal of American History*, vol. 74, no. 3 (December 1987), pp. 798–813, quoted at p. 809.

    ["Liberty of the Press"]: quoted in Rossiter, *Seedtime*, p. 31.

33   [*"Their being true"*]: *Case and Trial of Zenger*, quoted at p. 62.

    [*"Truth is a greater sin"*]: *ibid.*, p. 71.

    [*"A right—the liberty"*]: *ibid.*, p. 99.

    [*"Personal freedom rests"*]: Katz, Introduction, in *ibid.*, quoted at p. 34.

    [*"Educated in the Belief"*]: *Pennsylvania Gazette*, June 10, 1731, in Franklin, *Papers*, Leonard W. Labaree, ed. (Yale University Press, 1959–   ), vol. 1, pp. 194–99, quoted at p. 195.

    [*"So far above dispute"*]: Rossiter, *Seedtime*, p. 377.

    [*"Political liberty consists"*]: quoted in *ibid.*, p. 385.

34   [*Praise of liberty as "jewel" etc.*]: see Davidson.

    [*"That second Magna Carta"*]: *Letter to the People of Pennsylvania* (1760), quoted in Schwartz, *Great Rights*, p. 21.

    [*"A constitution, once adopted"*]: Hillard, p. 8.

    [*Enactments of rights and liberties in colonial America*]: Schwartz, *Roots*, vol. 1, part 2, Maryland Act quoted at p. 68, Massachusetts Body of Liberties at p. 72, Carolina Constitutions at p. 123, Schwartz on Carolina Constitutions at p. 108.

35   [*"All men are originally equal"*]: quoted in McDonald, *Novus Ordo*, p. 54.

    [*Concentration of wealth and economic differentials in colonial America*]: see Aronson, pp. 35, 48–49.

    [*Wood on social distinctions*]: Wood, *Creation*, pp. 73–74.

36   [*"Capacity, disposition"*]: Democraticus, "Loose Thoughts on Government," June 7, 1776, in *American Archives*, Peter Force, ed., 4th series, vol. 6 (1846), pp. 730–31, quoted at p. 730.

    [*"Even the reins of state"*]: quoted in Wood, *Creation*, p. 71.

    [*Slave population, eve of revolution*]: see Stella H. Sutherland, *Population Distribution in Colonial America* (Columbia University Press, 1936), p. 271; Harry A. Ploski and Warren Marr II, *The Negro Almanac*, 3rd ed. (Bellwether, 1976), p. 364 (table 10).

37   [*"A special link"*]: Pole, "Equality: An American Dilemma," manuscript, p. 1.

    [*"Alone can inspire"*]: quoted in Wood, *Creation*, p. 73.

    [*"By nature, equal and free"*]: Wilson, *Considerations on the Nature and Extent of the Legislative Authority of the British Parliament* (1774), excerpted in John Braeman, ed., *The Road to Independence* (Putnam, 1963), pp. 205–12, quoted at p. 205.

38   [*"Cause of America"*]: *Common Sense*, in Paine, *Writings*, vol. 1, pp. 67–120, quoted at pp. 68, 99, 100, 101.

    [*Greene on Paine*]: Greene, "Paine," pp. 86–87, 90–92, and passim.

    [*"Establish a new social order"*]: quoted in *ibid.*, p. 91.

39   [*"Do not mechanicks"*]: March 14, 1776, quoted in Ryerson, p. 255.

40   [*"Masterly Pen"*]: John Adams, *Diary and Autobiography (Adams Papers, Series 1)*, L. H. Butterfield, ed. (Belknap Press of Harvard University Press, 1961), vol. 3, *Autobiography* quoted at p. 335.

    [*"Turned to neither book"*]: letter to James Madison, August 30, 1823, in

Jefferson, *Writings,* Paul Leicester Ford, ed. (Putnam, 1892–99), vol. 10, pp. 266–69, quoted at p. 268.

40 [*"Patriots who decapitated Charles I"*]: Dumbauld, *Declaration,* p. 22.

[*"Committee of five"*]: see Adams, *Diary and Autobiography,* vol. 3, p. 389.

[*Franklin on the hatter*]: Jefferson letter to Robert Walsh, December 4, 1818, in Jefferson, *Writings,* vol. 10, pp. 116–19 fn. (anecdote at p. 120).

AN ERUPTION OF RIGHTS

Jefferson and the pursuit of happiness: Garry Wills's *Inventing America* was a major source of the ideas and conclusions on this subject; see also Herbert L. Ganter, "Jefferson's 'Pursuit of Happiness' and Some Forgotten Men," *William and Mary Quarterly,* 2nd series, vol. 16, nos. 3 and 4 (July and October 1936), pp. 422–34, 558–85; Adrienne Koch, "Power and Morals and the Founding Fathers: Jefferson," *Review of Politics,* vol. 15, no. 4 (October 1953), pp. 470–90; Matthews; Caroline Robbins, " 'When It Is That Colonies May Turn Independent': An Analysis of the Environment and Politics of Francis Hutcheson," *William and Mary Quarterly,* 3rd series, vol. 11, no. 2 (April 1954), pp. 214–51; von Eckardt; White.

Articles of Confederation period: Richard Beeman, Stephen Botein, and Edward C. Carter II, eds., *Beyond Confederation: Origins of the Constitution and American National Identity* (University of North Carolina Press, 1987); Richard B. Morris, *The Forging of the Union, 1781–1789* (Harper, 1987); Robert A. Rutland, *The Birth of the Bill of Rights, 1776–1791* (University of North Carolina Press, 1955), chs. 4–5; Schwartz, *Roots,* vol. 2, part 4; Wood, *Creation,* parts 2–4; Gordon S. Wood, "Democracy and the Constitution," in Robert A. Goldwin and William A. Schambra, eds., *How Democratic Is the Constitution?* (American Enterprise Institute for Public Policy Research, 1980), pp. 1–17.

Shays's Rebellion: James MacGregor Burns, *The Vineyard of Liberty* (Knopf, 1982), pp. 13–21 passim, and sources therein cited; Jackson Turner Main, *The Antifederalists: Critics of the Constitution, 1781–1788* (University of North Carolina Press, 1961), pp. 59–64; Morris, pp. 258–66; J. R. Pole, "Shays's Rebellion: A Political Interpretation," in Jack P. Greene, ed., *The Reinterpretation of the American Revolution, 1763–1789* (Harper, 1968), pp. 416–34.

Constitutional convention and struggle over ratification: W. B. Allen and Gordon Lloyd, eds., *The Essential Antifederalist* (University Press of America, 1985); Walter Hartwell Bennett, ed., *Letters from the Federal Farmer to the Republican* (University of Alabama Press, 1978); Walter Berns, "Does the Constitution 'Secure These Rights'?," in Goldwin and Schambra, pp. 59–78, and *ibid.,* passim; Irving Brant, *James Madison: Father of the Constitution, 1787–1800* (Bobbs-Merrill, 1950), chs. 1–17; Richard D. Brown, "Shays's Rebellion and the Ratification of the Federal Constitution in Massachusetts," in Beeman et al., pp. 113–27; Burns, *Vineyard,* pp. 27–63 passim; Linda Grant De Pauw, *The Eleventh Pillar: New York State and the Federal Constitution* (Cornell University Press, 1966); Michael A. Gillespie and Michael Lienesch, eds., *Ratifying the Constitution* (University Press of Kansas, 1989); Alexander Hamilton, James Madison, and John Jay, *The Federalist,* Benjamin F. Wright, ed. (Belknap Press of Harvard University Press, 1961); J. Edwin Hendricks, "Joining the Federal Union," in Lindley S. Butler and Alan D. Watson, eds., *The North Carolina Experience* (University of North Carolina Press, 1984), pp. 147–70; Adrienne Koch, *Jefferson and Madison: The Great Collaboration* (Peter Smith, 1970), pp. 33–55; Morris, ch. 11; Ralph A. Rossum, *"The Federalist's* Understanding of the Constitution as a Bill of Rights," in Charles R. Kesler, ed., *Saving the*

Revolution: The Federalist Papers *and the American Founding* (Free Press, 1987), pp. 219–33; Rutland, *Bill of Rights,* chs. 6–8; Robert A. Rutland, *The Ordeal of the Constitution: The Antifederalists and the Ratification Struggle of 1787–1788* (University of Oklahoma Press, 1966); Rutland, "Vox Populi—The Ratification of the Constitution," in Robert S. Peck and Ralph S. Pollock, eds., *The Blessings of Liberty* (ABA Books, n.d.), pp. 29–41; Schwartz, *Great Rights,* chs. 4–5 passim; Schwartz, *Roots,* vol. 2, pp. 435–63, and vols. 3–4 passim; Herbert J. Storing, ed., *The Complete Anti-Federalist,* 7 vols. (University of Chicago Press, 1981), esp. vol. 1; Wood, *Creation,* chs. 7–8.

PAGE
40 [*Rights in colonial charters and laws*]: Schwartz, *Roots,* vol. 1, part 2.
    [*"Life, liberty, & property"*]: *Journals of the Continental Congress, 1774–1789* (U. S. Government Printing Office, 1904–37), vol. 1, pp. 63–73, quoted at p. 67.
    [*"Their lives, liberties"*]: *ibid.,* vol. 4, pp. 357–58, quoted at p. 357.
41 [*"Take every possible occasion"*]: Hints to Americans Travelling in Europe, June 1788, in Jefferson, *Papers,* Julian Boyd, ed. (Princeton University Press, 1950–), vol. 13, pp. 264–75, quoted at p. 269.
    [*"Absolutely incognito"*]: letter of April 11, 1787, in *ibid.,* vol. 11, pp. 283–85, quoted at p. 285.
42 [*"Happiness of the people"*]: Hints to Americans, p. 269.
    [*"Large numbers of men"*]: Hutcheson, *A System of Moral Philosophy* (1755), vol. 2, p. 309.
    [*"Efficient motive force"*]: Wills, *Inventing America,* p. 253.
    [*"General happiness"*]: Hutcheson, vol. 2, p. 226.
    [*"Hard political test"*]: Wills, *Inventing America,* p. 251.
    [*"Begun in a thousand taverns"*]: Ryerson, p. 256.
    [*Jefferson's draft declaration and slavery*]: reprinted in Henry Steele Commager and Richard B. Morris, eds., *The Spirit of 'Seventy-Six* (Harper, 1967), pp. 316–17; see also Wills, *Inventing America,* pp. 65–75.
43 [*"Vehement philippic"*]: letter to Timothy Pickering, August 6, 1822, in Commager and Morris, pp. 313–14, quoted at p. 314.
    [*"How did his Majesty's governors"*]: quoted in Wills, *Inventing America,* p. 73.
    [*State bills of rights*]: Schwartz, *Roots,* vol. 2, part 3, Schwartz quoted on "first true Bill" at p. 231; see also Hillard.
44 [*"Stream of revolution"*]: Jameson, *The American Revolution Considered as a Social Movement* (Princeton University Press, 1967), p. 9.
45 [*"Fundamental principles"*]: *Journals of the Continental Congress,* vol. 32, pp. 334–43, quoted at p. 339.
    [*"To render the constitution"*]: Morris, pp. 252–57, quoted at p. 257.
    [*What was man?*]: letter to David Humphreys, December 26, 1786, in Washington, *Writings,* John C. Fitzpatrick, ed. (U. S. Government Printing Office, 1931–44), vol. 29, pp. 125–29, esp. pp. 125–26.
    [*"For God's sake"*]: letter to David Humphreys, October 22, 1786, in *ibid.,* vol. 29, pp. 26–28, quoted at p. 27.
46 [*"Commotions of this sort"*]: *ibid.,* p. 27.
    [*Philadelphia Jew's petition*]: Jonas Phillips, September 7, 1787, reprinted in Schwartz, *Roots,* vol. 2, pp. 439–40.
    [*"No declaration of any kind"*]: quoted in Schwartz, *Great Rights,* p. 106.
47 [*"State Declarations of Rights"*]: *ibid.,* p. 104.
    [*"Are no security"*]: *ibid.,* p. 106.
    [*"With regard to rights"*]: James Bowdoin, at the Massachusetts ratifying convention, January 23, 1788, quoted in Schwartz, *Roots,* vol. 3, p. 686.

47 [*"America's greatest contribution"*]: quoted in Burns, *Vineyard,* p. 45.
48 [*"Misshapened heterogeneous monster"*]: Luther Martin, quoted in Schwartz, *Roots,* vol. 3, p. 497.
[*"O my countrymen"*]: James Sullivan ("Cassius"), quoted in *ibid.,* vol. 3, p. 538.
49 [*"Remove the fears"*]: quoted in Schwartz, *Great Rights,* p. 128.
[*"Rights of conscience"*]: June 5, 1788, quoted in Schwartz, *Roots,* vol. 4, p. 771.
[*"Licentiousness has seldom produced"*]: June 6, 1788, quoted in *ibid.,* vol. 4, p. 779.

JAMES MADISON'S POLITICAL SOMERSAULT

Madison, Jefferson, and the Bill of Rights: Koch, *Jefferson and Madison,* ch. 3; Levy, *Constitutional Opinions,* pp. 117–19; Malone, vol. 2, ch. 9; Matthews, esp. chs. 6–7; Jack N. Rakove, "The Madisonian Moment," *University of Chicago Law Review,* vol. 55, no. 2 (Spring 1988), pp. 473–505, esp. pp. 501–2; Schwartz, *Roots,* vol. 3, pp. 592–623, 724–28, and vol. 4, pp. 846–51, 919–31, and vol. 5, pp. 983–1005.

Jefferson and Lafayette: Louis Gottschalk and Margaret Maddox, *Lafayette in the French Revolution: Through the October Days* (University of Chicago Press, 1969), esp. pp. 13–16, and chs. 4–5, 10, 13, passim; Malone, vol. 2, esp. pp. 223–25.

Madison and the Bill of Rights: Brant, chs. 18, 21; Edward Dumbauld, *The Bill of Rights, and What It Means Today* (University of Oklahoma Press, 1957), pp. 33–50; Paul Finkelman, "James Madison and the Bill of Rights: A Reluctant Paternity" (draft manuscript, 1990); James H. Hutson, "'A Nauseous Project,'" *Wilson Quarterly,* vol. 15, no. 1 (Winter 1991), pp. 57–70 passim; Levy, *Constitutional Opinions,* pp. 119–24; Levy, *Emergence of a Free Press,* pp. 257–66; James Madison, *Papers,* Robert A. Rutland et al., eds. (University Press of Virginia, 1962–   ), vol. 12; Jack N. Rakove, "'Parchment Barriers' and the Politics of Rights: A Madisonian Interpretation," paper prepared for a Woodrow Wilson International Center workshop on the Bill of Rights, 1989; Rutland, *Bill of Rights,* ch. 9; Schwartz, *Great Rights,* pp. 156–59, and ch. 6; Schwartz, *Roots,* vol. 5 passim.

PAGE
51 [*"Colossal error"*]: Levy, *Constitutional Opinions,* pp. 113, 116.
[*"Infinitely more safe"*]: quoted in Schwartz, *Roots,* vol. 4, p. 825.
52 [*"A fatal objection"*]: letter of October 24, 1787, in Jefferson, *Papers,* vol. 12, pp. 270–84, quoted at p. 280.
[*"I will now add"*]: letter of December 20, 1787, in *ibid.,* vol. 12, pp. 438–42, quoted at p. 440.
[*"My own opinion"*]: letter of October 17, 1788, in *ibid.,* vol. 14, pp. 16–21, quoted at pp. 18, 19, 20.
53 [*"Half a loaf"*]: letter of March 15, 1789, in *ibid.,* vol. 14, pp. 659–62, quoted at pp. 660–61.
[*"Ardent wish"*]: letter to William Short, November 16, 1791, quoted in Gottschalk and Maddox, p. 15.
54 [*"This security for liberty"*]: letter to John Paul Jones, March 23, 1789, in Jefferson, *Papers,* vol. 14, pp. 686–89, quoted at p. 688.
55 [*"I am dogmatically attached"*]: letter of January 14, 1789, in Madison, *Papers,* vol. 11, pp. 417–18, quoted at p. 418.
[*"Ceased to be a friend"*]: letter to George Eve, January 2, 1789, in *ibid.,* vol. 11, pp. 404–5, quoted at pp. 404, 405.
[*"Desires of the body of the people"*]: letter to John G. Jackson, December 27,

1821, quoted in Drew R. McCoy, *The Last of the Fathers: James Madison and the Republican Legacy* (Cambridge University Press, 1989), p. 89.

55 [*Common calls of states for rights*]: see Schwartz, *Great Rights*, pp. 157-58 (table), Schwartz quoted on "consensus" at p. 157.

56 [*"Mere compiler"*]: *ibid.*, p. 159.
[*"Bring on the subject"*]: quoted in *ibid.*, p. 163.
[*"Characteristic rights of freemen"*]: inaugural address, April 30, 1789, in Washington, *Writings*, vol. 30, pp. 291-96, quoted at p. 295; on Madison's authorship of the address, see Brant, pp. 256-58.
[*"May occasion suspicions"*]: quoted in Schwartz, *Great Rights*, p. 164.
[*"Without revenue"*]: James Jackson of Georgia, quoted in Schwartz, *Roots*, vol. 5, p. 1018.
[*"Vessel just launched"*]: *ibid.*, vol. 5, pp. 1017, 1018.

57 [*Madison's proposals to the House*]: *ibid.*, vol. 5, pp. 1023-34, quoted at p. 1026.
[*"Resolved itself"*]: *ibid.*, vol. 5, p. 1066.
[*"Exceedingly wearisome"*]: letter to Edmund Randolph, August 21, 1789, in Madison, *Papers*, vol. 12, pp. 348-49, quoted at p. 348.
[*"Has been absolutely necessary"*]: *ibid.*, p. 349.
[*"Like it as far as it goes"*]: letter of August 28, 1789, in Jefferson, *Papers*, vol. 15, pp. 364-69, quoted at p. 367.

58 [*"Most valuable amendment"*]: quoted in Schwartz, *Great Rights*, p. 182.

60 [*Virginia Anti-Federalists on Bill of Rights as "inadequate"*]: Richard Henry Lee and William Grayson, quoted in *ibid.*, p. 188.
[*"Wrong to admit"*] quoted in Robinson, *Slavery in the Structure of American Politics*, pp. 245, 243 fn. respectively.

CONSENSUS AND CONFLICT

The United States and the French Revolution: Charles D. Hazen, *Contemporary American Opinion of the French Revolution* (Johns Hopkins Press, 1897), pp. 1-53; Lawrence S. Kaplan, *Jefferson and France* (Yale University Press, 1967), esp. chs. 2-4; Malone, vol. 2, chs. 10, 12, and vol. 3, chs. 3-9, esp. ch. 3; Merrill D. Peterson, *Adams and Jefferson: A Revolutionary Dialogue* (University of Georgia Press, 1976), ch. 2; see also Edward Handler, *America and Europe in the Political Thought of John Adams* (Harvard University Press, 1964).

Political warfare in the Federalist era: Brant, ch. 29; Richard Buel, Jr., *Securing the Revolution: Ideology in American Politics, 1789-1815* (Cornell University Press, 1972); James T. Flexner, *George Washington: Anguish and Farewell* (Little, Brown, 1972); Handler; Hazen, esp. part 2; Richard Hofstadter, *The Idea of a Party System* (University of California Press, 1969), esp. chs. 1, 3; John R. Howe, Jr., "Republican Thought and the Political Violence of the 1790s," *American Quarterly*, vol. 19, no. 2 (Summer 1967), pp. 147-65; Malone, vol. 2, chs. 25-28, and vol. 3 passim; John C. Miller, *Crisis in Freedom: The Alien and Sedition Acts* (Little, Brown, 1951), esp. chs. 1-2; Marshall Smelser, "George Washington and the Alien and Sedition Acts," *American Historical Review*, vol. 59, no. 2 (January 1954), pp. 322-34; Smelser, "The Jacobin Phrenzy: Federalism and the Menace of Liberty, Equality, and Fraternity," *Review of Politics*, vol. 13, no. 4 (October 1951), pp. 457-82; James Morton Smith, *Freedom's Fetters: The Alien and Sedition Laws and American Civil Liberties* (Cornell University Press, 1956), esp. chs. 1-2; Donald H. Stewart, *The Opposition Press of the Federalist Period* (State University of New York Press, 1969).

Whiskey Rebellion: Steven R. Boyd, ed., *The Whiskey Rebellion: Past and Present Perspectives* (Greenwood Press, 1985); Burns, *Vineyard*, pp. 97-99; Thomas P. Slaughter,

The Whiskey Rebellion: Frontier Epilogue to the American Revolution (Oxford University Press, 1986).

Naturalization, Alien and Alien Enemies, and Sedition Acts: Burns, *Vineyard,* pp. 125–31; Malone, vol. 3, chs. 23–24; Miller, *Crisis in Freedom;* John C. Miller, *The Federalist Era, 1789–1801* (Harper, 1960), ch. 13; Smelser, "Washington and the Alien and Sedition Acts"; Smith, *Freedom's Fetters.*

Opposition to the Alien and Sedition Acts: Frank M. Anderson, "Contemporary Opinion of the Virginia and Kentucky Resolutions," *American Historical Review,* vol. 5, nos. 1 and 2 (October 1899 and January 1900), pp. 45–63, 225–52; Brant, ch. 34; Koch, *Jefferson and Madison,* ch. 7; Adrienne Koch and Harry Ammon, "The Virginia and Kentucky Resolutions: An Episode in Jefferson's and Madison's Defense of Civil Liberties," *William and Mary Quarterly,* 3rd series, vol. 5, no. 2 (April 1948), pp. 145–76; Levy, *Constitutional Opinions,* ch. 8; Leonard W. Levy, *Jefferson & Civil Liberties: The Dark Side* (Belknap Press of Harvard University Press, 1963), pp. 50–56; Malone, vol. 3, chs. 25–26; James Morton Smith, "The Grass Roots Origins of the Kentucky Resolutions," *William and Mary Quarterly,* 3rd series, vol. 27, no. 2 (April 1970), pp. 221–45; *The Virginia and Kentucky Resolutions of 1798 and '99, with Jefferson's Original Draught Thereof* (Jonathan Elliot, 1832).

Development of two-party politics in the Federalist era: Richard Buel, Jr., "Freedom of the Press in Revolutionary America: The Evolution of Libertarianism, 1760–1820," in Bernard Bailyn and John B. Hench, eds., *The Press & the American Revolution* (American Antiquarian Society, 1980), pp. 59–97, esp. pp. 82–93; Buel, *Securing the Revolution;* Burns, *Vineyard,* pp. 134–39, 144–48, 151–55; Noble E. Cunningham, "Election of 1800," in Arthur M. Schlesinger, Jr., *History of American Presidential Elections, 1789–1968* (Chelsea House, 1971), vol. 1, pp. 101–56; Hofstadter, esp. chs. 1–4; Koch, *Jefferson and Madison,* ch. 6; Malone, vol. 3, esp. chs. 29–30, and vol. 4, ch. 1; Miller, *Federalist Era,* chs. 7, 14; Roy F. Nichols, *The Invention of the American Political Parties* (Macmillan, 1967), esp. chs. 11–15; Peterson, ch. 3; Smelser, "Jacobin Phrenzy"; Stewart.

President Jefferson and civil liberties: Noble E. Cunningham, *The Jefferson Republicans in Power: Party Operations, 1801–1809* (University of North Carolina Press, 1963), esp. ch. 10; Levy, *Constitutional Opinions,* ch. 9; Levy, *Jefferson & Civil Liberties,* passim; Malone, vol. 4, chs. 12–13, 19, and vol. 5, chs. 13–21, 26, 30–35 passim; Louis Martin Sears, *Jefferson and the Embargo* (Duke University Press, 1927).

Jefferson and the judiciary: John Agresto, *The Supreme Court and Constitutional Democracy* (Cornell University Press, 1984); Julian P. Boyd, "The Chasm That Separated Thomas Jefferson and John Marshall," in Gottfried Dietze, ed., *Essays on the American Constitution* (Prentice-Hall, 1964), pp. 3–20; Robert Lowry Clinton, *Marbury v. Madison and Judicial Review* (University Press of Kansas, 1989); Henry Steele Commager, *Majority Rule and Minority Rights* (Peter Smith, 1958); Richard E. Ellis, *The Jeffersonian Crisis: Courts and Politics in the Young Republic* (Oxford University Press, 1971), esp. chs. 1–7, 15–17; Robert K. Faulkner, *The Jurisprudence of John Marshall* (Princeton University Press, 1968), esp. pp. 173–92, and ch. 4; Elizabeth McCaughey, "*Marbury* v. *Madison:* Have We Missed the Real Meaning?," *Presidential Studies Quarterly,* vol. 19, no. 3 (Summer 1989), pp. 491–528; Malone, vol. 4, esp. chs. 7–8; Christopher Wolfe, *The Rise of Modern Judicial Review: From Constitutional Interpretation to Judge-Made Law* (Basic Books, 1986), esp. chs. 2–4. The treatment of *Marbury* is drawn in part from Burns, *Vineyard,* pp. 183–89.

PAGE
62   ["*Liberty of the whole earth*"]: letter to William Short, January 3, 1793, in Jefferson, *Writings,* vol. 6, pp. 153–57, quoted at p. 154.

62   ["*One of the most wonderful events*"]: letter to Catherine Macauley Graham,
      January 9, 1790, in Washington, *Writings*, vol. 30, pp. 495–98, quoted at
      pp. 497, 498.

63   ["*How the Union of the States*"]: letter to Alexander Hamilton, August 26,
      1792, in *ibid.*, vol. 32, pp. 132–34, quoted at p. 133.
      ["*Treacherous in private friendship*"]: letter published in *Alexandria Gazette*,
      February 18, 1797, quoted in Smelser, "Jacobin Phrenzy," p. 461.
      ["*Blood suckers*"]: Boston *Columbian Centinel*, February 24, 1790, quoted
      in *ibid.*, p. 459.
      ["*The French party*"]: *ibid.*, p. 458.
      ["*Laws be better supported*"]: letter to Edmund Pendleton, January 22,
      1795, in Washington, *Writings*, vol. 34, pp. 98–101, quoted at p. 99.

64   ["*Treasonable or secret machinations*"]: text of act in Smith, *Freedom's Fetters*,
      pp. 438–40, quoted at p. 438.
      ["*Any insurrection, riot*"]: text of act in *ibid.*, pp. 441–42, quoted at pp.
      441, 442.
      ["*Afraid of publishing*"]: John Nicholas, quoted in Levy, *Emergence of a Free
      Press*, pp. 301–2.
      ["*Most wicked and base*"]: quoted in Smith, *Freedom's Fetters*, p. 97.
      ["*Profligacy, falsehood*"]: quoted in Handler, p. 180; for Adams's later
      disclaimer, see Smith, *Freedom's Fetters*, pp. 92–93.

66   ["*Present critical situation*"]: July 4, 1798, quoted in Smith, "Grass Roots
      Origins," p. 222.
      ["*EQUAL RIGHT TO JUDGE*"]: *Virginia and Kentucky Resolutions*, p. 16.
      ["*INTERPOSE FOR ARRESTING*"]: *ibid.*, p. 5.

67   ["*As alternating parties*"]: Hofstadter, p. 8.

68   ["*Supreme form of generosity*"]: José Ortega y Gasset, *The Revolt of the Masses*
      (Norton, 1932), p. 83.
      ["*Advocated the exemption*"]: Levy, *Emergence of a Free Press*, p. 301.
      ["*We are all republicans*"]: March 4, 1801, in Jefferson, *Writings*, vol. 8, pp.
      1–6, quoted at p. 3.
      ["*Monarchical*" *Federalist leaders*]: see Burns, *Vineyard*, pp. 164–65; Ma-
      lone, vol. 3, p. 265.
      ["*Integrity of the presses*"]: letter to Governor Thomas McKean, February
      19, 1803, in Jefferson, *Writings*, vol. 8, pp. 216–19, quoted at p. 218.
      ["*Bear in mind*"]: *ibid.*, vol. 8, quoted at p. 2.

69   [Marbury]: *Marbury* v. *Madison*, 1 Cranch 137 (1803).

3. THE REVOLUTIONS OF RIGHTS

Paine and The Rights of Man: Edmund Burke, *Reflections on the Revolution in France*
(Dent, 1971); Eric Foner, *Tom Paine and Revolutionary America* (Oxford University
Press, 1976), ch. 7; Thomas Paine, *The Rights of Man*, in Paine, *Writings*, Moncure
Daniel Conway, ed. (Putnam, 1894–96), vol. 2, pp. 265–523; John Stevenson,
Popular Disturbances in England, 1700–1870 (Longman, 1979), pp. 140–41, 143;
E. P. Thompson, *The Making of the English Working Class* (Victor Gollancz, 1963),
esp. chs. 4–5 passim.

PAGE
71   ["*So taken up with their theories*"]: Burke, pp. 62, 59 respectively.
72   ["*Man has no property in man*"]: Paine, *Rights of Man*, p. 278.
      [*Estimate of* Rights of Man *sales*]: Thompson, *Making*, p. 108 fn. 1.
      ["*Thrust into the hands*"]: quoted in *ibid.*, p. 108.

72   [*"People having a strong hand"*]: Wordsworth, *The Prelude (Text of 1805)*,
      Ernest de Selincourt, ed. (Oxford University Press, 1933), p. 165 (book
      9, lines 530–32).
      [*"Its comin yet"*]: Burns, "For a' that and a' that," in Burns, *Poems and
      Songs*, James Kinsley, ed. (Oxford University Press, 1968), vol. 2, pp.
      762–63, quoted at p. 763.

INDUSTRIALIZING RIGHTS

The British Industrial Revolution and its effects: Craig Calhoun, *The Question of Class
Struggle: Social Foundations of Popular Radicalism during the Industrial Revolution* (Uni-
versity of Chicago Press, 1982); G. D. H. Cole and A. W. Filson, eds., *British
Working Class Movements: Select Documents, 1789–1875* (Macmillan, 1951); John
Fielden, *The Curse of the Factory System* (1836; reprinted by Frank Cass, 1969); John
Foster, *Class Struggle and the Industrial Revolution: Early Industrial Capitalism in Three
English Towns* (Weidenfeld & Nicolson, 1974); J. L. Hammond and Barbara Ham-
mond, *The Town Labourer, 1760–1832: The New Civilisation* (Longmans, Green,
1925); Christopher Hill, *Reformation to Industrial Revolution: A Social and Economic
History of Britain, 1530–1780* (Weidenfeld & Nicolson, 1967), ch. 4; E. J. Hobs-
bawm, *The Age of Revolution, 1789–1848* (World Publishing, 1962); E. L. Jones and
G. E. Mingay, eds., *Land, Labour and Population in the Industrial Revolution* (Edward
Arnold, 1967); Paul Mantoux, "The Destruction of the Peasant Village," in Philip
A. M. Taylor, ed., *The Industrial Revolution in Britain: Triumph or Disaster?* (D. C.
Heath, 1958), pp. 64–73; Mantoux, *The Industrial Revolution in the Eighteenth Cen-
tury*, Marjorie Vernon, trans. (Jonathan Cape, 1928); Dorothy Marshall, *Industrial
England, 1776–1851* (Routledge & Kegan Paul, 1973); E. Royston Pike, ed., *"Hard
Times": Human Documents of the Industrial Revolution* (Praeger, 1966); Arthur Red-
ford, *Labour Migration in England, 1800–1850*, W. H. Chaloner, ed., 2nd ed. (Manchester University Press, 1964); Thompson, *Making*.

Food riots: Stevenson, esp. ch. 5, and pp. 176–79.

Labor organization and protest: Asa Briggs, ed., *Chartist Studies* (Macmillan, 1959);
Bythell, chs. 8–9; Calhoun; Cole and Filson; Hammond and Hammond, esp. chs.
4–5, 7, 12, 14; Marshall, ch. 6 passim; Stevenson, chs. 6–12; Dorothy Thompson,
ed., *The Early Chartists* (University of South Carolina Press, 1971); Thompson,
Making; J. T. Ward, *Chartism* (Barnes & Noble, 1973).

Women in the Industrial Revolution: Sheila Lewenhak, *Women and Trade Unions: An
Outline History of Women in the British Trade Union Movement* (Ernest Benn, 1977),
esp. chs. 2–4; Pike, pp. 219–78; Ivy Pinchbeck, *Women Workers and the Industrial
Revolution, 1750–1850* (Routledge, 1930); Barbara Taylor, *Eve and the New Jerusa-
lem: Socialism and Feminism in the Nineteenth Century* (Pantheon, 1983); Thompson,
Early Chartists, pp. 115–30; Thompson, *Making*, esp. pp. 414–17; Mary Wollstone-
craft, *The Rights of Women* (originally *A Vindication of the Rights of Women*, 1792), and
John Stuart Mill, *The Subjection of Women* (Dent, 1970).

PAGE
74   [*"Dark Satanic Mills"*]: William Blake, "Milton," in Blake, *Writings*,
      G. E. Bentley, Jr., ed. (Oxford University Press, 1978), vol. 1, p. 318.
      [*"Idle or mischievous Engine Boy"*]: quoted in Hammond and Hammond,
      p. 27.
75   [*Cotton Spinner's address*]: in Thompson, *Making*, pp. 199–202, Thompson
      quoted at pp. 202–3.

75   [*Cobbett on rights*]: quoted in *ibid.*, p. 761.
76   [*"Reactionary radicalism"*]: Calhoun, pp. 7–8, and ch. 3, and passim.
      [*"Workmen in general"*]: quoted in Thompson, *Making*, pp. 200, 202.
      [*"Not only the diversity"*]: Friedmann, "Property," in Philip P. Wiener, ed.,
      Dictionary of the History of Ideas (Scribner, 1973), vol. 3, pp. 650–57,
      quoted at p. 652.
77   [*"Liberty or Death"*]: quoted in Stevenson, pp. 178, 179.
      [*"Some legitimising notion"*]: Thompson, *Making*, p. 68.
      [*Kershaw's mother and the slubber*]: Pike, pp. 129–30, quoted at p. 130.
78   [Rights of Infants]: in Thompson, *Making*, pp. 162–63.

CHANGING RIGHTS: PROPERTY AND HAPPINESS

Hutcheson and property: Thomas A. Horne, *Property Rights and Poverty: Political Argument in Britain, 1605–1834* (University of North Carolina Press, 1990), pp. 75–88; Francis Hutcheson, *A Short Introduction to Moral Philosophy* (Robert Foulis, 1747); Hutcheson, *A System of Moral Philosophy*, 2 vols. (1755), esp. vol. 1, book 2; W. L. Taylor, *Francis Hutcheson and David Hume as Predecessors of Adam Smith* (Duke University Press, 1965), esp. pp. 142–45.

Hume and property: Horne, pp. 88–101 passim; David Hume, *An Enquiry Concerning the Principles of Morals*, in Hume, *Philosophical Works*, Thomas H. Green and Thomas H. Grose, eds. (Longmans, Green, 1882–86; reprinted by Scientific Verlag Aalen, 1964), vol. 4, pp. 169–287, esp. sect. 3 ("Of Justice") passim; Hume, *A Treatise of Human Nature*, in *ibid.*, vols. 1–2, esp. vol. 2, book 2, part 2 passim; Richard Schlatter, *Private Property: The History of an Idea* (George Allen & Unwin, 1951), pp. 239–43; Taylor, esp. pp. 145–54.

Locke and property: Horne, pp. 48–65; John Locke, *Two Treatises of Government*, Peter Laslett, ed. (Cambridge University Press, 1988); C. B. Macpherson, *The Political Theory of Possessive Individualism: Hobbes to Locke* (Clarendon Press, 1962), esp. ch. 5; Alan Ryan, *Property and Political Theory* (Basil Blackwell, 1984), ch. 1; Schlatter, esp. ch. 7; Martin Seliger, *The Liberal Politics of John Locke* (Praeger, 1969), esp. chs. 5–6; James Tully, *A Discourse on Property: John Locke and His Adversaries* (Cambridge University Press, 1980).

Rousseau and property: Arthur Cobban, *Rousseau and the Modern State* (George Allen & Unwin, 1934), esp. ch. 7; Kennedy F. Roche, *Rousseau: Stoic & Romantic* (Methuen, 1974), esp. ch. 10; Jean Jacques Rousseau, *The Social Contract/Discourses* (Dent, 1955); Ryan, *Property and Political Theory*, ch. 2; Schlatter, pp. 207–14.

Burke and property: Burke, *Reflections;* George Fasel, " 'The Soul That Animated': The Role of Property in Burke's Thought," *Studies in Burke and His Time*, vol. 17, no. 1 (Winter 1976), pp. 27–41; Horne, pp. 160–63; Russell Kirk, "Burke and Natural Rights," *Review of Politics*, vol. 13, no. 4 (October 1951), pp. 441–56; Schlatter, pp. 178–81; Jeremy Waldron, ed., *"Nonsense upon Stilts": Bentham, Burke, and Marx on the Rights of Man* (Methuen, 1987), ch. 4.

Bentham: Jeremy Bentham, *Anarchical Follies*, in Bentham, *Works*, John Bowring, ed. (William Tait, 1843), vol. 2, pp. 489–534; Bentham, "Security and Equality of Property," in C. B. Macpherson, ed., *Property: Mainstream and Critical Positions* (University of Toronto Press, 1978), pp. 41–58; H. L. A. Hart, "Bentham and the United States of America," *Journal of Law & Economics*, vol. 19, no. 3 (October 1976), pp. 547–67; Horne, pp. 143–59; Douglas G. Long, *Bentham on Liberty: Jeremy Bentham's Idea of Liberty in Relation to His Utilitarianism* (University of Toronto Press,

1977); Long, "Bentham on Property," in C. B. Macpherson et al., *Theories of Property: Aristotle to the Present,* Anthony Parel and Thomas Flanagan, eds. (Calgary Institute for the Humanities, 1979), pp. 221–54; Wesley C. Mitchell, "Bentham's Felicific Calculus," in Bhikhu Parekh, ed., *Jeremy Bentham* (Frank Cass, 1974), pp. 168–86; Parekh, ed., *Bentham's Political Thought* (Barnes & Noble, 1973); Ryan, *Property and Political Theory,* ch. 4 passim; Robert Shackleton, "The Greatest Happiness of the Greatest Number: The History of Bentham's Phrase," *Studies on Voltaire and the Eighteenth Century,* Theodore Besterman, ed., vol. 90 (1972), pp. 1461–82, esp. pp. 1473–81; Waldron, ch. 3.

John Stuart Mill: Fred R. Berger, *Happiness, Justice and Freedom: The Moral and Political Philosophy of John Stuart Mill* (University of California Press, 1984); Graeme Duncan and John Gray, "The Left Against Mill," in Wesley E. Cooper et al., eds., *New Essays on John Stuart Mill and Utilitarianism* (Canadian Association for Publishing in Philosophy, 1979), pp. 203–29; John Gray, "John Stuart Mill on Liberty, Utility, and Rights," in J. Roland Pennock and John W. Chapman, eds., *Human Rights* (New York University Press, 1981), pp. 80–116; Gray, "John Stuart Mill on the Theory of Property," in Parel and Flanagan, pp. 257–80; John Stuart Mill, *Principles of Political Economy,* W. J. Ashley, ed. (Longmans, Green, 1909), esp. books 2, 4–5; Mill, *Utilitarianism/On Liberty/Essay on Bentham,* Mary Warnock, ed. (New American Library, 1974); Mill and Harriet Taylor, *Essays on Sex Equality,* Alice S. Rossi, ed. (University of Chicago Press, 1970); John C. Rees, *John Stuart Mill's* On Liberty (Oxford University Press, 1985); Alan Ryan, *J. S. Mill* (Routledge & Kegan Paul, 1974); Ryan, *Property and Political Theory,* pp. 142–60.

Hegel and Young Hegelians: G. W. F. Hegel, *Philosophy of Right,* T. M. Knox, trans. (Oxford University Press, 1942), esp. part 1, and part 3, subsects. 2–3; Lewis P. Hinchman, "The Origins of Human Rights: A Hegelian Perspective," *Western Political Quarterly,* vol. 37, no. 1 (March 1984), pp. 7–31; David MacGregor, *The Communist Ideal in Hegel and Marx* (University of Toronto Press, 1984), esp. chs. 1, 6–7 passim; David McLellan, *The Young Hegelians and Karl Marx* (Praeger, 1969); Ryan, *Property and Political Theory,* ch. 5; Peter G. Stillman, "Property, Freedom, and Individuality in Hegel's and Marx's Political Thought," in J. Roland Pennock and John W. Chapman, eds., *Property* (New York University Press, 1980), pp. 130–67; Waldron, pp. 119–23, 188.

Marx: Allen E. Buchanan, *Marx and Justice: The Radical Critique of Liberalism* (Rowman and Littlefield, 1982), esp. ch. 4; Steven Lukes, *Marxism and Morality* (Oxford University Press, 1987), esp. ch. 4 passim; L. J. Macfarlane, "Marxist Theory and Human Rights," *Government and Opposition,* vol. 17, no. 4 (1982), pp. 414–28; McLellan, *Young Hegelians and Marx,* pp. 48–84 passim; Karl Marx, *Critique of the Gotha Programme,* C. P. Dutt, ed. (International Publishers, 1938); Marx, *On the Jewish Question,* in Marx, *Early Writings,* T. B. Bottomore, ed. and trans. (McGraw-Hill, 1964), pp. 1–40; Ryan, *Property and Political Theory,* ch. 6; Schlatter, pp. 273–77; Stillman; Waldron, ch. 5.

PAGE
79   [*"Security of property!"*]: Wollstonecraft, *A Vindication of the Rights of Men,* 2nd ed. (1790; reprinted by Scholars' Facsimiles & Reprints, 1960), p. 24; see also Wollstonecraft, *Rights of Women.*
80   [*"Universal industry"*]: Hutcheson, *System of Moral Philosophy,* vol. 1, pp. 320, 321.
        [*"Slothful wretches"*]: Hutcheson, *Short Introduction,* p. 247.
        [*"Never to put in the ballance"*]: ibid., p. 296.
        [*"By mere occupation"*]: Hutcheson, *System of Moral Philosophy,* vol. 1, p. 326.

80   ["*Sole origin*"]: Hume, *Enquiry*, p. 179.
["*A man's art*"]: *ibid.*, p. 189.
["*Wherever we depart*"]: *ibid.*, p. 188.

81   ["*Highly conducive*"]: Hume, *Treatise*, vol. 2, p. 269.
["*Particular hardships*"]: Hume, *Enquiry*, p. 274.
["*Justice was left*"]: Horne, p. 94.
["*Great and* chief *end*"]: Locke, *Second Treatise*, in Locke, *Two Treatises*, quoted at pp. 350–51.
["*Life, Health, Liberty*"]: *ibid.*, p. 271.
["*Being all equal*"]: *ibid.*

82   ["*Locke's astonishing achievement*"]: Macpherson, *Possessive Individualism*, p. 199.
["*Tacit and voluntary consent*"]: Locke, *Second Treatise*, p. 302.
["*Wise Locke*"]: Rousseau, *Discourse on the Origin of Inequality*, in Rousseau, *Social Contract/Discourses*, p. 198.
["This is mine"]: *ibid.*, p. 192.
["*Most sacred of all the rights*"]: *A Discourse on Political Economy*, in *ibid.*, p. 254.

83   ["*Monstrous fiction*"]: Burke, *Reflections*, p. 35.
["*All men have equal rights*"]: *ibid.*, p. 56.

84   ["*Right of pursuit of happiness*"]: quoted in Hart, p. 555.
["Bawling *upon paper*"]: Bentham, *Anarchical Follies*, p. 494.
["Of two individuals"]: Bentham, "Security and Equality of Property," p. 47.
["*What is the wealth*"]: *ibid.*, p. 45.
["*No rights without law*"]: quoted in Schlatter, p. 246.
["*Particular and subordinate* ends"]: quoted in Mitchell, p. 181.

85   ["*Security and equality are in conflict*"]: Bentham, "Security and Equality of Property," p. 57.
["*Motives are innumerable*"]: quoted in Berger, p. 14.
["*Happiness is not an abstract idea*"]: Mill, *Utilitarianism*, p. 291.
["*When we call anything*"]: *ibid.*, p. 309.

86   ["*Love of liberty*"]: *ibid.*, p. 260.
["*Should be the general practice*"]: Mill, *Principles of Political Economy*, p. 950.
["*An absolute right*"]: *ibid.*, p. 366.
["*Ideal perfection*"]: Mill, *Utilitarianism*, p. 268.

87   ["*Greater involvement*"]: Waldron, p. 122.
["*Right to enjoy*"]: Marx, *On the Jewish Question*, p. 25.
["*So-called* rights of man"]: *ibid.*, p. 24.

88   ["*Vulgar economic apologists*"]: Marx, *Capital: A Critique of Political Economy*, Frederick Engels, ed. (Modern Library, 1936), p. 669 fn. 1.
["*Taken over the painful role*"]: letter to Dagobert Oppenheim, August 1842, in Marx, *Letters*, Saul K. Padover, ed. and trans. (Prentice-Hall, 1979), pp. 18–19, quoted at p. 19.

PROPERTY RIGHTS IN THE LAND OF EDEN

Industrial Revolution in the United States: Thomas C. Cochran, *Frontiers of Change: Early Industrialism in America* (Oxford University Press, 1981); Brooke Hindle and Steven Lubar, *Engines of Change: The American Industrial Revolution, 1790–1860* (Smithsonian Institution Press, 1986); Douglass C. North, *The Economic Growth of the United States, 1790–1860* (Prentice-Hall, 1961).

Jefferson and property rights: Stanley N. Katz, "Thomas Jefferson and the Right to Property in Revolutionary America," *Journal of Law & Economics,* vol. 19, no. 3 (October 1976), pp. 467–88; Staughton Lynd, *Intellectual Origins of American Radicalism* (Pantheon, 1968), ch. 3; Schlatter, pp. 195–99; William B. Scott, *In Pursuit of Happiness: American Conceptions of Property from the Seventeenth to the Twentieth Century* (Indiana University Press, 1977), chs. 3–4 passim; Jean Yarbrough, "Jefferson and Property Rights," in Ellen Frankel Paul and Howard Dickman, eds., *Liberty, Property, and the Foundations of the American Constitution* (State University of New York Press, 1989), pp. 65–83.

Cooper: James Fenimore Cooper, *The American Democrat* (1838; reprinted by Knopf, 1931); John P. McWilliams, Jr., *Political Justice in a Republic: James Fenimore Cooper's America* (University of California Press, 1972); John F. Ross, *The Social Criticism of Fenimore Cooper* (University of California Press, 1933); Arthur M. Schlesinger, Jr., *The Age of Jackson* (Little, Brown, 1945), pp. 375–80.

PAGE

88 [*Immigration to the U.S., 1790s and 1810s*]: Richard B. Morris, ed., *Encyclopedia of American History* (Harper, 1953), p. 445.

89 [*"Whenever there is"*]: letter of October 28, 1785, in Jefferson, *Papers,* Julian P. Boyd, ed. (Princeton University Press, 1950–), vol. 8, pp. 681–83, quoted at p. 682.

[*"Aristocracy of wealth"*]: Jefferson, "Autobiography, 1743–1790," in Jefferson, *Writings,* Paul Leicester Ford, ed. (Putnam, 1892–99), vol. 1, pp. 1–153, quoted at p. 49.

[*"Of full age"*]: Jefferson's third draft of a Virginia constitution, before June 13, 1776, in Jefferson, *Papers,* vol. 1, pp. 356–64, quoted at p. 362.

[*"Give all power"*]: Madison's observations on Jefferson's draft of a Virginia constitution, 1788, in *ibid.,* vol. 6, pp. 308–16, quoted at p. 310.

90 [*"Rights of property"*]: remarks in debate at Constitutional Convention, Philadelphia, August 7, 1787, in Madison, *Papers,* Robert A. Rutland et al., eds. (University of Chicago Press, 1962–), vol. 10, pp. 138–39, quoted at p. 139.

[*"Tendency of things"*]: Francis Childs's version of Hamilton's speech of June 21, 1788, in Hamilton, *Papers,* Harold C. Syrett, ed. (Columbia University Press, 1961–79), vol. 5, pp. 36–45, quoted at pp. 42, 43.

["Earth belongs in usufruct"]: letter to James Madison, September 6, 1789, in Jefferson, *Papers,* pp. 392–97, quoted at p. 392.

[*"Universal law"*]: letter to Isaac McPherson, August 13, 1813, in Saul K. Padover, ed., *The Complete Jefferson* (Tudor Publishing, 1943), pp. 1011–17, quoted at p. 1015.

[*"To take from one"*]: quoted in *ibid.,* pp. 372–73.

[*"Those who labour"*]: Jefferson, *Notes on Virginia,* in Jefferson, *Writings,* vol. 3, pp. 68–295, quoted at p. 268.

91 [*"Cultivators of the earth"*]: *ibid.,* p. 279.

[*"Let our work-shops"*]: *ibid.,* p. 269.

[*"Commercial avarice"*]: letter to Henry Middleton, January 8, 1813, in Jefferson, *Works,* H. A. Washington, ed. (Townsend MacCoun, 1884), vol. 6, pp. 90–91, quoted at p. 91.

[*"Slave owner who was also"*]: Vonnegut, *Breakfast of Champions* (Delacorte Press, 1973), p. 34.

[*"Right to property"*]: letter of April 24, 1816, in Dumas Malone, ed., *Correspondence between Thomas Jefferson and Pierre Samuel du Pont de Nemours,*

1798–1817, Linwood Lehman, trans. (Houghton Mifflin, 1930), pp. 181–87, quoted at p. 184.

92   [*"Tyranny" of "publick opinion"*]: see Cooper, *American Democrat,* pp. 64–65.
[*"As property is the base"*]: ibid., p. 127.

EQUAL RIGHTS: LAW AND POLITICS

Property rights and the Supreme Court, early nineteenth century: Maurice G. Baxter, *Daniel Webster & the Supreme Court* (University of Massachusetts Press, 1966), ch. 4; Joseph Dorfman, "John Marshall: Political Economist," in W. Melville Jones, ed., *Chief Justice John Marshall: A Reappraisal* (Cornell University Press, 1956), pp. 124–44; Robert K. Faulkner, *The Jurisprudence of John Marshall* (Princeton University Press, 1968), pp. 20–33; Francis N. Stites, *John Marshall: Defender of the Constitution,* Oscar Handlin, ed. (Little, Brown, 1981), pp. 111–15, 122–27; William F. Swindler, *The Constitution and Chief Justice Marshall* (Dodd, Mead, 1978), pp. 56–65.

Jackson: Robert V. Remini, *Andrew Jackson,* 3 vols. (Harper, 1977–84); Remini, *The Legacy of Andrew Jackson* (Louisiana State University Press, 1988), esp. ch. 1; Schlesinger, passim; Charles G. Sellers, Jr., "Andrew Jackson and the Historians," *Mississippi Valley Historical Review,* vol. 44, no. 4 (March 1958), pp. 615–34; see also James MacGregor Burns, *The Vineyard of Liberty* (Knopf, 1982), chs. 9–10 passim.

Jackson and the bank: Philip S. Foner, *History of the Labor Movement in the United States: From Colonial Times to the Founding of the American Federation of Labor* (International Publishers, 1947), pp. 144–53; Bray Hammond, *Banks and Politics in the United States: From the Revolution to the Civil War* (Princeton University Press, 1957), chs. 10–14 passim; Remini, *Andrew Jackson,* vol. 2, chs. 20, 22, and vol. 3, chs. 6–8, 10–11 passim; Schlesinger, chs. 7–9.

Taney as Chief Justice: Walker Lewis, *Without Fear or Favor: A Biography of Chief Justice Roger Brooke Taney* (Houghton Mifflin, 1965), ch. 21, and part 4, and passim; Schlesinger, pp. 322–29; Charles W. Smith, Jr., *Roger B. Taney: Jacksonian Jurist* (University of North Carolina Press, 1936), chs. 6, 8–9, and passim; Carl B. Swisher, *Roger B. Taney* (Macmillan, 1935), chs. 15, 17–27, esp. pp. 361–74.

Indian removal: Burns, *Vineyard,* pp. 451–54; Remini, *Andrew Jackson,* esp. vol. 2, chs. 12, 15, and vol. 3, ch. 20; Remini, *Jackson Legacy,* ch. 2; Michael Paul Rogin, *Fathers and Children: Andrew Jackson and the Subjugation of the American Indian* (Knopf, 1975).

Jackson and slavery: Richard E. Ellis, *The Union at Risk: Jacksonian Democracy, States' Rights, and the Nullification Crisis* (Oxford University Press, 1987), pp. 189–94, and passim; Remini, *Jackson Legacy,* ch. 3; Leonard L. Richards, "The Jacksonians and Slavery," in Lewis Perry and Michael Fellman, eds., *Antislavery Reconsidered: New Perspectives on the Abolitionists* (Louisiana State University Press, 1979), pp. 99–118.

American labor and the Industrial Revolution: Joseph Dorfman, *The Economic Mind in American Civilization, 1606–1865* (Viking, 1946–59), vol. 2, esp. chs. 23–24; Thomas Dublin, *Women at Work: The Transformation of Work and Community in Lowell, Massachusetts, 1826–1860* (Columbia University Press, 1979); Philip S. Foner, ed., *The Factory Girls* (University of Illinois Press, 1977); Foner, *History of the Labor Movement,* chs. 4–14; Foner, *Organized Labor and the Black Worker, 1619–1973* (Praeger, 1974), ch. 1; Foner, *Women and the American Labor Movement: From Colonial Times to the Eve of World War I* (Free Press, 1979), chs. 2–6; Walter Hugins, *Jacksonian*

Democracy and the Working Class: A Study of the New York Workingmen's Movement, 1829–1837 (Stanford University Press, 1960); Edgar W. Martin, *The Standard of Living in 1860: American Consumption Levels on the Eve of the Civil War* (University of Chicago Press, 1942); Edward Pessen, *Most Uncommon Jacksonians: The Radical Leaders of the Early Labor Movement* (State University of New York Press, 1967); Pessen, *Riches, Class, and Power before the Civil War* (D. C. Heath, 1973), esp. chs. 3, 8.

Workers' political parties and the Locofocos: Foner, *History of the Labor Movement,* ch. 8, and pp. 153–66; Hugins; Pessen, *Uncommon Jacksonians,* ch. 2, and passim; Schlesinger, chs. 11, 15–17 passim.

Utopianism: Jonathan Beecher, *Charles Fourier: The Visionary and His World* (University of California Press, 1986); Burns, *Vineyard,* pp. 438–44; V. F. Calverton, *Where Angels Dared to Tread* (Bobbs-Merrill, 1941); Foner, *History of the Labor Movement,* ch. 10; Charles Fourier, *Harmonian Man: Selected Writings,* Mark Poster, ed., Susan Hanson, trans. (Doubleday/Anchor, 1971); John F. C. Harrison, *Quest for the New Moral World: Robert Owen and the Owenites in Britain and America* (Scribner, 1969); Charles Nordhoff, *Communistic Societies of the United States* (Harper, 1875); Schlesinger, ch. 28.

PAGE

92   *["It is, sir"]*: quoted in Stites, p. 124.

93   [Dartmouth *decision*]: *Trustees of Dartmouth College* v. *Woodward,* 4 Wheaton 518 (1819).
["Unequivocal limitation"]: Swindler, p. 63.
[Fletcher]: 6 Cranch 87 (1810).

94   *[Maldistribution of wealth]*: see Pessen, *Riches, Class, and Power,* ch. 3 passim; see also Marvin Meyers, *The Jacksonian Persuasion: Politics and Belief* (Stanford University Press, 1957), pp. 81–91.
["Man of the land"]: Hartz, *The Liberal Tradition in America* (Harcourt, 1955), p. 115.
["Democratic autocrat"]: quoted in Sellers, p. 615.
["Trying to kill me"]: quoted in Remini, *Andrew Jackson,* vol. 2, p. 366.

95   *["Rich and powerful"]*: veto message, July 10, 1832, in *A Compilation of the Messages and Papers of the Presidents,* James D. Richardson, ed. (Bureau of National Literature, 1913), vol. 2, pp. 1139–54, quoted at p. 1153.
["Equal rights for all"]: see Swisher, pp. 366–67.
["Sacredly guarded"]: *Charles River Bridge* v. *Warren Bridge,* 11 Peters 420 (1837), quoted at 548; see also Stanley I. Kutler, *Privilege and Creative Destruction: The Charles River Bridge Case* (Norton, 1978).
["Just and liberal"]: in *Messages and Papers of the Presidents,* vol. 2, pp. 999–1001, quoted at p. 1001.
["My children"]: quoted in Remini, *Andrew Jackson,* vol. 3, p. 306.

96   *["Constitution recognises the right"]*: *Dred Scott* v. *Sandford,* 19 Howard 393 (1857), quoted at 451.
["Drawn by Charles Dickens"]: Pessen, *Uncommon Jacksonians,* p. 157.

97   ["Entitled to equal education"]: quoted in *ibid.,* p. 73.
["At birth entitled"]: George Henry Evans, quoted in *ibid.*
[Labor invocations of Declaration]: see Philip S. Foner, ed., *We, the Other People* (University of Illinois Press, 1976), Introduction, and pp. 47–76.
["Ardent believers"]: Pessen, *Uncommon Jacksonians,* p. 103.
["What are rights?"]: quoted in *ibid.,* p. 104.
["Artificial social institutions"]: *ibid.,* p. 103.

98   *["Pleasures of factory life"]*: see Foner, *Factory Girls,* p. 28.

98   [*Dickens at Lowell*]: Dickens, *American Notes for General Circulation,* in Dickens, *Works* (Estes & Lauriat, 1890), vol. 1, pp. 92–100.
[*"Freedom—freedom for all!"*]: women workers' appeals to freedom and rights quoted in Foner, *Factory Girls,* pp. 118, 128, 182, 246, 247.

99   [*"Deprive the citizen"*]: quoted in ibid., p. 232.
[*"Woman is upon your side"*]: ibid., p. 217.
[*"Grace and bounty"*]: quoted in Foner, *History of the Labor Movement,* p. 123.
[*"Fair income"*]: ibid., p. 125.

100   [*"Introduce an entire new State"*]: quoted in Calverton, pp. 180, 181.
[*Schlesinger on "associationism"*]: Schlesinger, p. 363.
[*"Reject all political"*]: in Marx and Engels, *Selected Works* (International Publishers, 1968), pp. 31–63, quoted at p. 60.
[*Fitzhugh on slavery*]: Fitzhugh, *Sociology for the South, or the Failure of Free Society* (1854), excerpted in Francis W. Coker, ed., *Democracy, Liberty, and Property* (Macmillan, 1942), pp. 531–41, quoted at p. 540; see also "Fisher's Report," in Philip S. Foner and Ronald L. Lewis, eds., *Black Workers* (Temple University Press, 1989), pp. 84–89.

4. CROSSING TO JERUSALEM

David Walker: Lerone Bennett, Jr., *Pioneers in Protest* (Johnson Publishing, 1968), pp. 69–80; Jane H. Pease and William H. Pease, *They Who Would Be Free: Blacks' Search for Freedom, 1830–1861* (Atheneum, 1974), pp. 108–11; Benjamin Quarles, *Black Abolitionists* (Oxford University Press, 1969), ch. 1; David Walker, *David Walker's Appeal,* Charles M. Wiltse, ed. (Hill and Wang, 1965).

PAGE
103   [*"Can our condition be any worse?"*]: Walker, pp. 2, 75, 11, 12, 63, 11, 12 respectively.
104   [*"An inspired work" and "diabolical Boston pamphlet"*]: quoted in Quarles, *Black Abolitionists,* p. 17.
[*Garrison on* Appeal]: quoted in Pease and Pease, *They Who Would Be Free,* p. 111.
105   [*"Either the man of color"*]: letter of August 11, 1831, reprinted in Carter G. Woodson, ed., *The Mind of the Negro as Reflected in Letters Written during the Crisis, 1800–1860* (1926; reprinted by Negro Universities Press, 1969), pp. 232–34, quoted at p. 234.
[*"Caused me to stray"*]: 1827 address, reprinted in Herbert Aptheker, ed., *A Documentary History of the Negro People in the United States: From the Colonial Period to the Establishment of the N.A.A.C.P.* (Citadel Press, 1969), pp. 87–88, quoted at p. 88.
[*"Blacks always believed"*]: Williams, "Alchemical Notes: Reconstructing Ideals from Deconstructed Rights," in Jules Lobel, ed., *A Less Than Perfect Union: Alternative Perspectives on the U.S. Constitution* (Monthly Review Press, 1988), pp. 56–70, quoted at p. 64.

WHICH ROAD TO FREEDOM?

Abolitionism and black abolitionists/rights activists: Aptheker, esp. parts 1–3 passim; William Wells Brown, *The Narrative of William W. Brown, a Fugitive Slave* (1847; Addison-Wesley, 1969); Aileen S. Kraditor, *Means and Ends in American Abolitionism*

(Pantheon, 1969); Leon Litwack and August Meier, eds., *Black Leaders of the Nineteenth Century* (University of Illinois Press, 1988); Pease and Pease, *They Who Would Be Free;* Quarles, *Black Abolitionists;* C. Peter Ripley, ed., *The Black Abolitionist Papers* (University of North Carolina Press, 1985–   ), vol. 2; Woodson.

Frederick Douglass: Frederick Douglass, *My Bondage and My Freedom* (1855), William L. Andrews, ed. (University of Illinois Press, 1987); Douglass, *Narrative of the Life of Frederick Douglass, an American Slave* (1845), Benjamin Quarles, ed. (Belknap Press of Harvard University Press, 1960); Douglass, *Papers,* John W. Blassingame, ed., series 1 (Yale University Press, 1979–   ), vols. 1–3; Philip S. Foner, ed., *The Life and Writings of Frederick Douglass,* 5 vols. (International Publishers, 1950–75); Waldo E. Martin, Jr., "Frederick Douglass: Humanist as Race Leader," in Litwack and Meier, pp. 59–84; Martin, *The Mind of Frederick Douglass* (University of North Carolina Press, 1984).

Henry Highland Garnet: David Walker, *Walker's Appeal,* with Henry Highland Garnet, *An Address to the Slaves of the United States of America* (1848; reprinted by Arno Press, 1969); Sterling Stuckey, "A Last Stern Struggle: Henry Highland Garnet and Liberation Theory," in Litwack and Meier, pp. 129–47.

John Mercer Langston: William Cheek and Aimee Lee Cheek, "John Mercer Langston: Principle and Politics," in Litwack and Meier, pp. 103–26; John Mercer Langston, *Freedom and Citizenship: Selected Lectures and Addresses* (Rufus H. Darby, 1883); Langston, *From the Virginia Plantation to the National Capitol* (American Publishing Co., 1894).

PAGE

105   [*"During all my slave life"*]: 1878 written statement, in John W. Blassingame, ed., *Slave Testimony: Two Centuries of Letters, Speeches, Interviews, and Autobiographies* (Louisiana State University Press, 1977), pp. 743–45, quoted at p. 744.

       [*"Came to the conclusion"*]: 1863 interview, in *ibid.,* pp. 395–96, quoted at p. 395.

106   [*"Gave me a soul"*]: letter of 1853, in Dorothy Sterling, ed., *We Are Your Sisters: Black Women in the Nineteenth Century* (Norton, 1984), p. 79.

       [*"When de day's work"*]: interview, in Norman R. Yetman, ed., *Voices from Slavery* (Holt, Rinehart and Winston, 1970), pp. 310–15, quoted at p. 312.

107   [*"Sought not merely social change"*]: Ginzberg, " 'Moral Suasion Is Moral Balderdash': Women, Politics, and Social Activism in the 1850s," *Journal of American History,* vol. 73, no. 3 (December 1986), pp. 601–22, quoted at p. 601.

108   [*"Inestimable and invaluable instrument"*]: manifesto reprinted in Aptheker, pp. 106–7, quoted at p. 106.

       [*Assemblies as "bridge"*]: Pease and Pease, *They Who Would Be Free,* p. 122.

109   [*"Douglass's influence"*]: Martin, "Frederick Douglass," p. 61.

       [*"A large portion"*]: address delivered in Lynn, Massachusetts, October 1841, in Douglass, *Papers,* vol. 1, pp. 3–5, quoted at p. 4.

       [*"Entered into the very idea"*]: address delivered in Manchester, New Hampshire, January 24, 1854, in *ibid.,* vol. 2, pp. 454–60, quoted at pp. 454, 455.

       [*"Right of property in man"*]: address delivered in New York City, May 8, 1849, in *ibid.,* vol. 2, pp. 174–76, quoted at p. 176.

       [*"Main work"*]: "What Are the Colored People Doing for Themselves?,"

July 14, 1848, in Foner, *Douglass,* vol. 1, pp. 314–20, quoted at pp. 314, 316.

110 [*"Appeal of Forty Thousand"*]: reprinted in Aptheker, pp. 176–86, quoted at p. 186.

111 [*Marbles story*]: quoted in Quarles, *Black Abolitionists,* p. 174.
[*"Ours is the battle"*]: quoted in Stuckey, p. 134.
[*"Awake, awake"*]: Garnet, *An Address to the Slaves,* p. 96.
[*"Walking and talking encyclopedia"*]: quoted in Cheek and Cheek, p. 108.

112 [*Elizabeth Jennings*]: Pease and Pease, *They Who Would Be Free,* p. 167; Sterling, pp. 223–24, quoted at p. 224.

113 [*"Hugged the seats"*]: quoted in Pease and Pease, *They Who Would Be Free,* p. 166.
[*"Equal school rights"*]: Nell remarks reprinted in Aptheker, pp. 376–78, quoted at p. 377.
[*"Would be free"*]: Garnet, p. 93.

THEMSELVES STRIKE THE BLOW

Fugitive rescues and Underground Railroad: Aptheker, part 3 passim; Charles L. Blockson, *The Underground Railroad* (Prentice-Hall, 1987); Jane H. Pease and William H. Pease, *The Fugitive Slave Law and Anthony Burns: A Problem in Law Enforcement* (Lippincott, 1975); Pease and Pease, *They Who Would Be Free;* Wilbur H. Siebert, *The Underground Railroad from Slavery to Freedom* (Russell & Russell, 1898); William Still, *The Underground Rail Road* (1872; reprinted by Arno Press, 1968).

Harriet Tubman: Sarah H. Bradford, *Harriet Tubman: The Moses of Her People* (Citadel Press, 1961); Earl Conrad, *Harriet Tubman: Negro Soldier and Abolitionist* (International Publishers, 1942); Benjamin Quarles, "Harriet Tubman's Unlikely Leadership," in Litwack and Meier, pp. 43–57.

Dred Scott case: Elbert William R. Ewing, *Legal and Historical Status of the Dred Scott Decision* (Cobden Publishing, 1909); Don E. Fehrenbacher, *The Dred Scott Case: Its Significance in American Law and Politics* (Oxford University Press, 1978).

African-Americans in the Civil War: W. E. B. Du Bois, *Black Reconstruction in America* (Atheneum, 1979); Leon F. Litwack, *Been in the Storm So Long: The Aftermath of Slavery* (Vintage, 1980); James M. McPherson, *The Negro's Civil War* (Pantheon, 1965).

PAGE

114 [*"Armistice of 1850"*]: quoted in Fehrenbacher, p. 163.
[*"Blacks were major shapers"*]: Pease and Pease, *They Who Would Be Free,* p. 206.
[*"Slavery has been nationalized"*]: July 5, 1852, in Foner, *Douglass,* vol. 2, pp. 181–204, quoted at pp. 195, 196.
[*"No legislation can"*]: October 14, 1850, in Douglass, *Papers,* vol. 2, pp. 243–48, quoted at p. 248.

115 [*"Liberty of more value"*]: January 7, 1851, in *ibid.,* vol. 2, pp. 273–78, quoted at pp. 277, 276 respectively.
[*"Business of catching slaves"*]: editorial of *The Impartial Citizen,* quoted in *The Liberator,* October 11, 1850, and reprinted in Aptheker, p. 306.
[*"People of Syracuse"*]: in *ibid.,* pp. 306–8, quoted at p. 307.
[*"Clear treason"*]: quoted in Pease and Pease, *They Who Would Be Free,* p. 221.

116   [*"No such rights"*]: "Letter to the American Slaves," September 1850, in Aptheker, pp. 299–305, quoted at p. 302.
117   [*"I had reasoned dis"*]: quoted in Bradford, p. 29.
       [*"Accomplished her purpose"*]: quoted in Conrad, p. 14.
       [*Quarles on Tubman*]: Quarles, "Tubman," p. 45.
       [*"One of the greatest forces"*]: Siebert, p. 358.
118   [Dred Scott *decision*]: *Dred Scott* v. *Sandford*, 60 U.S. 393 (1857), quoted at 404–5, 425.
       [*Fehrenbacher* on Dred Scott]: Fehrenbacher, p. 363.
       [*Newspaper headlines*]: quoted in James MacGregor Burns, *The Vineyard of Liberty* (Knopf, 1982), p. 576.
119   [*"No rights which the white man was bound to respect"*]: *Dred Scott*, 407.
       [*"Founded and administered in iniquity"*]: quoted in Aptheker, p. 392.
       [*"Judicial incarnation of wolfishness"*]: address delivered in New York City, May 1857, in Douglass, *Papers*, vol. 3, pp. 163–83, quoted at pp. 167, 168, 169.
120   [*"Forever free"*]: in Lincoln, *Collected Works*, Roy P. Basler, ed. (Rutgers University Press, 1953), vol. 6, pp. 28–30, quoted at p. 29.
       [*"Sound the loud timbrel"*]: quoted in Eric Foner, *Reconstruction: America's Unfinished Revolution, 1863–1877* (Harper, 1988), p. 1.
       [*"Transformed a war of armies"*]: ibid., p. 7.
       [*"Key of the situation"*]: quoted in *ibid.*, p. 5.
       [*"Has not the man who conquers"*]: *ibid.*, p. 10.
       [*"Record of the Negro soldier"*]: Du Bois, p. 104.
121   [*"Slavery chain done broke at last"*]: quoted in Litwack, *Been in the Storm So Long*, p. 169.
       [*"Work does not end"*]: "The Work of the Future," November 1862, in Foner, *Douglass*, vol. 3, pp. 290–93, quoted at p. 293.
       [*Foner on "freedom"*]: Foner, *Reconstruction*, p. 77.

BOTTOM RAIL ON TOP

Reconstruction: Aptheker, esp. parts 5–6 passim; John Dittmer, "The Education of Henry McNeal Turner," in Litwack and Meier, pp. 253–72; Du Bois; Eric Foner, "Black Reconstruction Leaders at the Grass Roots," in Litwack and Meier, pp. 219–34; Eric Foner, *Nothing But Freedom: Emancipation and Its Legacy* (Louisiana State University Press, 1983); Foner, *Reconstruction;* Lawrence W. Levine, *Black Culture and Black Consciousness* (Oxford University Press, 1977); Litwack, *Been in the Storm So Long;* Leon F. Litwack, " 'Blues Falling Down Like Hail': The Ordeal of Black Freedom," in Robert H. Abzug and Stephen E. Maizlish, eds., *New Perspectives on Race and Slavery in America* (University Press of Kentucky, 1986), pp. 109–27; James M. McPherson, *The Struggle for Equality: Abolitionists and the Negro in the Civil War and Reconstruction* (Princeton University Press, 1964); Howard N. Rabinowitz, "Three Reconstruction Leaders: Blanche K. Bruce, Robert Brown Elliott, and Holland Thompson," in Litwack and Meier, pp. 191–217.

Fourteenth Amendment: Derrick Bell, *And We Are Not Saved: The Elusive Quest for Racial Justice* (Basic Books, 1987); Harold Cruse, *Plural But Equal: A Critical Study of Blacks and Minorities and America's Plural Society* (Morrow, 1987); Joseph B. James, *The Ratification of the Fourteenth Amendment* (Mercer University Press, 1984); Lobel; William E. Nelson, *The Fourteenth Amendment: From Political Principle to Judicial Doctrine* (Harvard University Press, 1988); Bernard Schwartz, ed., *The Fourteenth Amendment: Centennial Volume* (New York University Press, 1970).

PAGE
121   ["Shoutin' an' carryin' on"]: quoted in Litwack, Been in the Storm So Long, p. 225.
122   ["To belong to ourselves"]: ibid., p. 226.
       ["We do understand Freedom"]: 1865 resolutions, in Aptheker, pp. 536–38, quoted at p. 538.
       ["De slaves, where I lived"]: quoted in Litwack, Been in the Storm So Long, p. 328.
       ["We soon found out"]: ibid., p. 449.
123   ["Foundation of freedom"]: Foner, Reconstruction, p. 160.
       ["Uncle Sam is rich enough"]: quoted in Litwack, Been in the Storm So Long, p. 402.
       ["Great motivating ideal"]: Du Bois, p. 469.
124   ["Become part of their natures"]: quoted in Foner, "Black Reconstruction Leaders," p. 224.
       ["Not the persuit of happiness"]: quoted in Foner, Reconstruction, p. 114.
       ["De worse kind of slavery"]: quoted in Litwack, Been in the Storm So Long, p. 329.
125   ["Fatal and total surrender"]: quoted in Foner, Reconstruction, p. 255.
126   ["Peace treaty"]: Nelson, pp. 110–11.
       [Fourteenth Amendment's ambiguity]: see ibid., pp. 117–23.
       [Bingham's intentions for Fourteenth Amendment]: Henry Steele Commager, "Historical Background of the Fourteenth Amendment," in Schwartz, pp. 14–28, esp. p. 23.
127   ["Let's have our rights"]: quoted in Foner, Reconstruction, p. 282.
       [South Carolina convention]: Du Bois, pp. 393–99.
130   ["Pushed Republicans to the outer limits"]: Foner, Reconstruction, p. 455.
       ["Whether our constitutional rights"]: in Aptheker, pp. 600–4, quoted at p. 603.
       ["Something more than a delusion"]: ibid., quoted at p. 604.
131   ["We are taxed"]: in ibid., pp. 513–15, quoted at p. 514.
       ["Encourage sound morality"]: League's constitution excerpted in ibid., pp. 525–26, quoted at p. 526.
       ["No distinction"]: Appeal from League's executive board, in ibid., pp. 526–28, League constitution quoted at p. 527.
       ["Grievances and wants"]: quoted in Cheek and Cheek, p. 115.
       ["Astonishing advances"]: Foner, Reconstruction, p. 471.
       ["Individual invasion"]: Civil Rights Cases, 109 U.S. 3 (1883), quoted at 11.

WHITHER THE PROMISED LAND?

Post-Reconstruction: Aptheker, esp. parts 6–8 passim; Stewart Burns, "The Populist Movement and the Cooperative Commonwealth" (Ph.D. dissertation, University of California, Santa Cruz, 1984), ch. 10 passim; Cruse; Litwack, " 'Blues Falling Down Like Hail' "; Nelson; C. Vann Woodward, Origins of the New South, 1877–1913 (Louisiana State University Press, 1951); Woodward, The Strange Career of Jim Crow, 3rd rev. ed. (Oxford University Press, 1974), chs. 1–3.

PAGE
132   ["Time of testing"]: Woodward, Strange Career of Jim Crow, p. 33.
       ["Seamless web of oppression"]: Foner, Reconstruction, p. 598.
133   [Plessy]: 163 U.S. 537 (1896), Harlan dissent at 562, 559 respectively.

133   [Williams]: 170 U.S. 213 (1898).
       [*"It is important and right"*]: in Aptheker, pp. 753–57, quoted at p. 756.
134   [*Rudé on "derived" and "inherent" elements in new ideologies*]: Rudé, *Ideology and Popular Protest* (Pantheon, 1980), ch. 2.
       [*Negative vs. positive liberty*]: see Isaiah Berlin, *Two Concepts of Liberty* (Clarendon Press, 1958).
135   [*"World of walls"*]: quoted in Samuel Bowles and Herbert Gintis, *Democracy and Capitalism: Property, Community, and the Contradictions of Modern Social Thought* (Basic Books, 1987), pp. 17, 16 respectively.
       [*Foner on free labor ideology*]: Foner, *Reconstruction*, p. 277.
136   [*Marx on French civil war*]: see Marx, *The Civil War in France*, in Robert C. Tucker, ed., *The Marx-Engels Reader* (Norton, 1972), pp. 526–76, esp. p. 554.
       [*"Were born equal"*]: Alexis de Tocqueville, *Democracy in America* (Doubleday/Anchor, 1969), vol. 2, p. 509.

5. BONDS OF WOMANHOOD

Chapter title: Sarah Grimké, *Letters on the Equality of the Sexes and Other Essays,* Elizabeth Ann Bartlett, ed. (Yale University Press, 1988), p. 103. Grimké signed letters "Thine in the bonds of womanhood."

Indispensable source for chapter: Notable American Women, 1607–1950, 3 vols. (Belknap Press of Harvard University Press, 1971), and *Notable American Women: The Modern Period* (Belknap Press of Harvard University Press, 1980).

Grimké sisters: Gilbert H. Barnes and Dwight L. Dumond, eds., *Letters of Theodore Dwight Weld, Angelina Grimké Weld and Sarah Grimké, 1822–1844* (Peter Smith, 1965), vol. 1; Catherine H. Birney, *The Grimké Sisters: The First American Women Advocates of Abolition and Woman's Rights* (Greenwood Press, 1969); Grimké; Gerda Lerner, *The Grimké Sisters from South Carolina* (Houghton Mifflin, 1967); Katharine Du Pre Lumpkin, *The Emancipation of Angelina Grimké* (University of North Carolina Press, 1974).

PAGE
137   [*"God strengthen you"*]: quoted in Lerner, p. 5.
       [*God's arm "to lean upon"*]: ibid., p. 6.
       [*"I stand before you"*]: ibid., pp. 373–74, 7 respectively.
138   [*"We are placed very unexpectedly"*]: letter of August 12, 1837, in *Weld-Grimké Letters,* vol. 1, pp. 414–19, quoted at pp. 415, 416.
       [*"The time to assert a right"*]: letter of August 20, 1837, in *ibid.,* vol. 1, pp. 427–32, quoted at pp. 428, 430.
139   [*"WHATSOEVER IT IS MORALLY RIGHT"*]: Grimké, p. 100; on *Letters,* see Lerner, pp. 192–94.
       [*"All rights spring out of the moral nature"*]: Grimké, p. 97.
140   [*"Women's discontent"*]: Ellen Carol DuBois, *Feminism and Suffrage: The Emergence of an Independent Women's Movement in America, 1848–1869* (Cornell University Press, 1978), p. 32.
       [*"For the Enlightenment"*]: Bartlett, Introduction, in Grimké, p. 18.

THE ARISTOCRACY OF SEX

Early women's rights movement: Mari Jo Buhle and Paul Buhle, eds., *The Concise History of Woman Suffrage* (University of Illinois Press, 1978); Ellen Carol DuBois,

ed., *Elizabeth Cady Stanton/Susan B. Anthony: Correspondence, Writings, Speeches* (Schocken, 1981), pp. 2–130; DuBois, *Feminism and Suffrage;* DuBois, "Outgrowing the Compact of the Fathers: Equal Rights, Woman Suffrage, and the United States Constitution, 1820–1878," *Journal of American History,* vol. 74, no. 3 (December 1987), pp. 836–62; Eleanor Flexner, *Century of Struggle: The Woman's Rights Movement in the United States* (Atheneum, 1970), chs. 3–10; Lori D. Ginzberg, " 'Moral Suasion Is Moral Balderdash': Women, Politics, and Social Activism in the 1850s," *Journal of American History,* vol. 73, no. 3 (December 1986), pp. 601–22; Ginzberg, *Women and the Work of Benevolence: Morality, Politics, and Class in the Nineteenth-Century United States* (Yale University Press, 1990); Anne F. Scott and Andrew M. Scott, *One Half the People: The Fight for Woman Suffrage* (Lippincott, 1975).

Elizabeth Cady Stanton: Lois W. Banner, *Elizabeth Cady Stanton: A Radical for Woman's Rights* (Little, Brown, 1980); DuBois, *Stanton/Anthony;* Elizabeth Griffith, *In Her Own Right: The Life of Elizabeth Cady Stanton* (Oxford University Press, 1984); Alma Lutz, *Created Equal: A Biography of Elizabeth Cady Stanton, 1815–1902* (John Day, 1940); Elizabeth Cady Stanton, *Eighty Years and More (1815–1897): Reminiscences of Elizabeth Cady Stanton* (European Publishing, 1898); Theodore Stanton and Harriot Stanton Blatch, eds., *Elizabeth Cady Stanton As Revealed in Her Letters, Diary and Reminiscences,* 2 vols. (Harper, 1922).

Susan B. Anthony: Kathleen Barry, *Susan B. Anthony: A Biography of a Singular Feminist* (New York University Press, 1988); DuBois, *Stanton/Anthony.*

PAGE

141   [*"Chosen means"*]: Ginzberg, " 'Moral Suasion,' " p. 602.
      [*Ginzberg on women feeling politically disfranchised*]: *ibid.,* pp. 603–16; Ginzberg, *Women and the Work of Benevolence,* Introduction, and chs. 3–4.
      [*"Torrent of my long-accumulating discontent"*]: Stanton, *Eighty Years and More,* p. 148.

142   [*"Asked to construct a steam engine"*]: report of Seneca Falls convention, in Buhle and Buhle, pp. 91–98, quoted at p. 92.
      [*"Borrow political legitimacy"*]: DuBois, *Feminism and Suffrage,* p. 23.
      [*"Declaration of Sentiments and Resolutions"*]: in Buhle and Buhle, pp. 94–97, quoted at pp. 94, 95, 96.

143   [*"Tall, gaunt black woman"*]: quoted in Olive Gilbert, ed., *Narrative of Sojourner Truth* (1878; reprinted by Arno Press, 1968), pp. 131–32.

144   [*"Dat man ober dar"*]: *ibid.,* pp. 133–34; on Truth, see also Arthur H. Fauset, *Sojourner Truth: God's Faithful Pilgrim* (1938; reprinted by Russell & Russell, 1971).
      [*"Like the magical influence"*]: quoted in Gilbert, p. 135.
      [*Married couple as "one person"*]: quoted in Buhle and Buhle, p. 152.
      [*"Very being or legal existence"*]: quoted in Barry, p. 13.
      [*"Man in his lust"*]: letter of March 1, 1853, in Stanton and Blatch, vol. 2, pp. 48–49, quoted at p. 49.

145   [*"I forged the thunderbolts"*]: Stanton, *Eighty Years and More,* pp. 165–66.
146   [*"Propulsive force"*]: quoted in Lutz, p. 169.
      [*"Rights of woman as an individual"*]: Buhle and Buhle, pp. 154–55.

147   [*"Strong arm and blue uniform"*]: letter to the *National Anti-Slavery Standard,* December 26, 1865, in *ibid.,* pp. 219–20 fn., quoted at p. 219 fn.
      [*"Bury the black man"*]: quoted in DuBois, "Outgrowing the Compact of the Fathers," p. 846.
      [*"This is the negro's hour"*]: Stanton letter of December 26, 1865, in Buhle and Buhle, quoted at p. 219 fn.

147 [*"Like the flying of the shuttle"*]: quoted in Barry, p. 176.
     [*Greeley's revenge*]: quoted in Lutz, p. 142.
148 [*"The few who had the prescience"*]: quoted in DuBois, *Feminism and Suffrage*,
     p. 172.
     [*"Intensify sexual inequality"*]: *ibid.*, p. 174.
     [*"Aristocracy of sex"*]: quoted in *ibid.*, p. 175.
     [*"If I have to answer"*]: May 9, 1867, in Buhle and Buhle, pp. 235–36,
     quoted at p. 235.
149 [*"Question of life and death"*]: AERA debates, May 12–14, 1869, in *ibid.*,
     pp. 257–74, quoted at p. 258.
     [*"We are lost"*]: *ibid.*, pp. 259, 260.
     [*"Transitional phase of suffragism"*]: DuBois, *Feminism and Suffrage*,
     p. 187.
150 [*"Question of precedence"*]: quoted in Barry, p. 192.
     [*"Steered the women's rights movement away"*]: DuBois, "Outgrowing the
     Compact of the Fathers," p. 852.

THE NEW DEPARTURE

"New departure" strategy: Buhle and Buhle, pp. 281–96.

Stanton's philosophy of rights and political theory: Zillah R. Eisenstein, *The Radical Future of Liberal Feminism* (Northeastern University Press, 1986), ch. 7.

Willard and the Woman's Christian Temperance Union: Mary Earhart, *Frances Willard: From Prayers to Politics* (University of Chicago Press, 1944); Barbara L. Epstein, *The Politics of Domesticity: Women, Evangelism, and Temperance in Nineteenth-Century America* (Wesleyan University Press, 1981); Norton Mezvinsky, "The White-Ribbon Reform, 1874–1920" (Ph.D. dissertation, University of Wisconsin, 1959); Samuel Unger, "A History of the National Woman's Christian Temperance Union" (Ph.D. dissertation, Ohio State University, 1933); Frances E. Willard, *Glimpses of Fifty Years: The Autobiography of an American Woman* (Woman's Temperance Publication Association, 1889).

PAGE
151 [*Woodhull on her right to love*]: Woodhull, "A Speech on the Principles of
     Social Freedom," November 20, 1871, in Madeleine B. Stern, ed., *The
     Victoria Woodhull Reader* (M&S Press, 1974), pp. 1–43, quoted at p. 23.
152 [*Anthony's jubilant report*]: quoted in Barry, p. 249.
     [*"We throw to the winds"*]: Anthony, "Constitutional Argument," 1872, in
     DuBois, *Stanton/Anthony*, pp. 152–65, quoted at p. 153.
     [*"I shall never pay a dollar"*]: report of Anthony trial, June 17–18, 1873,
     in Buhle and Buhle, pp. 293–96, quoted at p. 296.
     [Minor]: 88 U.S. 162 (1874).
153 [*"Only suitable commemoration"*]: Lutz, p. 236.
     [*"Slight request"*]: report of the Centennial celebration, July 4, 1876, in
     Buhle and Buhle, pp. 297–303, quoted at p. 297.
     [*"Declaration of Rights for Women"*]: in *ibid.*, pp. 300–3, quoted at pp.
     300, 303.
154 [*Letters to Anthony on woman suffrage*]: in DuBois, *Stanton/Anthony*, pp.
     201–7, Sobers quoted at pp. 202–3, Rathbun at p. 204, Pryor at p. 205,
     Pool at p. 207.
155 [*"Vestibule of woman's emancipation"*]: quoted in Lutz, p. 228.
     [*"Conservatism cries out"*]: Stanton, "Home Life," in DuBois, *Stanton/
     Anthony*, pp. 131–38, quoted at pp. 132, 133.

155   [*"Oppress the citizens"*]: quoted in DuBois, "Outgrowing the Compact of the Fathers," p. 862.
        [*"All history shows"*]: quoted in Eisenstein, p. 156.
156   [*"Her birthright"*]: "The Solitude of Self," January 18, 1892, in DuBois, *Stanton/Anthony*, pp. 247–54, quoted at pp. 247, 248.
        [*"Feminism uses the individualist stance"*]: Eisenstein, p. 154.
157   [*Sumner's Social Darwinism*]: see Sumner, *What Social Classes Owe to Each Other* (Harper, 1911).
158   [*"Losing its radical associations"*]: Ginzberg, " 'Moral Suasion,' " p. 621.
        [*"Support for the suffrage"*]: DuBois, *Stanton/Anthony*, p. 174.
159   [*"Universal sisterhood"*]: quoted in Griffith, p. 193.
        [*"Literary Clubs, Art Unions"*]: quoted in Barry, p. 284.
        [*Purvis's support of women's cause*]: ibid., p. 287.
160   [*South Dakota suffrage campaign*]: see Anna Howard Shaw, "Aunt Susan," 1890, in DuBois, *Stanton/Anthony*, pp. 218–21; report of South Dakota campaign, 1890, in Buhle and Buhle, pp. 321–24.

DEMOCRACY SHOULD BEGIN AT HOME

Charlotte Perkins Gilman: Charlotte Perkins Gilman, *The Living of Charlotte Perkins Gilman: An Autobiography* (1935; reprinted by Arno Press, 1972); Gilman, *Women and Economics,* Carl N. Degler, ed. (Harper Torchbooks, 1966); Mary A. Hill, *Charlotte Perkins Gilman: The Making of a Radical Feminist, 1860–1896* (Temple University Press, 1980); Gary Scharnhorst, *Charlotte Perkins Gilman* (Twayne, 1985); Barbara Scott Winkler, *Victorian Daughters: The Lives and Feminism of Charlotte Perkins Gilman and Olive Schreiner* (Michigan Occasional Paper No. 13, Winter 1980).

Later woman suffrage movement: Buhle and Buhle, part 3 passim; Carrie Chapman Catt and Nettie Rogers Shuler, *Woman Suffrage and Politics* (Scribner, 1923); Nancy F. Cott, *The Grounding of Modern Feminism* (Yale University Press, 1987); Ellen Carol DuBois, "Working Women, Class Relations, and Suffrage Militance: Harriot Stanton Blatch and the New York Woman Suffrage Movement, 1894–1909," *Journal of American History*, vol. 74, no. 1 (June 1987), pp. 34–58; Flexner, chs. 19–24; Sherna Gluck, ed., *From Parlor to Prison: Five American Suffragists Talk about Their Lives* (Vintage, 1976); Inez Haynes Irwin, *The Story of the Woman's Party* (Harcourt, 1921); Aileen S. Kraditor, *The Ideas of the Woman Suffrage Movement, 1890–1920* (Doubleday/Anchor, 1971); Christine A. Lunardini, *From Equal Suffrage to Equal Rights: Alice Paul and the National Woman's Party, 1910–1928* (New York University Press, 1986); Mary Gray Peck, *Carrie Chapman Catt* (H. W. Wilson, 1944); Scott and Scott; Doris Stevens, *Jailed for Freedom* (Boni & Liveright, 1920); Justina L. Wilson, *Woman Suffrage: A Study Outline* (H. W. Wilson, 1916); *Woman Suffrage, Arguments and Results* (pamphlet collection, National American Woman Suffrage Association, n.d.).

PAGE
161   [*"Smooth, swift, easy flow"*]: Gilman, *The Living of Charlotte Perkins Gilman,* p. 235.
        [*"Marx and Veblen"*]: quoted in Hill, p. 4.
        [*"Matriolatry"*]: Gilman, *Women and Economics,* p. 174.
        [*"Sexuo-economic relation"*]: ibid., p. 94.
162   [*"Principles of development"*]: ibid., pp. xxxiii–xxxiv.
        [*Gender-specific barriers to full citizenship*]: see discussion of "plebiscitarian" vs. "functional" rights in Reinhard Bendix, *Nation-Building and Citizenship* (University of California Press, 1977), pp. 66–126, and application of

"functional" rights concept to women in Sorca M. O'Connor, "Women's Labor Force Participation and Preschool Enrollment: A Cross-National Perspective, 1965–80," *Sociology of Education*, vol. 61, no. 1 (January 1988), pp. 15–28, esp. pp. 15–17.

162 [*"No cause for alarm"*]: Gilman, *Women and Economics*, pp. 267, 237, 293 respectively.
[*"We shall have far happier marriages"*]: quoted in *ibid.*, p. xxix.
[*Gilman's vision and its lack of relevance for lower-class women*]: Scharnhorst, p. 54.

163 [*"Where are the people?"*]: quoted in Lunardini, p. 29.
[*Blatch and Women's Political Union*]: DuBois, "Working Women"; Gluck, pp. 17, 200–3.

164 [*National Woman's Party political strategy*]: Kraditor, pp. 191–99.
[*"I have worked all my life"*]: quoted in Lunardini, p. 105.

165 [*"Swinging their trunks sadly"*]: Peck, p. 245.
[*"Women do not want the vote"*]: quoted in Catt and Shuler, p. 252.
[New York Times *report*]: quoted in Peck, p. 252.
[*"Living petition"*]: Catt and Shuler, p. 260.
[*"Crowded stuffy room"*]: quoted in Scott and Scott, p. 129.
[*"We must do both"*]: *ibid.*, p. 130.

166 [*"Solemn compact"*]: quoted in Catt and Shuler, p. 263.
[*"I felt like Moses"*]: quoted in Scott and Scott, p. 131.
[*"Biggest week's work"*]: quoted in Peck, p. 263.
[*"A great army in perfect discipline"*]: Catt and Shuler, p. 263.
[*NWP's "war policy"*]: Stevens, pp. 83–84.
[*"We shall fight"*]: quoted in Lunardini, p. 114.

167 [*"America is not a democracy"*]: *ibid.*, p. 115.
[*"Determined, organized effort"*]: Stevens, p. 175.
[*"Forlorn piece of paper"*]: *ibid.*, p. 177.

168 [*"Magic touchstone" of states' rights*]: Flexner, p. 310.
[*"Shall we admit them"*]: September 30, 1918, in Wilson, *Papers*, Arthur S. Link, ed. (Princeton University Press, 1966–   ), vol. 51, pp. 158–61, quoted at p. 159.
[*"Pauseless campaign"*]: quoted in Peck, p. 5.

169 [*"Women with widely divergent views"*]: Gluck, p. 23.
170 [*"Didn't want anything else"*]: *ibid.*, p. 175.
[*"Because of a great victory"*]: quoted in Lunardini, p. 159.
[*Impact of privatism and liberal individualism on the woman's movement*]: Cott, pp. 276, 282–83.
[*"No new quality"*]: Emma Goldman, "Woman Suffrage," in Goldman, *The Traffic in Women and Other Essays on Feminism* (Times Change Press, 1970), pp. 51–63, quoted at p. 63; see also Goldman, "The Tragedy of Woman's Emancipation," in Goldman, *Anarchism and Other Essays* (Mother Earth Publishing Association, 1910), pp. 219–31.
[*"Right to self-expression"*]: Goldman, *Living My Life* (Knopf, 1931), vol. 1, p. 56.

6. RIGHTS TO BREAD AND ROSES

1877 uprising: Jeremy Brecher, *Strike!* (Straight Arrow Books, 1972), pp. 1–24; Robert V. Bruce, *1877: Year of Violence* (Bobbs-Merrill, 1959); Philip S. Foner, *The Great Labor Uprising of 1877* (Monad Press, 1977).

Labor republicanism: Leon Fink, "The New Labor History and the Powers of Historical Pessimism: Consensus, Hegemony, and the Case of the Knights of Labor,"

Journal of American History, vol. 75, no. 1 (June 1988), pp. 115–36; Fink, *Working-men's Democracy: The Knights of Labor and American Politics* (University of Illinois Press, 1983), esp. ch. 1; Philip S. Foner, ed., *We, the Other People: Alternative Declarations of Independence by Labor Groups, Farmers, Woman's Rights Advocates, Social-ists, and Blacks, 1829–1975* (University of Illinois Press, 1976); Herbert G. Gutman, *Work, Culture, and Society in Industrializing America: Essays in American Working-Class and Social History* (Knopf, 1976); David Montgomery, *Beyond Equality: Labor and the Radical Republicans, 1862–1872* (Knopf, 1967); Montgomery, "Labor and the Republic in Industrial America, 1860–1920," *Le Mouvement Social* (April–June 1980), pp. 201–15; Terence V. Powderly, *Thirty Years of Labor, 1859–1889* (1890; reprinted by Augustus M. Kelley, 1967), pp. 31–58; Daniel T. Rodgers, *Contested Truths: Keywords in American Politics since Independence* (Basic Books, 1987), pp. 45–79.

PAGE

171   [*"Every man willing to perform"*]: "Proclamation," July 25, 1877, reprinted in Foner, *Great Labor Uprising,* p. 102.
       [*"Not for the company"*]: quoted in *ibid.,* pp. 44–45.
172   [*"Character of a general insurrection"*]: *ibid.,* p. 74.
       [*"Second American Revolution"*]: *ibid.,* p. 230.
       [*"Strikes have been put down"*]: entry of August 5, 1877, quoted in Bruce, p. 315.
       [*"Tocsin that sounded"*]: *ibid.,* p. 318.
       [*"Entire regions lay in their grip"*]: Foner, *Great Labor Uprising,* p. 14.
       [*Tocqueville on "industrial aristocracy"*]: Alexis de Tocqueville, *Democracy in America* (Doubleday/Anchor, 1969), vol. 2, p. 557.
173   [*Montgomery on workers' moral responsibility*]: Montgomery, "Labor and the Republic," p. 206.
       [*"Find capital as rigid"*]: Herbert G. Gutman, "Work, Culture, and Society in Industrializing America, 1815–1919," in Gutman, pp. 3–78, quoted at p. 52.
       [*"Secure to the toilers"*]: *Knights of Labor: Record of the Proceedings of the General Assembly, 1878–1879* (n.p., n.d.) (University of California Library, Berke-ley), p. 28.
       [*"Life implies the right"*]: *John Swinton's Paper* (New York), May 25, 1884.
       [*Steward and others on dependent wage slave*]: Montgomery, *Beyond Equality,* pp. 251–52; Montgomery, "Labor and the Republic," p. 205.
       [*Rights of "producer-as-citizen" and "citizen-as-producer"*]: Fink, *Workingmen's Democracy,* p. 4.
174   [*"Mere strand"*]: Fink, "New Labor History," p. 121.

FIGHTING FOR TIME

Eight-hour movement and labor rights: Marion Cotter Cahill, *Shorter Hours: A Study of the Movement since the Civil War* (Columbia University Press, 1932); Lemuel Dan-ryid, *History and Philosophy of the Eight-Hour Movement,* AFL Eight-Hour Series, no. 3, 5th ed. (American Federation of Labor, 1899); Philip S. Foner and Brewster Chamberlin, eds., *Friedrich A. Sorge's Labor Movement in the United States* (Green-wood Press, 1977); Samuel Gompers, *Seventy Years of Life and Labor: An Autobiogra-phy,* Nick Salvatore, ed. (ILR Press, 1984); George Gunton, *The Economic and Social Importance of the Eight-Hour Movement,* AFL Eight-Hour Series, no. 2 (American Federation of Labor, 1889); R. W. Jocelyn, *The Rights of Labor: An Inquiry as to the Relation, Employer and Employed* (Charles H. Kerr, 1894); *Labor: Its Rights and Wrongs* (Labor Publishing, 1886; reprinted by Hyperion Press, 1975); Labor Research

Association, *The History of the Shorter Workday* (International Publishers, 1942); George E. McNeill, *The Eight Hour Primer: The Fact, Theory and the Argument,* AFL Eight-Hour Series, no. 1, 3rd ed. (American Federation of Labor, 1907); Montgomery, *Beyond Equality;* Powderly, *Thirty Years of Labor,* pp. 85–87, 240–70; David R. Roediger and Philip S. Foner, *Our Own Time: A History of American Labor and the Working Day* (Greenwood Press, 1989).

Knights of Labor and the 1886 movement: Paul Avrich, *The Haymarket Tragedy* (Princeton University Press, 1984); Henry David, *The History of the Haymarket Affair* (Farrar & Rinehart, 1936); Fink, *Workingmen's Democracy;* Philip S. Foner, *History of the Labor Movement in the United States* (International Publishers, 1947–), vol. 2; Susan Levine, "Labor's True Woman: Domesticity and Equal Rights in the Knights of Labor," *Journal of American History,* vol. 70, no. 2 (September 1983), pp. 323–39; Terence V. Powderly, *The Path I Trod,* Harry J. Carman et al., eds. (1940; reprinted by AMS Press, 1968); Powderly, *Thirty Years of Labor.*

PAGE
174   ["*First fruit*"]: Marx, *Capital* (Vintage, 1977), vol. 1, p. 414.
["*Must succumb*"]: quoted in *ibid.,* vol. 1, p. 414 fn.
["*From selling themselves*"]: *ibid.,* vol. 1, p. 416.
175   ["*Ten-Hour Circular*"]: quoted in Roediger and Foner, p. 31.
["*Eight hours for work*"]: *ibid.,* p. 98; Roediger on the new rallying cry at *ibid.*
["*Citizenship time*"]: quoted in *ibid.,* p. 7.
["*Clearer conception*"]: Gompers, "The Eight-Hour Workday," *American Federationist* (Washington, D.C.), April 1897.
[*Minister on shorter hours*]: quoted in Roediger and Foner, p. 60.
176   [*Steward on leisure*]: *ibid.,* p. 95.
[*Steward compared with Marx*]: Montgomery, *Beyond Equality,* p. 251.
["*Success of our republican institutions*"]: quoted in *ibid.,* p. 177.
177   ["*Universal strike*"]: quoted in Roediger and Foner, p. 129.
[*FOTLU on mass organization*]: *ibid.,* p. 130.
["*Outstanding vehicle of Negro-White unity*"]: Sidney H. Kessler, "The Organization of Negroes in the Knights of Labor," *Journal of Negro History,* vol. 37, no. 3 (July 1952), pp. 248–76, quoted at p. 276.
["*Regenerate American life*"]: Leon Fink, "Labor, Liberty, and the Law: Trade Unionism and the Problem of the American Constitutional Order," *Journal of American History,* vol. 74, no. 3 (December 1987), pp. 904–25, quoted at pp. 911–12.
178   ["*We want to feel the sunshine*"]: quoted in Roediger and Foner, p. 139.
179   [Lochner]: 198 U.S. 45 (1905), quoted at 53, 61; on the Fourteenth Amendment as applied to the labor movement, see John P. Roche, "Entrepreneurial Liberty and the Fourteenth Amendment," *Labor History,* vol. 4, no. 1 (Winter 1963), pp. 3–31.
["*Such fundamental stature*"]: William E. Nelson, *The Fourteenth Amendment: From Political Principle to Judicial Doctrine* (Harvard University Press, 1988), p. 199.
[Muller]: 208 U.S. 412 (1908).
["*Decisive period*"]: quoted in Roediger and Foner, p. 177.

SOLIDARITY FOREVER

Homestead and Pullman strikes: Brecher, pp. 53–100; Foner, *History of the Labor Movement,* vol. 2, pp. 235–78; Ray Ginger, *Eugene V. Debs* (Collier, 1962); Nick Salvatore, *Eugene V. Debs: Citizen and Socialist* (University of Illinois Press, 1982).

The Wobblies: Melvyn Dubofsky, *"Big Bill" Haywood* (Manchester University Press, 1987); Dubofsky, *We Shall Be All: A History of the Industrial Workers of the World,* 2nd ed. (University of Illinois Press, 1988); Elizabeth Gurley Flynn, *The Rebel Girl: An Autobiography,* rev. ed. (International Publishers, 1973); Flynn, "The Shame of Spokane," *International Socialist Review* (Chicago, January 1910), pp. 610–11; Philip S. Foner, ed., *Fellow Workers and Friends: I.W.W. Free-Speech Fights as Told by Participants* (Greenwood Press, 1981); William D. Haywood, *Bill Haywood's Book* (International Publishers, 1929), pp. 174–89; "Haywood's Luminous Thought," *Miners Magazine* (Denver, September 7, 1905); Joyce L. Kornbluh, ed., *Rebel Voices: An I.W.W. Anthology* (University of Michigan Press, 1964); Press Committee, "Solidarity Wins in Fresno," *International Socialist Review* (Chicago, April 1911), pp. 634–36; Patrick Renshaw, *The Wobblies: The Story of Syndicalism in the United States* (Doubleday/Anchor, 1968); *Solidarity: Eastern Organ of the Industrial Workers of the World* (New Castle, Pa., 1910–13); Jack Whyte, " 'His Honor' Gets His," *International Socialist Review* (Chicago, October 1912), p. 320.

PAGE

181   [*"Pennsylvanians can hardly appreciate"*]: quoted in Brecher, p. 60.

182   [*"Supreme strategist"*]: quoted in Salvatore, p. 131.

183   [*"For calling a mass meeting"*]: "Women Are Fighters," speech before Central Labor Council of Cincinnati, Ohio, July 23, 1902, in Philip S. Foner, ed., *Mother Jones Speaks: Collected Writings and Speeches* (Monad Press, 1983), pp. 91–94, quoted at p. 92.
         [*"There is before you one question"*]: July 19, 1902, in Edward M. Steel, ed., *The Speeches and Writings of Mother Jones* (University of Pittsburgh Press, 1988), pp. 15–21, quoted at pp. 16, 21.
         [*"Continental Congress"*]: quoted in Haywood, p. 181.
         [*"The working class and the employing class"*]: *Solidarity,* February 26, 1910.

184   [*"Labor lieutenants of capitalism"*]: Dubofsky, *We Shall Be All,* p. 150.
         [*"No more binding"*]: quoted in *ibid.,* p. 165.
         [*"Passive resistance"*]: *Solidarity,* March 19, 1910.
         [*"On to Spokane!"*]: *ibid.,* February 26, 1910.
         [*"One of the most dangerous"*]: quoted in Flynn, *Rebel Girl,* p. 110.

185   [*"Makes all the trouble"*]: quoted in Dubofsky, *We Shall Be All,* p. 181.
         [*"Treaty of Spokane"*]: *Solidarity,* March 19, 1910.
         [*"Box car special"*]: Press Committee, "Solidarity Wins in Fresno," p. 635.
         [*"Hardest one"*]: Jacob Fuchsenberger, "Status of the Fight," *Solidarity,* May 11, 1912.
         [*"To hell with your courts"*]: Whyte, p. 320.
         [*"Direct action of open conflict"*]: quoted in Dubofsky, *We Shall Be All,* pp. 173–74.

186   [*"Weave the shroud of capitalism"*]: *ibid.,* p. 234.
         [*"We want bread and roses too"*]: quoted in Kornbluh, p. 195.
         [*"As we come marching"*]: Oppenheim, "Bread and Roses," reprinted in *ibid.,* p. 196.

187   [*"Children were clubbed"*]: Flynn, *Rebel Girl,* p. 138.
         [*"We are all leaders"*]: quoted in Dubofsky, *We Shall Be All,* p. 272.
         [*"Our plan of battle"*]: *ibid.*

LABOR'S EMERGING BILL OF RIGHTS

Gompers and the American Federation of Labor: American Federationist (Washington, D.C., 1896–1917); Foner, *History of the Labor Movement,* vol. 2; Samuel Gompers,

7. THE RECONSTRUCTION OF RIGHTS

Centennial celebrations: James MacGregor Burns, *The Workshop of Democracy* (Knopf, 1985), pp. 109–10; Joseph Gies and Frances Gies, *The Ingenious Yankees* (Thomas Y. Crowell, 1976), pp. 3–9; J. S. Ingram, *The Centennial Exposition* (Hubbard Bros., 1876); Michael Kammen, *A Machine That Would Go of Itself: The Constitution in American Culture* (Knopf, 1986), ch. 5; Kammen, *A Season of Youth: The American Revolution and the Historical Imagination* (Knopf, 1978), pp. 59–65 passim; John W. Oliver, *History of American Technology* (Ronald Press, 1956), pp. 300–2; for a survey of American thought in the latter part of the nineteenth century, see Clarence J. Karier, *The Individual, Society, and Education: A History of American Educational Ideas,* 2nd ed. (University of Illinois Press, 1986), esp. chs. 5–9 passim.

PAGE
197   [*Grant's speech at exposition*]: quoted in Ingram, pp. 91–92.
198   [*"One day bring order"*]: Karier, p. 103.

THE SHEPHERD AND THE WOLF

Civil liberties in the first half of the nineteenth century: Thomas I. Emerson et al., eds., *Political and Civil Rights in the United States,* 3rd ed. (Little, Brown, 1967), vol. 1, pp. 39–45; Donald G. Morgan, "The Marshall Court and Civil Liberties," in Milton R. Konvitz and Clinton Rossiter, eds., *Aspects of Liberty* (Cornell University Press, 1958; reprinted by Johnson Reprint, 1965), pp. 163–78; Paul L. Murphy, *The Meaning of Freedom of Speech: First Amendment Freedoms from Wilson to FDR* (Greenwood Publishing, 1972), pp. 11–17; Russel B. Nye, *Fettered Freedom: Civil Liberties and the Slavery Controversy, 1830–1860* (Michigan State University Press, 1963); Leon Whipple, *The Story of Civil Liberties in the United States* (Vanguard Press, 1927), pp. 31–123.

Lincoln and rights in the Civil War: Don E. Fehrenbacher, *Lincoln in Text and Context* (Stanford University Press, 1987), chs. 9–10; Harold M. Hyman, *A More Perfect Union: The Impact of the Civil War and Reconstruction on the Constitution* (Knopf, 1973), chs. 5–16 passim; Frank L. Klement, *The Limits of Dissent: Clement L. Vallandigham & the Civil War* (University Press of Kentucky, 1970); Mark E. Neely, Jr., *The Fate of Liberty: Abraham Lincoln and Civil Liberties* (Oxford University Press, 1991); James G. Randall, *Constitutional Problems under Lincoln* (D. Appleton, 1926); Randall and Richard N. Current, *Lincoln the President: Last Full Measure* (Dodd, Mead, 1955), ch. 11 passim; James M. Smith and Paul L. Murphy, eds., *Liberty and Justice* (Knopf, 1958), ch. 12 passim; Dean Sprague, *Freedom under Lincoln* (Houghton Mifflin, 1965).

Civil liberties between the Civil War and World War I: Emerson et al., vol. 1, pp. 48–55; Murphy, *Freedom of Speech,* pp. 18–22; Paul L. Murphy, *World War I and the Origin of Civil Liberties in the United States* (Norton, 1979), ch. 1; William Preston, Jr., *Aliens and Dissenters: Federal Suppression of Radicals, 1903–1933* (Harvard University Press, 1963), chs. 1–3 passim; Whipple, ch. 6.

Rights and liberties during World War I: Zechariah Chafee, Jr., *Free Speech in the United States* (Harvard University Press, 1941), chs. 2–3; Jeremy Cohen, *Congress Shall Make No Law: Oliver Wendell Holmes, the First Amendment, and Judicial Decision Making* (Iowa State University Press, 1989); Melvyn Dubofsky, *We Shall Be All: A History*

Labor and the Common Welfare, Hayes Robbins, ed. (E. P. Dutton, 1919); Gompers, *Labor and the Employer,* Hayes Robbins, ed. (E. P. Dutton, 1920); Gompers, *Seventy Years of Life and Labor;* Harold C. Livesay, *Samuel Gompers and Organized Labor in America* (Little, Brown, 1978); David Montgomery, *The Fall of the House of Labor: The Workplace, the State, and American Labor Activism, 1865–1925* (Cambridge University Press, 1987); John S. Smith, "Organized Labor and Government in the Wilson Era, 1913–1921," *Labor History,* vol. 3, no. 3 (Fall 1962), pp. 265–86.

Labor's legal rights and labor law reform: John R. Commons, ed., *Trade Unionism and Labor Problems,* 2nd series (Ginn, 1921); Milton Derber, "The Idea of Industrial Democracy in America, 1898–1935," *Labor History,* vol. 7, no. 3 (Fall 1966), pp. 259–86, and vol. 8, no. 1 (Winter 1967), pp. 3–29; Howard Dickman, *Industrial Democracy in America: Ideological Origins of National Labor Relations Policy* (Open Court, 1987), pp. 217–39; Fink, "Labor, Liberty, and the Law"; Staughton Lynd, "Communal Rights," *Texas Law Review,* vol. 62 (May 1984), pp. 1417–41; Lynd, "The Right to Engage in Concerted Activity after Union Recognition: A Study of Legislative History," *Indiana Law Journal,* vol. 50 (1975), pp. 720–56; Martin J. Sklar, *The Corporate Reconstruction of American Capitalism, 1890–1916: The Market, the Law, and Politics* (Cambridge University Press, 1988); Christopher L. Tomlins, *The State and the Unions: Labor Relations, Law, and the Organized Labor Movement in America, 1880–1960* (Cambridge University Press, 1985); Maurice S. Trotta, *Collective Bargaining: Principles, Practices, Issues* (Simmons-Boardman, 1961), pp. 8–15; James Weinstein, *The Corporate Ideal in the Liberal State, 1900–1918* (Beacon Press, 1969).

PAGE
188   *["What's all this"]*: reprinted in *Literary Digest,* vol. 67, no. 9 (November 27, 1920), p. 19.
189   *["Corporate reconstruction"]*: Sklar, p. 5.
       [Loewe]: 208 U.S. 274 (1908).
       [Supreme Court affirmation of "yellow-dog contracts"]: *Adair* v. *U.S.,* 208 U.S. 161 (1908).
       ["Unless all things are held"]: *Coppage* v. *Kansas,* 236 U.S. 1 (1915), quoted at 17.
190   *["The labor of a human being"]*: quoted in Smith, p. 273.
       ["Justice has been done"]: quoted in Livesay, p. 169.
       ["Labor's Magna Carta"]: *ibid.,* p. 168.
       [Livesay on Clayton Act]: *ibid.,* p. 169; see *Hitchman Coal & Coke* v. *Mitchell,* 245 U.S. 229 (1917), and *Duplex Printing Press Co.* v. *Deering,* 254 U.S. 443 (1921).
       ["Levels of strike participation"]: Montgomery, *Fall of the House of Labor,* p. 6.
191   *["All unions sooner or later"]*: quoted in Derber, *Labor History,* vol. 8, p. 25.
       ["Concerted activities"]: quoted in Dickman, pp. 238–39.
       [Bendix on citizenship rights]: Bendix, *Nation-Building and Citizenship* (University of California Press, 1977), pp. 92–126.
       ["One of the earliest results"]: *ibid.,* p. 95.
192   *["Offered legal sanction"]*: Fink, "Labor, Liberty, and the Law," p. 906.
       ["To engage in concerted activities"]: quoted in Lynd, "Communal Rights," p. 1423.
       [Lynd on communal rights]: *ibid.,* p. 1430.
       [Arendt's definition of power]: Arendt, *On Violence* (Harcourt, 1970), p. 44.
193   *["Possess rights in the same way"]*: Lynd, "Communal Rights," p. 1419.
       ["Self-sufficient monad" and "rights of the limited individual"]: Marx, "On the Jewish Question," in Jeremy Waldron, ed., *"Nonsense upon Stilts": Bentham, Burke, and Marx on the Rights of Man* (Methuen, 1987), pp. 137–50, quoted at p. 146.

of the Industrial Workers of the World (Quadrangle, 1969), esp. chs. 16–17 passim; Donald Johnson, *The Challenge to American Freedoms: World War I and the Rise of the American Civil Liberties Union* (University of Kentucky Press, 1963); Samuel J. Kanofsky, *The Legacy of Holmes and Brandeis: A Study in the Influence of Ideas* (Macmillan, 1956; reprinted by Da Capo Press, 1974), ch. 9; Murphy, *Origin of Civil Liberties;* H. C. Peterson and Gilbert C. Fite, *Opponents of War, 1917–1918* (University of Wisconsin Press, 1957); Richard Polenberg, *Fighting Faiths: The Abrams Case, the Supreme Court, and Free Speech* (Viking, 1987); Preston, chs. 4–7 passim; Fred D. Ragan, "Justice Oliver Wendell Holmes, Jr., Zechariah Chafee, Jr., and the Clear and Present Danger Test for Free Speech: The First Year, 1919," *Journal of American History,* vol. 58, no. 1 (June 1971), pp. 24–45.

Red Scare: Chafee, chs. 4–7 passim; Stanley Coben, "A Study in Nativism: The American Red Scare of 1919–1920," *Political Science Quarterly,* vol. 79, no. 1 (March 1964), pp. 52–75; Anthony Gengarelly, "Distinguished Dissenters: Opposition to the Red Scare, 1919–1920" (unpublished manuscript, 1987); Corinne Jacker, *The Black Flag of Anarchy: Antistatism in the United States* (Scribner, 1968), chs. 12–13; Johnson, chs. 5–6; Murray B. Levin, *Political Hysteria in America: The Democratic Capacity for Repression* (Basic Books, 1971); Robert K. Murray, *Red Scare, 1919–1920* (University of Minnesota Press, 1955); Murphy, *Freedom of Speech,* chs. 3–6; Preston, chs. 7–9 passim; Samuel Walker, *In Defense of American Liberties: A History of the ACLU* (Oxford University Press, 1990), chs. 1–2 passim, esp. pp. 42–45.

Opposition to the Red Scare: Gengarelly; Johnson, passim; Peggy Lamson, *Roger Baldwin, Founder of the American Civil Liberties Union* (Houghton Mifflin, 1976), esp. chs. 6–7; Charles L. Markmann, *The Noblest Cry: A History of the American Civil Liberties Union* (St. Martin's Press, 1965), chs. 2–3, and passim; Murphy, *Origin of Civil Liberties,* ch. 5; Walker, chs. 1–2 passim.

PAGE
199 [*"Never had a good definition"*]: April 18, 1864, in Lincoln, *Collected Works,* Roy P. Basler, ed. (Rutgers University Press, 1953), vol. 7, pp. 301–3, quoted at pp. 301, 302.
[Barron]: 7 Peters 243 (1833).
200 [*"Enormous diversity of opinion"*]: Roche, "American Liberty: An Examination of the 'Tradition' of Freedom," in Konvitz and Rossiter, pp. 129–62, quoted at pp. 134, 146.
201 [*"By general law"*]: letter to Albert G. Hodges, April 4, 1864, in Lincoln, *Collected Works,* vol. 7, pp. 281–82, quoted at p. 281.
[*"Many Northern Democrats"*]: Fehrenbacher, p. 133.
[*"Virtually appealing"*]: Randall, p. 22.
202 [*Randall on Lincoln's interpretation of war power*]: ibid., pp. 36–37.
[*Merryman*]: ex parte Merryman, 17 Fed. Cas. 144 (1861), no. 9487, reprinted in Samuel Tyler, *Memoir of Roger Brooke Taney,* 2nd ed. (John Murphy, 1876), pp. 640–59.
[*Ohio Democrats on "constitutional remedy"*]: letter of June 26, 1863, quoted in Lincoln, *Collected Works,* vol. 6, p. 301 fn. 1; Lincoln's reply to "Matthew Birchard and Others," June 29, 1863, in *ibid.,* vol. 6, pp. 300–6.
203 [*"Must I shoot"*]: letter to Erastus Corning and others, June 12, 1863, in *ibid.,* vol. 6, pp. 260–69, quoted at p. 266.
[*"War does not suspend"*]: quoted in Neely, p. 206.
[*Republican senator on arrests beyond war zone*]: Lyman Trumbull, cited in Fehrenbacher, p. 135.
[*"Shown some signs"*]: Randall and Current, p. 246.

203 [*"All the laws, but one"*]: message to Congress in Special Session, July 4, 1861, in Lincoln, *Collected Works,* vol. 4, pp. 421–41, quoted at p. 430.

204 [*"Prostitutes, procurers"*]: Preston, p. 19.
[*"Oftentimes most severe"*]: *Fong Yue Ting* v. *U.S.,* 149 U.S. 698 (1893), quoted at 740.
[*"Once lead this people"*]: see Jerold S. Auerbach, "Woodrow Wilson's 'Prediction' to Frank Cobb: Words Historians Should Doubt Ever Got Spoken," *Journal of American History,* vol. 54, no. 3 (December 1967), pp. 608–17, Wilson quoted at p. 616.

205 [*Mob incidents and civic bans*]: see Murphy, *Origin of Civil Liberties,* pp. 128–32; see also Peterson and Fite passim.
[*State sedition and criminal syndicalism laws*]: Murphy, *Origin of Civil Liberties,* pp. 86–87.
[*"Business man's war"*]: quoted in Chafee, p. 143.
[*"Extend the sphere"*]: Madison, *The Federalist,* No. 10, November 22, 1787, in *The Federalist,* Jacob E. Cooke, ed. (Wesleyan University Press, 1961), pp. 56–65, quoted at p. 64.
[*"He kept us out"*]: Arthur S. Link, *Wilson: Campaigns for Progressivism and Peace, 1916–1917* (Princeton University Press, 1965), p. 109.
[*"Safe for democracy"*]: address to a Joint Session of Congress, April 2, 1917, in Wilson, *Papers,* Arthur S. Link, ed. (Princeton University Press, 1966–), vol. 41, pp. 519–27, quoted at p. 525.

206 [*"By reason of his conduct"*]: quoted in Murphy, *Origin of Civil Liberties,* p. 74.
[*"Part of the zone"*]: quoted in Chafee, p. 38.
[*"Used as a shield"*]: letter to Arthur Brisbane, April 25, 1917, in Wilson, *Papers,* vol. 42, p. 129.
[*"Absolutely necessary"*]: letter to Edwin Yates Webb, May 22, 1917, in *ibid.,* vol. 42, pp. 369–70, quoted at p. 370; see *New York Times,* May 23, 1917, p. 1.
[*"Absolute censorship powers"*]: Murphy, *Origin of Civil Liberties,* p. 81.
[*Gregory on Espionage Act*]: Chafee, pp. 39–40; Murphy, *Origin of Civil Liberties,* p. 82.
[*"Shall be construed"*]: quoted in Murphy, *Origin of Civil Liberties,* p. 82.
[*"Most dangerous types"*]: *ibid.,* p. 83.

207 [*"No such repressive"*]: *ibid.*
[*"Willfully utter, print"*]: 40 Stat. 553 (1918).
[*"Wilful obstruction"*]: quoted in Murphy, *Origin of Civil Liberties,* p. 98.
[*Censorship of* Nation, *Catholic journal, Veblen*]: *ibid.,* p. 102; Chafee, p. 99.

208 [*"Certainly are worthy"*]: quoted in Dubofsky, p. 427.
[Schenck]: *Schenck* v. *U.S.,* 249 U.S. 47 (1919); Schenck's leaflet quoted in Cohen, p. 28; Holmes's opinion quoted at p. 52 in *Schenck.*

209 [*"Not necessarily ineffective"*]: *Debs* v. *U.S.,* 249 U.S. 211 (1919), quoted at 214; for Chafee on Debs's address, see Chafee, p. 85.
[*"(Between ourselves)"*]: letter of March 16, 1919, in *Holmes-Laski Letters,* Mark DeWolfe Howe, ed. (Harvard University Press, 1953), vol. 1, pp. 189–90, quoted at p. 190.

210 [*Hand and Freund criticism of* Debs]: Ragan, pp. 39–40; Ernst Freund, "The Debs Case and Freedom of Speech," *New Republic,* vol. 19, no. 235 (May 3, 1919), pp. 13–15.
[*"Took Holmes to task"*]: Murphy, *Origin of Civil Liberties,* p. 267; see also Ragan, pp. 40–43.
[Abrams]: *Abrams* v. *U.S.,* 250 U.S. 616 (1919); leaflet quoted in Emer-

son et al., vol. 1, pp. 80–81; majority opinion by John H. Clarke in *Abrams,* quoted at 623; Holmes's dissent in *ibid.* at 630.

211   [*"Included virtually everyone"*]: Walker, p. 42.
[*"Looked vaguely 'foreign' "*]: *ibid.,* p. 44.
[*"No time to waste"*]: quoted in *ibid.*

212   [*"Did you see what I did"*]: Webster Thayer, quoted in Jacker, p. 163.
[*"Never in our full life"*]: quoted in *ibid.,* p. 171.

213   [*Baldwin in jail*]: James MacGregor Burns conversation with Baldwin, July 1979, Chilmark, Martha's Vineyard, Massachusetts.
[*"Opposition to the course"*]: quoted in Johnson, p. 47.
[*"Jails Are Waiting for Them"*]: *New York Times,* July 4, 1917, p. 8.
[*"Form of government"*]: quoted in Chafee, p. 306.

EDUCATION: A BIRTHRIGHT?

Education in state constitutions: The Federal and State Constitutions, Colonial Charters, and Other Organic Laws of the United States, Benjamin Perley Poore, comp., 2 vols. (U. S. Government Printing Office, 1877); for education as a right in the North Carolina constitution of 1868, see vol. 2, p. 1421; for examples of the encouragement of and/or provision for education in nineteenth-century state constitutions, see Indiana (1816), vol. 1, p. 508; Maine (1820), vol. 1, p. 797; Maryland (1851), vol. 1, p. 840; Texas (1866), vol. 2, p. 1800; Arkansas (1868), vol. 1, p. 136; Pennsylvania (1838, 1873), vol. 2, pp. 1563, 1586; Alabama (1875), vol. 1, p. 93.

Education in the founding era: Howard K. Beale, *A History of Freedom of Teaching in American Schools* (Octagon Books, 1978), ch. 1; Robert L. Church and Michael W. Sedlak, *Education in the United States* (Free Press, 1976), ch. 1; Merle Curti, *The Social Ideas of American Educators,* 2nd ed. (Pageant Books, 1959), ch. 1; Allen Oscar Hansen, *Liberalism and American Education in the Eighteenth Century* (Macmillan, 1926; reprinted by Octagon Books, 1965); Roy J. Honeywell, *The Educational Work of Thomas Jefferson* (Russell & Russell, 1964), chs. 10–11, and passim; Karier, chs. 1–2; Gordon C. Lee, ed., *Crusade Against Ignorance: Thomas Jefferson on Education* (Teachers College Press, 1961); Frederick Rudolph, ed., *Essays on Education in the Early Republic* (Belknap Press of Harvard University Press, 1965); Rush Welter, *Popular Education and Democratic Thought in America* (Columbia University Press, 1962), part 1.

Education in nineteenth- and early-twentieth-century America: Roberta Sue Alexander, *North Carolina Faces the Freedmen: Race Relations during Presidential Reconstruction, 1865–67* (Duke University Press, 1985), ch. 7; Beale, chs. 3–6; Fred G. Burke, *Public Education: Who's in Charge?* (Praeger, 1990), pp. 15–22, and ch. 3 passim; Church and Sedlak, parts 2–3; George S. Counts, "Education as an Individual Right," *School and Society,* vol. 15, no. 382 (April 22, 1922), pp. 433–37; Lawrence A. Cremin, *The Transformation of the School: Progressivism in American Education, 1876–1957* (Knopf, 1961), part 1; Curti, passim; Ruth Miller Elson, *Guardians of Tradition: American Schoolbooks of the Nineteenth Century* (University of Nebraska Press, 1964), parts 4–5, and passim; Eleanor Flexner, *Century of Struggle: The Woman's Rights Movement in the United States* (Belknap Press of Harvard University Press, 1959), ch. 2; Karier, chs. 3–9 passim; Jonathan Messerli, *Horace Mann* (Knopf, 1972); Henry J. Perkinson, *The Imperfect Panacea: American Faith in Education, 1865–1965* (Random House, 1968); Dorothy Ross, "Socialism and American Liberalism: Academic Social Thought in the 1880's," *Perspectives in American History,* vol. 11 (1977–78), pp. 5–79; John L. Rury, "Vocationalism for Home and Work: Women's Education in the United States, 1880–1930," in B. Edward

McClellan and William J. Reese, eds., *The Social History of American Education* (University of Illinois Press, 1988), pp. 233–56; Donald Spivey, *Schooling for the New Slavery: Black Industrial Education, 1868–1915* (Greenwood Press, 1978); Joel H. Spring, *Education and the Rise of the Corporate State* (Beacon Press, 1972); David B. Tyack et al., *Law and the Shaping of Public Education, 1785–1954* (University of Wisconsin Press, 1987), passim; Welter, *Popular Education*, parts 2–3.

Dewey and progressive education: Richard J. Bernstein, *John Dewey* (Washington Square Press, 1966), ch. 10, and passim; Church and Sedlak, part 4; Cremin, passim; Curti, ch. 15; John Dewey, *The Child and the Curriculum/The School and Society* (University of Chicago Press, 1956); Dewey, *Democracy and Education* (Macmillan, 1916); Dewey and Evelyn Dewey, *Schools of To-Morrow*, in Dewey, *The Middle Works, 1899–1924*, Jo Ann Boydston, ed. (Southern Illinois University Press, 1976–83), vol. 8, pp. 205–404; Michaelson, pp. 140–49; Welter, *Popular Education*, part 4 passim.

PAGE

214   [*"Right to the privilege"*]: 1868 constitution, in *Federal and State Constitutions,* vol. 2, quoted at p. 1421; see also Alexander, ch. 7 passim.

[*"Education should not be left"*]: Robert Coram, "Political Inquiries: To Which Is Added, A Plan for the General Establishment of Schools throughout the United States," in Rudolph, pp. 79–145, quoted at p. 113.

[*Washington on education and public opinion*]: September 19, 1796, in Washington, *Writings,* John C. Fitzpatrick, ed. (U. S. Government Printing Office, 1931–44), vol. 35, pp. 214–38, esp. p. 230.

[*"In our American republics"*]: quoted in Tyack et al, p. 24.

[*Jefferson's 1779 education bill*]: reprinted in Honeywell, appendix A, quoted at p. 201.

215   [*"Main objects"*]: letter of February 26, 1810, in Jefferson, *Works,* H. A. Washington, ed. (Townsend MacCoun, 1884), vol. 5, pp. 506–9, quoted at p. 509.

[*"Important truths"*]: letter to George Ticknor, November 25, 1817, in Jefferson, *Writings,* Paul Leicester Ford, ed. (Putnam, 1892–99), vol. 10, pp. 94–96, quoted at p. 96.

[*Jefferson's 1818 report on education*]: reprinted in Honeywell, appendix J, quoted at pp. 249–50.

[*Extension of education in the nineteenth century*]: see Richard B. Morris, ed., *Encyclopedia of American History* (Harper, 1953), pp. 556, 558.

216   [*"Wisdom preside in the halls"*]: quoted in Cremin, p. 9.

[*"The business man"*]: quoted in Curti, p. 203.

[*"Draw up your specifications"*]: quoted in Church and Sedlak, pp. 307, 308.

217   [*"Not bestowing gifts"*]: Counts, p. 436.

[*Education as "great equalizer"*]: quoted in Cremin, p. 9.

[*"Elevation and equality"*]: Fayetteville *News,* quoted in Alexander, p. 155.

[*Enrollment of black children, 1870–1900*]: U. S. Bureau of the Census, *Historical Statistics of the United States: Colonial Times to 1970* (U. S. Department of Commerce, Bureau of the Census, 1975), part 1, p. 370 (series H 433-441).

218   [*Spending in Mississippi on white and black students*]: Perkinson, p. 40.

[*Virginian on education as "luxury"*]: Governor F. W. M. Holliday, quoted in *ibid.,* p. 33.

[*"Force that promoted"*]: *ibid.,* p. 43.

[*"Through his skill"*]: *ibid.,* pp. 47–48.

218   [*"Higher training"*]: *ibid.*, p. 53.
        [*Women enrolled in home economics, 1920s*]: Rury, pp. 239–40.
219   [*Rury on female industrial training*]: see *ibid.*, p. 247.
        [*Principals on female commercial education*]: *ibid.*, p. 245.
        [*"Develop in children"*]: Curti, p. 127.
        [*Mann on treason against free speech*]: *ibid.*
        [*Mann's teaching against rebellion*]: *ibid.*, pp. 128–29.
        [*Mann's opposition to teaching abolition*]: *ibid.*, pp. 130–31.
220   [*"Best and wisest parent"*]: Dewey, *School and Society*, p. 7.
        [*"Natural lives"*]: Dewey and Dewey, *Schools of To-Morrow*, p. 235.
        [*Pratt on her "conversion experience"*]: quoted in Cremin, pp. 204–5.
221   [*Principles of progressive education*]: see *ibid.*, pp. 240–45.
        [*"Elicited not only"*]: *ibid.*, pp. 206, 207.
222   [*"One of the worst limitations"*]: Beale, p. 169.
        [*Numbers of one-teacher schools and students, early twentieth century*]: Cremin,
        p. 291.
223   [*"Functionally liberal"*]: Burke, p. 30.

ROOT, HOG, OR DIE?

Classical liberalism and its dissenters, post–Civil War: Burns, *Workshop,* esp. pp. 154–62;
Bruce Curtis, *William Graham Sumner* (Twayne, 1981), esp. chs. 6–7; Sidney Fine,
Laissez Faire and the General-Welfare State (University of Michigan Press, 1956), chs.
2–11 passim; Charles Forcey, *The Crossroads of Liberalism: Croly, Weyl, Lippmann, and
the Progressive Era, 1900–1925* (Oxford University Press, 1961); Edwin L. Godkin,
Problems of Modern Democracy (Scribner, 1896); Richard Hofstadter, *Social Darwin-
ism in American Thought,* rev. ed. (Beacon Press, 1955); R. Jeffrey Lustig, *Corporate
Liberalism: The Origins of Modern American Political Theory, 1890–1920* (University of
California Press, 1982); Vernon L. Parrington, *The Beginnings of Critical Realism in
America, 1860–1920* (Harcourt, 1930), pp. 154–68, 197–211; William B. Scott, *In
Pursuit of Happiness: American Conceptions of Property from the Seventeenth to the Twentieth
Century* (Indiana University Press, 1977), ch. 8 passim; William Graham Sumner,
Social Darwinism: Selected Essays (Prentice-Hall, 1963); James Weinstein, *The Corpo-
rate Ideal in the Liberal State, 1900–1918* (Beacon Press, 1969).

George, Bellamy, and liberal divisions over property rights: Edward Bellamy, *Looking
Backward: 2000–1887* (Houghton Mifflin, 1926); Burns, *Workshop,* pp. 162–67;
Joseph Dorfman, *The Economic Mind in American Civilization, 1865–1918* (Viking,
1949), ch. 6; Fine, pp. 289–301; George R. Geiger, *The Philosophy of Henry
George* (1933; reprinted by Hyperion Press, 1975); Henry George, *Progress and
Poverty* (Robert Schalkenbach Foundation, 1979); Lustig, ch. 3; Scott, pp. 160–65,
181–85.

Croly: Herbert Croly, *The Promise of American Life* (Macmillan, 1910); Forcey, ch.
1, and passim; John B. Judis, "Herbert Croly's Promise," *New Republic,* vol. 201,
no. 19 (November 6, 1989), pp. 84–87; Lustig, chs. 5, 7 passim; Scott, pp. 170–75.

Dewey: Fine, pp. 284–88; Lustig, chs. 5–6 passim; Scott, pp. 175–80; and sources
cited, *supra,* in "Education: A Birthright?"

The Supreme Court and the Fourteenth Amendment: Edward S. Corwin, *Liberty Against
Government: The Rise, Flowering, and Decline of a Famous Judicial Concept* (Louisiana
State University Press, 1948), passim; Fine, ch. 5; Lustig, esp. pp. 90–97 passim;
William E. Nelson, *The Fourteenth Amendment: From Political Principle to Judicial Doc-
trine* (Harvard University Press, 1988), esp. chs. 7–8 passim; Donald J. Pisani,

"Promotion and Regulation: Constitutionalism and the American Economy," *Journal of American History*, vol. 74, no. 3 (December 1987), pp. 740–68; John P. Roche, "Entrepreneurial Liberty and the Fourteenth Amendment," *Labor History*, vol. 4, no. 1 (Winter 1963), pp. 3–31; John R. Schmidhauser, *Constitutional Law in American Politics* (Brooks/Cole Publishing, 1984), chs. 6–7 passim; Scott, esp. ch. 8; Benjamin R. Twiss, *Lawyers and the Constitution: How Laissez Faire Came to the Supreme Court* (Princeton University Press, 1942).

Holmes and Brandeis: Ralph H. Gabriel, *The Course of American Democratic Thought* (Ronald Press, 1940), ch. 29; Konefsky; Max Lerner, ed., *The Mind and Faith of Justice Holmes* (Halcyon House, 1948); Lustig, esp. pp. 116–20, 176–83, 223–25; Alpheus T. Mason, *Brandeis: A Free Man's Life* (Viking, 1946), esp. chs. 35–36; Philippa Strum, *Louis D. Brandeis: Justice for the People* (Harvard University Press, 1984), esp. ch. 16; Morton G. White, *Social Thought in America: The Revolt Against Formalism* (Viking, 1949), esp. ch. 5, and pp. 103–6, 172–79.

Gitlow: Chafee, ch. 9; Lerner, pp. 321–25; see also David Fellman, "The Nationalization of American Civil Liberties," in M. Judd Harmon, ed., *Essays on the Constitution of the United States* (Kennikat Press, 1978), pp. 49–60.

PAGE
224   *["To Govern Well"]:* quoted in Burns, *Workshop*, p. 70.
      ["Must get out"]: quoted in Parrington, p. 162.
      ["Try, Try Again"]: in Moses Rischin, ed., *The American Gospel of Success: Individualism and Beyond* (Quadrangle, 1965), p. 45.
      ["By the same title"]: Burns, *Workshop*, pp. 49–50, quoted at p. 50.
225   *["Root, hog, or die"]:* quoted in *ibid.*, p. 159.
226   *["Restore the American economy"]:* quoted in Fine, p. 386.
      ["Powers of acquisition"]: quoted in Lustig, pp. 96, 97.
      ["Man belongs to himself"]: George, p. 334.
      ["Receives without producing"]: *ibid.*, pp. 341–42.
      ["Fundamental wrong"]: *ibid.*, p. 341.
      ["Equal right of all men"]: *ibid.*, p. 338.
227   *[George on Jefferson's Declaration]:* see *ibid.*, p. 545.
228   *["Functions in a democratic political organism"]:* Croly, p. 278.
      [Roosevelt, Promise, and "new nationalism"]: Judis, p. 86.
      ["Question of good use"]: Lippmann, *Drift and Mastery* (Mitchell Kennerley, 1914), p. 109.
229   *["Cooperative property right"]:* Scott, p. 177.
      ["Dedicated to the proposition"]: Roche, "Entrepreneurial Liberty," p. 20.
230   *[Waite on corporations as "persons"]:* Corwin, p. 193.
      ["Discrimination against the negroes"]: *Slaughter-House Cases*, 83 U.S. 36 (1873), majority opinion quoted at 81, Field at 105, 106, Bradley at 116, 120, 116, 122 respectively.
      ["Affected with a public interest"]: *Granger Cases*, 94 U. S. 113 (1877), majority opinion quoted at 130, Field at 186.
231   *["Lawful use"]:* *Chicago, Milwaukee and St. Paul Railway Co.* v. *Minnesota*, 134 U. S. 418 (1890), quoted at 458.
      [Numbers of Fourteenth Amendment decisions, 1890–1910]: see Howard Zinn, *A People's History of the United States* (Harper Colophon, 1980), p. 255.
      ["Liberty of the individual"]: *Lochner* v. *New York*, 198 U. S. 45 (1905), quoted at 53, 64.
      ["Lay profane hands"]: Roche, "Entrepreneurial Liberty," p. 21.

231   [*"Right to Speech"*]: quoted in Strum, p. 322.
232   [*"Constitution is not intended"*]: *Lochner,* 75.
        [*"Wholesale social regeneration"*]: quoted in Mason, pp. 572–73.
        [*"If you deny"*]: letter of December 20, 1918, in *Holmes-Pollock Letters,*
        Mark DeWolfe Howe, ed. (Harvard University Press, 1941), vol. 1, pp.
        274–75, quoted at p. 275; Holmes's reply in letter of January 24, 1919,
        in *ibid.,* vol. 2, pp. 3–4, quoted at p. 3.
233   [*"Sneered at the natural rights"*]: letter of September 15, 1916, in *Holmes-
        Laski Letters,* vol. 1, pp. 20–22, quoted at p. 21.
        [*"Mass struggle"*]: quoted in Chafee, pp. 318–19.
        [*"Direct incitement"*]: *Gitlow* v. *New York,* 268 U. S. 652 (1925), quoted
        at 665.
        [*"Every idea is an incitement"*]: *ibid.,* 673.
        [*"We may and do assume"*]: *ibid.,* 666.
        [*Lerner on* Gitlow]: Lerner, p. 323.
234   [*Chafee on American "checkerboard"*]: see Chafee, p. 324.
        [*"Factional squabbles"*]: quoted in Lerner, p. 324.
        [*"More successful"*]: Gengarelly, p. 471.
        [*"I want my crowd"*]: quoted in *ibid.*
        [*"Not asking to change"*]: *ibid.,* p. 472.
235   [*"Tempted to ask"*]: *ibid.*

8. NEW DEAL—NEW RIGHTS?

Hoover: James MacGregor Burns, *Uncommon Sense* (Harper, 1972), pp. 100–1;
George W. Carey, "Herbert Hoover's Concept of Individualism Revisited," in
Ellis W. Hawley, ed., *Herbert Hoover as Secretary of Commerce: Studies in New Era
Thought and Practice* (University of Iowa Press, 1981), pp. 217–52; Walter F. Dexter, *Herbert Hoover and American Individualism* (Macmillan, 1932); Ellis W. Hawley
et al., *Herbert Hoover and the Crisis of American Capitalism* (Schenkman Publishing,
1973); Herbert Hoover, *American Individualism* (Doubleday, Page, 1922); Albert U.
Romasco, *The Poverty of Abundance: Hoover, the Nation, the Depression* (Oxford University Press, 1965); Arthur M. Schlesinger, Jr., *The Crisis of the Old Order, 1919–
1933* (Houghton Mifflin, 1957), ch. 11.

PAGE
237   [*"Business has a right"*]: quoted in Robert K. Murray, *The Harding Era:
        Warren G. Harding and His Administration* (University of Minnesota Press,
        1969), p. 172.
        [*"Property rights and personal rights"*]: quoted in Donald R. McCoy, *Calvin
        Coolidge: The Quiet President* (Macmillan, 1967; reprinted by University
        Press of Kansas, 1988), p. 54.
        [*"Solemn assurance"*]: quoted in Robert H. Elias, *"Entangling Alliances with
        None": An Essay on the Individual in the American Twenties* (Norton, 1973),
        p. 93.
        [*"History shows"*]: Charles N. Fay, quoted in James W. Prothro, *The Dollar
        Decade: Business Ideas in the 1920's* (Louisiana State University Press,
        1954), p. 65.
        [*"All rights"*]: *Duplex Printing Press Co.* v. *Deering,* 254 U.S. 443 (1921),
        dissent quoted at 488; see also Philippa Strum, *Louis D. Brandeis: Justice
        for the People* (Harvard University Press, 1984), chs. 16–17.
238   [*"Rapidly growing aggregation"*]: *Quaker City Cab Co.* v. *Pennsylvania,* 277
        U.S. 389 (1928), dissent quoted at 410.

238   ["*We may be able*"]: quoted in Strum, p. 347.
239   ["*Better, brighter, broader*"]: Hoover, *American Individualism*, pp. 66, 9
        respectively.

LEFT, RIGHT, AND CENTER

FDR's Commonwealth Club address and the 1932 campaign: Kenneth S. Davis, *FDR: The New York Years, 1928–1933* (Random House, 1985), chs. 9–11, esp. pp. 368–71; Raymond Moley, *After Seven Years* (Harper, 1939), pp. 58–59, and chs. 1–2 passim; Franklin D. Roosevelt, *Public Papers and Addresses*, Samuel I. Rosenman, ed. (Random House, 1938–50), vol. 1, pp. 742–56; Rexford Tugwell, *In Search of Roosevelt* (Harvard University Press, 1972), chs. 4, 7; Tugwell, *The Brains Trust* (Viking, 1968).

Early New Deal: David K. Adams, "The New Deal and the Vital Center: A Continuing Struggle for Liberalism," in Herbert D. Rosenbaum and Elizabeth Bartelme, eds., *Franklin D. Roosevelt: The Man, the Myth, the Era, 1882–1945* (Greenwood Press, 1987), pp. 103–17 passim; Alan Brinkley, "The New Deal and the Idea of the State," in Steve Fraser and Gary Gerstle, eds., *The Rise and Fall of the New Deal Order, 1930–1980* (Princeton University Press, 1989), pp. 85–121; James MacGregor Burns, *The Crosswinds of Freedom* (Knopf, 1989), chs. 1–2 passim; Burns, *Roosevelt: The Lion and the Fox* (Harcourt, 1956), part 3 passim; Marion Clawson, *New Deal Planning: The National Resources Planning Board* (Johns Hopkins University Press, 1981); Robert M. Collins, "Positive Business Responses to the New Deal: The Roots of the Committee for Economic Development, 1933–1942," *Business History Review*, vol. 52, no. 3 (Autumn 1978), pp. 369–91; Paul K. Conkin, *The New Deal*, 2nd ed. (Harlan Davidson, 1975), ch. 2; Arthur A. Ekirch, Jr., *The Decline of American Liberalism* (Longmans, Green, 1955), ch. 15; Ekirch, *Ideologies and Utopias: The Impact of the New Deal on American Thought* (Quadrangle, 1969), esp. chs. 2, 3; Otis L. Graham, Jr., *Toward a Planned Society: From Roosevelt to Nixon* (Oxford University Press, 1976), ch. 1 passim; Ellis W. Hawley, *The New Deal and the Problem of Monopoly* (Princeton University Press, 1966), parts 1–2 passim; James Holt, "The New Deal and the American Anti-Statist Tradition," in John A. Braeman et al., eds., *The New Deal: National Level* (Ohio State University Press, 1975), pp. 27–49; Kim McQuaid, "Corporate Liberalism in the American Business Community, 1920–1940," *Business History Review*, vol. 52, no. 3 (Autumn 1978), pp. 342–68; Theodore Rosenof, *Dogma, Depression, and the New Deal: The Debate of Political Leaders over Economic Recovery* (Kennikat Press, 1975); Arthur M. Schlesinger, Jr., *The Coming of the New Deal* (Houghton Mifflin, 1959), parts 1–3 passim; Howard Zinn, ed., *New Deal Thought* (Bobbs-Merrill, 1966), esp. parts 1–3.

Right-wing and business opposition to the New Deal: Gary Dean Best, *Herbert Hoover: The Postpresidential Years, 1933–1964* (Hoover Institution Press, 1983), vol. 1, esp. chs. 1–2; Robert F. Burk, *The Corporate State and the Broker State: The Du Ponts and American National Politics, 1925–1940* (Harvard University Press, 1990), chs. 7–15 passim; Helen M. Burns, *The American Banking Community and New Deal Banking Reforms, 1933–1935* (Greenwood Press, 1974), esp. ch. 4 passim; Burns, *Crosswinds*, pp. 41–45; Burns, *Lion and Fox*, esp. pp. 234–41; Ekirch, *Ideologies*, pp. 190–97; Herbert Hoover, *Addresses upon the American Road, 1933–1938* (Scribner, 1938), esp. pp. 45–62, 75–86; Hoover, *The Challenge to Liberty* (Scribner, 1934); Rosenof, esp. pp. 26–30, 35–39, 78–80, 106–12, 116–19 passim; Schlesinger, *Coming*, part 7 passim; George Wolfskill, *The Revolt of the Conservatives: A History of the American Liberty League, 1934–1940* (Houghton Mifflin, 1962); Wolfskill and John A. Hudson, *All But the People: Franklin D. Roosevelt and His Critics, 1933–39* (Macmillan, 1969), esp. ch. 6.

Left-wing opposition to the New Deal: Alfred M. Bingham and Selden Rodman, eds., *Challenge to the New Deal* (Falcon Press, 1934); Burns, *Lion and Fox,* pp. 242–44; Ekirch, *Ideologies,* pp. 178–84; John T. Flynn, "Business," in Harold E. Stearns, ed., *America Now* (Literary Guild of America, 1938), pp. 119–31; Bernard K. Johnpoll, *Pacifist's Progress: Norman Thomas and the Decline of American Socialism* (Quadrangle, 1970), chs. 4–6; Harvey Klehr, *The Heyday of American Communism: The Depression Decade* (Basic Books, 1984); Donald R. McCoy, *Angry Voices: Left-of-Center Politics in the New Deal Era* (University of Kansas Press, 1958); Donald L. Miller, *The New American Radicalism: Alfred M. Bingham and Non-Marxian Insurgency in the New Deal Era* (Kennikat Press, 1979); Arthur M. Schlesinger, Jr., *The Politics of Upheaval* (Houghton Mifflin, 1960), esp. chs. 6–7, 9–12 passim; Norman Thomas, "Socialism, Not Roosevelt's Pale Pink Pills," in Zinn, pp. 398–403; Wolfskill and Hudson, esp. ch. 5.

Long, Coughlin, and Townsend: David H. Bennett, *Demagogues in the Depression: American Radicals and the Union Party, 1932–1936* (Rutgers University Press, 1969), esp. parts 1, 4; Alan Brinkley, *Voices of Protest: Huey Long, Father Coughlin and the Great Depression* (Knopf, 1982); Burns, *Crosswinds,* pp. 57–63, 66–68, 78–86 passim; Huey P. Long, *Every Man a King* (National Book Co., 1933); McCoy, *Angry Voices,* ch. 5; Schlesinger, *Politics of Upheaval,* esp. chs. 2–5 passim; Charles J. Tull, *Father Coughlin and the New Deal* (Syracuse University Press, 1965).

PAGE

239 [*Commonwealth Club address*]: Roosevelt, *Papers,* vol. 1, quoted at pp. 753, 754, 755.

240 [*FDR's inaugural address*]: March 4, 1933, in Roosevelt, *Papers,* vol. 2, pp. 11–16, quoted at p. 12.
[*"Bold, persistent experimentation"*]: address at Oglethorpe University, May 22, 1932, in *ibid.,* vol. 1, pp. 639–47, quoted at p. 646.
[*"Concert of action"*]: address at Jefferson Day Dinner, St. Paul, April 18, 1932, in *ibid.,* vol. 1, pp. 627–39, quoted at p. 639.
[*"National community"*]: *ibid.,* p. 630.

241 [*"Our national security"*]: May 7, 1933, in *ibid.,* vol. 2, pp. 160–68, quoted at p. 161.
[*"Exploitative character"*]: MacIver, "The Ambiguity of the New Deal," in Zinn, pp. 56–63, quoted at p. 61.
[*Lippmann on collectivism in war and peace*]: see Lippmann, "Planning Will Lead to Oligarchy," in *ibid.,* pp. 95–102, esp. pp. 96–97.
[*FDR in campaign on need for planning*]: see Graham, *Toward a Planned Society,* pp. 18–21, quoted at p. 19.

242 [*"Cement our society"*]: address at Green Bay, August 9, 1934, in Roosevelt, *Papers,* vol. 3, pp. 370–75, quoted at p. 375. The congressman quoted by Roosevelt was Edward Burke.
[*"Essentially the outward expression"*]: Washington, D.C., October 24, 1934, in *ibid.,* vol. 3, pp. 435–40, quoted at p. 436.

243 [*Business on New Deal as "collectivistic" and on FDR as "dictator"*]: see Wolfskill and Hudson, ch. 6 passim.
[*Frenchman on FDR's dissociation of wealth and virtue*]: Burns, *Lion and Fox,* p. 240.
[*"Job-holding bureaucracies"*]: June 16, 1935, in Hoover, *Addresses 1933–1938,* pp. 48–57, quoted at pp. 53, 51–52 respectively.

244 [*"Teach the necessity"*]: Jouett Shouse, quoted in *New York Times,* August 23, 1934, p. 1.
[*"Radical has always reason"*]: Flynn, "Big Business and the NRA," in Bingham and Rodman, pp. 118–22, quoted at p. 119.

518 / Notes for Pages 244–246

244   [*Communist Party membership, 1934*]: Klehr, p. 153.
        [*"Industrial slavery act"*]: Earl Browder, quoted in *ibid.*, p. 94.
        [*Stachel on "Roosevelt program"*]: *ibid.*, p. 124.
245   [*"Central headquarters"*]: *ibid.*, pp. 179, 178 respectively.
        [*Thomas on FDR and New Deal*]: quoted in Johnpoll, pp. 102–4.
246   [*"Articulate, organized lobby"*]: quoted in Brinkley, *Voices of Protest*, pp.
        133–34.
        [*"Broken down Colossus"*]: quoted in Bennett, p. 230.

LABOR'S MAGNA CARTA?

Labor and the NRA: Irving Bernstein, *Turbulent Years: A History of the American Worker,
1933–1941* (Houghton Mifflin, 1969), chs. 1–6 passim; Burns, *Crosswinds*, pp. 33,
46; Melvyn Dubofsky and Warren Van Tyne, *John L. Lewis* (Quadrangle/New York
Times Book Co., 1977), chs. 9–10 passim; James A. Gross, *The Making of the
National Labor Relations Board, 1933–1937* (State University of New York Press,
1974), chs. 1–4 passim; Peter H. Irons, *The New Deal Lawyers* (Princeton University
Press, 1982), sect. 1 passim, and ch. 10; Frances Perkins, *The Roosevelt I Knew*
(Viking, 1946), chs. 17–20 passim; Frances Fox Piven and Richard A. Cloward,
Poor People's Movements: Why They Succeed, How They Fail (Pantheon, 1977), pp.
107–30 passim; Schlesinger, *Coming*, part 2, esp. ch. 9; Twentieth Century Fund,
Inc., *Labor and the Government*, Alfred L. Bernheim and Dorothy Van Doren, eds.
(McGraw-Hill, 1935); on labor and the New Deal see also David Brody, *Workers
in Industrial America* (Oxford University Press, 1980), ch. 4.

Wagner Act: James B. Atleson, *Values and Assumptions in American Labor Law* (University of Massachusetts Press, 1983), ch. 2; Irving Bernstein, *The New Deal Collective Bargaining Policy* (University of California Press, 1950); Bernstein,
Turbulent Years, chs. 5, 7; Cletus E. Daniel, *The ACLU and the Wagner Act* (Cornell
Studies in Industrial and Labor Relations, 1980); R. W. Fleming, "The Significance of the Wagner Act," in Milton Derber and Edwin Young, eds., *Labor and
the New Deal* (University of Wisconsin Press, 1961), pp. 121–55; Gross, *Making*,
ch. 5; J. Joseph Huthmacher, *Senator Robert F. Wagner and the Rise of Urban Liberalism* (Atheneum, 1968), chs. 10–11 passim; Irons, ch. 11; "Labor's Struggle for
Rights" (editorial), *American Federationist*, vol. 42, no. 8 (August 1935), pp.
801–4; Perkins, pp. 239–44; Piven and Cloward, pp. 130–33; Schlesinger, *Coming*, ch. 24; "Shall Labor Have Rights?" (editorial), *American Federationist*, vol.
42, no. 5 (May 1935), pp. 465–66; Christopher L. Tomlins, *The State and the
Unions: Labor Relations, Law, and the Organized Labor Movement in America, 1880–
1960* (Cambridge University Press, 1985), ch. 4.

La Follette Committee: Jerold S. Auerbach, *Labor and Liberty: The La Follette Committee
and the New Deal* (Bobbs-Merrill, 1966); see also Richard C. Wilcock, "Industrial
Management's Policies toward Unionism," in Derber and Young, pp. 275–315.

NLRB and implementation of the Wagner Act: Atleson, passim; Bernstein, *Turbulent
Years*, esp. ch. 13; James MacGregor Burns, "A New House for the Labor Board,"
Journal of Politics, vol. 3, no. 4 (November 1941), pp. 486–508; J. Michael Eisner,
William Morris Leiserson (University of Wisconsin Press, 1967), ch. 7; Leon Fink,
"Labor, Liberty, and the Law: Trade Unionism and the Problem of the American
Constitutional Order," *Journal of American History*, vol. 74, no. 3 (December 1987),
pp. 904–25, esp. pp. 921–25; Gross, *Making*, chs. 6–7 passim; James A. Gross,
*The Reshaping of the National Labor Relations Board: National Labor Policy in Transition,
1937–1947* (State University of New York Press, 1981), esp. chs. 1–6 passim;
Irons, chs. 12–13; Staughton Lynd, "The Right to Engage in Concerted Activity
after Union Recognition: A Study of Legislative History," *Indiana Law Journal*, vol.

50 (1975), pp. 720–56 passim; Lynd, "Thesis and Antithesis: Section 7 of the NLRA, the First Amendment and Workers' Rights," in Jules Lobel, ed., *A Less Than Perfect Union* (Monthly Review Press, 1988), pp. 151–73; Harry A. Millis and Emily Clark Brown, *From the Wagner Act to Taft-Hartley: A Study of National Labor Policy and Labor Relations* (University of Chicago Press, 1950), part 1 passim; Doris E. Pullman and L. Reed Tripp, "Collective Bargaining Developments," in Derber and Young, pp. 317–60; Tomlins, chs. 4–6 passim.

Union campaigns in auto and steel: Bernstein, *Turbulent Years*, esp. chs. 10–11 passim; Robert R. R. Brooks, *As Steel Goes . . . : Unionism in a Basic Industry* (Yale University Press, 1940); Dubofsky and Van Tyne, ch. 12, and pp. 312–15; Sidney Fine, *Sit-Down: The General Motors Strike of 1936–1937* (University of Michigan Press, 1969); J. Woodford Howard, Jr., *Mr. Justice Murphy* (Princeton University Press, 1968), chs. 6–7 passim; Harry A. Millis, ed., *How Collective Bargaining Works: A Survey of Experiences in Leading American Industries* (Twentieth Century Fund, 1942; reprinted by Arno Press, 1971), chs. 10–11 passim; Perkins, pp. 319–24; Piven and Cloward, pp. 133–47. The treatment of these events is drawn in part from Burns, *Crosswinds*, pp. 96–100.

Counterattacks on unionism: Bernstein, *Turbulent Years*, pp. 478–98, 663–71; Brooks, ch. 6; Burns, *Crosswinds*, p. 100; Burns, "A New House"; Bruce J. Dierenfield, *Keeper of the Rules: Congressman Howard W. Smith of Virginia* (University Press of Virginia, 1987), pp. 84–105; Eisner, ch. 7; Gilbert J. Gall, "CIO Leaders and the Democratic Alliance: The Case of the Smith Committee and the NLRB," *Labor Studies Journal*, vol. 14, no. 2 (Summer 1989), pp. 3–27; Gross, *Reshaping*, chs. 7–12 passim; Earl Latham, *The Communist Controversy in Washington: From the New Deal to McCarthyism* (Harvard University Press, 1966), ch. 5; Harvey A. Levenstein, *Communism, Anticommunism, and the CIO* (Greenwood Press, 1981), chs. 2–5 passim; Millis and Brown, ch. 8 passim.

PAGE

247   [*"Full freedom of association"*]: quoted in Irving Bernstein, *The Lean Years: A History of the American Worker, 1920–1933* (Houghton Mifflin, 1960), p. 398.
       [*"Lone bright star"*]: *ibid.*, p. 415.
       [*Depression unemployment and union membership*]: *ibid.*, pp. 506, 84, 335 respectively.
       [*"Employees shall have the right"*]: quoted in Bernstein, *Turbulent Years*, p. 34.

248   [*"LABOR MUST ORGANIZE"*]: quoted in Schlesinger, *Coming*, p. 139.
       [*"ROOSEVELT WANTS YOU"*]: quoted in Burns, *Lion and Fox*, p. 216.
       [*"In nineteen hundred an' thirty-three"*]: quoted in Schlesinger, *Coming*, p. 139.
       [*"More drama than truth"*]: Perkins, p. 231.
       [Schechter]: *Schechter Poultry Corp.* v. *U.S.*, 295 U.S. 495 (1935).

249   [*Schlesinger on FDR and unions*]: Schlesinger, *Coming*, p. 402.
       [*"Resisting progress"*]: Tugwell, *The Industrial Discipline and the Governmental Arts* (Columbia University Press, 1933), pp. 134–35, quoted at p. 135.
       [*Perkins on labor's lack of ideas*]: see Schlesinger, *Coming*, p. 403.
       [*Perkins on Wagner and Wagner Act*]: Perkins, p. 239.

250   [*"Inequality of bargaining power"*]: National Labor Relations Act, 74th Congress, 1st Session, July 5, 1935, ch. 372, 49 Stat. 449, quoted at 449, 452.
       [*FDR on Wagner Act*]: July 5, 1935, in Roosevelt, *Papers*, vol. 4, pp. 294–95, quoted at p. 294.

250   [*Hughes on Wagner Act*]: NLRB v. Jones & Laughlin, 301 U.S. 1 (1937), quoted at 33.
        [*"Full freedom"*]: National Labor Relations Act, 450.
251   [*Weir on Wagner Act*]: quoted in Schlesinger, *Coming*, pp. 404–5.
        [*"Out-STALIN Stalin"*]: ibid., p. 405.
252   [*"Violations of the rights"*]: quoted in Auerbach, p. 1.
        [*Results of La Follette investigations*]: ibid., chs. 5–6 passim, Republic vice president quoted at p. 101, GM worker at p. 109, rabbi at p. 133.
253   [*"Traditional political forms"*]: quoted in Tomlins, p. 135.
        [*"Claims based on anything"*]: ibid.
254   [*"Regulatory ambit"*]: ibid., p. 147.
        [*Numbers of sit-downs, 1937*]: Fine, *Sit-Down*, p. 331.
255   [*"Had not asked for it"*]: David Brody, "The New Deal and the Labor Movement," in Brody, pp. 138–46, quoted at p. 141.
        [*"When they tie the can"*]: quoted in Fine, *Sit-Down*, p. 164.
        [*SWOC membership, January 1937*]: Bernstein, *Turbulent Years*, p. 465.
256   [*"Communists Rule the CIO"*]: quoted in Piven and Cloward, p. 165.
        [*NAM photo of Lewis*]: ibid.
        [*Numbers of union members, 1941*]: Bernstein, *Turbulent Years*, p. 769.
257   [*Derber on tolerance of dissidents*]: Derber, "The Idea of Industrial Democracy in America: 1915–1935," *Labor History*, vol. 8, no. 1 (Winter 1967), pp. 3–29, quoted at p. 29.
        [*"White shop"*]: see Raymond Wolters, *Negroes and the Great Depression: The Problem of Economic Recovery* (Greenwood Publishing, 1970), p. 184.
        [*"If labor organizations"*]: quoted in ibid., p. 178.
        [*Unionized women, 1940*]: Philip S. Foner, *Women and the American Labor Movement: From World War I to the Present* (Free Press, 1980), p. 333.
        [*"Froze the existing pattern"*]: ibid., p. 332.
258   [*"Orderly institutionalization"*]: quoted in Tomlins, p. 249.

TOWARD AN ECONOMIC BILL OF RIGHTS

Liberty League: Burk, chs. 8–14 passim; Burns, *Crosswinds*, pp. 42–43, 81–82; Frederick Rudolph, "The American Liberty League, 1934–1940," *American Historical Review*, vol. 56, no. 1 (October 1950), pp. 19–33; Wolfskill, *Revolt;* American Liberty League pamphlets in the collection of Sawyer Library, Williams College, Williamstown, Massachusetts.

Hoover in the 1930s: Best, vol. 1, esp. chs. 1–2; Dexter; Hoover, *Addresses 1933–1938;* Hoover, *Challenge;* Hoover, *Memoirs: The Great Depression, 1929–1941* (Macmillan, 1952), chs. 32–45.

The right to security and the New Deal idea of the state: see Adams; Arthur J. Altmeyer, *The Formative Years of Social Security* (University of Wisconsin Press, 1966); Irving Bernstein, *A Caring Society* (Houghton Mifflin, 1985), ch. 2; Eveline M. Burns, *Toward Social Security* (Whittlesey House, 1936); Brinkley, "New Deal and the Idea of the State"; Sidney Fine, *Laissez Faire and the General-Welfare State* (University of Michigan Press, 1956), p. 397; Daniel R. Fusfeld, "The New Deal and the Corporate State," in Rosenbaum and Bartelme, pp. 137–51 passim; Holt; Leonard Krieger, "The Idea of the Welfare State in Europe and the United States," *Journal of the History of Ideas*, vol. 24, no. 4 (October–December 1963), pp. 553–68; Roy Lubove, *The Struggle for Social Security, 1900–1935* (Harvard University Press, 1968); National Resources Planning Board, *Security, Work, and Relief Policies* (U.S. Government Printing Office, 1942); Jill Quadagno, *The Transformation of Old Age*

Security: Class and Politics in the American Welfare State (University of Chicago Press, 1988), esp. chs. 5–6; Gaston V. Rimlinger, *Welfare Policy and Industrialization in Europe, America, and Russia* (Wiley, 1971), esp. ch. 6; I. M. Rubinow, *The Quest for Security* (Holt, 1934); Maurice Stark, "The Meaning of Social Security," in William Haber and Wilbur J. Cohen, eds., *Readings in Social Security* (Prentice-Hall, 1948), pp. 41–45; Edwin E. Witte, "Organized Labor and Social Security," in Derber and Young, pp. 239–74.

PAGE

258   [*Hoover and the Liberty League*]: see Wolfskill, *Revolt*, p. 33.
259   [*Names originally proposed for Liberty League*]: see Burk, pp. 136, 138.
       [*Hays's queries to Liberty League*]: quoted in Wolfskill, *Revolt*, p. 30.
       [*"I can subscribe to that"*]: *ibid.*, pp. 30, 31.
       [*"Uphold two"*]: *ibid.*, pp. 34, 35.
260   [*"Too much stress"*]: quoted in Burk, p. 146.
       [*"All the big guns"*]: letter to William C. Bullitt, August 29, 1934, in *F.D.R.: His Personal Letters, 1928–1945*, Elliott Roosevelt, ed. (Duell, Sloan and Pearce, 1950), vol. 1, pp. 416–17, quoted at p. 417.
       [*FDR's 1936 State of the Union*]: January 3, 1936, in Roosevelt, *Papers*, vol. 5, pp. 8–18, quoted at p. 14.
       [*Mayflower banquet*]: Wolfskill, *Revolt*, pp. 142–53 passim, quoted at pp. 151, 152.
261   [*"Government by organized money"*]: October 31, 1936, in Roosevelt, *Papers*, vol. 5, pp. 566–73, quoted at p. 568.
       [*"Who may define"*]: Hoover, *Challenge*, p. 2.
262   [*FDR on postwar objectives*]: see press conference no. 658, July 5, 1940, in Roosevelt, *Papers*, vol. 9, pp. 281–85, esp. p. 285; see also James MacGregor Burns, *Roosevelt: The Soldier of Freedom* (Harcourt, 1970), p. 33.
263   [*"Those, who would give up"*]: Annual Message, January 6, 1941, in Roosevelt, *Papers*, vol. 9, pp. 663–72, quoted at pp. 665, 672.
       [*FDR's January 1944 address*]: State of the Union, January 11, 1944, in *ibid.*, vol. 13, pp. 32–42, quoted at pp. 40–41, as modified by comparison with a recording of the address.
265   [*"Antisocial license"*]: Henry Wallace and Robert Wagner, quoted in Holt, p. 42.
       [*"No civilized community"*]: *ibid.*, p. 43.
       [*"Interferences with personal freedom"*]: John Dickenson, quoted in *ibid.*, p. 43.
       [*"Left unresolved"*]: *ibid.*
       [*"Security for the individual"*]: Message to Congress, June 8, 1934, in Roosevelt, *Papers*, vol. 3, pp. 287–93, quoted at p. 288.
266   [*"First and continuing task"*]: Annual Message to Congress, January 4, 1935, in *ibid.*, vol. 4, pp. 15–25, quoted at p. 17.
       [*FDR on security in 1936 campaign*]: see, for example, *ibid.*, vol. 5, pp. 459–60, 479, 499, 500–1, 567, 574–75.
       [*"I am not for a return"*]: September 30, 1934, in *ibid.*, vol. 3, pp. 413–22, quoted at p. 422.

9. HOT WAR, COLD WAR: RIGHTS BESIEGED

[*FDR's appeal to Hitler and Hitler's response*]: A Message to Chancellor Adolf Hitler and Premier Benito Mussolini, April 14, 1939, in Roosevelt, *Public Papers and*

Addresses, Samuel I. Rosenman, ed. (Random House, 1938–50), vol. 8, pp. 201–5, quoted at pp. 201, 203 (see also press conference no. 539, April 15, 1939, in *ibid.,* pp. 208–17); William L. Shirer, *The Rise and Fall of the Third Reich: A History of Nazi Germany* (Simon and Schuster, 1960), pp. 469–75, Hitler quoted at pp. 473, 474, 475; James MacGregor Burns, *The Crosswinds of Freedom* (Knopf, 1989), pp. 149–52.

PAGE

268   [*"Reich Government were themselves"*]: quoted in Shirer, p. 470.
269   [*"What we face"*]: January 3, 1940, in Roosevelt, *Papers,* vol. 9, pp. 1–10, quoted at pp. 8–9.
       [Gobitis]: *Minersville School District* v. *Gobitis,* 310 U.S. 586 (1940), quoted at 595.

"ARMS IN THE DEFENSE OF LIBERTY"

FDR-Hoover relationship: Francis Biddle, *In Brief Authority* (Doubleday, 1962), pp. 164–68, 257–61; Frank J. Donner, *The Age of Surveillance* (Knopf, 1980), pp. 52–68, 241–44 passim; Morton H. Halperin et al., *The Lawless State: The Crimes of the U.S. Intelligence Agencies* (Penguin, 1976), pp. 91–101; Richard E. Morgan, *Domestic Intelligence: Monitoring Dissent in America* (University of Texas Press, 1980), pp. 30–40; Paul L. Murphy, *The Constitution in Crisis Times, 1918–1969* (Harper, 1972), pp. 213–17; Kenneth O'Reilly, "A New Deal for the FBI: The Roosevelt Administration, Crime Control, and National Security," *Journal of American History,* vol. 69, no. 3 (December 1982), pp. 638–58; Athan G. Theoharis, "Dissent and the State: Unleashing the FBI, 1917–1985," paper prepared for the Organization of American Historians' annual meeting, Washington, D.C., March 1990, esp. pp. 4–11; Theoharis, *Spying on Americans: Political Surveillance from Hoover to the Huston Plan* (Temple University Press, 1978), pp. 40–44, 66–76, 97–99, 156–60, 197–98 passim; Theoharis and John S. Cox, *The Boss: J. Edgar Hoover and the Great American Inquisition* (Temple University Press, 1988), chs. 8–9 passim.

HUAC: Martin Dies, *The Trojan Horse in America* (Dodd, Mead, 1940); Walter Goodman, *The Committee* (Farrar, Straus and Giroux, 1968), chs. 1–5 passim; Murphy, pp. 214–18; Richard Polenberg, "Franklin Roosevelt and Civil Liberties: The Case of the Dies Committee," *Historian,* vol. 30, no. 2 (February 1968), pp. 165–78.

1940 Alien Registration Act: Zechariah Chafee, Jr., *Free Speech in the United States* (Harvard University Press, 1941), ch. 12; Donner, pp. 61–64; Jack Peltason, *Constitutional Liberty and Seditious Activity: Individual Liberty and Government Security* (Carrie Chapman Catt Memorial Fund, 1954), ch. 8.

FDR, his critics, and sedition trial: Biddle, ch. 15; Wayne S. Cole, *Roosevelt & the Isolationists, 1932–45* (University of Nebraska Press, 1983), esp. chs. 30, 33 passim; Edward S. Corwin, *Total War and the Constitution* (Knopf, 1947), pp. 111–16; Sander A. Diamond, *The Nazi Movement in the United States, 1924–41* (Cornell University Press, 1974), esp. parts 3–4 passim; Robert E. Herzstein, *Roosevelt & Hitler: Prelude to War* (Paragon House, 1989); Glen Jeansonne, *Gerald L. K. Smith: Minister of Hate* (Yale University Press, 1988), esp. ch. 5; Richard Polenberg, *War and Society: The United States, 1941–1945* (Lippincott, 1972), pp. 45–48; Leo P. Ribuffo, *The Old Christian Right: The Protestant Far Right from the Great Depression to the Cold War* (Temple University Press, 1983), esp. ch. 5; Geoffrey S. Smith, *To Save a Nation: American Countersubversives, the New Deal, and the Coming of World War*

II (Basic Books, 1973); Richard W. Steele, "Franklin D. Roosevelt and His Foreign Policy Critics," *Political Science Quarterly*, vol. 94, no. 1 (Spring 1979), pp.
15–35; Theoharis, *Spying*, pp. 157–59; Samuel Walker, *In Defense of Civil Liberties:
A History of the ACLU* (Oxford University Press, 1990), pp. 153–58.

Aliens in World War II: Biddle, chs. 6, 12; Morton Grodzins, *Americans Betrayed:
Politics and the Japanese Evacuation* (University of Chicago Press, 1949), pp. 231–53
passim; Polenberg, *War and Society*, pp. 41–43.

Conscientious objection in World War II: American Civil Liberties Union, *Freedom in
Wartime* (ACLU, June 1943), pp. 37–39; American Civil Liberties Union, *In Defense
of Our Liberties* (ACLU, June 1944), pp. 34–38; J. Garry Clifford and Samuel R.
Spencer, Jr., *The First Peacetime Draft* (University Press of Kansas, 1986), ch. 8
passim, and pp. 221–23; Polenberg, *War and Society*, pp. 54–61; Mulford Q. Sibley
and Philip E. Jacob, *Conscription of Conscience: The American State and the Conscientious
Objector, 1940–1947* (Cornell University Press, 1952), chs. 3–4, and passim; Lillian
Schlissel, ed., *Conscience in America* (E. P. Dutton, 1968), part 6.

African-Americans and World War II: Biddle, pp. 152–60; James MacGregor Burns,
Roosevelt: The Soldier of Freedom (Harcourt, 1970), pp. 54–55, 123–24, 264–66,
462–63, 471–72; Lee Finkle, "The Conservative Aims of Militant Rhetoric: Black
Protest during World War II," *Journal of American History*, vol. 60, no. 3 (December
1973), pp. 692–713; Polenberg, *War and Society*, ch. 4; Louis Ruchames, *Race, Jobs,
& Politics: The Story of FEPC* (Columbia University Press, 1953); Patrick S. Wash-
burn, *A Question of Sedition: The Federal Government's Investigation of the Black Press
during World War II* (Oxford University Press, 1986); Neil A. Wynn, *The Afro-
American and the Second World War* (Holmes & Meier, 1976).

Japanese internment: ACLU, *Freedom in Wartime*, pp. 24–30; Biddle, ch. 13; Burns,
Crosswinds, pp. 189–90; Corwin, pp. 91–100; Gavan Daws, *Shoal of Time: A History
of the Hawaiian Islands* (Macmillan, 1968), esp. pp. 344–57; Charles Fairman, "The
Supreme Court on Military Jurisdiction: Martial Rule in Hawaii and the Yamashita
Case," *Harvard Law Review*, vol. 54, no. 6 (July 1946), pp. 833–82; Audrie Girdner
and Anne Loftis, *The Great Betrayal: The Evacuation of the Japanese Americans during
World War II* (Macmillan, 1969); Grodzins; Peter H. Irons, *Justice at War* (Oxford
University Press, 1983); Murphy, pp. 232–42; Polenberg, *War and Society*, pp.
61–72; Jacobus tenBroek et al., *Prejudice, War and the Constitution* (University of
California Press, 1954); Walker, pp. 136–49.

PAGE

270   [*"Free Americans"*]: in Roosevelt, *Papers*, vol. 10, pp. 554–57, quoted at
pp. 554, 555, 557.

271   [*"I have in mind"*]: Polenberg, "Roosevelt and Civil Liberties," pp. 174–
76, quoted at pp. 175–76; see also Goodman, pp. 111–13.

272   [*"Most drastic restrictions"*]: Chafee, p. 441.
        [*"Advocate, abet, advise"*]: quoted in Corwin, pp. 108, 111.
        [*"Hardly be considered"*]: quoted in Donner, p. 61.

273   [*"Anti-war talk"*]: Biddle, p. 238.
        [*"When are you going to indict"*]: quoted in *ibid.*
        [*"Native Fascists"*]: *ibid.*, p. 239.
        [*"Persons of Hebrew blood"*]: quoted in *ibid.*, p. 236.
        [*"Masses wake up"*]: quoted in Ribuffo, p. 202.
        [*"That any federal court"*]: Corwin, p. 116.

274   [*FDR's reassurance on alien registration*]: June 29, 1940, in Roosevelt, *Papers*,
vol. 9, pp. 274–75.
        [*"Reason of religious training"*]: quoted in Polenberg, *War and Society*, p. 54.

275   [*"Contemplates recognition"*]: quoted in Sibley and Jacob, p. 68.
         [*"Wildly disparate standards"*]: Polenberg, *War and Society*, p. 54.
         [*"For the government to require"*]: quoted in *ibid.*, p. 56.
         [*Polenberg on alternative service*]: *ibid.*
         [*"Set back the progress"*]: quoted in Ruchames, p. 17.
276   [*FDR's 1941 order on black employment*]: Executive Order no. 8802, June
         25, 1941, in Roosevelt, *Papers*, vol. 10, pp. 233–35.
         [*"I am a corporal"*]: quoted in Biddle, pp. 155–56.
277   [*"Most drastic invasion"*]: Corwin, p. 91.
278   [*"Personally directed"*]: tenBroek et al., p. 331.
         [*FDR on Japanese-American camps*]: Girdner and Loftis, pp. 237–38.
         [*"What must be done"*]: Biddle, p. 219.
         [*Congressman's objection to relocation*]: Earl C. Michener, quoted in Grod-
         zins, p. 340; Andrew J. May quoted on "extremely urgent" situation at
         ibid.
279   [*"Nobody's constitutional rights"*]: quoted in Ronald Steel, *Walter Lippmann
         and the American Century* (Atlantic Monthly Press/Little, Brown, 1980),
         p. 394.
         [*"To hell with habeas corpus"*]: Grodzins, pp. 387–88, quoted at p. 388.
         [*"A clear violation"*]: *Korematsu* v. *U.S.*, 323 U.S. 214 (1944), quoted
         at 225.
         [*"Approve all that the military"*]: *ibid.*, 244–45.
         [*"War-making branches"*]: *Hirabayashi* v. *U.S.*, 320 U.S. 81 (1943), quoted
         at 99.

THE PURSUIT OF NATIONAL SECURITY

FDR, Truman, Eisenhower administrations and Hoover's FBI: Alan Barth, *The Loyalty
of Free Men* (Viking, 1951), esp. ch. 7; Halperin et al., pp. 91–116; Kenneth
O'Reilly, "The FBI and the Origins of McCarthyism," *Historian*, vol. 45, no. 3
(May 1983), pp. 372–93; O'Reilly, "New Deal for the FBI"; Theoharis, "Dissent
and the State," passim; Theoharis, *Spying*, passim; Theoharis and Cox, *The Boss*,
chs. 8–11 passim; see also Thomas I. Emerson, "The FBI and the Bill of Rights,"
in Pat Watters and Stephen Gillers, eds., *Investigating the FBI* (Doubleday, 1973),
pp. 412–37; William W. Keller, *The Liberals and J. Edgar Hoover: Rise and Fall of a
Domestic Intelligence State* (Princeton University Press, 1989), esp. chs. 1–2 passim;
Athan G. Theoharis, ed., *Beyond the Hiss Case: The FBI, Congress, and the Cold War*
(Temple University Press, 1982).

Truman administration, Cold War, and civil liberties: Barth; Ralph S. Brown, Jr., *Loyalty
and Security: Employment Tests in the United States* (Yale University Press, 1958); David
Caute, *The Great Fear: The Anti-Communist Purge under Truman and Eisenhower* (Simon
and Schuster, 1978), esp. chs. 1–3, 13 passim; Fred J. Cook, *The Nightmare Decade:
The Life and Times of Senator Joe McCarthy* (Random House, 1971), chs. 3–4 passim;
Richard M. Fried, *Nightmare in Red: The McCarthy Era in Perspective* (Oxford Univer-
sity Press, 1990), esp. chs. 3–4 passim; Goodman, chs. 7–10 passim; Alan D.
Harper, *The Politics of Loyalty: The White House and the Communist Issue, 1946–1952*
(Greenwood Publishing, 1969); Mary S. McAuliffe, *Crisis on the Left: Cold War
Politics and American Liberals, 1947–1954* (University of Massachusetts Press, 1978);
Edward E. Palmer, ed., *The Communist Problem in America* (Thomas Y. Crowell,
1951), esp. pp. 385–99; Athan Theoharis, "The Escalation of the Loyalty Pro-
gram," in Barton J. Bernstein, ed., *Politics and Policies of the Truman Administration*
(Quadrangle, 1970), pp. 242–68; Theoharis, "The Rhetoric of Politics: Foreign

Policy, Internal Security, and Domestic Politics in the Truman Era, 1945–1950," in *ibid.*, pp. 196–241; Theoharis, *Seeds of Repression: Harry S. Truman and the Origins of McCarthyism* (Quadrangle, 1971); Theoharis, *Spying*, pp. 45–55, 199–209; Theoharis, "The Threat to Civil Liberties," in Thomas G. Paterson, ed., *Cold War Critics: Alternatives to American Foreign Policy in the Truman Years* (Quadrangle, 1971), pp. 266–98; Theoharis and Cox, *The Boss*, chs. 10–11 passim; John C. Wahlke, ed., *Loyalty in a Democratic State* (D. C. Heath, 1952); Walker, ch. 8 passim.

Internal Security Act: Barth, pp. 42–47; Harper, ch. 7; McAuliffe, pp. 77–80; Palmer, pp. 423–71; Peltason, ch. 9; William R. Tanner and Robert Griffith, "Legislative Politics and 'McCarthyism': The Internal Security Act of 1950," in Griffith and Athan Theoharis, eds., *The Specter* (New Viewpoints, 1974), pp. 172–89; Wahlke, pp. 65–83.

McCarthy and McCarthyism: Burns, *Crosswinds*, pp. 243–53, 258–59; Cook, *Nightmare Decade;* Richard M. Fried, *Men Against McCarthy* (Columbia University Press, 1976); Fried, *Nightmare*, esp. ch. 5; Robert Griffith, *The Politics of Fear: Joseph R. McCarthy and the Senate* (University Press of Kentucky, 1970); Harper, ch. 6; Earl Latham, *The Communist Controversy in Washington: From the New Deal to McCarthy* (Harvard University Press, 1966), esp. chs. 10–13 passim; McAuliffe, ch. 7 passim; Allen J. Matusow, ed., *Joseph R. McCarthy* (Prentice-Hall, 1970); Thomas C. Reeves, *The Life and Times of Joe McCarthy* (Stein & Day, 1982); Richard H. Rovere, *Senator Joe McCarthy* (Harcourt, 1959); Theoharis, *Seeds of Repression*, esp. ch. 8; Theoharis and Cox, *The Boss*, pp. 280–300.

Business, labor, and the Fear: Caute, part 5; Bert Cochran, *Labor and Communism: The Conflict That Shaped American Unions* (Princeton University Press, 1977), chs. 10–12 passim; Peter H. Irons, "American Business and the Origins of McCarthyism: The Cold War Crusade of the United States Chamber of Commerce," in Griffith and Theoharis, *The Specter*, pp. 72–89; McAuliffe, esp. ch. 4; David M. Oshinsky, "Labor's Cold War: The CIO and the Communists," in Griffith and Theoharis, *The Specter*, pp. 116–51; see also David Horowitz, ed., *Corporations and the Cold War* (Monthly Review Press, 1969).

Churches and the Fear: Cook, *Nightmare Decade*, pp. 288–91; Donald F. Crosby, *God, Church, and Flag: Senator Joseph R. McCarthy and the Catholic Church, 1950–1957* (University of North Carolina Press, 1978), ch. 10, and passim; Ralph Lord Roy, *Communism & the Churches* (Harcourt, 1960), chs. 10–21, and pp. 418–29 passim.

Education and the Fear: Barth, ch. 9; Caute, chs. 22–23; Sigmund Diamond, "The Arrangement: The FBI and Harvard University in the McCarthy Period," in Theoharis, *Beyond the Hiss Case*, pp. 341–71; Fried, *Nightmare*, esp. pp. 100–3; Sidney Hook, "Academic Freedom and Communism," in Wahlke, pp. 84–89; Alexander Meiklejohn, "Should Communists Be Allowed to Teach?," in *ibid.*, pp. 89–95; Ellen W. Schrecker, "Academic Freedom and the Cold War," *Antioch Review*, vol. 38, no. 3 (Summer 1980), pp. 313–27; Schrecker, *No Ivory Tower: McCarthyism and the Universities* (Oxford University Press, 1986).

PAGE
280   [*Press self-censorship in World War II*]: see Byron Price, "War Censorship," in Price and Elmer Davis, *War Information and Censorship* (American Council on Public Affairs, 1943), pp. 56–79; Robert E. Summers, ed., *Wartime Censorship of Press and Radio* (H. W. Wilson, 1942).
281   [*"Pious idea"*]: quoted in Fried, *Nightmare*, p. 51.
          [*"Specially watched"*]: Theoharis, "Dissent and the State," pp. 6–9, Roosevelt quoted at p. 8.

281   [*"Between national security"*]: Fried, *Nightmare,* p. 51.
        [*"Stir up among the rank and file"*]: quoted in Theoharis, *Spying,* p. 162.
        [*"A trespass"*]: ibid., p. 107.
282   [*"Ignorance and anticommunism"*]: *ibid.*
        [*"Scurrilous attacks"*]: quoted in *ibid.,* p. 166.
        [*FBI surveillance of Eleanor Roosevelt*]: see Theoharis and Cox, *The Boss,* pp.
        191–93 fn., "White Woman in the Kitchen" quoted at p. 192 fn.;
        Theoharis, "Dissent and the State," pp. 9–11.
        [*FBI microphone installations, 1953–55*]: Theoharis, *Spying,* p. 111.
        [*FBI "Security Index," 1954*]: *ibid.,* p. 55.
        [*New York agents assigned to "Communism," 1959*]: O'Reilly, "The FBI and
        the Origins of McCarthyism," p. 372 fn. 1.
284   [*"So as to serve"*]: quoted in Harper, appendix 1, p. 262.
        [*Organizations on attorney general's list*]: see Fried, *Nightmare,* pp. 70–71;
        Palmer, pp. 475–87.
        [*Instances of abuse and denials of procedural safeguards in loyalty investigations*]:
        Fried, *Nightmare,* pp. 71–72; Leonard A. Nikolorić, "The Government
        Loyalty Program," in Wahlke, pp. 50–58.
        [*"Think back"*]: quoted in Nikolorić, p. 52.
285   [*Richardson on loyalty program results*]: Cook, *Nightmare Decade,* p. 258.
286   [*"Here in my hand"*]: quoted in Reeves, p. 224.
        [*Truman on atmosphere of repression*]: Fried, *Nightmare,* p. 113.
287   [*Truman's McCarran veto message*]: September 22, 1950, in Truman, *Public
        Papers* (U.S. Government Printing Office, 1961–66), vol. 6, pp. 645–53,
        quoted at pp. 645, 649, 645, 650, 653 respectively.
288   [*"Cream-puff special"*]: quoted in Tanner and Griffith, p. 184.
        [*"Reason to believe"*]: ibid., p. 183.
        [*"Act with speed"*]: ibid., p. 184.
        [*"Most irreconcilable"*]: quoted in Steel, pp. 482, 481 respectively.
289   [*"Top Russian espionage agent"*]: quoted in Reeves, p. 261.
        [*"Extremely bad security risk"*]: ibid., p. 251.
        [*"Do you feel that you should be walking"*]: ibid., p. 522.
290   [*"There is no loyalty"*]: ibid., p. 623.
        [*"Front man for traitors"*]: quoted in Griffith, *Politics of Fear,* p. 114.
        [*"The rights you have"*]: quoted in Caute, p. 97.
        [*"It is pretty clear"*]: quoted in Goodman, p. 251.
        [*"I just will not"*]: quoted in David M. Oshinsky, *A Conspiracy So Immense:
        The World of Joe McCarthy* (Free Press, 1983), p. 260.
        [*"Massive retaliatory power"*]: address to the Council on Foreign Re-
        lations, January 12, 1954, in *Documents on American Foreign Relations,
        1954,* Peter V. Curl, ed. (Harper, 1955), pp. 7–15, quoted at pp. 9, 10,
        9 respectively.
291   [*Cases of Oklahoma librarian and Girl Scouts*]: Fried, *Nightmare,* p. 161.
        [*Burning of* Annals]: Cook, *Nightmare Decade,* p. 423.
        [*"Mighty lonesome"*]: quoted in *ibid.,* p. 15.
        [*"Russia's best friend"*]: quoted in Irons, "Business and McCarthyism," p. 76.
        [*"Set up some firing squads"*]: ibid., p. 79.
        [*"War of aggression"*]: Francis P. Matthews, quoted in *ibid.*
292   [*"Largest single group"*]: quoted in Reeves, p. 499.
        [*"Your Child is Their Target"*]: quoted in Fried, *Nightmare,* p. 100.
        [*"Anti-subversion crusades meshed"*]: *ibid.*
        [*Purges of New York City schoolteachers*]: ibid., pp. 104, 153.
        [*"Nothing in the nature"*]: quoted in Schrecker, "Academic Freedom and
        the Cold War," p. 318.

292   [*"Unfit to discharge"*]: quoted in Schrecker, *No Ivory Tower*, p. 112.
        [*"Card-holding members"*]: *ibid.*, p. 111.
293   [*"No witch-hunts at Yale"*]: *ibid.*

CENTERS OF INTOLERANCE

American-Soviet relations and American popular attitudes toward the Soviet Union and Communists since 1917: see Fried, *Nightmare*, ch. 2 passim.

Interpretations of Cold War Red Fear
Mass responsibility for Fear: see Daniel Bell, *The End of Ideology: On the Exhaustion of Political Ideas in the Fifties*, rev. ed. (Free Press, 1962), esp. ch. 6; Bell, ed., *The New American Right* (Criterion Books, 1955); Robert B. Fowler, *Believing Skeptics: American Political Intellectuals, 1945–1964* (Greenwood Press, 1978), esp. chs. 1, 6 passim; Richard Hofstadter, *Anti-Intellectualism in American Life* (Knopf, 1963), esp. chs. 1, 15 passim; Herbert H. Hyman and Paul B. Sheatsley, "Trends in Public Opinion on Civil Liberties," *Journal of Social Issues*, vol. 9, no. 3 (1953), pp. 6–16; William Kornhauser, *The Politics of Mass Society* (Free Press, 1959); Seymour Martin Lipset and Earl Raab, *The Politics of Unreason: Right-Wing Extremism in America, 1790–1970* (Harper, 1970), ch. 6, and passim; Richard H. Pells, *The Liberal Mind in a Conservative Age: American Intellectuals in the 1940s and 1950s* (Harper, 1985), esp. pp. 328–39; Nelson W. Polsby, "McCarthyism at the Grass Roots" (1960), in Earl Latham, ed., *The Meaning of McCarthyism*, 2nd ed. (D. C. Heath, 1973), pp. 153–65; Edward A. Shils, *The Torment of Secrecy: The Background and Consequences of American Security Policies* (Free Press, 1956); Samuel A. Stouffer, *Communism, Conformity, and Civil Liberties: A Cross-section of the Nation Speaks Its Mind* (1955; reprinted by Peter Smith, 1963), esp. ch. 2; John L. Sullivan, James Piereson, and George E. Marcus, *Political Tolerance and American Democracy* (University of Chicago Press, 1982), esp. chs. 1–2, 4, 6, 9; Martin A. Trow, *Right-Wing Radicalism and Political Intolerance: A Study of Support for McCarthy in a New England Town* (1957; published by Arno Press, 1980).

Elite responsibility for Fear: see Peter Bachrach, *The Theory of Democratic Elitism: A Critique* (Little, Brown, 1967); Caute, chs. 1–2; James L. Gibson, "Political Intolerance and Political Repression during the McCarthy Red Scare," *American Political Science Review*, vol. 82, no. 2 (June 1988), pp. 511–29; Griffith, *Politics of Fear;* Harper, *Politics of Loyalty;* Levin, chs. 5–7 passim; Michael Paul Rogin, *The Intellectuals and McCarthy: The Radical Specter* (MIT Press, 1967); Stouffer, esp. ch. 3; Athan Theoharis, "The Politics of Scholarship: Liberals, Anti-Communism, and McCarthyism," in Griffith and Theoharis, *The Specter*, pp. 262–80; Theoharis, *Seeds of Repression;* Trow, esp. chs. 1, 9.

_____

Intellectuals and Fear: Bachrach; Bell, *End of Ideology;* Thomas I. Cook, *Democratic Rights versus Communist Activity* (Doubleday, 1954); Fowler; Keller, ch. 2; McAuliffe, chs. 5, 7, and passim; Herbert Marcuse, "Repressive Tolerance," in Robert P. Wolff, Barrington Moore, Jr., and Marcuse, *A Critique of Pure Tolerance* (Beacon Press, 1965), pp. 81–117; Norman Markowitz, "A View from the Left: From the Popular Front to Cold War Liberalism," in Griffith and Theoharis, *The Specter*, pp. 90–115; Pells, esp. chs. 3, 5; James W. Prothro and Charles M. Grigg, "Fundamental Principles of Democracy: Bases of Agreement and Disagreement," *Journal of Politics*, vol. 22, no. 2 (May 1960), pp. 276–94; David Riesman and Nathan Glazer, "The Intellectuals and the Discontented Classes," in Bell, *New American*

Right, pp. 56–90; Rogin, esp. chs. 1–2, 9 passim; Arthur M. Schlesinger, Jr., *The Vital Center: The Politics of Freedom* (Houghton Mifflin, 1949); Edward A. Shils, "Ideology and Civility: On the Politics of the Intellectual," *Sewanee Review,* vol. 66, no. 3 (July–September 1958), pp. 450–80; Shils, *Torment of Secrecy;* Sullivan, Piereson, and Marcus, ch. 1 passim; Theoharis, "Politics of Scholarship"; Walker, ch. 9 passim.

Judiciary and Fear: Michael R. Belknap, "Cold War in the Courtroom: The Foley Square Communist Trial," in Belknap, ed., *American Political Trials* (Greenwood Press, 1981), pp. 233–62; Caute, esp. chs. 7, 9–10; Fried, *Nightmare,* pp. 90–91, 114–16, 184–88; Allen Guttmann and Benjamin Munn Ziegler, eds., *Communism, the Courts and the Constitution* (D. C. Heath, 1964); Murphy, chs. 8–10 passim; C. Herman Pritchett, *Civil Liberties and the Vinson Court* (University of Chicago Press, 1954); Peter L. Steinberg, *The Great "Red Menace": United States Prosecution of American Communists, 1947–1952* (Greenwood Press, 1984), passim.

PAGE

294   *[State bans on Communists]:* see Gibson, pp. 513–15; see also Caute, chs. 4, 17; Walter Gellhorn, ed., *The States and Subversion* (Cornell University Press, 1952); James Truett Selcraig, *The Red Scare in the Midwest, 1945–1955: A State and Local Study* (UMI Research Press, 1982).
["Little doubt"]: Gibson, p. 514.

295   *[Estimates of Americans affected by loyalty programs]:* Brown, *Loyalty and Security,* pp. 181–82.
["Enormous hostility"]: Hofstadter, "The Pseudo-Conservative Revolt," in Bell, *New American Right,* pp. 33–55, quoted at p. 47.

296   *["Elites, not masses"]:* Gibson, p. 511.
["Postwar liberals had functioned"]: Pells, p. 339.
["Potential for intolerance"]: Sullivan, Piereson, and Marcus, p. 260.

297   *["Where one wants to go"]:* Bell, *End of Ideology,* p. 405.
["Living dangerously"]: Schlesinger, "The Politics of Democracy," *Partisan Review,* vol. 18, no. 2 (March–April 1951), pp. 245–52, quoted at p. 246.

298   *["Repressive spirit"]:* Bendiner, "Civil Liberties and the Communists: Checking Subversion Without Harm to Democratic Rights," *Commentary,* vol. 5, no. 5 (May 1948), pp. 423–31, quoted at p. 429.
["Legitimate dissenting groups"]: quoted in Pells, p. 268.
["Riddle wrapped"]: radio broadcast of October 1, 1939, quoted in Martin Gilbert, *Winston S. Churchill: Finest Hour, 1939–1941* (Houghton Mifflin, 1983), p. 50.

299   *[Postwar Communist Party membership]:* see Caute, p. 185; Steinberg, p. 82.
["No documentation"]: Caute, p. 54.
["Society, group"]: quoted in Belknap, "Cold War in the Courtroom," p. 238.

300   *["Destruction of the Fifth Column"]:* quoted in Goodman, p. 99 fn.
["No more than project"]: defense attorney Abraham Isserman, quoted in Steinberg, p. 174.
["I find as a matter of law"]: quoted in Caute, p. 193.
["Whether the gravity"]: quoted in Belknap, "Cold War in the Courtroom," p. 251.
["Highly organized conspiracy"]: *Dennis* v. *U.S.,* 341 U.S. 494 (1951), Vinson quoted at 511, 509 respectively, Douglas at 589, 590.

301   *[1952 deportation of Italian-American]:* *Mascitti* v. *McGrath,* with *Harisiades* v. *Shaughnessy,* 342 U.S. 580 (1952).

301   [*"Roll the repression along"*]: John P. Frank, quoted in Murphy, p. 294.
        [*"Inquire into private affairs"*]: Quinn v. U.S., 349 U.S. 155 (1955), quoted
        at 161.
        [*Service*]: Service v. Dulles, 354 U.S. 363 (1957).
302   [*"No congressional power"*]: Watkins v. U.S., 354 U.S. 178 (1957), quoted
        at 200.
        [*New Hampshire and left-wing editor*]: Sweezy v. New Hampshire, 354 U.S. 234
        (1957).
        [*Yates*]: Yates v. U.S., 354 U.S. 298 (1957), decision quoted at 320, 321,
        Black at 339.
        [*Smith Act convictions and prosecutions after* Yates]: Caute, p. 208.
        [*"In calmer times"*]: Dennis, 581.

1 0 . E V E R Y B O D Y   S I N G   F R E E D O M

Montgomery bus boycott: Taylor Branch, *Parting the Waters: America in the King Years,
1954–63* (Simon and Schuster, 1988), chs. 4–5; David J. Garrow, *Bearing the Cross:
Martin Luther King, Jr., and the Southern Christian Leadership Conference* (Vintage,
1988), ch. 1; Martin Luther King, Jr., *Stride Toward Freedom: The Montgomery Story*
(Harper, 1986); Steven M. Millner, "The Montgomery Bus Boycott: A Case Study
in the Emergence and Career of a Social Movement," in David J. Garrow, ed.,
The Walking City: The Montgomery Bus Boycott, 1955–1956 (Carlson Publishing,
1989), pp. 381–605; Aldon D. Morris, *The Origins of the Civil Rights Movement: Black
Communities Organizing for Change* (Free Press, 1984), ch. 3; Howell Raines, *My Soul
Is Rested: Movement Days in the Deep South Remembered* (Penguin, 1983), pp. 37–65;
Jo Ann Gibson Robinson, *The Montgomery Bus Boycott and the Women Who Started It:
The Memoir of Jo Ann Gibson Robinson,* David J. Garrow, ed. (University of Tennes-
see Press, 1987); J. Mills Thornton III, "Challenge and Response in the Mont-
gomery Bus Boycott of 1955–1956," in Garrow, *Walking City,* pp. 323–79.

PAGE
305   [*"Life history of being rebellious"*]: quoted in Raines, p. 44.
        [*"When I had been pushed"*]: Parks radio interview by Sidney Roger, Mont-
        gomery, Alabama, 1956 (cassette recording from Pacifica Radio Archive,
        Los Angeles).
306   [*"Most militant man in town"*]: quoted in Stephen B. Oates, *Let the Trumpet
        Sound: The Life of Martin Luther King, Jr.* (Mentor, 1985), p. 60.
        [*Robinson's recollection of leaflet distribution*]: Robinson, pp. 46–47.
307   [*"We are determined to apply our citizenship"*]: "First Mass Meeting of the
        Montgomery Improvement Association," audiotape, December 5, 1955
        (Box 107, King Library and Archives, King Center, Atlanta).
        [*"We really were the ones"*]: Allen interview by Steven Millner, in Millner,
        p. 522.
308   [*"We, the Negro citizens of Montgomery"*]: King, "Statement to the National
        Democratic Platform Committee," August 11, 1956 (Martin Luther
        King, Jr., Papers, Mugar Library, Boston University).

FREEDOM NOW!

NAACP history and Brown v. Board of Education: Philip Elman, "The Solicitor
General's Office, Justice Frankfurter, and Civil Rights Litigation, 1946–1960: An
Oral History" (interviewed by Norman Silber), *Harvard Law Review,* vol. 100, no.

4 (February 1987), pp. 817–52; Randall Kennedy, "A Reply to Philip Elman," *Harvard Law Review*, vol. 100, no. 8 (June 1987), pp. 1938–48; Richard Kluger, *Simple Justice: The History of* Brown v. Board of Education *and Black America's Struggle for Equality* (Knopf, 1975); Mark V. Tushnet, "Commentary," in Charles W. Eagles, ed., *The Civil Rights Movement in America* (University Press of Mississippi, 1986), pp. 117–25; Tushnet, *The NAACP's Legal Strategy Against Segregated Education, 1925–1950* (University of North Carolina Press, 1987); J. Harvie Wilkinson III, *From* Brown *to* Bakke: *The Supreme Court and School Integration, 1954–1978* (Oxford University Press, 1979), chs. 1–4.

King and Southern Christian Leadership Conference: Branch; Adam Fairclough, *To Redeem the Soul of America: The Southern Christian Leadership Conference and Martin Luther King, Jr.* (University of Georgia Press, 1987); Garrow, *Bearing the Cross;* David L. Lewis, *King* (University of Illinois Press, 1978).

Student sit-in movement, freedom rides, and SNCC: Clayborne Carson, *In Struggle: SNCC and the Black Awakening of the 1960s* (Harvard University Press, 1981); James Farmer, *Lay Bare the Heart: An Autobiography of the Civil Rights Movement* (Arbor House, 1985); James Forman, *The Making of Black Revolutionaries* (Open Hand Publishing, 1985); Mary King, *Freedom Song: A Personal Story of the 1960s Civil Rights Movement* (Morrow, 1987); Susan Kling, *Fannie Lou Hamer* (Chicago: Women for Racial and Economic Equality, 1979); James Peck, *Freedom Ride* (Simon and Schuster, 1962); Raines, *My Soul Is Rested;* Howard Zinn, *SNCC: The New Abolitionists* (Beacon Press, 1965), chs. 1–3.

Albany and Birmingham movements: Branch, chs. 14–16, 18–20 passim; Garrow, *Bearing the Cross,* chs. 4–5; Martin Luther King, Jr., *Why We Can't Wait* (Harper, 1964); Morris, ch. 10.

Freedom songs: Bernice Johnson Reagon, "In Our Hands: Thoughts on Black Music," *Sing Out!,* vol. 24 (January–February 1976), pp. 1–5; Reagon, "Songs of the Civil Rights Movement, 1955–1965: A Study in Culture History" (Ph.D. dissertation, Howard University, 1975), esp. chs. 2, 3, 5.

School desegregation: Albert P. Blaustein and Clarence Clyde Ferguson, Jr., *Desegregation and the Law: The Meaning and Effect of the School Segregation Cases* (Vintage, 1962); Kluger; Wilkinson.

1964 Civil Rights Act: Carl M. Brauer, *John F. Kennedy and the Second Reconstruction* (Columbia University Press, 1977), chs. 9–10, and Conclusion; Debbie Louis, *And We Are Not Saved: A History of the Movement as People* (Doubleday, 1970), pp. 377–401; James L. Sundquist, *Politics and Policy: The Eisenhower, Kennedy, and Johnson Years* (Brookings Institution, 1968), ch. 6.

PAGE

309   [*Piven and Cloward on peasantry to proletariat*]: Piven and Cloward, *Poor People's Movements: Why They Succeed, How They Fail* (Pantheon, 1977), p. 192.

        [*Supreme Court rulings on "white primaries," restrictive covenants, and graduate school segregation*]: see *Smith* v. *Allwright,* 321 U.S. 649 (1944); *Shelley* v. *Kraemer,* 334 U.S. 1 (1948); *Gaines* v. *Canada,* 305 U.S. 337 (1938); *Sweatt* v. *Painter,* 339 U.S. 629 (1950); *McLaurin* v. *Oklahoma State Regents,* 339 U.S. 637 (1950).

        [*Brown*]: 347 U.S. 483 (1954), quoted at 494, 495.

        [*"Considerable complexity"*]: *ibid.,* 495.

        [*"With all deliberate speed"*]: 349 U.S. 294 (1955), quoted at 301.

310   [*"Born in protest"*]: James H. Cone, *Black Theology and Black Power* (Seabury Press, 1969), p. 94.

311   [*"Common church culture"*]: Morris, p. 11.
       [*Morris on SCLC strengths*]: ibid., pp. 46, 89.
       [*"We don't serve you here"*]: quoted in Raines, p. 76.
312   [*"Like a fever"*]: quoted in Carson, p. 12.
       [*Carson on high proportion of protesting students*]: ibid.
       [*"Right to direct their own affairs"*]: Baker interview by Clayborne Carson,
       New York, May 5, 1972, unpublished transcript.
       [*"Group-centered leadership"*]: report by Baker of the Raleigh conference,
       in *Southern Patriot* (May 1960), reprinted in Forman, pp. 217–18, quoted
       at p. 218; see also Ella Baker, "Developing Community Leadership," in
       Gerda Lerner, ed., *Black Women in White America* (Pantheon, 1972), pp.
       345–52, esp. p. 352.
313   [*Supreme Court ruling on segregated terminals*]: Boynton v. *Virginia*, 364 U.S.
       454 (1960).
       [*"Putting the movement on wheels"*]: Raines, p. 110.
       [*"Cooling off for 350 years"*]: quoted in Farmer, pp. 205–6; see also Robert
       Kennedy, *In His Own Words: The Unpublished Recollections of the Kennedy
       Years*, Edwin O. Guthman and Jeffrey Shulman, eds. (Bantam, 1988),
       p. 89.
314   [*"Self-consciously radical southern student movement"*]: Carson, p. 37.
       [*"Half a loaf"*]: Lewis, p. 163.
       [*"Set the pace"*]: quoted in Morris, p. 251.
       [*"If we can crack Birmingham"*]: quoted in Sundquist, p. 259.
       [*"Soul of the movement"*]: King, *Why We Can't Wait*, p. 57.
       [*"Differences among us"*]: Reagon, "In Our Hands," p. 1.
315   [*"Get on board, children, children"*]: Guy Carawan and Candie Carawan,
       eds., *Sing for Freedom: The Story of the Civil Rights Movement through Its Songs*
       (Sing Out Corporation, 1990), quoted at p. 86.
       [*"I submit that an individual"*]: King, "Letter from Birmingham Jail,"
       reprinted in King, *Why We Can't Wait*, pp. 77–100, quoted at p. 86.
316   [*Eisenhower's attitude toward* Brown]: Stephen E. Ambrose, *Eisenhower: The
       President* (Simon and Schuster, 1984), p. 190.
       [*"No one can gainsay the fact"*]: May 18, 1963, in Kennedy, *Public Papers*
       (U.S. Government Printing Office, 1962–64), vol. 3, pp. 406–9, quoted
       at p. 408.
       [*"Old as the scriptures"*]: June 11, 1963, in *ibid.*, vol. 3, pp. 468–71, quoted
       at p. 469.
317   [*"Washington has not seen"*]: quoted in Sundquist, p. 268.
       [*"Jim Crow as a legal entity was dead"*]: Woodward, *The Strange Career of Jim
       Crow*, 3rd rev. ed. (Oxford University Press, 1974), p. 186.
318   [*CORE analysis of Civil Rights Act*]: CORE Legal Department, "The 1964
       Civil Rights Law—A Hard Look," reprinted in Louis, pp. 377–402 (ap-
       pendix 4), quoted at p. 378.
       [*"Expand the civil-rights struggle"*]: Malcolm X, "The Ballot or the Bullet,"
       in George Breitman, ed., *Malcolm X Speaks* (Grove Press, 1966), pp.
       23–44, quoted at p. 34.
       [*"Only a valve, a vent"*]: Malcolm X, "Prospects for Freedom in 1965,"
       in *ibid.*, pp. 147–56, quoted at p. 151.

IS THIS AMERICA?

SNCC voter registration organizing: Carson, chs. 4, 6–9; Fannie Lou Hamer, *To
Praise Our Bridges: An Autobiography* (Jackson, Miss.: KIPCO, 1967); Kling; Bob

Moses, "Mississippi: 1961–1962," *Liberation* (January 1970), pp. 6–17; Zinn, chs. 4–12.

Mississippi Freedom Summer and MFDP: Sally Belfrage, *Freedom Summer* (Viking, 1968); Carson, chs. 8–9; Hamer; Len Holt, *The Summer That Didn't End* (Morrow, 1965); Kling; Leslie Burl McLemore, "The Mississippi Freedom Democratic Party: A Case Study of Grass-Roots Politics" (Ph.D. dissertation, University of Massachusetts, 1971); Zinn, ch. 12.

Selma movement and 1965 Voting Rights Act: Charles E. Fager, *Selma, 1965: The March That Changed the South* (Beacon Press, 1985); Garrow, *Bearing the Cross*, ch. 7; David J. Garrow, *Protest at Selma: Martin Luther King, Jr., and the Voting Rights Act of 1965* (Yale University Press, 1978).

PAGE

319   [*Black voter registration statistics*]: Garrow, *Protest at Selma*, pp. 11, 19.
        [*"You are a public official"*]: quoted in Branch, p. 480.
321   [*"Have you freedom-registered?"*]: Belfrage, p. 187.
        [*"Straight out of tarpaper shacks"*]: ibid., p. 201.
        [*"'Til my hands was as navy blue"*]: Raines, p. 254.
        [*"All of this is on account"*]: "The Life of Fannie Lou Hamer," Pacifica radio program (cassette recording from Pacifica Radio Archive, Los Angeles).
322   [*"Any honorable compromise"*]: quoted in Carson, p. 127.
        [*"We didn't come all this way"*]: quoted in Forman, p. 395.
323   [*"At times history and fate meet"*]: March 15, 1965, in Johnson, *Public Papers* (U.S. Government Printing Office, 1965–70), vol. 2, part 1, pp. 281–87, quoted at pp. 281, 284.
        [*Reactions of SCLC leaders to LBJ's address*]: interview with C. T. Vivian, in Henry Hampton and Steve Fayer, eds., *Voices of Freedom: An Oral History of the Civil Rights Movement from the 1950s through the 1980s* (Bantam, 1990), p. 236.
        [*"Mudcaked pilgrims"*]: Fager, p. 158.
        [*"How long?"*]: quoted in *ibid.*, p. 162.
324   [*"Climate of public opinion"*]: quoted in Garrow, *Protest at Selma*, p. 113.
        [*Reasons for limited electoral success*]: Fager, pp. 221–24.

Portions of the introduction and the first two sections of this chapter are drawn from Stewart Burns, *Social Movements of the 1960s: Searching for Democracy* (Twayne, 1990), ch. 1.

ECONOMIC JUSTICE

Black freedom movement and economic rights: Jervis Anderson, *A. Philip Randolph* (Harcourt, 1973); William H. Chafe, "The End of One Struggle, the Beginning of Another," in Eagles, pp. 127–48; Daniel S. Davis, *Mr. Black Labor: The Story of A. Philip Randolph, Father of the Civil Rights Movement* (E. P. Dutton, 1972); Fairclough, chs. 10–14; Garrow, *Bearing the Cross*, chs. 8–11; Charles V. Hamilton and Dona C. Hamilton, "Social Policies, Civil Rights, and Poverty," in Sheldon H. Danziger and Daniel H. Weinberg, eds., *Fighting Poverty: What Works and What Doesn't* (Harvard University Press, 1986), pp. 288–311; August Meier and Elliott Rudwick, *CORE: A Study in the Civil Rights Movement, 1942–1968* (Oxford University Press, 1973), chs. 7–12; Bayard Rustin, *Down the Line: The Collected Writings of*

Bayard Rustin (Quadrangle, 1971); Rustin, *Strategies for Freedom: The Changing Patterns of Black Protest* (Columbia University Press, 1976); Nancy J. Weiss, "Whitney M. Young, Jr.: Committing the Power Structure to the Cause of Civil Rights," in John Hope Franklin and August Meier, eds., *Black Leaders of the Twentieth Century* (University of Illinois Press, 1982), pp. 331–58; Whitney M. Young, Jr., "Should There Be 'Compensation' for Negroes?," *New York Times Magazine* (October 6, 1963), pp. 43, 128–29, 131; Young, *To Be Equal* (McGraw-Hill, 1964).

"War on poverty": Carl M. Brauer, "Kennedy, Johnson, and the War on Poverty," *Journal of American History,* vol. 69, no. 1 (June 1982), pp. 98–119; Kenneth Clark and Jeannette Hopkins, *A Relevant War Against Poverty: A Study of Community Action Programs and Observable Social Change* (Harper Torchbooks, 1970); Richard A. Cloward and Frances Fox Piven, *The Politics of Turmoil: Essays on Poverty, Race, and the Urban Crisis* (Vintage, 1975); Herbert J. Gans, *More Equality* (Pantheon, 1973); Michael Harrington, *The Other America: Poverty in the United States* (Macmillan, 1962); Robert H. Haveman, ed., *A Decade of Federal Antipoverty Programs: Achievements, Failures, and Lessons* (Academic Press, 1977); Hugh Heclo, "The Political Foundations of Antipoverty Policy," in Danziger and Weinberg, pp. 319–21; Sar A. Levitan, *The Great Society's Poor Law: A New Approach to Poverty* (Johns Hopkins Press, 1969); Daniel P. Moynihan, *Maximum Feasible Misunderstanding: Community Action in the War on Poverty* (Free Press, 1969); James T. Patterson, *America's Struggle Against Poverty, 1900–1980* (Harvard University Press, 1981), esp. parts 3–4; James L. Sundquist, ed., *On Fighting Poverty: Perspectives from Experience* (Basic Books, 1969).

Welfare rights movement: Richard A. Cloward and Frances Fox Piven, "Birth of a Movement" and "A Strategy to End Poverty," in Cloward and Piven, *The Politics of Turmoil,* pp. 89–106, 127–40; Nick Kotz and Mary Lynn Kotz, *A Passion for Equality: George A. Wiley and the Movement* (Norton, 1977); Lawrence M. Mead, *Beyond Entitlement: The Social Obligations of Citizenship* (Free Press, 1986); Daniel P. Moynihan, *The Politics of a Guaranteed Income: The Nixon Administration and the Family Assistance Plan* (Random House, 1973); Piven and Cloward, *Poor People's Movements,* chs. 2, 5; Frances Fox Piven and Richard A. Cloward, *Regulating the Poor: The Functions of Public Welfare* (Pantheon, 1971), esp. ch. 10; Guida West, *The National Welfare Rights Movement: The Social Protest of Poor Women* (Praeger, 1981).

Critiques of the black movement and economic rights: Derrick Bell, *And We Are Not Saved: The Elusive Quest for Racial Justice* (Basic Books, 1987), esp. chs. 1–2, 5–7; Harold Cruse, *Plural But Equal: A Critical Study of Blacks and Minorities and America's Plural Society* (Morrow, 1987); William Julius Wilson, *The Truly Disadvantaged* (University of Chicago Press, 1987).

PAGE

326   [*"Discrimination gap"*]: Young, *To Be Equal,* p. 22.

327   [*"Domestic Marshall Plan"*]: *ibid.,* pp. 27–28.

           [*"Radical programs for full employment"*]: Rustin, "From Protest to Politics: The Future of the Civil Rights Movement," *Commentary,* vol. 39, no. 2 (February 1965), pp. 25–31, quoted at p. 28.

328   [*"They tried to open up doors"*]: Patterson, p. 136.

           [*"Assure income as a matter of right"*]: quoted in *ibid.,* p. 143.

           [*"Maximum feasible participation"*]: quoted in Moynihan, *Maximum Feasible Misunderstanding,* p. 89.

           [*"Involvement of the poor"*]: *ibid.,* p. 97.

           [*"Charade"*]: Clark and Hopkins, p. 248.

           [*"Have so far not resulted"*]: *ibid.,* p. 249.

329   [*"It looked like the city had been bombed"*]: quoted in National Advisory
        Commission on Civil Disorders, *Report* (E. P. Dutton, 1968), p. 92.
        [*"Our nation is moving"*]: *ibid.*, p. 107.
        [*"Unprecedented levels of funding"*]: *ibid.*, pp. 1–2.
        [*"Reconstruction of the entire society"*]: quoted in Oates, p. 426.
        [*"Socially-conscious democracy"*]: King, *Where Do We Go from Here: Chaos or
        Community?* (Beacon Press, 1968), p. 187.
330   [*"Waves of the nation's poor"*]: quoted in Garrow, *Bearing the Cross*,
        p. 582.
        [*Cloward and Piven 1965 working paper*]: Cloward and Piven, "A Strategy
        to End Poverty."
331   [*Rise in welfare clients, 1960s*]: Patterson, p. 178.
        [*"Accompanying the rise in expectations"*]: *ibid.*, p. 183.
        [*"We all need to adopt"*]: quoted in *ibid.*, p. 188.
        [*Wiley on frustrations and potentials*]: quoted in Kotz and Kotz, p. 198.
332   [*"We feed our children bread and beans"*]: *ibid.*, p. 190.
        [*"Social protest of women"*]: West, p. xiii.
        [*"Jobs or income now!"*]: quoted in Kotz and Kotz, p. 200.
        [*"Street strategy"*]: West, p. 375.
        [*"Mountains of paperwork"*]: John Kifner, "The Deepening Welfare Cri-
        sis," *New York Times*, August 1, 1968, p. 23.
        [*Supreme Court ruling on welfare clients' right to privacy*]: see *Wyman* v. *James*,
        400 U.S. 309 (1971).
333   [*"Religion was the language"*]: quoted in Kotz and Kotz, p. 253.
        [*"In virtually every area of life"*]: Bell, p. 45.
        [*"Guarantee the right to a decent life"*]: quoted in Piven and Cloward, *Poor
        People's Movements*, p. 349.

                         PLURAL BUT EQUAL

Nineteenth-century black nationalism: Jane H. Pease and William H. Pease, *They Who
Would Be Free: Blacks' Search for Freedom, 1830–1861* (Atheneum, 1974), ch. 12.

Black Power: Robert L. Allen, *Black Awakening in Capitalist America: An Analytic
History* (Doubleday, 1969); Floyd B. Barbour, ed., *The Black Power Revolt* (Porter
Sargent, 1968); Breitman; Stokely Carmichael and Charles V. Hamilton, *Black
Power: The Politics of Liberation in America* (Vintage, 1967); Carmichael, *Stokely
Speaks: Black Power Back to Pan-Africanism* (Vintage, 1971); Carson; Philip S. Foner,
ed., *The Black Panthers Speak* (Lippincott, 1970); Forman; Hampton and Fayer;
Gene Marine, *The Black Panthers* (New American Library, 1969); Cleveland Sel-
lers, *The River of No Return: The Autobiography of a Black Militant and the Life and Death
of SNCC* (Morrow, 1973).

PAGE
335   [*"Ever-present but usually latent"*]: Allen, p. 97.
        [*"Make up a cultural nation"*]: "The Quotable Karenga," in Barbour, pp.
        162–70, quoted at p. 165.
        [*"Domestic colonialism"*]: Allen, p. 2, and ch. 1 passim.
336   [*"One-way street"*]: Carmichael and Hamilton, p. 55.
        [*"Meaningful only to a small chosen class"*]: Carmichael, *Stokely Speaks*, p. 43.
        [*"The racial and cultural personality"*]: *ibid.*, p. 39.
337   [*"Our major political objective"*]: "Black Panther Party Platform and Pro-
        gram: What We Want/What We Believe," in Foner, pp. 2–4, quoted at
        pp. 3–4.

337   [*"To create our own terms"*]: Carmichael, *Stokely Speaks,* p. 32.
338   [*Cruse on doctrine of "plural but equal"*]: Cruse, pp. 249, 252.

11. RIGHTS TO LIBERATION:

WOMEN AT THE CUTTING EDGE

PAGE

339   [*Rhode on women leaving labor force*]: Rhode, *Justice and Gender: Sex Discrimination and the Law* (Harvard University Press, 1989), p. 32.
340   [*"Core of the problem"*]: Friedan, *The Feminine Mystique,* 20th anniversary edition (Norton, 1983), p. 77.
       [*"Problem that has no name"*]: *ibid.,* p. 15.

ARE EQUAL RIGHTS ENOUGH?

NOW, the "older branch," and women's rights: Stewart Burns, *Social Movements of the 1960s: Searching for Democracy* (Twayne, 1990), pp. 119–25; Maren Lockwood Carden, *The New Feminist Movement* (Russell Sage, 1974); Barbara Sinclair Deckard, *The Women's Movement: Political, Socioeconomic, and Psychological Issues,* 3rd ed. (Harper, 1983); Jo Freeman, *The Politics of Women's Liberation* (Longman, 1975); Betty Friedan, *"It Changed My Life": Writings on the Women's Movement* (Norton, 1985); Jane De Hart Mathews, "The New Feminism and the Dynamics of Social Change," in Mathews and Linda K. Kerber, eds., *Women's America: Refocusing the Past* (Oxford University Press, 1982), pp. 397–425; Mary Lou Thompson, ed., *Voices of the New Feminism* (Beacon Press, 1975).

Sex discrimination law and public policy reform: Barbara Allen Babcock et al., *Sex Discrimination and the Law: Causes and Remedies* (Little, Brown, 1975); Ellen Boneparth, ed., *Women, Power, and Policy* (Pergamon Press, 1982); Eve Cary and Kathleen Willert Peratis, *Woman and the Law* (National Textbook, 1977); Kenneth M. Davidson, Ruth Bader Ginsburg, and Herma Hill Kay, *Sex-Based Discrimination: Text, Cases, and Materials* (West Publishing, 1974); Cynthia Harrison, *On Account of Sex: The Politics of Women's Issues, 1945–1968* (University of California Press, 1988); Wendy Kaminer, *A Fearful Freedom: Women's Flight from Equality* (Addison-Wesley, 1990); Catharine A. MacKinnon, *Feminism Unmodified: Discourses on Life and Law* (Harvard University Press, 1987), esp. Introduction, and chs. 1–2; Mary Ann Mason, *The Equality Trap* (Simon and Schuster, 1988); Martha Minow, *Making All the Difference: Inclusion, Exclusion, and American Law* (Cornell University Press, 1990); Susan Cary Nicholas, Alice M. Price, and Rachel Rubin, *Rights and Wrongs: Women's Struggle for Legal Equality* (Feminist Press, 1979); Debbie Ratterman, "Liberating Feminist Jurisprudence: Remaking the Tools, Re-Visioning Rights," *off our backs,* vol. 20, no. 9 (October 1990), pp. 12–13; Donald Allen Robinson, "Two Movements in Pursuit of Equal Employment Opportunity," *Signs,* vol. 4 (Spring 1979), pp. 413–33; Susan Deller Ross and Ann Barcher, *The Rights of Women: The Basic ACLU Guide to a Woman's Rights* (Bantam, 1983).

Radical feminism: Burns, pp. 116–19, 125–35; Alice Echols, *Daring to Be Bad: Radical Feminism in America, 1967–1975* (University of Minnesota Press, 1989); Zillah R. Eisenstein, *Feminism and Sexual Equality: Crisis in Liberal America* (Monthly Review Press, 1984); Eisenstein, *The Radical Future of Liberal Feminism* (Longman, 1981); Shulamith Firestone, *The Dialectic of Sex: The Case for Feminist Revolution* (Bantam, 1971); Freeman; Leah Fritz, *Dreamers & Dealers: An Intimate Appraisal of the Women's*

Movement (Beacon Press, 1980); Carol Hanisch, "The Liberal Takeover of Women's Liberation," in Redstockings, *Feminist Revolution* (Random House, 1978), pp. 163–67; Anne Koedt, Ellen Levine, and Anita Rapone, eds., *Radical Feminism* (Quadrangle/New York Times Book Co., 1973); Barbara Leon, "Separate to Integrate," in Redstockings, *Feminist Revolution*, pp. 152–57; Kate Millett, *Sexual Politics* (Doubleday, 1970); Robin Morgan, ed., *Sisterhood Is Powerful* (Vintage, 1970); Gayle Graham Yates, *What Women Want: The Ideas of the Movement* (Harvard University Press, 1975).

Equal Rights Amendment: Mary Frances Berry, *Why ERA Failed* (Indiana University Press, 1986); Joan Hoff-Wilson, ed., *Rights of Passage: The Past and Future of the ERA* (Indiana University Press, 1986); Jane J. Mansbridge, *Why We Lost the ERA* (University of Chicago Press, 1986); Rhode, ch. 4; Lisa Cronin Wohl, "White Gloves and Combat Boots: The Fight for ERA," *Civil Liberties Review*, vol. 1, no. 4 (Fall 1974), pp. 77–86.

PAGE

341   [*"Seething underground of women"*]: Friedan, *Feminine Mystique,* p. 383.
       [*"Ladies Day in the House"*]: quoted in Freeman, p. 54.
       [*"Conceived out of wedlock"*]: quoted in Robinson, p. 423.

342   [*"Unless women march on Washington"*]: quoted in Friedan, *"It Changed My Life,"* p. 77.
       [*"If Esther Peterson"*]: *ibid.,* p. 83.
       [*NOW statement of purpose*]: "NOW Statement of Purpose," in *ibid.,* pp. 87–91, quoted at pp. 87, 90.

343   [*"Rights, Not Roses"*]: quoted in *ibid.,* p. 108.
       [*"Largest oppressor of women workers"*]: quoted in Freeman, p. 189.
       [*"Magna carta for female workers"*]: Robinson, pp. 427, 429.
       [*"The right of every woman"*]: quoted in Friedan, *"It Changed My Life,"* p. 102.

344   [*"Come join us, sisters"*]: *New York Times,* August 27, 1970, pp. 1, 30, quoted at p. 30.
       [*"A federal policy of equal opportunity"*]: Freeman, p. 171.
       [*"While women's roles as workers"*]: Boneparth, p. 121.

345   [*"Women are measured"*]: MacKinnon, p. 34.
       [*"The difference difference makes"*]: Rhode, p. 313.

347   [*"For most American women"*]: Evans, *Personal Politics: The Roots of Women's Liberation in the Civil Rights Movement and the New Left* (Vintage, 1980), p. 218.
       [*"Superficial symptoms of sexism"*]: Firestone, p. 32.
       [*"Liberal equation"*]: Eisenstein, *Radical Future of Liberal Feminism,* p. 181.
       [*Evans on Friedan's critique of housewifery*]: Evans, p. 19.

348   [*"Full participation in the mainstream"*]: "NOW Statement of Purpose," p. 87.
       [*"Primary class system"*]: The Feminists, quoted in Yates, p. 93.
       [*"Male supremacy is the oldest"*]: "Redstockings Manifesto," in Morgan, pp. 533–36, quoted at p. 534.
       [*"A great deal more in common"*]: "Editorial: Notes from the Third Year," December 1971, reprinted in Koedt, Levine, and Rapone, pp. 300–1, quoted at p. 301.
       [*"Equality of rights"*]: quoted in Mansbridge, p. 1.

349   [*"Wipe out a wife's right to support"*]: quoted in Wohl, p. 81.
       [*"A stand-in for more fundamental concerns"*]: Rhode, pp. 69–70.
       [*Berry on prerequisite for amending Constitution*]: Berry, p. 3.

350   [*Mansbridge critique of ERA's lack of substance*]: Mansbridge, chs. 3–4.
       [*More "a catalyst than a source of change"*]: Rhode, p. 79.

TO OWN THE FLESH WE STAND IN

Abortion and reproductive rights: Ninia Baehr, *Abortion Without Apology: A Radical History for the 1990s* (South End Press, 1990); Lucinda Cisler, "Abortion Law Repeal (sort of): A Warning to Women," in Koedt, Levine, and Rapone, pp. 151–64; Cisler, "Unfinished Business: Birth Control and Women's Liberation," in Morgan, pp. 245–89; Sherrill Cohen and Nadine Taub, eds., *Reproductive Laws for the 1990s* (Humana Press, 1989); Susan E. Davis, *Women under Attack: Victories, Backlash and the Fight for Reproductive Freedom* (South End Press, 1988); Ronald Dworkin, "The Great Abortion Case," *New York Review of Books,* vol. 36, no. 11 (June 29, 1989), pp. 49–53; Zillah R. Eisenstein, *The Female Body and the Law* (University of California Press, 1988); Laura Flanders, "Abortion: The Usable Past," *Nation,* vol. 249, no. 5 (August 7–14, 1989), pp. 175–77; Faye D. Ginsburg, *Contested Lives: The Abortion Debate in an American Community* (University of California Press, 1989), esp. chs. 1–2; Linda Gordon, *Woman's Body, Woman's Right: A Social History of Birth Control in America* (Penguin, 1977), esp. ch. 14; Beverly Wildung Harrison, *Our Right to Choose: Toward a New Ethic of Abortion* (Beacon Press, 1983); Kristin Luker, *Abortion and the Politics of Motherhood* (University of California Press, 1984); James C. Mohr, *Abortion in America: The Origins and Evolution of National Policy, 1800–1900* (Oxford University Press, 1978); Rosalind Pollack Petchesky, *Abortion and Woman's Choice: The State, Sexuality, and Reproductive Freedom* (Longman, 1984); Petchesky, "Giving Women a Real Choice: Abortion Politics in the '90s," *Nation,* vol. 250, no. 21 (May 28, 1990), pp. 732–35; Katha Pollitt, "Checkbook Maternity: When Is a Mother Not a Mother?," *Nation,* vol. 251, no. 23 (December 31, 1990), pp. 825, 840–46; Hyman Rodman, Betty Sarvis, and Joy Walker Bonar, *The Abortion Question* (Columbia University Press, 1987); Becky Sarah, " 'Surrogate Motherhood': A Class Issue," *Somerville Community News* (Somerville, Massachusetts, February 1991), p. 3; Diane Schulder and Florynce Kennedy, *Abortion Rap* (McGraw-Hill, 1971); Jennifer Terry, "The Body Invaded: Medical Surveillance of Women as Reproducers," *Socialist Review,* vol. 19, no. 3 (July–September 1989), pp. 13–43.

Right-to-life movement: Ginsburg, ch. 3; Harrison, *Our Right to Choose,* ch. 7; Luker, chs. 6–9; John T. Noonan, Jr., *A Private Choice: Abortion in America in the Seventies* (Free Press, 1979); Connie Paige, *The Right to Lifers* (Summit Books, 1983); Petchesky, *Abortion and Woman's Choice,* ch. 7.

PAGE
351   [*Mohr and Luker on physicians' antiabortion crusade*]: Mohr, ch. 6; Luker, ch. 2.
352   [*"When we talk about women's rights"*]: quoted in Luker, p. 97.
       [*Ginsburg on redefining abortion as a personal right*]: Ginsburg, p. 40.
       [*Redstockings protest at legislative hearing*]: *New York Times,* February 14, 1969, p. 42.
353   [*Redstockings abortion "speak-out"*]: *Village Voice,* vol. 14, no. 24 (March 27, 1969), pp. 1, 29; Echols, pp. 140–42.
       [*"Confront the spurious personal-political distinction"*]: quoted in Echols, p. 142.
       [*Echols on radical view of abortion rights*]: ibid., p. 285.
       [*"Without the full capacity"*]: Cisler, "Unfinished Business," p. 246.

353   [Roe]: *Roe* v. *Wade*, 410 U.S. 113 (1973).
[*"Arbitrary"*]: Bob Woodward, "The Abortion Papers," Washington *Post*, January 22, 1989, pp. D1–2.

354   [Griswold *as precedent*]: 381 U.S. 479 (1965); Dworkin, "Great Abortion Case," p. 51.
[*"Concept of personal liberty"*]: *Roe*, 153.
[*"Organizational infrastructure"*]: Paige, p. 51.

355   [*"626-month-old fetus"*]: quoted in *ibid.*, p. 111.
[*Supreme Court decision upholding Hyde Amendment*]: *Harris* v. *McRae*, 448 U.S. 297 (1980).

356   [*Harrison critique of right-to-life perspective*]: Harrison, *Our Right to Choose*, pp. 208–30, quoted at pp. 227–28.

357   [*"Place and meaning of motherhood"*]: Luker, pp. 193, 200.
[*Supreme Court decision striking down Akron law*]: *Akron* v. *Akron Center for Reproductive Health, Inc.*, 462 U.S. 416 (1983).
[*"Who hope to overturn"*]: Ginsburg, p. 54.
[*Supreme Court affirmation of "Operation Rescue" ban*]: *Randall Terry* v. *New York State NOW*, 89-1408 (May 1990).

358   [*Black woman at Atlanta abortion clinic*]: quoted in Petchesky, "Giving Women a Real Choice," p. 735.
[Webster]: 492 U.S. 490 (1989).
[*"Slowly, in the post-Webster world"*]: Goodman, "Abortion Politics," San Francisco *Chronicle*, July 7, 1989.

359   [*O'Connor on fetal viability*]: *Akron*, 452–59, esp. 458.
[*"Loss of rights for women"*]: letter to Stewart Burns, December 3, 1990.
[*"Prenatal surveillance technologies"*]: Terry, p. 34.
[*"Whole new jurisprudence"*]: quoted in Harrison, *Our Right to Choose*, p. 236.

360   [*"Has come to mean"*]: *ibid.*, p. 50.
[*Harrison and Petchesky on transforming conditions of reproduction*]: *ibid.*, pp. 50–56, 244–56; Petchesky, *Abortion and Woman's Choice*, pp. 1–18; Petchesky, "Giving Women a Real Choice," p. 734, quoted at *ibid.*

THE EXPANDING UNIVERSE OF RIGHTS

Chavez and the United Farm Workers: Jacques E. Levy, *Cesar Chavez: Autobiography of La Causa* (Norton, 1975); Peter Matthiessen, *Sal Si Puedes: Cesar Chavez and the New American Revolution* (Delta, 1969).

Chicano movement: Carlos Munoz, Jr., *Youth, Identity, Power: The Chicano Movement* (Verso, 1989).

American Indians: Charles F. Wilkinson, *American Indians, Time, and the Law: Native Societies in a Modern Constitutional Democracy* (Yale University Press, 1987); Howard Zinn, *A People's History of the United States* (Harper Colophon, 1980), pp. 513–26.

Gay and lesbian rights: Sidney Abbott and Barbara Love, *Sappho Was a Right-on Woman: A Liberated View of Lesbianism* (Stein & Day, 1973); Barry D Adam, *The Rise of a Gay and Lesbian Movement* (Twayne, 1987); Charlotte Bunch, *Passionate Politics: Feminist Theory in Action* (St. Martin's Press, 1987); Arthur S. Leonard, "Gay/ Lesbian Rights: Report from the Legal Front," *Nation*, vol. 251, no. 1 (July 2, 1990), pp. 12–15; Nancy Myron and Charlotte Bunch, eds., *Lesbianism and the Women's Movement* (Diana Press, 1975); Randy Shilts, *The Mayor of Castro Street: The Life & Times of Harvey Milk* (St. Martin's Press, 1982); Thomas B. Stoddard et al., *The Rights of Gay People,* rev. ed. (Bantam, 1983).

Affirmative action: Derrick Bell, *And We Are Not Saved: The Elusive Quest for Racial Justice* (Basic Books, 1987), esp. chs. 5–7; Marshall Cohen, Thomas Nagel, and Thomas Scanlon, eds., *Equality and Preferential Treatment* (Princeton University Press, 1977); Ronald Dworkin, *A Matter of Principle* (Harvard University Press, 1985), chs. 14–16; Nathan Glazer, *Affirmative Discrimination: Ethnic Inequality and Public Policy* (Basic Books, 1975); Hugh Davis Graham, *The Civil Rights Era: Origins and Development of National Policy, 1960–1972* (Oxford University Press, 1990), chs. 4, 7–13, 17; Kathanne W. Greene, *Affirmative Action and Principles of Justice* (Greenwood Press, 1989); Charles Murray, *Losing Ground: American Social Policy, 1950–1980* (Basic Books, 1984); Shelby Steele, "A Negative Vote on Affirmative Action," *New York Times Magazine* (May 13, 1990), pp. 46–49, 73–75; Phyllis A. Wallace, "A Decade of Policy Developments in Equal Opportunities in Employment and Housing," in Robert H. Haveman, ed., *A Decade of Federal Antipoverty Programs: Achievements, Failures, and Lessons* (Academic Press, 1977), pp. 329–67; J. Harvie Wilkinson III, *From* Brown *to* Bakke: *The Supreme Court and School Integration, 1954–1978* (Oxford University Press, 1979), chs. 10–11.

PAGE

361   [*"Ready from within"*]: Clark, *Ready from Within: Septima Clark and the Civil Rights Movement* (Wild Trees Press, 1986), p. ix.

362   [*"Created a lot of first amendment law"*]: letters to authors, July 9, 1990, and August 2, 1990.
        [*"A mighty pulverizing engine"*]: quoted in Wilkinson, *American Indians,* p. 19.
        [*Indians' legal victories from late 1950s*]: ibid., ch. 1.

363   [*1973 Wounded Knee occupation*]: Zinn, pp. 523–25.
        [*"Homophile" organizations*]: Adam, pp. 62–64.
        [*"Primary cornerstone of male supremacy"*]: Myron and Bunch, p. 10.
        [*"Talked optimistically about new ideas"*]: Shilts, p. 42.

364   [Bowers]: 478 U.S. 186 (1986).
        [*"Our Holocaust"*]: quoted in San Francisco *Chronicle,* March 13, 1989, p. A6.

366   [Griggs]: 401 U.S. 424 (1971), quoted at 431, 432.
        [*Glazer and Murray on redefinition of equal opportunity*]: Glazer, pp. 48–49; Murray, pp. 221–23.
        [Bakke]: *Regents of the University of California v. Bakke,* 438 U.S. 265 (1978), Marshall in dissent on Court's "full circle" at 402.
        [*"It is this policy watershed"*]: Graham, p. 456.

367   [*"Supremacy of the procedural principle"*]: quoted in Wilkinson, *From* Brown *to* Bakke, p. 290.
        [*"Morality of process"*]: ibid.
        [*"Congress's overarching substantive purpose"*]: Graham, p. 461.
        [*"Distinctly American ethic"*]: Mason, p. 40.
        [*Wilson on the black underclass*]: Wilson, *The Truly Disadvantaged* (University of Chicago Press, 1987).

368   [*Schaar on "equal opportunity"*]: Schaar, "Equality of Opportunity, and Beyond," in Schaar, *Legitimacy in the Modern State* (Transaction Books, 1981), pp. 193–209, quoted at p. 200; see also Schaar, "Some Ways of Thinking about Equality," *Journal of Politics,* vol. 26, no. 4 (November 1964), pp. 867–95.
        [*Bell on affirmative action*]: Bell, p. 154.

369   [*"New definitions of work and leisure"*]: Rustin, "From Protest to Politics: The Future of the Civil Rights Movement," *Commentary,* vol. 39, no. 2

(February 1965), reprinted in Rustin, *Down the Line: The Collected Writings of Bayard Rustin* (Quadrangle, 1971), p. 118.

369 [*"Non-reformist" reform*]: André Gorz, *Strategy for Labor: A Radical Proposal* (Beacon Press, 1967), pp. 5, 7–8.

12. THE CROSSFIRE OF RIGHTS

FIRST AMENDMENT: THE FIXED STAR?

Religious freedom and the First Amendment: Henry J. Abraham, *Freedom and the Court: Civil Rights and Liberties in the United States,* 5th ed. (Oxford University Press, 1988), ch. 6; Walter Berns, *The First Amendment and the Future of American Democracy* (Basic Books, 1970), esp. chs. 1–2; James MacGregor Burns, J. W. Peltason, and Thomas E. Cronin, *Government by the People,* 14th ed. (Prentice-Hall, 1990), pp. 74–77; Jaye B. Hensel, ed., *Church, State, and Politics* (Roscoe Pound–American Trial Lawyers Foundation, 1981); Nat Hentoff, *The First Freedom: The Tumultuous History of Free Speech in America* (Delacorte Press, 1980), part 5; Philip B. Kurland, *Religion and the Law: Of Church and State and the Supreme Court* (Aldine, 1962); Leonard W. Levy, *The Establishment Clause: Religion and the First Amendment* (Macmillan, 1986); papers prepared for the National Symposium on the First Amendment Religious Liberty Clauses, Charlottesville, Virginia, April 11–13, 1988 (Williamsburg Charter Foundation, 1988); Leo Pfeffer, *God, Caesar, and the Constitution: The Court as Referee of Church-State Confrontation* (Beacon Press, 1975); Pfeffer, *Religion, State and the Burger Court* (Prometheus Books, 1984); David A. J. Richards, *Toleration and the Constitution* (Oxford University Press, 1986), part 2; William George Toupey, *Judicial Doctrines of Religious Rights in America* (University of North Carolina Press, 1948); Samuel Walker, *In Defense of American Liberties: A History of the ACLU* (Oxford University Press, 1990), pp. 72–77, 81, 107–10, 219–27, 342–46; *Williamsburg Charter Survey on Religion and Public Life* (Williamsburg Charter Foundation, 1988).

Free speech and the courts in the twentieth century: Abraham, esp. ch. 5; William Bailey, "The Supreme Court and Communications Theory: Contrasting Models of Speech Efficacy," in Thomas L. Tedford, John J. Makay, and David L. Jamison, eds., *Perspectives on Freedom of Speech* (Southern Illinois University Press, 1987), pp. 90–106; Berns, ch. 4; Burns, Peltason, and Cronin, pp. 78–82, 88–90; Francis Canavan, *Freedom of Expression: Purpose as Limit* (Claremont Academic Press, 1984), esp. chs. 1, 7; Zechariah Chafee, Jr., *Free Speech in the United States* (Harvard University Press, 1941); Jeremy Cohen, *Congress Shall Make No Law: Oliver Wendell Holmes, the First Amendment, and Judicial Decision Making* (Iowa State University Press, 1989); Everette E. Dennis, Donald M. Gilmoor, and David L. Grey, eds., *Justice Hugo Black and the First Amendment* (Iowa State University Press, 1978); Norman Dorsen, "The Need for a New Enlightenment: Lessons in Liberty from the Eighteenth Century," in James Brewer Stewart, ed., *The Constitution, the Law, and Freedom of Expression, 1787–1987* (Southern Illinois University Press, 1987), pp. 22–41; William I. Gorden and Richard Goodman, "A Rhetoric of Ritual and Desecration," in Tedford, Makay, and Jamison, pp. 154–69; Kent Greenawalt, *Speech, Crime, and the Uses of Language* (Oxford University Press, 1989), passim; Hentoff, part 5; Harry Kalven, Jr., *A Worthy Tradition: Freedom of Speech in America,* Jamie Kalven, ed. (Harper, 1988), esp. chs. 9–16 passim; Herbert Mitgang, *Dangerous Dossiers: Exposing the Secret War Against America's Greatest Authors* (Donald I. Fine, 1988); Paul L. Murphy, *The Meaning of Freedom of Speech: First Amendment Freedoms from Wilson to FDR* (Greenwood Publishing, 1972), ch. 13, and passim;

Richards, part 3 passim; Martin Shapiro, *Freedom of Speech: The Supreme Court and Judicial Review* (Prentice-Hall, 1966); Walker; Tinsley E. Yarbrough, *Mr. Justice Black and His Critics* (Duke University Press, 1988), esp. chs. 4–5.

Censorship: Paul S. Boyer, *Purity in Print: The Vice-Society Movement and Book Censorship in America* (Scribner, 1968); Heywood Broun and Margaret Leech, *Anthony Comstock: Roundsman of the Lord* (Albert & Charles Boni, 1927); Burns, Peltason, and Cronin, pp. 90–92; Harry M. Clor, ed., *Censorship and Freedom of Expression: Essays on Obscenity and the Law* (Rand McNally, 1971); Morris L. Ernst and Alan U. Schwartz, *Censorship: The Search for the Obscene* (Macmillan, 1964); Robert W. Haney, *Comstockery in America: Patterns of Censorship and Control* (Beacon Press, 1960); Richard H. Kuh, *Foolish Figleaves?: Pornography in—and out of—Court* (Macmillan, 1967); Grant S. McClellan, ed., *Censorship in the United States* (H. W. Wilson, 1967), passim; Jeff Rosen, " 'Miller' Time," *New Republic,* vol. 203, no. 14 (October 1, 1990), pp. 17–19; Bruce Shapiro, "From Comstockery to Helmsmanship," *Nation,* vol. 251, no. 10 (October 1, 1990), pp. 335–38.

PAGE

375 [*"Very real threat"*]: *Wisconsin* v. *Yoder,* 406 U.S. 205 (1972), quoted at 218.
[*"Mere opinion"*]: *Reynolds* v. *U.S.,* 98 U.S. 145 (1878), quoted at 164, 167.
[*"Admission to applicants"*]: *Bob Jones University* v. *U.S.,* 461 U.S. 574 (1983), quoted at 581, 604.
[*"Binding tie"*]: *Minersville School District* v. *Gobitis,* 310 U.S. 586 (1940), Frankfurter quoted at 596, 599, 598, 600 respectively, Stone at 604.

376 [*"Any fixed star"*]: *West Virginia State Board of Education* v. *Barnette,* 319 U.S. 624 (1943), Jackson quoted at 642, Frankfurter at 646, 647, 656.
[*"Wall of separation"*]: see *Reynolds,* Jefferson quoted at 164; see also *Everson* v. *Board of Education,* 330 U.S. 1 (1947), esp. 15–16.

377 [*"Secular legislative purpose"*]: *Lemon* v. *Kurtzman,* 403 U.S. 602 (1971), esp. 612–13, quoted at 612, 613.
[*"Require complete separation"*]: *Lynch* v. *Donnelly,* 465 U.S. 668 (1984), quoted at 673.
[*"We have done better"*]: Burns, Peltason, and Cronin, p. 78.

378 [*Poll on free speech*]: ibid.
[*"Important case involving"*]: Fred M. Vinson, writing for the Court, *Dennis* v. *U.S.,* 341 U.S. 494 (1951), quoted at 503.
[*"Proletarian revolution"*]: text of Gitlow's "Left Wing Manifesto" in *Gitlow* v. *New York,* 268 U.S. 652 (1925) at 655 fn.
[*"Fundamental personal rights"*]: *ibid.,* 666.

379 [*"Sharp sword"*]: Chafee, p. 325.
[*"Were not cowards"*]: *Whitney* v. *California,* 274 U.S. 357 (1927), quoted at 377.
[*Fiske*]: *Fiske* v. *Kansas,* 274 U.S. 380 (1927).
[*Chafee on* Fiske]: Chafee, p. 352.
[*"Truth, popularity"*]: *N.A.A.C.P.* v. *Button,* 371 U.S. 415 (1963), quoted at 445.
[*"No such thing"*]: *Gertz* v. *Welch,* 418 U.S. 323 (1974), quoted at 339.

380 [*"Liberal and comprehensive construction"*]: quoted in Walker, p. 79.
[*"Clear and present danger"*]: *Schenck* v. *U.S.,* 249 U.S. 47 (1919), quoted at 52.
[*"No danger flowing"*]: *Whitney,* 377, 378, 377 respectively.

381 [*"There are governmental interests"*]: *Hynes* v. *Mayor of Oradell,* 425 U.S. 610 (1976), quoted at 628.

381   [*"Delicate and vulnerable"*]: *N.A.A.C.P.* v. *Button,* 433.
        [*"Either forbids or requires"*]: *Lanzetta* v. *New Jersey,* 306 U.S. 451 (1939),
        quoted at 453.
        [*"At the heart"*]: *First Bank of Boston* v. *Bellotti,* 435 U.S. 765 (1978), quoted
        at 776.
        [*"Reduced constitutional value"*]: *Dun & Bradstreet, Inc.* v. *Greenmoss Builders,*
        472 U.S. 749 (1985), quoted at 761.
382   [*"What was said?"*]: Burns, Peltason, and Cronin, p. 82.
        [*"We would not have"*]: *Republic,* in Plato, *Five Great Dialogues,* B. Jowett,
        trans., and Louise Ropes Loomis, ed. (Walter J. Black, 1942), quoted at
        pp. 288, 289.
        [*"On the Sabbath"*]: quoted in Ernst and Schwartz, p. 5.
        [*"Composing, writing"*]: quoted in Donna A. Demac, *Liberty Denied: The
        Current Rise of Censorship in America* (PEN American Center, 1988), p. 39.
383   [*Comstock's haul in first year as special agent*]: Broun and Leech, p. 153.
        [*State antiobscenity laws, by 1900*]: Demac, *Liberty Denied,* pp. 39–40.
        [*Leaves of Grass and Comstockery*]: Francis Winwar, *An American Giant:
        Walt Whitman and His Times* (Harper, 1941), pp. 304–6.
        [*Mencken and* The *"Genius"*]: see W. A. Swanberg, *Dreiser* (Scribner,
        1965), pp. 203–17, 259–63 passim.
384   [*"I question"*]: quoted in Haney, p. 24.
        [Fanny Hill]: *Memoirs* v. *Massachusetts,* 383 U.S. 413 (1966).
        [Roth *and* Alberts]: *Roth* v. *U.S., Alberts* v. *California,* 354 U.S. 476 (1957).
        [Miller]: 413 U.S. 15 (1973).
385   [*"To conclude that juries"*]: *Jenkins* v. *Georgia,* 418 U.S. 153 (1974), quoted
        at 160, 161.

THE PEOPLE'S RIGHT TO KNOW

Freedom of the press and the people's right to know: Herbert Agar, "Rights Are Respon-
sibilities," in Harold L. Ickes, ed., *Freedom of the Press Today* (Vanguard Press,
1941), pp. 19–25; Ben H. Bagdikian, *The Effete Conspiracy and Other Crimes by the
Press* (Harper, 1972), esp. ch. 2; Burns, Peltason, and Cronin, pp. 86–88; James
W. Carey, "The Press and the Public Discourse," *The Center Magazine,* vol. 20, no.
2 (March–April 1987), pp. 4–16; Commission on Freedom of the Press, *A Free and
Responsible Press* (University of Chicago Press, 1947); Harold L. Cross, *The People's
Right to Know: Legal Access to Public Records and Proceedings* (Columbia University
Press, 1953); Kenneth S. Devol, ed., *Mass Media and the Supreme Court: The Legacy
of the Warren Years* (Hastings House, 1971); Franklyn S. Haiman, *Speech and Law
in a Free Society* (University of Chicago Press, 1981), esp. ch. 14; Evan Hendricks,
ed., *Former Secrets: Government Records Made Public through the Freedom of Information
Act* (Campaign for Political Rights, 1982); Hentoff, part 6; Ralph Ingersoll, "A
Free Press—For What?," in Ickes, pp. 137–42; Gerald W. Johnson, *Peril and
Promise: An Inquiry into Freedom of the Press* (Harper, 1958); Garth S. Jowett, "The
Selling of the Pentagon: Television Confronts the First Amendment," in John E.
O'Connor, ed., *American History, American Television: Interpreting the Video Past* (Fred-
erick Ungar, 1983), pp. 256–78; M. Ethan Katsh, *The Electronic Media and the
Transformation of Law* (Oxford University Press, 1989); Hiller Krieghbaum, *Pres-
sures on the Press* (Thomas Y. Crowell, 1972); J. Fred MacDonald, *Television and the
Red Menace: The Video Road to Vietnam* (Praeger, 1985); John C. Merrill, *The Dialectic
in Journalism: Toward a Responsible Use of Press Freedom* (Louisiana State University
Press, 1989); Kathryn C. Montgomery, *Target: Prime Time: Advocacy Groups and the
Struggle over Entertainment Television* (Oxford University Press, 1989); Thomas R.

Nilsen, "Free Speech, Persuasion, and the Democratic Process," in Tedford, Makay, and Jamison, pp. 229–40; Ithiel de Sola Pool, *Technologies of Freedom* (Belknap Press of Harvard University Press, 1983); Lucas A. Powe, Jr., *American Broadcasting and the First Amendment* (University of California Press, 1987); Powe, *The Fourth Estate and the Constitution* (University of California Press, 1991); Austin Ranney, *Channels of Power: The Impact of Television on American Politics* (Basic Books, 1983); Norman L. Rosenberg, *Protecting the Best Men: An Interpretive History of the Law of Libel* (University of North Carolina Press, 1986), esp. ch. 10; Bernard Rubin, *Media, Politics, and Democracy* (Oxford University Press, 1977); Harrison Salisbury, *Without Fear or Favor:* The New York Times *and Its Times* (Times Books, 1980), pp. 137–64 passim; Benno C. Schmidt, Jr., *Freedom of the Press vs. Public Access* (Praeger, 1976); Joseph Tussman, *Government and the Mind* (Oxford University Press, 1977); Peter Wyden, *Bay of Pigs* (Jonathan Cape, 1979), esp. pp. 45–47, 142–46, 152–55.

Hollywood censorship and self-censorship: Vincent Canby, "A New Movie Code," in McClellan, pp. 158–61; Ira H. Carmen, *Movies, Censorship, and the Law* (University of Michigan Press, 1966); Ernst and Schwartz, esp. ch. 22; Haney, ch. 9; Leonard J. Leff and Jerold L. Simmons, *The Dame in the Kimono: Hollywood, Censorship, and the Production Code from the 1920s to the 1960s* (Grove Weidenfeld, 1990); Olga J. Martin, *Hollywood's Movie Commandments: A Handbook for Motion Picture Writers and Reviewers* (H. W. Wilson, 1937; reprinted by Arno Press, 1970); Richard S. Randall, *Censorship of the Movies: The Social and Political Control of a Mass Medium* (University of Wisconsin Press, 1968).

PAGE

386   ["*Notion that human beings*"]: Koffler, "The New Seditious Libel," in Richard O. Curry, ed., *Freedom at Risk: Secrecy, Censorship, and Repression in the 1980s* (Temple University Press, 1988), pp. 140–61, quoted at p. 161; Meiklejohn quoted at *ibid.*
    ["*Has always meant*"]: Merrill, p. 34.

387   ["*Whose side are you on?*"]: quoted in Krieghbaum, p. 86.
    ["*Castro doesn't need agents*"]: quoted in Wyden, p. 155.
    ["*Maybe if you had printed*"]: *ibid.,* p. 155 fn.

388   ["*Historic turning point*"]: quoted in Krieghbaum, p. 55.
    ["*If government is to be*"]: *ibid.*
    ["*Bureaucratic ingenuity*"]: Ralph Nader, quoted in *ibid.*
    ["*Block citizen understanding*"]: *ibid.,* p. 56.
    ["*No longer open to doubt*"]: *Near* v. *Minnesota,* 283 U.S. 697 (1931), quoted at 707, 713.

389   ["*Irreparable harm*"]: quoted in Krieghbaum, p. 33.
    ["*Heavy presumption*"]: *New York Times* v. *U.S.,* 403 U.S. 713 (1971), quoted at 714, 729, 728 respectively.
    [" '*Actual malice*' "]: *New York Times* v. *Sullivan,* 376 U.S. 254 (1964), quoted at 280, 279, 270 respectively.

390   ["*Subject of public or general interest*"]: *Rosenbloom* v. *Metromedia,* 403 U.S. 29 (1971), quoted at 43, 51.
    ["*Of all the forms of communication*"]: *F.C.C.* v. *Pacifica Foundation,* 438 U.S. 726 (1978), quoted at 748.
    ["*Ample play*"]: quoted in Krieghbaum, p. 66.
    ["*Evident that broadcast licensees*"]: *ibid.,* pp. 66–67.

391   ["*People as a whole retain*"]: *Red Lion* v. *F.C.C.,* 395 U.S. 367 (1969), quoted at 390.
    ["*Even in 1969*"]: Powe, *Broadcasting and the First Amendment,* p. 39.

392   [*Warren on political censorship of films*]: Times Film Corporation v. Chicago, 365
        U.S. 43 (1961), esp. 69–73.
        [*1915 and 1948 Court rulings on film and the First Amendment*]: Mutual Film
        Corporation v. Ohio Industrial Commission, 236 U.S. 230 (1915), esp. 241–
        45; *U.S.* v. Paramount Pictures, 334 U.S. 131 (1948), esp. 166.
393   [*1929 film censorship*]: see Leff and Simmons, p. 8.
        [*"Though regarding motion pictures"*]: reprinted in *ibid.*, pp. 283–92, quoted
        at pp. 284–86.
394   [*"Don't give a damn"*]: quoted in *ibid.*, p. 99.
        [*"Action of Scarlett belching"*]: *ibid.*, p. 91.
        [*"Put brassieres on"*]: Hal Wallis, quoted in *ibid.*, p. 38.
        [*"I believe in censorship"*]: *ibid.*, p. 54.
        [*"Almost impossible to face"*]: *ibid.*, p. 81.
395   [*Kubrick on Lolita*]: *ibid.*, p. 223.
        [*"Encourage artistic expression"*]: quoted in *ibid.*, p. 271.
        [*"Monumental self-righteousness"*]: Canby, "Will They Censor the Teeny-
        bopper?," *New York Times*, March 22, 1970, sect. 2, pp. 1, 22, quoted at
        p. 22.
        [*"Psychologists, psychiatrists"*]: quoted in Leff and Simmons, p. 277.

TOWARD A CULTURAL BILL OF RIGHTS?

Rights of artists and public access to the arts: Edward Arian, *The Unfulfilled Promise: Public
Subsidy of the Arts in America* (Temple University Press, 1989); Edward C. Ban-
field, *The Democratic Muse: Visual Arts and the Public Interest* (Basic Books, 1984);
W. J. Baumol and W. G. Bowen, "Arguments for Public Support of the Perform-
ing Arts," in Mark Blaug, ed., *The Economics of the Arts* (Westview Press, 1976), pp.
42–57; Livingston Biddle, *Our Government and the Arts: A Perspective from Inside* (ACA
Books, 1988); Schuyler Chapin and Alberta Arthurs, "A Bill of Rights for Arts,"
New York Times, October 29, 1987, p. A31; Steven C. Dubin, *Bureaucratizing the
Muse: Public Funds and the Cultural Worker* (University of Chicago Press, 1987);
Bruno S. Frey and Werner W. Pommerehne, *Muses and Markets: Explorations in the
Economics of Art* (Basil Blackwell, 1989), esp. ch. 9; Charles J. Haughey, "Art and
the Majority," in Stephen A. Greyser, ed., *Cultural Policy and Arts Administration*
(Harvard Summer School in Arts Administration, 1973), pp. 57–79; Deborah A.
Hoover, *Supporting Yourself as an Artist: A Practical Guide,* 2nd ed. (Oxford University
Press, 1989); Robert Hughes, "Art and Politics," in Frederick Woodard and
Robert Hobbs, eds., *Human Rights/Human Wrongs: Art and Social Change* (Univer-
sity of Iowa Museum of Art, 1986), pp. 211–27; Daniel J. Kornstein, "A Cultural
Bill of Rights," *New York Law Journal,* February 26, 1988; Gary O. Larson, *The
Reluctant Patron: The United States Government and the Arts, 1943–1965* (University of
Pennsylvania Press, 1983); Hellmut Lehmann-Haupt, *Art under a Dictatorship* (Ox-
ford University Press, 1954), esp. pp. 236–48; William F. McDonald, *Federal Relief
Administration and the Arts* (Ohio State University Press, 1969); Richard D. McKin-
zie, *The New Deal for Artists* (Princeton University Press, 1973); Jerre Mangione,
The Dream and the Deal: The Federal Writers' Project, 1935–1943 (Little, Brown, 1972);
Charles C. Mark, *A Study of Cultural Policy in the United States* (UNESCO, 1969); Jane
De Hart Mathews, *The Federal Theatre, 1935–1939: Plays, Relief and Politics* (Prince-
ton University Press, 1967); Paul Mattick, Jr., "Arts and the State," *Nation,* vol.
251, no. 10 (October 1, 1990), pp. 348–58; Mitgang; Kevin V. Mulcahy, "Govern-
ment and the Arts in the United States," in Milton C. Cummings, Jr., and Richard
S. Katz, eds., *The Patron State: Government in the Arts in Europe, North America, and
Japan* (Oxford University Press, 1987), pp. 311–32; Dick Netzer, *The Subsidized*

Muse: Public Support for the Arts in the United States (Cambridge University Press, 1978); Gifford Phillips et al., *The Arts in a Democratic Society* (Center for the Study of Democratic Institutions, 1966); T. Scitovsky, "What's Wrong with the Arts Is What's Wrong with Society," in Blaug, pp. 58–69; Michael Straight, *Nancy Hanks: The Creation of a National Commitment to the Arts* (Duke University Press, 1988); Lynne Warren, *Alternative Spaces: A History in Chicago* (Museum of Contemporary Art, 1984).

Serrano, Mapplethorpe, and other controversies, and cultural rights: Robert Brustein, "The First Amendment and the NEA," *New Republic*, vol. 201, no. 11 (September 11, 1989), pp. 27–29; Robin Cembalest, "Imperfect Moment," *ARTnews*, vol. 89, no. 6 (Summer 1990), pp. 51–53; Douglas Davis, "Art & Contradiction: Helms, Censorship, and the Serpent," *Art in America*, vol. 78, no. 5 (May 1990), pp. 55–61; Sylvia Hochfield, "Art and the NEA: Caught in the Crossfire," *ARTnews*, vol. 89, no. 1 (January 1990), pp. 146–49; Gary Indiana, "Democracy, Inc.," *Artforum*, vol. 28, no. 1 (September 1989), pp. 11–12; Tom Mathews, "Fine Art or Foul?," *Newsweek*, vol. 116, no. 1 (July 2, 1990), pp. 46–52; Charles L. Mee, Jr., "When in Trouble, Start More," *New York Times*, July 8, 1990, sect. 2, pp. 5, 25; "Mixed Signals on Obscenity," *Newsweek*, vol. 116, no. 16 (October 15, 1990), p. 74. Judd Tully, "Read His Lips," *ARTnews*, vol. 89, no. 6 (Summer 1990), pp. 53–54; Carole S. Vance, "Misunderstanding Obscenity," *Art in America*, vol. 78, no. 5 (May 1990), pp. 49–55.

PAGE

396   ["*Work* very hard"]: letter to Thomas Poole, December 11, 1796, in Coleridge, *Collected Letters*, Earl Leslie Griggs, ed. (Clarendon Press, 1956–71), vol. 1, p. 160.

397   ["*Surge with energy*"]: quoted in Arian, p. 109.

398   ["*Even greater superiority*"]: Representative Jacob Javits, quoted in Larson, p. 77.
       ["*Avenues of propaganda*"]: Representative Fred E. Busbey, quoted in *ibid.*, p. 30.
       ["*Stabbing our glorious American art*"]: Representative George Dondero, quoted in *ibid.*, p. 34.
       ["*Freedom of the arts*"]: *ibid.*, pp. 96–97.
       ["*The well-being, the happiness*"]: *ibid.*, p. 167.

399   ["*Recognize the importance*"]: Arian, p. 61.

400   ["*Remember ancient Egypt*"]: quoted in Banfield, p. 57.
       ["*With federal funding*"]: quoted in Netzer, p. 36.
       ["*Not to shape national policy*"]: quoted in Arian, p. 58.
       [*Numbers of arts groups and artists, 1969*]: Mark, p. 32.

401   ["*Requires only subsistence*"]: quoted in Haughey, p. 70.
       ["*Make the arts more widely available*"]: quoted in Netzer, p. 19.
       ["*Something intrinsically abhorrent*"]: *ibid.*
       [*Subsidized arts attendance, 1970–71*]: *ibid.*

402   [*Arts attendance by income, 1973*]: *ibid.*, p. 20.
       ["*6.2 percent of the nation's arts organizations*"]: quoted in Mulcahy, p. 328.
       [*NEA funds for mass constituencies, 1981*]: Arian, p. 44 (figure 4).
       [*Numbers of community arts programs, 1967*]: *ibid.*, p. 120.

403   ["*Talent is in the community*"]: quoted in *ibid.*, p. 119.
       ["*Everyone has the right*"]: in *Human Rights: A Compilation of International Instruments of the United Nations* (United Nations, 1973), pp. 1–3, quoted at p. 3.
       [*A "jerk"*]: quoted in Indiana, p. 11.

404   [*"Write nasty things"*]: quoted in Brustein, p. 27.
       [*"No artist has a First Amendment right"*]: TRB, "Tea and Toleration," *New Republic*, vol. 201, no. 8 (August 21, 1989), p. 6.
       [*Feiffer caricature*]: Brustein, p. 27.
       [*Brustein on subsidies*]: ibid.
       [*"Our intention"*]: H. Louis Sirkin, quoted in *Newsweek*, vol. 115, no. 16 (April 16, 1990), p. 27.
       [*"Mapplethorpe was an important artist"*]: quoted in *New York Times*, October 6, 1990, p. 6.
405   [*Poll on public attitudes toward censorship and arts subsidies*]: *Newsweek*, vol. 116, no. 1 (July 2, 1990), p. 50.
       [*"Alter its audience's perception"*]: Hughes, pp. 216, 226.
       [*"Artists belong out front"*]: Mee, p. 25.

RONALD REAGAN'S BILL OF RIGHTS

The First Amendment in the Reagan era: Curry, passim; Donna A. Demac, *Keeping America Uninformed: Government Secrecy in the 1980's* (Pilgrim Press, 1984); Demac, *Liberty Denied*, passim; Norman Dorsen and Joel Gora, "The Burger Court and Freedom of Speech," in Vincent Blasi, ed., *The Burger Court: The Counter-Revolution That Wasn't* (Yale University Press, 1983), pp. 28–45; Thomas Emerson, "Freedom of the Press under the Burger Court," in *ibid.*, pp. 1–27; Hendricks; Mark Hertsgaard, *On Bended Knee: The Press and the Reagan Presidency* (Farrar, Straus and Giroux, 1988); Robert Emmet Long, ed., *Censorship* (H. W. Wilson, 1990), esp. parts 2–3; Walker, pp. 359–62.

The religious right in the Reagan era: Steve Bruce, *The Rise and Fall of the New Christian Right: Conservative Protestant Politics in America, 1978–1988* (Clarendon Press, 1988); Demac, *Liberty Denied*, esp. chs. 2, 4 passim; Robert Booth Fowler, *A New Engagement: Evangelical Political Thought, 1966–1976* (William B. Eerdmans, 1982); Gara LaMarche, "Some Censorship Trends in Censor-less America, 1989," paper prepared for a workshop on censorship, University of Wisconsin at Madison, June 15–18, 1989, esp. pp. 3–5; Robert C. Liebman and Robert Wuthnow, eds., *The New Christian Right: Mobilization and Legitimation* (Aldine, 1983); Matthew C. Moen, *The Christian Right and Congress* (University of Alabama Press, 1989); Alan Peshkin, *God's Choice: The Total World of a Fundamentalist Christian School* (University of Chicago Press, 1986); Pfeffer, *Religion, State, and the Burger Court*, esp. ch. 3 passim; Walker, pp. 342–46.

1990 flag-burning controversy: Fred Barnes, "Shell Conservatism," *New Republic*, vol. 203, nos. 2 and 3 (July 9 and 16, 1990), pp. 9–10; Alan Brinkley, "Old Glory: The Saga of a National Love Affair," *New York Times*, July 1, 1990, sect. 4, p. 2; Michael Kinsley, "Stars and Snipes," *New Republic*, vol. 203, nos. 2 and 3 (July 9 and 16, 1990), p. 4; "Value Judgments," *Newsweek*, vol. 115, no. 26 (June 25, 1990), pp. 16–18; *New York Times*, July 15, 1990, p. A12.

Defendants' rights revolution and counterrevolution: Abraham, chs. 3–4 passim; Christopher Byron, "Sweatshirt Justice," *New York*, vol. 22, no. 39 (October 2, 1989), pp. 42–54; David Fellman, *The Defendant's Rights Today* (University of Wisconsin Press, 1976); Fellman, "The Nationalization of American Civil Liberties," in M. Judd Harmon, ed., *Essays on the Constitution of the United States* (Kennikat Press, 1978), pp. 49–60; Stephen Gillers, "The Meese Lie," *Nation*, vol. 244, no. 7 (February 21, 1987), p. 205; Yale Kamisar, "The Swing of the Pendulum," *Nation*, vol. 239, no. 9 (September 29, 1984), pp. 271–74; Kamisar, "The Warren Court (Was It

Really So Defense-Minded?), the Burger Court (Is It Really So Prosecution-Oriented?), and Police Investigatory Practices," in Blasi, pp. 62–91; Deborah Kelly, "Victim Participation in the Criminal Justice System," in Arthur J. Lurigio et al., eds., *Victims of Crime: Problems, Policies and Programs* (Sage, 1990), pp. 172–87; Patrick A. Malone, " 'You Have the Right to Remain Silent': *Miranda* after Twenty Years," *American Scholar*, vol. 55, no. 3 (Summer 1986), pp. 367–80; Gary T. Marx, *Undercover: Police Surveillance in America* (University of California Press, 1988), esp. ch. 3; "Reagan's Days in Court," *Newsweek*, vol. 104, no. 3 (July 16, 1984), pp. 57–60; Jeffrey Toobin, "Viva Miranda: Ed Meese Tangles with the Law," *New Republic*, vol. 196, no. 7 (February 16, 1987), pp. 11–12; Arnold S. Trebach, *The Rationing of Justice: Constitutional Rights and the Criminal Process* (Rutgers University Press, 1964); "A 'Victim's Bill of Rights,' " *Newsweek*, vol. 99, no. 24 (June 14, 1982), p. 64; Walker, pp. 246–54; Robert L. Weinberg, "A Democratic Retreat: Comprehensive Crime Control," *Nation*, vol. 243, no. 1 (July 5 and 12, 1986), pp. 12–15; "When the Police Blunder a Little," *Time*, vol. 121, no. 11 (March 14, 1983), pp. 56, 61; Welsh S. White, *The Death Penalty in the Eighties* (University of Michigan Press, 1987), esp. ch. 1.

Reagan and the judiciary: Ethan Bronner, *Battle for Justice: How the Bork Nomination Shook America* (Norton, 1989); Ronald Dworkin, "The Bork Nomination," *New York Review of Books*, vol. 34, no. 13 (August 13, 1987), pp. 3–10; Jamie Kalven, "The Reagan Administration and the Federal Judiciary," in Curry, pp. 315–34; William Lasser, *The Limits of Judicial Power: The Supreme Court in American Politics* (University of North Carolina Press, 1988), pp. 222–45 passim; Stephen Macedo, *The New Right v. the Constitution* (Cato Institute, 1987); Walter F. Murphy, "Reagan's Judicial Strategy," in Larry Berman, ed., *Looking Back on the Reagan Presidency* (Johns Hopkins University Press, 1990), pp. 207–37; Herman Schwartz, *The New Right and the Constitution: Turning Back the Legal Clock* (Northeastern University Press, 1990); Schwartz, *Packing the Courts: The Conservative Campaign to Rewrite the Constitution* (Scribner, 1988); "Supreme or Not Supreme," *Time*, vol. 128, no. 18 (November 3, 1986), p. 46.

PAGE

407   [*"Faith in the miracle"*]: "Why Johnny Can't Speak" (editorial), *Nation*, vol. 246, no. 4 (January 30, 1988), p. 1.

[*"Responsibility to be right"*]: quoted in Koffler, p. 140.

[*"Close surveillance"*]: Demac, *Liberty Denied*, pp. 79–80.

[*"Just because information"*]: James Faurer, quoted in *ibid.*, p. 17.

408   [*Findings via FOIA*]: see Hendricks, pp. 39, 52, 141, 66, 189, 117, 158, 171 respectively.

[*"Attempted to cripple it"*]: Diana M. T. K. Autin, "The Reagan Administration and the Freedom of Information Act," in Curry, pp. 69–85, quoted at pp. 69–70.

[*"As if information"*]: quoted in Demac, *Keeping America Uninformed*, p. 140.

[*"Surrogates of the public stuff"*]: quoted in Hertsgaard, p. 40.

409   [*"Most skillful practitioner"*]: Demac, *Liberty Denied*, p. 135.

[*"Movement has also received"*]: *ibid.*, p. 14.

[*1962 Court decision barring school prayer*]: Engel v. Vitale, 370 U.S. 421 (1962).

[*"Hope I live to see"*]: quoted in Demac, *Liberty Denied*, p. 14.

410   [*"People of all races"*]: *ibid.*, p. 16.

[*"Purely secular"*]: *ibid.*

[*"Seeks to employ"*]: Edwards v. Aguillard, 482 U.S. 578 (1987), quoted at 597.

410   [*"Strongest blow yet"*]: Demac, *Liberty Denied*, p. 17.
411   [*"Scottsboro boys"*]: *Powell* v. *Alabama*, 287 U.S. 45 (1932).
        [*1936 Court ruling on confessions extracted by torture*]: *Brown* v. *Mississippi*, 297
        U.S. 278 (1936).
412   [Massiah]: *Massiah* v. *U.S.*, 377 U.S. 201 (1964), White quoted at 212.
        [Gideon]: *Gideon* v. *Wainwright*, 372 U.S. 335 (1963).
        [Escobedo]: 378 U.S. 478 (1964), majority opinion quoted at 492, White
        at 496.
        [Miranda]: *Miranda* v. *Arizona*, 384 U.S. 436 (1966).
413   [*"Dangerous experimentation"*]: quoted in Abraham, p. 160.
        [*Philadelphia "Miranda card"*]: reprinted in *ibid.*, p. 161 (figure 4.1).
414   [*Mr. Dooley on the Court*]: Finley Peter Dunne, "The Supreme Court's
        Decisions," in Dunne, *Mr. Dooley's Opinions* (R. H. Russell, 1901), pp.
        21–26, quoted at p. 26.
415   [*"Scarcely any political question"*]: Tocqueville, *Democracy in America*, Phil-
        lips Bradley, ed. (Knopf, 1945), vol. 1, p. 280.

13. A GLOBAL BILL OF HUMAN RIGHTS

UNESCO commission and its survey: Richard McKeon, "Philosophy and History in
the Development of Human Rights," in Howard E. Kiefer and Milton K. Munitz,
eds., *Ethics and Social Justice* (State University of New York Press, 1970), pp.
300–22; UNESCO, ed., *Human Rights: Comments and Interpretations* (Columbia University Press, 1949); see also Jeanne Hersch, "Is the Declaration of Human Rights
a Western Concept?," in Kiefer and Munitz, pp. 323–32; H. Lauterpacht, *An
International Bill of the Rights of Man* (Columbia University Press, 1945), part 1
passim; William Draper Lewis, ed., *Essential Human Rights, Annals of the American
Academy of Political and Social Science*, vol. 243 (January 1946).

Historical background of international human rights: Evan Borchard, "Historical Back-
ground of International Protection of Human Rights," in Lewis, *Essential Human
Rights*, pp. 112–17; Tom J. Farer, "The United Nations and Human Rights: More
than a Whimper, Less than a Roar," *Human Rights Quarterly*, vol. 9, no. 4 (1987),
pp. 550–53; Charles H. Fairbanks, Jr., and Eli Nathans, "The British Campaign
Against the Slave Trade," in Marc F. Plattner, ed., *Human Rights in Our Time*
(Westview Press, 1984), pp. 30–68; David P. Forsythe, *Human Rights and World
Politics*, 2nd ed. (University of Nebraska Press, 1989), pp. 7–10; Evan Luard, "The
Origins of International Concern over Human Rights," in Luard, ed., *The Interna-
tional Protection of Human Rights* (Praeger, 1967), pp. 7–21; Ellery C. Stowell,
Intervention in International Law (John Byrne, 1921).

PAGE
416   [*"Intellectual and historical circumstances"*]: "The Grounds of an Interna-
        tional Declaration of Human Rights," in UNESCO, *Human Rights*, pp.
        258–72, quoted at p. 262.
        [*"Common formulation"*]: "Memorandum and Questionnaire," in *ibid.*, pp.
        251–57, quoted at p. 255.
        [*"Illiterate but wise mother"*]: Gandhi, "A letter addressed to the Director-
        General of Unesco," in *ibid.*, p. 18.
        [*"Any kind of totalitarian leader"*]: Riezler, "Reflections on Human
        Rights," in *ibid.*, pp. 156–57, quoted at p. 157.
        [*Huxley on socialist governments*]: Huxley, "The Rights of Man and the Facts
        of the Human Situation," in *ibid.*, pp. 199–204, esp. pp. 200–1.

417   [*"Main purpose of liberty"*]: Tchechko, "The Conception of the Rights of Man in the U.S.S.R. based on Official Documents," in *ibid.,* pp. 158–76, quoted at p. 169.

[*"Either empty or arbitrary"*]: Croce, "The Rights of Man and the Present Historical Situation," in *ibid.,* pp. 93–95, quoted at p. 94.

[*"Protestant powers sought rights"*]: Luard, "Origins of International Concern," p. 9.

[*Luard on British promotion of Latin American independence*]: *ibid.,* p. 10.

THE ROOSEVELT LEGACY

FDR and international human rights: James MacGregor Burns, "The Roosevelt-Hitler Battle of Symbols," *Antioch Review,* vol. 2, no. 3 (Fall 1942), pp. 407–21; M. Glen Johnson, "The Contributions of Eleanor and Franklin Roosevelt to the Development of International Protection for Human Rights," *Human Rights Quarterly,* vol. 9, no. 1 (1987), pp. 19–48, esp. pp. 20–27; Ruth B. Russell and Jeannette E. Muther, *A History of the United Nations Charter: The Role of the United States, 1940–1945* (Brookings Institution, 1958), esp. pp. 323–29; Theodore A. Wilson, *The First Summit: Roosevelt and Churchill at Placentia Bay, 1941* (Houghton Mifflin, 1969), chs. 9–13 passim.

Eleanor Roosevelt and UN Human Rights Commission: Blanche Wiesen Cook, " 'Turn toward Peace': ER and Foreign Affairs," in Joan Hoff-Wilson and Marjorie Lightman, eds., *Without Precedent: The Life and Career of Eleanor Roosevelt* (Indiana University Press, 1984), pp. 108–21; Farer, "United Nations and Human Rights"; Tamara K. Hareven, *Eleanor Roosevelt: An American Conscience* (1968; reprinted by Da Capo Press, 1975), ch. 12; Samuel Hoare, "The UN Commission on Human Rights," in Luard, *International Protection of Human Rights,* pp. 59–98; John P. Humphrey, *Human Rights and the United Nations: A Great Adventure* (Transnational Publishers, 1984), pp. 17–77 passim; Humphrey, "The UN Charter and the Universal Declaration of Human Rights," in Luard, *International Protection of Human Rights,* pp. 39–58; Johnson, esp. pp. 27–47; Joseph P. Lash, *Eleanor: The Years Alone* (Norton, 1972), esp. chs. 1–4, 6, 9–10 passim; H. Lauterpacht, *International Law and Human Rights* (Praeger, 1950), esp. ch. 17; A. Glenn Mower, Jr., *The United States, the United Nations, and Human Rights: The Eleanor Roosevelt and Jimmy Carter Eras* (Greenwood Press, 1979), part 1; Eleanor Roosevelt, *On My Own* (Harper, 1958), chs. 5, 7–9; Howard Tolley, Jr., *The U.N. Commission on Human Rights* (Westview Press, 1987), chs. 1–2 passim; United Nations, *These Rights and Freedoms* (UN Department of Public Information, July 1950).

PAGE

418   [*"Reaffirm faith"*]: Charter of the United Nations, reprinted in Russell and Muther, pp. 1035–53, quoted at p. 1035 (preamble).

[*"Realization of human rights"*]: *ibid.,* p. 1038 (article 13).

419   [*"Have good reason"*]: June 26, 1945, in Truman, *Public Papers* (U.S. Government Printing Office, 1961–66), vol. 1, pp. 138–44, quoted at p. 142.

[*"Authorize the United Nations"*]: Charter, p. 1036 (article 2).

[*"Every rogue regime"*]: Farer, "United Nations and Human Rights," p. 554.

[*"Senile or an ass"*]: quoted in Johnson, p. 22.

420   [*"Freedom from fear"*]: Atlantic Charter, August 14, 1941, in Roosevelt, *Public Papers and Addresses,* Samuel I. Rosenman, ed. (Random House, 1938–50), vol. 10, pp. 314–15, quoted at p. 315.

420   [*"Of necessity"*]: August 21, 1941, in *ibid.*, vol. 10, pp. 333–34, quoted at
       p. 334.
       [*"Faith in life"*]: August 14, 1942, in *ibid.*, vol. 11, p. 328.
       [*"Integral part"*]: Russell and Muther, p. 323.
       [*"Extremely vital"*]: quoted in Johnson, p. 24.
       [*Pegler on Eleanor Roosevelt*]: see Lash, p. 41.
421   [*"Second half of the decade"*]: Johnson, p. 20.
       [*"Ignore the sovereign rights"*]: quoted in Farer, "United Nations and
       Human Rights," p. 556.
422   [*"Common standard"*]: quoted in Lash, p. 65.
       [*"A carbon copy"*]: James P. Hendrick, quoted in *ibid.*, p. 62.
       [*"Corresponding to the laws"*]: *ibid.*, p. 75.
       [*"Theoretical conjecture"*]: *ibid.*, p. 74.
       [*"Weak and completely unacceptable"*]: *ibid.*, p. 77.
423   [*"International Magna Carta"*]: quoted in Lauterpacht, *International Law
       and Human Rights*, p. 394.
       [*"Whereas recognition"*]: reprinted in *Human Rights: A Compilation of Inter-
       national Instruments of the United Nations* (United Nations, 1973),
       pp. 1–3.

MORAL IMPERATIVES AND PRACTICAL NEEDS

Human rights and foreign policy in the American tradition: Forsythe, *Human Rights and
World Politics,* pp. 103–5; Norman A. Graebner, "Human Rights and Foreign
Policy: The Historic Connection," in Kenneth W. Thompson, ed., *The Moral
Imperatives of Human Rights: A World Survey* (University Press of America, 1980),
pp. 39–67, esp. pp. 39–45; Arthur M. Schlesinger, Jr., *The Cycles of American History*
(Houghton Mifflin, 1986), pp. 89–95; Sandy Vogelgesang, *American Dream, Global
Nightmare: The Dilemma of U.S. Human Rights Policy* (Norton, 1980), pp. 72–75; see
also George F. Kennan, "Morality and Foreign Policy," *Foreign Affairs,* vol. 64, no.
2 (Winter 1985–86), pp. 205–18.

Kissinger, the Nixon-Ford administration, and human rights: James Ring Adams, "From
Helsinki to Madrid," in Plattner, pp. 105–24; Roberta Cohen, "Human Rights
Decision-Making in the Executive Branch: Some Proposals for a Coordinated
Strategy," in Donald P. Kommers and Gilburt D. Loescher, eds., *Human Rights and
American Foreign Policy* (University of Notre Dame Press, 1979), pp. 216–46, esp.
pp. 217–22; David P. Forsythe, *Human Rights and U.S. Foreign Policy: Congress
Reconsidered* (University Presses of Florida, 1988); Forsythe, *Human Rights and
World Politics,* esp. pp. 105–10; Donald M. Fraser, "Congress's Role in the Making
of International Human Rights Policy," in Kommers and Loescher, pp. 247–55;
Henry Kissinger, "Moral Promise and Practical Needs," *Department of State Bulletin,*
vol. 75 (November 15, 1976), pp. 597–605; Kissinger, *Years of Upheaval* (Little,
Brown, 1982), esp. pp. 246–55, 985–98; William Korey, "Final Acts and Final
Solutions," in Abdul Aziz Said, ed., *Human Rights and World Order* (Praeger,
1978), pp. 117–25; Arfon Rees, "The Soviet Union," in R. J. Vincent, ed., *Foreign
Policy and Human Rights* (Cambridge University Press, 1986), pp. 61–83 passim;
A. H. Robertson, "The Helsinki Agreement and Human Rights," in Kommers
and Loescher, pp. 130–49; Andrei D. Sakharov, "A Letter to the Congress of the
United States," in *Sakharov Speaks,* Harrison E. Salisbury, ed. (Vintage, 1974), pp.
212–15; Schlesinger, pp. 95–97; H. Gordon Skilling, *Charter 77 and Human Rights
in Czechoslovakia* (George Allen & Unwin, 1981), esp. ch. 8 passim; Vogelgesang,
esp. pp. 120–35 passim.

Carter administration and human rights: Georgi A. Arbatov and Willem Oltmans, *The Soviet Viewpoint* (Dodd, Mead, 1983), esp. ch. 4; Zbigniew Brzezinski, *Power and Principle: Memoirs of the National Security Advisor, 1977–1981* (Farrar, Straus and Giroux, 1983), ch. 4, and pp. 149–56, and passim; David Carleton and Michael Stohl, "The Foreign Policy of Human Rights: Rhetoric and Reality from Jimmy Carter to Ronald Reagan," *Human Rights Quarterly,* vol. 7, no. 2 (1985), pp. 205–29; Jimmy Carter, *Keeping Faith* (Bantam, 1982), pp. 141–51, and passim; Cohen, "Human Rights Decision-Making," pp. 222–40; Roberta Cohen, "Human Rights Diplomacy: The Carter Administration and the Southern Cone," *Human Rights Quarterly,* vol. 4, no. 2 (1982), pp. 212–42; Richard W. Cottam, "Arms Sales and Human Rights: The Case of Iran," in Peter G. Brown and Douglas MacLean, eds., *Human Rights and U.S. Foreign Policy* (Lexington Books, 1979), pp. 281–301; Thomas Draper, ed., *Human Rights* (H. W. Wilson, 1982); Tom J. Farer, ed., *Toward a Humanitarian Diplomacy: A Primer for Policy* (New York University Press, 1980); Forsythe, *Human Rights and World Politics,* esp. pp. 110–14; Raymond L. Garthoff, *Détente and Confrontation: American-Soviet Relations from Nixon to Reagan* (Brookings Institution, 1985), esp. pp. 563–75, 609–12; Graebner, pp. 50–67; Mower, part 2 passim; Joshua Muravchik, *The Uncertain Crusade: Jimmy Carter and the Dilemmas of Human Rights Policy* (Hamilton Press, 1986); Barry M. Rubin and Elizabeth P. Spiro, eds., *Human Rights and U.S. Foreign Policy* (Westview Press, 1979), esp. parts 2–4 passim; Andrei D. Sakharov, *Alarm and Hope,* Efrem Yankelovich and Alfred Friendly, Jr., eds. (Knopf, 1978), esp. ch. 4; Schlesinger, pp. 97–104; Mark L. Schneider, "A New Administration's New Policy: The Rise to Power of Human Rights," in Brown and MacLean, pp. 3–13; Abraham M. Sirkin, "Can a Human Rights Policy Be Consistent?," in *ibid.,* pp. 199–213; Gaddis Smith, *Morality, Reason, and Power: American Diplomacy in the Carter Years* (Hill and Wang, 1986), ch. 2, and passim; Cyrus Vance, *Hard Choices* (Simon and Schuster, 1983); Vogelgesang, pp. 135–53, and passim.

Reagan administration and human rights: William P. Clark, "Personal Liberties and National Security" (address at San Francisco, August 6, 1982), *Department of State Bulletin,* vol. 82, no. 2069 (December 1982), pp. 35–38; Draper, passim; Barbara Epstein, "The Reagan Doctrine and Right-Wing Democracy," *Socialist Review,* vol. 19, no. 1 (January–March 1989), pp. 9–38; Forsythe, *Congress Reconsidered;* Forsythe, *Human Rights and World Politics,* esp. pp. 114–21; David P. Forsythe, "Socioeconomic Human Rights: The United Nations, the United States, and Beyond," *Human Rights Quarterly,* vol. 4, no. 4 (1982), pp. 433–49, esp. pp. 435–40; Tamar Jacoby, "The Reagan Turnaround on Human Rights," *Foreign Affairs,* vol. 64, no. 5 (Summer 1986), pp. 1066–86; Jeane J. Kirkpatrick, "Dictatorships and Double Standards," reprinted in Howard J. Wiarda, ed., *Human Rights and U.S. Foreign Policy: Theoretical Approaches and Some Perspectives on Latin America* (American Enterprise Institute for Public Policy Research, 1982), pp. 5–29; Henry A. Kissinger, "Continuity and Change in American Foreign Policy," in Said, pp. 154–67; Aryeh Neier, "A Matter of Principle: Human Rights and Politics," *Nation,* vol. 252, no. 15 (April 22, 1991), pp. 519–22; Schlesinger, pp. 103–6.

PAGE

424   [*"Going backwards"*]: quoted in Lash, p. 22.
      [*"Policy was collapsed"*]: Forsythe, *Human Rights and World Politics,* p. 104.
      [*"Unwilling to witness"*]: January 20, 1961, in Kennedy, *Public Papers* (U.S. Government Printing Office, 1962–64), vol. 1, pp. 1–3, quoted at p. 1.
      [*"Working to right"*]: September 20, 1963, in *ibid.,* vol. 3, pp. 693–98, quoted at p. 697.

425   [*"Moral promise"*]: Kissinger, "Moral Promise and Practical Needs," pp. 604, 600 respectively.

426   [*"Like a bleeding heart"*]: quoted in Vogelgesang, p. 126.
[*"Tell Popper"*]: quoted in Schlesinger, p. 96.
[*"Aiming at the manipulation"*]: *ibid.*, p. 95.
[*"Moral vacuum"*]: *ibid.*
[*"Governments which practice"*]: quoted in Cohen, "Human Rights Decision-Making," p. 218.

427   [*"President should deny"*]: quoted in Forsythe, *Congress Reconsidered,* p. 8.
[*"Extraordinary circumstances"*]: quoted in Vogelgesang, p. 129.
[*"Declaration of intentions"*]: Robertson, "Helsinki Agreement," p. 130.
[*"Respect human rights"*]: *ibid.*, appendix, pp. 145–46, quoted at p. 145.
[*"Our commitment to human rights"*]: January 20, 1977, in Carter, *Public Papers* (U.S. Government Printing Office, 1977–82), vol. 1, part 1, pp. 1–4, quoted at pp. 2, 3.

428   [*"No longer separate"*]: address at commencement exercises at the University of Notre Dame, May 22, 1977, in *ibid.*, vol. 1, part 1, pp. 954–62, quoted at p. 957.

429   [*Carter's pledge to Sakharov*]: reprinted in Sakharov, *Alarm and Hope,* p. 50.
[*"Very sharp rebuff"*]: Brzezinski, p. 155.
[*"Enemy of the Soviet state"*]: *ibid.*, pp. 154–55, quoted at p. 155.
[*"More harmonious resolution"*]: Carter, *Keeping Faith,* pp. 149–50.

430   [*"Inordinate fear"*]: Notre Dame address, p. 956.
[*"Abandoned the philosophy"*]: Smith, p. 48.

431   [*"Entirely unintended"*]: Cottam, p. 299.
[*"Tocquevillian void"*]: see James MacGregor Burns, *The Crosswinds of Freedom* (Knopf, 1989), pp. 125, 665.
[*"Did not fully grasp"*]: Carter, *Keeping Faith,* p. 144.
[*Reagan advisers on "abandonment" of rights emphasis*]: quoted in Jacoby, p. 1069.
[*Haig on terrorism and human rights*]: *ibid.*
[*"Evil empire"*]: address at annual convention of the National Association of Evangelicals, Orlando, Florida, March 8, 1983, in Reagan, *Public Papers* (U.S. Government Printing Office, 1982–), vol. 3, part 1, pp. 359–64, quoted at p. 364.

432   [*"Hypocritical show"*]: Jacoby, p. 1073.
[*"Promotion of human rights"*]: *ibid.*, p. 1084.

433   [*"Restrain the American role"*]: quoted in *ibid.*, p. 1078.
[*"Foster the infrastructure"*]: Reagan, address to British Parliament, June 8, 1982, in Reagan, *Papers,* vol. 2, part 1, pp. 742–48, quoted at p. 746.
[*"Equation of human rights"*]: Neier, p. 522.

434   [*"Second Reagan Administration"*]: Forsythe, *Human Rights and World Politics,* p. 120.
[*"Expansion of human rights"*]: Carter, *Keeping Faith,* p. 144.

THREE WORLDS OF RIGHTS

The West and human rights: Josiah A. M. Cobbah, "African Values and the Human Rights Debate: An African Perspective," *Human Rights Quarterly,* vol. 9, no. 3 (1987), pp. 309–31, esp. pp. 312–20; Maurice Cranston, *What Are Human Rights?* (Taplinger, 1973); Jack Donnelly, *Universal Human Rights in Theory and Practice* (Cornell University Press, 1989), esp. ch. 5, and pp. 68–75; Donnelly and Rhoda Howard, eds., *International Handbook of Human Rights* (Greenwood Press, 1987), pp. 29–47, 161–81, 209–26, 339–57, 429–56; Forsythe, *Human Rights and World Politics,* esp. pp. 68–75, 163–72, 183; Forsythe, "Socioeconomic Human Rights"; Louis Henkin, *The Age of Rights* (Columbia University Press, 1990), esp. chs. 9–10 passim; Henkin, *The Rights of Man Today* (Westview Press, 1978), esp. pp. 35–51; Francis G. Jacobs, *The European Convention on Human Rights* (Clarendon Press, 1975); William Draper Lewis, "Human Rights in England and the United States," in Lewis, *Essential Human Rights,* pp. 60–66; A. H. Robertson, "The European Convention on Human Rights," in Luard, *International Protection of Human Rights,* pp. 99–131; Vogelgesang, esp. pp. 180–98 passim; see also Luard, "Conclusions," in Luard, *International Protection of Human Rights,* pp. 304–24.

Communist world and human rights: Andrei Amalrik, "By Bread Alone? A Well-Fed Slave Is a Well-Fed Slave," *New York Times,* February 3, 1977, p. A33; Arbatov and Oltmans, ch. 4; Valery Chalidze, *To Defend These Rights: Human Rights and the Soviet Union,* Guy Daniels, trans. (Random House, 1974); V. Chkhikvadze, "Constitution of True Human Rights and Freedoms," *International Affairs* (Moscow) (October 1980), pp. 13–20; Cranston, esp. chs. 7–9; *Denial of Human Rights in Eastern Europe: The Tenth Anniversary of the Universal Declaration of Human Rights* (Assembly of Captive European Nations, 1958); Donnelly, *Universal Human Rights,* pp. 55–57, 77–80; Donnelly and Howard, *International Handbook,* pp. 75–97, 99–116, 301–21, 409–28; Forsythe, *Human Rights and World Politics,* esp. pp. 75–78, 172–74, 183–86; Henkin, *Age of Rights,* esp. ch. 10; Henkin, *Rights of Man Today,* esp. pp. 55–78; William L. McBride, "Rights and the Marxian Tradition," *Praxis International,* vol. 4, no. 1 (April 1984), pp. 57–74; Alice Erh-Soon Tay, "Marxism, Socialism and Human Rights," in Eugene Kamenka and Tay, eds., *Human Rights* (St. Martin's Press, 1978), pp. 104–12; Tchechko; Cathy Young, " 'Bomzh' Away," *New Republic,* vol. 202, no. 5 (January 29, 1990), pp. 18–21.

Third World and human rights: David H. Bayley, *Public Liberties in the New States* (Rand McNally, 1964); Peter L. Berger, "Are Human Rights Universal?," in Rubin and Spiro, pp. 3–12; Cobbah; Donnelly, *Universal Human Rights,* passim; Donnelly and Howard, *International Handbook,* passim; Forsythe, *Human Rights and World Politics,* esp. pp. 78–82, 175–77, 186–87; Henkin, *Age of Rights,* esp. pp. 174–78; Henkin, *Rights of Man Today,* esp. pp. 78–88; Rhoda Howard, "The Full-Belly Thesis: Should Economic Rights Take Priority over Civil and Political Rights? Evidence from Sub-Saharan Africa," *Human Rights Quarterly,* vol. 5, no. 4 (1983), pp. 467–90; Abdullahi Ahmed An-Na'im and Francis M. Deng, eds., *Human Rights in Africa: Cross-Cultural Perspectives* (Brookings Institution, 1990); Alison Dundes Renteln, "The Unanswered Challenge of Relativism and the Consequences for Human Rights," *Human Rights Quarterly,* vol. 7, no. 4 (1985), pp. 514–40; Salvatore Senese, "External and Internal Self-Determination," *Social Justice,* vol. 16, no. 1 (Spring 1989), pp. 19–25; "Universal Declaration of the Rights of People" (Algiers, 1976), reprinted in *ibid.,* pp. 155–58; Theo van Boven, "Can Human Rights Have a Separate Existence from People's Rights?," *ibid.,* pp. 12–18; Vogelgesang, passim; Claude E. Welch, Jr., and Ronald I. Meltzer, eds., *Human Rights and Development in Africa* (State University of New York Press, 1984); Eddison Jonas Mudadirwa Zvobgo, "A Third World View," in Kommers and Loescher, pp. 90–106; see also Myres S. McDougal, Harold D. Lasswell, and Lung-chu Chen, *Human Rights and World Public Order: The Basic Policies of an International Law of Human Dignity* (Yale University Press, 1980); Thompson, *Moral Imperatives.*

PAGE

434   [*"Right to be free"*]: speech on Law Day before the University of Georgia's Law School, April 30, 1977, reprinted in Rubin and Spiro, pp. 217–24, quoted at p. 218.

435   [*"List of freedoms"*]: Pierre-Henri Teitgen, quoted in Robertson, "European Convention," p. 101.

436 [*"Totally different moral dimension"*]: Cranston, pp. 68, 66, 65, 68 respectively.

437 [*"Never be higher"*]: Marx, *Critique of the Gotha Progamme*, C. P. Dutt, ed. (International Publishers, 1938), p. 10.
[*"Communist ideology emphasizes"*]: Arbatov and Oltmans, p. 157.

438 [*"Most important feature"*]: Chkhikvadze, p. 18.
[*"He who does not work"*]: quoted in Henkin, *Age of Rights*, p. 160.
[*"Conformity with the interests"*]: quoted in Tay, p. 111.
[*"Deep differences"*]: Arbatov and Oltmans, p. 156.

439 [*Soviet failures in securing socioeconomic rights*]: see Young, passim.
[*Amalrik on rights*]: Amalrik.

441 [*"What freedom has our subsistence farmer?"*]: quoted in Howard, "Full-Belly Thesis," p. 467.
[*"Economic independence"*]: Claude E. Welch, Jr., "Human Rights as a Problem in Contemporary Africa," in Welch and Meltzer, pp. 11–31, Nkrumah quoted at p. 25.
[*"Were not only alien"*]: Zvobgo, p. 97.

442 [*"Culturally sacrosanct family"*]: Howard, "Women's Rights in English-speaking Sub-Saharan Africa," in Welch, pp. 46–74, quoted at p. 60.
[*"Attack on public order"*]: James Silk, "Traditional Culture and the Prospect for Human Rights in Africa," in Na'im and Deng, pp. 290–328, quoted at p. 295.

443 [*"A mask"*]: *ibid.*, quoted at p. 302.
[*"Permanent exceptional circumstance"*]: *ibid.*, p. 295.
[*"Generally satisfactory"*]: Claude E. Welch, Jr., "Human Rights in Francophone West Africa," in *ibid.*, pp. 184–212, quoted at p. 196.
[*"Suspended public politics"*]: *ibid.*, p. 195.

14. TRANSFORMING RIGHTS

The following sources were helpful in preparing this chapter: Michael Albert et al., *Liberating Theory* (South End Press, 1986); Lisa Albrecht and Rose M. Brewer, eds., *Bridges of Power: Women's Multicultural Alliances* (New Society Publishers, 1990), esp. part 1; Joyce Appleby, "The American Heritage: The Heirs and the Disinherited," *Journal of American History*, vol. 74, no. 3 (December 1987), pp. 798–813; Robert N. Bellah et al., *Habits of the Heart: Individualism and Commitment in American Life* (Harper, 1986); Samuel Bowles and Herbert Gintis, *Democracy and Capitalism: Property, Community, and the Contradictions of Modern Social Thought* (Basic Books, 1986); Maude P. Brunstetter, "Women in Power: Meir, Thatcher, and Aquino," paper prepared for delivery at the annual meeting of the American Political Science Association, Atlanta, August 31–September 3, 1989; Charlotte Bunch, *Passionate Politics: Feminist Theory in Action* (St. Martin's Press, 1987); James MacGregor Burns, *Leadership* (Harper, 1978); Stewart Burns, "The Populist Movement and the Cooperative Commonwealth: The Politics of Non-Reformist Reform" (Ph.D. dissertation, University of California, Santa Cruz, 1984), chs. 13–14; Pamela Johnston Conover, Stephen T. Leonard, and Donald D. Searing, " 'Duty Is a Four-Letter Word': Responsibility, Rights and Identity in Democratic Citizenship," paper prepared for delivery at the Symposium on Democratic Theory and Practice, Williams College, Williamstown, Massachusetts, July 31–August 4, 1989; Jack Donnelly, *The Concept of Human Rights*

(Croom Helm, 1985); W. E. B. Du Bois, *The Souls of Black Folk* (Dodd, Mead, 1979); Carol Gilligan, *In a Different Voice: Psychological Theory and Women's Development* (Harvard University Press, 1982); Thomas L. Haskell, "The Curious Persistence of Rights Talk in the 'Age of Interpretation,'" *Journal of American History*, vol. 74, no. 3 (December 1987), pp. 984–1012; Virginia Held, "Mothering versus Contract," in Jane J. Mansbridge, ed., *Beyond Self-Interest* (University of Chicago Press, 1990), pp. 287–304; Martin Luther King, Jr., *Where Do We Go from Here: Chaos or Community?* (Beacon Press, 1968); Audre Lorde, "Age, Race, Class, and Sex: Women Redefining Difference," in Lorde, *Sister Outsider* (Crossing Press, 1984), pp. 114–23; Staughton Lynd, "Communal Rights," *Texas Law Review*, vol. 62 (May 1984), pp. 1417–41; Douglas MacLean and Claudia Mills, eds., *Liberalism Reconsidered* (Rowman & Allanheld, 1983); Jane J. Mansbridge, "The Rise and Fall of Self-Interest in the Explanation of Political Life," in Mansbridge, pp. 3–22; A. I. Melden, *Rights and Persons* (University of California Press, 1977); Chantal Mouffe, "Radical Democracy or Liberal Democracy?," *Socialist Review*, vol. 20, no. 2 (April–June 1990), pp. 57–66; Barbara J. Nelson, "Women and Politics Worldwide," *Humphrey Institute News*, vol. 14, no. 1 (January 1991), pp. 11–13; David Plotke, "What's So New about New Social Movements?," *Socialist Review*, vol. 20, no. 1 (January–March 1990), pp. 81–102; Bernice Johnson Reagon, "Coalition Politics: Turning the Century," in Barbara Smith, ed., *Home Girls: A Black Feminist Anthology* (Kitchen Table: Women of Color Press, 1983), pp. 356–68; Sue Tolleson Rinehart, "Gender and the Epistemology of Leadership," paper prepared for delivery at the annual meeting of the International Society of Political Psychology, Washington, D.C., July 11–14, 1990; Michael J. Sandel, ed., *Liberalism and Its Critics* (New York University Press, 1984); Sandel, "The Political Theory of the Procedural Republic," in Gary C. Bryner and Noel B. Reynolds, eds., *Constitutionalism and Rights* (Brigham Young University, 1987), pp. 141–55; Sandel, "The Procedural Republic and the Unencumbered Self," *Political Theory*, vol. 12, no. 1 (February 1984), pp. 81–96; Mark Satin, "Multiculturalism Will Make Us Whole," *New Options*, no. 68, pp. 1–4, 7–8; Clarence N. Stone, "Transactional and Transforming Leadership: A Re-examination," paper prepared for delivery at the annual meeting of the American Political Science Association, San Francisco, August 30–September 2, 1990; Students for a Democratic Society, "Port Huron Statement," June 1962, reprinted in James Miller, *"Democracy Is in the Streets": From Port Huron to the Siege of Chicago* (Simon and Schuster, 1987), pp. 329–74; L. W. Sumner, *The Moral Foundation of Rights* (Clarendon Press, 1987); Nan Van Den Bergh and Lynn B. Cooper, eds., *Feminist Visions for Social Work* (National Association of Social Workers, 1986); Jeremy Waldron, ed., *"Nonsense upon Stilts": Bentham, Burke, and Marx on the Rights of Man* (Methuen, 1987); Waldron, ed., *Theories of Rights* (Oxford University Press, 1984).

PAGE

445   [*Cobblestone leadership*]: James MacGregor Burns, *Cobblestone Leadership: Majority Rule, Minority Power* (University of Oklahoma Press, 1990), esp. pp. ix–x.

446   [*UN World Summit for Children*]: coverage and quotations from *New York Times*, October 1, 1990, pp. A1, A12–14; see also T. Berry Brazelton, "Why Is America Failing Its Children?," *New York Times Magazine* (September 9, 1990), pp. 40–42, 50, 90; Nancy Q. Keefe, " 'Suffer the Little Children . . . ,' " *Berkshire Eagle*, October 14, 1990, p. E3; Robert Pear, "U.S. to Support U.N. on Children, but Money for Programs Is Scant," *New York Times*, September 26, 1990, pp. A1, A7; UNICEF, *The State of the World's Children 1990* (Oxford University Press, 1990).

447   [*American children, 1990*]: Children's Defense Fund, *Children 1990: A Report Card, Briefing Book, and Action Primer* (Children's Defense Fund, 1990), quoted at pp. 3, 5.

NURTURING RIGHTS

PAGE

454   [*"Most ancient of all societies"*]: Rousseau, *The Social Contract*, in Rousseau, *The Social Contract/Discourses* (Dent, 1955), p. 4.
[*Mill on the family*]: Mill, *The Subjection of Women*, 2nd ed. (Frederick A. Stokes, 1911), p. 97.

455   [*"Not subject to political bargaining"*]: Rawls, *A Theory of Justice* (Belknap Press of Harvard University Press, 1971), p. 4.
[*"Instead of importing"*]: Held, "Mothering versus Contract," p. 294.

458   [*"Embedded in culture"*]: Rinehart, "Gender and the Epistemology of Leadership," p. 1.

459   [*"Dependent, submissive and conforming"*]: see Burns, *Leadership*, p. 50.

EMPOWERING RIGHTS

PAGE

461   [*"Morality of responsibility"*]: Gilligan, pp. 132, 147.
[*Lynd on communal rights*]: Lynd, passim.

462   [*"Outer frame"*]: Walzer, "Citizenship," in Terence Ball, James Farr, and Russell L. Hanson, eds., *Political Innovation and Conceptual Change* (Cambridge University Press, 1989), pp. 211–19, quoted at p. 216.
[*"We would replace power"*]: "Port Huron Statement," p. 333.

464   [*"Socially constructed"*]: see Peter L. Berger and Thomas Luckmann, *The Social Construction of Reality: A Treatise in the Sociology of Knowledge* (Doubleday/Anchor, 1967).
[*"We must recognize differences"*]: Lorde, pp. 122–23.
[*" 'One-woman coalitions' "*]: Charlotte Bunch, "Making Common Cause: Diversity and Coalitions," in Bunch, pp. 149–57, quoted at p. 156.
[*"Assumed to be competitive"*]: Cohen and Rogers, *On Democracy* (Penguin, 1983), p. 173.

465   [*"True alliance"*]: King, *Where Do We Go from Here*, p. 151.
[*"Enlightened self-interest"*]: quoted in Ron Curran, "The Left in Los Angeles Attempts a United Stand," *In These Times*, vol. 12, no. 25 (May 18, 1988), p. 8.
[*"Self-interest rightly understood"*]: Alexis de Tocqueville, *Democracy in America* (Vintage, 1945), vol. 2, pp. 129–32.
[*"Ongoing, long-term arrangements"*]: Lisa Albrecht and Rose M. Brewer, "Bridges of Power: Women's Multicultural Alliances for Social Change," in Albrecht and Brewer, *Bridges of Power*, pp. 2–22, quoted at p. 4; see also Davida J. Alperin, "Social Diversity and the Necessity of Alliances," in *ibid.*, pp. 23–33.
[*"Not work done in your home"*]: Reagon, "Coalition Politics," p. 359.
[*"Structural renewal"*]: Buber, *Paths in Utopia*, R. F. C. Hull, trans. (Routledge & Kegan Paul, 1949), p. 27.

466   [*"Power-over" vs. "power-with"*]: Albrecht and Brewer, "Bridges of Power," p. 5; see also Van Den Bergh and Cooper, pp. 5–6.
[*"Africanize America"*]: Du Bois, p. 3.

467   [*"O, let America"*]: Hughes, "Let America Be America Again," in William Rose Benét and Norman Cousins, eds., *The Poetry of Freedom* (Random House, 1945), pp. 537–40, quoted at pp. 539, 540.

EPILOGUE: THE ENDLESS STRUGGLE

PAGE
470   [*"Explicit sex"*]: Samuel Walker, *In Defense of American Liberties: A History of the ACLU* (Oxford University Press, 1990), p. 353.

ACKNOWLEDGMENTS

Milton Djuric played an indispensable role at every stage of producing this book. He worked closely with the authors in developing ideas, planning the shape and organization of the volume, conducting research, drafting material, critiquing chapters, editing the manuscript. His creativity, knowledgeability, grace under pressure, and, above all, his holding the authors to his own high professional standards helped make this a true collaboration among the three of us.

Diane North of the University of California at Davis and Larry Glickman and Michael Thompson of the University of California at Berkeley conducted extensive research on workers' rights and the American labor movement.

We are indebted to three scholars for their extensive comments on the entire manuscript: Philippa Strum of Brooklyn College, Paul L. Murphy of the University of Minnesota, and Howard Zinn of Boston University. Each brought a special perspective and expertise to the work.

Ellen Carol DuBois of the University of California at Los Angeles offered invaluable criticisms of Chapter 5 on women's rights and the woman suffrage movement. Diane North and Larry Glickman contributed helpful critiques of Chapter 6. Jane Benson, Becky Sarah, Peter Holloran, and Thomas Jackson commented thoughtfully on chapters in their areas of knowledge.

Judith Addington was a special source of encouragement and advice on women's leadership. Research by Lois L. Duke of Clemson University in women's and other rights areas contributed to the volume. Maurice Greenbaum played an important role in launching the project. We also thank Clayborne Carson and the staff of the Martin Luther King, Jr., Papers Project at Stanford University.

560 / *Acknowledgments*

Donna Chenail, Peggy Bryant, Shirley Bushika, and Lori Tolle of the Williams College faculty secretarial office went far beyond the call of duty in preparing successive drafts of the manuscript under severe pressures of time. The staff of Sawyer Library at Williams College and of Stanford University's Green Library made their skills and resources generously available to us.

Our editor at Knopf, Ashbel Green, brought both his editorial talents and a wide knowledge of American history to his review of the manuscript. Also at Knopf, Jenny McPhee efficiently and with cheerful patience guided us through the complexities of the production process, while Melvin Rosenthal, with his usual acute attention to detail, shepherded the manuscript into print.

Dewey, John, 198, 219–20, 221, 228–9
Diamond, William, 226
Dickens, Charles, 74, 96, 98
Dies, Martin, 256, 271, 272
Diggers movement, 24–5
Diggs, Annie, 160
Dilling, Elizabeth, 273
Dirksen, Everett, 317
Discourse on . . . Inequality among Men (Rousseau), 25
Douglas, Paul, 288
Douglas, William O., 282, 300, 301, 380, 381, 411
Douglass, Frederick, 108–10, 111–21 *passim*, 133, 143, 149, 151, 159
Dred Scott v. *Sandford* (1857), 95–6, 118–19, 124
DuBois, Ellen, 140, 142, 148, 149, 150, 158
Du Bois, W. E. B., 120, 123, 134, 218, 309, 326, 466
Dulles, Allen, 387
Dulles, John Foster, 290, 301, 420
Dumbauld, Edward, 40

Echols, Alice, 353
economic bill of rights, Franklin Roosevelt's, 262–4
Edelman, Marian Wright, 330, 447, 458
education: for African-Americans (1800s), 217–18; anti-Communist campaigns and, 292–3; conservative and liberal views on, 216–17; desegregation of, 113, 309–10, 315–16; Locke's views, 20; as potential social equalizer, 217; progressive education, 219–23; public school systems, 215–16, 223, 235; religion in schools, 409–10; right to education, 214–16, 222–3, 450; teachers' role, 221–2, 235; for women, 151, 160, 218–19
eight-hour-day crusade, 174–80
Eisenhower, Dwight D., 281, 288–9, 290, 297, 316, 398, 423–4
Eisenstein, Zillah, 156–7, 347
El Salvador, 432
Emancipation Proclamation (1863), 119–20

Engels, Friedrich, 96, 100
England: Civil War, 21–5, 75; Industrial Revolution, 74–9; voting rights, 22–3, 79, 164
Enlightenment, the, 18–28 *passim*
Enquiry Concerning the Principles of Morals (Hume), 80–1
Equal Employment Opportunity Commission (EEOC), 341–2, 343, 365
equality and egalitarianism, 24–5, 35–7, 44, 83, 84–5, 97, 217, 345–6, 349–50; *see also* opportunity, equality of
Equal Pay Act of 1963, 341
Equal Rights Amendment (ERA), 169, 343, 348–50
Equal Rights Party, 97, 151
Ernst, Morris, 380
Escobedo v. *Illinois* (1964), 412
Espionage Act of 1917, 206, 207
Essay on . . . the Passions and Affections (Hutcheson), 26–7
Evans, Sara, 347
exclusionary rule, 412, 413
Exodus: as prototype of revolution, 3–7; and rights, 5, 7

Fair Labor Standards Act of 1938, 179–80, 257, 449
fairness doctrine, 390–1
Falwell, Jerry, 355, 409
family as model for society, 454–6
Fanon, Frantz, 337
Farer, Tom, 419
Farmer, James, 313
farm workers, 361–2
Faubus, Orval, 316
Federal Bureau of Investigation (FBI), 271, 272, 280–3, 284, 285, 290, 337, 407, 408
Federalist, The, 47, 205
Federation of Organized Trades and Labor Unions (FOTLU), 177, 178
Fehrenbacher, Don E., 118, 201
Feiffer, Jules, 404
Feminine Mystique, The (Friedan), 340
feminism, *see* women's rights movement
Ferrin, Mary Upton, 145
Ferry, Thomas, 153
Field, Stephen, 230

A NOTE ABOUT THE AUTHORS

James MacGregor Burns received his B.A. from
Williams College in 1939 and his Ph.D. from Harvard
University. He taught political science at Williams from 1941 to 1989.
Among his books are *Roosevelt: The Lion and the Fox* (1956),
The Deadlock of Democracy (1963), *Roosevelt: The Soldier of Freedom* (1970),
which was awarded both the Pulitzer Prize and the National Book Award,
Leadership (1978), *The Vineyard of Liberty* (1982),
The Workshop of Democracy (1985), and *The Crosswinds of Freedom* (1989).
Currently he is Woodrow Wilson Professor of Government,
Emeritus, at Williams, and Senior Scholar,
Jepson School of Leadership Studies,
University of Richmond.

Stewart Burns is a social historian and Associate Editor of
the Martin Luther King, Jr., Papers at Stanford University. He is the
author of *Social Movements of the 1960s: Searching for Democracy* (1990). He
received his Ph.D. from the University of California, Santa Cruz, in 1984.
Burns has taught at the University of California, Santa Cruz and Berkeley,
and at Stanford, where he serves as a Resident Fellow.
He has been a political activist for many years.

A NOTE ON THE TYPE

This book was set in Baskerville. Linotype Baskerville is a facsimile
cutting from type cast from the original matrices of a face designed by John
Baskerville. The original face was the forerunner of the "modern" group of
type faces. John Baskerville (1706–1775) of Birmingham, England, was
a writing master with a special renown for cutting inscriptions in stone.

Composed, printed and bound by The Haddon Craftsmen
Scranton, Pennsylvania

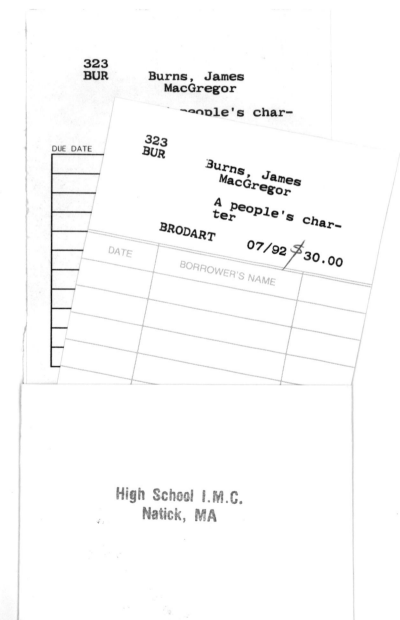